PRENTICE HALL

MIDDLE GRADES MATH
TOOLS FOR SUCCESS

Course 3

**PREPARING FOR
ALGEBRA AND GEOMETRY**

*Prentice Hall dedicates
this mathematics program
to all mathematics educators
and their students.*

AUTHORS

Suzanne H. Chapin

Mark Illingworth

Marsha S. Landau

Joanna O. Masingila

Leah McCracken

CONSULTING AUTHORS

Sadie Chavis Bragg

Bridget A. Hadley

Vincent O'Connor

Anne C. Patterson

PRENTICE HALL

MIDDLE GRADES MATH
TOOLS FOR SUCCESS

Course 3

**PREPARING FOR
ALGEBRA AND GEOMETRY**

Prentice
Hall

**Glenview, Illinois
Needham, Massachusetts
Upper Saddle River, New Jersey**

AUTHORS

Suzanne H. Chapin, Ed.D., Boston University, Boston, Massachusetts
Proportional Reasoning and Probability strands, and Tools for Problem Solving

Mark Illingworth, Hollis Public Schools, Hollis, New Hampshire
Graphing strand

Marsha S. Landau, Ph.D., Formerly, National Louis University, Evanston, Illinois
Algebra, Functions, and Computation strands

Joanna O. Masingila, Ph.D., Syracuse University, Syracuse, New York
Geometry strand

Leah McCracken, Lockwood School District, Billings, Montana
Data Analysis strand

CONSULTING AUTHORS

Sadie Chavis Bragg, Ed.D., Borough of Manhattan Community College, The City University of New York, New York, New York

Bridget A. Hadley, Mathematics Curriculum Specialist, Hopkinton, Massachusetts

Vincent O'Connor, Formerly, Milwaukee Public Schools, Milwaukee, Wisconsin

Anne C. Patterson, Volusia County Schools, Daytona Beach, Florida

ISBN: 0-13-043417-5

2 3 4 5 6 7 8 9 10 04 03 02 01 00

Prentice
Hall

We are grateful to our reviewers, who advised us in the development stages and provided invaluable feedback, ideas, and constructive criticism to help make this program one that meets the needs of middle grades teachers and students.

REVIEWERS

All Levels
Ann Bouie, Ph.D., Multicultural Reviewer, Oakland, California
Dorothy S. Strong, Ph.D., Chicago Public Schools, Chicago, Illinois

Course 1
Darla Agajanian, Sierra Vista School, Canyon Country, California
Rhonda Bird, Grand Haven Area Schools, Grand Haven, Michigan
Gary Critselous, Whittle Springs Middle School, Knoxville, Tennessee
Rhonda W. Davis, Durant Road Middle School, Raleigh, North Carolina
Leroy Dupee, Bridgeport Public Schools, Bridgeport, Connecticut
Jose Lalas, Ph.D., California State University, Dominguez Hills, California
Richard Lavers, Fitchburg High School, Fitchburg, Massachusetts
Lavaille Metoyer, Houston Independent School District, Houston, Texas

Course 2
Raylene Bryson, Alexander Middle School, Huntersville, North Carolina
Susan R. Buckley, Dallas Public Schools, Dallas, Texas
Sheila Cunningham, Klein Independent School District, Klein, Texas
Natarsha Mathis, Hart Junior High School, Washington, D.C.
Jean Patton, Clements Middle School, Covington, Georgia
Judy Trowell, Arkansas Department of Higher Education, Little Rock, Arkansas

Course 3
Michaele F. Chappell, Ph.D., University of South Florida, Tampa, Florida
Bettye Hall, Math Consultant, Houston, Texas
Joaquin Hernandez, Barbara Goleman Senior High, Miami, Florida
Steven H. Lapinski, Henrico County Public Schools, Richmond, Virginia
Dana Luterman, Lincoln Middle School, Kansas City, Missouri
Loretta Rector, Leonardo da Vinci School, Sacramento, California
Elias P. Rodriguez, Leander Middle School, Leander, Texas
Anthony C. Terceira, Providence School Department, Providence, Rhode Island

STAFF CREDITS
The people who made up the *Middle Grades Math* team—representing editorial, design, marketing, page production, editorial services, production, manufacturing, technology, electronic publishing, and advertising and promotion—and their managers are listed below. Bold type denotes core team members.
Barbara A. Bertell, Bruce Bond, Therese Bräuer, Christopher Brown, **Judith D. Buice**, Kathy Carter, Linda M. Coffey, Noralie V. Cox, Sheila DeFazio, Edward de Leon, Christine Deliee, Gabriella Della Corte, Jo DiGiustini, Robert G. Dunn, Barbara Flockhart, Audra Floyd, David B. Graham, Maria Green, Kristen Guevara, Jeff Ikler, Mimi Jigarjian, Elizabeth A. Jordan, Russell Lappa, Joan McCulley, Paul W. Murphy, Cindy A. Noftle, Caroline M. Power, Olena Serbyn, Dennis Slattery, Martha G. Smith, Kira Thaler Marbit, **Christina Trinchero**, **Stuart Wallace**, **Cynthia A. Weedel**, **Jeff Weidenaar**, **Mary Jane Wolfe,** Stewart Wood

We would like to give special thanks to National Math Consultants Ann F. Bell and Brenda Underwood for all their help in developing this program.

Contents

Integers and Variable Expressions

Problem Solving and Connections

...and More!

CHAPTER PROJECT

Theme: Weather
Weather or Not

Equations and Inequalities

Problem Solving and Connections

Transportation 116
Estimation 124
Animals 127
Money 129
Geography 134
Nature 144
Internet 158

...and More!

ASSESSMENT

CHAPTER PROJECT

Theme: Mobiles
Balancing Act

CHAPTER 4
Graphing in the Coordinate Plane

CHAPTER PROJECT

Theme: Recreation
Step Right Up!

CHAPTER

6 Applications of Proportions

CHAPTER PROJECT

Theme: Scale Models
Larger than Life

Problem Solving and Connections

...and More!

CHAPTER PROJECT

Theme: Savings
Invest in a Winner

ASSESSMENT

Problem Solving and Connections

...and More!

ASSESSMENT

CHAPTER PROJECT

Theme: Landscape Architecture
Great Escape

Geometry and Measurement

Problem Solving
and Connections

...and More!

ASSESSMENT

CHAPTER
PROJECT

Theme: Packaging
A Better Way?

**Problem Solving
and Connections**

Energy	**492**
Communications	**499**
Music	**500**
Transportation	**507**
Data Collection	**508**
Environment	**517**
Design	**519**

...and More!

CHAPTER PROJECT

Theme: Consumer Issues
How Much Dough?

CHAPTER 11 Probability

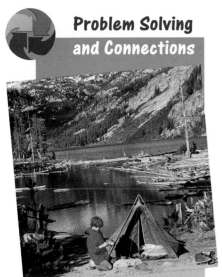
CHAPTER PROJECT

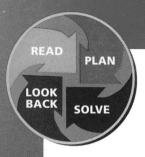

READ PLAN
LOOK BACK SOLVE

Tools for Problem Solving... An Overview

CONTENTS

To the Student:

The key to your success in math is your ability to use math in the real world—both now and in the future. To succeed you need math skill and some problem solving tools too. In this Problem Solving Overview, you'll learn how to use a four-step plan for problem solving, how to choose strategies for solving problems, how to best work in groups, and how to apply strategies to standardized tests.

As you work through the book, you'll find plenty of opportunities to improve your problem solving skills. The more you build on a skill, the better you'll get. And the better you get, the more confident you'll become. So keep at it!

Problem Solving Strategies

Draw a Diagram
Guess and Test
Look for a Pattern
Make a Table
Simulate the Problem
Solve a Simpler Problem
Too Much or Too Little
  Information
Use Logical Reasoning
Use Multiple Strategies
Work Backward
Write an Equation

The Four-Step Approach

Problem solving skills can help you in all areas of mathematics as well as in everyday life. How you approach a problem is one skill that can make a difference in whether or not you solve the problem. George Polya, a mathematician, devised a four-step method for solving problems.

POLYA'S FOUR-STEP APPROACH

1. Read and understand the problem.
2. Plan how to solve the problem. Try a strategy.
3. Solve the problem.
4. Look back.

To use Polya's four-step approach effectively, ask yourself questions about the problem as you try to solve it.

SAMPLE PROBLEM..

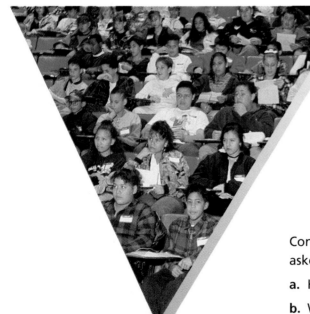

The seats in the auditorium at the Milton Middle School are numbered in an unusual pattern:

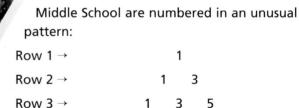

Row 1 →				1		
Row 2 →			1		3	
Row 3 →		1		3		5
Row 4 →	1		3		5	7
Row 5 →	1	3		5	7	9
Row 6 →	1	3	5	7	9	11

Confused by the arrangement of seats, the new principal asked students the following questions.

a. How many seats are in the 100th row?

b. What is the number of the last seat in the 100th row?

c. What is the sum of the seat numbers in the 100th row?

READ

Read for understanding. Summarize the problem.

Read the problem again. What information is given? What information is missing? What are you being asked to find or to do? You can start by making a list.

- **Information given** Each row has one more seat than the previous row, and seats are numbered with odd numbers.

- **Goals of the problem** Find the number of seats in the 100th row, the number of the last seat in the 100th row, and the sum of the seat numbers in the 100th row.

PLAN

Decide on a strategy.

Consider the strategies you know. Could you use one of them? Have you ever solved a similar problem? If so, try the same approach. However, you probably do not want to make a list of all 100 rows!

A problem of this sort might be solved by using the three strategies *Solve a Simpler Problem, Make a Table,* and *Look for a Pattern.*

SOLVE

Try the strategy.

Examine rows 1 through 6 and answer related questions for each row. Organize your work in a table so you can look for patterns.

Row	Number of Seats	Last Seat Number	Sum of Seat Numbers
1	1	1	1
2	2	3	4
3	3	5	9
4	4	7	16
5	5	9	25
6	6	11	36

Number of Seats The number of seats in a row is the same as the row number, so the 100th row has 100 seats.

Last Seat Number The last seat number in each row is one less than twice the row number. So the number of the last seat in the 100th row is $2 \cdot 100 - 1$, or 199.

Sum of Seat Numbers The sum of the seat numbers is a square number, the square of the row number. So, the sum of the seat numbers in row 100 is 100^2, or 10,000.

LOOK BACK

Think about how you solved the problem.

This is the most important step in solving problems. Check that you answered the original question. Ask yourself some questions.

- Is your answer reasonable?
- Does your answer make sense?
- Could you have solved the problem another way?

EXERCISES *On Your Own*

Use Polya's four-step method to solve each problem.
Remember that there are many ways to solve problems.

1. *Money* How many ways can you make change for 20 cents?

2. In the nursery rhyme "Jack and Jill," Jill fetches a pail of water. If Jill has only a 5-liter pail and a 3-liter pail, how can she fetch exactly one liter of water?

3. *Number Sense* What is the ones digit of 7^{36}?

4. Use the following clues to determine the number represented by MATH in the subtraction problem below.

   - Each letter represents a different digit.
   - The letters I and S represent digits 7 and 8, respectively.
   - Two of the three numbers are odd.
   - The digit 6 is not in any of the three numbers.

$$
\begin{array}{r}
\text{M A T H} \\
- \quad \text{I S} \\
\hline
\text{F U N}
\end{array}
$$

5. Molly is 4 years older than John. Four years ago, Molly was twice as old as John was then. How old is Molly now?

6. *Clocks* A grandfather clock chimes once at 1:00, twice at 2:00, three times at 3:00, and so on through 12:00. It also chimes once every quarter hour. How many times does the clock chime in one day?

7. The sum of 4 consecutive numbers is 594. What are the numbers?

Using Strategies

Knowing how to use several different problem solving strategies can help you become a great problem solver.

You already know some problem solving strategies from previous math classes. When planning how to solve a problem, consider some or all of these strategies:

Draw a Diagram   Guess and Test

Make a Table   Look for a Pattern

Write an Equation   Solve a Simpler Problem

Many problems can be solved in more than one way. Sometimes you can combine strategies or use one favorite approach. Any method that works is a good method!

SAMPLE PROBLEM..

Flying kites has been a popular pastime for over 2,000 years. All kites require a string, a body, and a tail. The tail of a kite steadies the kite in the air and helps keep the nose of the kite pointing upward.

One of the longest kites is the Chinese dragon kite. It must be launched by several people. The length of one particular dragon kite with its tail is 21 feet. If the tail is 15 feet longer than the kite body, how long is the kite body?

The three solutions that follow use *Draw a Diagram, Guess and Test* with *Make a Table,* and *Write an Equation* to solve the problem. As you examine the solutions, ask yourself, "Which strategy would I use?"

Solution 1

STRATEGY: *Draw a Diagram*

The *Draw a Diagram* strategy can help you see relationships in a problem. Draw a diagram to show that the kite and its tail are 21 feet long and the tail is 15 feet longer than the body.

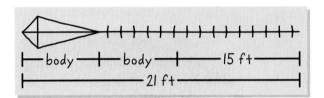

Subtracting 15 feet from 21 feet results in 6 feet, which is twice the length of the kite. So the kite body is 3 feet long.

Look Back If the body is 3 feet long, then the tail is 3 + 15, or 18 feet long. Together the body and the tail are 3 + 18, or 21 feet long. The answer makes sense.

Solution 2

STRATEGIES: *Guess and Test* and *Make a Table*

The *Guess and Test* strategy involves guessing the solution based on an estimation of a reasonable answer. Then you test your guess against the conditions in the problem.

To keep your guesses organized, use the *Make a Table* strategy with the *Guess and Test* strategy.

Guess the length of the kite body. Test your guess by calculating the length of the kite tail and the total length of the kite. Does your result fit the problem? If not, guess again.

Length of kite body (in feet)	Length of kite tail (in feet)	Total length (in feet)	Test
6	15 + 6 = 21	27	Too high
2	15 + 2 = 17	19	Too low
3	15 + 3 = 18	21	Exactly right

The body of the kite is 3 feet long.

Solution 3

STRATEGY: *Write an Equation*

To write and solve an equation, first define the variable. Let the variable represent the information you are asked to find.

Define the variable: Let x = the length of the kite body.

From the problem, you know that the tail is 15 feet longer than the kite body. Use this information to write an expression.

$$x + 15 = \text{length of kite tail}$$

You also know that together the kite body and the kite tail are 21 feet long. Use this information to write an equation.

kite body + kite tale = 21 ft	
$x + (x + 15) = 21$	⟵ Write an equation.
$2x + 15 = 21$	⟵ Combine like terms.
$2x = 6$	⟵ Subtract 15 from each side.
$x = 3$	⟵ Divide each side by 2.

The kite body is 3 ft long.

EXERCISES *On Your Own*

1. A pencil and an eraser together cost $2.00. The eraser costs $1.50 more than the pencil. How much does the eraser cost?

2. *Elections* In a local school committee election, 250 votes were cast for two candidates. Candidate A won the election by 10 votes. How many votes did Candidate A receive?

3. *Geometry* Suppose the staircase pattern shown below were continued. How many squares would you need to make the 12th staircase in the pattern?

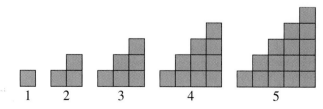

4. How many segments can be drawn that connect any 2 of 9 distinct points on a circle?

Working Together

This year you may be asked to work in a cooperative group. Working in a cooperative group is not just working at the same table with other students. In a cooperative group everyone shares ideas and is responsible for helping other group members. Sharing ideas with other students and learning how other students solve problems will help you to understand problems and become a better problem solver.

Usually classrooms have individual and group rules.

Individual rules

- You are responsible for your own work.
  - You are responsible for your own behavior.

Group rules

- You should help group members understand what you know and let them help you understand what they know.
  - You should try to answer questions within the group before asking a teacher for help.

Working in a cooperative group is especially useful when problems are confusing or complex. If the problem has many components, then members of the group can divide tasks in order to save time. For example, one person may make a graph while another writes an explanation of the graph. However, it is essential that members of a group tell the rest of the group what they did and how they did it.

Group members may also take on these group roles.

- The **recorder** takes notes and records information.
- The **researcher** tracks down information that is not immediately available.
- Each member of the group should have general supplies such as paper and pencil, a calculator, and a ruler. The **organizer** makes sure any unusual items, such as a stopwatch or masking tape, are available.
- The **presenter** explains the group's solution process to the rest of the class.

It is important to remember that even though students have different jobs, they all must contribute to solving the problem.

EXERCISES *On Your Own*

Work in a group. Assign a job to each member of your group. Then work together to solve the problems.

1. *Calculator* To change a fraction to a decimal, divide the numerator by the denominator.

   a. Change $\frac{1}{9}, \frac{2}{9}, \frac{3}{9}, \ldots, \frac{8}{9}$ to decimals and describe the pattern.

   b. What happens when the denominator is 99? Give examples and describe the pattern.

   c. What happens when the denominator is 999? Give examples and describe the pattern.

2. *Tickets* Adult theater tickets cost $3 more than student tickets. The total cost for 75 adults and 100 students is $925. Find the cost of a student ticket.

3. *Plumbing* A leaky faucet fills a 100-milliliter cup in 10 minutes.

   a. How much water is wasted in a day? A week? A year?

   b. How long does it take to waste a kiloliter of water? (*Hint:* 1 kiloliter = 1,000,000 milliliters)

4. *Woodworking* Kena is making a set of blocks for her baby sister. There will be one block in each of 5 different colors, 4 different shapes, and 3 different sizes. How many blocks will be in her set?

Preparing for Standardized Tests

In some multiple choice problems you are asked to compare values in two different columns. You use strategies to find the answer in each column and then compare the quantities.

SAMPLE PROBLEM...

Compare the quantity in Column A with the quantity in Column B. Then choose the appropriate letter from this list.

A. The quantity in Column A is greater.

B. The quantity in Column B is greater.

C. The two quantities are equal.

D. The relationship cannot be determined from the given information.

Column A	Column B
the number of different 3-digit numbers that can be made using the digits 1, 3, and 5, if no digit can be repeated in a number	6

Strategy: Make a list for the Column A problem.

The possible numbers are 135, 153, 315, 351, 513, 531. So 6 numbers are possible.

Compare: The quantities in Column A and Column B are equal. The answer is choice (C).

Strategies for the more conventional multiple choice questions include the following.

- estimating to eliminate some answer choices
- using *Work Backward* to see which answer choices fit the information given in the problem
- solving the problem and searching the choices for your answer

Some answer choices may mislead you. Once you decide on an answer, always check to make sure it answers the question.

Compare the quantity in Column A with the quantity in Column B. Then choose the best answer from this list.

A. The quantity in Column A is greater.

B. The quantity in Column B is greater.

C. The two quantities are equal.

D. The relationship cannot be determined from the given information.

	Column A	Column B
1.	the price per pound, if 7 lb costs $3.00	the price per pound, if 5 lb costs $2.00
2.	the number of factors of 24	the number of multiples of 12
3.	the next number in the pattern 1, 2, 4, 8, 16, . . .	the next number in the pattern 1, 4, 9, 16, . . .
4.	the product of a negative and a positive number	the product of two negative numbers
5.	x, if $0 < x < 32$ and x is divisible by 3 and 9	27

$$a > c, b > d$$
a, b, c, d are positive integers.

	Column A	Column B
6.	$\dfrac{a}{b}$	$\dfrac{c}{d}$
7.	$9 \cdot 682 \cdot 7$	$10 \cdot 682 \cdot 7$

Three gold coins and one silver coin are worth the same as 5 silver coins and 2 gold coins.

	Column A	Column B
8.	value of 4 silver coins	value of 1 gold coin

1 Drawing Conclusions from Statistical Data

| WHAT YOU WILL LEARN IN THIS CHAPTER | • How to organize data and interpret charts and graphs | • How to use technology to make appropriate graphs for data | • How to conduct a survey and find probabilities |

NEWS Flash

Has El Niño Arrived?

PRECIPITATION THIS YEAR

Heavy rainfall in the last four months has made up for a very dry winter. Is El Niño, the change in weather patterns caused by warmer waters off the Pacific coast of South America, responsible? Forecasters at the National Weather Service

Which news catches your eye? Do you notice graphs and charts in news magazines and newspapers? If a picture is worth a thousand words, a graph is worth a thousand numbers! Reporters use graphs to summarize data and to tell a story clearly and simply. Do they always do it accurately?

Create a Graph for a News Article
For your chapter project, you will analyze graphs and charts that appear in the news. Then, using a topic that you choose, you will write a news article and illustrate it with an appropriate graph.

• How to solve problems with too much or too little information

PROBLEM SOLVING

What You'll Learn

▼ To make bar graphs

▼ To make line graphs

...And Why

A visual display of data can tell an effective story.

Here's How

Look for questions that
- build understanding
- ✔ check understanding

THINK AND DISCUSS

▼ Making Bar Graphs

You can use a **bar graph** when comparing amounts. When you make a bar graph, be sure to use a title and to label each axis. One axis shows the categories. The other axis shows amounts.

■ **EXAMPLE 1**   *Real-World Problem Solving*

Sales Make a bar graph for the data in the table at the left.

┌─ The highest unit sale is 38 million. So a reasonable scale for
   the vertical axis is from 0 to 40 million. Label every 10 million,
   using equally spaced intervals.

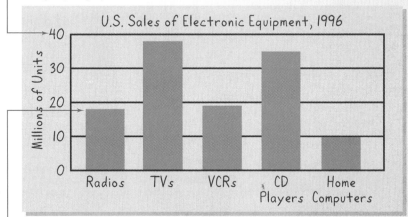

└─ To draw a bar on the graph, estimate its placement based
   on the vertical scale. The value 18 is about $\frac{3}{4}$ of the distance
   from 10 million to 20 million.

U.S. Sales of Electronic Equipment, 1996

Item	Units Sold (millions)
Radios	18
TVs	38
VCRs	19
CD players	35
Home computers	10

Source: Electronic Industries Association

1. **Look Back** Use the scale in Example 1. Explain how to estimate a bar height that represents 24 million units.

2. **✔ Try It Out** Make a bar graph for the number of hours each member of the swim team trained last week: Georgia, 7 h; Aaron, 14 h; Luis, 12 h; Felicia, 9 h; Danelle, 18 h.

A **stacked bar graph** has bars that are divided into categories. Each bar represents a total. Use a **key,** or *legend,* to identify each category within a bar.

A **sliding bar graph** shows two categories in each bar. The bars extend on either side of the center, which represents zero. Each side represents one category.

■ **EXAMPLE 2**   *Real-World Problem Solving*

Clubs The table at the right shows the number of girls and boys in the Environmental Club. Display these data in (a) a stacked bar graph and (b) a sliding bar graph.

Environmental Club Members

Grade	Girls	Boys
6	23	16
7	17	14
8	21	26

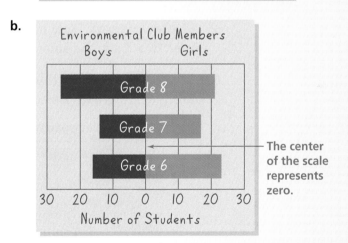

3. **a.** In which graph is it easier to see the total for grade 6?
   b. In which graph is it easier to compare the number of eighth-grade boys with the number of seventh-grade boys?

4. ■ *Look Back* What categories are listed in the key for the stacked bar graph? How are these categories shown in the sliding bar graph?

▼2 *Making Line Graphs*

**Sales of Cassettes
and CDs
(billions of dollars)**

Year	Cassettes	CDs
1990	3.7	3.5
1991	3.3	4.4
1992	3.4	5.4
1993	3.2	6.6
1994	3.3	8.5
1995	2.5	9.5

Source: Recording Industry
Association of America

Use a **line graph** to show changes over time. A **multiple line graph** shows more than one category changing over time.

■ **EXAMPLE 3**   *Real-World Problem Solving*

Entertainment Display the data in the table at the left in a multiple line graph.

The highest amount is $9.5 billion. Label the vertical axis with multiples of 2, from 0 to 12.

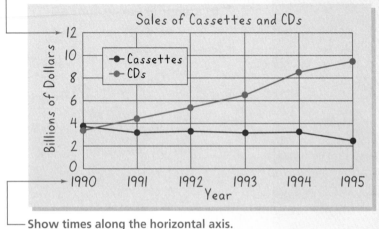

Show times along the horizontal axis.

5. ⸭ *Data Analysis* How have the sales of CDs changed over time? How have the sales of cassettes changed?

6. ✔ *Try It Out* Display the data from the table below in a multiple line graph. Be sure to include a key.

U. S. Newspaper Circulation (millions)

Type of Newspaper	1980	1985	1990	1995
Morning daily	29.4	36.4	41.3	43.1
Evening daily	32.8	26.4	21.0	15.1
Sunday	54.7	58.8	62.6	61.8

Source: Newspaper Association of America

Work Together
Making Bar Graphs

7. For each person in your group, record how many notebooks and how many pens you have. Have half your group use the data to make a stacked bar graph. Have the other half make a sliding bar graph. Compare your graphs.

1. *Entertainment* Use the graph and data from Example 3 on page 6. Display the data in a stacked bar graph and in a sliding bar graph.

Use the table at the right for Exercises 2–4.

2. Use the data to make a sliding bar graph.

3. Display the data in a multiple line graph.

4. What type of graph would you use to show that American eating habits are changing? Explain.

5. *Sports* Display the data below in a multiple line graph.

How Much Beef and Chicken Do Americans Eat Each Year?
(pounds per person)

Year	Beef	Chicken
1989	65	41
1990	64	42
1991	63	44
1992	63	46
1993	62	49
1994	64	50

Source: U.S. Department of Agriculture

Average Annual Salaries for Professional Athletes
(thousands of dollars)

Sport	1990	1991	1992	1993	1994	1995	1996
Football	365	425	492	683	636	714	765
Baseball	598	891	1,029	1,076	1,168	1,111	1,120

Sources: NFL Players Association and MLB Players Association

6. *Reasoning* What does this graph show about the relationship between education and earnings? Between education and unemployment?

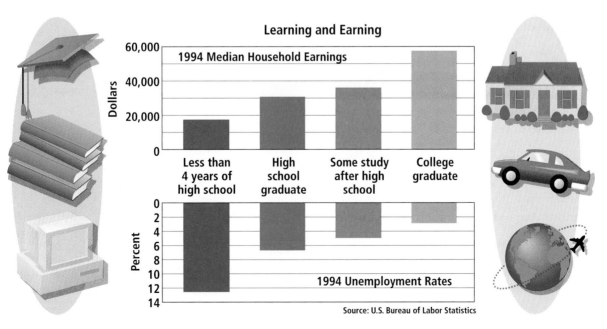

Learning and Earning

1994 Median Household Earnings

1994 Unemployment Rates

Source: U.S. Bureau of Labor Statistics

Use the graph at the right for Exercises 7 and 8.

What Happens To Our Garbage?

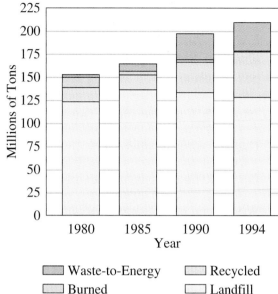

7. *Environment* About how many more million tons of garbage were recycled in 1994 than in 1980?

8. Which categories have shown growth since 1980? Which categories have stayed about the same? Which categories have decreased?

9. *Consumer Issues* Use the table below to make a stacked bar graph showing the cost of a meal in each country. Divide each bar into three categories: burger, drink, and dessert.

Source: Franklin Associates

Prices at an International Chain Restaurant

Country	Burger	Drink	Dessert
Japan	$1.65	$1.15	$1.80
Panama	$.70	$.70	$.80
United States	$1.34	$.93	$1.31

Source: *Scholastic Math*

10. *Writing* The double bar graph at the right displays the data for Example 2. Compare this graph to the stacked bar graph. Write a paragraph giving the advantages and disadvantages of each type of graph.

Environmental Club Members

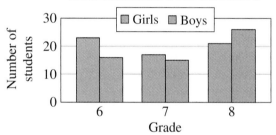

Mixed Review

Estimate. *(Previous course)*

11. 685 + 418   12. 732 · 7   13. 1789 ÷ 303

14. Together, Kim and Al earned $67.50 painting. Kim earned $5.50 more than Al. How much did Kim earn? *(Previous course)*

15. *Data Analysis* Use the circle graph at the right. Estimate the total number of women's and mixed leagues. About how many times greater is this than the number of men's leagues? *(Previous course)*

Bowling Leagues

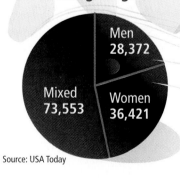

Men 28,372

Mixed 73,553

Women 36,421

Source: USA Today

Reading Graphs Critically

What You'll Learn

▼ 1 To recognize misleading graphs

▼ 2 To select an appropriate scale

...And Why

If you learn to read graphs critically, you won't be fooled by misleading graphs.

Here's How

Look for questions that
- ⊞ build understanding
- ✔ check understanding

THINK AND DISCUSS

1 *Recognizing Misleading Graphs*

The same data may be graphed in different ways. Sometimes, however, a graph gives a misleading visual impression. Look at the graphs below.

The graph at the left has a break symbol, ⋧, on the vertical axis. It shows that some of the values on the axis have been left out.

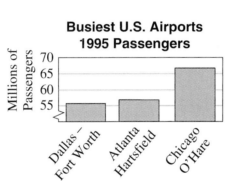

Source: Airport Council International

■ **EXAMPLE 1** *Real-World Problem Solving*

Travel Which graph shown above gives the impression that Chicago O'Hare Airport is twice as busy as Atlanta Hartsfield Airport? Explain.

In the graph with the break symbol, the bar that shows the number of passengers at Chicago O'Hare is more than twice as long as the bar for Atlanta Hartsfield. The visual display in this graph is misleading.

1. ✔ *Try It Out* Which graph makes the difference between the number of passengers at each airport appear smaller?

2. ⊞ *Analyze* Both graphs display the same data, but they do not give the same impression of the data. Explain why.

2 Selecting an Appropriate Scale

Statisticians sometimes use a break symbol to emphasize a trend or to show details in the data. First, they plan what scale to use.

■ **EXAMPLE 2** *Real-World Problem Solving*

Projected U.S. College Enrollment

Year	Students (millions)
1994	14.3
1995	14.2
1996	14.4
1997	14.6
1998	14.9
1999	15.2
2000	15.5

Source: U.S. National Center for Educational Statistics

Education Make two line graphs for the data shown at the left. In one of the graphs, use a break symbol.

The highest enrollment is 15.5 million. Label the vertical axis with multiples of 5, from 0 to 20.

The data range from about 14 million to 16 million. Label the vertical axis with multiples of 0.5, beginning with 14.0. Use a break symbol.

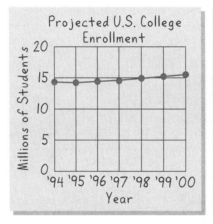

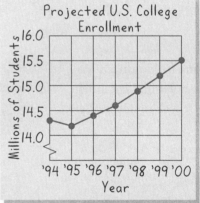

3. **Look Back** From which graph is it easier to read each year's enrollment? Explain.

4. Which graph shows the trend in enrollment more clearly? Why?

5. ✔ **Try It Out** Display the data shown below in a bar graph that uses a break symbol. First, plan the scale that you will use.

Number of Books Sold Annually

Year	1990	1991	1992	1993	1994
Books (millions)	2,005	2,040	2,041	2,079	2,127

Source: Book Industry Study Group, Inc.

Old Faithful Geyser in
Yellowstone National Park

Work Together
Creating Graphs to Tell a Story

Work in your group, using the data given below.

Visits to National Parks

Year	1991	1992	1993	1994	1995
Visits (millions)	267.8	274.7	273.1	268.6	269.6

Source: National Park Service

6. You want to write to Congress about the National Park Service. Create one graph that gives the visual impression of a large annual change in the number of visitors.

7. **Visual Thinking** Create a second graph that gives the impression of modest change.

8. Compare your graphs. From which graph can you make more accurate estimates of the number of visitors each year?

EXERCISES *On Your Own*

Use the graph at the right for Exercises 1–3.

1. **a.** Which magazine appears to have about twice the circulation of *Happy Homes and Gardens?*
   b. Which magazine actually has about twice the circulation of *Happy Homes and Gardens?*

2. **Writing** Explain why the graph gives a misleading visual impression of the data.

3. Redraw the graph to give an accurate impression of the data.

Circulation of Four Magazines

Happy Homes and Gardens
Geographic Life
Show Guide
Reader's World

7 8 9 10 11 12 13 14 15 16
Circulation (millions)

4. **Sports** Use the data below to create a bar graph that gives the visual impression that Pete Sampras earned many times more money than Andre Agassi and Steffi Graf.

1995 Professional Tennis Winnings

Pete Sampras	Andre Agassi	Steffi Graf
$5,415,066	$2,975,738	$2,538,620

Source: *Information Please Sports Almanac*

5. Using the data at the right, make a line graph that shows how the recycling rate has varied. Use a break symbol.

6. a. *Health* The graph below gives the impression that the percent of adult men who smoke has decreased to less than half the percent it was in 1970. Why is this impression incorrect?
   b. In 1994, was the percent of women who smoke about half the percent of men who smoke? Explain.
   c. Redraw the graph to give a more accurate impression of the data.

Recycling of Soft Drink Containers

Year	Percent Recycled
1990	52.4%
1991	54.1%
1992	60.0%
1993	57.6%
1994	60.6%
1995	57.4%

Source: National Soft Drink Association

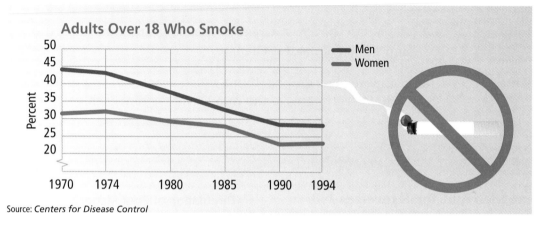

Source: *Centers for Disease Control*

Mixed Review

Use the data from the table at the right. *(Lesson 1-1)*

7. What type of graph would be best to compare the calories used during these activities?

8. Draw a graph to display the data.

Calories Burned During Activity

Sleeping	1 cal/min
Walking	5 cal/min
Swimming	8 cal/min
Running	10 cal/min

Estimate. Then find each answer. *(Previous course)*

9. $374 + 213 + 875$ 10. $124 - 76 + 236$ 11. $8 \times (93 - 44)$

CHAPTER PROJECT

PROJECT LINK: ANALYZING DATA

Find a graph that appears in an article or advertisement. If the graph is misleading, explain why it is. Then redraw it so it is not misleading. If it is not misleading, redraw it so that it is. Explain why it might be misinterpreted by someone.

Choose the best answer.

1. In 1994, there were 133,929,661 automobiles registered in the United States. What is this number rounded to the nearest hundred thousand?

   A. 130,000,000   **B.** 133,900,000
   C. 133,930,000   **D.** 134,000,000

Use the data below in Exercises 2 and 3.

Average Amount of Rain in July in Selected U.S. Cities

Atlanta, 4.7 in.	El Paso, 1.6 in.
Houston, 3.3 in.	Las Vegas, 0.5 in.
Miami, 6.0 in.	New York, 3.8 in.

2. If you were to list the three cities that get the least amount of rain in order from least to greatest, which cities would you choose?

   F. Las Vegas, El Paso, New York
   G. Las Vegas, El Paso, Houston
   H. Miami, Atlanta, New York
   J. Atlanta, Houston, Miami

3. To the nearest tenth of an inch, what is the average (mean) amount of rain for July for the six cities?

   A. 3.3   **B.** 3.5   **C.** 3.6   **D.** 5.5

4. How many students have 2 or more pets?

Pets in Students' Homes

Number of Pets	0	1	2	3	More than 3
Number of Students	11	16	9	11	6

   F. 6   **G.** 9   **H.** 26   **J.** 53

5. In a game, you get two points when the spinner lands on an odd number and no points for an even number. What is the probability that you will get two points on your next turn?

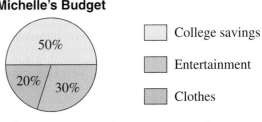

   A. $\frac{1}{8}$ **B.** $\frac{3}{8}$ **C.** $\frac{1}{2}$ **D.** $\frac{5}{8}$

Please note that items 6 and 7 have *five* answer choices.

6. Michelle receives $150 per month from a part-time job. This month, she bought a $50 sweater. By how much did she exceed her clothing budget this month?

Michelle's Budget

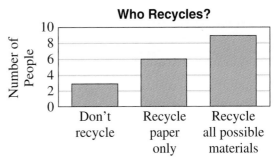

College savings

Entertainment

Clothes

   F. $20   **G.** $25   **H.** $30
   J. $50   **K.** $100

7. Room 201 collected data about recycling. How many people did they survey?

Who Recycles?

   A. 6   **B.** 9   **C.** 18
   D. 20   **E.** Not Here

What You'll Learn

▼1 To display frequency in a table or a line plot

▼2 To make a histogram using intervals

...And Why

You can use a histogram to summarize how often data items occur.

Here's How

Look for questions that
- build understanding
- ✔ check understanding

The great glory of American democracy is the right to protest for right.

The Rev. Martin Luther King, Jr. (1929–1968)

Work Together
Decoding a Message

QCF FJDXF CJR XJWZFZ.

1. Work with a partner. Use the hints below to break the coded message shown above. The message was spoken by astronaut Neil Armstrong from the moon on July 20, 1969.

- The letter that occurs most often represents *e*.
- The letter that occurs next most often represents *a*.
- The letters that represent *d, h*, and *l* each occur twice.
- The letters that represent *g, n, s*, and *t* each occur once.

THINK AND DISCUSS

▼1 *Making a Frequency Table or a Line Plot*

In breaking a coded message, an important clue is how often each letter occurs. The number of times a data item occurs is the **frequency** of the item. A **frequency table** lists each data item with its frequency.

■ EXAMPLE 1

Use the quotation at the left. Make a frequency table for the vowels that occur.

Make a tally mark for each vowel.

Letter	Tally	Frequency
a	||||	4
e	⁙||	6
i	||||	4
o	⁙||	6
u		0

The number of tally marks in each row is the frequency.

To display data in a **line plot,** place an ✗ for each response along a number line.

EXAMPLE 2

Human Body Temperatures (°F)

98, 98, 99, 97, 98, 96, 99, 98, 97, 100, 99, 98, 99

Make a line plot for the data shown at the left.

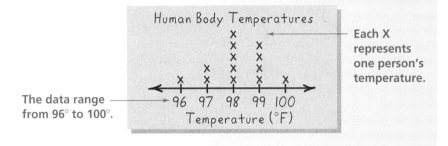

Human Body Temperatures

Each X represents one person's temperature.

The data range from 96° to 100°.

2. ✔ *Try It Out* Make a line plot for these cat body temperatures (°F): 101, 102, 101, 100, 102, 103, 102, 101, 101, 104, 101.

▼2 *Making a Histogram*

In making a frequency table, you sometimes group numerical data into intervals of equal size that do not overlap. This is helpful when there are many different values in the data.

EXAMPLE 3 *Real-World Problem Solving*

Hours of Battery Life

12, 9, 10, 14, 10, 11, 10, 18, 21, 10, 14, 22

Energy *Dynamath* and *Scholastic Math* magazines measured the battery life for different brands of portable stereos and CD players. Make a frequency table for the data shown at the left. Use intervals.

The data range from 9 to 22. Use equal-size intervals that begin with multiples of 5.

Battery Life		
Hours	Tally	Frequency
5–9	I	1
10–14	IIII III	8
15–19	I	1
20–24	II	2

3. a. ⁘*Analyze* Are the intervals 8−12, 13−15, 16−19, and 20−24 appropiate for the data in Example 3? Explain.
   b. Are the intervals 1−12 and 12−23 appropriate? Explain.
   c. Choose some new intervals that are appropriate for the data.

A **histogram** is a special type of bar graph used to show the frequency of data. In a histogram, there are no spaces between bars. The height of each bar gives the frequency of the data.

■ **EXAMPLE 4**

Make a histogram for the data from Example 3.

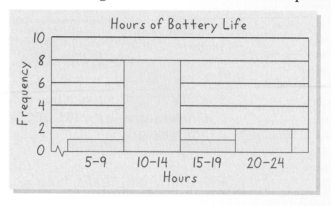

4. ■*Look Back* In the histogram above, which interval has the greatest frequency? In a sentence, describe what the bar for this interval represents.

5. ✔ *Try It Out* Use the data in Example 3. Choose equal-size intervals that are different from those in the Example. Use the intervals to make a frequency table and a histogram.

Make a line plot for each data set. Do not use intervals.

1. grades on a quiz: 90 95 90 70 85 80 100 95 80 85 90 75

2. cookies in a pound: 19 20 20 19 21 20 19 23 20 19 21 22 21 21 19 20 22 21 21

3. cost of a movie: $5.00, $6.00, $5.50, $7.00, $5.50, $7.00, $7.00, $7.50, $6.00, $5.00

4. hours spent on homework each night: 2 2 3 1 1 2 0 3 2 0 4 2 1 3 1 3 1 4 2 2

5. While shopping for school supplies, José compared the prices of binders. The prices he found are shown at the right.

   Prices for Binders
   $2.25, $3.89, $3.50, $7.49, $7.79, $3.69, $4.29, $2.49, $2.29

   a. Make a frequency table. Use intervals such as $2.00–$2.99.
   b. Use your frequency table to draw a histogram.
   c. José does not want to spend over $5.00 for a binder. He does not like the quality of the least expensive binders. In what price range(s) should he look? Explain.

15 KM INDIVIDUAL WOMAN

6. *Sports* Purnell says that the table of data at the right is a frequency table. Do you agree? Explain.

7. *Number Sense* Write the intervals described.
   a. intervals that begin with multiples of 5 for data that range from 17 to 43
   b. intervals that end with multiples of 10 for data that range from 58 to 100

8. **Choose A, B, C, or D.** Which intervals are appropriate for grouping data?

   A. 0–10, 10–20, 20–30   **B.** 0–10, 11–20, 21–29
   C. 1–10, 11–20, 21–30   **D.** 1–7, 8–18, 19–30

Distribution of Gold Medals 1994 Winter Olympics

Country	Medals
Russia	11
Norway	10
Germany	9
Italy	7
United States	6
South Korea	4
Austria	3
Canada	3
Sweden	2
Switzerland	2
Japan	1
Kazakhstan	1
Ukraine	1
Uzbekistan	1

Source: *U.S. Olympic Committee*

For each set of data in Exercises 9–11, choose intervals of equal size to group the data. Then make a frequency table and a histogram for the data.

9. ages of the members of the Seniors Hiking Club: 58 73 80 66 67 59 60 73 76 82 78 78 60 57 75 62

10. televisions sold at an appliance store each day: 7 8 9 13 14 18 5 9 11 16 5 6 14 12 10 9 7 9 2 21

11. grades on a test: 98, 83, 100, 94, 76, 87, 94, 62, 85, 73, 91, 89

12. a. *Transportation* Using intervals, make a frequency table of the number of cars per 100 people in selected parts of the world.
    b. Display the data in a histogram.

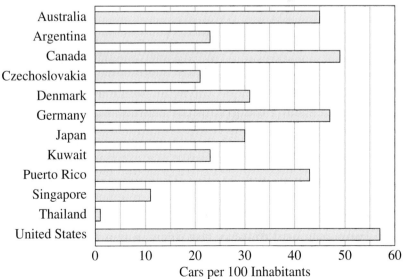

Who's On the Road?

Cars per 100 Inhabitants

Source: American Automobile Manufacturers Association

13. **a.** In the histogram shown at the right, which interval has the greatest frequency?
    b. How many students participated in the Read-a-thon?
    c. Estimate the total number of books read from the histogram.

14. *Writing* How will the appearance of a histogram change if you choose many small intervals instead of a few large intervals?

15. *Research* Choose a famous quotation of between 10 and 20 words. Make a frequency table for the occurrence of vowels.

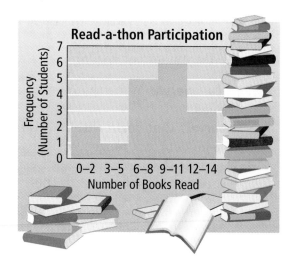

Read-a-thon Participation

Frequency (Number of Students) vs. Number of Books Read

0–2 3–5 6–8 9–11 12–14

Mixed Review

Use the data shown at the right. *(Lesson 1-2)*

Indianapolis 500 Winning Speeds

Driver	Speed (mi/h)
Arie Luyendyk (1990)	186.0
Rick Mears (1991)	176.5
Emerson Fittipaldi (1989)	167.6
Rick Mears (1984)	163.6

Source: Indianapolis Motor Speedway

16. Draw a graph that appears to make the fastest winning speed seem even faster when compared to the other speeds.

17. Redraw the graph to give a more accurate visual impression of the data.

Find each answer. *(Previous course)*

18. 18×4 **19.** 18×40 **20.** 180×400 **21.** $12,500 \div 25$ **22.** $40,000 \div 500$

✓ CHECKPOINT 1

Lessons 1-1 through 1-3

1. Use the data in the table at the right. Make a stacked bar graph and a sliding bar graph. Use one bar for each activity.

2. *Open-ended* Use these daily high temperatures (°F): 76, 83, 85, 79, 93, 88, 78. Decide how to present the data in a graph to show changes from day to day. Then draw the graph.

Weekly Leisure Time

Activity	Tobi	Ann
Reading	10 h	8 h
Listening to music	12 h	4 h
Sports	6 h	12 h

Below are the scores on a math test. For Exercises 3 and 4, choose intervals and display the data in the forms listed.

93 75 87 83 99 75 80 90 72 77 95 98 82 87 100 91 68

3. a frequency table   4. a histogram

Estimation Strategies

Before Lesson 1-4

When you make a *front-end estimate,* use only the digits having the largest place value. By *adjusting,* you can make a front-end estimate more accurate.

■ EXAMPLE 1

Estimate. Use front-end estimation with adjusting.

$6.79
  5.53
   .98
+ 3.49

$6 + $5 + $3 = $14 ← front-end estimate
$.79 + $.98 ≈ $2 ← adjustments
$.53 + $.49 ≈ $1
               $17 ← total estimate

∟ front-end digits

When the numbers in a sum are close to each other, you can use *clustering* to estimate the answer.

■ EXAMPLE 2

Estimate. Use clustering.

$$43,781 + 34,384 + 41,560 + 44,703 + 38,327$$

     All the numbers are near 40,000.

$$40,000 \times 5 = 200,000$$

Estimate. Use front-end estimation with adjusting.

1. 622	**2.** 7,935	**3.** 9,318	**4.** $8.39	**5.** $40.40	**6.** $6.77
802	1,516	2,504	4.65	19.53	1.94
575	1,704	809	2.19	1.68	3.62
957	+ 3,719	5,441	.79	9.79	+ 8.25
+ 132		+ 139	+ 6.85	+ 16.38	

Estimate. Use clustering.

7. $254 + 389 + 295 + 311$

8. $8,302 + 7,197 + 8,750 + 7,930$

9. $49 + 38 + 42 + 39 + 32 + 41 + 35$

10. $612 + 622 + 560 + 667 + 522 + 589$

11. $8 + 7 + 5 + 7 + 6 + 8 + 9 + 7$

12. $44,569 + 53,056 + 47,191$

13. $1,673 + 2,767 + 2,160 + 1,411$

14. $975 + 1,054 + 982 + 1,120 + 893 + 960$

Measures of Central Tendency

What You'll Learn

▼ ① To find measures of central tendency

▼ ② To choose the best measure of central tendency

...And Why

Meteorologists use the mean, the median, and the mode to describe weather patterns.

Here's How

Look for questions that
- ⊞ build understanding
- ✔ check understanding

Work Together

Analyzing Data

1. The data below show the shoe sizes for nine members of a basketball team. Make a line plot of the data.

   $$10 \quad 9 \quad 7\frac{1}{2} \quad 10 \quad 10 \quad 11 \quad 8\frac{1}{2} \quad 5 \quad 9$$

2. ⊞ **Data Analysis** Which shoe size occurs most often?

3. List the shoe sizes in order from least to greatest. Which size occurs in the middle of the list?

4. Add the shoe sizes in the data and divide the sum by nine. Does your answer represent a shoe size? Explain.

5. ⊞ **Think About It** Describe the "typical" shoe size for the athletes on the team. Explain your answer.

THINK AND DISCUSS

① Finding Measures of Central Tendency

The statistics mean, median, and mode are **measures of central tendency.** Consider the data in this set: 2, 3, 5, 7, 8, 8, 9.

2 3 5 7 **8 8** 9

The **mode** is the data item with the greatest frequency.

2 3 5 **7** 8 8 9

The **median** is the middle value when the data are in numerical order.

$2 + 3 + 5 + 7 + 8 + 8 + 9 = 42$

$\frac{42}{7} = 6$

mean $= \dfrac{\text{sum of the data}}{\text{total number of data items}}$

Typical Daily Temperature in San Francisco

Month	Temperature
January	49
February	52
March	53
April	56
May	58
June	62
July	63
August	64
September	64
October	61
November	55
December	49

Source: U.S. National Oceanic and Atmospheric Administration

■ **EXAMPLE 1**   *Real-World Problem Solving*

Weather Find (a) the mean, (b) the median, and (c) the mode of the temperature data shown at the left.

a. To find the mean, add the temperatures, then divide by 12.

686 ⊟ 12 ⊟ *57.16666667*

The mean is about 57.2.

b. To find the median, arrange the data in numerical order.

49 49 52 53 55 56 58 61 62 63 64 64

$\dfrac{56 + 58}{2} = 57$ ⟵ Since there are an even number of data items, add the two middle values and divide by 2.

The median is 57.

c. To find the mode, look for the number that occurs with the greatest frequency. Two numbers, 49 and 64, are listed twice. Therefore, there are two modes, 49 and 64.

6. ✔ *Try It Out* Find the mean, median, and mode of the data.
a. 3 4 5 5 6 7   **b.** 1 3 3 5 6 12

2 *Choosing the Best Measure*

Taisha's Juice Stand hires students for the summer. Taisha says the average hourly wage is $6.50. Some students disagree. They say most students make an hourly wage of $5.25. Here are the students' hourly wages in dollars.

5.25   5.25   5.25   5.25   5.25   6.00   6.00

6.00   6.25   7.00   7.00   7.00   13.00

7. ⬝⬝*Analyze* Which measure of central tendency are the students using to describe the data? Which is Taisha using?

8. Find the value of a third measure of central tendency that you could use to describe the data.

9. The student manager makes $13.00 per hour. She leaves and is replaced by a student who makes $7.00 per hour.
a. *Calculator* Find the new mean, median, and mode.
b. ⬝⬝*Reasoning* How does the change in this one data item affect the mean, median, and mode?

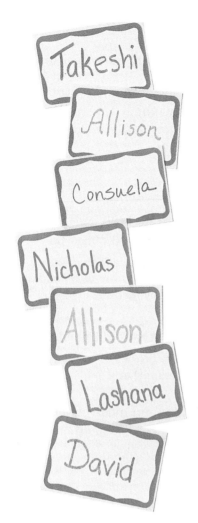

The mode of these names is
Allison.

If one data item is much higher or lower than the rest of the data, it is called an **outlier.** The $13.00 hourly rate is an example of an outlier. Outliers can have a big effect on the mean of the data, making the mean a poor representation of the data's center.

The median is not affected by an outlier, since half of the data are above the median and half of the data are below it.

Sometimes your data may not be numerical. If you ask seven people for their first names, the set of names is your data. Use the mode to describe the central tendency of nonnumerical data.

■ **EXAMPLE 2** *Real-World Problem Solving*

Is the mean, median, or mode the best measure of central tendency for each situation? Explain.

a. the favorite music video of your class

Mode; use the mode when the data are not numerical, or to identify the most popular item.

b. the ages of the students in your class

Mean or median; use the mean when there are no outliers to affect it.

c. the number of days absent from school

Median; use the median when an outlier may have too much influence on the mean. One student may have a high number of absences.

EXERCISES *On Your Own*

▦ *Choose* **Use a calculator, pencil and paper, or mental math. Find the mean, median, and mode of each of the following.**

1. hits per game
   0 0 0 0 1 1 2 2 3

2. test scores
   70   80   84   90   92   100

3. cost of lunch ($)
   1.25   1.75   1.25   1.75   1.35   1.25   1.75

4. hours of sleep
   7   8   8   9   9   9   9   10   10

5. a. Explain how each data set at the right has a mean of 8.
   b. Complete the data set 5, 6, 9, 10, ▩ so that the mean is 8.

   Set 1: 5, 5, 8, 11, 11
   Set 2: 7, 7, 7, 7, 12
   Set 3: −2, 0, 6, 18, 18

6. *Entertainment* The *Student News* rates movies by giving them one to five stars. Find the mean, median, and mode of the ratings data in the line plot at the right.

7. Choose A, B, or C. What is the best measure of central tendency for these typing rates (in words per minute)?
20 23 15 16 25 60 19
A. mean   **B.** median   **C.** mode

8. *Open-ended* Write a data set for which the mean, the median, and the mode are the same.

This Week's
Student News
Movie Ratings

What is the best measure of central tendency for each type of data? Explain.

9. allowance

10. favorite cereal

11. hours in school each day

12. spelling test scores

13. eye color

14. new car cost

15. *Writing* Describe situations in which one measure of central tendency is the most appropriate. Include one situation using the mean, one using the median, and one using the mode.

16. *Reasoning* You have one more math test. Here are your present scores: 89, 92, 78, 83, and 83.
a. What score must you get to raise the mean to 87?
b. What score must you get to raise the median to 85?

Mixed Review

Use the following data: 31, 28, 31, 30, 31, 30, 31, 31, 30, 31, 30, 31. *(Lesson 1-3)*

17. Make a frequency table.   **18.** Draw a line plot.   **19.** Draw a histogram.

20. Rob's heart rate is 72 beats/min. About how many beats per week is this? *(Previous course)*

CHAPTER PROJECT

PROJECT LINK: GATHERING DATA

Choose a topic that interests you, such as a sport or an environmental issue. Use an almanac or other resource to find data about your topic that you can graph. Write a news article for the data you have found.

Stem-and-Leaf Plots

What You'll Learn

▼ ① To make stem-and-leaf plots

▼ ② To use stem-and-leaf plots

...And Why

You can use a stem-and-leaf plot to arrange data visually.

Here's How

Look for questions that
- ⚏ build understanding
- ✔ check understanding

Percent of People Who Speak a Language Other Than English at Home

State	Percent
Connecticut	15
Massachusetts	15
Maine	9
New Hampshire	9
New Jersey	20
New York	23
Pennsylvania	7
Rhode Island	17
Vermont	6

Source: U.S. Census Bureau

THINK AND DISCUSS

① Making Stem-and-Leaf Plots

Do you speak a language other than English when you are at home? Have you ever wondered how many people do?

Look at the table at the left below. Using a stem-and-leaf plot can make working with the data easier. A **stem-and-leaf plot** shows data items in order. The choice of stems and leaves depends upon the type of data.

■ **EXAMPLE 1** *Real-World Problem Solving*

Make a stem-and-leaf plot for the data in the table at the left.

Step 1 Choose the stems. Look at the tens' place of the greatest and least numbers. The greatest value is 23; the least value is 6. Use stems 0, 1, and 2 to represent the tens' places.

stems   leaves

Step 2
```
0 | 6 7 9 9    ← The leaves are the ones' digits,
1 | 5 5 7        written in increasing order.
2 | 0 3
```
1 | 5 means 15 ← The key explains what the stems and leaves represent.

1. ⚏ **Look Back** What state is represented by the data with stem 0 and leaf 7? With stem 2 and leaf 0?

2. Why are there two 5's as leaves with the stem 1?

A stem can be more than one digit. It can be any number that helps you to organize your data. A leaf is usually one digit.

3. ✔ *Try It Out* Make a stem-and-leaf plot for the monthly record high temperatures in Death Valley, California. (*Hint:* Use the key "12|5 means 125.")

   87   91   101   111   120   125   134   126   120   113   97   86

❷ *Using Stem-and-Leaf Plots*

Because a stem-and-leaf plot displays data items in numerical order, it is easy to find the mode and the median.

■ **EXAMPLE 2**   *Real-World Problem Solving*

Sports Find the mode and the median of the finishing times (in seconds) for the 100-meter dash at a recent track meet.

```
13 | 6 7 9 9  ←  The 9's represent repeated leaves.
14 | 2 8          Use them for the mode.
15 | 2 7
                  There are eight times shown. Use the
                  fourth and fifth times for the median.
     13 | 6 means 13.6
```

The mode is 13.9 seconds. To find the median, average the two middle scores, 13.9 and 14.2. The median is 14.05 seconds.

The **range** of a set of numerical data is the difference between the greatest and least values in the set. You can use it with the mean, median, or mode to give a better picture of the data set.

4. ⬛*Data Analysis* Find the range of the data in Example 2.

EXERCISES *On Your Own*

Use this stem-and-leaf plot for Exercises 1–5.

```
20 | 0 0 0 7
21 | 2 3 3 6 9
22 |
23 | 2 7
     21 | 9 means 21.9
```

1. What numbers make up the stems?

2. What are the leaves for the first stem?

3. How many data items are shown in the stem-and-leaf plot?

4. Find the median, the mode, and the range.

5. *Reasoning* Suppose the key showed that 21|9 means 219. How would this change the median, the mode, and the range?

6. Recycling Make a stem-and-leaf plot for the data at the right.

Make a stem-and-leaf plot for each set of data.

7. 6 13 30 2 27 17 19 13 24 35 27 26 18 32 9

8. 3.7 5.0 6.9 3.2 4.5 6.3 6.7 5.8 5.2 6.9 5.0 4.3

Make a stem-and-leaf plot for each set of data, then find the median, the mode, and the range.

9. golf scores: 87 82 70 83 75 79 68 87 77 82 78 75

10. annual snowfall (inches): 38 77 56 38 40 29 45 32
47 45 51 24 36 58 45

Top 10 Cities in Recycling

City	Percent Recycled
Honolulu, Hi.	72
Jacksonville, Fla.	35
Los Angeles, Calif.	20
Minneapolis, Minn.	27
Newark, N.J.	51
Portland, Oreg.	38
St. Paul, Minn.	39
Seattle, Wash.	40
Virginia Beach, Va.	22
Washington, D.C.	20

Cars **A back-to-back stem-and-leaf plot compares two sets of data. Use the back-to-back plot at the right for Exercises 11–14.**

11. Find the range for highway driving.

12. Find the mode for city driving.

13. Which has the greater median, city driving or highway driving?

14. *Reasoning* Find the mean for highway driving. Explain your method.

15. *Writing* A set of data contains numbers in the 30's, 40's and 60's only. Is it necessary to put a 5 on the stem of a stem-and-leaf plot? Write a sentence justifying your answer.

New Car Mileage (mi/gal)

```
  City           Highway
9 8 8 | 1 |
7 4 2 | 2 | 4 5 7 8
    0 | 3 | 3 3
      | 4 | 0
```
means 27 ←— 7 | 2 | 8 —→ means 28

JOURNAL
How is a stem-and-leaf plot like a histogram? How is it different?

Mixed Review

For Exercises 16–19, use the following data: 95 85 65 100 55 90 60 80 65 65 70 75 80 70 65 95. *(Lessons 1-3 and 1-4)*

16. Find the mean, median, and mode.

17. Write intervals to group the data.

18. Make a frequency table, using intervals.

19. Draw a histogram.

20. Mel bought three shirts for $9.95 each and one tape for $5.75. How much change did he receive from $40? *(Previous course)*

Average Amount Spent by Visitors to the United States (dollars per person)

Country	Amount
Australia	2,279
Canada	330
France	1,703
Germany	1,778
Italy	1,973
Japan	2,381
Mexico	592
Netherlands	1,422
New Zealand	2,181
United Kingdom	1,596
Other countries	1,038

Source: *The World Almanac*

THINK AND DISCUSS

1 *Making Box-and-Whisker Plots*

A **box-and-whisker plot** shows the distribution of data along a number line.

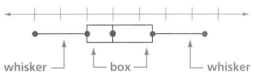

whisker — └ box ┘ — whisker

To make a box-and-whisker plot, you use values called quartiles. **Quartiles** divide the data into four equal parts. They are related to medians, which divide data into two equal parts.

330 592 **1038** 1422 1596 **1703** 1778 1973 **2181** 2279 2381

| lower quartile (median of the *lower half* of the data) | middle quartile (median of *all* the data) | upper quartile (median of the *upper half* of the data) |

■ **EXAMPLE 1**   *Real-World Problem Solving*

Travel Make a box-and-whisker plot for the travel data.

Step 1 Use a number line. Mark the least value and the greatest value. Then mark the quartiles.

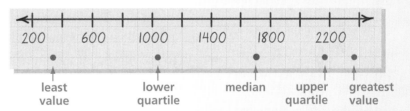

least value | lower quartile | median | upper quartile | greatest value

Step 2 Draw a box from the lower quartile to the upper quartile. Mark the median value with a vertical segment. Draw whiskers from the box to the least and greatest values.

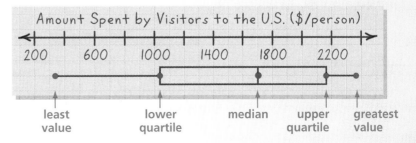

Amount Spent by Visitors to the U.S. ($/person)

least value | lower quartile | median | upper quartile | greatest value

1. **⚫Think About It** By looking at a box-and-whisker plot, can you determine the mean? The median? The mode? The range?

▼❷ *Comparing Two Sets of Data*

Box-and-whisker plots do not display every piece of data. Because they summarize data, box-and-whisker plots are useful with very large data sets or for making comparisons between data sets.

■ **EXAMPLE 2**   *Real-World Problem Solving*

Shopping The box-and-whisker plots below show prices for selected items at two clothing stores. Compare the data.

Clothing Prices ($)

Mall Store

Discount Store

Prices at the discount store are more tightly grouped around the median price of $25, with half the items costing about $18 to $35. At the mall store, the median price is about $32, with half the items costing $18 to $45.

For less-expensive items, there is not much difference in the prices at the two stores. For more-expensive items, the discount store offers lower prices.

2. **✔ Try It Out** The data below show students' heights in inches. Make two box-and-whisker plots. Then compare the data.

    Girls: 58 62 63 60 60 59 63 56 61 61

    Boys: 65 63 59 61 62 60 64 65 59 63

Work Together   *Collecting and Displaying Data*

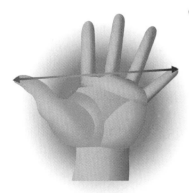

3. Measure the span of your hand to the nearest half centimeter. Record the measurement for each group member, making separate lists for boys and for girls. Combine data with other groups to make lists for the whole class.

4. **⚫Data Analysis** Make a box-and-whisker plot displaying boys' data and another displaying girls' data. Use the plots to compare the sets of data.

EXERCISES *On Your Own*

Use the box-and-whisker plot below to find each of the following.

Test Scores

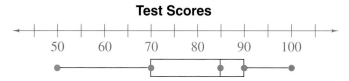

1. the median
2. the lower quartile
3. the upper quartile
4. the highest score
5. the lowest score
6. the range

7. Suppose you have an even number of data items in the lower half of your data. Describe how to find the lower quartile.

8. Make a box-and-whisker plot for the Daytona 500 data shown in the table at the right.

Average Speed of Daytona 500 Winners

Year	Speed (mi/h)
1986	148
1987	176
1988	138
1989	148
1990	166
1991	148
1992	160
1993	155
1994	157
1995	142
1996	154

Source: *The Universal Almanac*

For Exercises 9–12, refer to data and the box-and-whisker plot found in Example 1 on page 27.

9. When a box-and-whisker plot has a long box like the one shown in the Example, what do you know about the data?

10. Would the box change if the numbers 2,279 and 2,381 were replaced by greater numbers? Explain.

11. Why is the median not exactly in the middle of the box?

12. Does the box-and-whisker plot tell you how many pieces of data are included? Explain.

13. *Nature* The box-and-whisker plots below show speeds of the ten fastest fish and mammals. Compare the sets of data.

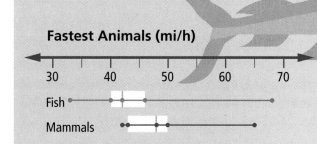

Writing For Exercises 14 and 15, make a box-and-whisker plot for each set of data. Use a single number line. Write a paragraph comparing the two sets of data.

14.
Home Runs Hit by League Leaders (1996 Season)

American League	52	50	49	48	47	44	44	40	39	39
National League	47	42	42	41	40	40	40	40	36	36

15.
Median Age at First Marriage (Census Years 1910–1990)

Women	21.6	21.2	21.3	21.5	20.3	20.3	20.8	22.0	23.9
Men	25.1	24.6	24.3	24.3	22.8	22.8	23.2	24.7	25.9

16. *Open-ended* Write two different sets of data that have identical box-and-whisker plots.

17. **Choose A, B, or C.** Identify the box-and-whisker plot for the data given below.

70 76 80 74 78 56 86 80 80 81 40 75 98 101 103

A. 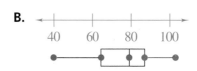 B. C.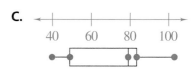

18. *Research* Gather data on a topic of your choice. Make a box-and-whisker plot to display the data. Write a paragraph to interpret the data that you find.

Mixed Review

For Exercises 19–24, use the following data: 31, 45, 50, 52, 45, 32, 33, 45, 50, 38.

19. Make a stem-and-leaf plot. *(Lesson 1-5)*   20. Find the range. *(Lesson 1-5)*

21. Find the median. *(Lesson 1-4)*   22. Find the mode. *(Lesson 1-4)*

23. Make a frequency table. *(Lesson 1-3)*   24. Make a line plot. *(Lesson 1-3)*

25. A town with a population of 28,000 people discards an average of 4 lb of waste per person each day. About how many tons of waste does the town discard in a week? *(Previous course)*

Graphing Data

Before Lesson 1-7 ➡

You can use a spreadsheet program to create many types of graphs. First, enter the category labels and the data in a spreadsheet.

■ EXAMPLE

Enter the data as shown at the right. Use the spreadsheet program to create a graph.

	A	B	C
1		Discount Price	List Price
2	Stereo	$178	$229
3	Television	$224	$299
4	CD Player	$119	$160

A spreadsheet has no title.

Row 2 contains prices for stereos.

Cell B3 contains the discount price for a television.

Column A contains the items being compared.

After entering the data, you will need to pick an appropriate type of graph. Choose from among those that your spreadsheet program can create. A double bar graph is an appropriate way to display these data.

Enter each set of data in a spreadsheet. Create a graph.

1. the data in the Example above

2. **Annual Spending per Child by Middle Income Families (1994)**

Age of Child	1	4	7	10	13	16
Amount Spent (dollars)	7,070	7,460	7,660	7,160	7,590	8,500

Source: U.S. Department of Agriculture

3. *Writing* What types of graphs are there in your spreadsheet program? Which types are appropriate to display the data in each exercise above? Explain.

1-7 Making Predictions from Scatter Plots

What You'll Learn

▼ To make scatter plots
▼ To use scatter plots to find trends

...And Why

A scatter plot can reveal trends in data and help you make predictions.

Here's How

Look for questions that
- build understanding
✔ check understanding

THINK AND DISCUSS

▼ Making Scatter Plots

Does the length across your outstretched arms have anything to do with your height?

A scatter plot can help you decide whether one thing is related to another. In a **scatter plot,** related data from two different sets are graphed as points.

■ EXAMPLE 1

Make a scatter plot for the data in the spreadsheet below.

	A	B	C
1	Name	Height (cm)	Arm Span (cm)
2	Manuel	192	191
3	Bridget	157	160
4	Chantrell	176	180
5	Rosa	158	156
6	Miyoko	142	147
7	George	170	168

Step 1 Use graph paper. Choose a scale along one axis to represent height measurements. Choose a scale along the other axis to represent arm-span measurements.

Step 2 Plot each data pair.

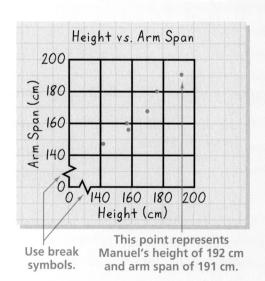

Use break symbols.

This point represents Manuel's height of 192 cm and arm span of 191 cm.

2 Using Scatter Plots to Find Trends

The data on height and arm span are related. As height increases, so does arm span.

To show a trend, draw a **trend line** that closely fits the data points in the scatter plot.

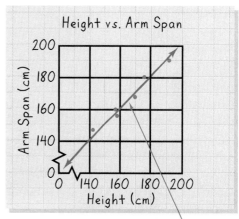

Height vs. Arm Span

About as many points should be above the trend line as below it.

■ **EXAMPLE 2** *Real-World Problem Solving*

Weather Use the scatter plot and trend line shown below.

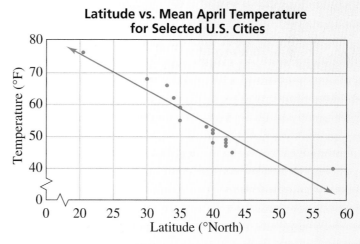

Latitude vs. Mean April Temperature for Selected U.S. Cities

a. Describe the trend in the data.

As the latitude of the city increases, the mean April temperature decreases.

b. Predict the mean April temperature for a city at 25° north latitude.

Find 25° along the horizontal axis. At 25° north latitude, the trend line seems to go through the 70°F mark. The mean April temperature should be near 70°F.

1. ⣿ **Draw a Conclusion** Do you think that predictions made from a trend line will always be accurate? Why or why not?

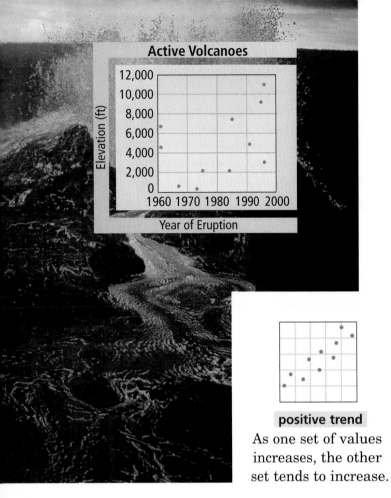

Active Volcanoes

Elevation (ft) vs. Year of Eruption

2. ♣ *Go a Step Further* Use the scatter plot at the left.
   a. Does this scatter plot show a clear trend? Explain.
   b. Does it make sense to try to fit a line to the data points? Why or why not?

The next three scatter plots summarize the types of relationships two sets of data may have.

positive trend
As one set of values increases, the other set tends to increase.

negative trend
As one set of values increases, the other set tends to decrease.

no trend
The points show no relationship.

3. ✔ *Try It Out* Do the data in Example 2 on page 33 show a positive trend, a negative trend, or no trend? Explain.

Work Together
Analyzing Trends in Data

4. ♣ *Data Collection* Estimate the number of hours you slept last night and the number of minutes of homework you did yesterday. Collect the same data from other students. Make a scatter plot of the data. If there is a trend, draw a trend line.

EXERCISES *On Your Own*

Make a scatter plot for each of the following sets of data.

1. **Number of Roommates vs. Monthly Rent**

Roomates	3	2	3	2	4
Rent	$100	$180	$80	$145	$70

2. **Softball Game Results**

Hits	7	8	4	11	8	2	5	9	1	4
Runs	3	2	2	7	4	2	1	3	0	1

3. Cars Make a scatter plot for the data shown in the table at the right.

4. Data Collection Toss a coin 20 times. After each toss, record the total number of heads and tails to that point. For example, after 13 tosses, you might have 6 heads and 7 tails. Draw a scatter plot for the data pairs.

5. Use the scatter plot shown in Example 2 on page 33.
  a. Predict the mean April temperature for a city at 45° north latitude.
  b. Predict the latitude of a city having a mean April temperature of 60°F.

What's a Car Worth?
Average Value of a Mid-size Sedan

Age (yr)	Value ($)	Age (yr)	Value ($)
3	11,000	1	15,000
2	12,000	4	8,000
7	3,000	5	7,000
8	1,000	3	6,000
2	10,000	4	8,000
2	14,000	1	13,000

6. Sports Display the data below in a scatter plot. If there is a trend, draw a trend line.

Chicago Bulls 1997 NBA Championship Series

	Jordan	Pippen	Kukoc	Longley	Williams
Average Points per Game	32.3	20.0	9.3	6.8	5.5
Most Points in One Game	39	27	16	12	10

Source: National Basketball Association

Tell whether each scatter plot in the given Exercise shows a trend. If it does, draw a trend line.

7. the scatter plot in Exercise 1

8. the scatter plot in Exercise 2

9. the scatter plot in Exercise 3

10. the scatter plot in Exercise 4

Open-ended **What type of trend does each scatter plot show? Describe a real-world situation that each scatter plot could represent.**

11.
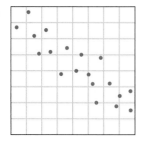

12.
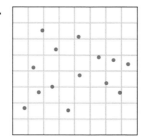

13.
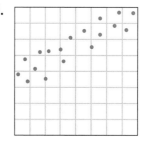

14. Farming Use the farm data at the right. Make a scatter plot showing the number of farms on one axis and the average number of acres on the other axis. If there is a trend, draw a trend line.

Writing For each topic described below, decide whether a scatter plot of data would be likely to show a positive trend, a negative trend, or no trend. Explain your choice.

15. grades and study time

16. age of owner and number of pets owned

17. outdoor temperature and layers of clothing

18. level of education and income (*Hint:* See graph on page 7.)

19. Choose A, B, or C. What kind of trend does the following statement describe? *As the mosquito population increases, the sale of insect repellent increases.*

    A. positive trend   **B.** negative trend   **C.** no trend

20. Reasoning As the number of women holding jobs increased, the record time in the women's 200-m run decreased. Does this negative trend mean that one set of data *caused* the other to occur? Explain.

Number and Size of U.S. Farms 1910–1990

Year	Number of Farms (thousands)	Average Size (acres)
1910	6,366	139
1920	6,454	149
1930	6,295	157
1940	6,102	175
1950	5,388	216
1960	3,962	297
1970	2,954	373
1980	2,440	426
1990	2,146	460

Source: *The Universal Almanac*

JOURNAL
What types of graphs can you use to represent two sets of data that are related to each other? Give examples. When is it appropriate to use a scatter plot?

Mixed Review

For Exercises 21 and 22, use the data on farms at the top of this page. (*Lesson 1-1*)

21. Make a line graph to display the number of farms for each year.

22. Make a sliding bar graph to display the number of farms and the average size of a farm. Use the years 1910, 1950, and 1990.

Estimate. Then find each answer. (*Previous course*)

23. 25% of 396   **24.** 10% of 841   **25.** 51% of 200   **26.** 33% of 89

27. 20% of 61   **28.** 74% of 80   **29.** 48% of 120   **30.** 68% of 305

Choosing an Appropriate Graph

What You'll Learn

▼ To read a circle graph

▼ To choose an appropriate graph for a set of data

...And Why

The right visual display of data will make your presentation of the data more effective.

Here's How

Look for questions that
- build understanding
- ✔ check understanding

THINK AND DISCUSS

▼ *Reading a Circle Graph*

Is rock music more popular than any other type? You can tell by looking at a circle graph that displays data about music sales. A **circle graph** shows parts of a whole. When the data are shown in percents, the total is 100%.

■ **EXAMPLE 1** *Real-World Problem Solving*

Music Use the circle graph. Which type of music had about one third of the sales?

Percent of 1995 Music Sales by Type

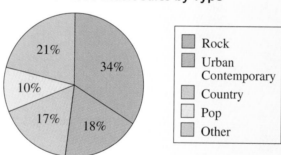

21%   34%

10%

17%   18%

☐ Rock
☐ Urban Contemporary
☐ Country
☐ Pop
☐ Other

Source: *Recording Industry Association of America*

Since $\frac{1}{3} \approx 33\%$, rock music, with 34% of the sales, had about one third of the sales.

1. ■ *Mental Math* Suppose the total of all music sales in 1995 was $12 billion. Estimate the sales for rock music.

2. ■ *Think About It* Explain why the graph at the right is not an appropriate display of data.

Graduation Rates for New Eng and

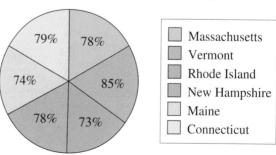

79%   78%

74%   85%

78%   73%

☐ Massachusetts
☐ Vermont
☐ Rhode Island
☐ New Hampshire
☐ Maine
☐ Connecticut

Make-up of 1995 School Enrollment

Age	Number Enrolled
5–6	7,901,000
7–9	11,555,000
10–13	15,448,000
14–15	7,651,000
16–17	6,997,000
18–19	4,274,000

Source: U.S. Department of Commerce

❷ *Choosing an Appropriate Graph*

Once you have gathered data, you must decide how to display them. The type of graph you choose depends on the type of data and the idea you want to communicate.

■ **EXAMPLE 2**   *Real-World Problem Solving*

Education Use the data at the left. Decide whether each type of graph is appropriate for the data. If it is appropriate, draw the graph.

a. a bar graph   **b.** a circle graph   **c.** a stem-and-leaf plot

a. It is easy to compare amounts on a bar graph.

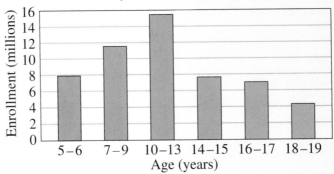

b. It is easy to see parts of a whole on a circle graph.

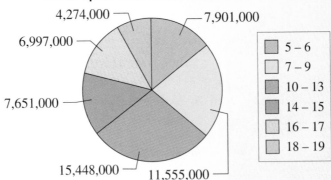

c. A stem-and-leaf plot is not appropriate. A stem-and-leaf plot would not show the age level for each number enrolled.

New England High School Graduation Rates

State	Percent Graduating
Massachusetts	78
Vermont	85
Rhode Island	73
New Hampshire	78
Maine	74
Connecticut	79

Source: U.S. Department of Education

3. ✔ *Try It Out* Explain whether each type of graph would be appropriate for the data at the left.

a. a bar graph   **b.** a line graph   **c.** a scatter plot

Work Together
Summarizing Types of Graphs

Here are the types of graphs you have studied in this chapter:

bar graph	histogram
stacked bar graph	stem-and-leaf plot
sliding bar graph	box-and-whisker plot
line graph	scatter plot
multiple line graph	circle graph
line plot	

  4. Use a spreadsheet program or note cards. Show an example for each type of graph. Then tell whether the graph is appropriate for each of the following.
  • to show frequency of data   • to show changes over time
  • to compare sets of data   • to show parts of a whole

EXERCISES *On Your Own*

Cars **Use the circle graph shown at the right.**

1. What category contains about half the cost?

2. What two categories are about equal in cost?

3. What category represents $\frac{1}{5}$ of the cost?

4. Suppose the cost of interest is $700 per year. Estimate the cost of a license and registration.

5. Suppose gas, oil, and maintenance cost $1100 per year. Estimate the total cost to own a car.

What You'll Spend on a Car

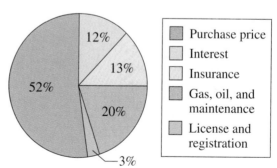

Source: American Automobile Manufacturers Association

Use the graph of Erika's budget shown at the right.

6. For what item does Erika budget twice as much as for recreation?

7. Suppose Erika earns $90 a month baby-sitting. How much of this does she budget for clothes?

Erika's Budget

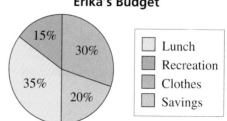

Decide which of the two types of graphs is an appropriate display for the data given. Explain your choice.

8. line graph or circle graph?
   percent of city dwellers in the United States each year from 1985 to 1999

9. histogram or scatter plot?
   inches of rain and the high temperature for each day in May

10. stem-and-leaf plot or circle graph?
    where people go on vacation

11. bar graph or scatter plot?
    life spans of selected animals

Decide which of the two types of graphs is an appropriate display for the data given. Then draw the graph.

12. circle graph or line graph?
    the personal computer data at the right

13. scatter plot or bar graph?

Temperature (°F)	55	57	63	68	70	73	80
Number of Students Wearing Jackets	10	11	8	5	4	2	0

14. bar graph or line graph?
    test scores: Amy, 93; Joy, 87; Tran, 91; Leah, 82; Jeb, 78

15. *Open-ended* Make a graph to illustrate the article below. Use a graph that compares two sets of data.

16. *Writing* Describe data you can collect that can be displayed in both a bar graph and a circle graph.

17. What type of graph should you choose when you have too much data to graph each data item, but you want to display the median and the highest and lowest data items?

Percent of U.S. Homes with Personal Computers

Year	Percent
1988	20
1989	21
1990	22
1991	25
1992	27
1993	30
1994	33
1995	37
1996	40

Source: Electronic Industries Association

How Do Americans Get to Work?

In 1990, 78% of Americans got to work by driving alone, 14% used a car pool, 5% used public transportation, and 3% used other methods such as walking or biking. But if they could choose the method they prefer, only 56% of Americans say they would drive to work alone. What would the rest do? 17% would choose to be in a car pool, 12% would like to use public transportation, and 15% would use other methods such as walking or biking.

Compare. Use <, >, or =. *(Previous course)*

18. 60% ▨ 50%   **19.** $\frac{1}{3}$ ▨ $\frac{1}{2}$ **20.** 0.4 ▨ 40%   **21.** $\frac{3}{4}$ ▨ 0.7

22. The value of certain business stocks is reported daily in the Dow Jones Average.
   a. Make a line graph that shows details of the data for a recent week shown at the right. Use a break symbol.
   b. Make a line graph for the data that does not use a break symbol. *(Lesson 1-2)*

Dow Jones Average

Day	Closing Value
Monday	7,604
Tuesday	7,758
Wednesday	7,690
Thursday	7,654
Friday	7,688

23. On Saturday the softball team practices at 9:00 A.M. It takes Jodie 35 min to get dressed and have breakfast, 1 h 25 min to do her paper route, and $\frac{3}{4}$ h to get from home to the field. For what time must Jodie set her alarm? *(Previous course)*

CHAPTER PROJECT

PROJECT LINK: PRESENTING DATA

How can you illustrate your news article? Decide on an appropriate graph to present the data you found on page 23. Use spreadsheet technology or other tools to make the graph.

✓ CHECKPOINT 2
Lessons 1-4 through 1-8

For Exercises 1–5, use the following data: 80, 83, 88, 88, 90, 106, 100, 101, 110, 109, 85.

1. Find the mean.   **2.** Find the median.   **3.** Find the mode.

4. Find the range.   **5.** Draw a box-and-whisker plot.

6. Make a stem-and-leaf plot for the data below.

   116 115 120 125 132 117 129 135 110 129 135

7. Choose A, B, C, or D. Select the appropriate type of graph for the data shown at the right. Then make the graph.

   A. a box-and-whisker plot   **B.** a scatter plot
   C. a line graph   **D.** a bar graph

Percent of Eye-Chart Symbols Identified

Distance (ft)	Percent Identified
20	85
24	73
32	58
40	50
58	31
63	12

1-9

Conducting a Survey

What You'll Learn

1. To plan a survey
2. To write survey questions

...And Why

You can gather reliable information with well-written survey questions.

Here's How

Look for questions that
- build understanding
- ✔ check understanding

THINK AND DISCUSS

1 Planning a Survey

What sport do you play? How much do you exercise? Questions like these are often asked in surveys. Statisticians collect information about specific groups. Any group of objects or people is called a **population.**

A **sample** is a part of the population. When you conduct a survey, you should take a sample from the population you want to study.

In a **random sample,** each object in the population has an equal chance of being selected.

■ **EXAMPLE 1**   *Real-World Problem Solving*

School You think that your school bus stops are too far apart. You want to see if riders on all the buses agree. Tell whether each survey plan describes a good sample.

a. Interview 50 students who enter the school building.

This sample will probably include students who are not bus riders. It is not a good sample because it is not taken from the population you want to study.

b. Interview several friends on your bus.

Your friends all ride the same bus. They may not represent the views of students on other buses. This is not a good sample because it is not random.

c. Pick four buses at random. Interview every fifth rider as he or she gets off the bus.

This is a good sample. It is selected at random from the population you want to study.

1. a. ✔ *Try It Out* To find out the type of music people prefer, you survey people at random at a local art museum. What's wrong with this survey plan?
   b. Describe a better survey plan.

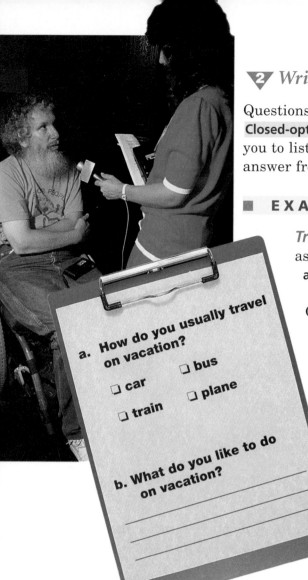

✌ *Writing Survey Questions*

Questions for a survey can be closed-option or open-option. **Closed-option** questions, such as multiple-choice questions, limit you to listed choices. **Open-option** questions allow you to answer freely.

■ **EXAMPLE 2**   *Real-World Problem Solving*

> **Travel** Look at the clipboard. Describe each question as closed-option or open-option.
>   a. closed-option   b. open-option

Often closed-option questions include the choice "other."

2. **⁝ Go a Step Further** Rewrite each open-option question as a closed-option question.
   a. What do you like to do on vacation?
   b. How many hours do you watch television each day?

Unfair questions are **biased questions.** They can make assumptions that may or may not be true. Biased questions can also make one answer seem better than another.

■ **EXAMPLE 3**

Explain why each of the following questions is biased.
a. How do you like your eggs cooked?
   The question assumes that you like eggs.

b. Do you like the luxurious car A, or the cheaper model, car B?
   The question makes car A seem more desirable.

3. **✔ Try It Out** Explain why each survey question is biased.
   a. Which shoes would you buy: the high-priced brand-name shoes or the well-made discount pair?
   b. What kind of dog do you prefer to have as a pet?

On the clipboard:
a. How do you usually travel on vacation?
   ☐ car   ☐ bus
   ☐ train   ☐ plane

b. What do you like to do on vacation?

In your group, decide on a topic for a survey at your school.

4. Write a description of the population you want to study. Does it include just students? Is it limited to certain classes?

5. Plan your survey. How will you get a good sample of your population? Write out your plan.

6. Write at least two unbiased survey questions. Make one question closed-option and the other open-option.

7. Conduct the survey and display the data results.

EXERCISES *On Your Own*

Suppose you want to find out how often teenagers in your town go to movies. For Exercises 1–4, tell whether each survey plan describes a good sample. Justify your answer.

1. You select a theater at random. One night, you interview all the teenagers who attend.

2. You select teenagers at random from a list of town residents. Then you interview them.

3. You interview every student in your English class.

4. You go to your favorite movie theater. You ask people near you how often they attend.

Describe each question as *closed-option* or *open-option*. Then rewrite it in the other form.

5. What is your favorite musical group?

6. Which type of book do you most like to read: mystery, romance, adventure, biography, science fiction, or other?

7. How much money do you spend on lunch each week?

Explain why each question is biased.

8. Is your brother one of your closest friends?

9. Do you think that warm, cuddly, little kittens are nicer than drooling puppies?

10. *Writing* Describe a survey situation for which an open-option question is appropriate. Then describe one for which a closed-option question is appropriate. Explain your choices.

11. *Open-ended* Give an example of a closed-option, biased survey question. Rewrite the question to ask for the same information in an unbiased way.

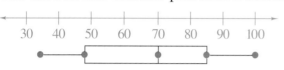

Estimate. Then find each answer. *(Previous course)*

12. $5 \times \$4.99$ 13. $7 \times \$3.29$ 14. $\$9.98 \div 2$ 15. $\$17.34 \div 5$ 16. $\$8.79 + \$3.98$

17. Use the box-and-whisker plot shown below. *(Lesson 1-6)*

```
   30   40   50   60   70   80   90   100
```

   a. Find the median.
   b. Find the upper quartile.
   c. Find the least value.
   d. Find the range.

18. Brenda received a gift certificate for $35. If she also has $7.50 cash, how many $9 tapes can she buy? *(Previous course)*

Math at Work

ARCHAEOLOGIST

Are you interested in discovering more about the world and who or what lived here long, long ago? If so, then you might consider a career as an archaeologist. As an archaeologist, you might travel to another country and work at a dig site, using special tools to search very carefully for evidence of other civilizations, such as shards of pottery or fossils. Archaeologists, like most scientists, use mathematics to help them conduct their research. Dating a piece of evidence, or dividing the floor of a dig site, or classifying their discoveries are just some of the ways that archaeologists use mathematics as a tool to help them.

For more information about being an archaeologist, visit the Prentice Hall Web site: www.phschool.com

1-10

Too Much or Too Little Information

THINK AND DISCUSS

Sometimes you cannot solve a problem because you do not have enough information. Other times you may be given more information than you actually need. In either case, you need to decide which facts are important before you begin any calculations.

SAMPLE PROBLEM...

Recently, 28 students at Gates Middle School were surveyed. They were asked, "Rounded to the nearest hour, how many hours a week do you spend listening to music?" Their responses are summarized in the box-and-whisker plot below.

Hours of Music Listening per Week

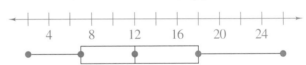

Find the mode and median of the students' responses.

....

READ

Read for understanding. Summarize the problem.

Read the problem carefully.

1. What facts are given?

2. What information are you asked to find?

PLAN

Decide on a strategy.

Look at the information in the problem and decide whether you have too much or too little information.

3. Is there enough information in the problem to allow you to find the mode? Explain your answer.

4. Is there enough information in the problem to allow you to find the median? Explain your answer.

5. What information is given that is not necessary for solving the problem?

SOLVE
Try the strategy.

You cannot find the mode. Because individual data items are not listed, you cannot tell which data item occurs most frequently.

The median is indicated by the dot on the vertical line in the box. The median number of hours is 12.

LOOK BACK
Think about how you solved the problem.

6. Name a method of presenting the data that would have allowed you to find the mode.

EXERCISES *On Your Own*

Solve each exercise, if possible. If an exercise cannot be solved, tell what information is needed.

1. Priya left her home at 8:20. She took a fifteen-minute bus ride, stopped at a bakery, and then walked to the library. If she spent twice as long walking as she did at the bakery, what time did she arrive at the library?

2. *Sports* In 1996, Andrés Galarraga and Mark McGwire led the major leagues in home runs. Their combined total of 99 homers equaled the total number of bases stolen by the Florida Marlins team. If McGwire hit five more homers than Galarraga, find the number of home runs Galarraga hit.

3. *Consumer Issues* Dan bought four packages of hot dogs on sale at $1.99 per package. They regularly sold for $2.49 per package. Rolls were on sale at two packages for one dollar. Dan bought four packages of rolls. How much did he save by buying the sale items?

4. A baby-sitter earned $4.25 per hour plus $7.00 for cab fare. He started working at 10 A.M. At what time did he finish if he received $41.00?

Andrés Galarraga of the Colorado Rockies

Use any strategy to solve each problem. Show all your work. If a problem cannot be solved, tell why.

5. In a collection of dimes and quarters, there are three more dimes than quarters. If the collection is worth $3.45, how many dimes and quarters are there?

6. *Sports* Eight teams are playing in a soccer tournament. Once a team loses a game, it is eliminated. If a team wins, it plays again. Each game consists of a ten-minute warm-up, two 30-minute halves, and a five-minute half-time. What is the latest time the tournament can start if it must end by 4:00 P.M. and there is only one field available?

7. *Transportation* A truck driver plans to drive 805 km. After 5 h, she has traveled 470 km. If she continues driving at this rate, will she arrive at her destination within 9 h of her starting time?

8. A drill team director wanted to arrange the team members in pairs. She found that she was one person short. She tried to arrange by fives and was still one person short. She finally arranged the team members by sevens. What is the least number of people on the drill team?

9. You are planning to set up chairs for the class play. The front row will have eight chairs. Each row thereafter will have three more chairs than the row in front of it. You know that there will be twelve rows. How many chairs will you need?

10. Examine the pattern at the right. In which row will the number 100 appear?

```
          1              row 1
       2     3           row 2
    4     5     6        row 3
  7    8     9    10     row 4
```

11. *Money* In how many different ways can you give change from a $100 bill for a $79 purchase if the customer will not accept coins or more than six $1 bills? Use $1-, $5-, and $10-bills.

Mixed Review

Write each fraction in simplest form. *(Previous course)*

12. $\frac{3}{9}$ 13. $\frac{8}{12}$ 14. $\frac{10}{25}$ 15. $\frac{7}{42}$

16. $\frac{14}{18}$ 17. $\frac{2}{50}$ 18. $\frac{27}{36}$ 19. $\frac{88}{110}$

20. Write a closed-option question to find out what students at your school do for lunch. *(Lesson 1-9)*

21. Decide whether a line graph or a bar graph is an appropriate display for the data shown at the right. Then draw the graph. *(Lesson 1-8)*

Typical Heights of Trees after 15 Years

Type of Tree	Height (ft)
Holly	10
Oak	25
Poplar	30
Juniper	10
Douglas fir	40
Yew	12
Weeping willow	30

Probability

What You'll Learn

▼ To find the probability that an event will occur

▼ To find a sample space

...And Why

You can use a sample space to analyze the probability that a family will have all girls or all boys.

Here's How

Look for questions that
- build understanding
- ✔ check understanding

THINK AND DISCUSS

▼ 1 *Finding a Probability*

Suppose there are six scarves in a drawer. Three of the scarves are blue, two are red, and one is green. If you choose a scarf at random, the probability that it will be green is 1 out of 6, or $\frac{1}{6}$.

In this situation, the six possible results (the six scarves) are called **outcomes.** An **event,** such as getting a green scarf, is any outcome or group of outcomes. When the outcomes each have the same chance of occuring, you can use the following formula.

$$\text{probability of an event} = \frac{\text{number of favorable outcomes}}{\text{number of possible outcomes}}$$

You can write the phrase *the probability of an event* as *P(event).*

■ EXAMPLE 1

Suppose you choose a scarf at random from the scarves shown at the left. Find (a) *P*(blue scarf) and (b) *P*(yellow scarf).

a. $P(\text{blue scarf}) = \frac{3}{6}$ — The three blue scarves represent favorable outcomes.

$= \frac{1}{2}$ — The six scarves represent the possible outcomes.

b. $P(\text{yellow scarf}) = \frac{0}{6}$ — Since there are no yellow scarves, there are no favorable outcomes.

$= 0$

1. ✔ *Try It Out* Find *P*(red scarf).

2. ⬛ *Analyze* Find the sum of these probabilities.
   P(blue scarf) + *P*(red scarf) + *P*(green scarf)

3. a. ⬛ *Reasoning* What is the probability of an event that is certain to happen?
   b. What is the probability of an event that cannot possibly happen?

Sometimes you can think of probability as the area of a region or as a percent.

■ **EXAMPLE 2**   *Real-World Problem Solving*

Pets Suppose you select a pet owner at random. Find the probability that the pet owner prefers to wash the pet indoors.

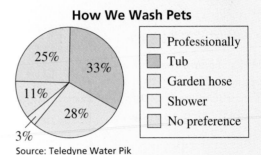

How We Wash Pets

25% 33% 11% 28% 3%

Professionally
Tub
Garden hose
Shower
No preference

Source: Teledyne Water Pik

In the graph, 33% of the area of the circle represents washing the pet in the tub. Also, 3% of the area represents washing the pet in the shower. Thus, $P(\text{prefers indoors}) = 36\%$, or $\frac{9}{25}$.

▼2 *Finding a Sample Space*

The set of all possible outcomes in a situation is called the **sample space.** Sometimes you can make a table to find the sample space.

■ **EXAMPLE 3**

Make a table to find the sample space for rolling two number cubes. Then find the probability that the two number cubes have a product of 12.

	1	2	3	4	5	6
1	(1, 1)	(2, 1)	(3, 1)	(4, 1)	(5, 1)	(6, 1)
2	(1, 2)	(2, 2)	(3, 2)	(4, 2)	(5, 2)	(6, 2)
3	(1, 3)	(2, 3)	(3, 3)	(4, 3)	(5, 3)	(6, 3)
4	(1, 4)	(2, 4)	(3, 4)	(4, 4)	(5, 4)	(6, 4)
5	(1, 5)	(2, 5)	(3, 5)	(4, 5)	(5, 5)	(6, 5)
6	(1, 6)	(2, 6)	(3, 6)	(4, 6)	(5, 6)	(6, 6)

There are 36 possible outcomes. Four of the outcomes, shown in red, have a product of 12. So, $P(\text{product of 12}) = \frac{4}{36}$, or $\frac{1}{9}$.

Need Help? For practice with fractions, see Skills Handbook page 610.

4. ✔ *Try It Out* Use the sample space in Example 3 to find each probability.
   a. $P(\text{sum is 8})$
   b. $P(\text{sum is odd})$
   c. $P(\text{difference is 0})$
   d. $P(\text{product is 21})$

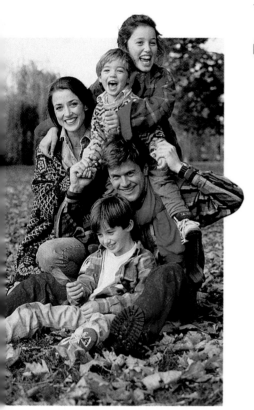

You can also draw a tree diagram to find the sample space.

■ EXAMPLE 4 *Real-World Problem Solving*

Biology How many boys and how many girls are likely to be in a family of three children? Draw a tree diagram to find the sample space. Then find the probability that there are at least two girls.

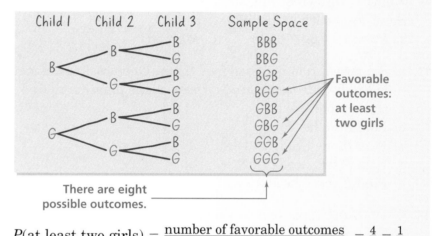

Child 1	Child 2	Child 3	Sample Space
B	B	B	BBB
		G	BBG
	G	B	BGB
		G	BGG
G	B	B	GBB
		G	GBG
	G	B	GGB
		G	GGG

Favorable outcomes: at least two girls

There are eight possible outcomes.

$$P(\text{at least two girls}) = \frac{\text{number of favorable outcomes}}{\text{number of possible outcomes}} = \frac{4}{8} = \frac{1}{2}.$$

5. ✔ *Try It Out* What's the probability that a family of three children will have exactly two girls? At least two boys?

EXERCISES *On Your Own*

1. Use the graph at the right. Find each probability.
   a. P(a person prefers music)
   b. P(a person prefers talk or ads)
   c. P(a person prefers anything but silence)

An eight-sided die has the numbers 1, 2, 3, 4, 5, 6, 7, and 8 on its faces. Find each probability if you roll the die once.

2. P(even number)   3. P(number less than 4)

4. P(multiple of 3)   5. P(number less than 10)

6. P(factor of 12)   7. P(negative number)

8. P(prime number)   9. P(composite number)

What We Prefer to Hear When on Hold

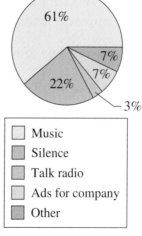

61%

7%

7%

22%

3%

☐ Music
☐ Silence
☐ Talk radio
☐ Ads for company
☐ Other

Source: *The Telephone Doctor*

Two four-sided dice each have the numbers 1, 2, 3, and 4 on their faces. Make a table to find the sample space for rolling the two dice. Then find each probability.

10. P(sum of 7)

11. P(sum of 5)

12. P(sum greater than 8)

13. P(product of 4)

14. P(product less than 9)

15. P(both numbers even)

16. A dart is thrown at random at the game board shown at the right. Find each probability.
   a. P(red)   **b.** P(blue)   **c.** P(green)

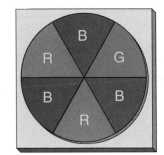

17. a. Suppose a coin is tossed four times. One possible outcome is *heads-tails-heads-heads*. Draw a tree diagram to find the sample space.
   b. Find P(no heads).
   c. Find P(one head).
   d. Find P(two heads).
   e. Find P(three heads).

18. *Gardening* A package of wildflower seeds contains 50 daisy seeds, 80 sunflower seeds, 100 black-eyed Susan seeds, and 20 lupine seeds. What is the probability that a seed selected at random will be a daisy seed?

19. *Writing* Can the fraction $\frac{5}{4}$ represent a probability? What numbers can be used to represent probabilities? Explain.

PORTFOLIO
Select one or two items from your work for this chapter. Consider:
• corrected work
• diagrams, graphs or charts
• a journal entry
Explain why you have included each selection.

Mixed Review

Choose A, B, C, or D. For Exercises 20–23, choose which type of graph is appropriate for each set of data. *(Lesson 1-8)*

A. circle graph   **B.** line graph   **C.** scatter plot   **D.** box-and-whisker plot

20. daily high temperatures during May in Phoenix

21. points vs. rebounds for each member of a basketball team

22. 100 store prices for 12-ounce drinks

23. percent of students in each of three grades

24. To find out whether students at your school like to read mystery novels, you plan to interview 50 students selected at random. Is this a good sample? Explain. *(Lesson 1-9)*

CHAPTER PROJECT

NEWS *Flash*

Create a Graph for a News Article The Project Link questions on pages 12, 23, and 41 should help you to complete your project. Here is a checklist to help you gather the parts of your project together.

- ✔ a news article or advertisement that contains a graph
- ✔ your analysis of whether the original graph is misleading, and your version of the graph
- ✔ a news article describing data about your topic
- ✔ a graph that presents the data for your news article

Arrange your news article and graph to look like a page from a magazine or newspaper. Write a title or headline for your article.

Reflect and Revise

Is your news article clear and convincing? Do your graphs use accurate scales and have appropriate labels and titles? Ask a friend to review your work for you. If necessary, make changes to improve your project.

Web Extension

Prentice Hall's Internet site contains information you might find helpful as you complete your project. Visit www.phschool.com/mgm3/ch1 for some links and ideas related to the news.

Organizing and Displaying Data 1-1, 1-2

A **stacked bar graph** has bars that are divided into categories. Each bar represents a total. A **sliding bar graph** shows two categories as bars graphed in opposite directions. A **multiple line graph** shows more than one category changing over time.

School Chorus Members

Year	Girls	Boys
1994	35	41
1995	32	40
1996	35	43
1997	34	37
1998	32	39

1. Make a stacked bar graph and a sliding bar graph using the data shown at the right. Let each bar represent a year.

2. Use the data at the right to draw a multiple line graph that appears to exaggerate the difference between the number of boys and the number of girls.

Frequency and Measures of Central Tendency 1-3, 1-4

A **frequency table** lists each data item with the number of times it occurs. Data from a frequency table can be displayed in a **line plot** or a **histogram.**

The **mean** of a set of numbers is the sum of the numbers divided by the number of data items. The **median** is the middle value in a set of numbers in numerical order. The **mode** is the data item that occurs most often.

For Exercises 3 and 4, use the following data on the ages of members of the Over 50 Bowling League.

53 57 78 64 68 72 77 58 60 78 80 81 55 70 52 63 65 79

3. Choose intervals to group the data. Then make a frequency table and a histogram.

4. Find the mean, median, and mode.

5. *Open-ended* Write a data set for which the median is a better measure of central tendency than the mean.

Stem-and-Leaf Plots and Box-and-Whisker Plots 1-5, 1-6

A **stem-and-leaf plot** displays each data item in order. A **box-and-whisker plot** shows the distribution of data in four equal parts along a number line. The **range** of a set of numbers is the difference between the greatest and the least values in the set.

For Exercises 5 and 6, use the data listed below showing juice prices (in cents) at various stores.

89 79 85 79 85 67 75 99 79 63 90 72 78 65 78

6. Make a stem-and-leaf plot.

7. Make a box-and-whisker plot.

Scatter Plots and Appropriate Graphs   1-7, 1-8

In a **scatter plot**, related data from two sets are graphed as points. If the points on a scatter plot show a trend, you can draw a **trend line.** The type of graph you choose depends on the type of data you have collected and the idea you want to communicate.

8. Make a scatter plot for the data shown at the right. If there is a trend, draw a trend line.

9. Choose A, B, or C. Choose the most appropriate graph to display data on changes in a child's height over a ten-year period.
   A. circle graph **B.** line graph **C.** scatter plot

Length (miles) and Water Flow (1000 ft³/s) of United States Rivers

Length	Flow	Length	Flow
2,540	76	1,290	56
2,340	593	1,240	265
1,980	225	1,040	57
1,900	348	886	68
1,460	41	774	67
1,420	58	724	67
1,310	281	659	41

Conducting a Survey, Problem Solving, and Probability   1-9, 1-10, 1-11

A **sample** is part of the population, or group, being studied. In a **random sample,** each item has an equal chance of being selected.

Survey questions can be **closed-option** (with limited choices of response) or **open-option. Biased questions** are unfair questions.

When outcomes each have the same chance of occuring, you can use the following formula to find the **probability of an event.**

$$P(\text{event}) = \frac{\text{number of favorable outcomes}}{\text{number of possible outcomes}}$$

The set of all possible outcomes is the **sample space.**

10. *Writing* Write an open-option, unbiased survey question to determine people's favorite type of fruit.

11. Suppose a coin is tossed three times.
   a. Find the sample space.
   b. Find P(exactly two heads).
   c. Find P(at least two heads).
   d. Find P(no heads).

Solve the following problem. If there is too little information, describe the information that is needed.

12. Minowa left home at 6:45 A.M. and drove for 2 h 10 min. She stopped for breakfast and then drove for 3 h 5 min before stopping for gas. At what time did she stop for gas?

1. In what year was the population of the United States about twice what is was in 1930?

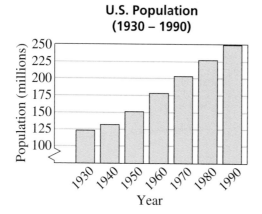

U.S. Population (1930 – 1990)

2. Decide whether a scatter plot, a bar graph, or a line graph would be the best way to display the data below. Explain your reasoning and draw your graph.

   Average daily water use (in gal/person):

   United States, 188; Canada, 142; France, 84; Spain, 102; Japan, 114; Germany, 50

   Source: *The Information Please Environmental Almanac*

3. Make a frequency table and a line plot for the following data.

   Subscribers (in millions) of the top 10 cable television networks:

   68 68 68 67 67 67 66 66 65 65

   Source: *The Universal Almanac*

4. Make a box-and-whisker plot for each set of data. Use a single number line. Then compare the two sets of data.

   Career earnings in millions of dollars of the top male and female golfers:

   M: 10.4 9.7 8.2 7.9 7.8 7.7 7.7 7.2 7.1

   F: 5.5 5.4 5.1 5.1 4.4 3.5 3.2 2.9 2.9

   Source: *The Universal Almanac*

5. Find the mean, median, and mode of the following data.

   36 17 41 25 19 33 25 44 41

6. *Writing* Write a closed-option, unbiased survey question to find the favorite subject of students in your school.

7. You have a set of data with five data items. The median is 23, the mean is 23, the mode is 26, and the range is 7. Find the five data items.

8. **Choose A, B, C, or D.** Which one of the following values can be determined using the box-and-whisker plot shown below?

   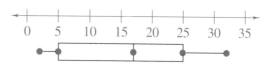

   A. the sample size   B. the mean
   C. the third quartile   D. the mode

9. Describe any trend you find in the scatter plot below.

   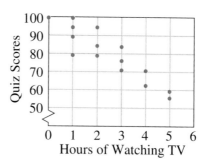

10. Suppose you roll two cubes. Each cube has the numbers 1, 2, 3, 4, 5, and 6 on its faces.
    a. Use a table to find the sample space.
    b. Find P(sum greater than 8).
    c. Find P(product is even).
    d. Find P(the numbers differ by 2).

Choose A, B, C, or D.

1. Find the median and the mode of the data in the line plot at the right.

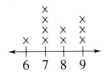

   A. 7 and 8   **B.** 8 and 9
   C. 7.5 and 7   **D.** 7.5 and 8

2. Which measure of central tendency would you use to describe data on your classmates' favorite brand of sneakers?

   A. mode   **B.** median
   C. mean or median   **D.** mean

3. Find two numbers whose sum is 10 and whose product is 24.

   A. 5 and 6   **B.** 3 and 8
   C. −2 and 12   **D.** 6 and 4

4. On one day of Russ's beach vacation, high tide occurred at 11:36 A.M., and low tide occurred at 6:39 P.M. How much time elapsed between high and low tide?

   A. 7 h 3 min   **B.** 7 h 15 min
   C. 6 h 15 min   **D.** 6 h 39 min

5. At a middle school gymnastics competition, the scores for the floor exercises were 5.1, 5.6, 5.3, 5.1, 4.8, 4.6, and 5.2. Find the mean (to the nearest tenth) and the median.

   A. 5.1 and 5.3   **B.** 5.2 and 5.2
   C. 5.2 and 5.1   **D.** 5.1 and 5.1

6. What are the missing numbers in the pattern below?

   2, 3, 5, 8, 12, ▧, 23, ▧, . . .

   A. 18 and 28   **B.** 17 and 30
   C. 15 and 26   **D.** 19 and 26

7. In a stem-and-leaf plot, which of the following can a stem represent?

   A. a units' digit   **B.** a tens' digit
   C. a tenths' digit **D.** any of these

8. At the Armstrong School, the student-to-teacher ratio is 12 : 1. If there are 30 teachers in the school, how many students are there?

   A. 42   **B.** 360
   C. 300   **D.** 250

9. Describe the relationship in the scatter plot shown below.

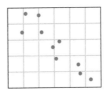

   A. positive trend
   B. negative trend
   C. no trend
   D. positive and negative trend

10. Which type of graph shows different items changing over time?

    A. stacked bar   **B.** sliding bar
    C. line   **D.** multiple line

11. Suppose you choose a whole number from 1 to 50 at random. Find the probability that the number you choose contains the digit 5.

    A. $\frac{1}{5}$ **B.** $\frac{1}{10}$ **C.** $\frac{3}{25}$ **D.** $\frac{1}{50}$

12. Sarah has four pairs of jeans and three shirts. How many different outfits can she choose?

    A. 7   **B.** 10   **C.** 12   **D.** 64

Integers and Variable Expressions

2

WEATHER
or NOT

Would you go swimming in 32° water? Is –2° a good temperature setting for a home freezer? The answer to both questions is, "That depends!" Are you using the Celsius or Fahrenheit scale? Water that is 32°C feels like a bath! As for a freezer, –2°C is barely below freezing, while –2°F is a deep freeze! Both the Fahrenheit and Celsius scales are used in North America, so it pays to know the difference.

Prepare a Report For your chapter project, you will examine weather data for a state or region of your choice. Your final project will be a report on temperature data, using both scales.

- How to use the *Guess and Test* strategy to solve problems

PROBLEM SOLVING

59

2-1 Integers and Absolute Value

What You'll Learn

▼ 1 To find the absolute value of an integer

▼ 2 To compare and order integers

...And Why

You can use integers to describe many quantities, such as earnings and expenses.

Here's How

Look for questions that
- ⊞ build understanding
- ✔ check understanding

THINK AND DISCUSS

1 Graphing and Absolute Values

Numbers that are the same distance from zero on a number line but in opposite directions are called **opposites.**

−4 and 4 are opposites.

Integers are the set of whole numbers and their opposites. The *sign* of an integer is positive if the number is greater than 0 and negative if the number is less than 0.

Integers: ... −4, −3, −2, −1, 0, 1, 2, 3, 4, 5, ...

negative integers   zero   positive integers

You can use positive and negative integers in discussing money.

■ **EXAMPLE 1** *Real-World Problem Solving*

Budgeting Teresa earns money by doing odd jobs such as washing windows. She records her earnings and expenses in a notebook. Graph these amounts on a number line.

Date	Earnings	Expenses
6/12	$ 12	
6/12		$ 6
6/13		$ 9
6/15	$ 9	

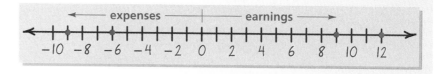

1. ✔ *Try It Out* What integer could you use to represent 500 feet below sea level?

2. ⊞ *Open-ended* Name some other examples of real-world uses of positive and negative numbers.

A number's distance from zero on the number line is called its **absolute value.** You write "the absolute value of 4" as |4|.

■ EXAMPLE 2

a. Find |6|.

On the number line, 6 is 6 units from 0. This means |6| = 6.

b. Find |−8|.

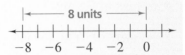

On the number line, −8 is 8 units from 0. This means |−8| = 8.

3. ✔ Try It Out Name two integers whose absolute value is 12.

4. ⁂ Number Sense Can the absolute value of a number be negative? Explain your answer.

GRAPHING CALCULATOR HINT

To find |−3|, enter this key sequence:

ABS (−) 3 ENTER .

2 *Comparing and Ordering Integers*

You can use a number line to compare and order positive and negative integers. Numbers increase from left to right on a number line.

■ EXAMPLE 3   *Real-World Problem Solving*

Weather Refer to the table. Which climate zone has a colder winter: subarctic or tundra?

To compare the temperatures −22°C and −18°C, you can graph the integers −22 and −18 on a number line.

The integer −22 is to the left of −18, so −22 < −18. Therefore, the subarctic climate is colder, on average, than the tundra.

5. ✔ Try It Out Which climate in the table has the lowest average winter temperature? Explain your answer.

6. ⁂ Go a Step Further Order all the climate zones in the chart from highest to lowest average winter temperature.

Climate Zone	Average Winter Temperature
Arid	13°C
Humid continental	−6°C
Ice cap	−25°C
Mediterranean	11°C
Subarctic	−22°C
Subtropical	8°C
Tropical	26°C
Tundra	−18°C

Write an integer to represent each situation.

1. a gain of 3 points   **2.** a $65 withdrawal   **3.** a $1,000 raise

4. a loss of 7 pounds   **5.** a profit of $50   **6.** 200 feet above sea level

7. *Weather* The lowest outdoor temperature ever recorded was 129°F below zero, in Vostok, Antarctica, in 1983.

8. *Geography* The lowest point in Africa, Lake Assal in Djibouti, is 571 ft below sea level.

Find each absolute value.

9. $|52|$ **10.** $|-6|$ **11.** $|0|$ **12.** $|-1.5|$ **13.** $|4 + 6|$ **14.** $|18 - 9|$

Compare. Write >, <, or =.

15. $|-14|$ ▪ $|14|$ **16.** 3 ▪ -4 **17.** -6 ▪ -8 **18.** $|-3|$ ▪ $|-6|$

19. $|-25|$ ▪ $|-1|$ **20.** 0 ▪ $|-5|$ **21.** $|75|$ ▪ $|-210|$ **22.** $|1|$ ▪ 0

Data Analysis **Use the information in the graph at the right to answer the questions.**

23. The lowest outdoor temperature ever recorded in Texas, $-31°C$, occurred on February 8, 1931. Was it ever that cold in Kansas? Explain.

24. Which state on the graph had a temperature of 48°C below zero at some time?

25. Which state on the graph experienced the coldest temperature?

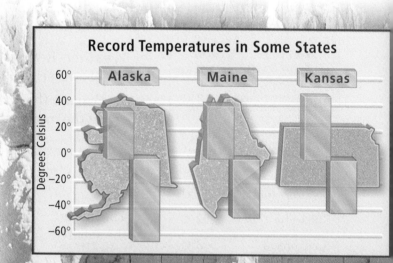

Record Temperatures in Some States

Alaska   Maine   Kansas

Degrees Celsius: 60° 40° 20° 0° −20° −40° −60°

Order the integers in each set from least to greatest.

26. $-9, 5, 2, -8, 0, 10, -12$ **27.** $-13, -16, 11, -6, 7, 2, -4$ **28.** $7, 3, -15, -7, 13, -1, 1$

Weather **Choose the point on the number line that describes each record low temperature.**

29. Van Buren, Maine
Jan. 19, 1925: $-48°$F

30. Tallahassee, Florida
Feb. 13, 1899: $-2°$F

31. Mauna Kea, Hawaii
May 17, 1979: $12°$F

32. Seminole, Texas
Feb. 8, 1933: $-23°$F

Algebra **State three numbers that you could substitute for x to make the inequality true.**

33. $|x| \geq 3$

34. $x < |-1|$

35. *Chemistry* The boiling point of oxygen is $-297°$F and the boiling point of nitrogen is $-320°$F. Which element has the higher boiling point?

36. *Writing* Explain how the set of whole numbers {0, 1, 2, . . . } is related to the set of integers. Use the Venn diagram.

37. **Choose A, B, C or D.** Which of the following contains only integers?

A. $-6, 0, \frac{1}{2}, 3, |-16|, 2$ **B.** $-3.2, -5, -1, -0.1, -4$
C. $2, -2, 2.5, -2.5, 3, -3$ **D.** $-9, 0, 2, -3, 1, 100, -8$

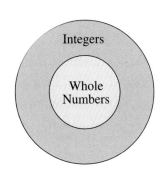

Integers

Whole Numbers

Mixed Review

38. a. Display the data in the table in a multiple line graph.
  b. Display the data in a double bar graph.
  c. *Writing* Describe the advantages and disadvantages of each type of graph. *(Lesson 1-1)*

Mental Math **Estimate using mental math.** *(Previous Course)*

39. 28% of 60   **40.** 50% of 71   **41.** 81% of 80

42. Mallory catalogued 24 shelves of books. Each shelf held 47 books. How many books did she catalogue? *(Previous Course)*

Temperatures in Detroit for One Summer Week

Day	High	Low
Sun.	86°	62°
Mon.	82°	61°
Tues.	80°	59°
Wed.	75°	64°
Thurs.	77°	68°
Fri.	73°	64°
Sat.	70°	61°

2-2 Writing and Evaluating Variable Expressions

What You'll Learn

1. To write variable expressions for word phrases
2. To evaluate variable expressions by using the rules for order of operations

...And Why

You can use variable expressions to calculate how much money you will earn for different work schedules.

Here's How

Look for questions that
- build understanding
- ✔ check understanding

THINK AND DISCUSS

1 Writing Variable Expressions

A **variable** is a letter or symbol that stands for a number. A **variable expression** is a group of numbers, variables, and operations.

You can translate word phrases such as "twice as much" and "half as heavy" into variable expressions. Study the table below.

Word Phrase	Variable Expression
three more than a number	$x + 3$
the quotient of a number and 8	$k \div 8$ or $\frac{k}{8}$
6 times a number	$6 \cdot y$ or $6y$
15 less than a number	$z - 15$

1. ⬡ **Algebra** Use each of the words or phrases below to rewrite one of the phrases in the table above.
   a. sum
   b. product
   c. decreased by
   d. divided by
   e. increased by
   f. minus

■ **EXAMPLE 1** *Real-World Problem Solving*

Money Aaron's after-school job pays $6 an hour. He works a different number of hours every week. Write a variable expression for his weekly earnings.

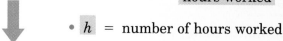

Words • $6 per hour · Number of hours worked

• h = number of hours worked

Expression • $6 \cdot h$ or $6h$

A variable expression for Aaron's weekly earnings is $6h$.

2. ✔ *Try It Out* At the ball game, a glass of soda costs $1.50. Write a variable expression for the cost of n glasses of soda.

2 *Using the Order of Operations*

You can **evaluate** a variable expression by substituting a number for each variable and then performing the indicated calculations. In Example 1, Aaron's earnings were represented by the variable expression $6h$. To find out how much Aaron earns in 25 hours, you evaluate $6h$ for $h = 25$.

$$6h = 6(25) = 150 \quad \longleftarrow \text{Substitute 25 for } h, \text{ then multiply.}$$

Aaron earns $150 in 25 hours.

3. ✔ Try It Out Evaluate the expression you wrote in Question 2 for $n = 5$.

To evaluate an expression containing more than one operation, use the rules for **order of operations.**

ORDER OF OPERATIONS

1. Work inside grouping symbols.
2. Multiply and divide from left to right.
3. Add and subtract from left to right.

Mathematicians developed these rules to help avoid the confusion of getting different answers to the same problem.

4. ⬡ Analyze Use the expression $1 + 2 \times 3$ to explain why the rules for order of operations are needed.

■ EXAMPLE 2

Algebra Evaluate each expression for $n = 8$.

a. $n + (13 - n) \div 5$

$\quad = 8 + (13 - 8) \div 5 \quad \longleftarrow \text{Substitute 8 for } n.$

$\quad = 8 + 5 \div 5 \quad\quad\quad \longleftarrow \text{Work within parentheses.}$

$\quad = 8 + 1 \quad\quad\quad\quad \longleftarrow \text{Divide.}$

$\quad = 9 \quad\quad\quad\quad\quad\quad \longleftarrow \text{Add.}$

b. $\dfrac{n + 24}{2n}$

$\quad = \dfrac{8 + 24}{2(8)} \quad \longleftarrow \text{Substitute 8 for } n.$

$\quad = \dfrac{32}{16} \quad \longleftarrow \begin{array}{l}\text{The fraction bar acts as a grouping symbol.}\\ \text{Evaluate above and below the fraction bar.}\end{array}$

$\quad = 2 \quad \longleftarrow \text{Divide.}$

5. ✔ Try It Out Evaluate each expression for $x = 12$.

   a. $3 \cdot x + (x \div 3)$ **b.** $\frac{x + 4}{14 - x} + x$

■ **EXAMPLE 3**   *Real-World Problem Solving*

Money The cost of an n–mile trip using Rod's Limo Service is given by the expression $\$5.00 + \$3.50n$. How much would a 12-mile trip cost?

Evaluate $5 + 3.5n$ for $n = 12$.

$$5 + 3.5n = 5 + 3.5(12) \quad \longleftarrow \text{Substitute 12 for } n.$$
$$= 5 + 42 \quad \longleftarrow \text{Multiply.}$$
$$= 47 \quad \longleftarrow \text{Add.}$$

A 12-mile trip costs $47.

6. ✔ Try It Out How much would a 20-mile trip cost using Rod's Limo Service?

EXERCISES *On Your Own*

Write a variable expression for each word phrase.

1. 27 plus a number

2. 13 less than a number

3. twice a number

4. the sum of -12 and a number

5. the product of -4 and a number

6. the sum of a number and and its opposite

7. the quotient of a number and negative 10

8. 14 more than 3 times a number

9. 7 more than the absolute value of a number

Write a variable expression for each situation.

10. the number of minutes in s seconds

11. the cost of x cartons of juice at $.75 each

12. the number of months old Bo is on his nth birthday

13. the number of calories in 3 slices of bread, where each slice has c calories

14. Kim's height if she is 6 inches shorter than her mother, who is x inches tall

15. Mike's age if Mike is 3 years older than Chandre, who is n years old

16. the number of heartbeats per minute if you count x beats in 15 seconds

17. the number of cars owned by n thousand inhabitants of Japan if there are 241 cars per 1,000 inhabitants

18. the number of miles your car gets per gallon if you use y gallons to travel 523 miles

⊞ Choose Use a calculator, paper and pencil, or mental math to evaluate each expression for $n = 3$, $x = 5$, and $y = 2$.

19. $7x - 8$

20. $7(n + 4)$

21. $12x + 4$

22. $13y - 16$

23. $2y - x$

24. $\dfrac{x + n}{y}$

25. $xy + n$

26. $\dfrac{3n + 3y}{x}$

27. $\dfrac{24}{4 - y} \cdot n$

28. $(30 \div x) + 9$

29. $(24 \div 4 - y) \cdot n$

30. $24 \div 4 - y \cdot n$

31. $x + 13 - 2 \cdot n$

32. $8 \div y + y \cdot 3$

33. $\dfrac{20n + 2x}{4n - y}$

34. $8y - 3x \div 2n$

Write a word phrase that can be represented by each variable expression.

35. $n \div 3$

36. $3 + a$

37. $-x$

38. $7h$

39. $w - 5$

For Exercises 40–44, match each sentence with one of the expressions given below.

A. $35 - 7$ **B.** $35x$ **C.** $m - 35$ **D.** $n + 35$ **E.** $(7)5$

40. A car was traveling 35 miles per hour for a number of hours.

41. Beshon ran 7 times a week for 5 weeks.

42. The plumber added an extra $35 to her bill.

43. Thirty-five fewer people came than the number expected.

44. Mark is 7 years younger than his 35-year-old sister.

45. *Ballooning* A hot-air balloon begins to descend toward the ground. Its height, in feet, after m minutes is given by the expression $2{,}250 - 150m$.
   a. What is the height of the balloon after 12 min?
   b. How many minutes will pass from the start of the balloon's descent until the time it lands? (*Hint:* Use *Guess and Test.*)

46. a. *Sales* A store sells one model of bicycle for $150. Write a variable expression for the amount of money the store will receive if it sells b of these bicycles.
   b. If $b = 2$, how much will the store receive from the sales?

47. Writing Why do you think that mathematicians often use symbols rather than words?

48. Research Choose a mathematical symbol and find out who introduced it and when it was first used.

Mixed Review

Write each mixed number as an improper fraction.
(Previous Course)

49. $4\frac{7}{10}$ **50.** $3\frac{3}{8}$ **51.** $8\frac{2}{7}$ **52.** $12\frac{5}{17}$ **53.** $7\frac{9}{16}$ **54.** $9\frac{5}{12}$

Mental Math **Evaluate each expression mentally. Explain your method.** *(Previous Course)*

55. $15.47 + $4.99   **56.** $62.50 + $37.85   **57.** $5.88 − $2.18   **58.** $26.99 − $11.49

59. The attendance at a series of medical lectures was 342 on Monday and 1,257 on Tuesday. Find the total attendance. *(Previous Course)*

60. Choose a Strategy It takes Cara 12 min to walk to school. She needs to get to school 15 min early to meet with the swimming coach. What time should she leave her house if school starts at 8:00 A.M.?

Math at Work

COMPUTER PROGRAMMER

Do you have a logical mind? If so, a career as a computer programmer may be the right one for you. Computer programmers write the detailed instructions called "programs" or "software" that computers use to carry out their functions. Applications programmers often work directly with experts to create programs that are used for desktop publishing, financial planning, and computer-aided designing. Systems programmers maintain the software that controls the operation of an entire computer system.

For more information about a career as a computer programmer, visit the Prentice Hall Web site: www.phschool.com

Adding Integers

What You'll Learn

▼ To use models to add integers

▼ To use a rule for adding integers

...And Why

You can add integers to find the total number of yards gained in a football game.

Here's How

Look for questions that

⚓ build understanding

✔ check understanding

THINK AND DISCUSS

▼ *Using Models to Add Integers*

The home football team has four downs to move the ball forward 10 yards toward the opponent's goal line. On the first down, the quarterback hands the ball to the running back, who is tackled for a 5-yard loss. On the second down, though, the team gains 7 yards.

You can chart the team's progress by adding integers. Use a number line to find the total number of yards the home team gains.

1st Down Begin at 0. To show a loss of 5 yards, move *left* 5 units to −5.

2nd Down Begin at −5. To show a gain of 7 yards, move *right* 7 units to 2.

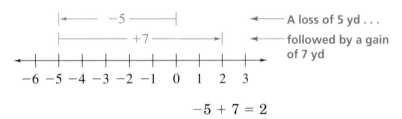

A loss of 5 yd . . .

followed by a gain of 7 yd

$$-5 + 7 = 2$$

The home team gained 2 yards.

1. ✔ *Try It Out* Use a number line to find each sum.
   a. $-9 + (-3)$ b. $6 + (-13)$ c. $-9 + 12$

If a football team loses 12 yd and then gains 12 yd, the team is back where it started: $(-12) + 12 = 0$. Since (-12) and 12 are opposites, their sum is 0, and they are called **additive inverses.**

2. ⚓ *Explain* What is the additive inverse of 6? Justify your answer by writing an equation.

Algebra tiles can help you add integers. A ▢ tile represents +1 or 1. A ◼ tile represents −1. Since 1 and −1 are additive inverses, an equal number of ▢ and ◼ tiles represents 0.

EXAMPLE 1

Use algebra tiles to add $6 + (-4)$.

$$6 \quad + \quad (-4) \quad = \quad 0 \quad + \quad 2 \quad = \quad 2$$

← Group and remove the zero pairs.

3. ✔ *Try It Out* Use algebra tiles to find each sum.

a. $5 + (-11)$ **b.** $-8 + (-6)$ **c.** $-7 + 14$

▼2 *Using a Rule for Adding Integers*

4. ⁂ *Think About It* Think about the number of tiles that you used to show each sum in Question 3.

a. If you use more positive tiles than negative tiles, then the sum is ___?___.

b. If you use more negative tiles than positive tiles, then the sum is ___?___.

This pattern suggests the following rules for adding integers.

ADDING TWO INTEGERS

Same Sign The sum of two positive integers is positive. The sum of two negative integers is negative.

Different Signs To add two integers with different signs, find the difference of their absolute values. The sum has the sign of the integer with the greater absolute value.

CALCULATOR HINT

To find $6 + (-15)$, enter this key sequence:
6 ⊞ 15 ⁺⁄₋ ≡ .

EXAMPLE 2

Find each sum.

a. $-9 + (-23) = -32$ ← Both -9 and -23 are negative, so the sum is negative.

b. $6 + (-15)$

$15 - 6 = 9$ ← Find the difference of $|-15|$ and $|6|$.

$6 + (-15) = -9$ ← $|-15| > |6|$, so the sum is negative.

5. ✔ *Try It Out* Find each sum.

a. $-62 + (-30)$ **b.** $33 + (-48)$ **c.** $-140 + 60$

Work Together

Work in groups of two or four. You will need a standard deck of cards. Use these rules for assigning values to the cards.

- Number cards are worth their face value. Aces are worth 1.
- The values of face cards are jacks, 11; queens, 12; kings, 13.
- All black cards represent positive integers.
- All red cards represent negative integers.

Each player should take two cards. Find the sum of your two cards. For example, if you pick a king of spades and a 7 of diamonds, your sum would be $13 + (-7) = 6$. The player with the highest sum collects everyone else's cards.

Continue playing until the last card is drawn. The person with the most cards wins the game.

EXERCISES *On Your Own*

Write the addition expression and sum that is represented by each model.

1.
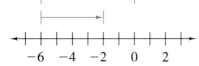

2.
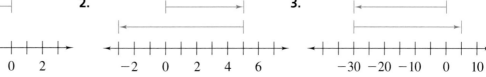

3.
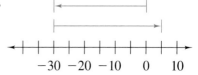

4.

5.

6.

Modeling **Draw a model and find each sum.**

7. $-7 + 5$ **8.** $-9 + (-6)$ **9.** $-3 + 5$ **10.** $-4 + (-7)$

Write an expression to describe each situation.

11. A scuba diver dove 53 ft below the surface of the ocean. She then rose 28 ft.

12. A tour group began the day at 415 ft below sea level. At the end of the day, they had gained 2,055 ft in elevation.

13. *Weather* The temperature at sunrise was $-24°F$. By noon, the temperature had risen 8 degrees.

Find each sum.

14. $13 + (-12)$ **15.** $-45 + (-67)$ **16.** $-17 + 18$ **17.** $14 + (-62)$

18. $-23 + 15$ **19.** $-9 + (-3)$ **20.** $-31 + (-39)$ **21.** $-83 + |-13|$

22. $|-98| + |-36|$ **23.** $|-11 + (-89)|$ **24.** $85 + (-47)$ **25.** $-58 + 27$

Number Sense **Refer to the number line. Is each sum positive or negative?**

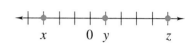

26. $x + y$ **27.** $x + z$ **28.** $x + x$ **29.** $x + y + z$

Algebra **Evaluate each expression for $n = -24$.**

30. $n + 32$ **31.** $15 + n$ **32.** $n + (-86)$ **33.** $98 + n$ **34.** $-24 + n$

35. *Hiking* A spelunker, or cave explorer, is 5,256 ft below Earth's surface at the lowest point of the Gouffre Jean Bernard cave in France. A mountain climber is at the top of Mount Everest in Nepal. The elevation of the mountain climber is 34,284 ft greater than that of the spelunker. Find the height of Mount Everest.

36. a. *Entertainment* To win a computer game, the total of the points scored must be positive. The chart at the right shows the points scored in each round. Did the player win? Explain.
   b. By how many points did the player win or lose?
   c. *Writing* Explain how you could use mental math or estimation to answer part (a).

Round	Points
1	−3,700
2	3,300
3	−3,200
4	2,900
5	1,800

Mixed Review

Compare. Use >, <, or =. *(Previous Course)*

37. $1.01 \blacksquare 0.95$ **38.** $0.100 \blacksquare 0.99$ **39.** $3.01 \blacksquare 3.016$ **40.** $7.300 \blacksquare 7.3$

Write a variable expression for each phrase. *(Lesson 2-2)*

41. Toshio's age, if Toshio is 7 years older than his brother, who is n years old

42. the number of hours Janelle worked if she earned $28 and makes $x per hour

43. Ramon kept a record of how he used his allowance. What kind of graph could he draw to show how the amount he saved relates to the total allowance? Explain. *(Lesson 1-8)*

Subtracting Integers

What You'll Learn

1. To use models to subtract integers
2. To use a rule to subtract integers

...And Why

You can subtract integers to find changes in temperature.

Here's How

Look for questions that
- build understanding
- ✔ check understanding

THINK AND DISCUSS

1 Using Models to Subtract Integers

Mountain climbers need to be prepared for changes in temperature due to the increase in altitude. Calculating difference in temperatures involves subtracting integers.

■ **EXAMPLE 1** *Real-World Problem Solving*

Mountain Climbing The graph shows temperatures at various altitudes. When you climb from 4,500 meters to 6,000 meters, how much colder does the temperature get?

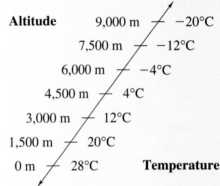

Altitude	Temperature
9,000 m	−20°C
7,500 m	−12°C
6,000 m	−4°C
4,500 m	4°C
3,000 m	12°C
1,500 m	20°C
0 m	28°C

The difference in the temperatures at 4,500 meters and 6,000 meters is given by the expression $4 - (-4)$.

You can use algebra tiles to find $4 - (-4)$.

←— Start with 4 positive tiles.

←— There are no negative tiles to subtract. Bring in 4 zero pairs.

←— Take away 4 negative tiles. There are 8 positive tiles left.

$4 - (-4) = 8$

It is 8°C colder at 6,000 meters than it is at 4,500 meters.

1. ✔ *Try It Out* Use algebra tiles to find each difference.

a. $3 - 6$ b. $-6 - (-4)$ c. $8 - (-3)$
d. $-5 - 8$ e. $-3 - (-7)$ f. $6 - 8$

▼2 *Using a Rule to Subtract Integers*

2. Use algebra tiles to find each difference and sum.

a. $4 - 2$	**b.** $5 - (-2)$	**c.** $-6 - 3$
$4 + (-2)$	$5 + 2$	$-6 + (-3)$

3. ⁂ *Patterns* What do you notice about each pair of sums and differences in Question 2? Write a rule about subtracting integers.

In Questions 2 and 3, you discovered the following rule about subtracting integers.

S U B T R A C T I N G   T W O   I N T E G E R S

To subtract an integer, add its opposite.

Example $40 - (-5) = 40 + 5 = 45$

■ **EXAMPLE 2**   *Real-World Problem Solving*

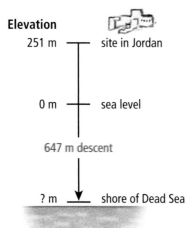

Elevation
- 251 m —— site in Jordan
- 0 m —— sea level
- 647 m descent
- ? m ▼ shore of Dead Sea

Geography A group of archaeologists leaves a site in Jordan and descends 647 meters to the shore of the Dead Sea. If their initial elevation is 251 meters above sea level, what is the elevation of the Dead Sea?

The diagram shows that the elevation of the Dead Sea is given by the expression $251 - 647$.

$$251 - 647 = 251 + (-647)$$ ⟵ To subtract 647, add its opposite, –647.

$$= -396$$ ⟵ $|-647| - |251| = 396$
The sign is negative because $|-647| > |251|$.

The elevation of the Dead Sea is 396 meters below sea level.

4. ✔ *Try It Out* Find each difference.

a. $38 - (-8)$	**b.** $-21 - 30$	**c.** $1 - 24$

Modeling **Draw a model and find each difference.**

1. $9 - (-1)$
2. $5 - 8$
3. $6 - 9$
4. $-10 - (-2)$

Number Sense **Without performing the subtraction, state whether each difference will be positive or negative.**

5. $5 - 11$
6. $81 - 73$
7. $10 - (-14)$
8. $-18 - 5$

9. $-14 - (-22)$
10. $-27 - 54$
11. $-76 - (-29)$
12. $62 - (-47)$

Write an equivalent addition expression for each subtraction expression. Then find the difference.

13. $27 - 52$
14. $19 - (-12)$
15. $-10 - (-8)$
16. $11 - (-25)$

17. $|-12| - 17$
18. $-28 - 28$
19. $-28 - (-28)$
20. $|-17| - |-12|$

21. $-36 - |29|$
22. $90 - (-78)$
23. $-55 - 21$
24. $42 - |-24|$

25. $56 - 28$
26. $26 - 56$
27. $95 - (-39)$
28. $27 - (-58)$

Patterns **Write the next four numbers in each pattern.**

29. $27, 20, 13, \blacksquare, \blacksquare, \blacksquare, \blacksquare$
30. $8, 5, 2, -1, \blacksquare, \blacksquare, \blacksquare, \blacksquare$
31. $14, 7, 0, -7, \blacksquare, \blacksquare, \blacksquare, \blacksquare$

32. $3, 5, 2, 4, 1, \blacksquare, \blacksquare, \blacksquare, \blacksquare$
33. $7, 14, 6, 12, 5, \blacksquare, \blacksquare, \blacksquare, \blacksquare$
34. $-4, 0, -2, 2, 0, 4, \blacksquare, \blacksquare, \blacksquare, \blacksquare$

35. *Banking* Arnold has $151 in his checking account. On Saturday, he writes a check for $248. How much does Arnold need to deposit into his account to prevent the account balance from dipping below $0?

36. Two different numbers are selected at random from the set $\{-10, 10, 20\}$. What is the probability that the difference between the first number selected and the second number selected is positive?

Choose **Use a calculator, paper and pencil, or mental math to evaluate each expression for $x = 4$, $y = -2$, and $z = -3$.**

37. $x + y$
38. $10 - z$
39. $y - z$
40. $x + y - z$
41. $y - 2 + x$

42. $35 - z + x$
43. $|y| - |z|$
44. $z + |y|$
45. $y - (-z)$
46. $x - z - |y|$

47. *Writing* Explain the relationship between adding a positive integer and subtracting a negative integer. Give examples.

48. *Probability* A bag contains 2 clear, 1 solid, and 5 cat's-eye marbles. What is the probability that a marble selected at random will be a cat's-eye? A solid? *(Lesson 1-11)*

Evaluate each expression. *(Lesson 2-2)*

49. $6 + 18 \div 3 \times 2$

50. $8 - 3 + 4 \times 5$

51. Extra prints at a photo shop cost \$.07 each. How much will 12 additional prints cost? *(Previous Course)*

52. Each question on a test is worth 3 points. Ken has 21 points. How many correct answers did he have? *(Previous Course)*

CHAPTER PROJECT

PROJECT LINK: ORGANIZING

Create a chart that compares the Celsius and Fahrenheit temperature scales. Indicate real-life situations, such as snowstorms, boiling water, beach weather, and so on. Include the chart in your report. What temperature is the same on both scales? Does this temperature ever occur in the region covered by your report?

✓ CHECKPOINT 1

Lessons 2-1 through 2-4

Compare. Use >, <, or =.

1. $13 \blacksquare 26$ **2.** $-19 \blacksquare 16$ **3.** $-9 \blacksquare -19$ **4.** $|76| \blacksquare 76$ **5.** $-19 \blacksquare |-23|$

Write a variable expression for each phrase.

6. the product of -3 and a number   **7.** a number divided by 12

Find each sum or difference.

8. $-7 + (-12)$ **9.** $-15 + 8$ **10.** $-32 - (-11)$ **11.** $12 - (-16)$ **12.** $23 - (-14)$

Evaluate each expression for $a = 19$ and $b = -3$.

13. $-a + 13$ **14.** $a - b + (-1)$ **15.** $a - b + 8$ **16.** $17 + b - a$

Multiplying and Dividing Integers

What You'll Learn

▼ To multiply integers
▼ To divide integers

...And Why

To find averages of sets containing negative numbers, you need to know how to divide integers.

Here's How

Look for questions that
▪ build understanding
✔ check understanding

Factor	Factor	Product
−30 ·	2 =	−60
−30 ·	1 =	−30
−30 ·	0 =	0
−30 ·	(−1) =	30
−30 ·	(−2) =	60

Work Together — *Preparing to Multiply Integers*

1. Copy and complete the table below. The first row is done for you. Recall that you can write $3 \cdot -4$ as $3(-4)$ or $(3)(-4)$.

Multiplication	Repeated Addition	Sum
$3(-2)$	$-2 + (-2) + (-2)$	-6
$5(-3)$	▪	▪
$4(-8)$	▪	▪
$2(-4)$	▪	▪
$3(-10)$	▪	▪

2. What do you notice about the sum in each case?

3. ▪ *Patterns* What does the pattern suggest about the product of one negative integer and one positive integer?

4. a. ▪ *Patterns* Look at the multiplication table at the left. What does the pattern suggest about the product of two negative integers?
   b. Use the pattern to predict the product of -30 and -3.

THINK AND DISCUSS

▼ *Multiplying Integers*

In the Work Together you discovered two rules for multiplying integers.

MULTIPLYING INTEGERS

The product of two integers with the same sign is positive.
Examples $8 \cdot 3 = 24$ $-8 \cdot (-3) = 24$

The product of two integers with opposite signs is negative.
Examples $6 \cdot (-5) = -30$ $-6 \cdot 5 = -30$

■ EXAMPLE 1

a. *Mental Math* Without computing, tell whether the product $-2 \cdot 3 \cdot (-5)$ is positive or negative. Explain your answer.

$$-2 \cdot 3 \quad \cdot \quad (-5)$$

negative • negative ← The product of the first two factors is negative.

positive ← The product of the two negative numbers is positive.

b. Find the product $(-2)(3)(-5)$ mentally.

$(-2)(3)(-5) = (-6)(-5) = 30$

5. ✔ *Try It Out* Find each product mentally.
  a. $(-8)(3)$ **b.** $(-6)(-4)$ **c.** $(-4)(-2)(-2)$ **d.** $(-3)(4)(-2)$

▼2 *Dividing Integers*

You know that division and multiplication are opposite operations. Look for a pattern in this group of multiplication equations and their related division equations.

Multiplication	Related Division Equations	
$(-6)(3) = -18$	$-18 \div 3 = -6$	$-18 \div (-6) = 3$
$(6)(-3) = -18$	$-18 \div (-3) = 6$	$-18 \div 6 = -3$
$(-6)(-3) = 18$	$18 \div (-3) = -6$	$18 \div (-6) = -3$

6. a. ⁙ *Patterns* What do you notice about the quotient of two negative integers?
  b. What do you notice about the quotient of a negative integer and a positive integer?

The rules for dividing integers are similar to the rules for multiplying integers.

DIVIDING INTEGERS

The quotient of two integers with the same sign is positive.
Examples $56 \div 8 = 7$ $-56 \div (-8) = 7$

The quotient of two integers with opposite signs is negative.
Examples $36 \div (-9) = -4$ $-36 \div 9 = -4$

7. ✔*Try It Out* Find each quotient.

    a. $-56 \div 4$ **b.** $-24 \div (-3)$ **c.** $48 \div (-6)$

■ **EXAMPLE 2**   *Real-World Problem Solving*

Money The average daily balance of Jane's checking account must remain positive for her to avoid a penalty fee. What was Jane's average daily balance for the week shown? Will she have to pay a penalty fee?

Balance of Checking Account	
Sunday	$34
Monday	−$28
Tuesday	−$28
Wednesday	−$28
Thursday	$16
Friday	$16
Saturday	$4

To find the average, divide the sum of the daily balances by the number of days, or 7.

$$\frac{34 + (-28) + (-28) + (-28) + 16 + 16 + 4}{7}$$

$$= \frac{-14}{7} \quad \longleftarrow \text{Find the sum in the numerator.}$$

$$= -2 \quad \longleftarrow \begin{array}{l}\text{The quotient of a negative integer}\\\text{and a positive integer is negative.}\end{array}$$

Jane's average daily balance was −$2. Jane will have to pay a penalty fee.

8. ✔*Try It Out* The low temperatures in Barrow, Alaska during one week were 11°F, 6°F, −2°F, −5°F, −8°F, −6°F, and −3°F. What was the mean low temperature for that week?

🖩 *CALCULATOR HINT*

To evaluate the expression in Example 3, enter this key sequence:

5 ⊠ 3 ⊞ ⊟ ⟦ 6 ⊟ 2 ⟧ ⊟ 2 ⊟ .

■ **EXAMPLE 3**

Evaluate the expression $5 \cdot (-3) - (6 - 2) \div 2$.

$5 \cdot (-3) - (6 - 2) \div 2$

$= 5 \cdot (-3) - 4 \div 2 \quad \longleftarrow \text{Work inside grouping symbols.}$

$= -15 - 2 \quad \longleftarrow \text{Multiply and divide.}$

$= -17 \quad \longleftarrow \text{Subtract.}$

9. ✔*Try It Out* Evaluate each expression.

    a. $-7 - (4 \cdot (-2) + 3)$ **b.** $(-4 + 9 \div (-3)) \cdot (-2)$

Number Sense **Determine the sign of each product.**

1. (negative number)(negative number) **2.** (positive number)(negative number)

3. $n \cdot n$, where $n \neq 0$ **4.** $y \cdot y \cdot y$, where $y < 0$

Mental Math **Find each product.**

5. $-3 \cdot 6$ **6.** $-6 \cdot (-9)$ **7.** $-7 \cdot 10$ **8.** $6 \cdot (-7)$ **9.** $-5 \cdot 12$

10. $-2 \cdot (-8)$ **11.** $3 \cdot (-15)$ **12.** $8 \cdot (-5)$ **13.** $(-7)(-2)(-1)$ **14.** $(-3)(3)(2)$

Write two related division equations for each multiplication equation.

15. $18 \cdot (-3) = -54$ **16.** $-12 \cdot 4 = -48$ **17.** $3 \cdot (-4) = -12$ **18.** $-7 \cdot (-2) = 14$

Algebra **Suppose x and y are positive, a and b are negative, $x \neq y$, and $a \neq b$. Determine the sign of each quotient.**

19. $\frac{x}{a}$ **20.** $\frac{y}{b}$ **21.** $\frac{a}{b}$ **22.** $\frac{x}{y}$ **23.** $\frac{a}{x + y}$ **24.** $\frac{b + a}{x}$

Mental Math **Find each quotient.**

25. $-50 \div 5$ **26.** $-45 \div 9$ **27.** $-64 \div 8$ **28.** $-54 \div (-9)$ **29.** $-12 \div (-3)$

30. $-32 \div 4$ **31.** $-18 \div 6$ **32.** $-28 \div (-7)$ **33.** $45 \div 5$ **34.** $72 \div (-8)$

35. *Number Sense* Find two integers whose sum is -5 and whose product is 4.

36. *Writing* Use examples to show how can you find the sign of a product when there are more than two factors.

37. *Finance* Jamal's stock rose $2, and then fell $1 for the next three days. If the stock rose $5 on the next day, what would his average gain or loss be for this 5-day period?

Find the value of each expression.

38. $-4 \cdot (-6) + 7 \cdot 2$ **39.** $-84 \div (-3 \cdot 4)$ **40.** $-5 \cdot (-4 - 2)$

41. $48 \div (-19 + 11)$ **42.** $15 \div (-3) - (6 - 2)$ **43.** $6 - 7 \cdot (-9) + 18 \div 3$

44. Reading About Math

   a. What integer represents the depth of the *Mahi*?

   b. What integer represents a descent of 20 ft/min?

   c. If a diver descends at a rate of 20 ft/min, does she reach the ship in 5 min? Explain.

45. Geology To explore Earth's crust, scientists began drilling in Zapolarny in arctic Russia on May 24, 1970. By April 1992, they had reached a depth of 40,230 ft.

   a. Write an integer to represent this depth.

   b. Estimation Estimate the depth they had drilled to the nearest mile. (1 mi = 5,280 ft)

Diving in Hawaii

THE WRECK OF THE *Mahi* is a favorite site for divers off the island of Oahu, in Hawaii. The *Mahi* is a 165-foot minesweeper that was sunk purposely in 1983. It is located 95 feet below the ocean's surface. A diver can explore the interior of the ship, which houses many different moray eels—some 6 feet long—and a variety of tropical fish.

46. Choose A, B, C, or D. Suppose you borrow $8 from each of 6 friends. Which number sentence best represents your debt?

   A. $-6 \cdot 8 = -48$ **B.** $-8 \cdot 6 = -48$ **C.** $-48 \div 6 = -8$ **D.** $-8 + 6 = -2$

Evaluate each expression for $x = 2$ and $y = -3$.

47. $(3x - 4) \cdot 4y$ **48.** $3x - (3 \cdot 2y)$ **49.** $3(x - y) - (-10)$ **50.** $3x - (y - (-13))$

Mixed Review

Find the opposite of each expression. *(Lesson 2-1)*

51. 9   **52.** -2 **53.** $|-6|$ **54.** 2   **55.** 7   **56.** -10

Estimation Estimate the value of each expression. *(Previous Course)*

57. $32 \cdot 1,098$ **58.** $352 + 347$ **59.** $496 \cdot 0.11$ **60.** $36,023 \div 410$

61. Tiwa sleeps about 7 hours each night. At the end of a year, about how many hours has she slept? *(Previous Course)*

2-6 Exponents and Multiplication

What You'll Learn

▼ **1** To use exponents in expressions and formulas

▼ **2** To multiply powers with the same base

...And Why

Using exponents is an efficient way to write products of a repeated factor.

Here's How

Look for questions that

⬚ build understanding

✔ check understanding

Work Together _____ *Investigating Exponents*

1. Complete the table.

Exponential Form	Read	Product of a Repeated Factor	Standard Form
2^1	2 to the 1st power	2	2
2^2	2 to the 2nd power or 2 squared	(2)(2)	4
2^3	2 to the 3rd power or 2 cubed	■	8
2^4	2 to the 4th power	(2)(2)(2)(2)	■
2^5	2 to the 5th power	■	■

2. ⬚ *Patterns* Compare the exponent of 2 in the first row of the table to the number of times the factor 2 is repeated. Does this relation hold for all rows of the table?

THINK AND DISCUSS

▼ **1** *Using Exponents*

You can use exponents to represent a repeated factor in multiplication. The repeated factor is called the **base.** The **exponent** tells how many times the factor is repeated or multiplied by itself.

$$\underbrace{2 \cdot 2 \cdot 2 \cdot 2 \cdot 2}_{\text{5 factors of 2}} = 2^5 \longleftarrow \text{5 is the exponent.}$$

2 is the base.

Any expression written in exponential form, such as 2^5 or a^3, is called a **power.** A power with an exponent of 1 means that the base is a factor only once. For example, $3^1 = 3$.

When you write a power with a negative number as the base, it is important to use grouping symbols to avoid confusion.

$$(-4)^4 = (-4)(-4)(-4)(-4) = 256$$

$$-4^4 = -(4)(4)(4)(4) = -256 \longleftarrow -4^4 \text{ is the opposite of } 4^4.$$

■ EXAMPLE 1

Evaluate each power.

a. x^2 for $x = -5$

$$x^2 = (x)(x)$$

$= (-5)(-5)$ ←——Substitute.——→

$= 25$ ←——Multiply.——→

b. x^3 for $x = 4$

$$x^3 = (x)(x)(x)$$

$= (4)(4)(4)$

$= 64$

3. ✔ *Try It Out* Evaluate each power.

a. y^3 for $y = 2$

b. y^2 for $y = -2$

You can use the $\boxed{y^x}$ key on a calculator to find the value of a number raised to a power. For example, 17^3 would be entered as 17 $\boxed{y^x}$ 3 $\boxed{=}$.

■ EXAMPLE 2

Use a calculator to evaluate.

a. $(-8)^5$ 8 $\boxed{+/-}$ $\boxed{y^x}$ 5 $\boxed{=}$ *-32768*

b. -15^4 15 $\boxed{y^x}$ 4 $\boxed{=}$ $\boxed{+/-}$ *-50625*

4. ⊕ *Think About It* Explain why you press the $\boxed{+/-}$ key *last* when evaluating -15^4.

⊞ *GRAPHING CALCULATOR HINT*

To find $(-8)^5$ on a graphing calculator, enter this key sequence:

$\boxed{(}$ $\boxed{(-)}$ 8 $\boxed{)}$ $\boxed{\wedge}$ 5 $\boxed{ENTER}$.

To find -15^4, enter this key sequence:

$\boxed{(-)}$ 15 $\boxed{\wedge}$ 4 $\boxed{ENTER}$.

② *Multiplying Powers with the Same Base*

To understand what it means to multiply powers with the same base, consider the product $5^3 \times 5^4$.

$5^3 \times 5^4 = (5)(5)(5) \times (5)(5)(5)(5)$ ←——Write the factors for each power.

$= (5)(5)(5)(5)(5)(5)(5) = 5^7$ ←——Write the product in exponential form.

So, $5^3 \times 5^4 = (5)(5)(5) \times (5)(5)(5)(5) = 5^{(3+4)} = 5^7$. This pattern suggests the following rule.

MULTIPLYING POWERS WITH THE SAME BASE

To multiply numbers or variables with the same base, add the exponents.

Arithmetic

$3^2 \cdot 3^5 = 3^{(2+5)} = 3^7$

Algebra

$a^m \cdot a^n = a^{(m+n)}$

2-6 Exponents and Multiplication   **83**

■ **EXAMPLE 3**

Write each expression using a single exponent.

a. $8^4 \cdot 8^7$

$= 8^{(4+7)}$ ⟵ Add the exponents. ⟶

$= 8^{11}$

b. $a^3 \cdot a^4$

$= a^{(3+4)}$

$= a^7$

5. ⬛ *Summarize* List the factors of a^3 and a^4 and show why $a^3 \cdot a^4 = a^7$.

EXERCISES *On Your Own*

Write each expression using a single exponent.

1. $7 \cdot 7 \cdot 7 \cdot 7$ 2. $(-5)(-5)(-5)$ 3. $(-x)(-x)(-x)(-x)$ 4. $3(-b)(-b)(-b)(-b)(-b)$

Write each expression as a product of a repeated factor.

5. 3^2 6. 10^5 7. -7^2 8. $(-9)^3$ 9. b^2 10. $-x^7$

Evaluate each power.

11. $(-3)^2$ 12. 6^3 13. -8^2 14. 1^{15} 15. 7^3 16. 151^1

17. *Writing* Barbara thinks that $3^4 = 4^3$ because $3 \cdot 4 = 4 \cdot 3$. Is she right? Explain.

Evaluate each expression for the given value.

18. $2a^3$ for $a = 2$ 19. $(2a)^3$ for $a = 2$

20. $-3n^2$ for $n = 3$ 21. $(-3n)^2$ for $n = 3$

Write each expression using a single exponent.

22. $4^4 \cdot 4^2$ 23. $a^3 \cdot a^5$ 24. $1^2 \cdot 1^7$

25. $(-5)^2 \cdot (-5)^7$ 26. $-n^3 \cdot n^5$ 27. $-b^3 \cdot -b^7$

28. *Computers* Computers store information in bits. If 2^3 bits equals 1 byte, and 2^{10} bytes equals 1 kilobyte, how many bits are in 1 kilobyte?

Complete each sentence with the correct base or exponent.

29. $64 = 8^{\blacksquare}$

30. $25 = \blacksquare^2$

31. $81 = 9^{\blacksquare} = 3^{\blacksquare}$

32. $16 = \blacksquare^2 = \blacksquare^4$

▦ *Choose* **Use a calculator, paper and pencil, or mental math to evaluate each expression.**

33. -4^3

34. 1^8

35. 9^6

36. $(-5)^2$

37. 5^3

38. 25^3

39. *Geometry* The formula for the area of a square is $A = s^2$. What is the area of a square whose sides measure 12 cm?

40. *Geometry* The formula for the volume of a cube is $V = s^3$. What is the volume of a cube whose sides measure 9 cm?

Mixed Review

41. Make a stem and leaf plot for this set of data: 23, 67, 45, 35, 16, 25, 29, 35, 41, 36, and 32. *(Lesson 1-5)*

Choose an appropriate type of graph to display the data described in each situation. *(Lesson 1-8)*

42. points vs. rebounds for each member of a basketball team

43. daily high temperatures in Phoenix during May

44. percent of students in each grade at a school

Write a variable expression for each phrase. *(Lesson 2-2)*

45. the quotient of a number and -2

46. a number decreased by -5

47. *Choose a Strategy* John has $18.98. Amy has three cents less than twice as much as John. If they pool their resources, how much do John and Amy have together?

CHAPTER PROJECT

PROJECT LINK: RESEARCHING

For the state, country, or region you select, research the historic temperature extremes. Report on the highest and lowest temperatures ever recorded. Include data on monthly or seasonal highs and lows as well. You may choose to present the data using a bar graph.

Using a Graphing Calculator

Before Lesson 2-7

You can use a graphing calculator to evaluate any expression.

■ EXAMPLE 1

Use a graphing calculator to evaluate $-3x^2 - x + 14$ for $x = -7$.

Keystrokes	**Explanation**	**Screen**
(−) 7 STO▶ ALPHA X ENTER	←— Store the value −7 to the —→ variable X.	−7→X −7
(−) 3 ALPHA X x^2 − ALPHA X + 14 ENTER	←— Enter and evaluate the expression. —→	−3X² −X+14 −126

To evaluate the expression in Example 1 for another value of x, start by storing that value to x. Press 2nd ENTER *twice* to recall the expression $-3x^2 - x + 14$ from memory. Then press ENTER.

You can use the TABLE function to evaluate an expression for many values of a variable.

■ EXAMPLE 2

Evaluate the expression in Example 1 for whole number values of x from 1 to 7.

Press Y=. Enter the expression $-3x^2 - x + 14$ next to y_1. Use the TblSet function to set TblMin to 1 and △Tbl to 1. Then press 2nd TABLE to view the table.

X	Y1
1	10
2	0
3	−16
4	−38
5	−66
6	−100
7	−140

Y1 = −3X² −X+14

Use a graphing calculator to evaluate each expression for the given values.

1. $x^2 - 2x + 5$ **a.** $x = 8$ **b.** $x = -10$ **c.** $x = 10$

2. $\frac{5}{9}(F - 32)$ **a.** $F = -40$ **b.** $F = 98.6$ **c.** $F = 212$

3. $-4x^2 + 34x - 42$ **a.** $x = 2$ **b.** $x = 12$ **c.** $x = 25$

4. Exercise 2 is the expression for converting °F to °C. Write another expression and evaluate it for three different values of the variable.

2-7 Evaluating Expressions With Exponents

What You'll Learn

1. To evaluate numerical expressions with exponents
2. To evaluate variable expressions with exponents

...And Why

Knowing how to evaluate variable expressions with exponents can help you when solving a problem with a formula.

Here's How

Look for questions that
- build understanding
- ✔ check understanding

THINK AND DISCUSS

1 Evaluating Numerical Expressions with Exponents

When you evaluate numerical expressions that have both exponents and grouping symbols, perform your calculations according to the order of operations.

ORDER OF OPERATIONS

1. Work inside the grouping symbols.
2. Evaluate the exponents.
3. Multiply and divide from left to right.
4. Add and subtract from left to right.

You can use the phrase "**P**lease **E**xcuse **M**y **D**ear **A**unt **S**ally" to help you remember the order of operations. (**P**arentheses first, **E**xponents next, then **M**ultiply and **D**ivide, and lastly **A**dd and **S**ubtract.)

■ EXAMPLE 1

Evaluate $26 - (5 \cdot 2)^2$.

$26 - (5 \cdot 2)^2$
$= 26 - (10)^2$ ←—Work inside the grouping symbols.
$= 26 - 100$ ←—Evaluate the power.
$= -74$ ←—Subtract.

1. a. Evaluate $26 - 5 \cdot 2^2$.
   b. ■ *Explain* Why is the value of the expression in part (a) different from the value of the expression in Example 1?

2. ✔ *Try It Out* Evaluate each expression.
   a. $(3 \cdot 2)^2 + 5$ b. $3^2 \cdot 2 + 5$ c. $-4^2 + 6 \cdot 3^2$

▼ 2 *Evaluating Variable Expressions with Exponents*

To evaluate a variable expression with exponents, replace each variable with a number, and then follow the order of operations.

■ **EXAMPLE 2**

Algebra Evaluate each expression for $x = 2$.

a. $5x^3$

$= 5(x)(x)(x)$

$= 5(2)(2)(2)$ ←——Substitute——→

$= 40$ ←——Multiply.——→

b. $(5x)^3$

$= (5x)(5x)(5x)$

$= (5 \cdot 2)(5 \cdot 2)(5 \cdot 2)$

$= (10)(10)(10)$

$= 1000$

3. ✔ *Try It Out* Evaluate each expression for $a = 3$.

a. $(6a)^2$ **b.** $6a^2$ **c.** $-2a^3$ **d.** $(-2a)^3$

Sometimes variable expressions contain more than one variable.

■ **EXAMPLE 3**   *Real-World Problem Solving*

Construction If you want to construct an arched doorway like the one shown here, you can use this formula to find the radius of the arch.

$$r = \frac{s^2 + h^2}{2h}$$

If the doorway has the dimensions $s = 4$ feet and $h = 2$ feet, find the radius r.

$$r = \frac{s^2 + h^2}{2h}$$

$$= \frac{4^2 + 2^2}{2 \cdot 2}$$ ←——Substitute 4 for *s* and 2 for *h*.

$$= \frac{16 + 4}{2 \cdot 2}$$ ←——The fraction bar acts as a grouping symbol. Evaluate the powers above the fraction bar.

$$= \frac{20}{4}$$ ←——Simplify above and below the fraction bar.

$$= 5$$ ←——Divide.

The radius of the arch is 5 feet.

4. ✔ *Try It Out* You can use the formula $h = 160t - 32t^2$ to estimate the number of feet a rocket reaches at t seconds. How high is a rocket 2 seconds after take-off?

EXERCISES *On Your Own*

Evaluate each expression.

1. $(-3)^2 + 12 \cdot 5$

2. $-3^2 + 12 \cdot 5$

3. $(3 \cdot 2)^2 + 5$

4. $3^2 \cdot 2 + 5$

5. $4 + (8 - 6)^2$

6. $4 + 8 - 6^2$

7. $(-3)^2 + 4^3 - 4$

8. $-3^2 + 4^3 - 4$

9. $3^2 + (6 - 2) \cdot 5 - 4^3$

Evaluate each expression for the given values.

10. $4k^2$ for $k = 3$

11. $-10c^3$ for $c = 6$

12. $x^2 - 8x + 16$ for $x = -4$

13. $15 - a^3$ for $a = 2$

14. $-3t^2 \div 9$ for $t = -3$

15. $\dfrac{n^2 + 5}{n^2}$ for $n = 2$

16. $-2x^2y$ for $x = 5, y = 10$

17. $7a + b^2$ for $a = -3, b = 5$

18. $6w^3 - 2x$ for $w = -2, x = -6$

19. $3^x + (3 + 1)^y$ for $x = 3, y = 2$

▦ **Choose** Use a calculator, pencil and paper, or mental math. **Evaluate each expression for $a = 2.5$, $b = -5$, and $c = 5$.**

20. $b^3 + 5$

21. $a^3 - 5$

22. $5 - b^3$

23. $5c^3 - 5$

24. $b^2 + b + 5$

25. $20a^3b^3$

26. $a^3b^3c^3$

27. $(b \div c)^3$

28. $a^2 - c^2$

29. $(a - c)^2$

30. *Writing* Pick two expressions in Exercises 20−29 that you evaluated mentally. Explain the method(s) you used.

31. *Geometry* The area of a square with side length s is given by the equation $A = s^2$. Write an equation for the area of a square with sides that are twice as long. Compare the areas of the two squares. Is the area of the new square twice as large? Explain.

32. *Sports* The distance a skydiver falls before she opens her parachute depends on how long she waits. If you ignore air resistance, the formula that relates distance to time is $d = 16t^2$, where $d = $ distance in feet and $t = $ number of seconds in free fall. How far does a skydiver fall in 3 seconds?

33. _Geometry_ The volume of a cylinder can be found by using the formula $V = \pi r^2 h$, where r is the radius of the base and h is the height of the cylinder. Find the volume of the cylinder shown. Use $\pi = 3.14$.

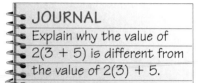

6 cm

30 cm

Estimation **Estimate the value of each expression for the given value of the variable.**

34. $3 + 2p^2$ for $p = 4.3$ **35.** $5r^3 - 4r$ for $r = 0.2$

36. $3n^3 + 2n$ for $n = -1.9$ **37.** $z^2 - 4z + 3$ for $z = 5.1$

38. $\dfrac{n^2 + n}{n + 1}$ for $n = 2.7$ **39.** $3m^2 + 18 \div 6$ for $m = 3.3$

JOURNAL
Explain why the value of $2(3 + 5)$ is different from the value of $2(3) + 5$.

Mixed Review

Evaluate each expression. _(Lesson 2-2)_

40. $2(3 + 6) \div 4 - 2$ **41.** $3 \times 6 + (10 \div 5)$ **42.** $9 \times (4 + 3 - 7) - 7$

Find the mean, median, and mode. _(Lesson 1-4)_

43. 14, 31, 33, 14, 50   **44.** 8, 17, 34, 17, 19   **45.** 12, 18, 15, 15, 17

Write a variable expression for each situation. _(Lesson 2-2)_

46. Bob's weight if he is 17 pounds lighter than Drake, who weighs n pounds

47. Danzell's height if he is 6 inches shorter than his father, who is h inches tall

48. Casandra's score if she scored 15 points more than Kyle, who scored p points

49. Vuthy's salary if he makes $12,500 more than Pete, who makes s dollars per year

50. Ralonda earns $40 for an 8-hour workday. How many hours does she have to work to earn enough to buy a $7.50 movie ticket? _(Previous Course)_

CHAPTER PROJECT

PROJECT LINK: MODELING

Develop a simple rule for mentally estimating the Fahrenheit temperature given the Celsius temperature. Give the rule in words or as a formula, and include it in your report.

Mental Math and Properties of Numbers

What You'll Learn

▼ To use the properties of numbers to find sums and differences mentally

▼ To use the properties of numbers to find products mentally

...And Why

The properties of addition and multiplication can help you find an answer quickly when you do not have a calculator or pencil and paper.

Here's How

Look for questions that

⊞ build understanding

✔ check understanding

THINK AND DISCUSS

▼ *Evaluating Sums and Differences Mentally*

Maybe you've heard a friend say something like this: "Let's see, I need 4 pencils at \$.89 each, so that's \$3.56 and I'll get \$1.44 change from my \$5.00."

Were you surprised by how fast your friend figured this out without a calculator? Chances are your friend knows how to use mathematical properties to make these calculations simple enough to do mentally.

PROPERTIES OF ADDITION AND MULTIPLICATION

Arithmetic	**Algebra**
Commutative Property	
$3 + 2 = 2 + 3$	$a + b = b + a$
$3(2) = 2(3)$	$ab = ba$
Associative Property	
$(2 + 3) + 4 = 2 + (3 + 4)$	$(a + b) + c = a + (b + c)$
$(2 \cdot 3) \cdot 4 = 2 \cdot (3 \cdot 4)$	$(a \cdot b) \cdot c = a \cdot (b \cdot c)$
Identity Property	
$6 + 0 = 6$	$a + 0 = a$
$6(1) = 6$	$a(1) = a$

---

1. ⊞ *Think About It* Which property allows you to change how factors or addends are grouped?

2. Which property allows you to add three negative numbers in any order?

When you add groups of numbers, look for combinations that equal 0, 10, or a multiple of 10 to make your calculations easier.

■ EXAMPLE 1

Evaluate each sum mentally.

a. $5 + (-7) + (-5)$

$= 5 + (-5) + (-7)$ ← Use the commutative property to move opposites 5 and –5 together.

$= 0 + (-7)$ ← Add $5 + (-5)$.

$= -7$ ← Use the identity property.

b. $23 + 16 + 37$

$= 23 + 37 + 16$ ← Use the commutative property to move 23 and 37 together to form a multiple of ten.

$= 60 + 16 = 76$ ← Add.

3. ✔ Try It Out Evaluate $125 + 62 + 75$ mentally.

You can make adding integers easier by grouping positive numbers and negative numbers and then looking for opposites.

■ EXAMPLE 2

Evaluate $(-6) + 46 + 17 + (-11)$ mentally.

$(-6) + 46 + 17 + (-11)$

$= 46 + 17 + (-11) + (-6)$ ← Use the commutative property to move the negative addends together.

$= 46 + 17 + (-17)$ ← Add $(-11) + (-6)$.

$= 46$ ← Use the identity property.

4. ✔ Try It Out Evaluate each sum mentally.

a. $20 + (-8) + 12 + (-16)$ b. $-19 + 7 + 23 + (-31)$

▼2 *Evaluating Products Mentally*

When you multiply a group of numbers, look for combinations that equal 10 or a multiple of 10 to make your calculations easier.

■ EXAMPLE 3

Evaluate $5 \cdot 7 \cdot 8$ mentally.

$5 \cdot 7 \cdot 8$

$= 5 \cdot 8 \cdot 7$ ← Use the commutative property to move factors 5 and 8 together to form a multiple of ten.

$= 40 \cdot 7 = 280$ ← Multiply.

5. ✔ *Try It Out* Evaluate each product mentally.
   a. $4 \cdot 356 \cdot 25$ **b.** $8 \cdot (-4) \cdot (-10)$

The distributive property combines multiplication with addition or subtraction.

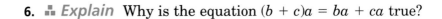

DISTRIBUTIVE PROPERTY	
Arithmetic	**Algebra**
$2(3 + 4) = (2 \cdot 3) + (2 \cdot 4)$	$a(b + c) = ab + ac$
$9(15 - 3) = (9 \cdot 15) - (9 \cdot 3)$	$a(b - c) = ab - ac$

6. ⬚ *Explain* Why is the equation $(b + c)a = ba + ca$ true?

You can use the distributive property to rewrite one factor as a sum of two numbers.

■ **EXAMPLE 4**

Evaluate 25(14) mentally.

$$25(14) = 25(10 + 4) \quad \longleftarrow 14 = 10 + 4$$
$$= 25(10) + 25(4) \quad \longleftarrow \text{Use the distributive property.}$$
$$= 250 + 100 \quad \longleftarrow \text{Multiply.}$$
$$= 350 \quad \longleftarrow \text{Add.}$$

Sometimes rewriting one factor as the difference of two numbers can help you with a mental calculation.

■ **EXAMPLE 5**   *Real-World Problem Solving*

Consumer Issues Carlos finds a calculator that costs $8.90. Mentally calculate how much it will cost him if he buys one for each of his four children.

$$4(8.9) = 4(9 - 0.1) \quad \longleftarrow 8.9 = 9 - 0.1$$
$$= 4(9) - 4(0.1) \quad \longleftarrow \text{Use the distributive property.}$$
$$= 36 - 0.4 \quad \longleftarrow \text{Multiply.}$$
$$= 35.6 \quad \longleftarrow \text{Subtract.}$$

The four calculators will cost Carlos $35.60.

7. ✔ *Try It Out* Evaluate each product mentally.
   a. $6 \cdot 15$ **b.** $8 \cdot 53$ **c.** $5(7.8)$

Evaluate each sum mentally. Explain your method.

1. $-3 + 14 + (-7) + 6$

2. $-5 + 2 + 18 + (-45)$

3. $4 + (-3) + 6 + (-7)$

4. $87 + 32 + 13$

5. $5 + (-2) + 5 + (-8)$

6. $55 + 63 + 25$

7. $70 + 333 + 430$

8. $178 + 288 + 22$

9. $540 + 160 + 28 - 10$

Evaluate each product mentally. Explain your method.

10. $(-2)(43)(-5)$

11. $5 \cdot 245 \cdot 20$

12. $(20)(34)(-5)$

13. $(8)(-4)(-10)$

14. $-2(5 \cdot 46)$

15. $2(13 + 50)$

16. $5 \times 168 \times 20$

17. $(40)(29)(-10)$

Rewrite each product so you can use the distributive property. Evaluate mentally.

18. $25(198)$

19. $1.8(5)$

20. $(4)(\$1.99)$

21. $(103)(\$22)$

22. $4(522)$

Reasoning **Decide whether each equation is true or false. Explain your reasoning.**

23. $7 \cdot 6 + 4 = 7 \cdot 4 + 6$

24. $-6(9 - 2) = 6(11)$

25. $13 \cdot 9 = 10 \cdot 9 + 3 \cdot 3$

Refer to the sample at the right. It shows how to adjust numbers in a sum to make them easier to total. Use this method to calculate each sum below mentally. Check your answers with a calculator.

Sample:

$$\begin{array}{rcl} 496 + 4 & \longrightarrow & 500 \\ +246 - 4 & \longrightarrow & + 242 \\ \hline & & 742 \end{array}$$

26. $398 + 247$

27. $\$2.98 + \$1.98$

28. $\$5.99 + \$2.41$

29. $603 + 398$

30. a. Use the table at the right. If the low temperature was 32°F on Sunday, what was it by the end of the day on Thursday?

b. *Analyze* Which properties could help you solve this problem mentally?

Day	Change in Low Temperature (°F)
Mon.	+11
Tues.	−14
Wed.	+9
Thurs.	−6

31. a. Copy and complete. $16 + ((-8) - 20) = (16 + (-8)) - \blacksquare$.

b. *Analyze* What property or properties did you use?

32. *Writing* Explain how you would use the properties in this lesson to evaluate $(-68) + 6(-99) + (-32)$.

Consumer Issues **Use the illustration for Exercises 33–35.**

33. Shayna bought 4 notebooks for school. If she gave the cashier a $10 bill, how much change did she get?

34. Rebecca buys 5 packages of ten folders. How much money does she spend? How much of her $8.50 is left?

35. Kyle bought 1 box of markers, 1 package of lined paper, and 5 packages of folders. How much did he spend in all?

Spiral Notebook $1.89

Package of Ten folders $.79

Package of Lined paper $1.19

Box of Eight markers $3.49

Mixed Review

Write a variable expression for each phrase. *(Lesson 2-1)*

36. 5 times a number

37. 5 more than a number

38. the sum of 5 and a number

Evaluate each expression. *(Lesson 2-2)*

39. $-6b$ for $b = -2$

40. $12 - g$ for $g = -4$

41. $3c + 7$ for $c = -1$

42. $12 - 2w$ for $w = 3$

43. The median of three numbers is 7. The range is 14. The mean is 11. What are the three numbers? *(Lesson 1-4)*

✓ CHECKPOINT 2   *Lessons 2-5 through 2-8*

Evaluate each expression.

1. $(13)(-32)$

2. $-4 \div (-1)$

3. $(-2)^3 \cdot 3^2$

4. -3^3

5. $-30 \div (-3)(2)$

Evaluate each expression for $x = 2$ and $y = 4$.

6. $19 - x - y$

7. $y - 10 - (-x)$

8. $(x^3)(y)$

9. $-x^2 - y^2$

10. **Choose A, B, C, or D.** Six friends have five marbles each. Which expression represents the total number of marbles?

   A. 6^5 B. $5 \cdot 6$ C. $6 + 5$ D. $\frac{6}{5}$

11. *Open-ended* Write an expression that includes grouping symbols, and three different operations. Then evaluate it.

Extra Practice, Lesson 2-8, page 583   2-8 Mental Math and Properties of Numbers

2-9

Guess and Test

THINK AND DISCUSS

To *Guess and Test* means you begin with a guess that you think makes sense. You test the guess to see if it gives you an answer that fits the problem. If your first guess does not solve the problem, use the results to help you make a better guess the next time. You continue to guess and test until you find the answer.

SAMPLE PROBLEM...

Eighty-nine scientists of the planet Leggus held a meeting to study a strange creature discovered on the planet Earth.

"It seems strange," the Centaurians said, "that this creature can maneuver on only two legs, when using four legs as we do is so much better."

"Indeed," the three-legged Tripodians replied. "It's a wonder they don't fall without a third leg for balance."

The 89 Centaurian and Tripodian scientists at this gathering had a total of 319 legs. Now, all you fine detectives out there, how many were Centaurians and how many were Tripodians?

READ

Read for understanding. Summarize the problem.

1. Read the problem again. Think about the information.
   a. What is the total number of scientists?
   b. How many legs does a Centaurian have? How many does a Tripodian have?
   c. What is the total number of legs?
   d. Summarize what the problem is about and what it is asking you to find.

PLAN
Decide on a strategy.

Guess and Test is a good strategy for this problem. Begin by guessing the number of scientists in one group. First guess that there are 45 Centaurians (about half the scientists).

 **SOLVE**
Try the strategy.

2. a. How many Tripodians would there be?
  b. How many legs would all the Centaurians have?
  c. How many legs would all the Tripodians have?
  d. Does the guess satisfy the conditions of the problem? Explain.

3. Would your next guess be more or fewer Centaurians? Why?

Try another number for the Centaurians. Repeat Questions 2 and 3 until you find the solution. You can use a table like the one shown to keep track of your guesses.

Aliens	Number Attending	Number of Legs
Centaurians	45	■
Tripodians	44	■
Totals	89	■

 LOOK BACK
Think about how you solved the problem.

4. a. How many Centaurians and Tripodians were there?
  b. Discuss any pattern you found or shortcut you used that helped you solve the problem.

EXERCISES *On Your Own*

Use the *Guess and Test* strategy to solve each problem.

1. On the two days before a swim meet, Jesse swam a total of 2,050 meters. The second day she swam 250 meters more than the first day. How many meters did she swim on each day?

2. Al's Grooming Salon is very busy. The groomer must clip the nails of 40 birds and cats. There are 110 animal feet in all. How many birds are there? How many cats are there?

3. In a math class of 26 students, each girl drew a triangle and each boy drew a rectangle. If there were 92 sides in all, how many girls and how many boys were in the class?

4. Two integers have a sum of -9 and a difference of 5. What are the integers?

Use any strategy to solve each problem. Show your work.

5. Rosa drove a total of 1,000 mi during three days. On the second day she drove the same number of miles as she did on the first and third days combined. How many miles did she drive on the second day?

6. A sporting goods store manager ordered twice as many pairs of basketball sneakers as tennis sneakers. He ordered 96 pairs in all. How many pairs of each kind did he order?

7. a. At a hospital, 40 of the babies born this year were members of either triplets or twins. Could there have been only one set of triplets and all the rest twins? Explain.

b. How many different combinations of twins and triplets could there be?

8. Jeanne Louise Calment of France lived to be the oldest human on record. Carrie White of the United States lived 6 years less than Calment. If the sum of their ages is 238 years, how old did each person live to be?

9. *Sports* Claudia defeated six opponents to become the town tennis champion. The loser of each match dropped out of the competition. The winner moved on to the next level. What is the greatest possible number of players in this tournament?

Mixed Review

Estimate using rounding. *(Previous Course)*

10. $16{,}327 + 8{,}104$ **11.** $43{,}212 - 21{,}605$ **12.** $627 - 244$ **13.** $4{,}649 + 8{,}768$

For Exercises 14–16, use the following data: 89 75 93 76 89 92 84 98 72 88. *(Lesson 1-4)*

14. Find the mean, median, and mode.   **15.** Make a frequency table, using intervals.

16. *Estimation* The area of the United States is 3,618,787 mi^2. The area of Bermuda is 20.6 mi^2. About how many times larger is the United States? *(Previous Course)*

2-10 Exponents and Division

What You'll Learn

▼ **1** To divide powers with the same base

▼ **2** To evaluate expressions with zero and negative exponents

...And Why

You can write very small numbers by using negative exponents.

Here's How

Look for questions that
- build understanding
✔ check understanding

A magnified view of an animal cell.

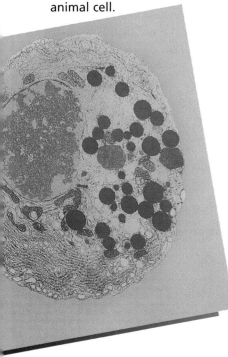

THINK AND DISCUSS

1 *Dividing Powers with the Same Base*

You might read in a biology textbook that the diameter of a cell is 6×10^{-4} mm. What does the negative exponent mean? To find out, first explore the connection between division and exponents.

■ **EXAMPLE 1**

Find $7^5 \div 7^3$.
$$7^5 \div 7^3 = \frac{7^5}{7^3} = \frac{\overset{1}{\cancel{7}} \cdot \overset{1}{\cancel{7}} \cdot \overset{1}{\cancel{7}} \cdot 7 \cdot 7}{\underset{1}{\cancel{7}} \cdot \underset{1}{\cancel{7}} \cdot \underset{1}{\cancel{7}}} = \frac{7 \cdot 7}{1} = 7^2 = 49$$

1. ✔ *Try It Out* Find each quotient.
   a. $3^7 \div 3^3$ **b.** $4^7 \div 4^5$ **c.** $2^7 \div 2^6$ **d.** $5^4 \div 5$

Example 1 above suggests the following rule.

DIVIDING POWERS WITH THE SAME BASE

To divide numbers or variables with the same base, subtract the exponents.

Arithmetic	**Algebra**
$\dfrac{7^5}{7^3} = 7^{(5-3)} = 7^2$	$\dfrac{a^m}{a^n} = a^{(m-n)}$, where $a \neq 0$

■ **EXAMPLE 2**

Simplify $n^{12} \div n^5$.
$$n^{12} \div n^5 = n^{(12-5)} \qquad \longleftarrow \text{Subtract the exponents.}$$
$$= n^7 \qquad\qquad \longleftarrow \text{Simplify.}$$

2. ✔ *Try It Out* Complete each equation.
   a. $2^9 \div 2^7 = 2^{\blacksquare}$ **b.** $r^9 \div r^6 = r^{\blacksquare}$ **c.** $c^4 \div c^{\blacksquare} = c^2$

▼2 *Using Zero and Negative Exponents*

To understand what it means to have zero as an exponent, consider these two methods of evaluating the quotient $\frac{3^5}{3^5}$.

$$\frac{3^5}{3^5} = 3^{(5-5)} = 3^0 \quad \longleftarrow \text{Subtract the exponents.}$$

$$\frac{3^5}{3^5} = \frac{\overset{1}{\cancel{3}} \cdot \overset{1}{\cancel{3}} \cdot \overset{1}{\cancel{3}} \cdot \overset{1}{\cancel{3}} \cdot \overset{1}{\cancel{3}}}{\underset{1}{\cancel{3}} \cdot \underset{1}{\cancel{3}} \cdot \underset{1}{\cancel{3}} \cdot \underset{1}{\cancel{3}} \cdot \underset{1}{\cancel{3}}} = \frac{1}{1} = 1 \quad \longleftarrow \begin{array}{l}\text{Factor the numerator and}\\ \text{denominator. Then simplify.}\end{array}$$

Since $\frac{3^5}{3^5} = 3^0$ and $\frac{3^5}{3^5} = 1$, you know that $3^0 = 1$. This suggests the following definition of zero as an exponent.

ZERO AS AN EXPONENT

For any nonzero number a, $a^0 = 1$.

■ EXAMPLE 3

a. Evaluate $(-8)^0$.

$(-8)^0 = 1 \quad \longleftarrow \begin{array}{c}\text{Definition of zero}\\ \text{as an exponent.}\end{array} \longrightarrow$

b. Simplify m^0.

$m^0 = 1$

3. ✔ Try It Out Simplify each expression.

a. $(-32)^0$ **b.** $2n^0$ **c.** $m^4 \div m^4 = m^{\blacksquare}$

To understand what it means to have a negative exponent, consider these two methods of evaluating the quotient $\frac{6^2}{6^4}$.

$$\frac{6^2}{6^4} = 6^{(2-4)} = 6^{-2} \quad \longleftarrow \text{Subtract the exponents.}$$

$$\frac{6^2}{6^4} = \frac{\overset{1}{\cancel{6}} \cdot \overset{1}{\cancel{6}}}{\underset{1}{\cancel{6}} \cdot \underset{1}{\cancel{6}} \cdot 6 \cdot 6} \quad \longleftarrow \begin{array}{l}\text{Factor the numerator and}\\ \text{denominator.}\end{array}$$

$$= \frac{1}{6 \cdot 6} = \frac{1}{6^2} \quad \longleftarrow \text{Simplify.}$$

Since $\frac{6^2}{6^4} = 6^{-2}$ and $\frac{6^2}{6^4} = \frac{1}{6^2}$, you know that $6^{-2} = \frac{1}{6^2}$. This suggests the following definition of negative exponents.

NEGATIVE EXPONENT

For any nonzero number a and any integer n, $a^{-n} = \frac{1}{a^n}$.

Wolf spiders are hairy spiders that are most often dark brown in color. They are nocturnal hunting spiders that run rapidly after prey. Wolf spiders do not construct webs.

■ **EXAMPLE 4**   *Real-World Problem Solving*

Biology A common house spider weighs about 10^{-4} kilogram. Express this weight as a fraction and as a decimal.

$$10^{-4} = \frac{1}{10^4} \quad \longleftarrow \text{Definition of a negative exponent.}$$

$$= \frac{1}{10,000} \quad \longleftarrow \text{Simplify.}$$

$$= 0.0001 \quad \longleftarrow \text{Rewrite as a decimal.}$$

4. ✔ *Try It Out* Write each expression as a fraction.
   a. 3^{-1} **b.** 2^{-3} **c.** -3^{-2} **d.** $(-2)^{-3}$

5. ⁂ *Go a Step Further* Complete each equation.
   a. $y^{-4} = \frac{1}{y^{\blacksquare}}$ **b.** $\frac{1}{2}x^{\blacksquare} = \frac{1}{2x^2}$

6. Write two equivalent expressions for each quotient. One should have a positive exponent and one a negative exponent.
   a. $\frac{7^4}{7^6}$ **b.** $\frac{2}{2^8}$ **c.** $\frac{w^4}{w^8}$ **d.** $\frac{6x^3}{-2x^8}$

Work Together
Patterns and Negative Exponents

7. **a.** Find the missing terms: 16, 8, 4, 2, 1, ▨, ▨, ▨.
   b. Each term in part (a) can be written as a power of 2. Complete: $2^4, 2^3, 2^2, 2^1, \blacksquare^{\blacksquare}, \blacksquare^{\blacksquare}, \blacksquare^{\blacksquare}, \blacksquare^{\blacksquare}$.

8. Work with a partner to create a pattern like the one above using 10 as a base.

EXERCISES *On Your Own*

Write each expression as an integer.

1. $1^{20} \div 1^{10}$ 2. $\frac{6^5}{6^4}$ 3. $\frac{-3^8}{-3^5}$ 4. $10^{12} \div 10^8$ 5. $(-3)^7 \div (-3)^4$

Simplify each expression.

6. $g^{12} \div g^9$ 7. $m^8 \div m$ 8. $\frac{c^9}{c^7}$ 9. $\frac{s^{10}}{s^6}$ 10. $\frac{8d^7}{-2d^4}$

Is each statement *true* or *false*? Explain your reasoning.

11. $4^0 = 4^1$ 12. $8^0 = (-8)^0$ 13. $1^{-5} = (-1)^5$ 14. $2^1 \div 2^{-1} = 2^0$

Write each expression as an integer or simple fraction.

15. $(-5)^{-3}$ 16. -2^{-4} 17. $\dfrac{4^0}{4^2}$ 18. $\dfrac{1}{2^{-4}}$ 19. $\dfrac{(-4)^6}{-4^6}$ 20. $\dfrac{(-2)^3}{(-2)^6}$

Simplify each expression. Use only positive exponents.

21. x^{-4} 22. $2y^{-3}$ 23. $2^{-2}y^2$ 24. 3^0g 25. $4^{-1}d^0$

26. $a^{10} \div a^{15}$ 27. $2m^9 \div m^9$ 28. $\dfrac{10h^3}{5h^7}$ 29. $\dfrac{y^4}{y^9}$ 30. $8(2n)^{-2}$

Complete each equation.

31. $\dfrac{3^{14}}{3^{\blacksquare}} = 3^7$ 32. $\dfrac{x^5}{x^{\blacksquare}} = x^3$ 33. $\dfrac{10z^{12}}{5z^4} = 2z^{\blacksquare}$ 34. $\dfrac{1}{6^5} = 6^{\blacksquare}$ 35. $\dfrac{1}{(-4)^8} = (-4)^{\blacksquare}$

36. $\dfrac{1}{c^7} = c^{\blacksquare}$ 37. $\dfrac{1}{-8} = (-2)^{\blacksquare}$ 38. $\dfrac{1}{100} = 10^{\blacksquare}$ 39. $\dfrac{y^{\blacksquare}}{y^{12}} = y^{-2}$ 40. $\dfrac{y^3}{y^{\blacksquare}} = y^{-9}$

41. *Open-ended* Write three expressions equivalent to $4^7 \div 4^3$.

42. *Writing* Explain why the value of -4^0 is negative and the value of $(-4)^0$ is positive.

43. *Reasoning* When is a^{-3} a negative number? A positive number? Explain.

Write each underlined number as a power of 10.

Sample: $0.01 = \dfrac{1}{100} = \dfrac{1}{10^2} = 10^{-2}$

44. A snowflake weighs <u>0.000001</u> gram.

45. An influenza virus measures <u>0.0001</u> millimeter across.

46. A nanosecond is <u>0.000000001</u> of a second.

47. The diameter of a hydrogen atom is <u>0.00000001</u> millimeter.

> JOURNAL
> How are the rules for multiplying and dividing powers of the same base alike? How are they different?

Mixed Review

Make a line plot for each set of data. *(Lesson 1-3)*

48. 10, 18, 8, 10, 13, 11, 10, 8, 13, 12   49. 175, 180, 155, 220, 175, 175, 200, 200, 180

Find each sum or difference. *(Lessons 2-3 and 2-4)*

50. $-6 + 4$ 51. $-8 + (-5)$ 52. $-2 + 6$ 53. $-4 - (-5)$ 54. $-2 - (-2)$

55. William's brother is one third his father's age. His father is three times William's age. If William is 16, how old is his brother? *(Previous Course)*

2-11 Scientific Notation

What You'll Learn

1 To write numbers using scientific notation

2 To write numbers in standard form

...And Why

You can use scientific notation to help you work with very large and very small numbers.

Here's How

Look for questions that
- build understanding
- ✔ check understanding

Work Together — *Preparing to Use Scientific Notation*

1. Copy and complete each statement. Use a calculator.

6.71×10^{3}	$= 6.71 \times 1{,}000 =$ ■	
6.71×10^{2}	$= 6.71 \times$ ■ $=$ ■	
6.71×10^{1}	$= 6.71 \times$ ■ $=$ ■	
6.71×10^{0}	$= 6.71 \times$ ■ $=$ ■	
6.71×10^{-1}	$= 6.71 \times \frac{1}{10} = 6.71 \times 0.1 =$ ■	
6.71×10^{-2}	$= 6.71 \times$ ■ $= 6.71 \times$ ■ $=$ ■	
6.71×10^{-3}	$= 6.71 \times$ ■ $= 6.71 \times$ ■ $=$ ■	

2. ⊞ *Patterns* What patterns do you see in your answers?

THINK AND DISCUSS

1 *Using Scientific Notation*

Scientific notation is a shorthand way to write very large and very small numbers. A number in **scientific notation** is written as the product of two factors. The first factor is a number greater than or equal to 1 and less than 10. The second is a power of 10.

■ **EXAMPLE 1** *Real-World Problem Solving*

Astronomy Earth is roughly spherical in shape. Its volume is very, very large—about 259,000,000,000 cubic miles! Write this number in scientific notation.

$$259{,}000{,}000{,}000.$$

You move the decimal point 11 places to get a factor greater than or equal to 1 and less than 10.

11 places

$$= 2.59 \times 100{,}000{,}000{,}000$$
$$= 2.59 \times 10^{11}$$ ← The exponent of 10 is 11.

3. ✔ *Try It Out* Write each number in scientific notation.
 a. 789,000 **b.** 256,000,000 **c.** 4,124,000

4. a. ⚏ *Look Back* Is the volume of Earth equal to 25.9×10^{10} mi^3? Explain.

b. Explain why the expression 25.9×10^{10} is *not* written in scientific notation.

Powers of Ten

10^4	$= 10,000$
10^3	$= 1,000$
10^2	$= 100$
10^1	$= 10$
10^0	$= 1$
10^{-1}	$= 0.1$
10^{-2}	$= 0.01$
10^{-3}	$= 0.001$
10^{-4}	$= 0.0001$

■ **EXAMPLE 2**

Write 0.000056 in scientific notation.

$$0.000056$$
5 places

You move the decimal point 5 places to get a factor greater than or equal to 1 and less than 10.

$$= 5.6 \times 0.00001$$
$$= 5.6 \times 10^{-5}$$

The exponent of 10 is −5.

5. ⚏ *Think About It* Explain why the exponent in Example 1 is positive, while the exponent in Example 2 is negative.

6. ✔ *Try It Out* Write each number in scientific notation.
a. 0.000789 **b.** 0.0000023 **c.** 0.004124

▼2 *Changing to Standard Form*

You can change numbers from scientific notation to **standard form** by working backward.

■ **EXAMPLE 3**

Write (a) 1.9×10^5 and (b) 4.519×10^{-4} in standard form.

a. $1.9 \times 10^5 = 1.90000$
5 places
$$= 190,000$$

A positive exponent indicates a large number. Move the decimal point 5 places to the right.

b. $4.519 \times 10^{-4} = 0004.519$
4 places
$$= .0004519$$

A negative exponent indicates a small number. Move the decimal point 4 places to the left.

7. How does the number of places you need to move the decimal point compare to the absolute value of the exponent of 10 in Example 3?

8. ✔ *Try It Out* Write each number in standard form.
a. 2.354×10^9 **b.** -1.2×10^5 **c.** 5.8×10^{-6}

To compare and order numbers written in scientific notation, look at their exponents first.

■ **EXAMPLE 4**   *Real-World Problem Solving*

Science Order the items in the chart from smallest to largest.

Approximate Sizes (mm)	
Paint pigment	7.0×10^{-5}
Red blood cell	8.0×10^{-3}
Virus	2.5×10^{-5}
Atomic radius	1.2×10^{-7}
Ketchup particle	9.5×10^{-5}

- First, order the exponents.
  $$-7 \ < \ -5 \ < \ -3$$
  So, $10^{-7} < 10^{-5} < 10^{-3}$.

- Next, compare numbers with the same exponent.

  $2.5 < 7.0 < 9.5$
  So, $2.5 \times 10^{-5} < 7.0 \times 10^{-5} < 9.5 \times 10^{-5}$.

- Finally, write the items in order from smallest to largest.

  1.2×10^{-7} 2.5×10^{-5} 7.0×10^{-5} 9.5×10^{-5} 8.0×10^{-3}
  atomic   virus   paint   ketchup   red blood
  radius   pigment   particle   cell

9. ✔ *Try It Out* Order this set of data from least to greatest.
   $5.6 \times 10^{-10}, 7.5 \times 10^{-21}, 6.2 \times 10^{-10}, 9.2 \times 10^{-15}$

GRAPHING CALCULATOR HINT

On a graphing calculator, enter this key sequence:
3.9 [EE] [(-)] 14 [ENTER].
The display should read
3.9 E −14.

On a calculator, you can enter a number in scientific notation, such as 3.9×10^{-14}, by using the exponent key.

3.9 [EXP] 14 [+/-] [=] *3.9⁻¹⁴* or *3.9E−14*

10. ✔ *Try It Out* Write the number on each calculator display first in scientific notation, then in standard form.
    a. *3.⁻⁰²*   b. *5.6E9*   c. *2.1 ⁰³*

EXERCISES *On Your Own*

Write each number in scientific notation.

1. 45,600
2. 0.000000013
3. 80,000,000
4. 0.0002
5. 0.000981

6. 23,000
7. 0.0101
8. 8,100
9. 6,250,000
10. 0.003

11. **Choose A, B, C, or D.** Which of the following is 0.000072 written in scientific notation?

   A. 72×10^{-6} B. 7.2×10^{5} C. 7.2×0.00001 D. 7.2×10^{-5}

Find each value of n.

12. $4{,}630 = 4.63 \times 10^n$ **13.** $0.00345 = 3.45 \times 10^n$ **14.** $90{,}000{,}000 = 9 \times 10^n$

15. $637{,}000 = n \times 10^5$ **16.** $0.0045 = n \times 10^{-3}$ **17.** $0.00000003008 = n \times 10^{-8}$

Write each number in scientific notation.

18. The temperature inside the sun is greater than $16{,}000{,}000°$C.

19. The diameter of the thinnest copper wire is 0.0005 in.

20. *Astronomy* The closest we get to the planet Venus is $25{,}700{,}000$ miles.

21. *Biology* The smallest flowering and fruiting plant weighs 0.00001 ounces.

Write each number in standard form.

22. 7×10^{-9} **23.** 1.362×10^8 **24.** 4.02×10^{-5} **25.** 4×10^3 **26.** 7.89×10^6

27. 9.5×10^{-1} **28.** 1.32×10^5 **29.** 5×10^{-4} **30.** 7×10^7 **31.** 3.6×10^{-3}

Number Sense **Decide which expression is greater. Explain how you know.**

32. 2×10^6 or 8×10^5 **33.** 9×10^{-4} or 9×10^{-5} **34.** 3.0×10^{-4} or 3.2×10^{-4}

35. Choose A, B, C, or D. Which number is equal to 6×10^{-4}?

    A. $-60{,}000$ **B.** 0.00006 **C.** $\dfrac{6}{10{,}000}$ **D.** -0.0006

Order each set of numbers from least to greatest.

36. 10^3, 10^{-10}, 10^7, 10^{-9}, 10^0

37. 3.1×10^3, 5.7×10^3, 9.5×10^3, 8.6×10^3

38. 7.2×10^5, 7.2×10^6, 7.02×10^6, 7.1×10^6

39. 2.15×10^{-7}, 3.1×10^{-5}, 4.2×10^{-8}, 5.678×10^{-5}

40. *Astronomy* Order the planets in the chart at the right, starting with the planet closest to the sun.

Write the number on each calculator display first in scientific notation, then in standard form.

41. 7.892^{-10} **42.** $6.^{13}$ **43.** $4.9E{-}12$

44. 5.97^{-5} **45.** $3.491E7$ **46.** $5.6E{-}9$

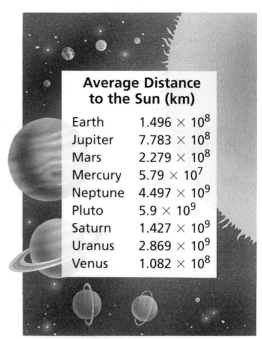

Average Distance to the Sun (km)	
Earth	1.496×10^8
Jupiter	7.783×10^8
Mars	2.279×10^8
Mercury	5.79×10^7
Neptune	4.497×10^9
Pluto	5.9×10^9
Saturn	1.427×10^9
Uranus	2.869×10^9
Venus	1.082×10^8

Sizes of planets and sun are not to scale.

47. *Biology* One liter (L) equals 10^6 cubic millimeters (mm^3). There are 5×10^6 red blood cells in 1 mm^3 of blood. Use scientific notation to write the number of red blood cells in 1 L of human blood.

48. *Biology* A human being has about 2.5×10^{13} red blood cells in his or her bloodstream. There are about 2 white blood cells for every 1,000 red blood cells. How many white blood cells are in a human's bloodstream?

49. *Reasoning* When a number is written in scientific notation, what does a positive power of ten indicate about the size of the number? What does a negative power of ten indicate?

50. *Writing* A number written in scientific notation is doubled. Explain why the exponent of 10 may or may not change.

PORTFOLIO
Select one or two items from your work for this chapter. Consider:
• corrected work
• work you found challenging
• a journal entry
Explain why you have included each selection that you make.

Mixed Review

Evaluate each expression for $x = 2$ and $y = 4$. *(Lesson 2-2)*

51. $xy - 5$

52. $x + 5 - y$

53. $19 - x - y$

54. $y - 10 - (-x)$

Find the next four numbers in each pattern. *(Lesson 2-4)*

55. 100, 50, 70, 20, ■, ■, ■, ■

56. 1, 11, 21, 31, ■, ■, ■, ■

Evaluate each expression. *(Lesson 2-6)*

57. $(14 - 16)^3 + 10$

58. $-4 \cdot (2 - 8)^2$

59. $(-7 - 8)^2 \cdot 20$

60. *Choose a Strategy* Bart saves a nickel every five days and a penny every two days. On July 1, he saves a penny and a nickel. How much money will he have on July 31?

CHAPTER PROJECT

PROJECT LINK: WRITING

The Fahrenheit scale is widely used in the United States. However, American scientists almost always use the Celsius scale in their work. Explain why this is so, and include your explanation in your report.

Choose the best answer.

1. How would you write these elevations from lowest point to highest point?

Death Valley, CA	−282 ft
Guadalupe Peak, TX	8,749 ft
New Orleans, LA	−8 ft
Pike's Peak, CO	14,110 ft

   A. −8 ft, −282 ft, 8,749 ft, 14,110 ft
   B. −282 ft, −8 ft, 8,749 ft, 14,110 ft
   C. 14,110 ft, 8,749 ft, −282 ft, −8 ft
   D. 14,110 ft, 8,749 ft, −8 ft, −282 ft

2. Which is equivalent to $\dfrac{2^9}{2^3}$?

   F. 1^3 G. 1^6 H. 2^3 J. 2^6

3. Which is equivalent to $2^5 \cdot 4^3$?

   A. $2 \cdot 2 \cdot 2 \cdot 2 \cdot 2 \cdot 4 \cdot 4 \cdot 4$
   B. $(5 \cdot 2) + (4 \cdot 3)$
   C. $5 \cdot 5 \cdot 4 \cdot 4 \cdot 4$
   D. $10 \cdot 12$

4. Which of these is *not* equivalent to 4(99)?

   F. $4(100) - 4(1)$ G. $4(100) - 1$
   H. $4(100 - 1)$ J. $400 - 4$

5. *Astronomy* On average, Earth is about 9.3×10^7 miles from the sun. What is another way to express this measure?

   A. 9,300,000,000   B. 930,000,000
   C. 93,000,000   D. 9,300,000

6. *Biology* A human red blood cell is 0.000008 m in diameter. What is this number written in scientific notation?

   F. 8×10^{-7} G. 0.8×10^{-6}
   H. 8×10^{-6} J. 8×10^{-5}

Please note that items 7–11 have *five* answer choices.

7. Tomas is on a diet and loses 2 pounds a month. If he started dieting at 190 pounds, how much will he weigh after 8 months?

   A. 206 pounds   B. 188 pounds
   C. 174 pounds   D. 173 pounds
   E. 172 pounds

8. Shondel started on the third floor, rode an elevator up 9 floors, then down 5 floors, and then down 3 more floors. On what floor was she then?

   F. 1   G. 4   H. 7
   J. 8   K. 17

9. *Money* Josh began $250 in debt. Each month he increased his debt $50. After 4 months, how much did he owe?

   A. $50   B. $250   C. $300
   D. $400   E. $450

10. The temperature in Chicago is −1°F at noon. A 10 degree drop is predicted for the afternoon. What will the temperature be then?

    F. 11°F   G. 9°F   H. −9°F
    J. −10°F   K. −11°F

11. *Sports* During their first three downs in a recent football game, the Cougars gained 6 yards, lost 15 yards, and gained 4 yards. What was their net change in position?

    A. −25 yards   B. −5 yards
    C. 5 yards   D. 13 yards
    E. 17 yards

CHAPTER PROJECT

WEATHER or NOT

Prepare a Report The Project Link questions on pages 76, 85, 90, and 107 should help you complete your project. Here is a checklist to help you gather the parts of your project together.

✔ the chart comparing Celsius and Fahrenheit scales

✔ the region on which your report is based

✔ the temperature information for the region

✔ the graphs or maps used to display data

✔ the simple rule for converting Celsius to Fahrenheit degrees

Be prepared to present your report to a group of travel agents. You'll want to be interesting, factual, and instructive. Include maps, charts, and graphs to make your information as clear as possible. Explain clearly the two temperature scales in use.

Reflect and Revise

Review your report with a family member. Is your data clear and easy to understand? Is your conversion rule easily applied mentally? If necessary, make changes to improve your report.

Web Extension

Prentice Hall's Internet site contains information you might find helpful as you complete your project. Visit www.phschool.com/mgm3/ch2 for some links and ideas related to weather.

Integers and Absolute Value 2-1

Integers are the set of whole numbers and their opposites. The **absolute value** of a number is its distance from zero.

Compare. Write >, <, or =.

1. -8 ■ -1 2. -7 ■ 2 3. $|-3|$ ■ 1 4. $|-4|$ ■ $|4|$

Adding and Subtracting Integers 2-3, 2-4

Numbers that are opposites are called **additive inverses.** Their sum is zero. The sum of two positive integers is positive. The sum of two negative integers is negative.

To add integers with *different* signs, *subtract* their absolute values and keep the sign of the integer with the greater absolute value. To subtract an integer, you add its opposite.

Find each sum or difference.

5. $(-9) + (-3)$ 6. $8 + (-3)$ 7. $(-11) - (-5)$ 8. $(-9) - 2$

Multiplying and Dividing Integers 2-5

The product or quotient of two integers with the *same* sign is *positive*. The product or quotient of two integers with *different* signs is *negative*.

Evaluate each expression.

9. $-3 \cdot 18$ 10. $(-34) \div (-2)$ 11. $-1{,}260 \div 45$ 12. $-15 \cdot (-4) \div (-12)$

13. *Writing* Explain how you would use the distributive property and the commutative and associative properties of addition to simplify $-8(99) + (-7) + (-93)$.

Variable Expressions 2-2, 2-7

A **variable expression** is a group of numbers, variables, and operations. To **evaluate** a variable expression, you replace the variable with a number and then compute, following the **order of operations.**

Write a variable expression for each phrase.

14. the sum of b and 7   **15.** 8 less than w **16.** 3 more than twice y

Evaluate each expression for $x = 2$.

17. $6 \cdot (x - 1)^2$ **18.** $40 \div x + 7.5$ **19.** $40 \div (x + 7.5)$ **20.** $x^2 - 7x$

Guess and Test, and Mental Math   2-8, 2-9

To evaluate an expression mentally, you may find the commutative property, associative property, identity property, or the distributive property helpful.

Evaluate each expression mentally. Explain your method.

21. $(-5)(168)(20)$ **22.** $125 + 394 + 575$ **23.** $4(18 + 25)$ **24.** $(-9) + (-3) + (-1)$

Sometimes the best way to solve a problem is to guess, test your guess, and make a better guess. Making a table is a good way to organize your guesses so that you can look for a pattern.

25. The length of a rectangle is 6 m greater than the width, and the area is 55 m^2. What are the dimensions?

26. A box contains 30 triangles and squares. There are 103 sides altogether. How many of each figure are there?

Exponents and Scientific Notation   2-6, 2-10, 2-11

Any expression in exponential form, such as 2^5 is called a **power.** To multiply powers with the same base, add the exponents. To divide powers with the same base, subtract the exponents.

$$\underbrace{2 \cdot 2 \cdot 2 \cdot 2 \cdot 2}_{5 \text{ factors of } 2} = 2^5 \quad \longleftarrow 5 \text{ is the exponent.}$$
$$\quad\quad\quad\quad\quad\quad\quad\searrow 2 \text{ is the base.}$$

Evaluate or simplify each expression.

27. $2^3 \cdot 2^2$ **28.** $-4^2 + 1^3 + (-15)^0$ **29.** $\dfrac{t^7}{t^9}$ **30.** $\dfrac{4}{4^{-2}}$ **31.** $\dfrac{-2^4}{-2^6}$

A number in **scientific notation** is written as the product of two factors. The first factor is a number greater than or equal to 1 and less than 10. The second factor is a power of 10.

Write each number in scientific notation.

32. 295.6   **33.** 0.0083   **34.** 90,560   **35.** 0.03   **36.** 0.5987

1. Compare. Write $>$, $<$, or $=$.
   a. -12 ▦ 12
   b. $|-4|$ ▦ -4
   c. 0 ▦ -1
   d. $-(-2)$ ▦ $|-2|$

2. Evaluate each expression.
   a. $-15 + (-11)$
   b. $26 - (-14)$
   c. $-9(-6)$
   d. $|-21| \div (-3)$

3. *Writing* Explain the difference between the *opposite* of a number and the *absolute value* of a number.

4. *Algebra* Write a variable expression for each phrase.
   a. 15 more than a number
   b. the quotient of a number and -10
   c. 7 less than twice a number
   d. the product of a number and -13

5. Evaluate.
   a. $-8(15) + 12 \div (-4)$
   b. $(-14) \div 2 - (-5) \cdot (-10)$
   c. $3^2 + 6 \div (-2)$
   d. $(-24) \cdot 2 - (-13) \cdot 2$

6. Write each number in standard form.
   a. 9.35×10^3
   b. 1.53×10^{-4}
   c. 918×10^0
   d. 6.125×10^{-1}

7. Write each expression using exponents.
   a. $(-7)(-7)(x)(x)(x)$
   b. $8 \cdot 8 \cdot 8 \cdot 8 \cdot y \cdot y$
   c. $(a)(a)(a)(a)(-2)(-2)(-2)$

8. Write each expression using a single exponent.
   a. $t^2 \cdot t^3 \cdot t$
   b. $2^5 \cdot 2^6 \cdot 2^4$

9. Write each number in scientific notation.
   a. 0.00459
   b. 18 million
   c. 7,590
   d. 0.03

10. **Choose A, B, C, or D.** Which of the following equations are true?
    I. $8^5 \cdot 8^4 = 8^{20}$
    II. $(-1)^3 \cdot 1^2 = 1$
    III. $(-5)^2 - |-5| = 10^2 \div 5$
    IV. $3^4 \cdot 3^5 = 3^9$

    A. I only
    B. II and III only
    C. III and IV only
    D. I, II, III, and IV

11. *Algebra* Evaluate each variable expression for the given values of the variables.
    a. $-19b$ for $b = -3$
    b. x^3 for $x = 10$
    c. $|-5 - t|$ for $t = -6$
    d. $-b^2 - 4b$ for $b = -3$
    e. $-8abc$ for $a = -5$, $b = 7$, $c = -4$

12. Evaluate each expression.
    a. -5^3
    b. $\dfrac{4^5}{4^2}$
    c. $2^0 \cdot 6^{-1}$
    d. $2^{-3} - \left(\dfrac{1}{2}\right)^3$

13. Use the distributive property to complete. Then evaluate either side of the equation mentally.
    a. $28 \cdot (-6) = (30 - $ ▦ $)(-6)$
    b. $15 \cdot 1.97 = 15(2 - $ ▦ $)$

14. A department store was selling ten-speed bikes at \$120 each and CDs at \$10 each. During the first five minutes of the opening-day sale, 13 of the items were sold. The total cost of the items was \$680. How many bikes and CDs were sold?

15. *Writing* Explain how to determine the *sign* of the product of a group of positive and negative integers without computing the product.

Choose the best answer.

1. Which survey question is an example of a non-biased, closed-option question?

   A. What is your favorite TV show?
   B. Are you under voting age or are you old enough to vote?
   C. Do you prefer canned or fresh spinach ?
   D. Are you in 7th or 8th grade?

2. What information *cannot* be determined from the box-and-whisker plot shown?

   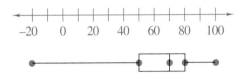

   A. the median   B. the range
   C. the quartiles   D. the outliers

3. Which expression does *not* equal 5(2.99)?

   A. $5(3) - 0.01$ B. $5(3) - 5(0.01)$
   C. $5(2) + 5(0.99)$ D. $\frac{10(2.99)}{2}$

4. Which expression does *not* equal $\frac{9}{16}$?

   A. $32 \cdot 4^{-2}$ B. $3^2 \div 4^2$
   C. $9 \cdot 2^{-4}$ D. $3^2 \cdot 4^{-2}$

5. How many integers are there whose absolute value is less than 3?

   A. 4   B. 5   C. 6   D. 3

6. What can the expression $12k$ represent?

   A. the cost (in cents) of a dozen cans of juice if each can costs 12 cents
   B. the cost (in cents) of k photocopies if each photocopy costs 12 cents
   C. the time it took Alana to run 1 mi if she ran 12 mi in k min
   D. Darrin's age, if Darrin is k years older than his 12-year-old brother

7. Jake recieved these grades on his math tests: 83, 86, 95, 95, 90, 82, 85, 82, 87, 82. What is his median test score?

   A. 82   B. 86   C. 85.5   D. 86.7

8. For the school bottle-and-can drive, the class officers brought in the following number of cans: 36, 40, 85, 63. Find the average (mean) number of cans.

   A. 40   B. 51.5   C. 56
   D. There is no mean.

9. Which expression has the same value as $8 - 11$?

   A. $8 - (-11)$ B. $|8 - 11|$
   C. $-8 + 11$ D. $8 + (-11)$

10. Which expression is equivalent to $2^4 \times 2^2$?

    A. 4^8 B. 4^6 C. 2^8 D. 2^6

11. Althea has $3.50 to spend for lunch each week. She always buys milk, which costs $.25. A full lunch (including milk) costs $1.35. How many days a week can she buy a full lunch?

    A. 1   B. 2   C. 3   D. 4

12. According to the graph shown, when did the stock fund earn the most?

    Earnings of Two Investments

    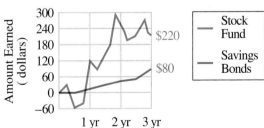

    A. the 1st year   B. the 2nd year
    C. the 3rd year   D. Not Here

Equations and Inequalities

3

Balancing ACT

Mobiles are a popular form of art that you may see anywhere: in people's homes, in large office buildings, and in parks. The objects on a mobile float gently on currents of air. Mobiles were first popularized by American sculptor Alexander Calder (1898–1976). Calder is considered the founder of kinetic art, or art that is in motion.

Make a Mobile For your chapter project, you will explore techniques for constructing a mobile. Your concern will be that the objects on the mobile hang in balance. You will use equations to model the relationships in your mobile.

- How to solve problems by writing an equation

What You'll Learn

▼1 To combine like terms

▼2 To simplify expressions

...And Why

You can use variable expressions to model transportation problems and geometry problems.

Here's How

Look for questions that
- 🔧 build understanding
- ✔ check understanding

QUICKreview

▫ represents 1.

◼ represents −1.

THINK AND DISCUSS

▼1 Combining Like Terms

Six students from San Jose Middle School bicycled to a game. The rest came in three buses. Seven students from Mission Hill School bicycled. The rest came in two buses. If you know that each bus carried the same number of students, then you can model the total number of students by using algebra tiles.

◼ = x, the number of students on a bus

▫ = a student arriving by bicycle

San Jose Middle School

Mission Hill School

1. How many buses were there in all? How many students bicycled in all?

2. 🔧 **Think About It** Write a variable expression that represents the total number of students who came by bus.

3. Write a variable expression that represents the total number of students who came to the game.

When you modeled the school bus problem, you used algebra tiles to model the terms. A **term** is part of a variable expression. For example, the expression $-3x + 5y + 10$ has three terms: $-3x$, $5y$, and 10.

Terms with the same variable(s) are called **like terms.** In the expression $2x + 7 + 4x$, $2x$ and $4x$ are like terms. You use tiles with the same size and shape to represent like terms. When you add or subtract like terms, you are **combining like terms.**

■ **EXAMPLE 1**

Combine like terms in the expression $5m + 9m$.

$$5m + 9m = 5 \cdot m + 9 \cdot m$$
$$= (5 + 9)m \qquad \longleftarrow \text{distributive property}$$
$$= 14m \qquad \longleftarrow \text{Add.}$$

4. ✓ *Try It Out* Combine like terms.
   a. $4x + 7x$ **b.** $3b - b$ **c.** $c - 5c$

▼2 *Simplifying Expressions*

You can **simplify** an expression by combining like terms and performing as many operations within the expression as possible.

■ **EXAMPLE 2**

Simplify $2s + 4t + s$.

$$2s + 4t + s = 2s + s + 4t \qquad \longleftarrow \text{commutative property}$$
$$= (2s + s) + 4t \qquad \longleftarrow \text{associative property}$$
$$= (2 + 1)s + 4t \qquad \longleftarrow \text{distributive property}$$
$$= 3s + 4t \qquad \longleftarrow \text{All like terms are combined.}$$

5. ✓ *Try It Out* Simplify.
   a. $2m + 3 + 6m$ **b.** $4b + x + 2x - b$
   c. $4a + 7 - 2a + 3$ **d.** $6x + y + 3x - 5y$

You can use the distributive property to simplify an expression.

■ **EXAMPLE 3**

Simplify $2(x + 3)$.

$$2(x + 3) = 2(x) + 2(3) \qquad \longleftarrow \text{distributive property}$$
$$= 2x + 6 \qquad \longleftarrow \text{All like terms are combined.}$$

6. ⬚*Modeling* Explain how the tiles below are a model of Example 3. (*Hint:* The black line stands for "equals.")

7. ✓ *Try It Out* Simplify $5(x - 7) + 4x$.

EXERCISES *On Your Own*

Write a variable expression for each model.

1.   2.   3.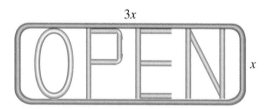

Combine like terms.

4. $8b + 3b$ 5. $9z - 4z$ 6. $3b - 7b$ 7. $-5t + 2t$ 8. $m + m$

9. $j - 4j$ 10. $-8v - 2v$ 11. $-6h + 5h$ 12. $x - 10x$ 13. $2k + k$

14. $-5s + 2s$ 15. $7q - 6q$ 16. $8n - n$ 17. $-2j - 7j$ 18. $-6j + j$

19. A "neon" sign is made from bent lengths of glass tubes filled with gas. The kind of gas inside a tube determines its color. Write a simplified variable expression that represents the perimeter of the rectangular sign at the right.

Complete with the appropriate numbers or variables.

20. $5(h + 12) = ■ \cdot h + 5 \cdot ■ = 5h + ■$

21. $(■ - 3)■ = ■ \cdot 6 - ■ \cdot 6 = 6z - ■$

Simplify each expression.

22. $12(d - 6)$ 23. $9(m + 7)$ 24. $3a + 2 + a$ 25. $x + 3y + x + y$

26. $2x + 1 + 3x$ 27. $(q + 1)5$ 28. $5n - 6 + 4n + 3$ 29. $-6 + 5(1 + r)$

30. $3 + 5(a - 4)$ 31. $x + 2(x - y)$ 32. $n + 4n - 3n$ 33. $7b + 5 - 9b + c$

34. $2z - 3 - 8z + 1$ 35. $4(b + 8) - 7b$ 36. $5x + y - 4x - 9$ 37. $-5u + 6 + u + 4u$

38. *Writing* Your best friend was absent when combining like terms was explained in class. Write an explanation you might give to him or her over the telephone. Give examples.

39. *Reasoning* Write two different expressions that can be simplified to $3m + 8$. One expression should have three terms, and the other should have four terms.

40. Here are five steps in a number trick.
   Step 1   Choose a number.
   Step 2   Double the chosen number.
   Step 3   Add 3 to the result.
   Step 4   Multiply the result by 5.
   Step 5   Subtract 6 from the result.
   a. If someone tells you the result of Step 5, how can you tell what number he or she chose in Step 1?
   b. Let n represent the number chosen in Step 1. Write a simplified expression that represents what happens at each step. Record your expressions in a table like the one at the right
   c. Using the expressions, explain why the trick works.

Step	Expression
1	n
2	$2n$
3	$2n + 3$
4	■
5	■

Mixed Review

41. a. Display the data at the right in a bar graph. *(Lesson 1-1)*
   b. Which two cities have about the same population?
   c. Which city has the greatest number of people?
   d. Which city is the least populated?

1994 Populations

Los Angeles	3,449,000
Philadelphia	1,524,000
Chicago	2,732,000
Detroit	992,000
New York	7,330,000
Houston	1,702,000

Graph the numbers on a single number line. *(Lesson 2-1)*

42. -8 **43.** 3 **44.** 0

45. -6 **46.** -1.5 **47.** $|-5|$

48. There are 4 ten-dollar bills, 6 five-dollar bills, and 4 one-dollar bills in a wallet. You draw out one bill at random. Find the probability of each event. *(Lesson 1-11)*
   a. $P(\text{one })$ **b.** $P(\text{not ten})$ **c.** $P(\text{five or one })$

3-2 Solving Equations by Subtracting or Adding

What You'll Learn

1 To solve equations by subtracting
2 To solve equations by adding

...And Why

You can use subtraction and addition to solve money and temperature problems.

Here's How

Look for questions that
- build understanding
- ✔ check understanding

THINK AND DISCUSS

1 Solving Equations by Subtracting

A mathematical sentence with an equal sign is an **equation.** Like a scale, both sides must be equal for it to balance.

In an equation like $x + 2 = 5$, a value of the variable that makes the equation true is called a **solution.** You can solve $x + 2 = 5$ by using algebra tiles.

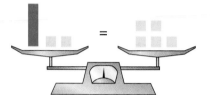

1. What do you get if you remove two yellow tiles from each side of the scale? What is the solution of the equation?

To solve an equation, you use opposite, or inverse, operations to isolate the variable. To "undo" addition, use subtraction.

SUBTRACTION PROPERTY OF EQUALITY

If you subtract the same number from each side of an equation, the two sides remain equal.

Arithmetic	Algebra
$10 = (5)(2)$	$a = b$
$10 - 4 = (5)(2) - 4$	$a - c = b - c$

Need Help? For practice with subtracting decimals, see Skills Handbook page 603.

■ EXAMPLE 1

Solve $n + 3.4 = 8$. Check the solution.

$$n + 3.4 = 8$$
$$n + 3.4 - 3.4 = 8 - 3.4 \longleftarrow \text{Subtract 3.4 from each side.}$$
$$n = 4.6 \longleftarrow \text{Simplify.}$$

Check $\quad n + 3.4 = 8 \qquad \longleftarrow \text{Use the original equation.}$
$$4.6 + 3.4 \overset{?}{=} 8 \qquad \longleftarrow \text{Replace } n \text{ with 4.6.}$$
$$8 = 8 \checkmark \qquad \longleftarrow \text{The solution checks.}$$

2. **⸬Look Back** Why was 3.4 subtracted from each side of the equation?

3. **⸬Modeling** Draw a model of $x + 3 = 10$ using a balance scale. Use the model to solve the equation.

4. **✓ Try It Out** Solve and check each equation.
   a. $x + 10 = 8$ **b.** $m + 2 = 3\frac{1}{2}$ **c.** $3 + j = -1$

▼2 *Solving Equations by Adding*

You can use addition to "undo" subtraction.

ADDITION PROPERTY OF EQUALITY

If you add the same number to each side of an equation, the two sides remain equal.

Arithmetic	**Algebra**
$10 = (5)(2)$	$a = b$
$10 + 4 = (5)(2) + 4$	$a + c = b + c$

You can use an equation to help you solve an everyday problem.

■ **EXAMPLE 2**   *Real-World Problem Solving*

Money Sven withdrew $35.00 from his bank account. The new balance was $243.25. What was the previous balance?

Words • $\boxed{\text{previous balance}} - \boxed{\text{withdrawal}} = \boxed{\text{new balance}}$

⬇

• Let $\boxed{p}$ = previous balance

Equation • $\boxed{p} - \boxed{35} = \boxed{243.25}$

$$p - 35 = 243.25$$
$$p - 35 + 35 = 243.25 + 35 \quad \longleftarrow \text{Add 35 to each side.}$$
$$p = 278.25 \quad \longleftarrow \text{Simplify.}$$

The previous balance in Sven's account was $278.25.

5. **✓ Try It Out** Solve and check each equation.
   a. $n - 7 = 10$ **b.** $-2 = j - 5$ **c.** $m - 9 = -8$

Work Together — *Using Models to Solve Equations*

- Work in a group. Write an equation for each model given below. The tiles on each side of the black line are equal.

- Use the model to solve the equation. Take the same number of tiles away from each side of the equation to get the variable alone on one side of the equation. (*Hint:* You may have to add zero pairs to one side before you can take tiles away.)

6.

7.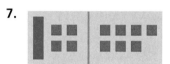

8.

9.

EXERCISES *On Your Own*

Write an equation for each model. Then solve the equation.

1.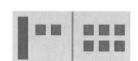

2.

3.

Solve each equation. Check the solution.

4. $a + 15 = -9$

5. $64 = n + 34$

6. $x + 3.6 = -4.1$

7. $7 = w + 9$

8. $k + 3 = 0$

9. $c + \frac{1}{2} = 8$

10. $-9 = v + (-3)$

11. $x + 350 = -72$

12. $x + 6 = \frac{1}{2}$

13. $0.3 = p + 1.5$

14. $2 = b + 6$

15. $-19 = h + (-47)$

16. $m - \frac{2}{3} = 7$

17. $1{,}570 = x + 215$

18. $n + (-7) = -53$

19. $3.2 = b + 7.5$

20. Choose A, B, C, or D. José sold one of his baseball cards for $9.30. This was $3.75 more than he originally paid for the card. If a represents the amount José originally paid, which equation *cannot* be used to find this amount?

A. $a + 3.75 = 9.30$

B. $9.30 - a = 3.75$

C. $9.30 = 3.75 + a$

D. $a - 3.75 = 9.30$

Mental Math **Solve each equation. Check the solution.**

21. $y + 7 = 12$

22. $n - 8 = -2$

23. $20 = -7 + k$

24. $b + 14 = 5$

25. $7 = d - 14$

26. $g - \frac{1}{2} = -\frac{1}{2}$

27. $6 + q = -8$

28. $-1 = w + 17$

Write an equation for each problem. Solve the equation. Then give the solution of the problem.

29. *Education* According to the United States Census, the average high school graduate earns $18,700 a year. This is $13,900 less than the average college graduate earns each year. How much does the average college graduate earn each year?

30. Yesterday Jena mailed some invitations for a party. Today she mailed eight more invitations. If Jena mailed 52 invitations in all, how many did she mail yesterday?

31. *Health* In 1959, dentists in the United States performed 34 tooth extractions for every 100 people in the population. By 1990, that rate had dropped by 16 extractions. For every hundred people, how many teeth were pulled in 1990?

32. The temperature at 6:00 P.M. was 12°F. At 6:00 A.M. it was 15 degrees cooler. What was the temperature at 6:00 A.M.?

Choose **Use a calculator, paper and pencil, or mental math. Solve each equation. Check the solution.**

33. $z - 4 = -11$

34. $-15 = 6 + m$

35. $3 + w = 12.09$

36. $n - 3.5 = 9$

37. $f + \frac{1}{2} = 5$

38. $7 + b = -13$

39. $x - 1.75 = 19$

40. $156 = b - (-29)$

41. $12 + k = 1.93$

42. $p + (-4) = 7\frac{1}{2}$

43. $0 = n + 20$

44. $-9.32 = x - 5.07$

45. *Writing* Write a problem that you can solve using the equation $a + 8.40 = 11.55$.

Reasoning **Choose from** $-3, -2, -1, 0, 1, 2,$ **and** 3. **Find** *all* **the numbers that are solutions of each equation.**

46. $n = 3$

47. $|n| = 3$

48. $|n| = -3$

49. $|n| = 0$

50. $|n| + 1 = 2$

51. $|n + 1| = 2$

Estimation **Estimate the solution of each equation.**

52. $r + 8.019 = -11.57$

53. $-3.9004 = y - 61.41$

54. $j - 0.0155 = 3.029$

55. $-14.8 + p = 2.03$

56. $n - 5.876 = -17.092$

57. $-8\frac{7}{8} = b - 4\frac{1}{8}$

JOURNAL

Explain how an equation is like a balance scale. Give an example of an equation. Show how you would solve the equation using a balance scale as a model.

58. *Reasoning* Consider the equation $x + 15 = x + 9 + 6$.
  a. What happens when you try to solve the equation?
  b. For what values of x is the original equation true?
  c. *Open-ended* Write an equation that is true for all values of the variable you use.

Mixed Review

Use the following data for Exercises 59 and 60:
22, 26, 25, 25, 27, 22, 23, 25, 24, 26, 23, 27. *(Lesson 1-3)*

59. Make a frequency table. Do not use intervals.

60. Draw a line plot.

Find each sum. *(Lesson 2-3)*

61. $-5 + 2$

62. $-7 + (-3)$

63. $-4 + (-10)$

64. $3 + (-7)$

65. *Choose a Strategy* Use each of the digits from 1 to 5 exactly once. Find the two numbers made from these digits that give you the greatest possible product. Explain why you believe you have found the greatest product.

CHAPTER PROJECT

PROJECT LINK: CALCULATING

In this project, you will consider mobiles on which objects hang to the left or right of a main support wire. Suppose you want to construct the mobile at the right. You want to find the weight x that will make the mobile balance. Write and solve an equation to represent your conclusion.

$x + 3 = 5; 2$ oz

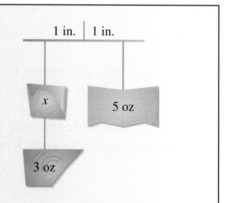

EXPLORATION

Magic Squares with Integers

After Lesson 3-2

A **magic square** is a table with the same number of rows as columns. Each row, column, and diagonal in a magic square has the same sum. At the right is a 3-by-3 magic square. What is the sum of each row, column, and diagonal?

8	3	4
1	5	9
6	7	2

up a diagonal:
$6 + 5 + 4 = 15$

across the second row:
$1 + 5 + 9 = 15$

down the third column:
$4 + 9 + 2 = 15$

■ EXAMPLE

Write and solve an equation to find each missing value in the magic square at the right.

-4	-6	b
6	-2	-10
a	2	0

Use the middle row to find the sum: $6 + (-2) + (-10) = -6$.

Write and solve an equation for the first column.

$$-4 + 6 + a = -6$$
$$a + 2 = -6$$
$$a + 2 - 2 = -6 - 2$$
$$a = -8$$

Write and solve an equation for the first row.

$$-4 + (-6) + b = -6$$
$$b - 10 = -6$$
$$b - 10 + 10 = -6 + 10$$
$$b = 4$$

Write and solve an equation to find each missing value in the magic squares below.

1.

2	b	-2
a	-1	c
0	1	-4

2.

17	x	7
12	22	z
w	y	27

3.

a	11	8
c	b	-7
e	d	14

4.

-6	4	5	-9
2	x	-1	-3
-5	1	y	0
w	-7	-8	z

5. *Open-ended* Use one of the magic squares on this page. Multiply each entry by -2. Is the result still a magic square? Explain.

6. *Writing* In a 3-by-3 magic square, what is the least number of values you must know in order to use equations to complete the square? Explain.

What You'll Learn

▼ To solve equations by dividing

▼ To solve equations by multiplying

...And Why

You can use multiplication and division to solve problems about business and money.

Here's How

Look for questions that

▪ build understanding

✔ check understanding

Work Together
Using Models to Solve Equations

You have three weeks to save $27 for a ticket to a concert. You want to know how much you need to save each week.

1. Explain how the tiles below are a model of this situation. What do the green tiles represent? The yellow tiles?

2. The tiles on each side are divided into three equal groups. What is the solution of the equation? How much should you save each week?

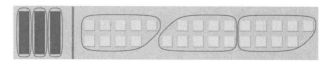

3. ▪ *Modeling* Use tiles to model and solve each equation.

   a. $2x = -8$ b. $4y = 12$ c. $-14 = 7z$

THINK AND DISCUSS

▼ *Solving Equations by Dividing*

You solved an equation by dividing tiles into equal groups. Similarly, you can isolate a variable by dividing to undo multiplication.

DIVISION PROPERTY OF EQUALITY

If you divide each side of an equation by the same nonzero number, the two sides remain equal.

Arithmetic

$$10 = 6 + 4$$
$$\frac{10}{3} = \frac{6 + 4}{3}$$

Algebra

$$a = b$$
$$\frac{a}{c} = \frac{b}{c}, c \neq 0$$

■ **EXAMPLE 1** *Real-World Problem Solving*

Animals A circus has 6 adult tigers that perform in its acts. Their trainer orders 40.8 kilograms of meat for them each day. Each tiger receives the same amount. How much meat does each tiger eat in a day?

Words • | number of tigers | · | pounds of meat per tiger | = | total number of pounds of meat |

• Let n = pounds of meat per tiger

Equation • $6 \cdot n = 40.8$

$$6n = 40.8$$
$$\frac{6n}{6} = \frac{40.8}{6} \quad \longleftarrow \text{Divide each side by 6.}$$
$$n = 6.8 \quad \longleftarrow \text{Simplify.}$$

Each tiger eats 6.8 kilograms of meat in a day.

Need Help? For practice with dividing decimals by whole numbers, see Skills Handbook page 606.

4. ✓ *Try It Out* Solve and check each equation.
   a. $7w = 280$ **b.** $27 = -3d$ **c.** $12x = -48$

2 *Solving Equations by Multiplying*

You can solve an equation by multiplying to undo division.

> **MULTIPLICATION PROPERTY OF EQUALITY**
>
> If you multiply each side of an equation by the same number, the two sides remain equal.
>
> | **Arithmetic** | **Algebra** |
> | :---: | :---: |
> | $10 = 6 + 4$ | $a = b$ |
> | $10(3) = (6 + 4)(3)$ | $ac = bc$ |

■ EXAMPLE 2

QUICKreview

$-7\left(\dfrac{x}{-7}\right) = \dfrac{-7 \cdot x}{-7} = x$

Solve $\dfrac{x}{-7} = 15$. Check the solution.

$$\dfrac{x}{-7} = 15$$

$$-7\left(\dfrac{x}{-7}\right) = -7(15) \quad \longleftarrow \text{Multiply each side by } -7.$$

$$x = -105 \quad \longleftarrow \text{Simplify.}$$

Check $\dfrac{x}{-7} = 15 \quad \longleftarrow \text{Start with the original equation.}$

$$\dfrac{-105}{-7} \overset{?}{=} 15 \quad \longleftarrow \text{Replace } x \text{ with } -105.$$

$$15 = 15 \checkmark \quad \longleftarrow \text{The solution checks.}$$

5. ✓ *Try It Out* Solve and check each equation.

a. $\dfrac{x}{5} = 8$ b. $\dfrac{b}{-3} = 6$ c. $-40 = \dfrac{n}{4}$

EXERCISES *On Your Own*

Write and solve an equation using each model.

1.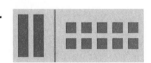

2.

3.

Solve each equation. Check the solution.

4. $8t = 56$ **5.** $6p = -30$ **6.** $-4b = 76$ **7.** $12 = -3s$ **8.** $280 = -7w$

9. $-5.4 = -0.9g$ **10.** $10s = -5$ **11.** $204 = -17x$ **12.** $-35d = -140$ **13.** $100m = 5{,}000$

14. $-x = 11$ **15.** $20b = -460$ **16.** $5m = 0$ **17.** $3 = 9b$ **18.** $1.25 = -5t$

19. Money The cost of a bicycle is $180. Write and solve an equation for each problem. Then give the solution of the problem.

    a. Tran plans to buy the bicycle nine weeks from now. He wants to know how much money he must save per week.

    b. Andrea knows she can save $12 per week. She wants to know how many weeks it will take to save the $180.

Solve each equation. Check the solution.

20. $\frac{x}{4} = 5$

21. $\frac{n}{-2} = 12$

22. $10.1 = \frac{s}{-8}$

23. $24 = -3s$

24. $\frac{c}{-4} = -64$

25. $-2 = \frac{d}{20}$

26. $30 = \frac{w}{15}$

27. $-1 = \frac{-t}{7}$

28. $3.5 = -5x$

29. $-24k = 144$

30. $\frac{m}{-15} = -10$

31. $\frac{y}{-9} = 2$

32. $\frac{m}{8} = 0$

33. $700 = -35x$

34. $32 = \frac{-c}{5}$

One of the greatest recent innovations in bicycles is a "two-wheel drive" bike invented by Billie Joe Becoat of Illinois. His company holds the patent rights on the bike in 32 countries.
Source: *Ebony*

Write an equation for each problem. Solve the equation. Then give the solution of the problem.

35. Eight pens cost $9.84 in all. What is the price of one pen?

36. Business The median number of calls to a toll-free customer service line doubled from 1992 to 1995. In 1992 the median was 1,500 calls per week. What was the median in 1995?

37. Surveys In a recent survey, adults were asked to name inventions that they couldn't live without. Automobiles were named about eight times more often than computers. Eight percent of those surveyed mentioned computers. What percent mentioned automobiles?

Mental Math **Is −5 a solution of each equation?**

38. $25v = -5$

39. $\frac{15}{m} = -3$

40. $-15 = \frac{d}{-3}$

41. $10 = -2t$

42. $-5p = 25$

43. Writing Write a real-life problem in which you know the length of a side of a square and you want to find its perimeter. Draw a diagram and give the equation you use to solve the problem.

Mixed Review

Indianapolis 500 Winning Speeds

Year	Miles per Hour
1993	157.2
1994	160.9
1995	153.6
1996	148.0

44. Use the table at the right. Draw a graph that appears to exaggerate the 1994 winning speed. *(Lesson 1-2)*

Round to the underlined place-value. *(Previous Course)*

45. 5.6̲45   **46.** 85.99̲9   **47.** 0.0029̲3   **48.** 1̲8.235

Write an expression for each situation. *(Lesson 2-2)*

49. Maria's father is 5 years older than 3 times Maria's age. Maria is *n* years old.

50. the number of plastic forks if you bought 3 packages, each containing *x* forks

---

CHAPTER PROJECT

PROJECT LINK: EXPERIMENTING

To construct a mobile you hang one disk 5 inches to the left of the main support wire. You want to hang two equal-size disks on one string to the right of the main support wire. Solve the equation $2x = 5(1)$ to find out how far away from the support wire they should be. Write a similar problem describing how to hang an unequal number of disks on each side of a mobile. Write and solve the equation you use. Experiment to test your conclusions.

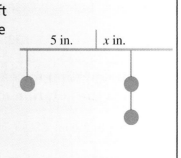

Math at Work

RESEARCH SCIENTIST

If you have an inquisitive mind and enjoy solving problems, you might consider a career as a research scientist. There are opportunities in agriculture, biotechnology, chemical and nuclear technology, manufacturing, and forensic science. Research scientists develop new products and technologies. If you choose this career, you will make observations, calculate and record results, and interpret graphs and statistics.

For more information about a career as a research scientist, visit the Prentice Hall Web site: www.phschool.com

What You'll Learn

1 To solve two-step equations

2 To use two-step equations to solve problems

...And Why

You can use two-step equations to solve problems involving air travel.

Here's How

Look for questions that
- build understanding
- ✔ check understanding

QUICK**review**

To solve an equation, you use inverse operations to isolate the variable.

Work Together   *Using Models to Solve Equations*

Work in groups. Use this model of the equation $2x - 3 = 7$.

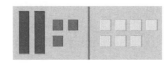

1. Add three yellow tiles to each side. Then simplify by removing zero pairs. Write an equation to represent the result.

2. Divide the tiles on each side into two groups of equal size. Remove one group from each side. What is the solution of the equation?

3. *Modeling* Use algebra tiles to solve each equation.
     a. $3x - 4 = 2$ **b.** $-7 = 2y + 1$ **c.** $4b - 3 = 9$

THINK AND DISCUSS

1 *Solving Two-step Equations*

The equation $-3y + 5 = 26$ involves two steps. The variable is multiplied by -3. Then 5 is added. To solve the equation, work backward. First undo the addition by subtracting 5 from each side. Then undo the multiplication by dividing each side by -3.

■ **EXAMPLE 1**

Solve $-3y + 5 = 26$. Check your solution.

$$-3y + 5 = 26$$
$$-3y + 5 - 5 = 26 - 5 \quad \longleftarrow \text{Subtract 5 from each side.}$$
$$-3y = 21 \quad \longleftarrow \text{Simplify.}$$
$$\frac{-3y}{-3} = \frac{21}{-3} \quad \longleftarrow \text{Divide each side by } -3.$$
$$y = -7 \quad \longleftarrow \text{Simplify.}$$

Check $-3y + 5 = 26$ $\longleftarrow$ Start with the original equation.
$$-3(-7) + 5 \stackrel{?}{=} 26 \quad \longleftarrow \text{Replace } y \text{ with } -7.$$
$$26 = 26 \checkmark \quad \longleftarrow \text{The solution checks.}$$

4. ✓ *Try It Out* Solve each equation. Check your solution.
a. $6m - 4 = 14$ **b.** $3x + 7 = 10$ **c.** $-9 = 8k - 1$

▼ *Using Two-Step Equations to Solve Problems*

You can use two-step equations to solve everyday problems.

■ **EXAMPLE 2**   *Real-World Problem Solving*

Recreation Three friends shared equally the cost of renting a boat. Each person rented a life preserver for $4, and each paid $20 in all. What was the cost of renting the boat?

Words • $\left(\boxed{\begin{array}{c} \text{cost} \\ \text{of boat} \end{array}} \div 3 \right) + \boxed{\begin{array}{c} \$4 \text{ per} \\ \text{preserver} \end{array}} = \boxed{\begin{array}{c} \$20 \text{ cost} \\ \text{per person} \end{array}}$

• Let $\boxed{c}$ = cost of boat

Equation • $\left(\boxed{c} \div 3 \right) + \boxed{4} = \boxed{20}$

$$\frac{c}{3} + 4 = 20$$
$$\frac{c}{3} + 4 - 4 = 20 - 4 \quad \longleftarrow \text{Subtract 4 from each side.}$$
$$\frac{c}{3} = 16 \quad \longleftarrow \text{Simplify.}$$
$$3\left(\frac{c}{3}\right) = 3(16) \quad \longleftarrow \text{Multiply each side by 3.}$$
$$c = 48 \quad \longleftarrow \text{Simplify.}$$

The cost of renting the boat was $48.

EXERCISES *On Your Own*

Solve each equation. Check your solution.

1. $3s - 4 = 8$

2. $\frac{k}{5} + 1 = 6$

3. $-7 = 9 + 2g$

4. $-5 = \frac{x}{2} - 5$

5. $\frac{n}{-8} + 2 = -3$

6. $-5 + 10b = -75$

7. $4m - 12 = 0$

8. $\frac{1}{2} = 9y + 4\frac{1}{2}$

9. $5 + \frac{k}{9} = -31$

10. $30 = 18 + 2b$

11. $11z - 6 = 335$

12. $\frac{x}{-8} - 7 = -9$

13. $4m + 8 = 4$

14. $-11 = 1 + 3n$

15. $3 + \frac{m}{-10} = 6$

16. $\frac{t}{-2} - 8 = 10$

17. $1.2 = 3s - 1.8$

18. $\frac{y}{40} - 9 = 30$

19. $15 = 15x + 15$

20. $\frac{j}{300} - 2 = -9$

21. $\frac{n}{4} - 1 = 10$

22. $10 = 3q - 2$

23. $-2z + 1 = -9$

24. $-20 = \frac{x}{2} + 7$

25. **Choose A, B, C, or D.** Your soccer team plans to rent a bus to go to a professional game. The total cost of the trip will be $555. If the team plans to use the $72 in its treasury toward the cost, how much will each of the 23 members have to pay? Choose the equation that represents this situation.

   A. $72x + 23 = 555$ **B.** $23x - 72 = 555$ **C.** $23x + 72 = 555$ **D.** $72x - 23 = 555$

26. *Writing* Describe how the process of solving $3v - 9 = 12$ is different from solving $3v = 12$.

27. Chanika ordered four tapes by mail. Each tape cost the same amount. With a $5 shipping charge, the total cost was $33. Write and solve an equation to find the cost of one tape.

28. *Nutrition* Around the world, different food organizations recommend different daily allowances of nutrients. In France, the recommended daily allowance of protein is 135 grams, which is 27 grams less than twice Spain's recommended daily allowance of protein. Solve an equation to find the recommended daily allowance of protein in Spain.

FLYING SOARS

The number of people taking airline flights is increasing steadily each year. With an expanding global economy, people are flying more both for business and for pleasure. The number of people flying on international flights increased from 374 million in 1995 to 404 million in 1996.

Airlines are not the only businesses benefiting from increased air travel. In 1996, Boeing, an aircraft manufacturer in the United States, had an exceptionally busy year with orders for 645 new planes.

29. *Reading About Math* 1996 was a record year for Airbus, a European aircraft manufacturer, but its orders didn't even come close to those of Boeing. Boeing had 27 more than double the number of orders Airbus had. Write and solve an equation to find the number of orders that Airbus had.

30. Six families split the cost of a family-reunion party. Each family also spent $65 for a motel room. Each family's share of the cost of the party plus the motel room came to $160. Write and solve an equation to find the cost of the party.

31. Open-ended Write a problem that you could represent with the equation $7b + 3 = 101$. Then solve the equation and show your solution to the problem.

Mixed Review

Simplify each expression. *(Lesson 2-10)*

32. $5^3 \div 5^2$ **33.** 3^{-1} **34.** 9^{-2} **35.** $\dfrac{6^4}{6^6}$ **36.** 8^0

Find the least common multiple (LCM) for each set of numbers. *(Previous Course)*

37. 10, 15   **38.** 6, 9   **39.** 4, 20   **40.** 8, 12   **41.** 11, 22, 33

42. Geography Mount McKinley is 20,320 feet above sea level. Death Valley is 282 feet below sea level. What is the difference between these two elevations? *(Lesson 2-4)*

✓ CHECKPOINT 1   Lessons 3-1 through 3-4

Simplify each expression.

1. $9(4 + d)$ **2.** $-3m + 4 - 5m$ **3.** $2h + 4(h - 5)$ **4.** $2x + 3y + x$

Solve each equation. Check the solution.

5. $-7 + q = 4$ **6.** $16 = -2v$ **7.** $x - 78 = 1,375$ **8.** $-9 = b - 12$

9. $2s + 5 = 12$ **10.** $\dfrac{b}{-12} = -3$ **11.** $49 = 5z - 26$ **12.** $20 = \dfrac{m}{2} + 7$

13. Julio bought pencils that cost $.39 each and a notebook that cost $1.19. The total cost was $3.92. Write and solve an equation to find the number of pencils Julio bought.

14. Open-ended Write two different equations for which -2 is the solution. One should be a one-step equation and the other should be a two-step equation.

3-5

Write an Equation

Problem Solving Strategies

Draw a Diagram
Guess and Test
Look for a Pattern
Make a Table
Simulate the Problem
Solve a Simpler Problem
Too Much or Too Little
  Information
Use Logical Reasoning
Use Multiple Strategies
Work Backward
✔ Write an Equation

THINK AND DISCUSS

You can solve many types of problems by writing equations.

SAMPLE PROBLEM........................

John wants to buy a camera that costs $269.95. He plans to make a down payment of $100. He will pay the rest of the cost in five equal payments over the next five months. How much will each payment be?

 READ

Read for understanding. Summarize the problem.

1. Think about the information you are given and what you need to find.
   a. What is the cost of the camera that John wants to buy?
   b. What does it mean to make a "down payment" of $100?
   c. Summarize the goal of the problem in your own words.

 PLAN

Decide on a strategy.

Writing an equation is a good strategy for solving this problem. Translate the important words and phrases of the problem into the symbols of an equation.

Words   • $\boxed{\text{down payment}} + \left(5 \cdot \boxed{\text{amount of each payment}}\right) = \boxed{\text{total cost}}$

   • Let p = amount of each payment

Equation • $\boxed{100} + (5 \cdot \boxed{p}) = \boxed{269.95}$

SOLVE

Try the strategy.

2. What operation(s) will you use to solve the equation? In which order will you use them?

3. What is the solution of the equation? Of the problem?

 LOOK BACK

Think about how you solved the problem.

4. Use substitution to check your solution of the *equation*.

5. Use estimation to check that your solution of the *problem* is reasonable.

6. ✓ *Try It Out* Look back at the problem about the camera.
   a. Suppose that John made three equal payments instead of five. What would be the amount of each payment?
   b. Suppose that John made a down payment of $100, but could only afford payments of $20 each month. About how many months would it take to pay for the camera?

EXERCISES *On Your Own*

Write an equation to solve each problem. Check the solution.

1. *Sports* You are training for the cross-country team. The coach recommends that you run an average of 35 miles each week. If you plan to take two days off each week, how many miles should you average on the days you run?

2. *Savings* For the past eight months, Donesha saved the same amount each month for her class trip. Just before the trip, her grandmother gave her $45. Donesha had a total of $325. How much did she save each month?

3. *Electricity* Electrical appliances create electric fields that are measured in volts per meter (V/m). A refrigerator creates an electric field of 60 V/m. This is 4 V/m less than four times the field created by a vacuum cleaner. What is the strength of the electric field created by a vacuum cleaner?

4. If you add 236 to half a number, the result is 950. What is the number?

Use any strategy to solve each problem. Show your work.

5. The product of the page numbers on two facing pages of a book is 4,160. What are the page numbers?

6. When 18 gallons of water are poured into an empty tank, the tank is filled to three fourths of its capacity. What is the total number of gallons that the tank can hold?

7. *Jobs* Asheesh and two friends shoveled snow for three hours. They divided their earnings equally. Asheesh spent $11 of his share, and then deposited the remaining $15 in the bank. What was the total amount the friends earned?

8. *Budget* The student council's budget for a party is shown at the right. They need to increase the amount for music to $725, but they must keep the same total amount. They want to decrease the amount for each of the other items equally. Make a revised budget for the party.

Item	Amount
Music	$500
Refreshments	$750
Decorations	$325
Supplies	$120

9. Nathan has an after-school job delivering groceries. He usually works 15 hours per week and earns $4 per hour. When he works more than 15 hours in a week, he earns $6 per hour for each hour of overtime. How many hours must Nathan work in one week to earn at least $100 in that week?

10. The length of a board is 48 in. Dyani cuts the board into two pieces so that one piece is 8 in. longer than the other. How long is each piece?

Mixed Review

You are conducting a survey of favorite TV programs.
(Lesson 1-9)

11. Write an open-option unbiased survey question.

12. Write a closed-option biased survey question.

Write each percent as a decimal. *(Previous Course)*

13. 0.35%   14. 7.8%   15. 35.9%   16. 0.08%   17. 14.26%   18. 0.632%

19. *Choose a Strategy* Find two numbers whose difference is 42 and whose product is -405.

CHAPTER PROJECT

PROJECT LINK: INVESTIGATING

You are constructing a mobile. You hang a 2-ounce disk six inches from the main support wire. You want to hang a different-sized disk four inches away on the other side of the support wire. Experiment to find out how much the disk should weigh for the mobile to balance. Write an equation to represent your conclusion.

Simplifying and Solving Equations

What You'll Learn

▼1 To combine like terms and use the distributive property to solve equations

▼2 To solve equations with variables on both sides of the equal sign

...And Why

You can use equations like those in this lesson to solve problems involving geometry.

Here's How

Look for questions that
⊞ build understanding
✔ check understanding

Work Together — Using Models to Solve Equations

These tiles model $4x + (3 + x) = 18$.

1. How is this equation different from ones you have solved?

2. Regroup the tiles so that all the x tiles are together.
   a. Write an equation for the regrouped tiles.
   b. What is the solution of your new equation?

3. ⊞ *Modeling* Use algebra tiles to solve each equation.
   a. $3n + 4n = 14$ b. $8 = 2x - 1 + x$

THINK AND DISCUSS

▼1 *Simplifying Before Solving an Equation*

An equation may have like terms on one or both sides of the equal sign. To solve the equation, you want to isolate the variable. The first step is to combine like terms.

■ EXAMPLE 1

Solve $3n + 9 + 4n = 2$. Check the solution.

$$3n + 9 + 4n = 2$$
$$3n + 4n + 9 = 2 \qquad \longleftarrow \text{commutative property}$$
$$7n + 9 = 2 \qquad \longleftarrow \text{Combine like terms.}$$
$$7n + 9 - 9 = 2 - 9 \qquad \longleftarrow \text{Subtract 9 from each side.}$$
$$7n = -7 \qquad \longleftarrow \text{Simplify.}$$
$$\frac{7n}{7} = \frac{-7}{7} \qquad \longleftarrow \text{Divide each side by 7.}$$
$$n = -1 \qquad \longleftarrow \text{Simplify.}$$

Check $\quad 3n + 9 + 4n = 2 \qquad \longleftarrow$ Use the original equation.
$$3(-1) + 9 + 4(-1) \overset{?}{=} 2 \qquad \longleftarrow \text{Replace } n \text{ with } -1.$$
$$2 = 2 \checkmark \qquad \longleftarrow \text{The solution checks.}$$

QUICKreview

Like terms are terms with the same variable(s).

4. ✓ *Try It Out* Solve each equation. Check the solution.
  a. $n + 7n - 2 = 22$ **b.** $-15 = 5b + 12 - 2b$

If an equation has parentheses, you must first use the
distributive property.

■ **EXAMPLE 2**   *Real-World Problem Solving*

Fund-raising The 24 students in your class have pledged
to collect 1,200 returnable bottles to raise money for the
library. During the first week, each student collected
34 bottles. How many more bottles must each student
collect?

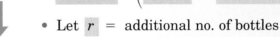

Words • [24 students] · ([34 bottles] + [additional no. of bottles]) = [1,200 bottles]

⬇ • Let r = additional no. of bottles

Equation • [24] ([34] + [r]) = [1,200]

$$24(34 + r) = 1,200$$
$$816 + 24r = 1,200 \quad \longleftarrow \text{distributive property}$$
$$816 - 816 + 24r = 1,200 - 816 \quad \longleftarrow \text{Subtract 816 from each side.}$$
$$24r = 384 \quad \longleftarrow \text{Simplify.}$$
$$\frac{24r}{24} = \frac{384}{24} \quad \longleftarrow \text{Divide each side by 24.}$$
$$r = 16 \quad \longleftarrow \text{Simplify.}$$

Each student must collect 16 more bottles.

5. ✓ *Try It Out* Solve each equation. Check the solution.
  a. $2(n - 8) = 22$ **b.** $6(4 - 3k) = 42$

▼2 *Equations with Variables on Both Sides*

These tiles model the equation $2x + 6 = 5x$.

6. a. ⬥ *Modeling* Remove two variable tiles from each side.
   Write an equation for the resulting model.
  b. Divide each side of the model into three equal groups.
   What is the solution of the equation?

If an equation has variables on both sides, you can use properties of equality to remove the variable from one side of the equation.

■ **EXAMPLE 3**

Solve $7 + 3h = -1 + 5h$. Check the solution.

$$7 + 3h = -1 + 5h$$
$$7 + 3h - 3h = -1 + 5h - 3h \quad \longleftarrow \text{Subtract } 3h \text{ from each side.}$$
$$7 = -1 + 2h \quad \longleftarrow \text{Combine like terms.}$$
$$7 + 1 = -1 + 2h + 1 \quad \longleftarrow \text{Add 1 to each side.}$$
$$8 = 2h \quad \longleftarrow \text{Simplify.}$$
$$\frac{8}{2} = \frac{2h}{2} \quad \longleftarrow \text{Divide each side by 2.}$$
$$4 = h \quad \longleftarrow \text{Simplify.}$$
Check $7 + 3h = -1 + 5h \quad \longleftarrow \text{Use the original equation.}$
$$7 + 3(4) \stackrel{?}{=} -1 + 5(4) \quad \longleftarrow \text{Replace } h \text{ with 4.}$$
$$19 = 19 \checkmark \quad \longleftarrow \text{The solution checks.}$$

7. ✓ *Try It Out* Solve each equation. Check the solution.
a. $7b - 2 = b + 10$ **b.** $2(n + 9) = n - 2$

EXERCISES *On Your Own*

Solve the equations modeled below.

1.

2.

Solve each equation. Check the solution.

3. $-8 = z + 3z$

4. $40 = 5(d - 2)$

5. $2(z - 1) = 16$

6. $5h + 2 - h = 22$

7. $9(d - 1) + d = 11$

8. $3b + b + 8 = 0$

9. $3a + 12 - 6a = -9$

10. $15 = -3(c - 1) + 9$

11. $19 = 4(k + 1) - k$

12. $2(z - 20) + 3z = 10$

13. $9 - x - 4x = 11$

14. $5s - 2 + 3(s - 11) = 5$

15. $-3m + 4 + 5m = -6$

16. $j + 5(j - 1) = 13$

17. $3c + 12 - c = 78$

18. *Writing* Write a summary of the methods you have learned for solving equations. Be sure to include examples.

Write an equation for each problem. Solve the equation. Then give the solution of the problem.

19. *Sports* A croquet ball weighs 460 g. Together a golf ball and a croquet ball weigh the same as eleven golf balls. How much does a golf ball weigh?

20. Eight less than twice a number is sixteen less than three times the number. What is the number?

Solve each equation. Check the solution.

21. $14z = -8 + 6z$

22. $-5y = 12 - 9y$

23. $22 + x = 37 + 6x$

24. $7m = 9(m + 4)$

25. $8(4 - y) = 2y$

26. $6d + 1 = 15 - d$

27. $2(1.5a + 4) - 6a = -7$

28. $5y = y - 40$

29. $9(k - 10) = -k$

30. $3t + 14 = 42 - t$

31. $x + 8 + 4x = 28$

32. $8 - 3(p - 4) = 2p$

For Exercises 33 and 34, write an equation for the given diagram. Then find the unknown lengths.

33.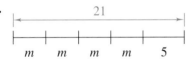

34.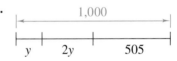

Mixed Review

35. Describe a situation that shows a positive trend, one that shows a negative trend, and one that shows no trend.
(Lesson 1-7)

Evaluate each expression. *(Lesson 2-6)*

36. 3^2

37. 6^3

38. 5^4

39. 1^{10}

40. $(-8)^2$

41. -8^2

42. *Choose a Strategy* Doreen has the same number of sisters as brothers. Her brother Oscar has twice as many sisters as brothers. How many children are in the family?

3-7 Formulas

What You'll Learn

▼ To use formulas to solve problems

② To solve formulas for another variable

...And Why

You can use formulas to find perimeters, areas, and rates in sports events.

Here's How

Look for questions that

⣿ build understanding

✔ check understanding

THINK AND DISCUSS

▼ *Using Formulas to Solve Problems*

A **formula** is an equation that shows a relationship between two or more quantities. The quantities are represented by variables.

1. You can use a formula to find the number of feet f in a given number of inches i. Complete: $f = \blacksquare \, i$.

2. ⣿ *Open-ended* From your everyday experience, describe two other quantities that you can relate with a formula. Choose variables to represent the quantities and write a formula.

A list of formulas for perimeters and areas is on page 596. Recall that the **perimeter** of a figure is the distance around it. The **area** of a figure is the amount of space that it encloses.

3. ⣿ *Think About It* Tell whether each measure could be a *perimeter*, an *area*, or *neither of these*.
   a. 14 ft^2 **b.** 19.3 m **c.** 5 cm^3 **d.** 0.5 in.^2

4. Find the perimeter of a rectangle 5 m wide and 6 m long.

QUICKreview

The variables b_1 and b_2 stand for "base 1" and "base 2." The lowered 1 and 2 are called subscripts.

■ EXAMPLE 1

Geometry Find the area of the trapezoid shown at the right.

$b_1 = 4.3 \text{ cm}$

$h = 4.0 \text{ cm}$

$b_2 = 9.1 \text{ cm}$

$A = \frac{1}{2} h(b_1 + b_2)$ ⟵ Trapezoid area formula

$A = \frac{1}{2}(4.0)(4.3 + 9.1)$ ⟵ Substitute.

$A = \frac{1}{2}(4)(13.4) = 2(13.4) = 26.8$ ⟵ Simplify.

The area of the trapezoid is 26.8 cm^2.

5. ✔*Try It Out* Find the area of each figure.
   a. rectangle: $\ell = 7 \text{ m}, w = 6 \text{ m}$
   b. trapezoid: $b_1 = 5 \text{ m}, b_2 = 11 \text{ m}, h = 7 \text{ m}$

To use a formula, you may need to apply properties of equality.

■ **EXAMPLE 2**   *Real-World Problem Solving*

Sports   The Iditarod is a 1,159-mile sled-dog race from Anchorage, Alaska to Nome, Alaska. Susan Butcher is a four-time winner of the race. Her average time was about 11 days. Find her average rate in miles per day.

Use the distance formula $d = rt$, where d is the distance traveled, r is the rate of travel, and t is the time spent traveling.

$$d = rt \qquad \longleftarrow \text{distance formula}$$
$$1{,}159 = r \cdot 11 \qquad \longleftarrow \text{Substitute 1,159 for } d \text{ and 11 for } t.$$
$$\frac{1{,}159}{11} = \frac{r \cdot 11}{11} \qquad \longleftarrow \text{Divide each side by 11.}$$
$$\frac{1{,}159}{11} = r \qquad \longleftarrow \text{Simplify the right side.}$$
$$r = 1159 \boxed{\div} 11 \boxed{=} \; \mathit{105.36363}$$

Susan Butcher traveled at an average rate of about 105 miles per day.

▼2 *Transforming Formulas*

Sometimes you need to transform a formula to make it easier to use. To do so, use properties of equality to isolate the variable.

■ **EXAMPLE 3**

Geometry   Write a formula for finding the width of a rectangle when the length and perimeter are known.

Use the perimeter formula $P = 2\ell + 2w$. Isolate the variable w.

$$P = 2\ell + 2w \qquad \longleftarrow \text{rectangle perimeter formula}$$
$$P - 2\ell = 2\ell + 2w - 2\ell \qquad \longleftarrow \text{Subtract } 2\ell \text{ from each side.}$$
$$P - 2\ell = 2w \qquad \longleftarrow \text{Simplify the right side.}$$
$$\frac{P - 2\ell}{2} = \frac{2w}{2} \qquad \longleftarrow \text{Divide each side by 2.}$$
$$\frac{P - 2\ell}{2} = w \qquad \longleftarrow \text{Simplify the right side.}$$

6. ✔*Try It Out*   Many famous Egyptian pyramids are rectangular pyramids. The formula for the volume of a rectangular pyramid is $V = \frac{1}{3}\ell wh$. Solve this formula for h, the height of the pyramid.

Geometry **Find the perimeter of each figure.**

1.

$s = 9$ cm

2.
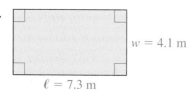
$w = 4.1$ m
$\ell = 7.3$ m

3.
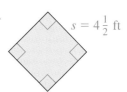
$s = 4\frac{1}{2}$ ft

Geometry **Find the area of each figure.**

4. square: side = 6.2 cm

5. rectangle: 8 m by 2.5 m

6. trapezoid: $b_1 = 12$ ft, $b_2 = 20$ ft, $h = 8.5$ ft

7.
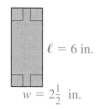
$\ell = 6$ in.
$w = 2\frac{1}{2}$ in.

8.
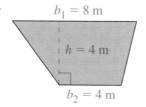
$b_1 = 8$ m
$h = 4$ m
$b_2 = 4$ m

9.

$s = 0.5$ cm

10. The perimeter of a rectangular picture frame is 48 in. The width is 10 in. Find the length.

11. **Geometry** What is the length of one side of a square with area 144 m^2?

12. **Aviation** An airplane flew for 90 min at an average speed of 475 mi/h. How far did it fly?

13. **Writing** How is transforming a formula similar to solving an equation with just one variable? How is it different?

14. The Jacksons left home at 7:00 A.M. and drove directly to their vacation spot 240 mi away. They arrived at noon.
   a. What was their average speed?
   b. Three days later, the Jacksons began the return trip at 4:00 P.M. They drove at an average speed of 50 mi/h and made a 30-min rest stop. When did they arrive home?

15. **Nature** When a cricket chirps n times per minute, you can find the temperature F in degrees Fahrenheit by using the formula $F = \frac{n}{4} + 37$. Write a formula to find the number of times a cricket chirps per minute when you know the temperature.

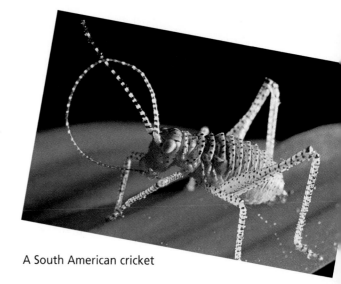
A South American cricket

Solve each formula for the variable indicated in red.

16. $A = bh$

17. $d = rt$

18. $C = 2\pi r$

19. $A = \frac{1}{2} d_1 d_2$

20. $I = prt$

21. $P = 2\ell + 2w$

22. $V = \ell wh$

23. $y = mx + b$

24. $y = mx + b$

25. a. Write a formula for finding the height, h, of a trapezoid when the area and the lengths of the bases are known.

b. The area of a trapezoid is 133 ft^2. The bases are 11 ft and 17 ft long. Use your formula to find the height.

26. You use the formula $F = \frac{9}{5}C + 32$ to find a temperature F in degrees Fahrenheit given the temperature C in degrees Celsius.

a. Write a formula for finding the temperature in degrees Celsius when given a temperature in degrees Fahrenheit.

b. Use your formula to find the Celsius temperature that corresponds to a comfortable room temperature of 68°F.

c. *Research* Three scales used for measuring temperature are Fahrenheit, Celsius, and Kelvin. Find out where or in what circumstances each scale is commonly used. Find the boiling and freezing point of water on each scale.

Mixed Review

Write each number in standard form. *(Lesson 2-11)*

27. 2.03×10^6

28. 4.29×10^{-5}

29. 3.24×10^{-3}

30. 5.35×10^6

31. 7.98×10^{-2}

Use the following data for Exercises 32–34:
105, 90, 112, 83, 97, 98, 94, 139, 127, 100, 134, 125. *(Lesson 1-5)*

32. Make a stem-and-leaf plot.

33. Use the stem-and-leaf plot to find the median of the data.

34. Find the range of the data.

35. *Choose a Strategy* How can you make change for a ten-dollar bill using an equal number of nickels, dimes, and quarters?

Formulas in Spreadsheets

After Lesson 3-7

You can use a spreadsheet to evaluate formulas. Spreadsheets use the symbols + and − for addition and subtraction, but they use different symbols for other operations, as shown in the table.

Operators in Spreadsheets

Symbol	Meaning	Example
*	Multiplication	$2*4 = 8$
/	Division	$12/3 = 4$
^	Exponent	$6\wedge 2 = 36$

■ EXAMPLE

Evaluate the formula $P = 2\ell + 2w$ for $\ell = 3$ and for whole-number values of w from 8 to 11.

Row 1 describes what is in each column. Enter the values of ℓ and w into the first two columns.

	A	B	C
1	L	W	2L + 2W
2		3	8	
3		3	9	
4		3	10	
5		3	11	

Now you need to enter an expression into cell C2. Start by writing the formula.

$$P = 2\ell + 2w$$
$$= 2(A2) + 2(B2) \quad \longleftarrow \text{Substitute cell names for the variables.}$$

In cell C2, enter the expression $= 2*A2 + 2*B2$. The spreadsheet evaluates the expression automatically. Copy this expression down into rows 3–5. The spreadsheet automatically adjusts the expression when you copy it.

× ✓	= 2* A2 + 2* B2		
	A	B	C
1	L	W	2L + 2W
2		3	8	22
3		3	9	24
4		3	10	26
5		3	11	28

Suppose the values of a, b, and c are in cells A2, B2, and C2 of a spreadsheet. Write the expression you would use to enter each formula in the spreadsheet.

1. $P = a + b + c$

2. $x = \dfrac{3a + 5b}{8}$

3. $A = \frac{1}{2}ab$

4. $A = c^2$

Use a spreadsheet to evaluate the formula $A = \frac{1}{2} bh$ for the values listed.

5. $b = 8$; $h = 10, 11, 12, 13, 14,$ and 15

6. $b = 8, 9, 10, 11,$ and 12; $h = 10$

7. Open-ended Use a spreadsheet to evaluate the formula $r = \dfrac{d}{t}$ for several values of d and t. How does the value of r change when t increases? When d increases?

Inequalities

What You'll Learn

▼ To write inequalities
▼ To graph inequalities

...And Why

You can use inequalities to represent everyday situations.

Here's How

Look for questions that
⊞ build understanding
✔ check understanding

QUICKreview

$<$ is less than
$>$ is greater than
$\leq$ is less than or equal to
$\geq$ is greater than or equal to

Work Together

Writing Inequalities

1. Work in a group. Define a variable and write an inequality to represent each sign.

   a.
   b.
   c.

   CARPOOLS ONLY
   2 OR MORE PERSONS PER VEHICLE

   GENERAL ADMISSION 750
   SENIOR CITIZENS 450
   CHILDREN UNDER 12 450
   BARGAIN 450
   GIFT CERTIFICATES 1500

   OVER 10′-9″ HIGH

2. Write an inequality for each situation. Tell what your variable stands for.
   a. No more than 10 people are allowed in the elevator.
   b. For the tour bus to run, at least six people must sign up.
   c. The most you can pay for a jacket is $75.

3. ⊞ *Open-ended* Describe four situations that you can model with inequalities. Write an inequality for each situation.

THINK AND DISCUSS

▼ *Writing Inequalities*

An **inequality** is a statement that compares two expressions. Some inequalities contain a variable, such as $y \geq -3$. A **solution** of an inequality is any value of the variable that makes the inequality true. So, 2 is a solution of $y \geq -3$ because $2 \geq -3$.

4. Tell whether each number is a solution of $y \geq -3$.
   a. -4 b. -1 c. -3 d. 0 e. $\frac{1}{2}$ f. 4.2

■ EXAMPLE 1

Define a variable and write an inequality to describe this situation: There are no more than 20 students in the class.

Words   •   number of students in class | is no more than   20

• Let n = number of students in class

Inequality   • n ≤   20

Check Try values *less than* or *equal to* 20 in the original statement.

19 is no more than 20. ✓ True.
20 is no more than 20. ✓ True.
So the inequality $n \leq 20$ is correct.

5. ✓ *Try It Out* Define a variable and write an inequality to describe each situation.
   a. Fewer then 150 students saw the play.
   b. No less than 100 tickets were sold.
   c. There were at most 250 seats in the auditorium.
   d. You should order a minimum of 5 dozen cookies.

▼ 2 Graphing Inequalities

You cannot *list* all the solutions of an inequality like $y \geq -3$. You can *show* the solutions, however, by graphing them.

■ EXAMPLE 2

Graph each inequality.
   a. $x < 2$

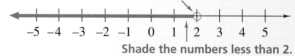

An open dot means 2 is *not* a solution.

Shade the numbers less than 2.

   b. $x \geq -3$

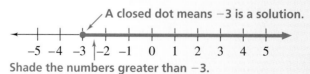

A closed dot means −3 is a solution.

Shade the numbers greater than −3.

6. ✓ *Try It Out* Graph each inequality.
   a. $y \geq -1$ **b.** $m < 5$ **c.** $n \leq 0$

When a variable is on the right side of an inequality, you can rewrite it. For example, you can rewrite $-5 < m$ as $m > -5$. Notice that the direction of the inequality symbol is reversed.

7. ✓ *Try It Out* Rewrite each inequality so that the variable is on the left. Then graph the inequality.
   a. $1 \leq y$ **b.** $-3 > x$ **c.** $-4 < t$

EXERCISES *On Your Own*

State whether each number is a solution of $x > -1$.

1. -4 2. 6 3. 0 4. $-6\frac{1}{2}$ 5. -1 6. 3.2

Write an inequality for each sentence.

7. A number k is not positive.

8. The wage w must be no less than $6.75.

9. The price p is not more than $40.

10. The number d is at least a dozen.

Define a variable and write an inequality to describe each situation.

11. The delivery truck makes more than 85 stops each day.

12. In a densely populated area, a car's speed should not exceed 35 mi/h.

13. A child must be at least 50 in. tall to ride on the roller coaster.

14. The bakery had fewer than 8 loaves of bread left.

15. We expect at most 400 students to attend the football game.

16. The class must raise no less than $85 to go to the museum.

17. The bus can hold a maximum of 65 students.

18. You will need a minimum of 30 extra chairs for the performance.

Write an inequality for each graph.

19.

20.

21.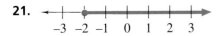

22.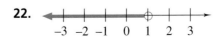

Graph each inequality on a number line.

23. $c \le -4$ **24.** $z > 6$ **25.** $t \ge -3$ **26.** $3 < b$

27. $r \ge -1$ **28.** $n > 0$ **29.** $q < 4$ **30.** $-5 > n$

31. $5 < t$ **32.** $q \le -3$ **33.** $0 \le z$ **34.** $-6 \ge a$

Reasoning **Write > or < to make each statement true.**

35. If $a > b$, then b ■ a.   **36.** If $x > y$ and $y > z$, then x ■ z.

37. Choose A, B, C, or D. Which inequality has the same solution as $-4 < m$?

   A. $m < -4$ **B.** $m > -4$ **C.** $m \ge -4$ **D.** $m \le -4$

38. *Writing* Describe how the solution of an inequality and the solution of an equation are alike. How are they different?

39. *Open-ended* Use the symbols $<$, $>$, $\le$, and $\ge$ to write four different inequalities. Graph the inequalities on separate number lines.

Summer Heat and Exercise

When is it too hot to exercise safely? The graph at the right shows that the danger zone begins at about 82°F and 78% humidity. When conditions are in that zone, exercising increases your chances of heat exhaustion and heat stroke.

When weather conditions are in the danger or emergency zones, you are advised not to exercise. Wait until conditions have improved.

If conditions are in the alert zone, exercise with caution.

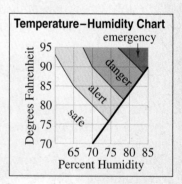

40. *Reading About Math* The temperature is 85°F. Write an inequality to represent the humidity levels h at which it is safe to exercise.

41. The humidity level is 70%. Write an inequality to represent the temperatures t at which exercise is dangerous.

42. *Temperature* According to the weather forecast, the temperature today will be greater than −4°C.

   a. Graph the possible temperatures on a number line.
   b. Write an inequality for the possible temperatures.
   c. Is −3.5°C a possible temperature for this day? Explain.
   d. How would the graph and the inequality be different if the forecast were for a temperature no less than −4°C?

 If you have trouble relating to temperatures in degrees Celsius, learning this little poem can help you.

30	hot
20	nice
10	cold
0	ice!

43. *Education* Define a variable and write an inequality for each sentence.

   a. There are more than 95,000 elementary and secondary schools in the United States.
   b. Since 1990, the total spending for these schools has exceeded $200 billion.
   c. There are at most 4,000 colleges and universities in the United States.
   d. The total number of people in the United States who attend college on a part-time basis does not exceed 7 million.

Mixed Review

Find the mean and median of each set of data. *(Lesson 1-4)*

44. 7, 9, 55, 41, 9, 52, 36, 33

45. 40, 98, 79, 77, 65, 74, 55, 90

Compare. Use >, <, or = . *(Previous Course)*

46. 4,951 ▧ 5,308   **47.** 0.06 ▧ 0.066   **48.** 3.0 ▧ 3.002   **49.** 0.05 ▧ 0.050

50. *Choose a Strategy* Lusita bought a baseball card for 20 cents and sold it for 45 cents. She then bought it back for 40 cents and sold it again for a dollar. How much money did she make?

CHAPTER PROJECT

PROJECT LINK: CREATING

Use wire, string, clothes hangers, or plastic straws to construct a mobile. Hang cardboard disks, figures made of clay, or other objects from your mobile. Use what you have learned to design the mobile so that it balances. Write any equations you used to build your mobile.

Choose the best answer.

1. Melanie wants to buy sod for her trapezoid-shaped garden. How many square feet of sod should she buy?

$A = \frac{1}{2} h(b_1 + b_2)$

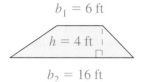

$b_1 = 6$ ft

$h = 4$ ft

$b_2 = 16$ ft

   A. 44 ft^2 **B.** 70 ft^2
   C. 88 ft^2 **D.** 176 ft^2

2. If $3x - 6 = 15$, what is the value of x?
   F. 3   **G.** 7   **H.** 9   **J.** 21

3. The formula $d = 16t^2$ relates the distance d in feet an object falls in the time t in seconds it takes to fall.

   A stone is dropped into a well. It takes 3 seconds for the stone to reach the bottom. How deep is the well?
   A. 2,304 ft   **B.** 154 ft
   C. 144 ft   **D.** 48 ft

4. Which graph shows the solution of $y > -4$?

   F.

   $-7 \; -6 \; -5 \; -4 \; -3 \; -2 \; -1 \quad 0$

   G.

   $-7 \; -6 \; -5 \; -4 \; -3 \; -2 \; -1 \quad 0$

   H.

   $-7 \; -6 \; -5 \; -4 \; -3 \; -2 \; -1 \quad 0$

   J.

   $-7 \; -6 \; -5 \; -4 \; -3 \; -2 \; -1 \quad 0$

5. Which equation has the same solution as $\frac{a}{2} - 3 = 11$?
   A. $a - 3 = 22$
   B. $\frac{a}{2} - 3 + 3 = 11 - 3$
   C. $\frac{a}{2} - 3 + 3 = 11 + 3$
   D. $\frac{a - 3}{2} = 11$

Please note that items 6–8 each have *five* answer choices.

6. Jimisha was 30 points behind. After 2 moves, she is now 70 points ahead. What equation represents how much she scored to get ahead?
   F. $-30 + n = 70$
   G. $70 - 30 = n$
   H. $30 + n = 70$
   J. $-30 + 70 = n$
   K. $30 - n = 70$

7. Tom owes his brother $150. He pays back $70. If money owed is negative, which equation represents the result?
   A. $150 - 70 = d$
   B. $150 + 70 = d$
   C. $-150 - 70 = d$
   D. $-150 + 70 = d$
   E. $150 = 70 + d$

8. Janice's checking account charges a fee of $3.50 per month on balances less than $250. She opened the account with $100 and didn't use it for 3 months. Which equation describes how much she had in the account at the end of 3 months?
   F. $3 \cdot 3.50 = b$
   G. $250 - 100 = b$
   H. $100 + 3 \cdot 3.50 = b$
   J. $100 - 3.50 = b$
   K. $100 - 3 \cdot 3.50 = b$

Solving Inequalities by Subtracting or Adding

What You'll Learn

▼ 1 To solve inequalities by subtracting

▼ 2 To solve inequalities by adding

...And Why

You can use addition or subtraction to solve inequalities involving money.

Here's How

Look for questions that
- ⸫ build understanding
- ✔ check understanding

THINK AND DISCUSS

▼ 1 Solving Inequalities by Subtracting

Consider the inequality $-3 \leq 1$. The number line shows what happens when you subtract 2 from each side of the inequality.

$$-3 \leq 1$$
$$-3 - 2 \leq 1 - 2$$
$$-5 \leq -1$$

Subtracting the same number from each side of an inequality does not change the relationship between the left and right sides.

SUBTRACTION PROPERTIES FOR INEQUALITIES

Arithmetic	Algebra
$7 > 3$, so $7 - 5 > 3 - 5$	If $a > b$, then $a - c > b - c$.
$2 < 9$, so $2 - 6 < 9 - 6$	If $a < b$, then $a - c < b - c$.

---

1. ⸫ **Think About It** What number would you subtract from each side of each inequality to get a simpler inequality?
   a. $n + 4 < 7$ **b.** $-5 > b + 3.5$ **c.** $x + 5\frac{1}{4} \geq 0$

It is easy to recognize the solutions of an inequality such as $y < 5$. To solve some other inequalities, you may need to first express them as simpler inequalities.

■ EXAMPLE 1

Solve $q + 6 \geq 5$. Graph the solution.
$$q + 6 \geq 5$$
$$q + 6 - 6 \geq 5 - 6 \quad \longleftarrow \text{Subtract 6 from each side.}$$
$$q \geq -1 \quad \longleftarrow \text{Simplify.}$$

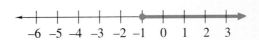

2. ✓ *Try It Out* Solve each inequality. Graph the solution.
 a. $y + 3 < 4$ **b.** $n + 7 > -4$ **c.** $-2 \leq d + 5$

▼2 *Solving Inequalities by Adding*

At the beginning of the year, DeJon is 62 inches tall and Anzu is 50 inches tall. Each of them grows three inches during the year.

3. a. Write inequalities comparing their heights at the beginning of the year and at the end of the year.
 b. ⁘*Go a Step Further* If DeJon and Anzu keep growing at the same rate, what will be true?

You can see that adding the same number to each side of an inequality does not change the relationship between the sides.

ADDITION PROPERTIES FOR INEQUALITIES	
Arithmetic	**Algebra**
$12 > 8$, so $12 + 4 > 8 + 4$	If $a > b$, then $a + c > b + c$.
$2 < 9$, so $2 + 6 < 9 + 6$	If $a < b$, then $a + c < b + c$.

■ **EXAMPLE 2** *Real-World Problem Solving*

Money You spent $12.50 on groceries. When you got home, you had at least $25 in your wallet. How much money did you have before you went shopping?

Words • money in wallet before shopping $- 12.50$ is at least 25

 • Let m = money in wallet before shopping

Inequality • m $- 12.50$ $\geq$ 25

$$m - 12.50 \geq 25$$
$$m - 12.50 + 12.50 \geq 25 + 12.50 \quad \longleftarrow \text{Add 12.50 to each side.}$$
$$m \geq 37.50 \quad \longleftarrow \text{Simplify.}$$

You had at least $37.50 before you went shopping.

4. ✓ *Try It Out* Solve each inequality. Graph the solution.
 a. $t - 5 < 12$ **b.** $y + 5 > -2$ **c.** $-5 \leq x + 2$

What number would you subtract from each side of each inequality to get a simpler inequality?

1. $p + 2 > -1$ **2.** $z + 4 > -5$ **3.** $3 \leq n + 8$ **4.** $-7 \geq x + 1.2$

5. a. Solve $x + 7 < 5$. Graph your solution.
   b. Choose a number less than -2 and a number greater than -2. Test each number to see if it is a solution to $x + 7 < 5$.
   c. Test -2 to see if it is a solution to $x + 7 < 5$.
   d. *Writing* Parts (b) and (c) serve as a check to your solution of the inequality in part (a). Write a general description of how you can use three steps as a way to check the solution of an inequality.
   e. *Open-ended* Give an example of an inequality that you can solve with addition or subtraction. Solve the inequality and check your solution.

Solve each inequality. Graph the solution.

6. $m + 4 < -2$ **7.** $s + 13 \geq -6$ **8.** $23 \leq x + 17$ **9.** $y + 200 > 1500$

10. $9 > d + 5$ **11.** $m + \frac{1}{2} < 3$ **12.** $x + 3.4 \geq -2.6$ **13.** $0 \leq n + 3$

14. $4.5 < n + 6$ **15.** $y + 78 \geq 54$ **16.** $2\frac{3}{4} > k + \frac{1}{2}$ **17.** $-3000 < b + 4200$

Write an inequality for each problem. Solve the inequality. Then give the solution of the problem.

18. The temperature has increased 17 degrees since 8:00 A.M. It is now above 65°F. What was the temperature at 8:00 A.M.?

19. A perfect score on a spelling test is 10. Amy scored 9, 8, 10, and 9 on her first four tests. What score must she get on the fifth test to have a total of at least 45 points?

Solve each inequality. Graph the solution.

20. $n - 3 > 8$ **21.** $x - 1 \geq -2$ **22.** $4 + f \geq -7$ **23.** $25 < b - 18$

24. $-16 \leq x + 72$ **25.** $r - 5 < -5$ **26.** $w + 1.5 \leq 2.5$ **27.** $w - 3.2 \geq 8.7$

28. $-5\frac{1}{2} > z - 3$ **29.** $950 + n \leq 2$ **30.** $2\frac{3}{4} \geq x - 1\frac{1}{4}$ **31.** $b - 2.1 \leq 0$

32. *Banking* You are opening a checking account that requires a $250 minimum balance. You will deposit a check for $218.63. Write and solve an inequality to find the additional amount you should deposit.

Mixed Review

33. Choose an appropriate graph and graph the data in the table at the right. *(Lesson 1-8)*

Evaluate each expression. *(Previous Course)*

34. $4^2 - 2^2$　　**35.** $458 - 85.6$　　**36.** $68.8 - 56.9$

37. $8 \times 7 \div 4$　　**38.** $4 \times 3 - 8$　　**39.** $5^2 \times 2$

40. *Choose a Strategy* You sold refreshments at a school play. A small juice was $.50, and a large was $.75. You made $103 by selling 162 juice drinks. How many large juice drinks and how many small juice drinks did you sell?

Results of a Class Survey of Students' Favorite Sports

Soccer	9
Tennis	5
Hockey	6
Softball	7
Other	3

✓ CHECKPOINT 2　　　　　　　*Lessons 3-5 through 3-9*

Solve each equation. Check your solution.

1. $-5 = 2x + 4 + x$　　**2.** $-8a = 2a - 30$　　**3.** $-15 = 5(g - 2)$

Solve each inequality. Graph the solution.

4. $n - 8 < -3$　　**5.** $b + 20 \geq 18$　　**6.** $-11 \leq k - 2$

7. A train traveled 240 mi in 5 h. Use the formula $d = rt$ to find the train's average speed.

8. Choose A, B, C, or D. Choose the inequality that best represents this sentence: The cost c is no less than $20.
 A. $c \geq 20$　　**B.** $c \leq 20$
 C. $c < 20$　　**D.** $c > 20$

9. Dan rented a sports car from EconoCar Rental. His bill for one day was $45.73. Write and solve an equation to find the number of miles he drove.

EconoCar Rental

Rent a sports car for **$27.95 per day** plus **14¢ per mile.**

Solving Inequalities by Dividing or Multiplying

What You'll Learn

▼ **1** To solve inequalities by dividing

▼ **2** To solve inequalities by multiplying

...And Why

You can multiply or divide inequalities to solve business problems such as the Internet problem in this lesson.

Here's How

Look for questions that
- ⊞ build understanding
- ✔ check understanding

Work Together

Solving Inequalities

1. Substitute 2 for a. Then use $<$ or $>$ to compare each pair of quantities.

a. $12 \ \blacksquare \ 8$

$12a \ \blacksquare \ 8a$

$\dfrac{12}{a} \ \blacksquare \ \dfrac{8}{a}$

b. $-9 \ \blacksquare \ -6$

$-9a \ \blacksquare \ -6a$

$\dfrac{-9}{a} \ \blacksquare \ \dfrac{-6}{a}$

2. ⊞ *Patterns* What pattern do you notice in your answers to Question 1? Complete: When you multiply or divide an inequality by the same *positive* number, the relationship between the sides of the inequality ___?___.

3. Substitute -3 for a in the inequalities in Question 1. Then use $<$ or $>$ to compare.

4. ⊞ *Patterns* What happens when you multiply or divide each side of an inequality by the same *negative* number?

THINK AND DISCUSS

▼**1** Solving Inequalities by Dividing

You discovered in the Work Together that dividing each side of an inequality by a positive number does not change the relationship between the sides of the inequality. Dividing by a negative number, however, *reverses* the relationship.

DIVISION PROPERTIES FOR INEQUALITIES

Arithmetic	Algebra
$12 > 9$, so $\dfrac{12}{3} > \dfrac{9}{3}$	If $a > b$ and $c > 0$, then $\dfrac{a}{c} > \dfrac{b}{c}$.
$6 < 14$, so $\dfrac{6}{2} < \dfrac{14}{2}$	If $a < b$ and $c > 0$, then $\dfrac{a}{c} < \dfrac{b}{c}$.
$16 > 8$, so $\dfrac{16}{-4} < \dfrac{8}{-4}$	If $a > b$ and $c < 0$, then $\dfrac{a}{c} < \dfrac{b}{c}$.
$10 < 15$, so $\dfrac{10}{-5} > \dfrac{15}{-5}$	If $a < b$ and $c < 0$, then $\dfrac{a}{c} > \dfrac{b}{c}$.

■ EXAMPLE 1

Solve $-3a \le 12$. Graph the solution.

$$-3a \le 12$$
$$\frac{-3a}{-3} \ge \frac{12}{-3} \quad \longleftarrow \text{Divide each side by –3 and reverse the direction of the inequality.}$$
$$a \ge -4 \quad \longleftarrow \text{Simplify.}$$

-6 -5 -4 -3 -2 -1 0 1 2 3

5. **▪Look Back** Check the solution to Example 1 by substituting values less than, equal to, and greater than -4 into the original inequality.

6. **✓ Try It Out** Solve each inequality and graph the solution.
   a. $-5b > 40$ **b.** $-60 < 12m$ **c.** $-9x \le -3$

■ EXAMPLE 2   *Real-World Problem Solving*

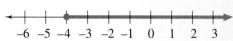

WebLink Internet Access
New Customer Special!
Unlimited monthly Internet access
for only $15 per month.

Click here for more information.

Internet The WebLink Company is advertising a deal for new customers. Its goal is to boost revenue by at least $450,000. How many new customers must the offer attract to meet the company's goal?

Words • number of new customers · $15 is at least $450,000

• Let n = number of new customers

Inequality • $n \cdot 15 \ge 450{,}000$

$$15n \ge 450{,}000$$
$$\frac{15n}{15} \ge \frac{450{,}000}{15} \quad \longleftarrow \text{Divide each side by 15. The direction of the inequality remains the same.}$$
$$n \ge 30{,}000 \quad \longleftarrow \text{Simplify.}$$

WebLink must attract at least 30,000 new customers.

▼2 *Solving Inequalities by Multiplying*

The multiplication properties for inequalities are similar to the division properties. When you multiply each side by a positive number, do not change the direction of the inequality. When you multiply by a negative number, reverse the direction.

MULTIPLICATION PROPERTIES FOR INEQUALITIES	
Arithmetic	**Algebra**
$5 > 3$, so $5(7) > 3(7)$	If $a > b$ and $c > 0$, then $ac > bc$.
$4 < 8$, so $4(7) < 8(7)$	If $a < b$ and $c > 0$, then $ac < bc$.
$8 > 2$, so $8(-5) < 2(-5)$	If $a > b$ and $c < 0$, then $ac < bc$.
$6 < 7$, so $6(-3) > 7(-3)$	If $a < b$ and $c < 0$, then $ac > bc$.

■ EXAMPLE 3

Solve $\frac{s}{-2} < 1$. Graph the solution.

$$\frac{s}{-2} < 1$$
$$-2\left(\frac{s}{-2}\right) > -2(1) \quad \longleftarrow \text{Multiply each side by } -2 \text{ and reverse the direction of the inequality.}$$
$$s > -2 \quad \longleftarrow \text{Simplify.}$$

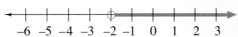

7. ✓ *Try It Out* Solve each inequality and graph the solution.

    a. $\frac{b}{-4} \geq 15$ **b.** $\frac{s}{8} \leq 20$ **c.** $-4 > \frac{s}{-2}$

EXERCISES *On Your Own*

Solve each inequality. Graph the solution.

1. $7p > 49$ **2.** $-6x \leq 24$ **3.** $12 < 3b$ **4.** $-2x \leq -14$ **5.** $5c < -10$

6. $-15 > 3q$ **7.** $-4t \geq 20$ **8.** $1200 > 150m$ **9.** $-144 \leq -18y$ **10.** $18 > 6j$

11. $3x \geq -42$ **12.** $30 < 15z$ **13.** $-2x > 12.4$ **14.** $3 \leq 0.5c$ **15.** $-x > -2$

16. *Writing* Write a paragraph to explain how solving $5x > -20$ is different from solving $-5x > 20$.

Solve each inequality. Graph the solution.

17. $\frac{d}{8} > 3$ **18.** $\frac{n}{-2} \le 11$ **19.** $-10 < \frac{r}{5}$ **20.** $6 \ge \frac{b}{-7}$ **21.** $-5m > 45$

22. $\frac{1}{10}j \le -9$ **23.** $32 > \frac{y}{100}$ **24.** $200 < -40k$ **25.** $\frac{y}{2} > 0$ **26.** $12 < \frac{d}{-8}$

27. $\frac{1}{-2}t < 1$ **28.** $16x \ge -96$ **29.** $-6 > \frac{n}{2}$ **30.** $\frac{x}{-3.6} \le 10$ **31.** $-625 > -25n$

Solve each two-step inequality. (*Hint:* **Use steps similar to those you would use for solving a two-step equation.**)

32. $2x + 5 < 17$ **33.** $\frac{n}{2} - 4 \ge -3$ **34.** $10 > 3m - 8$ **35.** $0 \le -b + 20$

Write an inequality for each problem. Solve the inequality. Then give the solution to the problem.

36. When a number is divided by -3, the result is not more than 15. What is the number?

37. Three friends washed cars together and shared their total earnings equally. They earned at least $150 one weekend. How much did each friend earn?

38. *Stereos* Hector wants to buy a new portable stereo. His parents agree to lend him $175 if Hector will pay them back at least $15 per month. How long will it take Hector to pay the money he owes?

39. *Estimation* You have $37.85, and you want to buy some tapes that each cost $4.95. Write and solve an inequality to estimate the greatest number of tapes that you can buy.

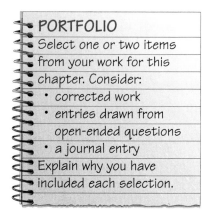

PORTFOLIO
Select one or two items from your work for this chapter. Consider:
• corrected work
• entries drawn from open-ended questions
• a journal entry
Explain why you have included each selection.

Mixed Review

Simplify. *(Lessons 2-3, 2-4, and 2-5)*

40. $17 - 24$ **41.** $-5 - (-6)$ **42.** $4(-12)$ **43.** $-220 \div 11$ **44.** $-63 \div (-7)$

Find the next three numbers in each pattern. *(Previous Course)*

45. $14, 21, 28, \ldots$ **46.** $18, 16, 14, \ldots$ **47.** $15, 25, 35, \ldots$ **48.** $3, 6, 12, 24, \ldots$

49. *Choose a Strategy* If you add 10 to one third of a number, the result is 20 less than the number. What is the number?

CHAPTER PROJECT

Balancing ACT

Making a Mobile The Project Link questions on pages 124, 130, 137, and 151 should help you to complete your project. Here is a checklist to help you gather the parts of your project together.

✔ equations used to model the mobiles in each Project Link

✔ a finished mobile to display for the class

✔ a summary of any equations you used in your completed mobile and an explanation of how you used them

Display your mobile in your classroom. Assemble the other parts of your project in a notebook. Write a summary telling what you learned about creating a mobile and how to keep it in balance.

Reflect and Revise

Review your project with a friend. Is your work complete? Does your mobile balance? Is your mobile attractive? If necessary, make any changes to improve your project.

Web Extension

Prentice Hall's Internet site contains information you might find helpful as you complete your project. Visit www.phschool.com/mgm3/ch3 for some links and ideas related to mobiles.

Simplifying Variable Expressions 3-1

The parts of a variable expression are **terms. Like terms** are terms with the same variable(s). You can **simplify** an expression by **combining like terms** and performing as many operations within the expression as possible. You can use the distributive property to simplify an expression.

Simplify each expression.

1. $8x + 3(x - 4)$ **2.** $3(a + 2) + 5(a - 1)$ **3.** $4(x - 3) - 3(x - 1)$

Solving Equations 3-2, 3-3, 3-4, 3-6

A value of the variable that makes an equation true is called a **solution.** An equation can be solved by adding the same quantity to each side, or by subtracting the same quantity from each side. An equation can also be solved by multiplying or dividing each side by the same quantity.

Solve each equation.

4. $x - 7 = 23$ **5.** $x + 3.1 = 4.6$ **6.** $x + 8.4 = -1.2$ **7.** $-14 + x = -5$

8. $-1.7y = -34$ **9.** $\frac{z}{4} = -2.1$ **10.** $2.5x = -8$ **11.** $\frac{w}{3.7} = 20$

To solve two-step equations, undo the addition or subtraction first. Then undo the multiplication or division.

Solve each equation.

12. $2x - 5 = 19$ **13.** $4 + 3q = -6.8$ **14.** $-1 = \frac{a}{5} + 2$ **15.** $\frac{c}{-3} - 1.6 = 2$

If an equation has variables on each side, simplify each side and isolate the variable on one side of the equation.

Solve each equation.

16. $4a + 3 - a = -7 + 2 + a$ **17.** $2b - 8 = -b + 7$ **18.** $18 = 2(3k + 1) - k$

19. *Writing* Briefly describe the steps, in order, for solving the equation $4(x - 5) = x + 4 - 5x$.

Writing an equation is a good strategy for solving a problem.

20. Randall bought bagels at 55¢ each and some cream cheese for $1.60. He spent $6.00. How many bagels did he buy?

21. Emilia gets her hair cut once every 4 weeks. She spends a total of $156 a year on haircuts. How much is one haircut?

Formulas 3-7

A **formula** is an equation that shows the relationship between two or more quantities. The **perimeter** of a figure is the distance around it. The **area** of a figure is the amount of space it encloses.

22. Find the perimeter and area of a rectangle with base 11 ft and height 5 ft.

23. Find the average rate of travel if a car travels 270 mi in 6 h.

24. **Choose A, B, C, or D.** Choose the formula that can be rewritten as $A = \frac{1}{2}bh$.

A. $b = \frac{2A}{h}$ **B.** $h = \frac{b}{2A}$ **C.** $h = A - 2b$ **D.** $b = h - 2A$

Inequalities 3-8

An **inequality** is a statement that compares two expressions.

25. Define a variable and write an inequality to describe the following: The class must raise at least $150.

Solving Inequalities 3-9, 3-10

A **solution** of an inequality is any value of the variable that makes the inequality true. Adding or subtracting the same number from each side does not change the direction of the inequality symbol. Multiplying or dividing each side by the same positive number does not change the direction of the inequality symbol. Multiplying or dividing each side by the same negative number reverses the direction of the inequality symbol.

Solve each inequality. Graph the solution.

26. $x - 7 > -12$ **27.** $32 \leq t + 8$ **28.** $5t \leq -35$ **29.** $72 > -9v$

1. Simplify each expression.
   a. $9 + 4r - 7$ **b.** $5 + (-12t) + 8t$
   c. $2(3m - 5) + 6$ **d.** $-4(7f + 2g) - 5$

2. *Writing* Describe how solving an inequality is like solving an equation. Describe how it is different. Include examples.

3. *Open-ended* Write a problem that you can solve using the equation $3k - 12 = 4$.

4. Solve each equation.
   a. $4m - 9 = 27$
   b. $-3(h + 7) = -18$
   c. $\frac{r}{-5} - 3 = 14$
   d. $6 + 2d = 3d - 4$

5. **Choose A, B, C, or D.** Which of the following equations has the same solution as $13s - 3 = 4s + 15$?

   I. $3s = 6$ **II.** $s - 2 = 0$ **III.** $17s = 18$

   A. I only
   B. II and III only
   C. I and III only
   D. I and II only

6. Write and solve an equation that describes each relationship.

   a.
   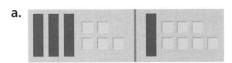

   b. You buy 15 apples and a $2.75 block of cheese. The bill is $6.20. How much did each apple cost?

7. Find how long it takes to bicycle 30 mi at 12 mi/h. Use the formula $d = r \cdot t$.

8. Find the area of each figure.
   a. square: $s = 13$ cm
   b. rectangle: $\ell = 2.5$ in., $w = 1.6$ in.
   c. trapezoid: $b_1 = 2.2$ m, $b_2 = 3.8$ m, $h = 4.5$ m

9. Solve each formula for the variable indicated in red.
   a. $P = 4s$
   b. $C = \pi d$
   c. $A = \frac{1}{2}bh$

10. Define a variable and write an inequality to describe each situation.
   a. Each driver must be at least 16 years old.
   b. You can have no more than 5 passengers in the car.
   c. There are fewer than 3 weeks until vacation.
   d. There are at most 75 tickets to the play still available.

11. When a number is multiplied by -3, the result is at least 15. Write and solve an inequality to describe the solution. Graph the solution.

12. **Choose A, B, C, or D.** The solution of which inequality is represented by the graph below?

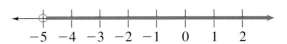

   A. $25 > -5w$ **B.** $3x \geq -15$
   C. $-4y > -20$ **D.** $2z < -10$

13. Solve each inequality. Graph the solution.
   a. $18 > w + 3$ **b.** $y - 12 > -7$
   c. $\frac{z}{3} \leq 5$ **d.** $-4s \geq 64$

Choose the best answer.

1. Which variable expression is not equivalent to $2(y + 3)$?

   A. $2(y) + 2(3)$ **B.** $(y + 3) + (y + 3)$
   C. $2y + 3$ **D.** $2(3 + y)$

2. What is the value of $3 + 2b^2$ when $b = -3$?

   A. 45   **B.** -15 **C.** 21   **D.** 39

3. Karen swam for a half hour on Monday. She increased her workout by the same number of minutes each day. On Friday, she swam for one hour. Which equation describes the number of minutes she increased her daily workout?

   A. $30 + 4m = 60$ **B.** $\frac{60}{m} = 4$
   C. $30 + 5m = 60$ **D.** $5m = 60$

4. Which equation does *not* have the solution $w = -1.5$?

   A. $\frac{9}{w} = -6$ **B.** $-10w = 15$
   C. $4 - 3w = 8.5$ **D.** $-1 - 2w = -4$

5. Which sum is greatest?

   A. $-15 + 7$ **B.** $22 + (-19)$
   C. $-8 + (-16)$ **D.** $|-11| + (-12)$

6. How much can you save on your grocery bill if you have 3 coupons, each for $1.00 off, and 2 coupons, each for $2.00 off?

   A. $3.00   **B.** $4.00
   C. $5.00   **D.** $7.00

7. What can you conclude if you know that $x > y$ and $y > z$? (All three variables x, y, and z are integers other than zero.)

   A. $z > x$ **B.** $z < x$
   C. $x > y + z$ **D.** $\frac{x}{y} > \frac{y}{z}$

8. Which group of numbers is in order from least to greatest?

   A. $-3, -4, 0, 1, 2$
   B. $-4, -3, 0, 1, 2$
   C. $0, 1, 2, -3, -4$
   D. $-4, -3, 2, 1, 0$

9. The local copy center charges $.08 per copy. What would it cost to make a copy of the school song for the 250 students in the school?

   A. $.20
   B. $2
   C. $20
   D. $200
   E. $2000

10. Six employees at Wolfe Inc. each earn $25,000 per year. The seventh employee, M. J. Wolfe, the General Manager, would not tell her salary. The company report said the average annual salary at Wolfe Inc. is $45,000. Which of these is a reasonable conclusion about the company report?

    A. The report uses the median income.
    B. The report uses the mode income.
    C. M. J. Wolfe's salary is $45,000.
    D. M. J. Wolfe's salary was not included in the average salary.
    E. M. J. Wolfe's salary was included in the average salary.

11. What is the perimeter of a rectangle with length 11 meters and width 7 meters?

    A. 18 m   **B.** 77 m
    C. 36 m   **D.** 38.5 m
    E. Not Here

Graphing in the Coordinate Plane

4

THEME:
RECREATION

Step Right Up!

Have you ever been to a carnival or fair? "Hit the bulls-eye and win a prize!" Is it skill? Or is it luck?

Design a Game Imagine that your class is putting on a fair to raise money for a class trip. For your chapter project you will invent a game in which a ball rolls down a ramp and comes to rest in a target area of you own design. Does a bulls-eye score 10, or maybe 100? Can the players vary the slope of the ramp? You decide, since you make up the rules! Your final product will be the game, along with written rules of play.

• How to solve problems using logical reasoning

What You'll Learn

▼ To graph points in the coordinate plane

...And Why

Graphic designers use coordinates to create computer images.

Here's How

Look for questions that
- build understanding
- ✔ check understanding

THINK AND DISCUSS

Computer artists create many of the images you see in movies and video games. The spaceship shown was drawn by instructing the computer to color specific points called pixels.

You can use a pair of numbers called **coordinates** to describe the location of a pixel. In the pair, the first value tells the location in the horizontal direction. The second value tells the location in the vertical direction.

■ EXAMPLE 1   *Real-World Problem Solving*

Graphic Design

What are the coordinates of the pixel at the far left edge of the spaceship?

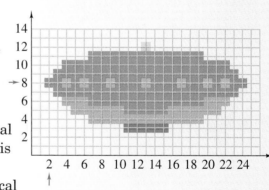

The horizontal value for this point is 2. The vertical value is 8. The coordinates are (2, 8).

1. ✔ *Try It Out* What are the coordinates of the pixel at the far right edge?

2. ▪ *Patterns* What are the coordinates of each orange pixel? What do these coordinates have in common?

The **coordinate plane** is a grid that uses two number lines to locate points.

The **y–axis** is a vertical number line.

The **x–axis** is a horizontal number line.

The axes divide the plane into four **quadrants.**

The axes intersect at the **origin.**

With the coordinate plane, you can use an **ordered pair** such as $(2, -5)$ to record coordinates. The first number in the pair is the **x-coordinate.** The second number is the **y-coordinate.**

3. ✔ *Try It Out* What are the x- and y-coordinates of $(2, -5)$? Which number tells you how far to move left or right of the origin? Which tells you how far to move up or down?

■ **EXAMPLE 2**

Graph point $A(-3, 2)$ on the coordinate plane.

Start at the origin. The x-coordinate of the point is -3, so move 3 units to the left, along the x-axis.

The y-coordinate is 2. Move 2 units up from the x-axis. Draw a dot. Label it A.

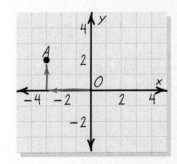

4. ✔ *Try It Out* Graph each point. Use one coordinate plane.
   a. $A(4, -2)$ b. $B(2, -4)$ c. $C(-4, -3)$ d. $D(0, -2)$

5. ▪ *Mental Math* In which quadrants would you find the points with these coordinates?
   a. $(-11, -7)$ b. $(18, -9)$ c. $(5, 8)$ d. $(-2, 7)$

6. Describe how to move from the origin to the point with the given coordinates. Then tell on which axis each point lies.
   a. $(0, -4)$ b. $(4, 0)$ c. $(-5, 0)$ d. $(0, 3)$

Work Together

The rotating blade of a milling machine cuts a straight path in a sheet of metal, wood, or plastic.

7. Use graph paper. Draw the shape that a milling machine would make given these instructions: Go to $(-7, 7)$. Lower blade. Cut to $(-7, 1)$. Raise blade. Go to $(-4, 7)$. Lower blade. Cut to $(-4, 1)$. Raise blade. Go to $(-7, 4)$. Lower blade. Cut to $(-4, 4)$. Raise blade. What is the shape?

8. Have each member of your group design one or more letters on a coordinate plane. Write step-by-step directions for a milling machine to cut the letters.

9. Test the directions written by another member of your group.

EXERCISES *On Your Own*

Name the point with the given coordinates in the graph at the right.

1. $(2, 1)$
2. $(-5, -2)$
3. $(-3, -3)$

4. $(0, 2)$
5. $(2, -4)$
6. $(-3, 1)$

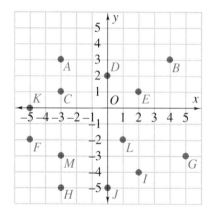

Name the coordinates of each point in the graph at the right.

7. J
8. A
9. K

10. G
11. L
12. B

In Exercises 13–23, state in which quadrant or on which axis you would find the point with the given coordinates.

13. $(12, 11)$
14. $(0, -15)$
15. $(-5, 8.9)$

16. $(40, -35)$
17. $(-3, -2.71)$
18. $(112, 0)$

19. $(0, 5)$
20. $(8, -2)$
21. $(-150, 200)$

22. (x, y) if $x > 0$ and $y < 0$
23. (x, y) if $x < 0$ and $y > 0$

 PROBLEM SOLVING HINT

For Exercises 22 and 23, try *Guess and Test*. Pick a point in a quadrant and test to see if its coordinates meet the conditions described.

24. *Geography* Degrees of longitude and latitude give locations of places on a map. For example, the longitude of Chicago is about 88° W and the latitude is about 42° N. Find the longitude and latitude of St. Paul and Lincoln.

Graph each point on the same coordinate plane.

25. $A(4, -5)$ **26.** $B(-3, -2)$ **27.** $C(4, 0)$ **28.** $D(0, -3)$

29. $F(1, -4)$ **30.** $G(-4, -5)$ **31.** $H(3, 4)$ **32.** $K(-3, 2)$

33. *Open-ended* Locate four points that are exactly 5 units from the origin. Are there any others? If so, what shape would they describe?

34. Choose A, B, C, or D. The coordinates of three vertices of a rectangle are $(1, -1)$, $(9, -1)$, and $(1, -10)$. What are the coordinates of the fourth vertex?

   A. $(9, 1)$ **B.** $(1, -9)$ **C.** $(9, -10)$ **D.** $(-10, -9)$

35. a. *Geometry* Graph each point on a coordinate plane. $(-3, 2)$, $(2, -3)$, $(5, 0)$, $(4, 1)$, $(2, -1)$, $(1, 0)$, $(2, 1)$, $(1, 2)$, $(0, 1)$, $(-1, 2)$, $(1, 4)$, $(0, 5)$, $(-3, 2)$

   b. Connect the points in order and describe the figure formed.

36. *Writing* Write step-by-step directions that will get the mouse through the maze to the cheese.

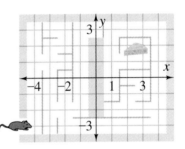

Mixed Review

37. Solve each problem using the graph. *(Lessons 1-1 and 1-2)*
   a. How many inches did Becky grow from age 2 to age 8?
   b. At what age was Becky twice as tall as she was at age 1?

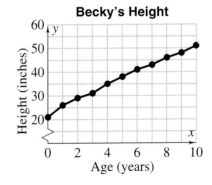

Find the value of each expression. *(Lesson 2-5)*

38. $-4 \times (-25) \times 3$ **39.** $-100 \times 0 + 6$ **40.** $90 \div (-15)$

41. $-51 \div 3 + (-3)$ **42.** $84 \div (-7) + 12$ **43.** $8 + (4 - 9)$

44. Suppose you take a true-false quiz that has three questions. Use a tree diagram to find how many sets of answers are possible. *(Lesson 1-11)*

Equations with Two Variables

What You'll Learn

▼ **1** To find solutions of equations with two variables

▼ **2** To graph solutions of equations with two variables

...And Why

Solutions to equations with two variables can help you make decisions about money.

Here's How

Look for questions that
- ∴ build understanding
- ✔ check understanding

THINK AND DISCUSS

▼ 1 *Finding Solutions*

Beth is buying peaches and plums. She plans to buy ten pieces of fruit.

1. How many of each type of fruit might she buy? Complete the table to show the possible answers.

Peaches	0	1	2	3	■	■	■	■	■	■	■
Plums	10	9	■	■	■	■	■	■	■	■	■

The equation below describes how many of each type of fruit Beth can buy.

$$x \quad + \quad y \quad = \quad 10$$

↑
x represents the number of peaches

↑
y represents the number of plums

When Beth changes the number of peaches that she buys, the number of plums changes also. Both quantities vary. So, the equation contains two variables.

When the values in an ordered pair make an equation with two variables true, the ordered pair is a **solution.** For example, $(1, 9)$ is a solution of $x + y = 10$.

■ EXAMPLE 1

Show that the ordered pair $(-3, 2)$ is a solution of the equation $y = 2x + 8$.

$$y = 2x + 8$$

Substitute 2 for *y*. ⟶ $2 \overset{?}{=} 2(-3) + 8$ ⟵ Substitute −3 for *x*.

$$2 = 2 ✓$$

$2 = 2$, so $(-3, 2)$ is a solution of $y = 2x + 8$.

2. ✔ *Try It Out* Show that (2, 14) is *not* a solution of
$y = 2x + 8$.

■ **EXAMPLE 2** **Real-World Problem Solving**

Savings Suppose you have $35 saved. You plan to add $4
each week to your savings. The equation $y = 35 + 4x$
relates the amount y that you have saved to the number of
weeks x that have passed. Complete the solution (6, ■) to
find how much will you have saved after 6 weeks.

$y = 35 + 4x$
$y = 35 + 4(6)$ ◀—Substitute 6 for x.
$y = 59$ ◀—Simplify the right side of the equation.

A solution of the equation is (6, 59). You will have $59 saved
after 6 weeks.

3. ▪ *Look Back* Use the equation in Example 2 to find how
much you will have saved after 10 weeks.

4. ✔ *Try It Out* Complete each solution for $y = 3x - 2$.
a. (2, ■) **b.** (1, ■) **c.** (0, ■) **d.** (−1, ■)

❷ *Graphing Solutions*

You have seen that an equation with two variables can have
many solutions. You can show these solutions on a graph.

GRAPHING CALCULATOR HINT

You can use the TABLE
feature of a graphing
calculator to find solutions of
$y = 2x + 3$.

■ **EXAMPLE 3**

Find and graph several solutions of $y = 2x + 3$.

Step 1 Make a table to find
solutions.

Choose several values for x.
↓
Substitute and simplify.

x	$2x + 3 = y$	(x, y)
−2	$2(-2) + 3 = -1$	$(-2, -1)$
−1	$2(-1) + 3 = 1$	$(-1, 1)$
0	$2(0) + 3 = 3$	$(0, 3)$
1	$2(1) + 3 = 5$	$(1, 5)$
2	$2(2) + 3 = 7$	$(2, 7)$

Step 2 Graph each
solution.

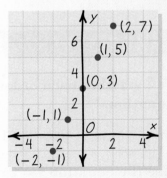

5. a. ⁂*Look Back* Study the pattern of the points on the graph in Example 3. What appears to be true?
   b. Complete the solution $(\frac{1}{2}, \blacksquare)$. How is it related to the other solutions?

An equation like $y = 2x + 3$ is a **linear equation** because the graph of its solutions consists of points that lie on a line.

6. ⁂*Draw a Conclusion* How many solutions do you think a linear equation has? How do you know?

To graph a linear equation, show all of its solutions. First, find and graph several solutions. Then draw a line through the points.

■ EXAMPLE 4

Graph the linear equation $y = -\frac{1}{2}x + 2$.

Step 1 Make a table.

Step 2 Graph the ordered pairs and draw a line through the points.

x	$-\frac{1}{2}x + 2 = y$	(x, y)
-2	$-\frac{1}{2}(-2) + 2 = 3$	$(-2, 3)$
0	$-\frac{1}{2}(0) + 2 = 2$	$(0, 2)$
2	$-\frac{1}{2}(2) + 2 = 1$	$(2, 1)$
4	$-\frac{1}{2}(4) + 2 = 0$	$(4, 0)$
6	$-\frac{1}{2}(6) + 2 = -1$	$(6, -1)$

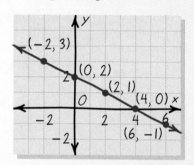

7. Why do you think only even numbers were substituted for x?

8. ✔*Try It Out* Graph each linear equation.
   a. $y = x + 3$ **b.** $y = -3x + 2$ **c.** $y = \frac{1}{2}x - 3$

EXERCISES *On Your Own*

Tell whether each ordered pair is a solution of the given equation.

1. $y = -7x + 10$; $(-3, 31)$, $(7, 59)$, $(0, 10)$ **2.** $y = \frac{1}{3}x - 2$; $(12, 6)$, $(-24, -10)$, $(99, 31)$

Use the equation $y = 2x - 4$. Complete each solution.

3. $(0, \blacksquare)$ **4.** $(-3, \blacksquare)$ **5.** $(50, \blacksquare)$ **6.** $(-200, \blacksquare)$ **7.** $(-17, \blacksquare)$ **8.** $(58, \blacksquare)$

9. **Entertainment** The equation $y = 3x + 12$ describes the cost y to rent x videos. Complete the solution $(8, \blacksquare)$. How much will it cost to rent 8 videos?

10. **Cars** The Quality Care Auto Repair Shop charges a $10 flat fee for work done plus $40 per hour for labor. Complete the solution $(2.5, \blacksquare)$ for the equation $y = 40x + 10$. What does this solution represent?

Graph each linear equation.

11. $y = 3x + 4$

12. $y = -x + 3$

13. $y = -3x - 5$

14. $y = \frac{1}{2}x - 4$

15. $y = \frac{3}{4}x - 1$

16. $y = \frac{2}{3}x + 1$

17. $y = x + 2$

18. $y = -4x$

19. $y = 4x - 6$

20. **Writing** Four of these ordered pairs are solutions of the same linear equation. Which one is not? Explain why.
$A(2, 1)$, $B(0, -4)$, $C(1, -2)$, $D(4, 4)$, $E(3, 2)$

21. **Design** In the design at the right, 12 squares enclose a row of 3 circles.

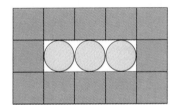

a. Use graph paper. Find the number of squares it takes to enclose rows of 1, 2, 3, 4, 5, and 6 circles. Keep track of your data in a table like the one shown.

b. Graph the ordered pairs from your table on a coordinate plane. Draw a line through all 6 points.

c. Use your graph to predict the number of squares it would take to enclose a row of 10 circles.

Number of Circles (x)	Number of Squares (y)	(x, y)
3	12	(3,12)
$\blacksquare$	$\blacksquare$	$\blacksquare$

Mixed Review

Solve each equation. *(Lesson 3-2)*

22. $x + 0.6 = 0.9$

23. $8.06 = 6.5 + y$

24. $z - 1.2 = 1.35$

25. $4.01 - t = -6.11$

Evaluate each expression. *(Lesson 2-6)*

26. $12^2 - 10^2$

27. $11^2 - 7^2 - 5^2$

28. $(997 - 999)^5$

29. $(3 \cdot 10^2) + (4 \cdot 10^1)$

30. **Choose a Strategy** A magazine ad costs $4.00 for the first two lines and $1.50 for each additional line. Bold print costs $.50 extra per line. How much does an ad cost if it has 8 lines, with 2 of the lines in bold print? *(Lesson 2-3)*

4-3 Understanding Slope

What You'll Learn

▼ 1 To find the slope of a line from a graph
▼ 2 To find slope from a table

...And Why

You can use slope to describe how temperature changes with an increase in altitude.

Here's How

Look for questions that
⁂ build understanding
✔ check understanding

Work Together
Exploring Slope

1. The drawing shows the cross section of a staircase. Note the *rise* and *run*. Work with your group to draw a staircase for each rise and run listed below. Use graph paper. Make each staircase 12 grid blocks high.
   a. rise = 1, run = 1
   b. rise = 4, run = 2
   c. rise = 2, run = 1
   d. rise = 2, run = 2
   e. rise = 3, run = 2
   f. rise = 2, run = 3

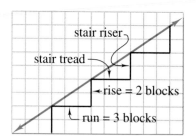

2. On each staircase, label the rise and run and draw a diagonal line along the stairs' edges. Cut out each staircase along the lines shown in red in the diagram.

3. **a.** ⁂*Visual Thinking* Order the staircases by steepness.
   b. Which staircase would be hardest to climb? Why?
   c. Does a larger rise always mean the staircase is steeper? Explain.
   d. What do you notice about the values of the rises and runs of the staircases that are equally steep?

THINK AND DISCUSS

▼ 1 Finding Slope From a Graph

Slope is a number indicating steepness. The slope of a staircase is the ratio of the rise to the run.

$$\textbf{slope} = \frac{\text{rise}}{\text{run}}$$

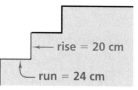

Need Help? For practice with writing equivalent fractions, see Skills Handbook page 610.

4. ✔*Try It Out* A staircase has risers that are 20 cm high and treads that are 24 cm deep. Express the slope in simplest form.

Slope also describes the steepness of lines in the coordinate plane.

$$\textbf{slope of a line} = \frac{\text{change in } y}{\text{change in } x} \quad \begin{matrix}\leftarrow\text{rise}\\ \leftarrow\text{run}\end{matrix}$$

■ EXAMPLE 1

Find the slope of the line.

Choose two points on the line. Count the units of change between the points.

$$\textbf{slope} = \frac{\text{change in } y}{\text{change in } x} = \frac{3}{6} = \frac{1}{2}$$

The slope is $\frac{1}{2}$.

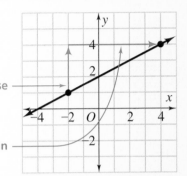

rise

run

The slope of a line tells you how quickly one variable changes in relation to the other variable.

■ EXAMPLE 2   *Real-World Problem Solving*

Meteorology
Find the slope of the line in the graph. How does air temperature change in relation to altitude?

$$\text{slope} = \frac{\text{change in } y}{\text{change in } x}$$

$$= \frac{-7 \text{ degrees}}{2,000 \text{ ft}}$$

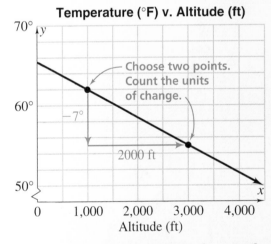

Temperature (°F) v. Altitude (ft)

Choose two points. Count the units of change.

$-7°$

2000 ft

Altitude (ft)

Air temperature decreases 7 degrees for every two thousand feet of altitude, or 3.5 degrees every thousand feet.

Mt. Kilimanjaro

It's cold at the peak and warm on the plain.

The following graphs show lines with various slopes.

Positive slope: the line moves upward from left to right.

Negative slope: the line moves downward from left to right.

Zero slope: the line is horizontal.

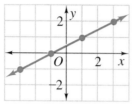

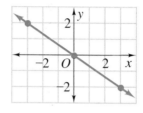

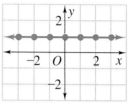

5. ✔ *Try It Out* Find the slope of each line shown above.

▼2 *Finding Slope from a Table*

The Student Exchange Club is holding a car wash to raise money. For each car the students wash, they raise $3. You can describe this situation with an equation containing two variables.

$$y = 3x$$

↑ y represents dollars raised

↑ x represents cars washed

6. ▪*Patterns* The table shows some solutions for the equation $y = 3x$. Complete the blanks showing how x and y change.

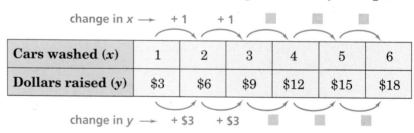

change in x →	+1	+1			
Cars washed (x)	1	2	3	4	5	6
Dollars raised (y)	$3	$6	$9	$12	$15	$18
change in y →	+$3	+$3			

When you graph the points from the table, the repeating pattern of changes causes the points to lie on a line.

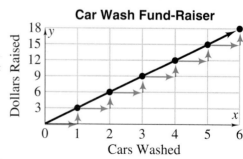

Car Wash Fund-Raiser

For the line in the graph,

$$\text{slope} = \frac{\text{change in } y}{\text{change in } x} = \frac{\$3}{1 \text{ car}} = \$3 \text{ per car.}$$

7. **⚏Reasoning** What relationship is there between the slope of the line and its equation, $y = 3x$?

■ EXAMPLE 3

The table below contains coordinates of several points on a line. Find the slope of the line. Then graph the line.

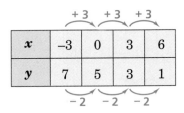

x	−3	0	3	6
y	7	5	3	1

$$\text{slope} = \frac{\text{change in } y}{\text{change in } x}$$

$$= \frac{-2}{3} \text{ or } -\frac{2}{3}$$

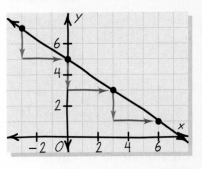

8. **✔ Try It Out** The points from each table lie on a line. Find the slope of the line. Then graph the line.

a.
x	−1	0	1	2
y	2	0	−2	−4

b.
x	−2	0	2	4
y	−3	−2	−1	0

EXERCISES *On Your Own*

Find the slope of each line.

1.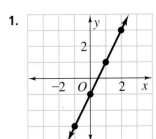

2.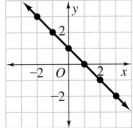

3.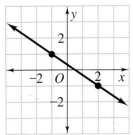

4.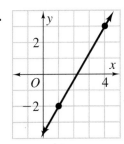

5. **Writing** Explain which roof is steeper: a roof with a rise of 5 and a run of 3 or a roof with a rise of 3 and a run of 5.

For each linear equation, make a table of solutions. Then graph the line and find the slope.

6. $y = 3x - 1$

7. $y = \frac{2}{3}x + 2$

8. $y = -\frac{1}{2}x - 3$

9. $y = x + 1$

10. a. *Reading About Math* Does a ramp with a slope of $\frac{1}{14}$ comply with federal guidelines? Explain.

b. If the ramp in part (a) reaches a doorway 2 ft above ground, how far from the building does it begin?

The points from each table lie on a line. Find the slope of the line. Then graph the line.

11.

x	4	5	6	7
y	-2	0	2	4

12.

x	-2	-1	0	1
y	3	2	1	0

13.

x	-4	-2	0	2
y	7	4	1	-2

14.

x	-2	1	4	7
y	2	3	4	5

Ramps Mean Access for All

Last night, local officials ruled that all public buildings must have wheelchair accessibility. According to federal guidelines, no ramp may have a slope greater than $\frac{1}{12}$. Building owners have until the last day of the year to comply with this new ordinance.

Find the slope of each line. Describe how one variable changes in relation to the other.

15.

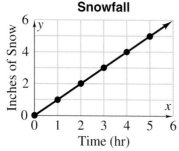

Snowfall

16.

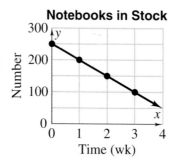

Notebooks in Stock

17.

Savings

Mixed Review

Evaluate. Let $a = 7$ and $b = -3$. *(Lesson 2-7)*

18. b^2

19. $-2a - b$

20. $a^2 + b^2$

21. $4a - 3b$

22. $7a^2 - 3b + b^2$

23. Demond types 40 words per minute. How many words does he type in $\frac{3}{4}$ hour? *(Lesson 3-5)*

CHAPTER PROJECT

PROJECT LINK: CALCULATING

Select the ramp and the type of ball or marble you will use. Then hold the ramp in various positions, measuring the rise and run for each position. Calculate each slope. What is meant by a slope of 1? A slope of 0? Explain how the concept of slope affects your game.

Graphing Lines

After Lesson 4-3

You can use a graphing calculator to graph equations and find solutions.

■ EXAMPLE

Graph $y = \frac{1}{2}x + 1$ and make a table of solutions.

Step 1 Use the WINDOW feature to set the range.

```
WINDOW FORMAT
Xmin = -6
Xmax = 6
Xscl = 1
Ymin = -4
Ymax = 4
Yscl = 1
```

Step 2 Use Y= to enter the equation.

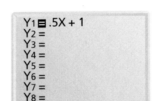

```
Y1 ▆ .5X + 1
Y2 =
Y3 =
Y4 =
Y5 =
Y6 =
Y7 =
Y8 =
```

Step 3 Use the GRAPH feature to view the graph.

Step 4 Use the TABLE feature to see solutions.

X	Y1
-3	-.5
-2	0
-1	.5
0	1
1	1.5
2	2
3	2.5

X=-3

Step 5 Sketch the graph and copy the table of solutions.

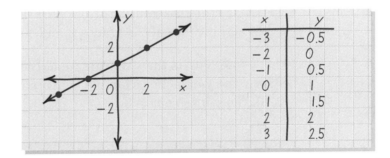

x	y
-3	-0.5
-2	0
-1	0.5
0	1
1	1.5
2	2
3	2.5

Use a graphing calculator to graph each equation and make a table of solutions.

1. $y = 0.8x - 3$
2. $y = 2x - 1.5$
3. $y = -\frac{2}{3}x + 2$
4. $y = -1.5x + 1.7$

5. **Writing** Use the table to find the slope of each line in Exercises 1–4. How is the slope related to each equation?

4-4 Using the y-intercept

What You'll Learn

1 To graph an equation using the slope and the *y*-intercept

2 To write an equation for a line

...And Why

You can graph lines more quickly by using the slope and the *y*-intercept.

Here's How

Look for questions that
- build understanding
- ✔ check understanding

THINK AND DISCUSS

1 *Graphing an Equation in Slope-Intercept Form*

How are the graphs of $y = \frac{2}{3}x + 3$ and $y = \frac{2}{3}x - 1$ related to their equations? You can see from the graphs below that they both have a slope of $\frac{2}{3}$. Do the values 3 and -1 have any special meaning? The next question will help you decide.

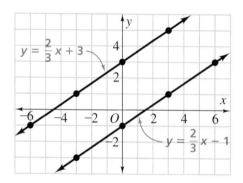

1. **a.** Complete the solution $(0, \blacksquare)$ for $y = \frac{2}{3}x + 3$ and for $y = \frac{2}{3}x - 1$.

   b. **Visual Thinking** Locate these solutions on the graph. On which axis do they lie?

   c. Use the two solutions from part (a) to explain the significance of the values 3 and -1 in the equations.

The **y-intercept** is the *y*-coordinate of the point where a line crosses the *y*-axis. For example, when a line crosses the *y*-axis at $(0, 3)$, the *y*-intercept is 3.

SLOPE-INTERCEPT FORM

An equation written in the form $y = mx + b$ is in **slope-intercept form.** The graph is a line with slope m and *y*-intercept b.

Example: In the equation $y = \frac{2}{3}x - 1$, the value $\frac{2}{3}$ is the slope of the line. The value -1 is the *y*-intercept of the line.

■ EXAMPLE 1

Identify the slope and y-intercept of each equation.

a. $y = \frac{1}{2}x$

$y = \frac{1}{2}x + 0$

↑   ↑

slope = $\frac{1}{2}$ y-intercept = 0

b. $y = x - 4$

$y = 1x - 4$

↑   ↑

slope = 1 y-intercept = −4

2. ✔ **Try It Out** Identify the slope and y-intercept of each equation.
    a. $y = -\frac{3}{4}x + 2$ **b.** $y = 2x - 3$ **c.** $y = -x$

When a linear equation is in slope-intercept form, you can graph the solutions without first making a table.

■ EXAMPLE 2   *Real-World Problem Solving*

Landscaping The Green Thumb Landscapers use the equation $y = \frac{3}{5}x + 4$ to predict the growth of 4-foot ornamental trees that they plant. In the equation, x represents time in years and y represents the height of the tree in feet. Graph the equation.

Step 1 Since the y-intercept is 4, graph (0, 4).

Step 2 Since the slope is $\frac{3}{5}$, move 3 units up from (0, 4). Then move 5 units right to graph a second point. Repeat the pattern to graph more points.

Step 3 Draw a line through the points.

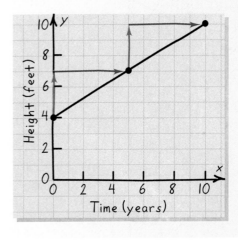

3. ■ *Predict* Use the graph above to predict the height of a tree after 10 years.

4. ✔ **Try It Out** Graph each equation. Use the y-intercept and the slope.
    a. $y = -3x + 4$ **b.** $y = x$ **c.** $y = \frac{1}{2}x - 3$

2 *Writing an Equation for a Line*

You can also use slope-intercept form to write an equation for a line.

■ EXAMPLE 3

Write an equation for the line shown in the graph.

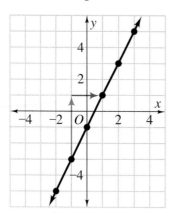

Step 1 Find the y-intercept and the slope.

y-intercept $= -1$

slope $= \dfrac{\text{change in } y}{\text{change in } x} = \dfrac{4}{2} = 2$

Step 2 Write the equation.

$y = mx + b$ ← Use slope-intercept form.

$y = 2x - 1$ ← Substitute 2 for m and -1 for b.

5. ✔ *Try It Out* Write an equation for line a and for line b in the graph at the left.

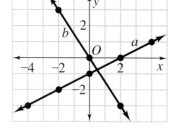

Horizontal and vertical lines have equations that contain only one variable.

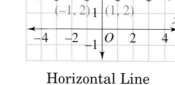

Horizontal Line
Equation: $y = 2$

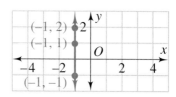

Vertical Line
Equation: $x = -1$

Look at the vertical line. Notice that, no matter what number you choose for the y-coordinate, the x-coordinate is always -1.

6. ⊞ *Go a Step Further* Write an equation for line ℓ and for line m in the graph at the left.

EXERCISES *On Your Own*

Identify the slope and y-intercept of each equation.

1. $y = 3x - 2$
2. $y = x + 5$
3. $y = -2x - 8$
4. $y = \dfrac{3}{5}x$

Graph each equation.

5. $y = -\frac{1}{3}x + 5$ **6.** $y = 4x + 3$ **7.** $y = \frac{2}{3}x - 6$ **8.** $y = -2x - 1$

9. $y = \frac{2}{5}x + 1$ **10.** $y = 3x$ **11.** $y = -x - 1$ **12.** $y = x + 4$

13. What are the slope and the y-intercept of $y = x$? Explain.

14. *Pets* Jerrod keeps track of how much cat food is in the house for his cat. The equation $y = -\frac{1}{2}x + 12$ relates y, the number of cans left, to x, the number of days since he bought 12 cans.
  a. Graph the equation. Be sure to label each axis.
  b. What is the slope of the graph? What does it represent?

15. *Writing* The equation $3x + 2y = 8$ is not in slope-intercept form. Explain the steps you would use to write it in slope-intercept form.

Write an equation for each line. Use slope-intercept form.

16. 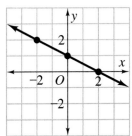   **17.** 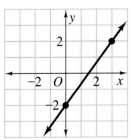   **18.** 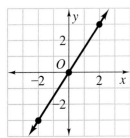   **19.**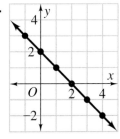

20. Choose A, B, C, or D. Which equation has a graph that passes through the origin?

  A. $y = 7x + 1$ **B.** $y = 7x - 7$ **C.** $y = 7x$ **D.** $y = x - 7$

21. *Writing* Explain why it is impossible for any point to lie on both $y = 3x + 5$ *and* on $y = 3x - 2$. Use a graph to illustrate your explanation.

Geometry **Use a term from geometry to describe the graphs of the pairs of lines.**

22. two lines with the same slope but different y-intercepts

23. two lines with the same y-intercept but different slopes

24. two lines with different slopes and different y-intercepts

JOURNAL
List the methods you have learned for graphing equations. For each method, write a set of instructions in the form of steps to follow, a recipe, or a script.

Solve each inequality. Graph the solution. *(Lesson 3-9)*

25. $x + 4 \geq 10$ **26.** $x - 5 \leq -5$ **27.** $x - 3 > 7$ **28.** $x + 9 < 6$

29. *Choose a Strategy* A clock strikes the number of hours each hour and once every half hour. How many times will the clock strike in a day?

✓ CHECKPOINT 1

Lessons 4-1 through 4-4

Graph each point on the same coordinate plane.

1. $B(4, -3)$ **2.** $C(0, 2)$ **3.** $D(-5, -3)$ **4.** $F(-3, 3)$

Graph each linear equation.

5. $y = 2x - 4$ **6.** $y = \frac{2}{3}x + 2$ **7.** $y = -x + 3$

8. Find the slope of each line in the graph at the right.

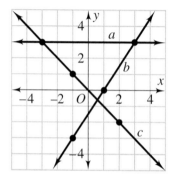

Math at Work

WEB PAGE DIRECTOR

If you enjoy writing and graphic design, then consider a career as a Web page director. Planning a Web page requires writing text, deciding on graphics, and finding other Web sites to link with. You will need to know HTML, or Hypertext Markup Language, to write and tag components on the page.

Proficiency at geometry will help when designing and using graphics. Also, it helps to know how to construct a flowchart for a site that consists of many different pages, links, and references!

For more information about being a Web site director, visit the Prentice Hall Web site: www.phschool.com

4-5 Use Logical Reasoning

THINK AND DISCUSS

You can use a **Venn diagram** to logically organize items by what they have in common.

SAMPLE PROBLEM..

The chart shows countries that produced at least 10 million metric tons of rice, corn, or wheat in 1994. How many countries produced at least 10 million tons of all three grains? How many countries produced 10 million tons of at least one grain?

Leading Producers of Rice, Corn, and Wheat

Rice	China, India, Indonesia, Bangladesh, Burma, Thailand, Japan, Brazil, Philippines
Corn	United States, China, Brazil, Mexico, France, South Africa, India, Argentina
Wheat	China, United States, India, Russia, France, Canada, Turkey, Germany, Pakistan, Ukraine, United Kingdom, Iran, Argentina

READ

Read for understanding. Summarize the problem.

1. Think about the information you are given.
   a. How many different crops do you have information about?
   b. Do some countries produce more than one crop? Explain.
   c. What does the problem ask you to find?

PLAN

Decide on a strategy.

You can use logical reasoning to place each country in a Venn diagram. First, draw a large rectangle. Inside it draw three loops that overlap. Label the loops R (for rice), C (for corn), and W (for wheat).

2. Suppose a country is placed in the overlap of the loops labeled R and C. What crops does the country produce? What does the overlap of all three loops represent?

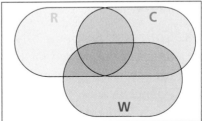

SOLVE

Try the strategy.

3. Which countries were leading producers of rice? Were any of these countries also leading producers of corn or wheat? Place each rice-producing country in the correct portion of your diagram. Complete the diagram by placing the remaining countries.

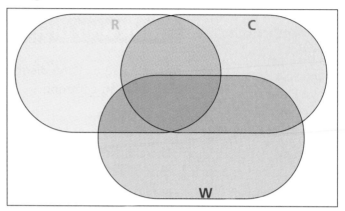

4. How many countries produced at least 10 million tons of all three grains? How many countries produced 10 million tons of at least one grain?

LOOK BACK

Think about how you solved the problem.

5. **a.** Why does one section of the diagram contain no countries?
   b. Describe the characteristics of a country that would be placed inside the rectangle, but outside all three loops.

EXERCISES *On Your Own*

Use logical reasoning to solve each problem.

1. Place the information at the right in a Venn diagram. What are the common factors of 40 and 30? What is the greatest common factor?

   Factors of 40 1, 2, 4, 5, 8, 10, 20, 40
   Factors of 30 1, 2, 3, 5, 6, 10, 15, 30

2. *Games* Keith asked 30 people whether they knew how to play whist or dominoes. Fifteen of them knew how to play whist and 20 knew how to play dominoes. Five people did not know how to play either game. How many knew how to play both games?

3. *Contests* A Science Olympiad team has 15 members. Ten members prepared for math and engineering events, 8 prepared for life science events, and 9 prepared for physical science events. If no student prepared in all three areas, how many students prepared in two out of the three areas?

Use any strategy to solve each problem. Show your work.

4. Pierre was born in the twentieth century and will be x years old in the year x^2. In what year was Pierre born?

5. The total of all the scores on an eighth-grade mathematics test was 2,145 points. The mean score was 82.5 points. If there are 14 girls in the class, how many boys are there?

6. A carpenter has exactly 36 meters of fencing to make a rectangular pen for a pig. Assume that both the length and the width must be a whole number of meters. What size rectangle will give the pig the most room?

7. **Patterns** The bleacher seats of Central Stadium are numbered as shown at the right. Suppose that the pattern continues for all the rows in the stadium. In which row would you find seat 100?

Seat Numbers

row 1	1				
row 2	2	3			
row 3	4	5	6		
row 4	7	8	9	10	
row 5	11	12	13	14	15

Mixed Review

Change each decimal to a fraction in simplest form.
(Previous Course)

8. 0.8   **9.** 0.75   **10.** 9.36   **11.** 0.008   **12.** 0.074   **13.** 0.375

Simplify each expression. *(Lessons 2-6 and 2-10)*

14. $(-6)^3$ **15.** $m \cdot m^2$ **16.** $x^5 \div x^3$ **17.** $4^2 + 4^0$ **18.** 3^{-2} **19.** $8^4 \div 8^2$

20. **Travel** The formula $d = rt$ relates a rate r, a distance d, and a time t. Find the rate for a car that traveled 264 miles in 4.8 hours. *(Lesson 3-7)*

CHAPTER PROJECT

PROJECT LINK: COLLECTING DATA

Using several different slopes, release the ball from the same point each time and measure the distance it rolls. Present your data in a table or graph. For what slope is the distance the greatest? What will be the slope in your game? Will the players be allowed to adjust the slope during play? Explain.

Using Graphs of Equations

What You'll Learn

1 To solve a problem by writing an equation

2 To graph an equation using intercepts

...And Why

When a problem has many solutions, you can use a graph to find the ones you need.

Here's How

Look for questions that

- build understanding
- ✔ check understanding

THINK AND DISCUSS

1 *Writing an Equation*

Sometimes you can write and graph an equation with two variables to describe a real-world situation.

■ **EXAMPLE 1**   *Real-World Problem Solving*

Jobs Suppose you are a server at a restaurant. Your salary is $10.00 for a four-hour shift. The customers you serve leave an average tip of $1.50 each. Write and graph an equation to represent your total earnings.

Words   • $\boxed{\text{total earnings}}$ = $10.00 + $1.50 × $\boxed{\text{number of customers}}$

   • Let y = total earnings
   • Let x = number of customers

Equation • $y = 10 + 1.5x$

Write the equation in slope-intercept form.

$$y = 1.5x + 10$$

$$\text{slope} = 1.5 = \frac{15}{10}$$

Graph the equation.

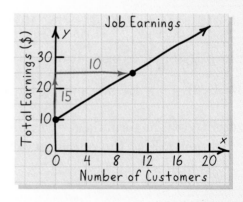

1. a. ■ **Visual Thinking** Use the graph to find how many customers you must serve to earn $40.
   b. Estimate your earnings if you serve 15 customers.

2. ■ **What If . . .** Explain how each change in pay would affect the slope or y-intercept of the graph.
   a. Your pay from the restaurant is raised to $12.
   b. Your average tip is now $2 per customer.

2 Using Intercepts to Graph an Equation

The **x-intercept** of a line is the *x*-coordinate of the point where the line crosses the *x*-axis.

3. **a.** Complete the solution (■, 0) for the equation $4x - y = 8$.
   b. On which axis does this solution lie?
   c. What is the *x*-intercept of the graph of $4x - y = 8$?

When a linear equation is not in slope-intercept form, you can use the *x*- and *y*-intercepts to graph the line.

■ **EXAMPLE 2**   *Real-World Problem Solving*

Exercise If you walk briskly, you burn 5 calories per minute. If you run, you burn 10 calories per minute. The equation $5x + 10y = 250$ describes combinations of walking for *x* minutes and running for *y* minutes to burn a total of 250 calories. Graph the equation.

Complete the solution (■, 0) to find the *x*-intercept.

$$5x + 10y = 250$$
$$5x + 10(0) = 250$$
$$5x = 250$$
$$x = 50$$

Complete the solution (0, ■) to find the *y*-intercept.

$$5x + 10y = 250$$
$$5(0) + 10y = 250$$
$$10y = 250$$
$$y = 25$$

Graph the intercepts.
Draw the line.

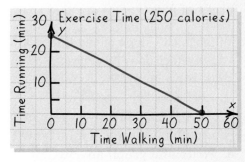

4. **a.** Find three solutions of the equation from Example 2.
   b. ⁂*Explain* What combination of walking and running does each solution represent?

5. **a.** Find the slope of the graph in Example 2. Include units.
   b. ⁂*Draw a Conclusion* Complete this statement: For every increase of one minute in the time you run, you can __?__ the time you walk by __?__ minutes.

6. ✔ *Try It Out* Use x- and y-intercepts to graph each equation.

a. $3x - 5y = 30$ **b.** $x + 4y = 12$

EXERCISES *On Your Own*

Use the given word model to write an equation with two variables for each problem. Then graph the equation.

1. total cost = \$3.50 × number of items

2. plant growth = $2.5 \frac{\text{in.}}{\text{day}}$ × number of days

3. hours awake = 24 − hours sleeping

4. total cost = cost of order + \$7 mailing fee

Use the graph below for Exercises 5–8.

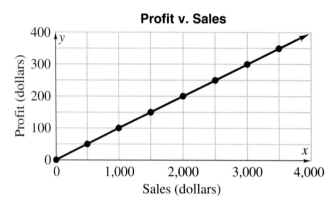

Profit v. Sales

5. What sales are needed to produce a profit of \$300?

6. What profit is produced by sales of \$2,000?

7. What is the slope of the line in the graph? What effect does an increase of \$500 in sales have on profit? Explain.

8. What is the y-intercept of the graph? What does it represent in terms of sales and profit?

9. *Jobs* A pizza delivery person earns \$20 for a four-hour shift. His customers tip him an average of \$2 per order.
  a. Write and graph an equation to represent his total earnings.
  b. Use the graph to find his earnings if he delivers 18 orders.
  c. How many customers must he serve to earn \$52?

Graph each equation by finding the x- and y-intercepts.

10. $x + y = 6$ **11.** $x - y = 4$ **12.** $2x - y = 6$ **13.** $-2x + y = 8$

14. $4x + 3y = 12$ **15.** $x - 4y = 20$ **16.** $6x - 7y = 42$ **17.** $5x + 3y = 300$

18. **Footwear** The length of a man's foot is related to his shoe size by the formula $s = 3\ell - 22$. The length ℓ is measured in inches. (The actual shoe size s is rounded to the nearest half unit.)

   a. Graph the formula. Place the length of the foot along the horizontal axis.
   b. In which quadrant(s) does your graph make sense? Explain.
   c. Use your graph to estimate the shoe size for a man whose foot measures 10.5 in.
   d. Alan wears size $8\frac{1}{2}$ shoes. Estimate the length of his foot.

19. **Entertainment** The Ballesteros family consists of 2 adults and 4 children. They spent $26 for circus tickets. The equation $2x + 4y = 26$ describes the cost x for each adult's ticket and the cost y for each child's ticket.
   a. Graph the equation.
   b. **Open-ended** Find two solutions of the equation. What ticket prices does each solution represent?

20. **Food** Suppose you have $60 to spend on shrimp and chicken wings for a party. Shrimp costs $10/lb. Wings cost $6/lb. The equation $10x + 6y = 60$ describes the amount of shrimp x and wings y you can buy.
   a. Graph the equation.
   b. Find three solutions. What combination of shrimp and wings does each solution represent?
   c. What is the slope of the graph? What does it represent in terms of buying shrimp and wings?

> **JOURNAL**
> Write a word model with two variables that describes something in your everyday life. Then write and graph an equation for your model. Interpret several solutions.

Mixed Review

Find the next three numbers in each pattern. *(Previous Course)*

21. 14, 28, 56, 112, . . . 22. 2, 12, 22, 32, . . . 23. 91, 9.1, 0.91, . . . 24. 20, 10, 5, . . .

Compare. Write >, <, or =. *(Lesson 2-1)*

25. $-15 \ \blacksquare \ -35$ 26. $19 \ \blacksquare \ -19$ 27. $9 \ \blacksquare \ -8$ 28. $|0| \ \blacksquare \ |-4|$

29. **Choose a Strategy** Mei-lin starts with $480. In the first week she withdraws half the money. In the second week she withdraws half of what is left. If she continues this pattern, in what week will she withdraw $15?

What You'll Learn

▼ To solve a problem by using two equations

...And Why

In business, you can use income and expense equations to learn when you will start to make a profit.

Here's How

Look for questions that
⊞ build understanding
✔ check understanding

THINK AND DISCUSS

You can make comparisons by placing the graphs of two linear equations on the same coordinate grid.

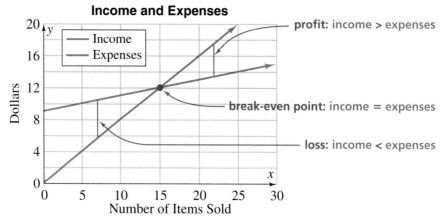

Income and Expenses

1. **a.** ⊞ *Visual Thinking* Use the graph shown above. If 5 items are sold, estimate the income. Estimate the expenses. Have you made a profit or a loss? About how much is it?
   b. Answer the same questions for 15 items and for 20 items.

■ **EXAMPLE** *Real-World Problem Solving*

Money Write and graph equations to represent income and expenses for the cake sale. Find the break-even point.

STUDENT COUNCIL CAKE SALE

EXPENSES

$20 to set up and
     decorate sales booth

$2 to make each cake

INCOME

$4 each cake sold

Words • income = $4 × number of cakes sold

⬇

• Let y = income
• Let x = number of cakes sold

Income Equation • $y = 4x$

Words • expenses = $2 × number of cakes sold + $20

⬇

• Let y = expenses
• Let x = number of cakes sold

Expenses Equation • $y = 2x + \$20$

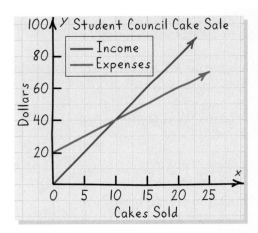

Student Council Cake Sale

— Income
— Expenses

The break-even point occurs where the two lines intersect. The coordinates are (10, 40). If the student council sells 10 cakes, the income and expenses will each be $40.

2. ✔ *Try It Out* Use the graph to find the profit or loss with the given sales.

    a. 5 cakes sold   **b.** 15 cakes sold   **c.** 25 cakes sold

Two or more related equations are called a *system of equations*.

Work Together   *Exploring the Break-even Point*

You and the rest of your school's Computer Club are designing software games to sell. For each game, you have expenses of $200 for development plus $3 for each disk copy that you make and sell.

3. How much should you charge for a copy of the game? Decide on two possible prices. Poll your classmates to see how many would buy a computer game at each price.

4. **a.** Write an equation to represent your expenses for one game.
    b. For each of the two possible selling prices, write an equation to represent income.
    c. On two separate graphs, show the expense equation with one of the income equations.
    d. Find the break-even point for each selling price.

Tenadar Software is a kid-based company that develops and markets inexpensive games and learning software for children of all ages. The company was founded in the spring of 1995.

5. ⚎ *Reasoning* What are some strategies that you could use to have the break-even point occur with fewer sales?

6. ⚎ *Reasoning* Would doubling the selling price guarantee a greater profit? Explain.

For Exercises 1–7, use the graphs of income and expenses at the right.

Key Chain Fund-Raiser

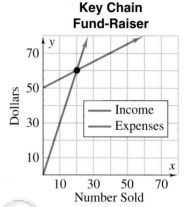

1. Suppose you sell 10 key chains. Will there be a profit or a loss? Explain.

2. What are the coordinates of the break-even point?

3. How many key chains must you sell to break even?

4. *Writing* Explain how to tell from the graph when there is a profit and when there is a loss.

5. a. Write an equation for the income line shown in the graph.
   b. What is the slope of this line?
   c. What is the selling price of one key chain?

6. a. Write an equation for the expense line shown in the graph.
   b. What are the slope and *y*-intercept of this line?
   c. *Open-ended* What might the slope and the *y*-intercept represent in terms of expenses?

7. Suppose you sell 40 key chains. What is the profit?

8. *Exercise* One weight lifter starts with a 3-lb dumbbell and increases the weight by 1 lb per month. Another starts with a 5-lb dumbbell and increases the weight by $\frac{1}{2}$ lb per month.
   a. For each weight lifter, write an equation that represents how much weight *y* she is lifting after *x* months.
   b. Graph both equations on the same coordinate grid. Where do the lines intersect? What do the coordinates of this point represent?
   c. After how many months will the two people be lifting the same amount?
   d. Will they ever be lifting the same amount again? Explain.

9. *Fund-raising* To make custom T-shirts, you spend $30 on decorating material and $5 for each plain T-shirt. You plan to sell the shirts for $8 each. Write and graph equations to represent income and expenses. Find the break-even point.

10. *Sales* You estimate that you can make muffins for $.30 each. Advertising will cost $18.00. You sell the muffins for $.75 each. Write and graph equations to represent income and expenses. Find the break-even point.

11. **Recreation** Two balloons are in the air. Balloon A is at an altitude of 1,000 ft and rising at the rate of 100 ft/min. Balloon B is at 2,500 ft and descending 200 ft/min.
    a. For each balloon, write an equation to relate the altitude of the balloon to the number of minutes that have passed.
    b. Graph both equations on the same coordinate grid. Where do the lines intersect? What do the coordinates of this point represent?

Mixed Review

Simplify each expression. *(Lesson 3-1)*

12. $8(z + 7) + 3z$ 13. $6x + 3x + 2$ 14. $4(p - 3p)$ 15. $3(y + 3) - 4$

16. **Choose a Strategy** Kelly has equal numbers of pennies, nickels, dimes, and quarters. The total is $6.15. How many of each type of coin does Kelly have?

CHAPTER PROJECT

PROJECT LINK: DESIGNING

Design the target area where the ball will come to rest and score points. Mark the point values for each region. You will want this design available as you explain the rules of your game. Estimate an average point score. For what score will you award a prize at the fair? How did the data you collected in the Project Link on page 189 affect the design of your target?

✓ CHECKPOINT 2   *Lessons 4-5 through 4-7*

1. **Music** In a poll of 25 students, 15 liked rock and 9 liked jazz. Four students liked both types of music. How many students didn't like either type of music?

2. The equation $y = 0.1x + 0.5$ represents the cost y (in dollars) of a long-distance telephone call lasting x minutes.
   a. Graph the equation.
   b. Find three solutions. What does each solution represent?

3. Use the graph at the right. Find the break-even point and tell what it means.

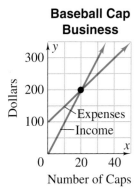

Baseball Cap Business

4-8 Translations

What You'll Learn

▼ To graph the image of a translation

▼ To describe a translation

...And Why

You can use translations to help make three-dimensional drawings.

Here's How

Look for questions that
- build understanding
- ✔ check understanding

THINK AND DISCUSS

1 Graphing a Translation

A **transformation** is a change of position, shape, or size of a figure. Three types of transformation that change position are a slide, a flip, and a turn.

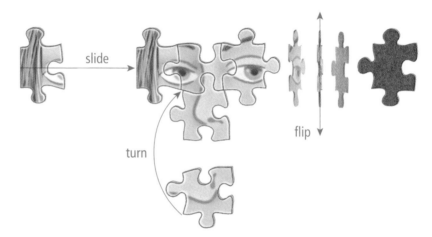

slide

turn

flip ▼

1. What are some other places in real life you have seen a slide? A flip? A turn?

The figure you get after a transformation is the **image** of the original figure. To identify the image of a point A, you can use the notation A' (read "A prime"). Another name for a slide is a **translation.**

■ EXAMPLE 1

Translate point $B(-2, -1)$ up 4 units. What are the coordinates of its image, B'?

Count up 4 units from point B. Graph B'. The coordinates of B' are $(-2, 3)$.

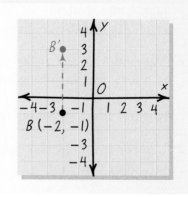

2. ✔ *Try It Out* Translate point B in Example 1 to the left 4 units. What are the coordinates of its image?

QUICKreview

Each corner of a triangle is a vertex (plural: vertices).

To translate a triangle, first slide the vertices of the triangle. Then connect the image points to complete the translation.

■ EXAMPLE 2

Translate $\triangle DEF$ to the right 5 units and down 3 units.

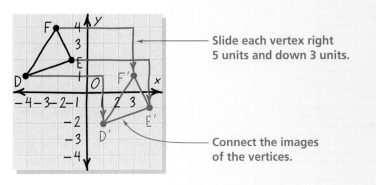

Slide each vertex right 5 units and down 3 units.

Connect the images of the vertices.

To show a translation, you can use arrow notation. You write $A \longrightarrow A'$. You read this as "point A goes to point A'."

3. Complete the arrow notation for the translation in Example 2: $\triangle DEF \longrightarrow$ __?__.

4. ✔ *Try It Out* Translate $\triangle DEF$ in Example 2 to the left 2 units and up 4 units.

▼ *Describing a Translation*

To find the coordinates of an image, you can add or subtract the amount of movement from the coordinates of the original figure.

5. ⸬ *Visual Thinking* Tell whether each movement affects the *x-coordinate* or the *y-coordinate*.
a. moving a point up or down **b.** moving a point left or right

6. ⸬ *What If . . .* Suppose that you translate a point to the left 1 unit and up 3 units. What would you do to the coordinates of the original point to find the coordinates of the image?

You can write a general rule to describe a translation. For example, $(x, y) \longrightarrow (x - 1, y + 3)$ describes a translation to the left 1 unit and up 3 units.

■ EXAMPLE 3

Write a rule to describe the translation of the black triangle to the blue triangle.

Each point has moved 3 units to the right and 2 units down. So the translation adds 3 to the *x*-coordinate and subtracts 2 from the *y*-coordinate. The rule is $(x, y) \longrightarrow (x + 3, y - 2)$.

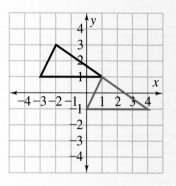

7. ✔*Try It Out* Suppose $Q(3, 9) \longrightarrow Q'(5, -2)$. Write a rule to describe the translation.

You can translate lines on the coordinate plane.

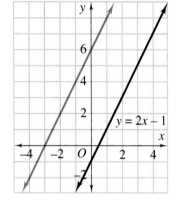

8. ⬥*Reasoning* In the graph at the left, the graph of $y = 2x - 1$ has been translated up 7 units.
   a. What is the *y*-intercept of the image?
   b. What is the slope of the image? How did you find it?
   c. What is the equation of the image?
   d. How does the equation of the image relate to the equation of the original line?

Work Together
Designing a Logo

Art You can use translations to draw three-dimensional (3-D) figures.

Step 1
Draw a figure on graph paper.

Step 2
Translate the figure.

Step 3
Connect each vertex with its image.

Step 4
Use dashes for sides that are not visible.

In your group, design a figure on graph paper that represents your school name or letters. Then use the steps shown above to create a 3-D design. Make several other 3-D designs by varying the length and direction of the translation you use. Decide which translations work best to create designs that look 3-D.

Use graph paper to graph the image of *STUV* after each translation. Name the coordinates of *S'*, *T'*, *U'*, and *V'*.

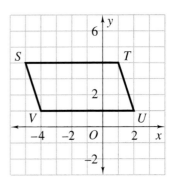

1. down 6 units

2. left 2 units

3. left 3 units, up 4 units

4. right 1 unit, down 3 units

5. *Mental Math* Translate point *N*(1, 5) right 3 units and up 7 units. Translate its image, point *N'*, left 3 units and down 7 units. What are the coordinates of the image of point *N'*?

Copy each figure. Then graph the image, using the given translation.

6.

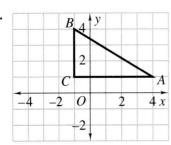

left 3 units, down 4 units

7.

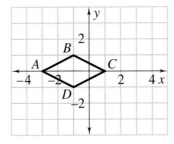

up 2 units

8.

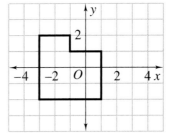

right 4 units, up 3 units

9. The graph shows an ice skater moving along the ice. How far and in what direction has the skater moved?

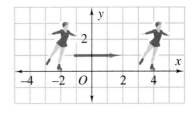

10. The vertices of △*MNP* are *M*(−4, 1), *N*(−2, 4), and *P*(−1, −1). The triangle is translated to the right 5 units and down 2 units. How would you find the coordinates of *M'*, *N'*, and *P'*?

Write a rule to describe the translation shown on each graph.

11.

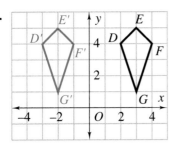

12.

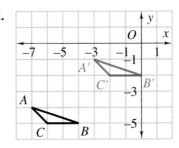

13.

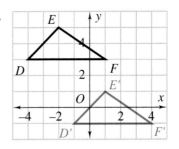

14. **Research** Find out the rules for moving the playing pieces in chess. How many different types of moves can you make? Describe each move as a translation.

15. Suppose $L(0, -4) \longrightarrow L'(7, 7)$. Write a rule to describe the translation.

16. **a.** The vertices of $\triangle HJK$ are $H(-4, 0)$, $J(2, 4)$, and $K(4, 1)$. Graph the triangle.
    b. Write a rule that will translate point H to the origin.
    c. Graph the image of $\triangle HJK$ using your rule from part (b).

17. **Writing** A shape is translated three times to form an image. The first translation is right 3 units and up 5 units. The second translation is right 7 units and up 11 units. The third is left 4 units and down 2 units. What shortcut can you use to form the same image in only one translation? Explain.

18. **a.** The diagram at the right shows the graph of the equation $y = \frac{1}{2}x$. Translate the line to the right 2 units and up 5 units. Graph its image.
    b. Find the equation of the image line.
    c. *Open-ended* Describe another translation that produces the same image line.

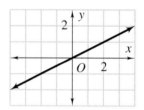

Mixed Review

Graph each linear equation. *(Lesson 4-2)*

19. $y = -4x + 5$ 20. $y = 2x - 3$ 21. $y = \frac{2}{5}x + 2$ 22. $y = -\frac{5}{3}x + 5$

Mental Math **Evaluate each expression.** *(Lesson 2-5)*

23. $(-14) \cdot (-4)$ 24. $(-343) \cdot 0$ 25. $(-48) \div 6$ 26. $(-75) \div (-5)$ 27. $(-3)5 \div (-3)$

28. Mr. Dunn tells his students that he is thinking of a number. If he multiplies the number by 5, subtracts 15, and adds 4, the result is 44. Find the number. *(Lesson 3-5)*

29. *Choose a Strategy* At 1 P.M., Mike and Kia start swimming from the same point. Mike swims east at a rate of 2 mi/h. Kia swims west at 4 mi/h. When will they be 9 miles apart?

Choose the best answer.

1. What ordered pair best represents the intersection of line ℓ and line m?

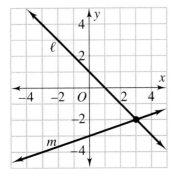

   A. $(-3, 2)$ B. $(-2, 3)$
   C. $(2, -3)$ D. $(3, -2)$

2. Which table of x- and y-values could have been created for $y = x - 2$?

F. x	y	G. x	y	H. x	y	J. x	y
-1	3	-1	3	-1	-3	-1	-1
0	2	0	2	0	-2	0	-2
1	1	1	3	1	-1	1	-3

3. What is the equation of line k?

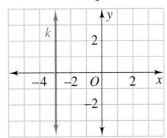

   A. $y = -3$ B. $x = -3$
   C. $y = 3$ D. $x = 3$

4. Which is equivalent to $3^4 4^2$?

   F. $12 \cdot 8$
   G. $(4 \cdot 3) + (2 \cdot 4)$
   H. $4 \cdot 4 \cdot 4 \cdot 2 \cdot 2 \cdot 2 \cdot 2$
   J. $3 \cdot 3 \cdot 3 \cdot 3 \cdot 4 \cdot 4$

5. Which equation has a graph containing the points $(0, 1)$, $(-2, -3)$ and $(2, 5)$?

   A. $y = 2x + 1$ B. $y = x + 1$
   C. $y = 2x - 1$ D. $y = x - 1$

6. Sixteen gigabytes of computer memory equals 1.6×10^{10} bytes. Which of these is equivalent to this number?

   F. 160,000,000   G. 1,600,000,000
   H. 16,000,000,000 J. 160,000,000,000

Please note that items 7–8 have *five* answer choices.

7. Chad went to a progressive dinner. He walked 8 blocks east for the appetizer. Then he walked 3 blocks west for the salad. The main course was 2 blocks north. Finally, the dessert was 4 blocks south of the salad. Which diagram shows how Chad walked?

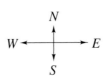

A.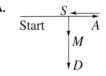

B.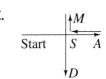

C.

D.

E.

8. The diving board is 4 ft above the pool. The pool is 15 ft deep. The total length of Jayna's dive is 10 ft. How far did she go below the surface of the water?

   F. 19 ft   G. 14 ft   H. 39 ft
   J. 6 ft   K. 5 ft

4-9 Reflections and Symmetry

What You'll Learn

▼ **1** To graph reflections
▼ **2** To identify lines of symmetry

...And Why

Reflections and symmetry in design make many objects more appealing.

Here's How

Look for questions that
▪▪ build understanding
✔ check understanding

Work Together   *Exploring Reflections*

1. Work with a partner. Fold a piece of tracing paper in half. Then unfold the paper and label the halves I and II. On half I, draw △*DEF*.

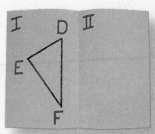

2. Refold the paper. On the back of half II, trace the triangle. Unfold the paper and trace this triangle onto the front of half II. Label the vertices of the last triangle *D'*, *E'*, and *F'* to correspond to the vertices of △*DEF*.

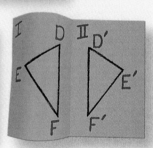

3. Compare the distances of *D* and *D'* from the fold. Do the same for the other vertices. What appears to be true?

THINK AND DISCUSS

▼ **1** *Graphing Reflections*

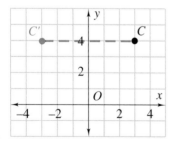

Another name for a flip is a **reflection.** In the diagram at the left, *C'* is the image of *C* after a reflection over the *y*-axis. The *y*-axis is the **line of reflection.**

In the Work Together, you discovered that a point and its reflection are the same distance from the line of reflection. In the diagram, *C* and *C'* are each 3 units from the *y*-axis.

Notice also in the diagram that the line of reflection is perpendicular to the segment connecting *C* and *C'*. That is, the *y*-axis and $\overline{CC'}$ intersect to form a 90° angle.

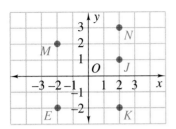

4. a. ⠿ *Think About It* J is *not* the reflection of K over the x-axis. Why isn't it?

b. M is *not* the reflection of N over the y-axis. Why isn't it?

c. For which two lettered points is the x-axis the line of reflection? Explain.

■ EXAMPLE 1

Graph the point $A(3, 2)$. Then graph its image after it is reflected over the x-axis. Name the coordinates of A'.

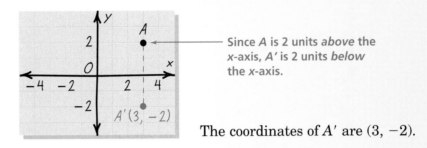

Since A is 2 units *above* the x-axis, A' is 2 units *below* the x-axis.

The coordinates of A' are $(3, -2)$.

5. ✔ *Try It Out* Graph $D(-2, 1)$ and its image after a reflection over the y-axis.

To reflect a triangle over a line, first reflect the vertices of the triangle. Then connect the image points.

■ EXAMPLE 2

Graph the image of $\triangle BCD$ after a reflection over the red line. Name the coordinates of the vertices of $\triangle B'C'D'$.

Since C is 5 units above the red line, C' is 5 units below the line.

Reflect the other vertices. Draw $\triangle B'C'D'$.

The coordinates of the vertices are $B'(-2, -4)$, $C'(1, -6)$, and $D'(2, -3)$.

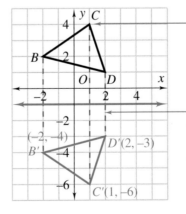

6. ✔ *Try It Out* Graph $\triangle JKL$ and its image after a reflection over each line.

a. the x-axis　　**b.** the blue line　　**c.** the red line

2 *Identifying Lines of Symmetry*

If a figure can be reflected over a line so that its image matches the original figure, the figure has **reflectional symmetry.** For example, the leaf at the left has reflectional symmetry. The green line is a **line of symmetry.**

■ EXAMPLE 3

Does the figure have reflectional symmetry? If it does, draw the line(s) of symmetry.

a. 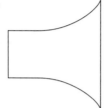 **b.**  **c.**

Yes, the figure matches over a horizontal line.

No, the figure is not symmetric.

Yes, the figure has three lines of symmetry.

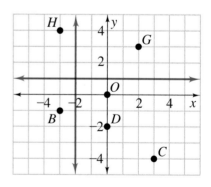

EXERCISES *On Your Own*

Graph the given point and its image after each reflection. Name the coordinates of the image.

1. $H(-3, 4)$ over the x-axis

2. $G(2, 3)$ over the y-axis

3. $B(-3, -1)$ over the red line

4. $D(0, -2)$ over the blue line

5. $C(3, -4)$ over the blue line

6. $O(0, 0)$ over the red line

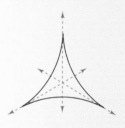

$\triangle MPS$ **has vertices** $M(4, 5)$, $P(1, 2)$, **and** $S(5, 1)$**. Graph** $\triangle MPS$ **and its image after a reflection over each line.**

7. the x-axis

8. the y-axis

9. the line through $(-1, 1)$ and $(-1, 3)$

10. **Writing** How do the signs of the coordinates change when you reflect a point over the *x*-axis? Over the *y*-axis?

11. **a.** **Geometry** The vertices of △*RST* are *R*(0, 4), *S*(0, 0), and *T*(−4, 0). Graph △*RST* on a coordinate plane.
    b. Reflect △*RST* over the *y*-axis. Then reflect the image over the *x*-axis. Finally, reflect the second image over the *y*-axis.
    c. Describe the figure formed by △*RST* and its images.

Does each figure have reflectional symmetry? If it does, state how many lines of symmetry it has.

12.

13.

14.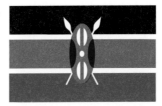

Flag of Kenya

Each diagram shows a shape folded along a red line of symmetry. Sketch the unfolded figure.

15.

16.

17.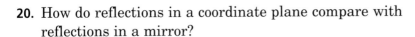

18. **a.** Graph the image of △*JKL* after a reflection over the red line. Name the coordinates of the vertices of △*J'K'L'*.
    b. **Reasoning** What do you notice about the *y*-coordinates of each vertex of △*JKL* and its image?
    c. What do you notice about the mean of the *x*-coordinates of each vertex of △*JKL* and its image?

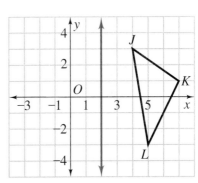

19. **a.** Graph these ordered pairs and connect the points in order: (−3, −3), (−4, −1), (−1, 2), (1, 1), (2, 5), and (4, 4).
    b. These segments form half a figure whose line of symmetry has the equation *y* = *x*. Complete the figure.

20. How do reflections in a coordinate plane compare with reflections in a mirror?

21. The words COB and BEE have reflectional symmetry. Find three other words with reflectional symmetry.

22. *Literature* "The Tiger" was written by the English poet William Blake (1757–1827). What symmetry do you see in a tiger?

23. *Reasoning* Suppose $T'(0, 6)$ is the reflection of $T(6, 0)$.
  a. How would you find the line of reflection?
  b. What is an equation for the line of reflection?

Open-ended **Draw four 6 × 6 squares on a piece of graph paper. Shade the boxes in each square to make designs with the given number of lines of symmetry.**

24. only 1   **25.** exactly 2   **26.** no lines   **27.** exactly 4

28. *Writing* How many lines of symmetry do you think a circle has? Explain.

*Tiger! Tiger! burning bright
In the forests of the night,
What immortal hand or eye
Could frame thy fearful
symmetry?*

Mixed Review

Mental Math **Find the value of each expression.** *(Lesson 2-8)*

29. $-7 + 8 + (-13) + 2$ **30.** $(-20)(-13)(-5)$ **31.** $(0.7 + 0.3) \times (13 - 4)$

Solve each inequality. Graph the solution. *(Lesson 3-10)*

32. $5t \leq 20$ **33.** $-3n \geq 18$ **34.** $\frac{w}{3} > -2$ **35.** $\frac{s}{-5} < 3$ **36.** $-7x \geq -35$

37. Theron measured the life of twelve different light bulbs. The data represent the number of days each bulb lasted: 19, 21, 20, 38, 42, 28, 24, 37, 33, 18, 26, 20. *(Lesson 1-6)*
  a. Make a box-and-whisker plot.
  b. Find the mean, median, mode, and range of the data.

CHAPTER PROJECT

PROJECT LINK: GRAPHING

Decide how much contestants at the fair will pay to play the game. Write and graph an equation that describes income. Then estimate your expenses. Include start-up costs such as advertising and materials. About how many games will be played for each prize? What will the prizes cost? Write and graph an equation for your expenses. Find the break-even point.

4-10 Exploring Rotations

What You'll Learn

1. To graph rotations
2. To identify rotational symmetry

...And Why

You can create artistic designs by using rotational symmetry.

Here's How

Look for questions that
- build understanding
- ✔ check understanding

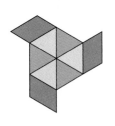

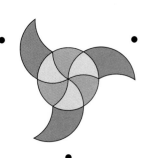

Here are some examples of designs you could make in the Work Together.

Work Together

Exploring Rotations

1. Begin with paper cut in squares about 4 inches on each side.

Step 1 Place a piece of the paper over the figure at the right. Trace eveything shown in black: the center point, the kite, and the vertices of the triangle.

Step 2 Place the point of your pencil on the center point. Rotate the paper until the vertices of the triangle again overlap. Trace the kite in its new location.

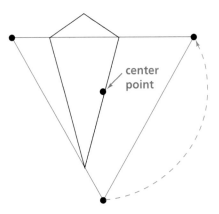

center point

Step 3 Repeat Step 2 until there are three kites on your paper. Check your drawing by comparing it with others in your group.

2. **Go a Step Further** Create your own design.
   a. On a blank piece of paper, trace the center point and the three vertices of the triangle from the diagram above. Then draw your own shape on the paper.
   b. Place the paper on your desktop. Use a new piece of paper to repeat the process in Question 1. Color your design. Create a display of your group's designs.

THINK AND DISCUSS

▼1 *Graphing Rotations*

A **rotation** is a transformation that turns a figure about a fixed point called the **center of rotation.** You can rotate a figure up to 360°. In this book, all rotations will be counterclockwise.

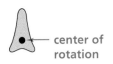
center of rotation

90°

180°

270°

360°

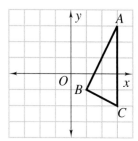

■ EXAMPLE 1

Draw the image of △ABC, shown at the left, after a rotation of 90° about the origin.

Step 1 Draw △ABC. Place a piece of tracing paper over your graph. Trace the vertices of the triangle, the x-axis, and the y-axis. Then place your pencil at the origin to rotate the paper.

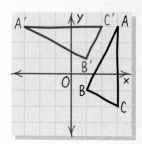

Step 2 Rotate the paper 90°. (The axes should line up.) Mark the position of each vertex by pressing through the paper.

Step 3 Remove the tracing paper. Complete the figure.

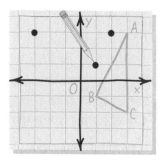

3. ✔ *Try It Out* Draw the image of △ABC after a rotation of 180° about the origin.

4. Rotate each point the given number of degrees about the origin. Give the coordinates of each image point.
   a. A(2, 3); 180°   **b.** F(−3, −1); 270°   **c.** D(0, 2); 90°

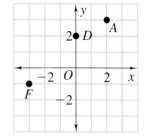

❷ *Identifying Rotational Symmetry*

If a figure can be rotated 180° or less so that its image matches the original figure, then the figure has **rotational symmetry.**

120°

The image matches the original figure after $\frac{1}{3}$ of a complete rotation.

$\frac{1}{3} \cdot 360° = 120°$

Design Which figures have rotational symmetry? For those that do, give the angle of rotation.

a.

b.

c.

The image matches the original after $\frac{1}{5}$ of a complete rotation.
$\frac{1}{5} \cdot 360° = 72°$

This figure does not have rotational symmetry.

The image matches the original after $\frac{1}{2}$ of a complete rotation.
$\frac{1}{2} \cdot 360° = 180°$

EXERCISES *On Your Own*

Each figure is an image formed by rotating the figure at the right. What is the angle of rotation of each?

1.

2.

3.

Copy each figure. Then draw the image of the figure after the given rotation about the origin.

4. 180°
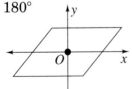

5. 90°
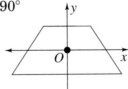

6. 270°
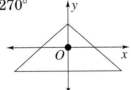

7. 180°
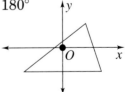

Graph each point. Then rotate it the given number of degrees about the origin. Give the coordinates of the image.

8. $L(3, 3)$; 90°   9. $M(-4, -2)$; 270°   10. $N(3, -5)$; 180°   11. $P(0, -4)$; 270°

12. Describe the symmetries of the figures in Exercises 4–7 as they relate to the *x*-axis, the *y*-axis, and the origin.

13. Choose A, B, C, or D. Which figure is a rotation of the figure at the right?

A.   B.   C. D.

Which figures have rotational symmetry? For those that do, give the angle of rotation.

14.    15.    16.    17.

18. Graph △*JKL* with vertices *J*(1, −3), *K*(6, −2), and *L*(6, −4). Draw the three images formed by rotating the triangle 90°, 180°, and 270° about the origin.

19. *Open-ended* Find a word that has either reflectional or rotational symmetry.

20. *Writing* Explain why triangle II is an image of triangle I after a rotation or after a reflection.

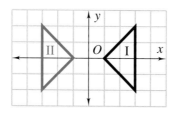

PORTFOLIO
Select one or two items from your work for this chapter. Consider:
• open-ended exercises
• graphs using the coordinate plane
• examples of transformations
Explain why you have included each selection.

Mixed Review

Evaluate each expression. *(Previous Course)*

21. $\frac{1}{2} + 2\frac{1}{2}$ 22. $2\frac{4}{5} - \frac{3}{5}$ 23. $\frac{5}{6} \times 18$ 24. $\frac{7}{8} \cdot 4$ 25. $\frac{3}{8} + \frac{2}{8} + \frac{3}{8}$

Solve each equation. *(Lesson 3-4)*

26. $284 - 35y = 4$ 27. $2x + 7 = -42$ 28. $500 = 10(x + 30)$ 29. $0 = -3x + (-15)$

30. *Choose a Strategy* Jimena and Tupi each have $.49. They also each have 12 coins. Jimena has a coin that Tupi doesn't have. What coins does each have?

CHAPTER PROJECT

Step Right UP!

Design a Game The Project Link questions on pages 180, 189, 197, and 208 should help you complete your project. Here is a checklist to help you gather the parts of your project together.

- ✔ the ramp, or a model or diagram of it
- ✔ the design of the target area
- ✔ the rules of play
- ✔ the expected income and expenses for the game

Demonstrate or describe your game to the class. Explain clearly the rules of play. Discuss how the profit for the class will depend on the number of players and the number of winners, and explain your calculations.

Reflect and Revise

Allow some of your friends to try out the game. Is it fun to play? Is there a reasonable chance of winning? If necessary, adjust the rules or the materials to improve the game.

Web Extension
Prentice Hall's Internet site contains information you might find helpful as you complete your project. Visit www.phschool.com/mgm3/ch4 for some links and ideas related to games.

④ WRAP UP

Graphing and Equations

4-1, 4-2

An **ordered pair** describes the location of a point on a coordinate plane. The first number in the pair is the **x-coordinate**. The second number is the **y-coordinate**.

When the values in an ordered pair make an equation with two variables true, the ordered pair is a **solution** of the equation. To graph a linear equation, graph several solutions and draw a line through the points.

Name the point with the given coordinates.

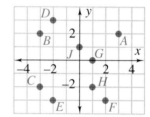

1. $(3, 2)$ **2.** $(2, -3)$ **3.** $(1, 0)$ **4.** $(-3, 2)$

Name the coordinates of each point.

5. C **6.** D **7.** H **8.** E

Graph each equation.

9. $y = x + 3$ **10.** $y = \frac{1}{4}x - 1$ **11.** $y = -2x + 1$ **12.** $y = -\frac{2}{3}x$

13. In which quadrant would you find the point $M(7, -4)$?

Slopes and y-intercepts

4-3, 4-4

The **y-intercept** is the y-coordinate of the point where the line crosses the y-axis. An equation written in the form $y = mx + b$ is in **slope-intercept form**. The graph is a line with a slope m and y-intercept b.

$$\textbf{slope} = \frac{\text{rise}}{\text{run}} = \frac{\text{change in } y}{\text{change in } x}$$

Identify the slope and y-intercept.

14. $y = \frac{3}{4}x + 6$ **15.** $y = 2x + 1$ **16.** $y = -2x + 3$

The points from each table lie on a line. Find the slope.

17.

x	0	1	2	3	4
y	-3	-1	1	3	5

18.

x	-2	-1	0	1	2
y	5	4	3	2	1

19.

x	-3	-1	1	3	5
y	7	4	1	-2	-5

20. *Writing* How can you tell if the graph of $y = -7x - 3$ is above or below the graph of $y = -7x + 1$?

Using logical reasoning and graphs can help you solve problems.

21. There are 450 students at Fuller Middle School. Of these, 200 study Spanish, 150 study French, and 150 do not study a foreign language. How many study both Spanish and French?

22. The equation $x + 3y = 12$ describes the number of soft drinks x and the number of sandwiches y you can buy for $12.
    a. Graph the equation.
    b. Find three solutions. Tell what each solution represents.

23. Charlene sells decorated barrettes. She spends $10 for basic supplies and $2 per barrette. She charges $4 per barrette.
    a. Write and graph an equation for expenses and an equation for income.
    b. Find the break-even point.

Translations, Reflections, and Rotations   4-8, 4-9, 4-10

A **transformation** is a change of position, shape, or size of a figure. The figure after a transformation is called the **image**. You can transform figures in a plane by **translation**, **reflection**, or **rotation**.

If a figure can be reflected over a line so that its image matches the original figure, the figure has **reflectional symmetry**. If a figure can be rotated 180° or less so that its image matches the original figure, it has **rotational symmetry**.

Figure II is the image of Figure I. Describe the transformation.

24.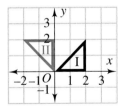

25.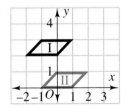

26.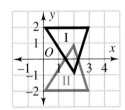

27.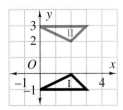

28. a. *Open-ended* Draw a figure that has reflectional symmetry.
    b. Draw a figure that has rotational symmetry.

Graph each point on a coordinate plane.

1. $A(4, -2)$ 2. $B(0, 5)$ 3. $C(-3, 2)$

4. In which quadrant would you find the point with coordinates $(-4, -2)$?

Tell whether the ordered pair $(-5, 8)$ is a solution of the given equation.

5. $x + y = 3$ 6. $2x - 10 = -2y$

Find the slope and the y-intercept. Graph each equation.

7. $y = 3x - 5$ 8. $y = -\frac{3}{4}x + 3$

Match each equation with its graph.

9. $y = 3x + 2$

10. $3x + y = -2$

11. $y = -2$

12. $x = 2$

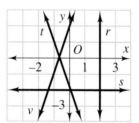

Choose A, B, C, or D.

13. A line on the coordinate plane falls from left to right. Which could *not* be the equation of the line?
   A. $x + y = 7$ B. $y = -2x + 5$
   C. $y = 2x - 1$ D. $y = -x + 3$

14. Expenses for a school dance are $100. Tickets are $3 each. Which equation correctly relates the profit y to the number of tickets sold x?
   A. $y = 3x + 100$ B. $y = 100 - 3x$
   C. $y = 100x + 3$ D. $y = 3x - 100$

15. Graph $4x + 3y = 12$ by finding the x- and y-intercepts.

16. *Writing* Describe a real-life situation for which you could use the equation $y = 1.25x + 0.50$.

17. To make a game, you spend $20 for set-up costs and $5 for material for each game. You plan to sell each game for $15. Write equations to represent income and expenses. Find the break-even point.

$\triangle JKL$ has vertices $J(4, 5)$, $K(6, 2)$, and $L(3, 2)$. Graph $\triangle JKL$ and its image after each transformation.

18. translation 6 units left

19. translation 4 units left and 3 units down

20. reflection over the x-axis

21. reflection over the line through $(1, -2)$ and $(1, 2)$

22. $90°$ rotation about the origin

23. $180°$ rotation about the origin

24. Write a rule to describe the translation shown on the graph.

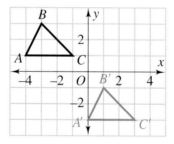

25. *Open-ended* Draw and describe a figure that has exactly three lines of symmetry.

Choose A, B, C, or D.

1. Which set of numbers satisfies the inequality $2x - 3 < -1$?

   A. $-2, -1, 0$ **B.** $-1, 0, 1$
   C. $0, 1, 2$ **D.** $1, 2, 3$

2. Which expression is *not* equivalent to $2^3 \cdot 2^5$?

   A. 2^8 **B.** $2^4 \cdot 2^3 \cdot 2$
   C. $2^4 \cdot 2^4$ **D.** 4^8

3. A sales manager must prepare a report for the president of her company. The report must compare the monthly sales of the current year with the monthly sales of the previous year. What would be the best way for her to display the data?

   A. a circle graph
   B. a line plot
   C. a double bar graph
   D. a box-and-whisker plot

4. Which of the following is the equation for a line with a positive slope?

   A. $y = -3x - 1$ **B.** $y = 2$
   C. $y = 5x + 4$ **D.** $y = -4x + 1$

5. Under a certain reflection, the image of $P(3, -1)$ is $P'(-1, -1)$. What are the coordinates of the image of $Q(-2, 4)$ under the same reflection?

   A. $(-2, -5)$ **B.** $(-6, 4)$
   C. $(-2, -4)$ **D.** $(4, 4)$

6. Which numbers, when included in the set $\{8, 8, 9, 12, 13\}$, will raise the values of *both* the mean and the median?

   A $5, 8$ **B.** $7, 15$
   C. $10, 15$ **D.** $9, 10$

7. A rectangle has perimeter 28 cm. Its length is 10 cm more than its width. Which equation could be used to find the dimensions of the rectangle?

   A. $w + (w + 10) = 28$
   B. $2w + 2(w + 10) = 28$
   C. $w(w + 10) = 28$
   D. $2w(w + 10) = 28$

8. In which quadrant are the x-coordinates of all ordered pairs positive and the y-coordinates all negative?

   A. I   **B.** II   **C.** III   **D.** IV

9. Which variable expression is *not* equivalent to $2(x - 3)$?

   A. $2(x) - 2(3)$
   B. $2(-3) + 2x$
   C. $(x - 3) + (x - 3)$
   D. $2x - 3$

10. How can $2 \cdot 2 \cdot 2 \cdot 5 \cdot 5 \cdot b \cdot b$ be written in exponential notation?

    A. $16b^2$ **B.** $2 \cdot 10^2 b^2$
    C. $2^3 5^2 b^2$ **D.** $2^2 5^3 b^2$

11. Which equation describes the line in the diagram?

    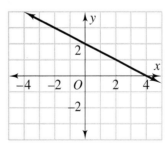

    A. $y = \frac{1}{2}x - 2$ **B.** $y = -\frac{1}{2}x - 2$
    C. $y = \frac{1}{2}x + 2$ **D.** $y = -\frac{1}{2}x + 2$

Rational Numbers and Irrational Numbers

5

| WHAT YOU WILL LEARN IN THIS CHAPTER | • How to identify rational and irrational numbers | • How to perform operations with rational numbers | • How to use the Pythagorean theorem |

A NEW NEW YEAR

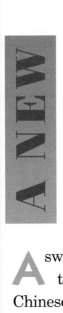

THEME:
TIME

A swirling dragon marks the start of the Chinese new year. The Chinese calendar is one of several calendars used throughout the world. Each calendar is a unique solution to the problem of how to keep track of time. The calendars are all different, yet they all work quite well.

Invent a New Calendar For your chapter project, you will invent a *new* calendar, defining weeks and months as you wish. Will your calendar have 10 months per year? Might it have 5-day weeks? The decisions are up to you. Your final product will be a new calendar and a description of the advantages of your new system.

Steps to help you complete the project:

- How to use the *Work Backward* strategy to solve problems

PROBLEM SOLVING

5-1 Factors

What You'll Learn

1 To identify prime and composite numbers

2 To find common factors and the greatest common factor

...And Why

You can use factors to arrange groups of people and organize supplies.

Here's How

Look for questions that
- build understanding
- ✔ check understanding

Work Together

Exploring Factors

The photograph at the right shows all the rectangles you can make with 12 tiles. Work with a partner. Make as many rectangles as you can with 36 tiles.

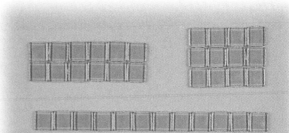

1. List the dimensions of all the rectangles you made. How many different rectangles did you make?

2. How many rectangles can you make with 2 tiles? With 3 tiles? With 5 tiles? With 11 tiles?

3. For each number from 2 to 20, decide whether you can make *one* or *more than one* rectangle with that number of tiles.

THINK AND DISCUSS

1 *Identifying Prime and Composite Numbers*

The diagram in the Work Together shows that the numbers 1, 2, 3, 4, 6, and 12 are all factors of 12. One number is a **factor** of a second number if it divides into that number with no remainder. You can say that the second number is **divisible** by the first.

You can use the following divisibility tests to see if a number is divisible by another number.

Number	Divisibility Test for Number
2	Ones' digit is even.
3	Sum of digits is divisible by 3.
5	Ones' digit is 0 or 5.
9	Sum of the digits is divisible by 9.
10	Ones' digit is 0.

In the Work Together you discovered that you can make only one rectangle with 11 tiles. So, the only factors of 11 are 1 and 11. Therefore, 11 is a prime number.

A **prime number** is a whole number greater than 1 with exactly two factors, 1 and itself. A whole number greater than 1 with more than two factors is a **composite number.**

■ **EXAMPLE 1**

Tell whether each number is prime or composite.
a. 117 **b.** 37

Use the divisibility tests to find out if each number is divisible by another number besides 1 and itself.

a. Since the sum of its digits is divisible by 3, 117 is divisible by 3. It has more than two factors, so it is composite.

b. The only divisors of 37 are 1 and 37, so 37 is prime.

4. ✓ *Try It Out* Tell whether each number is prime or composite. If the number is composite, list its factors.
    a. 39   **b.** 2   **c.** 550   **d.** 147   **e.** 97

Writing a composite number as a product of prime numbers is the **prime factorization** of the number. You can use a *factor tree* to find the prime factorization.

■ **EXAMPLE 2**

Use a factor tree to find the prime factorization of 315.

Step 1 Write the number as the product of two factors.

Step 2 Repeat Step 1 with any remaining composite factors.

Step 3 Write the prime factorization.

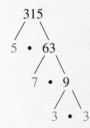

$$315 = 3 \cdot 3 \cdot 5 \cdot 7$$
$$= 3^2 \cdot 5 \cdot 7$$

5. ✓ *Try It Out* Find the prime factorization of each number.
    a. 48   **b.** 56   **c.** 72   **d.** 360   **e.** 204

6. ⬝ *Reasoning* How many factors does the square of a prime number have? Give an example.

2 *Finding the Greatest Common Factor*

You call the factors common to a set of numbers common factors. The greatest factor common to the numbers is the **greatest common factor** (GCF).

■ **EXAMPLE 3**   *Real-World Problem Solving*

Parades A band with 42 members is marching in a parade behind a band with 36 members. You want to arrange the bands into the same number of rows. What is the greatest number of rows in which you can arrange the two bands?

Begin by finding the factors of 42 and 36.

factors of 42: 1, 2, 3, 6, 7, 14, 21, 42
factors of 36: 1, 2, 3, 4, 6, 9, 12, 18, 36

The factors 1, 2, 3, and 6 are common to both numbers. The GCF is 6. So, the greatest number of rows in which you can arrange the two bands is 6.

You can also use prime factorization to find the greatest common factor of a set of numbers.

■ **EXAMPLE 4**

Find the GCF of 60 and 72.

Step 1   Find the prime factorization of each number.
$$60 = 2 \cdot 2 \cdot 3 \cdot 5 \qquad 72 = 2 \cdot 2 \cdot 2 \cdot 3 \cdot 3$$

Step 2   Identify the common prime factors.

Circle the common prime factors; or use a Venn diagram.

$60 = 2 \cdot 2 \cdot 3 \cdot 5$

$72 = 2 \cdot 2 \cdot 2 \cdot 3 \cdot 3$

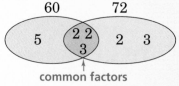

common factors

Step 3   Find the product of the common factors.
   The GCF of 60 and 72 is $2 \cdot 2 \cdot 3 = 12$.

7. ✓ *Try It Out* Find the GCF of each pair of numbers.
   a. 54, 90   b. 75, 125   c. 24, 64

8. ⁂ *Think About It* What is the GCF of any two prime numbers? Explain why.

EXERCISES *On Your Own*

List all the factors of each number.

1. 30   2. 31   3. 55   4. 64   5. 52   6. 81

7. 96   8. 144   9. 45   10. 75   11. 53   12. 100

Tell whether each number is *prime* or *composite*. If the number is composite, list its factors.

13. 21   14. 23   15. 93   16. 471   17. 47   18. 141

19. 97   20. 45   21. 87   22. 133   23. 198   24. 12

Write the prime factorization of each number.

25. 54   26. 150   27. 225   28. 186   29. 621

30. 750   31. 1,344   32. 504   33. 792   34. 3,240

35. *History* In 1742, the mathematician Christian Goldbach made a conjecture that every even number greater than 2 can be expressed as the sum of two prime numbers. Do you think this is true? Try to write each of the following numbers as the sum of two prime numbers.
   a. 6   b. 16   c. 24   d. 32   e. 60

36. *Writing* If a number is divisible by 3, is it also divisible by 9? If a number is divisible by 9, is it also divisible by 3? Explain.

37. *Open-ended* Name three numbers other than 1 that have an odd number of factors.

38. *Logging* Two pieces of timber have lengths 63 ft and 84 ft. A sawmill operator needs to cut the timber into logs of equal length. What is the greatest possible length of the logs?

Find the GCF of each pair of numbers.

39. 16, 36   **40.** 20, 125   **41.** 84, 136   **42.** 72, 126   **43.** 28, 70

44. 15, 18   **45.** 30, 15   **46.** 96, 81   **47.** 50, 135   **48.** 20, 28

49. Ms. Cabrera has the art supplies listed at the
right. She wants to give the supplies to as
many classes as possible. Each class must
receive an equal number of each item.
  a. What is the greatest number of classes that
  can get supplies?
  b. How many of each item will each class
  receive?

paint brushes   120
boxes of markers   78
packs of paper   24
sets of watercolors   54

50. *Reasoning* Why is 2 the only even prime
number?

Mixed Review

Solve each equation. Then check each solution. *(Lesson 3-2)*

51. $y + 7 = 5$ **52.** $x - 4 = -9$ **53.** $2 = a + 11$ **54.** $-1 = 3 + d$

55. $-14 = a - 6$ **56.** $3 + p = -15$ **57.** $-12 + t = -10$ **58.** $18 + x = 9$

Which ordered pairs are solutions of $y + 2x = 4$? *(Lesson 4-2)*

59. $(0, 4)$ **60.** $(1, 3)$ **61.** $(-4, 4)$ **62.** $(-1, 6)$ **63.** $(-8, 2)$ **64.** $(-5, -6)$

65. *Choose a Strategy* An auditorium can seat 525 people. If
four seats are occupied for every empty seat, how many
people are in the room?

CHAPTER PROJECT

PROJECT LINK: WRITING

Look at the calendar we use today. Are there exactly 52 weeks
in a year or exactly 4 weeks in a month? Explain. Is 365 a prime
number? Create a new system for a calendar. Define what you
might call a month and a week. Use mathematical terms such
as divisible, factor, and prime to describe your calendar.

Rational Numbers

What You'll Learn

1 To write rational numbers as fractions in simplest form

2 To identify rational numbers

...And Why

You can use rational numbers to describe everyday situations, such as temperature or sea level measurement.

Here's How

Look for questions that

⬝⬝ build understanding

✔ check understanding

The world's largest thermometer, which measures 134 feet, stands outside a restaurant in Baker, California.

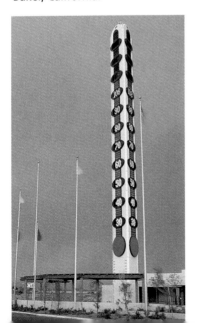

THINK AND DISCUSS

1 Writing Rational Numbers in Simplest Form

A **rational number** is a number you can write as a ratio of two integers in the form $\frac{a}{b}$, where $b \neq 0$. A rational number that is a fraction is in **simplest form** when the greatest common factor (GCF) of the numerator and denominator is 1.

■ EXAMPLE 1

Write $\frac{54}{60}$ in simplest form.

Method 1 Use the GCF.

$54 = 2 \cdot 3 \cdot 3 \cdot 3$ ⟵ The common prime factors are
$60 = 2 \cdot 2 \cdot 3 \cdot 5$ 2 and 3, so the GCF is $2 \cdot 3 = 6$.

$\frac{54}{60} = \frac{54 \div 6}{60 \div 6} = \frac{9}{10}$ ⟵ Divide the numerator and denominator by the GCF.

Method 2 Use prime factorization.

$$\frac{54}{60} = \frac{\overset{1}{2} \cdot \overset{1}{3} \cdot 3 \cdot 3}{\underset{1}{2} \cdot 2 \cdot \underset{1}{3} \cdot 5} = \frac{9}{10}$$

1. ✓ *Try It Out* Write each rational number in simplest form.

   a. $\frac{16}{40}$ b. $-\frac{45}{54}$ c. $\frac{36}{108}$ d. $-\frac{27}{45}$

2 Identifying Rational Numbers

Temperatures on a thermometer are an example of rational numbers. The following are all rational numbers.

proper fractions:	$\frac{2}{5}$	$-\frac{1}{2} = \frac{-1}{2}$	$-\frac{3}{8} = \frac{-3}{8}$
improper fractions:	$\frac{9}{4}$	$-\frac{24}{5} = \frac{-24}{5}$	$-\frac{3}{2} = \frac{3}{-2}$
mixed numbers:	$3\frac{1}{2} = \frac{7}{2}$	$-2\frac{4}{7} = \frac{-18}{7}$	
integers:	$33 = \frac{33}{1}$	$-450 = \frac{-450}{1}$	$0 = \frac{0}{1}$
some decimals:	$0.7 = \frac{7}{10}$	$-1.3 = \frac{-13}{10}$	$0.43 = \frac{43}{100}$

You can write negative rational numbers that are fractions in three ways.

Example: $-\frac{1}{2} = \frac{-1}{2} = \frac{1}{-2}$

■ EXAMPLE 2

Write each rational number in the form $\frac{a}{b}$. Write in simplest form.

Need Help? For practice with mixed numbers and improper fractions, see Skills Handbook page 611.

a. $-2\frac{4}{7} = -\frac{2 \cdot 7 + 4}{7} = \frac{-18}{7}$ ← Rewrite as an improper fraction.

b. $0.15 = \frac{15}{100}$ ← Write as a fraction with a denominator of 100.

$= \frac{15 \div 5}{100 \div 5} = \frac{3}{20}$ ← Write in simplest form.

c. $-1.4 = -\frac{14}{10} = \frac{-14}{10}$ ← Write as a fraction with a denominator of 10.

$= \frac{-14 \div 2}{10 \div 2} = \frac{-7}{5}$ ← Write in simplest form.

2. ■ *Think About It* In the expression $\frac{a}{b}$, why can b not equal 0?

3. ✓ *Try It Out* Write each rational number in the form $\frac{a}{b}$. Write in simplest form.

a. $10\frac{1}{3}$ b. $-1\frac{7}{10}$ c. 0.08 d. -6.5 e. 11

When you multiply a rational number by a fraction equal to 1, the result is an equivalent rational number.

■ EXAMPLE 3

Write three fractions equal to $-\frac{7}{8}$.

$-\frac{7}{8} = \frac{-7}{8} \cdot \frac{3}{3} = \frac{-21}{24}$ ← $\frac{3}{3}$ is equal to 1.

$-\frac{7}{8} = \frac{-7}{8} \cdot \frac{-2}{-2} = \frac{14}{-16}$ ← $\frac{-2}{-2}$ is equal to 1.

$-\frac{7}{8} = \frac{-7}{8} \cdot \frac{-10}{-10} = \frac{70}{-80}$ ← $\frac{-10}{-10}$ is equal to 1.

4. ✓ *Try It Out* Write three fractions equal to each rational number.

a. $\frac{1}{2}$ b. $-\frac{2}{5}$ c. $\frac{7}{6}$ d. 9

5. ■ *Look Back* What property of multiplication allows you to write equivalent fractions as you did in Example 3?

Choose Use a calculator, paper and pencil, or mental math to write each rational number in simplest form.

1. $\frac{55}{88}$ 2. $\frac{-72}{96}$ 3. $-\frac{12}{54}$ 4. $\frac{14}{98}$ 5. $\frac{24}{-60}$

6. $\frac{48}{64}$ 7. $\frac{-56}{80}$ 8. $\frac{9}{93}$ 9. $\frac{40}{50}$ 10. $\frac{120}{-252}$

11. **Choose A, B, C, D, or E.** Which is *not* in simplest form?

   A. $-\frac{8}{15}$ **B.** $\frac{13}{52}$ **C.** $\frac{32}{45}$ **D.** $-\frac{9}{49}$ **E.** $-\frac{21}{40}$

12. *Writing* Compare the two methods shown in Example 1 of writing a fraction in simplest form. Describe the method you prefer and explain why.

Algebra Evaluate each expression for the given value of the variables. Write as a fraction or mixed number in simplest form.

13. $\frac{x}{y}$ for $x = -36$ and $y = 54$

14. $\frac{x^2}{y^2}$ for $x = 4$ and $y = 8$

15. $\frac{x + y}{x}$ for $x = 18$ and $y = -3$

16. $\frac{x + y}{x - y}$ for $x = 18$ and $y = -3$

17. $\frac{x - y}{x}$ for $x = 10$ and $y = -2$

18. $\frac{5x}{x + y}$ for $x = -4$ and $y = -3$

Write a rational number for each situation.

19. The divers located the shipwreck 20.5 m below sea level.

20. Zakiya received two fifths of the votes.

21. The temperature fell to twelve degrees Celsius below zero.

22. The price of the stock rose two and three fourths points.

Jay Browning, from Palatka, Florida, has been helping his father's company excavate the 500-year-old wreck of a Spanish sailing ship in 20 feet of water off the Bahamas.

Source: *National Geographic World*

Write each rational number as a ratio in the form $\frac{a}{b}$.

23. -8 **24.** 0.93 **25.** 1.8 **26.** $-6\frac{1}{2}$ **27.** 0.2

28. 0 **29.** $4\frac{1}{3}$ **30.** -2.7 **31.** 1.75 **32.** -4.125

Write three fractions equal to each rational number.

33. $3\frac{1}{2}$ **34.** 5 **35.** $-\frac{25}{4}$ **36.** 1.1 **37.** 0

38. $-4\frac{2}{3}$ **39.** 0.6 **40.** $-\frac{3}{2}$ **41.** -2 **42.** -0.75

Identify each number using as many names as apply. Choose from *whole number*, *integer*, and *rational number*.

43. -24 **44.** 1.2 **45.** $\frac{-4}{7}$ **46.** 0

47. 0.66 **48.** $5\frac{1}{2}$ **49.** 8.9 **50.** -100

Find the absolute value and opposite of each rational number.

Samples: $\left|-\frac{5}{6}\right| = \frac{5}{6}$ $\left|\frac{5}{6}\right| = \frac{5}{6}$

$-\left(-\frac{5}{6}\right) = \frac{5}{6}$

51. $-\frac{4}{5}$ **52.** -3.7 **53.** 0.6 **54.** $2\frac{3}{4}$ **55.** $-\frac{1}{3}$

56. *Estimation* Estimate the rational number represented by each point on this number line. Write each answer as a fraction.

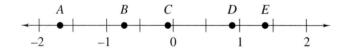

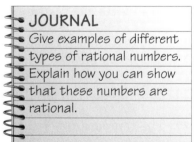

JOURNAL
Give examples of different types of rational numbers. Explain how you can show that these numbers are rational.

Mixed Review

Graph each inequality on a separate number line. *(Lesson 3-8)*

57. $x \le -5$ **58.** $y > 2$ **59.** $p < -1$ **60.** $q \ge -5$ **61.** $t \le 3$

62. Danzell left his home and jogged north 4 blocks, then east 3 blocks, and then south 4 blocks. How many blocks east of his home was he when he stopped jogging? *(Lesson 4-5)*

5-3 Equivalent Fractions and Decimals

What You'll Learn

▼1 To write fractions as decimals

▼2 To write repeating decimals as fractions

...And Why

Statisticians use fractions and decimals to report athletes' achievements and voting results.

Here's How

Look for questions that

⁙ build understanding

✔ check understanding

Roberto Clemente was a baseball player for the Pittsburgh Pirates from 1955 to 1972. In 1966, he was named the National League's MVP.

Source: Topps

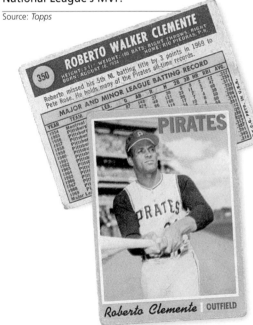

Roberto Clemente OUTFIELD

THINK AND DISCUSS

▼1 Writing Fractions as Decimals

In baseball, a batting average represents the fraction of times at bat that a player makes a hit. It is customary to give a player's batting average as a decimal to three places.

■ **EXAMPLE 1** *Real-World Problem Solving*

▦ **Sports** In 1967, Roberto Clemente earned his fourth National League batting title. He had 209 hits in 585 times at bat. What was his batting average that year?

Divide the number of hits by the number of at-bats.

Use paper and pencil, as shown at the right, or enter this key sequence on a calculator.

209 ÷ 585 ▤ *0.3572649*

Round the decimal to three places.

Clemente's batting average was 0.357.

$$
\begin{array}{r}
0.3572 \\
585 \overline{)209.0000} \\
\underline{1755} \\
3350 \\
\underline{2925} \\
4250 \\
\underline{4095} \\
1550 \\
\underline{1170} \\
380
\end{array}
$$

1. ✔ *Try It Out* Write each batting average as a decimal to three places.
   a. 5 hits in 16 times at bat
   b. 7 hits in 23 times at bat

You can write any fraction as a decimal by dividing the numerator by the denominator. If the division ends with a remainder of zero, the decimal is called a **terminating decimal.**

If the division does not end and produces a repeating pattern of nonzero remainders, the decimal is called a **repeating decimal.**

■ **EXAMPLE 2**

Write $\frac{26}{11}$ as a decimal.
Use a calculator or paper and
pencil to find $26 \div 11$.

$26 \; \boxed{\div} \; 11 \; \boxed{=} \; 2.3636364$

With either method, the quotient
suggests that *36* repeats
without end. Write a bar over
these digits.

$$\frac{26}{11} = 2.36363636 \ldots$$

$$\frac{26}{11} = 2.\overline{36}$$

```
          2.3636
   11 )26.0000
        22
        40
        33
        70
        66
        40
        33
        70
        66
         4
```

2. ▪ **Technology** On some calculators, the display for $\frac{26}{11}$ will
be 2.3636364. Why do you think this happens?

3. ▪ **Think About It** How can you use division to change $\frac{26}{11}$ to
a mixed number?

4. ✓ **Try It Out** Write each fraction as a decimal.

    a. $\frac{2}{3}$ **b.** $-\frac{1}{12}$ **c.** $5\frac{5}{6}$ **d.** $\frac{7}{9}$ **e.** $-3\frac{5}{11}$

▼ *Writing Repeating Decimals as Fractions*

To write a repeating decimal as a fraction, you can use algebra.

■ **EXAMPLE 3**

Algebra Write $0.\overline{45}$ as a fraction in simplest form.

Step 1 Let the variable n equal the given decimal.

$$n = 0.\overline{45}$$
$$100n = 45.\overline{45}$$

⟵ Multiply each side by 10^2, or 100,
because 2 digits repeat.

Step 2 Subtract to eliminate the repeating part, $0.\overline{45}$.

$$100n = 45.45454545 \ldots$$
$$- \quad n = 0.45454545 \ldots$$
$$99n = 45.00000000 \ldots$$

⟵ The subtraction property of
equality allows you to subtract
equal quantities from each side.

$$99n = 45$$

Step 3 Now solve the new equation.

$$99n = 45$$

$$\frac{99n}{99} = \frac{45}{99} \qquad \longleftarrow \text{Divide each side by 99.}$$

$$n = \frac{45}{99} \qquad \longleftarrow \text{Simplify.}$$

$$n = \frac{45 \div 9}{99 \div 9} = \frac{5}{11} \qquad \longleftarrow \text{Divide the numerator and denominator by the GCF.}$$

5. ✓ *Try It Out* Write each repeating decimal as a fraction in simplest form.

a. $0.\overline{7}$ **b.** $0.\overline{54}$ **c.** $0.\overline{2}$ **d.** $0.\overline{24}$

The set of rational numbers includes both terminating and repeating decimals, since all these decimals can be written in the form $\frac{a}{b}$.

Work Together
Looking For Decimal Patterns

Set 1

$\frac{1}{9}$ $\frac{2}{9}$ $\frac{3}{9}$ $\frac{4}{9}$ $\frac{5}{9}$

6. a. ⬛*Patterns* Work with a partner. Write each fraction in Set 1 at the left as a decimal. What pattern do you see?
    b. Use your pattern to predict what decimal is equal to $\frac{8}{9}$. Use a calculator to check your prediction.

Set 2

$\frac{1}{11}$ $\frac{2}{11}$ $\frac{3}{11}$ $\frac{4}{11}$ $\frac{5}{11}$

7. Repeat Question 6 with Set 2. This time, predict what decimal is equal to $\frac{8}{11}$.

8. Do you think there are other sets of fractions that have similar patterns? Make a conjecture. Then use a calculator to test it.

Share your patterns with the rest of the class.

EXERCISES *On Your Own*

Choose Use a calculator, paper and pencil, or mental math. Write each fraction or mixed number as a decimal.

1. $\frac{7}{12}$ **2.** $-4\frac{3}{20}$ **3.** $\frac{2}{3}$ **4.** $1\frac{3}{11}$ **5.** $-\frac{4}{5}$ **6.** $\frac{9}{16}$

7. $1\frac{7}{8}$ **8.** $-\frac{3}{10}$ **9.** $-\frac{1}{3}$ **10.** $2\frac{5}{6}$ **11.** $4\frac{2}{5}$ **12.** $-\frac{15}{13}$

13. $-18\frac{3}{4}$ **14.** $-\frac{8}{15}$ **15.** $-\frac{7}{9}$ **16.** $\frac{12}{11}$ **17.** $-\frac{3}{20}$ **18.** $-\frac{1}{12}$

19. The tables below contain commonly used fractions. Copy and complete the tables by finding the decimal equivalents.

Eighths, Fourths, and Halves

Fraction	$\frac{1}{8}$	$\frac{1}{4}$	$\frac{3}{8}$	$\frac{1}{2}$	$\frac{5}{8}$	$\frac{3}{4}$	$\frac{7}{8}$
Decimal	▪	▪	▪	▪	▪	▪	▪

Sixths, Thirds, and Halves

Fraction	$\frac{1}{6}$	$\frac{1}{3}$	$\frac{1}{2}$	$\frac{2}{3}$	$\frac{5}{6}$
Decimal	▪	▪	▪	▪	▪

Fifths

Fraction	$\frac{1}{5}$	$\frac{2}{5}$	$\frac{3}{5}$	$\frac{4}{5}$
Decimal	▪	▪	▪	▪

20. *Data Analysis* The circle graph at the right shows the size of American households in 1995. Write a fraction in simplest form for the part of American families in each category.
  a. two persons   **b.** three persons
  c. four persons   **d.** five or more persons

21. *Writing* Describe a situation in which you would use fractions and a situation in which you would use decimals.

22. *Open-ended* Give three examples of a denominator of a fraction that will always produce a terminating decimal when the fraction is expressed as a decimal.

23. *Calculator* Although you cannot see the repetition in the calculator display, there is a repeating block of digits in the decimal that is equal to $\frac{1}{7}$. Express $\frac{1}{7}$ as a repeating decimal.

American Families by Size 1995

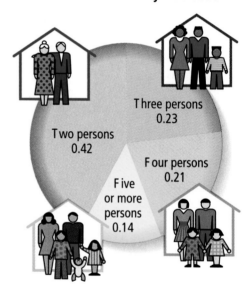

Rewrite each repeating decimal with a bar over the block of repeating digits.

24. 0.717171 . . .   **25.** 0.3144444 . . .   **26.** 0.528282828 . . .   **27.** 5.272727 . . .

Write each repeating decimal as a fraction or mixed number in simplest form.

28. $-5.\overline{2}$ **29.** $0.\overline{4}$ **30.** $13.\overline{32}$ **31.** $23.\overline{12}$ **32.** $7.\overline{48}$

33. $-1.\overline{7}$ **34.** $0.\overline{23}$ **35.** $2.\overline{8}$ **36.** $-3.\overline{5}$ **37.** $1.\overline{34}$

38. *Open-ended* Give three examples of commonly used repeating decimals. Write the fraction equivalent of each.

39. *Reasoning* Explain how you can find the sum of two repeating decimals. Give an example in your explanation.

Mixed Review

Write each equation in slope-intercept form. Name the slope and the *y*-intercept. *(Lesson 4-6)*

40. $x + y = -3$ **41.** $4x - 2y = -6$ **42.** $x + 5y = -15$ **43.** $-3x + 2y = -10$

44. $x - 4y = -4$ **45.** $4x = y + 2$ **46.** $y + 2 = 2x$ **47.** $3(y + 1) = 12x$

48. *Choose a Strategy* A group of three children worked all day cleaning a vacant lot. A fourth child worked for only half the day. The owner paid the group $70. How should they divide the money?

✓ CHECKPOINT 1   *Lessons 5-1 through 5-3*

Tell whether each number is *prime* or *composite*. If the number is composite, list its factors.

1. 19 **2.** 38 **3.** 57 **4.** 137 **5.** 365

Write the prime factorization of each number.

6. 160 **7.** 108 **8.** 847 **9.** 531 **10.** 650

Write each fraction or mixed number as a decimal. Write each decimal as a fraction or mixed number in simplest form.

11. $\frac{3}{4}$ **12.** $-4\frac{2}{3}$ **13.** $-\frac{5}{8}$ **14.** $6\frac{7}{20}$ **15.** $-12\frac{4}{5}$

16. 0.4 **17.** -3.16 **18.** 24.125 **19.** $0.\overline{54}$ **20.** $1.\overline{8}$

21. *Writing* Explain two different methods of finding the greatest common factor (GCF) of two numbers. Include an example in your explanation.

Comparing and Ordering Rational Numbers

THINK AND DISCUSS

1 Finding the Least Common Multiple

A **multiple** of a number is the product of that number and any nonzero whole number.

multiples of 4: 4, 8, ⑫, 16, 20, ㉔, 28, 32, ㊱, . . .

multiples of 6: 6, ⑫, 18, ㉔, 30, ㊱, 42, . . .

The circles around 12, 24, and 36 indicate multiples that are the same for both numbers. These are the common multiples of 4 and 6. The least multiple that is the same for both numbers is 12. So, 12 is the **least common multiple** (LCM) of 4 and 6.

1. ✓ *Try It Out* Find the LCM of 8 and 10.

You can find the LCM of a set of numbers by using prime factorizations.

■ EXAMPLE 1

Find the LCM of 36 and 30.

Method 1

- Write the prime factorization of each number.

$$36 = ②\cdot②\cdot③\cdot③$$
$$30 = 2 \cdot 3 \cdot ⑤$$

- Circle each different factor the greatest number of times it appears.

- Multiply the circled factors.

$$LCM = 2 \cdot 2 \cdot 3 \cdot 3 \cdot 5$$
$$= 180$$

Method 2

- Display all the prime factors of 36 and 30 in a Venn diagram.

- Multiply all factors in the diagram to find the LCM.

$$LCM = 2 \cdot 2 \cdot 3 \cdot 3 \cdot 5 = 180$$

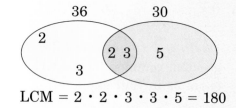

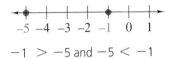

To compare integers such as
−5 and −1, think of a number
line. The integer farther to
the right is the greater
integer.

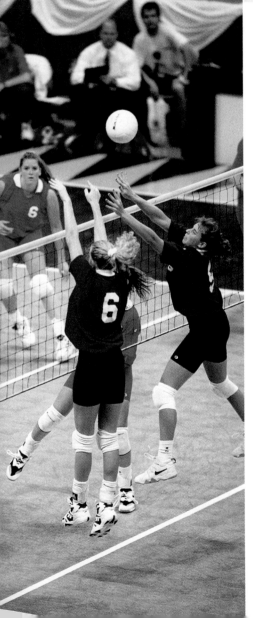

−1 > −5 and −5 < −1

2. ✓ *Try It Out* Find the LCM of each pair of numbers.
   a. 18, 32   **b.** 56, 72   **c.** 54, 84

❷ *Comparing and Ordering Rational Numbers*

To compare rational numbers that have the same denominator,
such as $-\frac{5}{8}$ and $-\frac{1}{8}$, just compare their numerators.

$$-\frac{5}{8} = \frac{-5}{8} \text{ and } -\frac{1}{8} = \frac{-1}{8} \qquad -5 < -1, \text{ so } -\frac{5}{8} < -\frac{1}{8}.$$

When the fractions have different denominators, you need to
rewrite the fractions with a common denominator. The **least
common denominator** (LCD) is the LCM of the denominators.

■ **EXAMPLE 2**   *Real-World Problem Solving*

Sports The red volleyball team won 4 out of 9 matches this
season. The blue team won 5 out of 12 matches. Which team
has the better record?

The red team has won $\frac{4}{9}$ of its matches. The blue team has
won $\frac{5}{12}$ of its matches. To find out which team has the better
record, you need to compare the fractions $\frac{4}{9}$ and $\frac{5}{12}$.

Step 1   Find the LCM of 9 and 12.
$$9 = \boxed{3 \cdot 3}$$
$$12 = \boxed{2 \cdot 2} \cdot 3$$
$$LCM = 2 \cdot 2 \cdot 3 \cdot 3 = 36$$

The LCM of 9 and 12 is 36.
So, the LCD of $\frac{4}{9}$ and $\frac{5}{12}$ is 36.

Step 2   Rewrite $\frac{4}{9}$ and $\frac{5}{12}$ as fractions with 36 as the
denominator.
$$\frac{4}{9} = \frac{4 \cdot 4}{9 \cdot 4} = \frac{16}{36} \qquad \frac{5}{12} = \frac{5 \cdot 3}{12 \cdot 3} = \frac{15}{36}$$

Step 3   Compare the numerators.
$$\frac{16}{36} > \frac{15}{36}, \text{ so } \frac{4}{9} > \frac{5}{12}.$$

The red team has the better record.

3. ✓ *Try It Out* Replace each ■ with <, >, or =.
   a. $\frac{3}{5}$ ■ $\frac{2}{3}$ **b.** $-\frac{7}{12}$ ■ $-\frac{3}{4}$ **c.** $-\frac{3}{8}$ ■ $-\frac{4}{9}$

4. ♣ *What If . . .* Suppose the blue team wins its next match,
   before the red team plays again. Which team will have the
   better record? Explain why.

To compare a fraction and a decimal, start by writing each number in the same form.

■ EXAMPLE 3

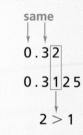

Compare 0.32 and $\frac{5}{16}$.

Need Help? For practice with comparing decimals, see Skills Handbook page 601.

• Use a calculator to find the decimal equal to $\frac{5}{16}$.

   5 ⊡ 16 ▤ *0.3125*

• Compare 0.32 and 0.3125, by lining up the decimal points and comparing the digits from left to right.

same

$$0.3\boxed{2}$$

$$0.3\boxed{1}25$$

So 0.32 > 0.3125, and $0.32 > \frac{5}{16}$.

2 > 1

5. ✓ *Try It Out* Compare -0.32 and $-\frac{5}{16}$.

6. ⬛ *Explain* Describe how to compare 0.32 and $\frac{5}{16}$ by writing 0.32 as a fraction. Which method do you prefer?

To order a set of rational numbers, you can use a number line.

■ EXAMPLE 4

Order $\frac{5}{8}$, -0.37, 1.12, $-\frac{29}{40}$, and 0.3 from least to greatest.

First write each fraction as a decimal.

$$\frac{5}{8} = 0.625 \qquad\qquad -\frac{29}{40} = -0.725$$

Then graph each decimal on a number line.

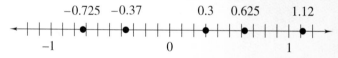

The order of the points from left to right gives the order of the numbers from least to greatest.

$-0.725 < -0.37 < 0.3 < 0.625 < 1.12$, so

$$-\frac{29}{40} < -0.37 < 0.3 < \frac{5}{8} < 1.12.$$

7. ✓ *Try It Out* Order each set of rational numbers from least to greatest.

a. $\frac{8}{5}$, $1\frac{1}{2}$, -0.625, $-\frac{7}{8}$, 1.6   **b.** $-\frac{5}{12}$, -0.4, $-\frac{1}{2}$, $-\frac{4}{9}$

Find the LCM of each pair of numbers.

1. 2, 15   **2.** 18, 45   **3.** 36, 24   **4.** 35, 50   **5.** 16, 20

6. 21, 56   **7.** 24, 30   **8.** 28, 48   **9.** 48, 64   **10.** 25, 45

11. 60, 75   **12.** 20, 72   **13.** 80, 100   **14.** 125, 625   **15.** 81, 144

16. *Sports* Jake scored 9 out of 12 field goals during a basketball game. Reggie scored 3 out of 5. Who has the better average for this game? Explain.

17. *Writing* Explain how finding an LCM is different from finding a GCF. Be sure to give examples.

Mental Math **Use mental math to compare each pair of numbers. Use >, <, or =.**

18. $-\frac{1}{11}$ ■ $-\frac{1}{9}$ **19.** $\frac{5}{7}$ ■ $\frac{5}{8}$ **20.** $\frac{1}{4}$ ■ 0.3 **21.** -0.6 ■ $-\frac{3}{5}$

Choose **Use a calculator, pencil and paper, or mental math to compare each pair of numbers. Use >, <, or =.**

22. 0.735 ■ $\frac{3}{4}$ **23.** $-\frac{9}{10}$ ■ -0.91 **24.** $-2\frac{4}{5}$ ■ $-2\frac{7}{9}$ **25.** $-\frac{7}{8}$ ■ -0.87

26. $-\frac{7}{12}$ ■ -0.7 **27.** $1\frac{11}{16}$ ■ 1.6875 **28.** $\frac{7}{9}$ ■ $\frac{5}{6}$ **29.** -0.375 ■ $-\frac{3}{8}$

30. **a.** Joe's Hot Dog stand buys hot dogs in packages of 36 and hot dog buns in packages of 20. What is the least number of hot dogs and buns Joe can buy to have an equal number of each? (*Hint:* Use common multiples.)

b. How many packages of hot dogs and buns will this be?

31. **Choose A, B, C, or D.** Which set of rational numbers is ordered from greatest to least?

A. $0.76, \frac{3}{4}, \frac{5}{8}, 0.65$ **B.** $-0.9, -\frac{7}{8}, -0.52, -\frac{1}{2}$

C. $\frac{12}{15}, \frac{2}{3}, 0.4, \frac{5}{16}$ **D.** $\frac{2}{3}, -0.61, -\frac{3}{8}, -0.01$

32. *Estimation* Match each rational number below with a point on the number line.

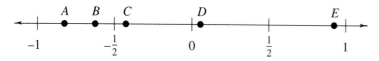

I. $-\dfrac{5}{8}$ II. 0.055 III. $\dfrac{15}{16}$ IV. $-\dfrac{5}{12}$ V. -0.8125

33. *Exercise* Karen exercises at the gym every 3 days. Her friend Mai exercises at the same gym every 5 days. They met at the gym June 1. When will they next meet at the gym?

Mixed Review

Super Bowl Scores

Football **Use the scores to complete Exercises 34–36.**
(Lesson 1-5)

34. Display the data in a stem-and-leaf plot.

35. Which 10-point interval of the stem-and-leaf plot contains the greatest number of scores?

36. Find the mean, median, mode, and range of the scores.

Compare. Use <, >, or =. *(Lesson 2-1)*

37. -12 ▦ 15 **38.** $|4|$ ▦ $|-9|$ **39.** $|-12|$ ▦ $|12|$

40. 8 ▦ $|-3|$ **41.** 0 ▦ -3 **42.** -53 ▦ -54

43. What is the greatest 5-digit number you can write if each digit must be odd and no numbers are repeated? *(Lesson 2-9)*

Game	Winner's Score
I	35
II	24
III	25
IV	16
V	32
VI	36
VII	21
VIII	27
IX	31
X	31
XI	35
XII	42
XIII	35
XIV	31

CHAPTER PROJECT

PROJECT LINK: RESEARCHING

The prefaces *sept-, oct-, nov-,* and *dec-* mean *seven, eight, nine,* and *ten.* Why aren't the months September through December the seventh through tenth months of the year? Research how the calendar has changed over the years. Use your research to write an introduction for your project.

Estimating with Fractions

Before Lesson 5-5

You can estimate a fraction by comparing its numerator to its denominator. Think of a number line as you estimate.

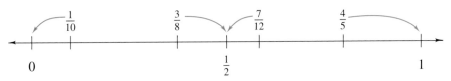

Round to 0 if the numerator is close to 0.

Round to $\frac{1}{2}$ if the denominator is about double the numerator.

Round to 1 if the numerator almost equals the denominator.

■ EXAMPLE 1

Estimate the sum $\frac{1}{8} + \frac{9}{10}$.

$$\begin{array}{ccc} \frac{1}{8} & + & \frac{9}{10} \\ \downarrow & & \downarrow \\ 0 & + & 1 \end{array}$$ ◄— Round the fractions.

$\frac{1}{8} + \frac{9}{10} \approx 0 + 1 = 1$

■ EXAMPLE 2

Estimate the product $2\frac{5}{6} \cdot 4\frac{4}{5}$.

$$\begin{array}{ccc} 2\frac{5}{6} & \cdot & 4\frac{4}{5} \\ & & \\ (2 + 1) & \cdot & (4 + 1) \end{array}$$ ◄— Round the mixed numbers.

$2\frac{5}{6} \cdot 4\frac{4}{5} \approx 3 \cdot 5 = 15$

Estimate each sum, difference, product, or quotient.

1. $\frac{7}{9} + \frac{1}{3}$

2. $\frac{3}{4} - \frac{1}{6}$

3. $\frac{11}{12} \cdot \frac{3}{8}$

4. $\frac{3}{10} \div \frac{7}{8}$

5. $\frac{2}{3} \cdot \frac{1}{9}$

6. $6\frac{4}{5} + 2\frac{1}{4}$

7. $2\frac{3}{20} - 1\frac{1}{9}$

8. $3\frac{8}{9} \cdot 7\frac{5}{6}$

9. $6\frac{7}{8} \div 1\frac{1}{5}$

10. $8\frac{1}{10} \div \frac{8}{9}$

11. $3\frac{1}{6} + 1\frac{4}{7}$

12. $2\frac{1}{2} - 1\frac{1}{3}$

13. $5\frac{1}{3} - 2\frac{3}{4}$

14. $3\frac{3}{4} \cdot 2\frac{4}{5}$

15. $4\frac{5}{8} + \frac{3}{5}$

5-5 Adding and Subtracting Like Fractions

What You'll Learn

▼1 To add or subtract fractions with like denominators

▼2 To add or subtract mixed numbers with like denominators

...And Why

You can add or subtract fractions with like denominators to find totals in a circle graph.

Here's How

Look for questions that
- build understanding
- ✔ check understanding

THINK AND DISCUSS

▼1 *Adding and Subtracting Like Fractions*

To add or subtract fractions with the same denominator, add or subtract the numerators. Then write the sum or difference over the denominator.

■ **EXAMPLE 1**   *Real-World Problem Solving*

Data Analysis The circle graph below shows the sizes and types of cars sold in the United States in 1995. What fraction of the sales were small and mid-size cars?

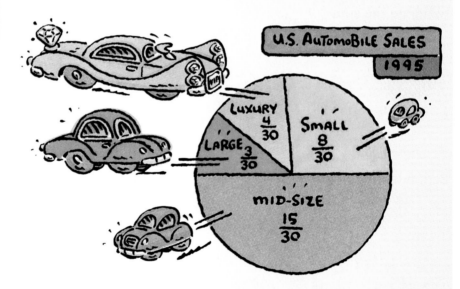

$$\frac{8}{30} + \frac{15}{30} = \frac{23}{30}$$ ← Add the numerators. Write the sum over the denominator.

Twenty-three thirtieths of the sales were small and mid-size cars.

1. a. ▪*Look Back* What fraction of the 1995 U.S. automobile sales were large and luxury cars?
   b. Use part (a) to find the difference between the fraction of the sales of small and mid-size cars and the fraction of the sales of large and luxury cars.

To add or subtract positive or negative fractions, you can use a process similar to adding or subtracting integers.

■ **EXAMPLE 2**

Need Help? For practice with adding and subtracting fractions with like denominators, see Skills Handbook page 612.

Find the difference $-\frac{7}{10} - \frac{9}{10}$.

$-\frac{7}{10} - \frac{9}{10} = -\frac{7}{10} + \left(-\frac{9}{10}\right)$ ← Change subtraction to addition of the opposite.

$= \frac{-7 + (-9)}{10}$ ← Write the sum of the numerators over the denominator.

$= \frac{-16}{10}$ ← Add the numerators.

$= \frac{-16}{10}$ ← Divide the numerator and denominator by the GCF of −16 and 10.

$= \frac{-8}{5} = -1\frac{3}{5}$ ← Rewrite the improper fraction as a mixed number.

2. ✓**Try It Out** Find each sum or difference. Write each answer in simplest form.

   a. $-\frac{5}{24} + \frac{23}{24}$ **b.** $\frac{5}{12} - \frac{7}{12}$ **c.** $-\frac{1}{3} - \left(-\frac{2}{3}\right)$ **d.** $-\frac{1}{8} + \left(-\frac{3}{8}\right)$

❷ Adding and Subtracting Like Mixed Numbers

Example 3 shows a vertical method for adding or subtracting rational numbers that are mixed numbers. You can use this method for sums and differences of positive numbers.

■ **EXAMPLE 3**

Find the difference $5\frac{1}{8} - 1\frac{3}{8}$.

Estimate: $5\frac{1}{8} - 1\frac{3}{8} \approx 5 - 1 = 4$

$\begin{aligned} 5\frac{1}{8} &= 4\frac{9}{8} \qquad\qquad \leftarrow 5\frac{1}{8} = 4 + 1\frac{1}{8} = 4\frac{9}{8} \\ -\quad 1\frac{3}{8} &= 1\frac{3}{8} \\ \hline 3\frac{6}{8} &= 3\frac{3}{4} \quad \leftarrow \text{Subtract the whole numbers, and then subtract the fractions.} \end{aligned}$

3. ⁂**Look Back** Compare the difference in Example 3 to the estimate. Explain why the answer is reasonable.

4. ✓**Try It Out** Find the sum or difference.

   a. $8\frac{1}{5} - 1\frac{4}{5}$ **b.** $9\frac{2}{3} + 3\frac{1}{3}$ **c.** $6\frac{5}{12} - 5\frac{7}{12}$

Example 4 shows another method that you can use to add or subtract rational numbers that are mixed numbers with unlike signs.

QUICK**review**

$6\frac{3}{4} = \frac{6 \cdot 4 + 3}{4} = \frac{27}{4}$

■ **EXAMPLE 4**

Find the sum $-3\frac{1}{4} + 6\frac{3}{4}$.

Estimate: $-3\frac{1}{4} + 6\frac{3}{4} \approx -3 + 7 = 4$

$$-3\frac{1}{4} + 6\frac{3}{4} = \frac{-13}{4} + \frac{27}{4}$$ ← Write each mixed number as an improper fraction.

$$= \frac{-13 + 27}{4}$$ ← Write the sum of the numerators over the denominator.

$$= \frac{14}{4}$$ ← Add the numerators.

$$= \frac{14}{4}$$ ← Divide the numerator and denominator by the GCF of 14 and 4.

$$= \frac{7}{2} = 3\frac{1}{2}$$ ← Rewrite the improper fraction as a mixed number.

5. ✓ *Try It Out* Find each sum and difference.

a. $-2\frac{1}{6} - 3\frac{5}{6}$ b. $7\frac{2}{5} + \left(-3\frac{3}{5}\right)$ c. $-1\frac{2}{9} - \left(-2\frac{5}{9}\right)$

EXERCISES *On Your Own*

Find each sum or difference. Write each answer as a fraction or mixed number in simplest form.

1. $\frac{5}{8} + \frac{7}{8}$ 2. $\frac{7}{10} + \left(-\frac{9}{10}\right)$ 3. $-\frac{1}{4} + \frac{3}{4}$ 4. $\frac{13}{16} + \left(-\frac{5}{16}\right)$ 5. $-\frac{11}{12} - \frac{7}{12}$

6. $-\frac{3}{4} - \frac{1}{4}$ 7. $-\frac{2}{3} - \frac{2}{3}$ 8. $-\frac{4}{9} - \frac{1}{9}$ 9. $\frac{17}{20} - \left(-\frac{13}{20}\right)$ 10. $\frac{2}{7} - \left(-\frac{4}{7}\right)$

11. $-7\frac{1}{10} - 3\frac{7}{10}$ 12. $-7\frac{3}{4} + 2\frac{1}{4}$ 13. $3\frac{1}{3} - 5\frac{2}{3}$ 14. $-7\frac{1}{10} - \left(-3\frac{7}{10}\right)$

15. $-9\frac{3}{12} + \left(-2\frac{1}{12}\right)$ 16. $-2 + \left(-1\frac{29}{60}\right)$ 17. $-3\frac{1}{8} - 6\frac{3}{8}$ 18. $8\frac{2}{9} + \left(-\frac{3}{9}\right)$

19. $5\frac{1}{5} - \left(-3\frac{2}{5}\right)$ 20. $4\frac{3}{20} + \left(-3\frac{7}{20}\right)$ 21. $-5\frac{1}{6} - \left(-4\frac{1}{6}\right)$ 22. $-1\frac{1}{12} + \left(-9\frac{5}{12}\right)$

23. **Pottery** Darryl is applying glaze to 16 ceramic bowls of equal size. He started with $2\frac{1}{2}$ cups of glaze. After glazing four bowls, he has $1\frac{3}{4}$ cups of glaze left. Do you think he will have enough for the remaining bowls? Explain.

24. **Writing** Maria added $-6\frac{2}{5}$ and $-1\frac{3}{5}$ and got $-7\frac{5}{5}$. Explain how she can simplify her answer.

Estimation **Estimate each answer.**

25. $\frac{3}{10} + \left(-\frac{9}{10}\right)$ **26.** $-\frac{4}{7} - \frac{1}{7}$ **27.** $\frac{19}{20} + \left(-\frac{11}{20}\right)$ **28.** $-\frac{4}{6} - \frac{1}{6}$

29. $7\frac{7}{8} + \left(-3\frac{1}{8}\right)$ **30.** $-8 - 1\frac{1}{2}$ **31.** $-9\frac{14}{15} + \left(-2\frac{7}{15}\right)$ **32.** $-6\frac{11}{12} - \left(-\frac{5}{12}\right)$

33. *Open-ended* Write a real-world problem involving addition or subtraction of fractions with like denominators. Estimate the answer and then solve the problem.

Mixed Review

Solve each inequality and graph the solution on a number line. *(Lessons 3-9 and 3-10)*

34. $12t > -6$ **35.** $-x \geq 5$ **36.** $6 \leq y - 4$ **37.** $-4 < r + 2\frac{1}{2}$ **38.** $\frac{p}{-3} \leq 15$

Simplify each numerical expression. *(Lessons 2-3, 2-4 and 2-5)*

39. $4 \div (-2)$ **40.** $-7 \cdot (-21)$ **41.** $-5 \cdot (-2) \cdot (-3)$ **42.** $3 \cdot 2 - 12$ **43.** $-169 \div 13$

44. *Choose a Strategy* Adrienne borrowed $10,000. She will pay back a total of $13,728, including interest. She has 48 equal payments. What is the amount of each payment?

Math at Work

NEWSPAPER REPORTER

Do you enjoy digging for information? Are you able to express your ideas in words? You may be interested in a career as a newspaper reporter. Newspaper reporters investigate leads, make observations, and interview people. Reporters can specialize in fields such as health, social events, business, or politics. They use math to lay out pages, edit, and gather statistical data. They work backward and use patterns to solve problems!

For more information about being a newspaper reporter, visit the Prentice Hall Web site: www.phschool.com

5-6 Adding and Subtracting Rational Numbers

What You'll Learn

▼1 To add and subtract rational numbers

▼2 To solve equations with rational numbers

...And Why

You can solve real-world problems such as problems involving rainfall or stocks.

Here's How

Look for questions that
⁛ build understanding
✔ check understanding

Work Together
Modeling Fraction Sums

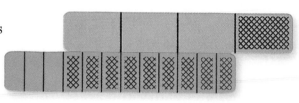

• Work in pairs. Find two models from a set of fraction models that form one whole.

• List as many combinations as you can whose sum is 1. Use the bars to help.

• Then, list as many combinations as you can whose sum is $1\frac{1}{2}$.

THINK AND DISCUSS

▼1 *Adding and Subtracting Rational Numbers*

To add or subtract fractions with unlike denominators, rewrite each fraction using the least common denominator (LCD).

■ **EXAMPLE 1**

Find the sum $-\frac{1}{4} + \frac{3}{7}$.

The LCM of 4 and 7 is 28, so the LCD of $-\frac{1}{4}$ and $\frac{3}{7}$ is 28.

$$-\frac{1}{4} + \frac{3}{7} = \frac{-1 \cdot 7}{4 \cdot 7} + \frac{3 \cdot 4}{7 \cdot 4}$$ ← Write equivalent fractions with a denominator of 28.

$$= \frac{-7}{28} + \frac{12}{28}$$ ← Simplify.

$$= \frac{-7 + 12}{28}$$ ← Write the sum over the common denominator.

$$= \frac{5}{28}$$ ← Simplify.

1. ⁛**Reasoning** Explain why the sum in Example 1 is a positive number.

2. ✔**Try It Out** Find each sum or difference.
   a. $\frac{3}{10} + \left(-\frac{2}{5}\right)$ b. $\frac{1}{3} - \frac{3}{4}$ c. $-\frac{2}{9} - \frac{2}{3}$

You can use the same method to add or subtract mixed numbers.

■ **EXAMPLE 2**

Find the difference $4\frac{2}{3} - 6\frac{1}{2}$.

Estimate: $4\frac{2}{3} - 6\frac{1}{2} \approx 5 - 7 = -2$

$$4\frac{2}{3} - 6\frac{1}{2} = \frac{14}{3} - \frac{13}{2}$$ ← Write improper fractions.

$$= \frac{14 \cdot 2}{3 \cdot 2} + \frac{-13 \cdot 3}{2 \cdot 3}$$ ← The LCD is 6.

$$= \frac{28}{6} - \frac{39}{6}$$ ← Write equivalent fractions with a denominator of 6.

$$= \frac{28 - 39}{6}$$ ← Write the difference over the common denominator.

$$= \frac{-11}{6} = -1\frac{5}{6}$$ ← Simplify.

3. **⊞ Look Back** Compare the difference in Example 2 with the estimate. Is the answer reasonable? Explain.

4. **✓ Try It Out** Find each sum or difference.

   a. $3\frac{1}{2} - 7\frac{4}{5}$ b. $-12\frac{3}{8} + 9\frac{11}{12}$ c. $5 - \left(-1\frac{2}{15}\right)$

▼2 Solving Equations with Rational Numbers

You can use addition or subtraction to solve many rational-number equations.

QUICKreview

Addition and subtraction are inverse operations. Subtraction can "undo" addition, and addition can "undo" subtraction.

■ **EXAMPLE 3**

Algebra Solve $m + \frac{7}{10} = \frac{4}{15}$.

$$m + \frac{7}{10} = \frac{4}{15}$$

$$m + \frac{7}{10} - \frac{7}{10} = \frac{4}{15} - \frac{7}{10}$$ ← Subtract $\frac{7}{10}$ from each side.

$$m = \frac{8}{30} - \frac{21}{30}$$ ← The LCD is 30.

$$m = \frac{8 - 21}{30}$$ ← Write the difference over the common denominator.

$$m = -\frac{13}{30}$$ ← Simplify.

5. **⊞ Look Back** Explain how you can check the answer to Example 3.

6. **✓ Try It Out** Solve each equation.

   a. $y + \frac{5}{8} = \frac{1}{2}$ b. $x - \frac{2}{3} = \frac{3}{4}$ c. $t - \frac{5}{6} = -\frac{1}{9}$

■ **EXAMPLE 4**   *Real-World Problem Solving*

Snowfall The 1994 annual snowfall in Norfolk, Virginia, was $7\frac{1}{2}$ inches. During the first three months, it snowed $6\frac{3}{5}$ inches. Then, it didn't snow again until December. Find the December snowfall.

Words   • $\boxed{\text{Jan.–Mar. snowfall}}$ + $\boxed{\text{Dec. snowfall}}$ = $\boxed{\text{Norfolk annual snowfall}}$

   • Norfolk annual snowfall = $7\frac{1}{2}$ in.
   Let $\boxed{s}$ = Dec. snowfall

Equation   • $\boxed{6\frac{3}{5}}$ + $\boxed{s}$ = $\boxed{7\frac{1}{2}}$

$$6\frac{3}{5} + s = 7\frac{1}{2}$$
$$6\frac{3}{5} - 6\frac{3}{5} + s = 7\frac{1}{2} - 6\frac{3}{5} \quad \longleftarrow \text{Subtract } 6\frac{3}{5} \text{ from each side.}$$
$$s = \frac{15}{2} - \frac{33}{5} \quad \longleftarrow \begin{array}{l}\text{Write the mixed numbers} \\ \text{as improper fractions.}\end{array}$$
$$s = \frac{75}{10} - \frac{66}{10} \quad \longleftarrow \text{The LCD is 10.}$$
$$s = \frac{75 - 66}{10} \quad \longleftarrow \begin{array}{l}\text{Write the difference over} \\ \text{the common denominator.}\end{array}$$
$$s = \frac{9}{10} \quad \longleftarrow \text{Simplify.}$$

The December 1994 snowfall in Norfolk, Virginia, was $\frac{9}{10}$ in.

EXERCISES *On Your Own*

Write each sum or difference as a fraction or mixed number in simplest form.

1. $\frac{3}{4} + \frac{1}{8}$
2. $\frac{7}{10} - \frac{3}{5}$
3. $\frac{5}{8} + \left(-\frac{1}{2}\right)$
4. $-\frac{3}{4} - \frac{1}{8}$
5. $\frac{5}{6} - \frac{2}{3}$

6. $-\frac{5}{8} + \frac{7}{12}$
7. $\frac{1}{2} - \left(-\frac{5}{6}\right)$
8. $-\frac{1}{2} + \left(-\frac{1}{5}\right)$
9. $-\frac{5}{12} - \frac{3}{4}$
10. $\frac{2}{3} - \frac{4}{7}$

11. $2\frac{2}{3} - 4\frac{1}{4}$
12. $4\frac{1}{3} - 6\frac{1}{4}$
13. $-7\frac{2}{5} + \left(-2\frac{3}{4}\right)$
14. $-5\frac{1}{2} + 8\frac{2}{3}$
15. $7\frac{4}{5} + \left(-11\frac{1}{3}\right)$

16. $-10 - 7\frac{7}{9}$
17. $8 - 5\frac{3}{8}$
18. $4\frac{3}{4} - \left(-1\frac{2}{3}\right)$
19. $12\frac{9}{10} + 3\frac{4}{5}$
20. $7\frac{1}{6} + \left(-6\frac{5}{12}\right)$

21. **a.** *Crafts* For a craft project, Zia needs three pieces of wire with lengths $7\frac{1}{2}$ in., $5\frac{3}{4}$ in., and $6\frac{3}{8}$ in. What is the total length of wire that she needs?

   b. Zia bought a 24-in. length of wire for $.99. What length will remain after she cuts the three pieces from it?

Active Day *for* LOCAL STOCKS

Company	Opening Price	Closing Price
DeQ	$22\frac{1}{2}$	$26\frac{1}{8}$
HPG	$33\frac{3}{4}$	$29\frac{5}{8}$
MJC	$25\frac{1}{4}$	19
ZaC	$47\frac{3}{4}$	$54\frac{3}{4}$

The stock prices for several local companies changed dramatically yesterday. Stocks for DeQuintin Co. (DeQ) and Zamco Co. (ZaC) rose on reports of record yearly sales and earnings.

Although there was a decrease in the price of the stock of the Hicks-Porter Group (HPG), a company spokesperson was quick to point out that yesterday's closing price was $4\frac{1}{2}$ points above the closing price exactly one year ago.

22. *Reading About Math* Use the table in the media clip above. For each company, find the amount of change between the opening and closing prices.

23. What was the closing price of Hicks-Porter Group (HPG) stock one year ago?

Write each answer as a fraction or mixed number in simplest form. Then rewrite as a decimal.

24. $\frac{1}{3} + \left(-\frac{4}{9}\right) - \frac{2}{3}$

25. $-\frac{3}{8} + \frac{1}{16} - \frac{1}{4} + \left(-\frac{3}{16}\right)$

26. $-0.125 - \frac{1}{4} + 0.75 - \frac{3}{8}$

27. $-1.25 + \frac{5}{6} - 1.75 + 1\frac{1}{3}$

28. $\frac{3}{4} - \frac{7}{8} + 2.5 - 0.75$

29. $-12.6 - \frac{2}{5} + \frac{9}{10} - (-0.4)$

Algebra **Solve each equation.**

30. $x + \frac{4}{5} = -\frac{3}{10}$

31. $y - \frac{1}{3} = -\frac{3}{4}$

32. $t + \left(-\frac{5}{6}\right) = -\frac{1}{2}$

33. $k - \frac{7}{8} = \frac{1}{4}$

34. $s - 2\frac{1}{2} = -5$

35. $m + \frac{11}{12} = -\frac{1}{3}$

36. $x + 3\frac{3}{4} = -8\frac{1}{2}$

37. $d - 8.1 = -4.5$

38. $y - 0.28 = 1.5$

39. $\frac{1}{2} + c = -3\frac{1}{6}$

40. $-2\frac{7}{12} + z = 1\frac{2}{3}$

41. $6.9 + x = 2\frac{3}{5}$

42. *Writing* How is solving an equation that involves rational numbers similar to solving an equation that involves integers? How is it different? Be sure to give examples.

43. *Carpentry* The piece of wood that a carpenter calls a 2 by 4 is actually $1\frac{1}{2}$ in. thick by $3\frac{1}{2}$ in. wide. If two 2 by 4's are joined with their $3\frac{1}{2}$-in. surfaces touching, what is the thickness of the resulting piece of wood?

44. *Open-ended* Write a word problem involving rational numbers that can be solved using addition or subtraction. Estimate the solution to your problem, then solve. Compare your solution to your estimate.

45. Choose A, B, C, or D. Which equation has a positive solution?

A. $n - \frac{1}{5} = -\frac{1}{7}$ **B.** $p + \frac{5}{6} = -\frac{7}{8}$ **C.** $n - \left(-\frac{1}{2}\right) = -\frac{1}{4}$ **D.** $p + \left(-1\frac{3}{4}\right) = -2\frac{1}{8}$

Algebra **Choose from** $-2, -1\frac{1}{2}, -1, -\frac{1}{2}, 0, \frac{1}{2}, 1, 1\frac{1}{2},$ **and** $2.$
Find all the numbers that are solutions of each equation.

46. $|n| = \frac{1}{2}$ **47.** $\left|n + \frac{1}{2}\right| = 2$ **48.** $|n| + \frac{1}{2} = 2$ **49.** $|n - 1| = 1$

50. $|n| = 1\frac{1}{2}$ **51.** $\left|n - \frac{1}{2}\right| = \frac{1}{2}$ **52.** $|n + 1| = \frac{1}{2}$ **53.** $|n - 2| = 1$

Mixed Review

Probability **A bag contains two nickels, four dimes, and three quarters. One coin is chosen. What is the probability of each event?** *(Lesson 1-11)*

54. $P(\text{dime})$ **55.** $P(\text{nickel or dime})$ **56.** $P(\textit{not} \text{ nickel})$ **57.** $P(\text{dime or quarter})$

Solve each equation. Check the solution. *(Lesson 3-6)*

58. $3(p - 4) = 3$ **59.** $6q - 2q = 18 - (-2)$ **60.** $7r = 4^2 + 5$

61. $2t + 4t - 12 = 6^2$ **62.** $5(x + 1) = 65$ **63.** $7y + 3y = 5^2 - 3 \cdot 5$

64. An off-road motorcycle has a 3.3 gallon gas tank. It can travel 90 miles on a full tank. How many miles per gallon does it get? *(Lesson 2-5)*

CHAPTER PROJECT

PROJECT LINK: ANALYZING

What are leap years? Why are they necessary? In today's calendar, which years are leap years? Use the word *divisible* in your explanation. Decide whether to include a leap year in the calendar that you are creating. Include an explanation of your decision in your project.

5-7 Multiplying and Dividing Rational Numbers

5-7

What You'll Learn

1 To multiply rational numbers

2 To divide rational numbers

...And Why

Multiplying rational numbers allows you to find a fraction of or a part of any quantity.

Here's How

Look for questions that

- build understanding
- ✔ check understanding

THINK AND DISCUSS

1 *Multiplying Rational Numbers*

About $\frac{3}{4}$ of the world's fresh water is in glaciers. Antarctica has $\frac{9}{10}$ of the world's glaciers. To find the fraction of the fresh water that is in Antarctica's glaciers, you can use a model, or you can multiply $\frac{3}{4}$ by $\frac{9}{10}$.

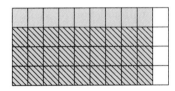

$$\frac{3}{4} \cdot \frac{9}{10} = \frac{3 \cdot 9}{4 \cdot 10} = \frac{27}{40}$$

About $\frac{27}{40}$ of the world's fresh water is in Antarctica's glaciers.

To find the product of rational numbers that are fractions, multiply the numerators and multiply the denominators.

■ EXAMPLE 1

Find the product $\frac{5}{8} \cdot \left(-\frac{7}{15}\right)$.

$$\frac{5}{8} \cdot \left(-\frac{7}{15}\right) = \frac{5}{8} \cdot \left(\frac{-7}{15}\right)$$

$$= \frac{\overset{1}{5} \cdot (-7)}{8 \cdot \underset{3}{15}} \quad \longleftarrow \text{Divide the numerator and denominator by their GCF.}$$

$$= -\frac{7}{24} \quad \longleftarrow \text{Find the products.}$$

1. ✔ *Try It Out* Find each product.

a. $-\frac{4}{5} \cdot \frac{3}{8}$ b. $-\frac{2}{5} \cdot \left(-\frac{5}{12}\right)$ c. $\frac{3}{4} \cdot \left(-\frac{8}{9}\right)$

To multiply rational numbers expressed as mixed numbers, write each mixed number as an improper fraction, and then multiply.

Need Help? For practice with multiplying fractions, see Skills Handbook page 613.

■ EXAMPLE 2

Find the product $-2\frac{1}{4} \cdot \left(-3\frac{3}{5}\right)$.

Estimate: $-2\frac{1}{4} \cdot \left(-3\frac{3}{5}\right) \approx -2(-4) = 8$

$-2\frac{1}{4} \cdot \left(-3\frac{3}{5}\right) = -\frac{9}{4} \cdot \left(-\frac{18}{5}\right)$ ←— Write improper fractions.

$= \frac{-9 \cdot (-\overset{-9}{\cancel{18}})}{\underset{2}{\cancel{4}} \cdot 5}$ ←— Divide the numerator and denominator by their GCF.

$= \frac{81}{10} = 8\frac{1}{10}$ ←— Find the products. Then write as a mixed number.

2. ✓ Try It Out Find each product.

    a. $2\frac{3}{4} \cdot \frac{7}{12}$ **b.** $4\frac{1}{8} \cdot \left(-5\frac{1}{3}\right)$ **c.** $-2\frac{7}{9} \cdot -45$

Two numbers whose product is 1 are called **reciprocals.** Here are three examples of reciprocals.

$$\frac{3}{4} \cdot \frac{4}{3} = 1 \qquad\qquad -\frac{7}{2} \cdot \left(-\frac{2}{7}\right) = 1 \qquad\qquad -5 \cdot \left(-\frac{1}{5}\right) = 1$$

The reciprocal of $\frac{a}{b}$ is $\frac{b}{a}$, where $a \neq 0$ and $b \neq 0$. The reciprocal of a nonzero number a is $\frac{1}{a}$, or a^{-1}. The reciprocal of a number is called its **multiplicative inverse.**

To solve rational-number equations involving multiplication, you can use reciprocals.

■ EXAMPLE 3

Algebra Solve $-\frac{1}{2}t = 2\frac{1}{3}$.

$$-\frac{1}{2}t = 2\frac{1}{3}$$

$\left(-\frac{2}{1}\right)\left(-\frac{1}{2}\right)t = \left(-\frac{2}{1}\right)\left(2\frac{1}{3}\right)$ ←— Multiply each side by the reciprocal of $-\frac{1}{2}$.

$1 \cdot t = \left(-\frac{2}{1}\right)\left(\frac{7}{3}\right)$ ←— Write $2\frac{1}{3}$ as an improper fraction.

$t = \frac{-14}{3}$ ←— Find the products.

$t = -4\frac{2}{3}$ ←— Write as a mixed number.

3. ✓ Try It Out Solve each equation.

    a. $\frac{2}{3}y = -4$ **b.** $-1\frac{3}{4}x = 14$ **c.** $-\frac{1}{6}k = -\frac{1}{2}$

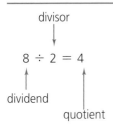

2 Dividing Rational Numbers

To divide rational numbers that are fractions, multiply by the reciprocal of the divisor. When division involves mixed numbers or integers, first rewrite the numbers as improper fractions.

■ EXAMPLE 4

Find the quotient $10\frac{2}{3} \div (-3)$.

Estimate: $10\frac{2}{3} \div (-3) \approx 12 \div (-3) = -4$

Need Help? For practice with dividing mixed numbers, see Skills Handbook page 613.

$$10\frac{2}{3} \div (-3) = \frac{32}{3} \div \left(-\frac{3}{1}\right) \quad \longleftarrow \text{Write improper fractions.}$$

$$= \frac{32}{3} \cdot \left(-\frac{1}{3}\right) \quad \longleftarrow \text{Multiply by the reciprocal of } -\frac{3}{1}.$$

$$= \frac{32 \cdot (-1)}{3 \cdot 3} \quad \longleftarrow \begin{array}{l}\text{Multiply the numerators.}\\\text{Multiply the denominators.}\end{array}$$

$$= \frac{-32}{9} \quad \longleftarrow \text{Find the products.}$$

$$= -3\frac{5}{9} \quad \longleftarrow \begin{array}{l}\text{Write as a mixed number.}\\\text{Compare with your estimate.}\end{array}$$

4. ✓ **Try It Out** Find each quotient.

a. $7\frac{7}{8} \div \left(-1\frac{3}{4}\right)$ b. $-2\frac{1}{2} \div \frac{1}{4}$ c. $-12 \div \left(-5\frac{1}{6}\right)$

EXERCISES *On Your Own*

Write each product in simplest form.

1. $\frac{8}{9} \cdot \left(-\frac{3}{4}\right)$ 2. $-\frac{1}{2} \cdot \frac{2}{3}$

3. $\frac{9}{10} \cdot \left(-\frac{2}{3}\right)$ 4. $-\frac{34}{35} \cdot (-7)$

5. $-4\frac{5}{6} \cdot 2\frac{1}{4}$ 6. $-\frac{4}{5} \cdot \left(-2\frac{1}{2}\right)$

7. $2\frac{2}{3} \cdot 3\frac{3}{8}$ 8. $-6 \cdot 5\frac{1}{3}$

9. $-3\frac{3}{4} \cdot \left(-3\frac{1}{3}\right)$ 10. $8 \cdot \left(-6\frac{2}{5}\right)$

11. $-4\frac{4}{5} \cdot \left(-\frac{5}{6}\right)$ 12. $\frac{4}{9} \cdot \left(-2\frac{1}{4}\right)$

13. *Banners* The cheerleaders need $1\frac{3}{4}$ yd of fabric to make one banner. How many yards of material do they need to make 5 banners?

Algebra **Solve each equation.**

14. $\frac{1}{2}j = \frac{2}{3}$

15. $-\frac{5}{8}x = 10$

16. $-\frac{3}{4}y = 2\frac{2}{5}$

17. $\frac{3}{10}r = -2\frac{1}{4}$

18. $-\frac{4}{5}t = -16$

19. $-1\frac{1}{2}m = 4\frac{1}{2}$

20. $\frac{11}{12}x = -3\frac{1}{7}$

21. $3\frac{1}{5}d = -\frac{1}{4}$

Find each quotient.

22. $\frac{1}{2} \div \left(-\frac{3}{4}\right)$

23. $-\frac{8}{9} \div \left(-\frac{1}{6}\right)$

24. $-5 \div \frac{1}{8}$

25. $-\frac{5}{6} \div \left(-\frac{2}{3}\right)$

26. $-3\frac{2}{3} \div 1\frac{1}{4}$

27. $-5\frac{5}{6} \div 2\frac{1}{3}$

28. $-8\frac{9}{10} \div \frac{1}{10}$

29. $5\frac{1}{2} \div \left(-\frac{1}{2}\right)$

30. $-12 \div \frac{1}{3}$

31. $-\frac{4}{5} \div \left(-1\frac{3}{5}\right)$

32. $\frac{2}{3} \div (-6)$

33. $-8 \div \left(-\frac{2}{5}\right)$

Prize Winning Molasses-Bran Muffins

$\frac{3}{4}$ c milk	• Heat oven to 400°F.
1 egg	• Pour milk on cereal and let stand 1 minute.
$\frac{1}{3}$ c molasses	• Beat in egg, oil, and molasses.
3 tsp baking powder	• Stir in remaining ingredients all at once.
$1\frac{1}{2}$ c wheat bran cereal	• Mix until flour is just moistened.
$\frac{1}{2}$ c vegetable oil	• Pour into greased muffin pan.
$1\frac{1}{4}$ c whole wheat flour	• Bake for 20 minutes.
1 tsp salt	Makes 12 muffins.

---

34. *Cooking* One pound of flour contains about four cups. About how many molasses-bran muffins can you make from a 5-lb bag of flour using the recipe above?

35. The information panel on a 16-oz box of wheat bran cereal indicates that it contains sixteen $\frac{2}{3}$-cup servings. Is this enough cereal to make four dozen molasses-bran muffins? Explain.

36. How much of each ingredient would you need to make $2\frac{1}{2}$ dozen molasses-bran muffins?

37. *Writing* Explain how you can use division of fractions to find how many quarters are in $30 and to find how many half-dollars are in $75.

38. **Choose A, B, C, or D.** Which quotient is *not* equal to 1?

A. $-\frac{7}{2} \div \left(-3\frac{1}{2}\right)$

B. $-0.25 \div \left(-\frac{1}{4}\right)$

C. $1\frac{2}{3} \div \frac{5}{3}$

D. $\frac{1}{2} \div 2$

Geometry Find the perimeter and area of each square.

39.

$1\frac{7}{8}$ in.

40.
$1\frac{3}{4}$ in.

41.

$1\frac{3}{5}$ in.

42.
$1\frac{1}{2}$ in.

Mixed Review

Write a variable expression for each phrase. *(Lesson 2-2)*

43. the number of days in w weeks

44. the number of inches in y feet

45. Bill's age next year if he was x years old last year

46. the amount of money in your pocket if you have n quarters

47. *Choose a Strategy* A square, a circle, and a triangle are different colors. The figure that is yellow has four congruent sides. The figure that is round is not green. One of the figures is blue. Find the color of each figure.

✓ CHECKPOINT 2

Lessons 5-4 through 5-7

Compare. Use >, <, or =.

1. $\frac{7}{9} \blacksquare \frac{5}{6}$

2. $-0.35 \blacksquare -\frac{4}{15}$

3. $\frac{15}{24} \blacksquare \frac{10}{16}$

4. $-\frac{2}{3} \blacksquare -0.65$

5. $-0.12 \blacksquare -\frac{1}{8}$

Write each answer as a fraction or mixed number in simplest form.

6. $-\frac{1}{6} + \frac{5}{6}$

7. $-3\frac{2}{5} + \left(-2\frac{1}{3}\right)$

8. $\frac{11}{12} - \left(-\frac{3}{4}\right)$

9. $-\frac{3}{8} \cdot \left(-\frac{14}{15}\right)$

10. $-8\frac{1}{2} \div 4\frac{1}{4}$

Solve each equation.

11. $y + \frac{3}{4} = -\frac{2}{3}$

12. $y - 4\frac{5}{6} = -6\frac{1}{8}$

13. $-\frac{8}{9}x = \frac{5}{6}$

14. $-2\frac{1}{4}k = \frac{3}{12}$

15. **Choose A, B, C, or D.** Which product is *not* equal to 1?

   A. $\frac{2}{5} \cdot 2\frac{1}{2}$ **B.** $-4 \cdot \left(-\frac{1}{4}\right)$ **C.** $-\frac{3}{8} \cdot \frac{24}{9}$ **D.** $-1 \cdot (-1)$

16. *Open-ended* Write a word problem involving rational numbers that can be solved using multiplication. Show the solution.

Extra Practice, Lesson 5-7, page 586   **5-7** Multiplying and Dividing Rational Numbers   **253**

5-8 Work Backward

Problem Solving Strategies

Draw a Diagram
Guess and Test
Look for a Pattern
Make a Table
Simulate the Problem
Solve a Simpler Problem
Too Much or Too Little
  Information
Use Logical Reasoning
Use Multiple Strategies
✔ Work Backward
Write an Equation

THINK AND DISCUSS

To solve some problems, you may need to work backward.

SAMPLE PROBLEM

International spies Cara Brimhat and Rex Coattails accidentally left clues to their whereabouts when they deposited money in several banks. At the start of their mission, they deposited half of their money in Paris. Then they deposited $5,000 in Cairo. Their mission next took them to Istanbul, where they deposited half their remaining money. Now they have $7,500 left. What amount did they have at the start of their mission?

READ

Read for understanding. Summarize the problem.

1. a. What amount do Cara and Rex have now?
   b. In which cities did Cara and Rex make deposits?
   c. Describe their deposit in each city.
   d. Summarize the goal of the problem in your own words.

PLAN

Decide on a strategy.

In this problem, you know a *final* amount of money. To find the *starting* amount, work backward. Begin with $7,500 and undo the deposits.

SOLVE

Try the strategy.

2. Complete each sentence.
   a. The final amount, $7,500, is $\frac{1}{2}$ the amount they had when they got to Istanbul. So, when they got to Instanbul they had 2 · $7,500, or ■.
   b. The amount they took to Istanbul was $5,000 less than what they had when they got to Cairo. So, when they got to Cairo they had $5,000 more, or ■.
   c. The amount they took to Cairo was only $\frac{1}{2}$ the amount they had when they began in Paris. So, when they began in Paris they had twice as much, or ■.

3. What is the solution of the problem?

LOOK BACK

Think about how you solved the problem.

When you work backward to solve a problem, you can check your solution by working *forward*.

4. a. Use your solution of the problem. Take $\frac{1}{2}$ of that amount. What is the result?
   b. Subtract $5,000. What is the result?
   c. Take $\frac{1}{2}$ of that amount. Is the result $7,500?

EXERCISES *On Your Own*

Work backward to solve each problem.

1. a. If you start with a number, subtract 8, multiply by $\frac{1}{2}$, add 5, and then divide by 11, the result is 5. Find the number.
   b. *Reasoning* What operations did you use to solve this problem? How are they related to the operations mentioned in the problem?

2. *Jobs* Lanora returned home from mowing lawns at 3:00 P.M. on Saturday. It took $1\frac{1}{2}$ h to mow the first lawn. It took twice as long to mow the next lawn. After a half-hour break, it took $1\frac{1}{4}$ h to mow one more lawn. At what time did she start?

3. *Business* Bert bought a case of pens. On Monday he sold half the pens. On Tuesday he sold 30 more. On Wednesday he sold half the pens that were left. On Thursday he sold the remaining 40 pens. How many pens were in the case?

4. Niabi is thinking of a number. If you divide it by 2, square the result, subtract 4, and then divide by 6, the result is 10. What is the number?

Use any strategy to solve each problem. Show all your work.

5. Each house on Future Road is painted white, blue, brown, or gray. The front door can be red, green, or yellow. Suppose that the builder used the pattern shown at the right. Describe the next house in the pattern.

6. *Shopping* You can buy balloons in packs of 25 or packs of 75. Jill bought eight packs and had 450 balloons in all. How many packs of each size did she buy?

7. *Patterns* Find the next three numbers in each pattern.
   a. $\frac{1}{32}, \frac{1}{8}, \frac{1}{16}, \frac{1}{4}, \frac{1}{8}, \frac{1}{2}, \frac{1}{4}, \ldots$
   b. $-54, -18, -6, -2, \ldots$

8. *Farming* Red Apple Farm has 32 rows of apple trees in its orchard. Each row contains 28 trees. This year's harvest is 17,920 bushels of apples. What is the average number of bushels of apples that each tree produces?

9. *Money* The vending machine in the school cafeteria takes quarters, dimes, and nickels only. Right now, a small light indicates that you must use exact change.
   a. Suppose you want to buy crackers that cost 65¢. How many different combinations of coins could you use?
   b. If you use exactly six coins, what coins do you use?

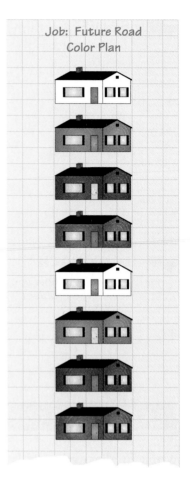

Job: Future Road Color Plan

Mixed Review

Write a rule to describe each translation. *(Lesson 4-8)*

10. $P(3, 2) \longrightarrow P'(-1, -2)$ 11. $A(1, 10) \longrightarrow A'(-4, 2)$ 12. $D(7, -2) \longrightarrow D'(-1, 2)$

Order each set of numbers from least to greatest. *(Lesson 2-1)*

13. $-2, -8, 10, -12, 4, -6$ 14. $46, -48, -28, 12, -18, -47$ 15. $23, 18, -98, 2, -85, 24$

16. $-12, 5, 0, -1, 23, -15$ 17. $-15, -22, -2, 16, -38$ 18. $-13, 10, -9, 0, -10, 17$

19. A diver was 78 ft below the surface of the water. She rose 50 ft and then descended 16 ft. At what level is she now?
    (Lesson 3-4)

Using a Calculator with Fractions

Before Lesson 5-9

You can use a scientific calculator to add, subtract, multiply, and divide fractions.

■ EXAMPLE 1

Find the sum $\frac{7}{8} + \frac{3}{5}$.

Estimate: $\frac{7}{8} + \frac{3}{5} \approx 1 + \frac{1}{2} = 1\frac{1}{2}$

Enter the following keystrokes on a scientific calculator.

7 [a^b/c] 8 [+] 3 [a^b/c] 5 [=] 1_19_40

$\frac{7}{8} + \frac{3}{5} = 1\frac{19}{40}$

■ EXAMPLE 2

Find the quotient $2\frac{3}{4} \div 1\frac{5}{8}$.

Estimate: $2\frac{3}{4} \div 1\frac{5}{8} \approx 3 \div 1\frac{1}{2} = 3 \div \frac{3}{2} = 3 \cdot \frac{2}{3} = 2$

Enter the following keystrokes on a scientific calculator.

2 [a^b/c] 3 [a^b/c] 4 [÷] 1 [a^b/c] 5 [a^b/c] 8 [=] 1_9_13

$2\frac{3}{4} \div 1\frac{5}{8} = 1\frac{9}{13}$

Use a scientific calculator to perform the indicated operation.

1. $\frac{2}{3} + \frac{3}{8}$
2. $\frac{3}{5} - \frac{1}{4}$
3. $\frac{3}{5} \cdot \frac{1}{2}$
4. $\frac{2}{5} \div \frac{5}{8}$
5. $15 \cdot \frac{1}{6}$

6. $\frac{7}{20} - \frac{1}{12}$
7. $\frac{8}{9} \cdot 5$
8. $\frac{7}{8} \div 3$
9. $\frac{3}{5} + \frac{1}{4}$
10. $\frac{1}{3} \div \frac{9}{8}$

11. $\frac{1}{6} + \frac{4}{7}$
12. $2\frac{1}{2} - \frac{1}{3}$
13. $7 \cdot 5\frac{1}{4}$
14. $5\frac{1}{3} - 2\frac{3}{4}$
15. $2\frac{1}{2} \div \frac{3}{4}$

16. $4\frac{5}{8} + \frac{3}{5}$
17. $\frac{9}{16} \div \frac{3}{8}$
18. $1\frac{1}{12} + 9\frac{3}{8}$
19. $12 \div \frac{3}{4}$
20. $20 \cdot 1\frac{2}{5}$

21. $\frac{9}{10} \cdot 1\frac{1}{2}$
22. $8 \div \frac{3}{7}$
23. $7\frac{1}{2} \cdot 6$
24. $8 \div 2\frac{4}{5}$
25. $3 - 1\frac{2}{3}$

26. *Writing* Explain how you could use a scientific calculator to change a fraction to simplest form.

What You'll Learn

▼ **1** To find square roots of numbers

▼ **2** To classify real numbers

...And Why

You can use a calculator to find square roots.

Here's How

Look for questions that

🔹 build understanding

✔ check understanding

THINK AND DISCUSS

▼ **1** *Finding Square Roots*

Sixteen square tiles can form a square with 4 tiles on each side. A number like 16 that is the square of a whole number is a **perfect square**.

$16 = 4^2$

1. List the perfect squares from 0 to 150.

The opposite of squaring a number is finding its **square root**. Because $16 = 4^2$, a square root of 16 is 4. You can use the square root symbol, $\sqrt{}$, to write this as $\sqrt{16} = 4$.

■ EXAMPLE 1

Estimate the value of $\sqrt{28}$ to the nearest whole number.

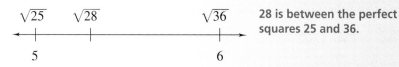

28 is between the perfect squares 25 and 36.

Since 28 is closer to 25 than 36, $\sqrt{28}$ is closer to 5 than 6. So, $\sqrt{28} \approx 5$.

2. ✓ *Try It Out* Estimate the value of each expression to the nearest whole number.

a. $\sqrt{38}$ **b.** $\sqrt{105}$ **c.** $\sqrt{54}$ **d.** $\sqrt{95}$

You can use a calculator to find square roots.

■ EXAMPLE 2

Find $\sqrt{47}$ and $-\sqrt{75}$ to the nearest tenth.

47 $\boxed{\sqrt{x}}$ *6.8556546* ≈ 6.9 75 $\boxed{\sqrt{x}}$ $\boxed{+/-}$ *-8.660254* ≈ -8.7

3. ✓ *Try It Out* Find each square root to the nearest tenth.

a. $\sqrt{7}$ **b.** $-\sqrt{40}$ **c.** $\sqrt{72}$ **d.** $-\sqrt{90}$

▼2 *Classifying Real Numbers*

In Lesson 5-3, you learned how to write terminating decimals and repeating decimals as fractions. These decimals are rational numbers. There are other decimals that do not terminate and do not repeat. These nonrepeating, nonterminating decimals are called **irrational numbers.**

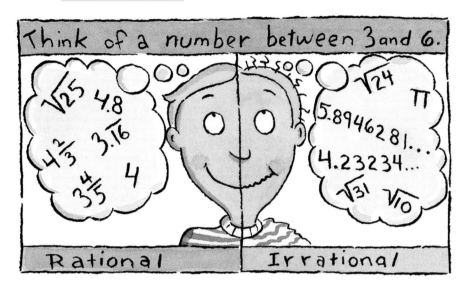

Irrational numbers include the square root of any positive integer that is not a perfect square.

Rational	Irrational
$\sqrt{4}$ $\sqrt{9}$ $\sqrt{256}$	$\sqrt{2}$ $\sqrt{3}$ $\sqrt{8}$ $\sqrt{27}$ $\sqrt{42}$

4. ⠿*Calculator* Find the value of each irrational number listed above. Round to the nearest thousandth.

5. ⠿*Reasoning* List the numbers in the form $\sqrt{x}$ that are *not* whole numbers for whole-number values of x less than 10.

Irrational numbers also include decimals that have a pattern in their digits and do not terminate or repeat. One such decimal is shown below.

$$0.02022022202222 \ldots$$

6. a. ⠿*Patterns* Describe the pattern of 0's and 2's in the decimal above.
   b. Explain why the decimal is not a repeating decimal.
   c. ⠿*Open-ended* Write a decimal similar to the one above that involves the digits 5 and 9.

QUICKreview

A rational number is a number that can be written as a ratio of two integers in the form $\frac{a}{b}$, where $b \neq 0$.

■ **EXAMPLE 3**

Tell whether each number is *rational* or *irrational*. Explain your reasoning.

    a. $0.818118111\ldots$ **b.** $0.\overline{81}$ **c.** $1\frac{2}{9}$

    a. $0.818118111\ldots$ is an irrational number because it is a nonrepeating, nonterminating decimal.

    b. $0.\overline{81}$ is a rational number because it can be written as $\frac{81}{99}$.

    c. $1\frac{2}{9}$ is a rational number because it can be written as $\frac{11}{9}$.

7. ✓ *Try It Out* Identify each number as *rational* or *irrational*.
    a. $0.\overline{6}$ **b.** $5.23438392\ldots$ **c.** $\sqrt{144}$ **d.** $\sqrt{200}$

Rational and irrational numbers together form the set of **real numbers.** The Venn diagram below shows the relationships among these and other sets of numbers that you have studied.

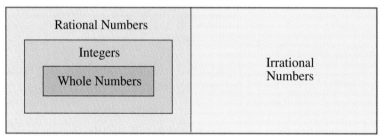

Real Numbers

8. ⊞ *Go a Step Further* *Natural numbers* are the following set of numbers.

    $1, 2, 3, 4, 5, 6, \ldots$

Where would you place the set of natural numbers in the Venn diagram of the real number system? Explain.

9. a. If a number is irrational, can it also be rational? Explain.
    b. If a number is an integer, can it also be a real number? Explain.

10. Name two numbers that fit each description.
    a. a real number that is not a rational number
    b. a rational number that is not an integer
    c. an integer that is not a whole number
    d. a square root that is a rational number
    e. a square root that is an irrational number

Find each square root. If a number is not a perfect square, approximate the square root to the nearest tenth.

1. $\sqrt{169}$ 2. $\sqrt{53}$ 3. $-\sqrt{89}$ 4. $\sqrt{0.27}$ 5. $\sqrt{2{,}704}$ 6. $\sqrt{3{,}481}$

7. $\sqrt{289}$ 8. $-\sqrt{191}$ 9. $\sqrt{\frac{4}{16}}$ 10. $\sqrt{800}$ 11. $\sqrt{3{,}025}$ 12. $\sqrt{6.4}$

Estimate the value of each expression.

13. $\sqrt{56}$ 14. $\sqrt{94}$ 15. $\sqrt{125}$ 16. $\sqrt{54}$ 17. $\sqrt{148}$ 18. $\sqrt{175}$

19. $\sqrt{110}$ 20. $\sqrt{34}$ 21. $\sqrt{84}$ 22. $\sqrt{19}$ 23. $\sqrt{105}$ 24. $\sqrt{78}$

25. *Geometry* Find the area of the smaller square in the figure. The area of the larger square is 49 in.^{2}.

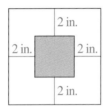

26. *Writing* Explain why you cannot find the square root of a negative number.

Explain why each number is rational or irrational.

27. $\sqrt{12}$ 28. $0.6666\ldots$ 29. $1.5435415\ldots$ 30. $\sqrt{225}$ 31. 4.365

For each number, write all the categories to which it belongs. Choose from *real number, rational number, irrational number, integer,* and *whole number.*

32. $-\frac{3}{5}$ 33. $0.1\overline{53}$ 34. $\sqrt{100}$ 35. 3.14 36. $0.333333\ldots$

37. $4\frac{1}{2}$ 38. 0 39. $-\sqrt{36}$ 40. $\sqrt{104}$ 41. $5.121231234\ldots$

42. *Aviation* Aviators can calculate the distance to the horizon in miles by multiplying 1.23 times the square root of the altitude in feet. If a plane is at an altitude of 40,000 ft, what is the distance to the horizon?

Algebra **Find two integers that make each equation true.**

43. $x^2 = 100$ **44.** $y^2 = 121$ **45.** $t^2 = 169$ **46.** $x^2 = 1$ **47.** $y^2 = 625$

48. *Reasoning* Is the sum of the two irrational numbers shown below a rational or irrational number? Explain.

$$0.01001000100001\ldots$$
$$+\ 0.10110111011110\ldots$$

49. *Calculator* Write a simplified expression for each product. Then, use a calculator to find the value of each expression.

Sample: $\sqrt{8} \cdot \sqrt{6} = \sqrt{8 \cdot 6} = \sqrt{48} \approx 6.9$

a. $\sqrt{2} \cdot \sqrt{5}$ **b.** $\sqrt{3} \cdot \sqrt{6}$ **c.** $\sqrt{2} \cdot \sqrt{8}$
d. $\sqrt{3} \cdot \sqrt{12}$ **e.** $\sqrt{5} \cdot \sqrt{15}$ **f.** $\sqrt{5} \cdot \sqrt{20}$

50. a. Which products in Exercise 49 are rational numbers?
   b. *Open-ended* Write two other square roots that are irrational numbers, but whose product is a rational number.

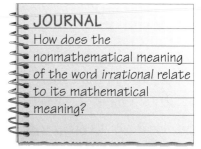

JOURNAL
How does the nonmathematical meaning of the word *irrational* relate to its mathematical meaning?

Mixed Review

Evaluate each expression for $a = -3$, $b = -5$, and $c = -1$.
(Lesson 2-7)

51. $b^2 - a$ **52.** $a + bc$ **53.** $c^9 \div a^2$ **54.** $(b - a)^4$ **55.** $\dfrac{abc}{a}$ **56.** $\dfrac{a + b}{2}$

Graph points A–F on one coordinate plane. *(Lesson 4-1)*

57. $A(2, 3)$ **58.** $B(-2, 5)$ **59.** $C(0, -3)$ **60.** $D(1, 0)$ **61.** $E(4, -3)$ **62.** $F(-5, -4)$

63. *Choose a Strategy* Agnes mailed letters and postcards for a total of $3.07. If postage costs 32 cents for each letter and 19 cents for each postcard, how many of each did she mail?

CHAPTER PROJECT

PROJECT LINK: DESIGNING

Design your calendar. Create one poster displaying the whole year. Use art work or photos for each month or time interval.

5-10

The Pythagorean Theorem

What You'll Learn

▼ 1 To use the Pythagorean theorem

▼ 2 To identify right triangles

...And Why

You can use the Pythagorean theorem to find distances.

Here's How

Look for questions that

⣿ build understanding

✔ check understanding

QUICKreview

A right triangle is a triangle with a right angle.

Work Together

Exploring Right Triangles

Work with a partner to explore how the lengths of the sides of a right triangle are related.

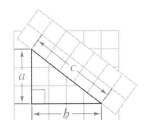

1. Find a, b, and c in the right triangle shown. Record the lengths in a table like the one below.

Side Lengths			Squares		
a	b	c	a^2	b^2	c^2
⬛	⬛	⬛	⬛	⬛	⬛
6	8	⬛	⬛	⬛	⬛
5	12	⬛	⬛	⬛	⬛

2. On graph paper, draw two other right triangles using the lengths a and b shown in the table. Use the edge of a piece of graph paper to find the length c. Record the lengths.

3. Complete the table by finding the squares of the lengths of the sides of each triangle.

4. ⣿*Patterns* Look for a pattern in the table. Complete this equation: $\blacksquare^2 + \blacksquare^2 = \blacksquare^2$.

THINK AND DISCUSS

▼1 *Using the Pythagorean Theorem*

In a right triangle, the side opposite the right angle is the **hypotenuse.** The other sides are the **legs** of the right triangle.

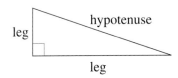

5. Which side of a right triangle is always the longest side?

In the Work Together you investigated some cases of the Pythagorean theorem.

THE PYTHAGOREAN THEOREM

In any right triangle, the sum of the squares of the lengths of the legs is equal to the square of the length of the hypotenuse.

$$a^2 + b^2 = c^2$$

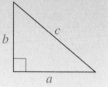

■ **EXAMPLE 1**   *Real-World Problem Solving*

Transportation Commuters can take a ferry from Bay Harbor across the bay to Hampton. What is the distance the ferry travels?

$$a^2 + b^2 = c^2 \quad \longleftarrow \text{Use the Pythagorean theorem.}$$
$$3.4^2 + 4.2^2 = c^2 \quad \longleftarrow \text{Substitute } a = 3.4 \text{ and } b = 4.2.$$
$$\sqrt{3.4^2 + 4.2^2} = c \quad \longleftarrow \text{Find the square root of each side.}$$

3.4 ⬚x² ➕ 4.2 ⬚x² 🟰 ⬚√x̄ 5.4037024

The ferry travels about 5.4 kilometers.

6. a. What is the distance from Bay Harbor to Hampton if a commuter takes Collins Avenue onto the Causeway?
b. How many kilometers shorter is the ferry ride than the car ride?

You can use the Pythagorean theorem to find the length of a leg of a right triangle when you know the length of the hypotenuse and the other leg.

QUICKreview

BC means "the distance from *B* to *C*" or the length of $\overline{BC}$.

■ **EXAMPLE 2**

Find *BC* in the triangle at the right.

$$AB^2 + BC^2 = AC^2$$ ◄——Use the Pythagorean theorem.
$$8^2 + BC^2 = 10^2$$ ◄——Substitute *AB* = 8 and *AC* = 10.
$$64 + BC^2 = 100$$ ◄——Simplify.
$$BC^2 = 36$$ ◄——Subtract 64 from each side.
$$\sqrt{BC^2} = \sqrt{36}$$ ◄——Find the square root of each side.
$$BC = 6$$ ◄——Simplify.

BC is 6 centimeters.

7. ✓ *Try It Out* The lengths of two sides of a right triangle are given. Find the length of the third side to the nearest tenth of a unit.

a. legs: 7 m and 4 m   **b.** leg: 3 ft; hypotenuse: 8 ft

▼2 *Identifying Right Triangles*

You can substitute the lengths of the sides of a triangle into the equation $a^2 + b^2 = c^2$ to find out whether the triangle is a right triangle. The triangle is a right triangle if the equation is true.

■ **EXAMPLE 3**

Is a triangle with sides 7 in., 25 in., and 24 in. a right triangle?

$$a^2 + b^2 = c^2$$ ◄——Write the Pythagorean theorem.
$$7^2 + 24^2 \stackrel{?}{=} 25^2$$ ◄——Substitute *a* = 7, *b* = 24, and *c* = 25. The longest side is *c*.
$$49 + 576 \stackrel{?}{=} 625$$ ◄——Simplify.
$$625 = 625 ✓$$ ◄——Compare.

The triangle is a right triangle.

8. ✓ *Try It Out* Is a triangle with the given side lengths a right triangle? Explain.

a. 8 cm, 10 cm, 12 cm   **b.** 8 in., 9 in., 10 in.

Name the hypotenuse and legs of each right triangle.

1.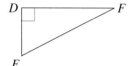

2.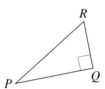

3.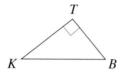

4.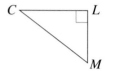

Find the missing side length to the nearest tenth of a unit.

5.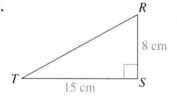

6.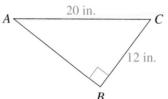

7.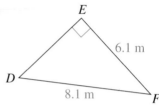

8.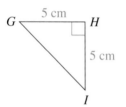

9.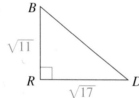

10.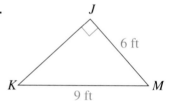

Calculator **The lengths of two sides of a right triangle are given. Find the length of the third side to the nearest tenth of a unit.**

11. legs: 9 ft and 6 ft

12. legs: 3.9 km and 5.4 km

13. leg: 15 in.; hypotenuse: 18 in.

14. leg: 5.1 m; hypotenuse: 9.8 m

15. leg: 20 mi; hypotenuse: 24 mi

16. leg: 2.8 cm; hypotenuse: 3.5 cm

17. *Writing* Jarrod is standing at point A in the diagram at the right. Explain how he can find the distance across the pond.

18. *Hobbies* Two hikers started their trip from a camp by walking 1.5 km due east. They then turned due north, walking 1.7 km to a large pond. To the nearest tenth of a kilometer, how far is the pond from the camp?

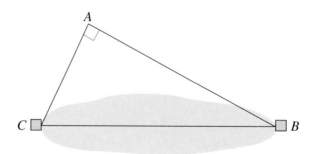

Algebra **Find the value of _n_ in each diagram. Give your answer as a square root.**

19. 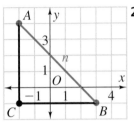 **20.** 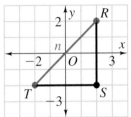 **21.** 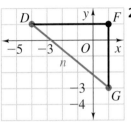 **22.**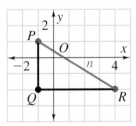

23. *Oceanography* A diver swims 20 m underwater to the place where a buoy is anchored 10 m below the surface of the water. On the surface, how far is the buoy located from the place where the diver started?

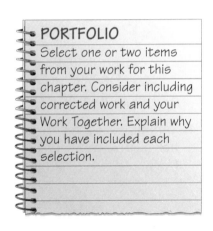

Is a triangle with the given side lengths a right triangle? Explain.

24. 16 in., 63 in., 65 in.

25. 15 cm, 35 cm, 40 cm

26. 2.9 m, 2.0 m, 2.1 m

27. 2.8 cm, 5.3 cm, 4.5 cm

28. 1.6 km, 1.2 km, 1.2 km

29. $\sqrt{56}$, 9, 5

30. $\sqrt{5}$, $\sqrt{3}$, $\sqrt{4}$

31. $\sqrt{15}$, $\sqrt{24}$, 3

PORTFOLIO
Select one or two items from your work for this chapter. Consider including corrected work and your Work Together. Explain why you have included each selection.

32. Any three natural numbers that make $a^2 + b^2 = c^2$ true form a Pythagorean triple. For example, 3, 4, 5 is a Pythagorean triple. Use the *Guess and Test* strategy to find the Pythagorean triple for each value of _c_.
  a. $c = 10$ **b.** $c = 13$ **c.** $c = 17$

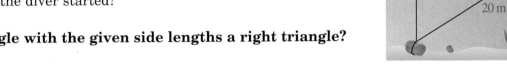

Mixed Review

Write each sum or product in scientific notation and then in standard form. *(Lessons 2-3, 2-5, and 2-11)*

33. 99,999,999 + 1

34. 55,000 + 65,000

35. 8,000,000 + 8,000,000

36. 100,000 × 1,000,000

37. 99,999,000 × 1,000

38. 23,000 × 46,100

39. *Choose a Strategy* Find two numbers whose sum is 46 and whose difference is 12.

Choose the best answer.

1. Which of these shows the fractions in order from least to greatest?

   A. $\frac{5}{8}, \frac{3}{4}, \frac{5}{6}, \frac{11}{12}$

   B. $\frac{3}{4}, \frac{5}{6}, \frac{5}{8}, \frac{11}{12}$

   C. $\frac{11}{12}, \frac{5}{8}, \frac{5}{6}, \frac{3}{4}$

   D. $\frac{3}{4}, \frac{5}{8}, \frac{5}{6}, \frac{11}{12}$

2. Which fraction is equivalent to 0.75?

   F. $\frac{13}{20}$ G. $\frac{3}{4}$ H. $\frac{7}{5}$ J. $7\frac{5}{10}$

3. The drawing shows a side view of a car ramp. What is the height of the ramp?

   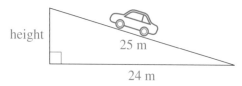

   A. 1 m   B. 7 m   C. 10 m   D. 35 m

4. Tanika wants to puts a diagonal brace on her picture frame. What is the length of the brace?

   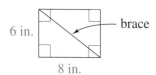

   F. 4 in.   G. 5 in.   H. 10 in.   J. 14 in.

5. If $\frac{1}{3}x - 1\frac{1}{2} = 3$, what is the value of x?

   A. $13\frac{1}{2}$ B. $9\frac{1}{2}$ C. $4\frac{1}{2}$ D. 2

6. Lemar needs 5 tbsp of milk for a recipe. He only has measuring cups. There are 16 tbsp in 1 cup. Which measuring cup is closest to 5 tbsp?

   F. $\frac{1}{8}$ c   G. $\frac{1}{4}$ c   H. $\frac{1}{3}$ c   J. $\frac{1}{2}$ c

7. Which fraction is equivalent to $\frac{2}{3}$?

   A. $\frac{4}{9}$ B. $\frac{16}{48}$ C. $\frac{24}{36}$ D. $\frac{21}{32}$

8. Which fraction is greater than $\frac{3}{5}$?

   F. $\frac{5}{8}$ G. $\frac{6}{11}$ H. $\frac{8}{15}$ J. $\frac{6}{10}$

Please note that items 9–13 have *five* answer choices.

9. Liane wants to cut $5\frac{1}{3}$ ft of ribbon into 4 equal pieces. How long should each piece be?

   A. $1\frac{1}{4}$ ft   B. $1\frac{1}{3}$ ft   C. $20\frac{1}{3}$ ft

   D. $21\frac{1}{3}$ ft   E. Not Here

10. Carlos jogs on a $\frac{1}{4}$-mile track. If he does 18 laps, how far has he jogged?

    F. 72 miles   G. 18 miles   H. 9 miles

    J. $4\frac{1}{2}$ miles   K. $4\frac{1}{4}$ miles

11. Siri's plant was $3\frac{1}{2}$ in. high on Monday and grew $\frac{1}{4}$ in. each day. How tall was the plant after 5 days?

    A. $1\frac{1}{4}$ in.   B. $3\frac{3}{4}$ in.   C. $4\frac{1}{4}$ in.

    D. $4\frac{3}{4}$ in.   E. $5\frac{3}{4}$ in.

12. Nancy is baking for a bake sale. She needs quite a bit of flour: $2\frac{1}{2}$ c for cookies, $4\frac{1}{3}$ c for muffins, and $3\frac{3}{4}$ c for a cake. How much flour does she need?

    F. $9\frac{5}{9}$ c   G. $10\frac{3}{8}$ c   H. $10\frac{5}{12}$ c

    J. $10\frac{1}{2}$ c   K. $10\frac{7}{12}$ c

13. Mitsu needs $1\frac{1}{2}$ c of chopped pecans. He has $\frac{3}{8}$ c. How much more does he need?

    A. $\frac{1}{8}$ c   B. $\frac{7}{8}$ c   C. $1\frac{1}{8}$ c

    D. $1\frac{2}{6}$ c   E. $1\frac{7}{8}$ c

CHAPTER PROJECT

A NEW NEW YEAR

Invent a New Calendar The Project Link questions on pages 224, 238, 248, and 262 should help you complete your project. Here is a checklist to help you gather the parts of your project together.

✔ an introduction

✔ the definitions of *week* and *month*, and the names of the months and days

✔ a description of how your calendar works

✔ the design of the calendar

Pretend you are presenting your proposed calendar to an international commission that is considering revising the calendar. Explain the advantages of the calendar you invented, and why it should be adopted. Be sure your calculations are accurate, and your arguments are clear and effective.

Reflect and Revise

Explain the calendar you invented to a friend, and review all your calculations. If necessary, make changes to improve your proposal.

Web Extension
Prentice Hall's Internet site contains information you might find helpful as you complete your project. Visit www.phschool.com/mgm3/ch5 for some links and ideas related to calendars.

Factors, and Comparing and Ordering Rational Numbers   5-1, 5-4

A **prime number** is a whole number greater than 1 with exactly two factors, 1 and itself. The greatest factor common to a set of numbers is the **greatest common factor** (GCF).

The **least common multiple** (LCM) of a group of numbers is the least multiple that is the same for the group of numbers.

To order rational numbers, write the numbers as fractions with a common denominator and compare the numerators, or write the fractions as decimals and compare.

Find the GCF and LCM of each pair of numbers.

1. 16, 20   **2.** 45, 90   **3.** 28, 56   **4.** 20, 75   **5.** 24, 36

Write the prime factorization of each number.

6. 360   **7.** 700   **8.** 1,440   **9.** 378   **10.** 7,020

Compare. Use >, <, or =.

11. $\frac{3}{5}$ ▇ $\frac{7}{9}$ **12.** -4.66 ▇ $-\frac{14}{3}$ **13.** $\frac{5}{6}$ ▇ $\frac{8}{9}$ **14.** 0.625 ▇ $\frac{5}{8}$

Rational Numbers, Equivalent Fractions and Decimals   5-2, 5-3

A **rational number** is a number that can be written as a ratio of two integers in the form $\frac{a}{b}$, where $b \neq 0$. **Terminating decimals** and **repeating decimals** are rational numbers.

Write each rational number as a ratio in the form $\frac{a}{b}$.

15. 0.125 **16.** -3.5 **17.** -9 **18.** $2\frac{1}{3}$ **19.** $-\frac{3}{4}$

Write each decimal as a fraction or mixed number in simplest form. Write each fraction or mixed number as a decimal.

20. 0.36 **21.** $-\frac{9}{10}$ **22.** $\frac{4}{5}$ **23.** $-4\frac{2}{3}$ **24.** 1.65

25. $\frac{4}{11}$ **26.** $-1\frac{5}{8}$ **27.** $-\frac{2}{3}$ **28.** $1.\overline{3}$ **29.** $6.\overline{24}$

Adding and Subtracting Rational Numbers
5-5, 5-6

To add or subtract fractions with like denominators, add or subtract the numerators.

If the denominators are different, write equivalent fractions using the LCD.

Find each sum or difference.

30. $-\frac{7}{8} + \frac{3}{4}$

31. $-2\frac{4}{5} - \left(-1\frac{3}{10}\right)$

32. $-\frac{5}{9} - \frac{2}{3}$

33. $-3\frac{1}{6} + 2\frac{1}{2}$

Multiplying and Dividing Rational Numbers
5-7

To multiply fractions, multiply numerators and multiply denominators. To divide, multiply by the reciprocal of the divisor.

To multiply or divide mixed numbers, change each mixed number to an improper fraction, then multiply or divide.

Find each product or quotient.

34. $\frac{4}{5} \cdot \frac{5}{8}$

35. $-\frac{1}{6} \cdot \left(-\frac{3}{8}\right)$

36. $2\frac{1}{2} \div \frac{10}{13}$

37. $-4\frac{2}{3} \div 2\frac{2}{9}$

Work Backward
5-8

Many problems can be solved by working backward.

38. If you multiply a number by -8 and then divide by $-\frac{1}{3}$, the result is -6. Find the number.

Square Roots, Irrational Numbers, Pythagorean Theorem
5-9, 5-10

Nonrepeating, nonterminating decimals are **irrational numbers.** The square of a whole number is a **perfect square.** The opposite of squaring a number is findings its **square root.**

If a and b are the lengths of the legs of a right triangle, and c is the length of the hypotenuse, then $a^2 + b^2 = c^2$.

Find each square root. If a number is not a perfect square, round to the nearest tenth.

39. $\sqrt{196}$

40. $-\sqrt{\frac{25}{36}}$

41. $\sqrt{57}$

42. $\sqrt{1.6}$

43. $\sqrt{225}$

44. The foot of a 20-ft ladder is 12 ft from the base of a house. How far up the side of the house does the ladder reach?

1. Write a rational number for each point on the number line.

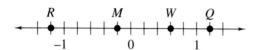

a. R b. W
c. M d. Q

2. Determine whether each number is rational or irrational.
   a. $2.\overline{79}$ b. $-\sqrt{10}$
   c. $-1\frac{5}{6}$ d. $\sqrt{49}$

3. *Writing* Describe the differences between rational and irrational numbers.

4. Write the prime factorization of each number, using long division or a factor tree.
   a. 90   b. 120
   c. 280   d. 432

5. Compare. Use $>$, $<$, or $=$.
   a. $\frac{3}{8}$ ▨ 0.4 b. $-\frac{1}{2}$ ▨ $-\frac{5}{12}$
   c. -0.89 ▨ $-\frac{9}{10}$ d. $\frac{4}{9}$ ▨ $0.\overline{4}$

6. Find the GCF and LCM of each set.
   a. 12, 16   b. 6, 25
   c. 9, 24   d. 32, 48

7. Write each fraction or mixed number as a decimal.
   a. $\frac{2}{5}$ b. $-3\frac{3}{8}$
   c. $1\frac{4}{15}$ d. $\frac{7}{11}$

8. Write each decimal as a fraction or mixed number in simplest form.
   a. 0.64 b. $2.\overline{3}$

9. Write each sum or difference in simplified form.
   a. $-\frac{3}{5} - \frac{1}{3}$ b. $\frac{1}{12} - \frac{5}{12}$
   c. $-3\frac{1}{4} + \left(-2\frac{2}{3}\right)$ d. $\frac{11}{12} - \frac{3}{4}$
   e. $2\frac{1}{5} + 3\frac{1}{3}$ f. $-16\frac{1}{10} + \left(-2\frac{1}{2}\right)$

10. Write each product or quotient in simplified form.
    a. $-\frac{2}{5} \cdot \frac{7}{8}$ b. $-2\frac{3}{4} \cdot \frac{8}{9}$
    c. $-\frac{5}{8} \div \left(-\frac{1}{2}\right)$ d. $1\frac{1}{2} \div \left(-\frac{5}{12}\right)$

11. **Choose A, B, C, or D.** In which set are all three values equal?
    A. $\frac{5}{11}$, 0.45, $\frac{45}{99}$ B. $\frac{3}{4}$, 0.72, $\frac{75}{100}$
    C. $\frac{2}{9}$, 0.022, $0.\overline{2}$ D. $\frac{1}{8}$, 0.125, 0.1250

12. Solve each equation.
    a. $x + \frac{5}{6} = -\frac{1}{2}$ b. $-\frac{9}{10}y = -\frac{3}{4}$
    c. $-1\frac{4}{5}n = -\frac{7}{9}$ d. $2\frac{1}{2}k = -10$

13. Find each square root.
    a. $\sqrt{144}$ b. $\sqrt{1.21}$
    c. $-\sqrt{400}$ d. $\sqrt{200}$

14. The lengths of two sides of a right triangle are given. Find the third length if c is the length of the hypotenuse.
    a. $c = 5, a = 3$
    b. $b = 30, c = 34$
    c. $a = 5, b = 12$
    d. $a = 48, c = 60$

15. After each bounce of a ball, it bounces $\frac{2}{3}$ as high as on the previous bounce. After the second bounce, the ball's highest point is 12 in. off the floor. How high was the ball before the first bounce?

Choose A, B, C, or D.

1. Which statement is *true*?

   A. $\frac{2}{7} + \frac{2}{5} = \frac{2}{7 + 5}$

   B. $\frac{5}{6} \div \frac{3}{4} = \left(\frac{5}{6} \div 3\right) \div 4$

   C. $\frac{2}{3} \cdot \frac{8}{3} = \frac{2 \cdot 8}{3}$

   D. $\frac{11}{8} - \frac{7}{8} = \frac{11 - 7}{8}$

2. Evan is twice as old as Ben. Four years ago, the sum of their ages was 10 years. How old is Evan now?

   A. 10 y   B. 12 y   C. 14 y   D. 16 y

3. A point P is reflected over the y-axis and then this image is reflected over the x-axis. This image is (2, 1). What are the coordinates of point P?

   A. $(-1, -2)$ B. $(-2, 1)$

   C. $(-2, -1)$ D. $(2, -1)$

4. Which statement is *false*?

   A. $6^0 = 1^0$ B. $(-1)^2 = 1^{-2}$

   C. $2^{-4} = 4^{-2}$ D. $(-3)^3 = 3^{-3}$

5. How many different prime factors does the number 504 have?

   A. 3   B. 5   C. 7   D. 9

6. Paul wants to put a metal strip around a rectangular piece of wood that is 6 in. by 9 in. How much metal strip should he buy?

   A. 15 in.   B. 30 in.   C. 36 in.   D. 54 in.

7. What is the best estimate for $6\frac{2}{3} \div \left(-\frac{5}{6}\right)$?

   A. $6 \cdot \left(-\frac{1}{2}\right) = -3$

   B. $7 \cdot (-2) = -14$

   C. $6 \div (-1) = -6$

   D. $7 \div (-1) = -7$

8. What is the range of the data given in the stem-and-leaf plot?

   $$
   \begin{array}{c|ccccccc}
   3 & 1 & 2 & 2 & 2 & & & \\
   4 & 3 & 4 & 5 & 5 & 9 & & \\
   5 & 0 & 0 & 2 & 3 & 6 & 8 & \\
   \end{array}
   $$
   $3 \mid 1$ means 31

   A. 58   B. 49   C. 27   D. 32

9. The data given in the stem-and-leaf plot above could most likely represent which quantity?

   A. birth weights in pounds

   B. heights of professional basketball players in inches

   C. numbers of hours spent exercising in one day

   D. numbers of minutes students spend studying for a test

10. If $x - 12 = -8$, what is the value of x?

    A. -20 B. -4 C. 4   D. 20

11. Which equation has a graph containing the points $(-3, 3)$, $(0, 1)$, and $(6, -3)$?

    A. $y = -x + 1$ B. $y = -3x + 1$

    C. $2x + 3y = 3$ D. $y = -\frac{2}{3}x$

12. What is the slope of the line in the graph?

    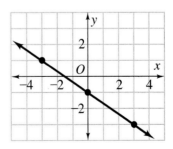

    A. $\frac{3}{2}$ B. $-\frac{3}{2}$ C. $\frac{2}{3}$ D. $-\frac{2}{3}$

6

Applications of Proportions

THEME:
SCALE
MODELS

Larger _than_ Life

Mount Rushmore is an example of a scale model that is larger than the objects on which it was based—much larger! Other types of scale models, such as some toys, are smaller than the objects on which they are based.

Build a Scale Model For your chapter project, you will build your own scale model. First, you will choose an object to model. Use your imagination! Your model can be larger or smaller than the actual object—you choose the scale. Finally, you will select building materials and assemble the model.

Steps to help you complete the project:

• **How to solve problems by drawing a diagram**

PROBLEM SOLVING

Exploring Ratios and Rates

What You'll Learn

1 To write ratios and express them in simplest form

2 To find unit rates

...And Why

You can use unit rates to compare gasoline consumption of different cars.

Here's How

Look for questions that
- build understanding
- ✔ check understanding

THINK AND DISCUSS

1 *Exploring Ratios*

In the United States, 2 out of every 5 people have brown eyes. In this statement, 2 and 5 form a ratio. A **ratio** is a comparison of two quantities by division. You can write ratios in several ways.

Arithmetic	**Algebra**
2 to 5 2 : 5 $\frac{2}{5}$	a to b $a : b$ $\frac{a}{b}(b \neq 0)$

1. ⬛ *Think About It* Give examples of ratios in everyday life.

You can use a ratio to compare a *part* to another *part*, a *part* to the *whole*, or the *whole* to a *part*.

■ EXAMPLE 1

Write three ratios using the jar of colored marbles.

$\frac{\text{part}}{\text{part}} \longrightarrow \frac{\text{blue}}{\text{yellow}} = \frac{7}{9}$

$\frac{\text{part}}{\text{whole}} \longrightarrow \frac{\text{blue}}{\text{total}} = \frac{7}{16}$

$\frac{\text{whole}}{\text{part}} \longrightarrow \frac{\text{total}}{\text{yellow}} = \frac{16}{9}$

2. ✔ *Try It Out* Write three other ratios for the jar of marbles.

To write a ratio in simplest form, you write it as a fraction and find the simplest form of the fraction.

Need Help? For practice writing equivalent fractions, see Skills Handbook page 610.

■ EXAMPLE 2

Write the ratio 48 seconds to 2 minutes in simplest form.

$\frac{48 \text{ s}}{2 \text{ min}} = \frac{48 \text{ s}}{120 \text{ s}}$ ⟵ Convert minutes to seconds so that both measures are in the same units.

$\frac{48}{120} = \frac{48 \div 24}{120 \div 24} = \frac{2}{5}$ ⟵ Divide the numerator and the denominator by the GCF, 24.

The ratio of 48 seconds to 2 minutes is $\frac{2}{5}$.

3. ✔ *Try It Out* Express each ratio in simplest form.

    a. $\frac{15}{33}$ **b.** $7 : 35$ **c.** 8 in. to 3 ft

▼2 *Finding Unit Rates*

A **rate** is a ratio comparing two different types of quantities, such as miles to gallons or feet to seconds. A **unit rate** is a rate that has a denominator of 1. To find a unit rate, divide both the numerator and the denominator by the denominator.

■ **EXAMPLE 3**   *Real-World Problem Solving*

Advertising An ad in the classified section of a newspaper costs $9 for six lines of copy. Find the unit rate.

$$\frac{\text{cost in dollars}}{\text{number of lines}} = \frac{9}{6} \quad \longleftarrow \begin{array}{l}\text{Write a rate comparing}\\ \text{dollars to lines.}\end{array}$$

$$= \frac{9 \div 6}{6 \div 6} \quad \longleftarrow \begin{array}{l}\text{Divide numerator and}\\ \text{denominator by 6.}\end{array}$$

$$= \frac{1.5}{1} \quad \longleftarrow \text{Simplify.}$$

The unit rate is $1.50 per line, or $1.50/line.

4. ⬛ *Calculator* The unit price of an item at a grocery store is a familiar example of a unit rate. Find the unit price of each box of cereal.

    a. $3.95 for 20 oz   **b.** $4.29 for 24 oz   **c.** $2.25 for 12 oz

It is easy to compare rates when they are expressed as unit rates.

■ **EXAMPLE 4**   *Real-World Problem Solving*

Consumer Issues Elena drove her car 224 miles on 9 gallons of gas. Manuel drove his car 330 miles on 14 gallons of gas. Which car got more miles per gallon?

$\frac{\text{miles}}{\text{gallon}} \longrightarrow \frac{224}{9} \approx 24.9 \text{ mi/gal} \quad \longleftarrow$ Find the unit rate for Elena's car.

$\frac{\text{miles}}{\text{gallon}} \longrightarrow \frac{330}{14} \approx 23.6 \text{ mi/gal} \quad \longleftarrow$ Find the unit rate for Manuel's car.

Elena's car got more miles per gallon than Manuel's car.

5. ✔ *Try It Out* A 1-liter bottle of apple juice costs $1.19. A 1.3-liter bottle costs $1.49. Which is the better buy?

Write three ratios that each model can represent.

1.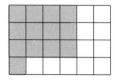

2.

3.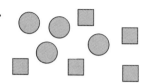

4. Write four ratios that are equal to the ratio 6 : 9.

Write each ratio in simplest form.

5. 4 : 28

6. $\frac{27}{9}$

7. 10 out of 16

8. $\frac{30}{45}$

9. 12 to 8

10. $\frac{35}{100}$

11. 11 out of 17

12. $\frac{48}{144}$

13. 4 to 18

14. $\frac{9}{30}$

15. 1 ft to 1 yd

16. 25 min to 2h

17. 8 in. to 4 ft

18. 12 min to 1 h

19. 10 s to 1 min

20. *Art* To make the color rose, you mix drops of food coloring. You use 5 drops of red, 1 drop of blue, and 2 drops of yellow.
    a. What is the ratio of yellow drops to the total number of drops, written in simplest form?
    b. How many drops of each color will you need to use if you use 24 drops of food coloring in all?

21. a. Today, Leneice is 16 years old and Josh is 12 years old. What is the ratio of Leneice's age to Josh's age?
    b. Will the ratio be the same two years from now? Explain.
    c. What happens to the ratio as they get older?

22. *Reasoning* A bag contains 7 red marbles and 5 black marbles. You must add 60 marbles to the bag, but the ratio of red to black marbles must remain the same. How many of each color should you add?

The table at the right shows the results of a survey. Write each of the ratios below as a fraction in simplest form and as a decimal rounded to the nearest hundredth.

23. *For* to *Against*

24. *Against* to *For*

25. *For* to the total

26. *Against* to the total

Choose Use a calculator, paper and pencil, or mental math to find each unit rate.

27. 20 gal in 4 min

28. $21 for 12 roses

29. 200 m in 22 s

30. 52 deliveries in 8 h

31. 36 people for 3 rooms

32. 780 mi in 3 days

33. 676 mi in 13 h

34. 412 words in 5 min

35. $66 for 8 h

36. *Cars* A midsize car can travel 200 mi on 7 gal of gasoline. A minivan can travel 350 mi on 12 gal. Which has the greater fuel efficiency? Explain.

37. *Consumer Issues* A carton of twelve cans of juice costs $3.99, while a carton of eight cans costs $2.79. Which is the better buy?

A SWEET *Spot*

VERMONT is one of the country's major producers of maple syrup. There are close to 2,500 maple growers in Vermont, each of whom taps an average of 1,000 trees. About 500,000 gallons of maple syrup are produced each year.

When the sap is running, growers collect it from their trees daily and boil it down to make the syrup.

Traditionally, the season for "sugaring," as this process is called, begins on the first Tuesday in March. In reality, though, the sap runs only when temperatures rise to 40°F–50°F during the day and fall to 20°F–30°F at night.

A grower can tap 7,000 gallons of sap from 1,000 trees per season, yielding 200 gallons of syrup, which is then sold at $4.50 per half-pint.

38. *Reading About Math* On average, how many trees are tapped per year in Vermont?

39. What is the ratio of the number of gallons of sap a grower taps to the number of gallons of syrup made from it, in simplest form?

40. Assume that a gallon of maple syrup sells at the same unit price as a half-pint. How much does a gallon of maple syrup cost? (1 gal = 8 pt)

41. a. *Open-ended* Calculate the unit price of a grocery item that you have in your home. Give the name of the item, the original price, and the original unit of measure.

   b. *Writing* Many states have laws requiring that the unit prices of grocery items be posted in stores. Explain why these laws were enacted.

Mixed Review

Write the prime factorization of each number. *(Lesson 5-1)*

42. 81   **43.** 2,400   **44.** 975   **45.** 914   **46.** 423   **47.** 144

In Exercises 48–53, state in which quadrant or on which axis you would find the point with the given coordinates.
(Lesson 4-1)

48. $(-4, 3)$ **49.** $(-6, -2)$ **50.** $(5, 0)$ **51.** $(4, -4)$ **52.** $(-2, 0.5)$ **53.** $(0, -3)$

54. *Choose a Strategy* Suppose you divide a number by -6, add 2, multiply by 10, and subtract 5. The result is 10. Find the number.

Math at Work

AUTOMOTIVE MECHANIC

If you have a good ability for diagnosing mechanical problems, you might consider a career as an automotive mechanic. An automotive mechanic must diagnose a car's problems and repair them. Mechanics also inspect and adjust the car's parts. An ability to reason and solve problems is a mathematical skill that an auto mechanic applies in diagnosing auto problems quickly and accurately. Mechanics also need to have good estimating skills when determining the approximate cost of a repair.

For more information about a career as an automotive mechanic, visit the Prentice Hall Web site: www.phschool.com

6-2 Units of Measurement

What You'll Learn

▼ To develop measurement sense

▼ To use dimensional analysis

...And Why

You can use dimensional analysis to express rates in different units of measure.

Here's How

Look for questions that
⊞ build understanding
✔ check understanding

Work Together
Developing Measurement Sense

Refer to the table at the bottom of this page. For each unit, describe something that you could reasonably measure using that unit. For instance, it would be reasonable to measure the weight of an elephant in tons, but not the weight of a raisin.

THINK AND DISCUSS

▼ *Developing Measurement Sense*

You are used to using two systems of measurement. The table below shows common customary and metric units.

Units of Measurement

Type	Unit	Equivalent
Length (customary)	inch (in.)	
	foot (ft)	1 ft = 12 in.
	yard (yd)	1 yd = 3 ft
	mile (mi)	1 mi = 5,280 ft
Length (metric)	centimeter (cm)	
	meter (m)	1 m = 100 cm
	kilometer (km)	1 km = 1,000 m
Volume (customary)	fluid ounce (fl oz)	
	cup (c)	1 c = 8 fl oz
	pint (pt)	1 pt = 2 c
	quart (qt)	1 qt = 2 pt
	gallon (gal)	1 gal = 4 qt
Volume (metric)	milliliter (mL)	
	liter (L)	1 L = 1,000 mL
Weight (customary)	ounce (oz)	
	pound (lb)	1 lb = 16 oz
	ton (t)	1 t = 2,000 lb
Mass (metric)	gram (g)	
	kilogram (kg)	1 kg = 1,000 g

When you measure an object, choose an appropriate unit.

■ **EXAMPLE 1** *Real-World Problem Solving*

What customary unit would you use for each measure?

a. weight of a truck   ton   ◄———A ton is a very large unit of weight.

b. volume of a juice box   fluid ounce ◄———A fluid ounce is a small unit of volume.

1. ✔ *Try It Out* What customary unit would you use for each measure?
   a. distance from coast to coast **b.** length of an insect wing

■ **EXAMPLE 2** *Real-World Problem Solving*

What metric unit would you use for each measure?

a. volume of a jug of cider   liter ◄———A liter is a large unit of volume.

b. mass of a serving of rice   gram ◄———A gram is a small unit of mass.

2. ✔ *Try It Out* What metric unit would you use for each measure?
   a. a child's height   **b.** volume of a thimble

▼ *Using Dimensional Analysis*

To convert units of measure, multiply by a ratio equal to 1, such as $\frac{5{,}280 \text{ ft}}{1 \text{ mi}}$. This process is called **dimensional analysis.**

3. ♣ *Think About It* Explain why the ratio $\frac{5{,}280 \text{ ft}}{1 \text{ mi}}$ is equal to 1.

4. For each pair of units, write a ratio that is equal to 1.
   a. feet and inches   **b.** kilometers and meters

■ **EXAMPLE 3**

Use dimensional analysis to convert 1.2 miles to feet.

$$1.2 \text{ mi} = \frac{1.2 \text{ mi}}{1} \cdot \frac{5{,}280 \text{ ft}}{1 \text{ mi}}$$ ◄———Multiply by a ratio that is equal to 1. Cancel matching units.

$$= \frac{(1.2)(5{,}280) \text{ ft}}{1}$$ ◄———Simplify.

$$= 6{,}336 \text{ ft}$$ ◄———Multiply.

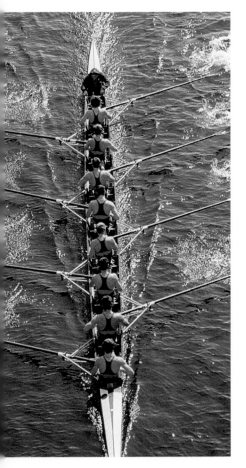

In Example 3, the ratio $\frac{5,280 \text{ ft}}{1 \text{ mi}}$ is called the *conversion factor.* If you are converting feet to miles, use the reciprocal of this ratio.

$$7,345 \text{ ft} = \frac{7,345 \text{ ft}}{1} \cdot \frac{1 \text{ mi}}{5,280 \text{ ft}} = \frac{7,345 \text{ mi}}{5,280} \approx 1.4 \text{ mi}$$

5. **⊞ Reasoning** Suppose that you need to convert a number of ounces to pounds. Explain how you decide whether to use $\frac{16 \text{ oz}}{1 \text{ lb}}$ or $\frac{1 \text{ lb}}{16 \text{ oz}}$ as a conversion factor.

6. ✔ **Try It Out** Use dimensional analysis to convert each measure.
   a. 72 oz = ▨ lb   b. 5 t = ▨ lb   c. 3.5 km = ▨ m

Sometimes you need to use two or more conversion factors. In Example 4, you will use two conversion factors to convert a rate.

■ **EXAMPLE 4**   *Real-World Problem Solving*

Rowing Princeton University won the 1996 Intercollegiate Rowing Association Regatta by completing the 2,000-m course at a rate of 6.07 m/s. Convert this rate to kilometers per minute.

$$\frac{6.07 \text{ m}}{1 \text{ s}} = \frac{6.07 \text{ m}}{1 \text{ s}} \cdot \frac{60 \text{ s}}{1 \text{ min}} \cdot \frac{1 \text{ km}}{1,000 \text{ m}}$$ ← Multiply by two ratios that are equal to 1. Cancel matching units.

$$= \frac{(6.07)(60)(1) \text{ km}}{1,000 \text{ min}}$$ ← Simplify.

6.07 ⊠ 60 ⊟ 1000 ⊟ *0.3642*   ← Use a calculator.

The Princeton team raced at a rate of 0.3642 km/min.

7. ✔ **Try It Out** Cantrell ran a road race at 0.15 mi/min. Convert his rate to feet per second.

You can also use dimensional analysis to estimate. Suppose you want to know approximately how many hours are in 126 min. Because you will use the conversion factor of $\frac{1 \text{ h}}{60 \text{ min}}$, round 126 to 120, an amount easily divisible by 60.

$$126 \text{ min} \approx 120 \text{ min} = \frac{120 \text{ min}}{1} \cdot \frac{1 \text{ h}}{60 \text{ min}} = \frac{120 \text{ h}}{60} = 2 \text{ h}$$

So, 126 min is about 2 h. Rounding numbers to make them easier to divide is an example of using *compatible numbers.*

8. **⊞ Estimation** Use compatible numbers to estimate the number of cups in 50 fl oz.

What customary unit would you use for each measure?

1. length of a pencil

2. weight of a plum

3. volume of a baby bottle

4. weight of a bookcase

5. volume of a gas tank

6. height of a ceiling

7. volume of a coffee cup

8. distance to Mexico

9. weight of a car

What metric unit would you use for each measure?

10. volume of a paper cup

11. length of a bowling lane

12. mass of an adult

13. mass of an apple

14. volume of a large pot

15. height of a person

16. length of an index card

17. mass of a cracker

18. distance to Toronto

Use dimensional analysis to convert each measure.

19. 32 in. = ■ ft

20. 2,500 cm = ■ m

21. 3 km = ■ m

22. 15,000 g = ■ kg

23. 300 yd = ■ ft

24. 12.5 L = ■ mL

25. $1\frac{1}{2}$ mi = ■ ft

26. 325 d = ■ h

27. 68 oz = ■ lb

28. 9 gal = ■ c

29. $5\frac{1}{2}$ qt = ■ fl oz

30. 64 fl oz = ■ gal

31. *World Facts* In 1990, there were approximately 141,542,000 babies born in the world. About how many births was this per day? Per hour? Per minute? Per second?

32. *Research* Find information about the use of the metric system in the United States. In what industries is it used? What is the federal government's policy with regard to the metric system?

33. *Business* On an average business day in the United States, there are 9.5 million minutes of telephone calls. Express this rate as hours of telephone calls per business day.

34. *Writing* Describe a method you could use to estimate how many times you blink your eyes in a day, in a week, and in a year.

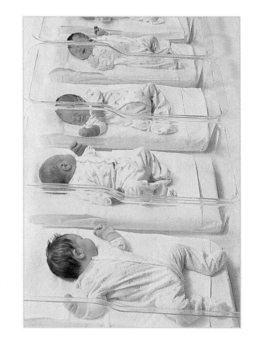

Use dimensional analysis to find an equal rate.

35. 90 in./min = ■ ft/min   **36.** $27/h = $■ /min   **37.** 12 cm/d = ■ cm/h

38. 12 qt/min = ■ gal/min   **39.** 60 mi/h = ■ ft/min   **40.** $6/h = ■ ¢/min

41. 14 cm/s = ■ m/h   **42.** 64 yd/h = ■ in./s   **43.** 90 km/h = ■ m/min

44. *Sports* Some pitchers can throw a baseball as fast as 95 mi/h. How many feet per second is this?

45. *Health* The average person needs $2\frac{1}{2}$ qt of water each day. How many gallons does the average person need per week?

46. a. *Nature* The cheetah, the fastest land animal, has been clocked at a speed at 92.4 ft/s. Convert the cheetah's speed to mi/h.
    b. *Reasoning* Do you think a cheetah actually can cover this distance in one hour? Explain.

Estimation **Use dimensional analysis to find a reasonable estimate.**

JOURNAL
About 41 foreign visitors arrive in the United States every minute. Explain how to express this rate as visitors per hour, visitors per day, and visitors per week.

47. 148 in. is about ■ ft.   **48.** 354 s is about ■ min.

49. 200 h is about ■ d.   **50.** 90 fl oz is about ■ c.

51. 500 min is about ■ h.   **52.** 3.04 mi is about ■ ft.

Mixed Review

Graph each linear equation. *(Lesson 4-2)*

53. $y = -x + 4$ **54.** $y = \frac{1}{2}x - 1$ **55.** $y = 2x - 2$ **56.** $y = -x + 3$ **57.** $y = 3x + 2$

Write each rational number as a ratio in the form $\frac{a}{b}$.
(Lesson 5-2)

58. -3 **59.** 0.56   **60.** 6.4   **61.** $8\frac{1}{2}$ **62.** 23   **63.** -0.27

64. *Food* A raisin has 4 calories and weighs 4×10^{-2} oz. Write this weight as a decimal. *(Lesson 2-11)*

65. *Biology* The diameter of each red blood cell in the human body is 0.0003 inch. Write this measurement in scientific notation. *(Lesson 2-11)*

6-3 Solving Proportions

What You'll Learn

1 To solve proportions

2 To use proportions to solve problems

...And Why

You can use proportions to calculate the amount of foreign currency you would receive in exchange for dollars.

Here's How

Look for questions that
- build understanding
- ✔ check understanding

Work Together
Finding Equal Rates

Here are three activities that you could do for one minute: hop on one foot, do jumping jacks, or recite the alphabet.

1. Choose one of the activities. Have one person perform the activity, another person count the number of times the activity is performed, and a third person keep time for one minute. Express your count as a rate per minute.

2. **Go a Step Further** Use your answer from Question 1. Express it as a rate for 2 minutes, 5 minutes, and 60 minutes. Explain how you found each answer.

THINK AND DISCUSS

1 *Solving Proportions*

The rates that you investigated in the Work Together are equal rates, even though they cover different periods of time. With any two of the rates from the Work Together, you can write a proportion. A **proportion** is a statement that two ratios are equal. You can write a proportion in words or as an equation.

Arithmetic	**Algebra**
6 is to 9 as 8 is to 12.	a is to b as c is to d.
$\frac{6}{9} = \frac{8}{12}$	$\frac{a}{b} = \frac{c}{d}, b \neq 0, d \neq 0$

The cross product property is a property of proportions.

CROSS PRODUCT PROPERTY

In a proportion the **cross products** of the terms are equal.

$$\frac{6}{9} = \frac{8}{12} \quad \begin{array}{l} 9 \cdot 8 = 72 \\ 6 \cdot 12 = 72 \end{array} \quad \text{cross products}$$

Often a proportion involves a variable. To solve the proportion, you find a value of the variable that makes the statement true.

■ **EXAMPLE 1**

Solve $\frac{7}{12} = \frac{z}{51}$.

Estimate: The ratio $\frac{7}{12}$ is about $\frac{1}{2}$, so the value of z is about $\frac{1}{2}$ of 51, or 25.

$$\frac{7}{12} = \frac{z}{51}$$

$7 \cdot 51 = 12z$ ←—Write the cross products.

$357 = 12z$ ←—Multiply.

$\frac{357}{12} = \frac{12z}{12}$ ←—Divide each side by 12.

$29.75 = z$ ←—Simplify.

3. ✔ *Try It Out* Solve each proportion.

   a. $\frac{x}{8} = \frac{3}{10}$ **b.** $\frac{4}{9} = \frac{15}{n}$ **c.** $\frac{5}{g} = \frac{8}{25}$

▼2 *Using Proportions to Solve Problems*

You can use proportions to solve many types of problems.

■ **EXAMPLE 2**   *Real-World Problem Solving*

Money–changing stores make a profit by charging a fee or by building a fee into the exchange rate they offer their customers.

▦ *Money* On a recent day, the exchange rate for dollars to French francs was 0.175. On this day, how many francs would you receive for 250 dollars?

Let f represent the number of francs.

dollars → $\frac{0.175}{1} = \frac{250}{f}$ ←— dollars
francs →   ←— francs

$0.175f = 1 \cdot 250$ ←—Write the cross products.

$\frac{0.175f}{0.175} = \frac{250}{0.175}$ ←—Divide each side by 0.175.

250 ▣ 0.175 ▤ *1428.5714* ←—Use a calculator.

You would receive about 1,429 francs.

4. ✔ *Try It Out* On a recent day, the exchange rate for dollars to British pounds was 1.6049. How many pounds would you receive for 250 dollars?

1. a. Write two proportions that the model at the right could represent.

   b. Draw a model to represent
   6 is to 16 as 3 is to 8.

Mental Math **Solve each proportion mentally.**

2. $\dfrac{2}{9} = \dfrac{10}{a}$

3. $\dfrac{k}{4} = \dfrac{21}{12}$

4. $\dfrac{45}{15} = \dfrac{y}{1}$

5. $\dfrac{12}{t} = \dfrac{8}{6}$

6. $\dfrac{16}{7} = \dfrac{8}{x}$

7. $\dfrac{100}{b} = \dfrac{150}{9}$

8. $\dfrac{12}{9} = \dfrac{w}{12}$

9. $\dfrac{x}{42} = \dfrac{9}{14}$

10. Choose A, B, C, or D. Which proportion does *not* have the same solution as the others?

   A. $\dfrac{3.9}{4.7} = \dfrac{n}{5}$

   B. $\dfrac{3.9}{n} = \dfrac{4.7}{5}$

   C. $\dfrac{n}{4.7} = \dfrac{5}{3.9}$

   D. $\dfrac{4.7}{3.9} = \dfrac{5}{n}$

11. Write three different proportions using the numbers 4, 12, 16, and 48.

Estimation **Estimate the solution of each proportion.**

12. $\dfrac{k}{20} = \dfrac{12}{47}$

13. $\dfrac{5}{2} = \dfrac{31}{b}$

14. $\dfrac{18}{5.9} = \dfrac{w}{7}$

15. $\dfrac{1.5}{r} = \dfrac{2.5}{4.97}$

16. $\dfrac{50}{r} = \dfrac{24}{7.8}$

17. $\dfrac{k}{19} = \dfrac{15}{7}$

18. $\dfrac{k}{4} = \dfrac{11}{45}$

19. $\dfrac{7}{3.6} = \dfrac{t}{21}$

Choose **Use a calculator, paper and pencil, or mental math to solve each proportion.**

20. $\dfrac{2}{5} = \dfrac{m}{45}$

21. $\dfrac{4}{k} = \dfrac{64}{264}$

22. $\dfrac{6}{25} = \dfrac{c}{30}$

23. $\dfrac{n}{27} = \dfrac{4.2}{9}$

24. $\dfrac{18}{11} = \dfrac{49.5}{s}$

25. $\dfrac{8}{0.5} = \dfrac{x}{5}$

26. $\dfrac{h}{12} = \dfrac{18}{45}$

27. $\dfrac{9}{4} = \dfrac{7}{k}$

28. 3 is to 8 as 50 is to *g*.   **29.** 6 is to 3 as *d* is to 7.   **30.** 8.1 is to 3 as *y* is to 1.

31. *Writing* In 3 hours, Jim can walk 14 miles. To find the time it would take to walk 25 miles, he wrote the proportion $\dfrac{3}{14} = \dfrac{25}{h}$. What was his mistake?

32. *Science* The seesaw shown at the right is balanced when $a : y = b : x$. Suppose that a 50-pound weight rests 29 inches from the fulcrum. You must place a 30-pound weight on the other side. How far from the fulcrum must you place it to balance the seesaw?

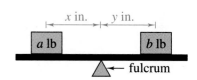

Write a proportion for each situation. Then solve.

33. *Shopping* Six oranges cost $1.00. What do 28 oranges cost?

34. *Exercise* Karla walks 1.5 miles in 22 minutes. How long will it take her to walk 4 miles?

35. *Business* Li Su paid $1.08 to make 18 copies at the Copy Shoppe. At that rate, how much would she pay for 40 copies?

36. *Nutrition* A 354-gram box of granola contains 20 grams of fat. The recommended serving size of granola is 55 grams. How many grams of fat does the recommended serving size contain?

37. *Money* On a particular day, the exchange rate for dollars to German marks was 0.5582. How many German marks would you receive in exchange for 350 dollars?

Mixed Review

Write each repeating decimal as a fraction or mixed number in simplest form. *(Lesson 5-3)*

38. $0.\overline{21}$ 　　39. $3.\overline{8}$ 　　40. $0.\overline{23}$ 　　41. $0.\overline{3}$ 　　42. $5.\overline{16}$ 　　43. $0.\overline{6}$

Solve each equation. Check the solution. *(Lesson 3-3)*

44. $368 = 2.3a$ 　　45. $3b = 54$ 　　46. $13c = 182$ 　　47. $64 = 4x$ 　　48. $4.8y = 15.36$

49. *Finance* Lovell's after-school business lost $12 a week for 4 weeks, broke even for 2 weeks, and made $30 a week for 2 weeks. Describe his profit at the end of 8 weeks. *(Lesson 2-5)*

CHAPTER PROJECT

PROJECT LINK: RESEARCHING

Decide which object you will model. Research (or measure) the real-life dimensions of that object, and list all of those dimensions. Then decide on the approximate size of your model.

Measuring Angles

Before Lesson 6-4

An **angle** is a geometric figure formed by two rays with a common endpoint. The rays are **sides** of the angle and the endpoint is the **vertex** of the angle. The angle at the right can be named in three different ways: $\angle A$, $\angle BAC$, or $\angle CAB$.

Angles can be classified by their measures.

Acute angle
less than 90°

Right angle
90°

Obtuse angle
greater than 90° but less than 180°

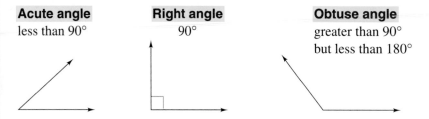

■ EXAMPLE

Measure the angle. Classify it as acute, right, or obtuse.

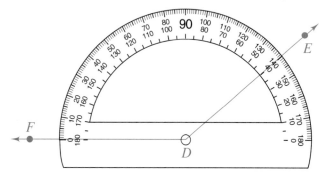

Read the number through which $\overrightarrow{DE}$ passes.

Line up side $\overrightarrow{DF}$ through 0° with D at the center of the protractor.

The measure of the angle is 140°. The angle is obtuse.

Measure each angle. Classify it as acute, right, or obtuse.

1.
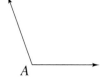

2.
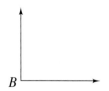

3.

4.
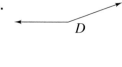

Draw an angle with the given measure.

5. 30°   **6.** 45°   **7.** 95°   **8.** 117°   **9.** 140°   **10.** 170°

6-4 Similar Figures and Proportions

QUICKreview

A polygon is a closed plane figure with at least three sides, each of which is a segment. Example:

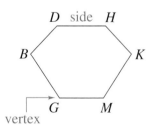

THINK AND DISCUSS

▼ 1 *Identifying Similar Polygons*

Figures that have the same shape but not necessarily the same size are **similar figures.** When you project a slide onto a screen, the image on the screen is similar to the image on the slide.

1. Name some other everyday examples of similarity.

The two triangles at the right are similar. The corresponding angles have equal measures. Angles that have equal measure are called **congruent angles.**

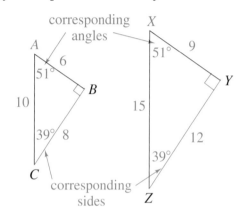

2. a. ▪ *Patterns* Find the ratios $\frac{AB}{XY}$, $\frac{BC}{YZ}$, $\frac{AC}{XZ}$, and $\frac{\text{perimeter of } \triangle ABC}{\text{perimeter of } \triangle XYZ}$. What do you notice?

b. Suppose you double the lengths of the sides of $\triangle ABC$. How would the perimeter change?

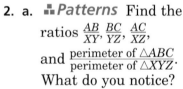

If two polygons are similar, then
- corresponding angles are congruent,
- corresponding sides are in proportion, and
- perimeters are in proportion to corresponding sides.

The symbol $\sim$ means *is similar to*. The symbol $\cong$ means *is congruent to*. For the triangles above, $\triangle ABC \sim \triangle XYZ$. You can identify these relationships among corresponding parts.

$\angle A \cong \angle X, \angle B \cong \angle Y, \angle C \cong \angle Z$ ← Corresponding angles are congruent.

$\dfrac{AB}{XY} = \dfrac{BC}{YZ} = \dfrac{AC}{XZ}$ ← Corresponding sides are in proportion.

■ EXAMPLE 1

Is rectangle *LMNO* similar to rectangle *HIJK*? Explain why or why not.

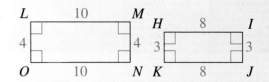

First, check to see if corresponding angles are congruent.

$\angle L \cong \angle H$
$\angle M \cong \angle I$
$\angle N \cong \angle J$ ⟵ All right angles have measure 90°.
$\angle O \cong \angle K$

Next, check to see if corresponding sides are in proportion.

$\dfrac{MN}{IJ} \stackrel{?}{=} \dfrac{LM}{HI}$ ⟵ $\overline{MN}$ corresponds to $\overline{IJ}$.
   $\overline{LM}$ corresponds to $\overline{HI}$.

$\dfrac{4}{3} \stackrel{?}{=} \dfrac{10}{8}$ ⟵ Substitute.

$4 \cdot 8 \stackrel{?}{=} 3 \cdot 10$ ⟵ Write the cross products.

$32 \neq 30$ ⟵ The cross products are not equal, so the sides are not in proportion.

Corresponding sides are not in proportion, so rectangle *LMNO* is *not* similar to rectangle *HIJK*.

▼2 Finding Unknown Lengths

You can use proportions to find unknown lengths in similar figures.

■ EXAMPLE 2

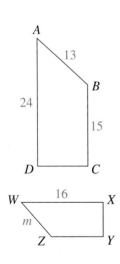

Given that trapezoid *ABCD* ~ trapezoid *WZYX*, find *m*.

$\dfrac{AD}{WX} = \dfrac{AB}{WZ}$ ⟵ $\overline{AD}$ corresponds to $\overline{WX}$.
   $\overline{AB}$ corresponds to $\overline{WZ}$.

$\dfrac{24}{16} = \dfrac{13}{m}$ ⟵ Substitute.

$24 \cdot m = 16 \cdot 13$ ⟵ Write the cross products.

$\dfrac{24m}{24} = \dfrac{208}{24}$ ⟵ Multiply. Then divide each side by 24.

$m = 8\dfrac{2}{3}$ ⟵ Simplify.

3. ✔ Try It Out Find the length of $\overline{YZ}$.

Example 3 involves overlapping similar polygons.

■ EXAMPLE 3

$\triangle JKL \sim \triangle GKH$. Find the value of t.

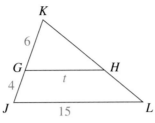

$$\frac{KG}{KJ} = \frac{GH}{JL} \qquad \leftarrow \begin{array}{l} \overline{KG} \text{ corresponds to } \overline{KJ}. \\ \overline{GH} \text{ corresponds to } \overline{JL}. \end{array}$$

$$\frac{6}{10} = \frac{t}{15} \qquad \leftarrow \text{Substitute. Notice that } KJ = 6 + 4 = 10.$$

$$6 \cdot 15 = 10 \cdot t \qquad \leftarrow \text{Write the cross products.}$$

$$\frac{90}{10} = \frac{10t}{10} \qquad \leftarrow \text{Multiply. Then divide each side by 10.}$$

$$9 = t \qquad \leftarrow \text{Simplify.}$$

4. ✔ **Try It Out** Suppose $KL = 15$. What is the length of $\overline{KH}$? The length of $\overline{HL}$?

EXERCISES *On Your Own*

Tell whether each figure contains a pair of similar polygons. If so, state the similarity.

1.
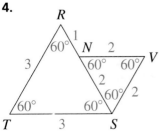

2.
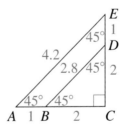

3.
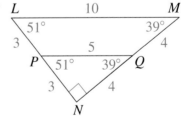

4.
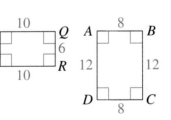

5.
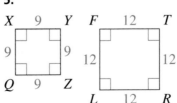

6.
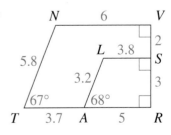

Each figure shows a pair of similar polygons. Find each unknown length.

7.

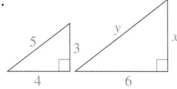

8.

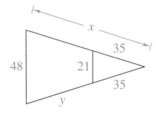

9.

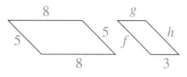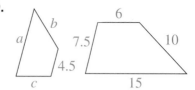

10.

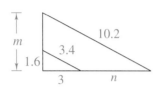

11.

12. **Theater** A frame of movie film is 35 mm wide and 26.25 mm high. The film is projected on a screen so that the image is 8 m high. How wide is the image?

13. **Writing** Suppose that two polygons have corresponding angles congruent and corresponding sides congruent. Are the polygons similar? Explain why or why not.

14. **Choose A, B, C, or D.** Which statement is *false?*
    A. All squares are similar.
    B. Corresponding angles of similar triangles are congruent.
    C. Not all circles are similar.
    D. Not all rectangles are similar.

15. **Open-ended** Give some real-life examples of objects or machines that produce similar figures.

16. A right triangle with sides of lengths 3 cm, 4 cm, and 5 cm is similar to a right triangle with side lengths 12 cm, 16 cm, and 20 cm. What is the perimeter of the larger triangle? Find the ratio of corresponding sides and the ratio of the perimeters. What do you notice?

Choose Use a calculator, pencil and paper, or mental math to compare each pair of numbers. Use >, <, or =. *(Lesson 5-4)*

17. $\frac{16}{20}$ ■ 0.8 **18.** $\frac{7}{8}$ ■ 0.85 **19.** $\frac{18}{12}$ ■ -1.5 **20.** $\frac{11}{50}$ ■ 0.25 **21.** $\frac{5}{14}$ ■ $-0.\overline{3}$

Find the slope and *y*-intercept of each equation.
(Lesson 4-4)

22. $y = 12x + 4$ **23.** $y = 4 - x$ **24.** $14x - 2y = 1$ **25.** $2x + y = -16$

26. *Choose a Strategy* Paulina places a long-distance call to her grandparents in London and talks for 45 minutes. The long-distance company bills the call at the rate of $0.10 per half minute. How much does the call cost Paulina?

CHAPTER
PROJECT

PROJECT LINK: WRITING

Choose the material from which you will construct your model. The material can be wood, papier-mâché, clay, or something else. Explain your choice, stating advantages and disadvantages of using various materials for the type of scale model you are building.

✓ CHECKPOINT 1   *Lessons 6-1 through 6-4*

1. *Business* It costs $38 to have eight pages of notes typed. What is the unit rate?

2. *Aviation* An airplane is flying at 455 miles per hour. What is its speed in feet per minute?

3. What metric unit would you use to measure the volume of a gasoline tank?

4. What customary unit would you use to measure the weight of a pumpkin?

Solve each proportion.

5. $\frac{2}{5} = \frac{n}{15}$ **6.** $\frac{0.7}{k} = \frac{7}{28}$ **7.** $\frac{16}{15} = \frac{4}{m}$

8. The figure at the right shows a pair of similar triangles. Find the value of each variable.

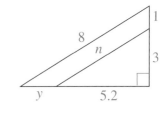

6-5

Similarity Transformations

What You'll Learn

▼ **1** To locate dilation images

▼ **2** To find the scale factor of a dilation

...And Why

You can use a similarity transformation to enlarge or reduce a logo to the desired size.

Here's How

Look for questions that

- ▪ build understanding
- ✔ check understanding

Work Together

Exploring Dilations

1. Have each member of your group plot $A(4, 2)$, $B(8, 2)$, $C(4, 5)$, and $O(0, 0)$ on graph paper. Draw $\triangle ABC$.

2. Use a different color to draw rays $\overrightarrow{OA}$, $\overrightarrow{OB}$, and $\overrightarrow{OC}$.

3. Use a compass to locate point A' on $\overrightarrow{OA}$ so that $\overline{AA'} \cong \overline{OA}$, as shown below. Locate points B' and C' in a similar manner.

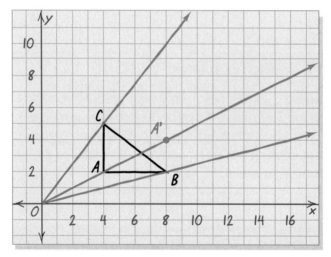

4. ▪ **Think About It** Draw $\triangle A'B'C'$. What appears to be true about $\triangle ABC$ and $\triangle A'B'C'$? Explain your answer.

THINK AND DISCUSS

1 Locating Dilation Images

The transformation in the Work Together is a dilation. Every **dilation** has a center and a scale factor. In the Work Together, the center of the dilation was the origin. The **scale factor** of a dilation describes the size of the change from the original figure to its image. The scale factor in the Work Together was 2.

As you noticed, the image of a figure after a dilation is similar to the original figure. A dilation is a similarity transformation.

This dilation has center C and scale factor 3, so $CR' = 3 \cdot CR$.

■ EXAMPLE 1

Find the image of
△*ABC* after a dilation
with center *A* and scale
factor $\frac{1}{2}$.

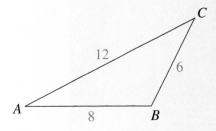

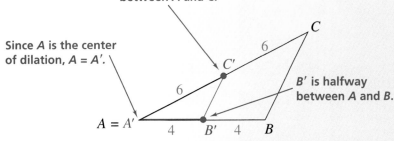

C' is halfway
between A and C.

Since A is the center
of dilation, A = A'.

B' is halfway
between A and B.

△*A'B'C'* is the image of △*ABC* after a dilation with
center *A* and scale factor $\frac{1}{2}$. △*ABC* ~ △*A'B'C'*

To find the image of a figure on the coordinate plane after a
dilation with center (0, 0), you multiply the *x*- and *y*-coordinates
by the scale factor. For example, for a dilation with scale factor 4,
you use the rule $(x, y) \longrightarrow (4x, 4y)$.

■ EXAMPLE 2

Find the coordinates of
the image of quadrilateral
KLMN after a dilation
with center at the origin
and scale factor $\frac{3}{2}$. Then
graph the image.

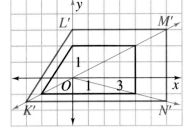

$$K(-2,-1) \longrightarrow K'\left(-3,-\tfrac{3}{2}\right)$$
$$L(0, 2) \longrightarrow L'(0, 3)$$
$$M(4, 2) \longrightarrow M'(6, 3)$$
$$N(4,-1) \longrightarrow N'\left(6,-\tfrac{3}{2}\right)$$

←— Multiply the *x*- and
y-coordinates of each
point by $\frac{3}{2}$.

5. ✔ Try It Out Find the coordinates of the image of
quadrilateral *KLMN* after a dilation with center at the origin
and scale factor 3.

2 Finding a Scale Factor

Notice that the image of △ABC in Example 1 is smaller than the original figure and that the image of *KLMN* in Example 2 is larger than the original figure. If the image is larger than the original figure, the dilation is an **enlargement.** If the image is smaller than the original figure, the dilation is a **reduction.**

6. ⋅ Look Back What scale factors produce enlargements? Reductions?

7. ⋅ Think About It What is true of the image of a figure after a dilation with scale factor 1?

■ EXAMPLE 3

The blue figure is a dilation of the red figure. Find the scale factor.

a.

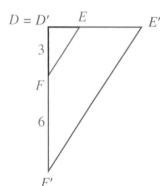

$$\frac{D'F'}{DF} = \frac{3+6}{3} = 3$$

b.

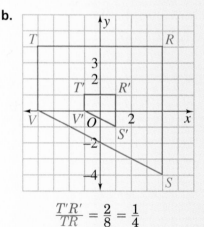

$$\frac{T'R'}{TR} = \frac{2}{8} = \frac{1}{4}$$

This large boot is located at the North Star Mall in San Antonio, Texas.

EXERCISES *On Your Own*

Copy △ABC and point O. Draw the image of △ABC under a dilation with the given center and scale factor.

1. center A, scale factor 2

2. center B, scale factor $\frac{1}{2}$

3. center O, scale factor 3

4. center C, scale factor 1.5

5. center A, scale factor $\frac{2}{3}$

6. center O, scale factor $\frac{1}{3}$

Graph quadrilateral *ABCD* and its image *A'B'C'D'* after a dilation with center (0, 0) and the given scale factor. Give the coordinates of the vertices of *A'B'C'D'*.

7. $A(-2, -1)$, $B(2, 0)$, $C(2, 2)$, $D(-1, 2)$; scale factor 2

8. $A(-3, 0)$, $B(1, -4)$, $C(5, 0)$, $D(1, 4)$; scale factor $\frac{1}{2}$

9. $A(0, 1)$, $B(2, 3)$, $C(1, 4)$, $D(-1, 2)$; scale factor 3

Each blue figure is a dilation of the adjacent red figure. Find the scale factor and classify each dilation as an enlargement or a reduction.

10.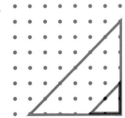

11.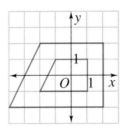

12.

13.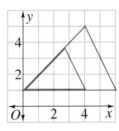

14.

15.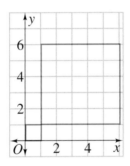

16.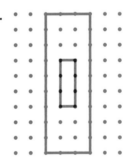

17.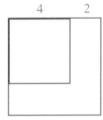

18. **a.** Graph a square with vertices $A(1, 1)$, $B(4, 1)$, $C(4, 4)$, and $D(1, 4)$.
   b. Find the area of $ABCD$.
   c. Graph $A'B'C'D'$, the image of $ABCD$ after a dilation with center (0, 0) and scale factor 2.
   d. Find the area of $A'B'C'D'$.
   e. Find the ratio of the area of $A'B'C'D'$ to the area of $ABCD$.
   f. Repeat parts (b)–(e) with $A''B''C''D''$, the image of $ABCD$ after a dilation with center (0, 0) and scale factor 3.
   g. *Writing* Explain how the area of the image of a square under a dilation with scale factor r compares to the area of the original square.

19. *Business* You have a copy of your company logo that is 6.2 cm wide. You need to make a reduced color copy of the logo that is 3.4 cm wide. What scale factor should you choose on the copy machine?

20. *Geometry* A triangle has three 60° angles and three sides of length 60 cm. The triangle is dilated with a scale factor of 1.75.
    a. What are the lengths of the sides of the image?
    b. What are the measures of the angles of the image?

21. △*A'B'C'* is the image of △*ABC* after a dilation. *AB* = 7 cm, *AC* = 8 cm, *A'B'* = 14 cm, and *B'C'* = 18 cm.
    a. What is the scale factor of the dilation?
    b. Find *BC* and *A'C'*.
    c. Find the perimeter of △*ABC* and of △*A'B'C'*.
    d. How do the two perimeters compare?

Mixed Review

Graph each equation by finding the *x*- and *y*-intercepts.
(Lesson 4-6)

22. $3x + 4y = 12$ 23. $x - 5y = 10$ 24. $4x - 3y = 24$ 25. $7x + 2y = 42$

Find each sum or difference. Write each answer as a fraction or mixed number in simplest form. *(Lesson 5-5)*

26. $\frac{5}{17} + \frac{15}{17}$ 27. $\frac{12}{21} + \frac{2}{21}$ 28. $-\frac{3}{8} - \frac{7}{8}$ 29. $\frac{7}{13} + \frac{6}{13}$ 30. $\frac{9}{11} - \frac{2}{11}$

31. *Business* Vinay takes a job at a local computer store at a salary of $180 per week plus a $35 commission on every computer that he sells. Compute his pay for a week in which he sells 7 computers. *(Lesson 3-6)*

CHAPTER PROJECT

PROJECT LINK: CALCULATING

Is your scale model an enlargement or a reduction of the actual object? Give the scale factor. Then, for each dimension listed in the Project Link on page 295, calculate the corresponding dimension of the scale model.

Geometry Software and Dilations

After Lesson 6-5

You can use dynamic geometry software to dilate a figure. To do so, use the dilation command. The software will prompt you to specify a center of dilation and a scale factor.

■ EXAMPLE

Use dynamic geometry software to draw a triangle $\triangle ABC$, and then draw a point D on $\overline{AB}$. Create the image of $\triangle ABC$ after a dilation with center D and scale factor 2.5.

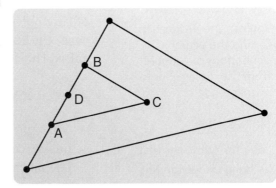

The result of following the instructions above is shown at the right. When you use your mouse to move point D, the entire image will move, too. When you move any of the vertices of $\triangle ABC$, the image will change, too.

Use geometry software to draw a triangle $\triangle EFG$, and then draw a point H not on the triangle. Create the image of $\triangle EFG$ after a dilation with center H and scale factor 1.75. Label the image $\triangle IJK$.

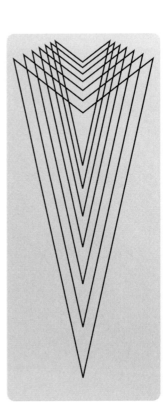

1. Describe the relationship between $\triangle EFG$ and $\triangle IJK$ when point H is moved anywhere inside of $\triangle EFG$.

2. Move point H outside of $\triangle EFG$. When H is outside of $\triangle EFG$, is it possible for $\triangle EFG$ and $\triangle IJK$ to have no points in common? One point in common? Two points in common? More than two points in common? Print an example of each case.

3. Describe the location of point H if points E and F are on $\overline{IJ}$.

4. Describe the location of point H if point F is on $\overline{IJ}$ and point G is on $\overline{IK}$.

5. *Design* Draw a figure, then dilate it repeatedly to create a design. You may want to include other transformations, such as rotations, in your design. Print the design, then color it.

6-6 Using Proportions to Solve Problems

What You'll Learn

▼ Using proportions to solve problems

...And Why

You can use proportions to find the actual dimensions of a figure from the dimensions of a scale model.

Here's How

Look for questions that
- build understanding
- ✔ check understanding

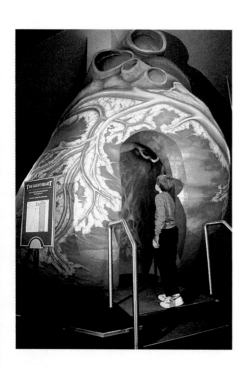

THINK AND DISCUSS

A **scale model** of an object is similar to the actual object. Many scale models, such as trains and doll houses, are smaller than the objects they represent. Other models are larger scale models of tiny objects, such as insects and microorganisms. In either case, the ratio of the length of the model to the actual length is called the **scale** of the model.

■ **EXAMPLE**   *Real-World Problem Solving*

Museums The Museum of Science and Industry in Chicago has a scale model of a human heart that is large enough for people to walk through. The height of the scale model is 16 ft. The scale used is 1 ft : $\frac{9}{32}$ in. What is the height of the actual heart on which the model is designed?

Let h = height of the actual heart.

Write a proportion.

$$\underset{\text{actual height (in.)}}{\overset{\text{model height (ft)}}{\longrightarrow}} \ \frac{1}{\frac{9}{32}} = \frac{16}{h} \ \underset{\longleftarrow \text{ actual height (in.)}}{\overset{\longleftarrow \text{ model height (ft)}}{}}$$

$$1 \cdot h = 16 \cdot \frac{9}{32} \qquad \longleftarrow \text{Write the cross products.}$$

$$h = \cancel{16}^{1} \cdot \frac{9}{\cancel{32}_{2}} \qquad \longleftarrow \text{Divide by the GCF.}$$

$$h = \frac{9}{2} \qquad \longleftarrow \text{Simplify.}$$

$$h = 4\frac{1}{2} \qquad \longleftarrow \begin{array}{l}\text{Write the improper fraction}\\\text{as a mixed number.}\end{array}$$

The height of the actual heart is $4\frac{1}{2}$ in.

1. ✔ *Try It Out* The width of the actual heart on which the model is designed is $3\frac{3}{4}$ in. What is the width of the scale model?

2. ▪ *Reasoning* Is it possible to use a different proportion to solve the problem? Explain.

1. **Construction** A builder wants to make a model of the farm silo pictured at the right. The scale of the model will be 1 in. : $2\frac{1}{2}$ ft.
   a. What will be the height of the model silo?
   b. What will be the diameter of the model silo?
   c. Suppose that the scale of the model is changed to 1 in. : 6 ft. What will be the height and the diameter of the model?
   d. A competing builder made a model of the silo that is 20 in. high. What is the scale of this model? (Give your answer in the form 1 in. : ■ ft.)

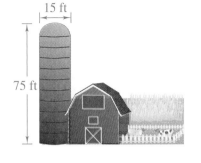

15 ft

75 ft

Architecture The diagram at the right is an architect's plan for a bedroom and bath area. Measure the blueprint with an inch ruler to answer the questions.

2. How many feet wide are the doors leading into the bedroom and into the bath?

3. How wide is the widest part of the bedroom?

4. **Writing** Could a bed 6 feet long and 3 feet wide fit into the narrow section of the bedroom? Explain why or why not.

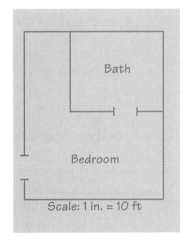

Bath

Bedroom

Scale: 1 in. = 10 ft

Models Model trains built on the HO scale are $\frac{1}{87}$ the size of real trains. Models built on the N scale are $\frac{1}{160}$ the size of real trains. Use this information for Exercises 5–7.

5. Which models are larger, HO- or N-scale models?

6. A locomotive on a real train is about 50 ft long. How long is a model made on the HO scale? On the N scale?

7. A full-size passenger car is 80 ft long. A model of the car is $\frac{1}{2}$ ft long. On which scale was the model made?

8. **Open-ended** Choose an item such as a calculator, a pair of scissors, or a pen. Make a scale drawing. Be sure to include the scale.

9. **Sports** A tennis court is 36 ft wide and 78 ft long. Use an inch ruler to measure the scale drawing at the right. Find the scale used.

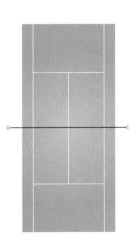

SCALE: 1 cm = 100 km

Maps **Use the map above and a metric ruler.**

10. **a.** What is the map distance between Abilene and Houston?
    b. What is the actual distance in kilometers?

11. How far is it from Lubbock to Austin in kilometers?

12. What city on the map is about 290 km from Ft. Worth?

13. *Theater* Suppose you want to make an actor 5 ft tall appear to be shrunk to the height of a tissue box. A regular tissue box is $9\frac{1}{2}$ in. long, $4\frac{3}{4}$ in. wide, and 4 in. tall. What must be the dimensions of your stage model?

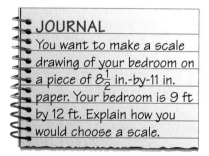

JOURNAL
You want to make a scale drawing of your bedroom on a piece of $8\frac{1}{2}$ in.-by-11 in. paper. Your bedroom is 9 ft by 12 ft. Explain how you would choose a scale.

Mixed Review

$A(3, 8)$, $B(6, 4)$, $C(2, 2)$, and $D(1, 5)$ are the vertices of a quadrilateral. Graph each of the following. *(Lesson 4-10)*

14. a 90° rotation of *ABCD* about the origin   15. a 180° rotation of *ABCD* about the origin

Estimate to the nearest whole number. *(Lesson 5-9)*

16. $\sqrt{54}$ 17. $\sqrt{98}$ 18. $\sqrt{256}$ 19. $\sqrt{401}$ 20. $\sqrt{65}$ 21. $\sqrt{220}$

22. *Choose a Strategy* A garage charges $3 for the first hour and $.75 for each additional hour. Todd parks at 9:00 A.M. If he pays $5.25, during what time period does he return?

6-7 Draw a Diagram

Problem Solving Strategies

- ✔ Draw a Diagram
- Guess and Test
- Look for a Pattern
- Make a Model
- Make a Table
- Simulate the Problem
- Solve a Simpler Problem
- Too Much or Too Little Information
- Use Logical Reasoning
- Use Multiple Strategies
- Work Backward
- Write an Equation

THINK AND DISCUSS

Diagrams can help you to picture the facts in problems involving distances and lengths.

SAMPLE PROBLEM..

Calvin and Shawn are 200 feet apart. A flagpole is halfway between them. Both boys begin walking at the same speed toward one another. Halfway to the flagpole, Calvin realizes that he dropped his keys at his starting point. He goes back, picks up his keys, and walks toward the pole again. How far are Calvin and Shawn from the flagpole when they finally meet?

....

 READ

Read for understanding. Summarize the problem.

Think about what you know and what you need to find out.

1. How far apart are the boys at the start?

2. How far from the flagpole is each boy at the start? How do you know?

3. Is it important to know that the boys walk at the same speed? Explain why or why not.

 PLAN

Decide on a strategy.

The problem involves movement and distances, so drawing a diagram might be a good strategy. Since Calvin and Shawn are walking along the same line, the diagram can involve a line. Since the boys do not always move in the same direction, the diagram should show the changes in direction.

 SOLVE

Try the strategy.

Draw a line. Show the starting positions, the position of the flagpole, and the distance the boys are apart at the start.

Next, draw Calvin's and Shawn's movements in order.

Step 1 They walk halfway to the flagpole.

Step 2 Calvin returns. Shawn continues toward Calvin.

Step 3 Calvin starts again. Shawn continues.

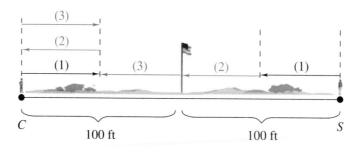

4. How far are the boys from the flagpole when they meet?

5. Use your diagram to determine how far each boy walked. What should be true about these distances?

LOOK BACK

Think about how you solved the problem.

6. Suppose Calvin and Shawn were 400 feet apart at the beginning of the problem. How would the outcome change?

EXERCISES *On Your Own*

Use diagrams to solve each problem.

1. A ball is dropped from a height of 64 ft. With each bounce, the ball reaches a height that is half the height of the previous bounce. After which bounce will the ball rebound to a maximum height of 6 in.?

2. Jane leaves New York on a cross-country car trip at 7 A.M. She averages 40 mi/h. Alice plans to take exactly the same route but does not leave until 8 A.M. She averages 50 mi/h. At what time will she pass Jane?

3. Snoozles are always born as twins, and each snoozle always moves in the opposite direction from its twin. Twin snoozles are at the origin. One follows the path (0, 0) to (1, 3) to (2, 2) to (4, 7). What path will its twin follow?

4. A delivery truck leaves a store and travels in the following directions: 6 km east, then 4 km south, then 2 km west, and then 7 km north. At the end of the route, how far is the truck from the store?

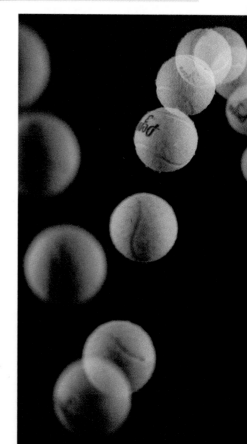

Use any strategy to solve each problem. Show your work.

5. Two 24-gal water tanks are next to each other. Tank A is half full, and tank B is one-third full. A pump transfers water from tank A to tank B at the rate of 8 gal/min. Another pump transfers water from tank B back to tank A at 6 gal/min.
   a. Which tank is losing water? Which tank is gaining?
   b. How many gallons per minute are being added to the tank that is being filled?
   c. Which tank will be empty or full first? Explain.

6. Could you restack the blocks at the right to form a cube? If so, how many blocks would be along each edge of the cube?

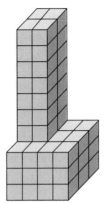

7. Alicia has started a business making toy trucks. Ten people work on the trucks in three steps: sanding, attaching the wheels, and painting. One person can sand 30 trucks per day, one person can attach wheels to 12 trucks per day, and one person can paint 20 trucks per day.
   a. How many employees should Alicia assign to each step so that no parts are left over at the end of the day?
   b. How many finished trucks can they produce in one day?

8. Eddie failed to study for his first quiz of the marking period, and he got only 1 point out of 10. If he gets a perfect 10 on all the other quizzes, how many more quizzes will it take him to bring his mean score up to a 9?

Mixed Review

Is a triangle with each given set of side lengths a right triangle? Explain. *(Lesson 5-10)*

9. 15 ft, 8 ft, 17 ft   10. 5 yd, 8 yd, 5 yd   11. 12 cm, 16 cm, 20 cm

Find the coordinates of the image point. *(Lesson 4-8)*

12. a translation of $P(3, -2)$ to the left 8 units and up 2 units

13. a translation of $Q(2, -3)$ to the right 2 units and down 8 units

14. *Videotapes* A videotape will record at most 6 hours of programs. Nancy has recorded $2\frac{2}{3}$ hours of a movie. Her friend Hideo wants to record $3\frac{1}{2}$ hours more of a football game on the same tape. Can he do this? Explain. *(Lesson 5-6)*

Choose the best answer.

1. In Room 109, 8 students are left-handed. 28 students are right-handed. What is the ratio of left-handed to right-handed?

   A. 2 to 5   **B.** 2 to 7   **C.** 5 to 2   **D.** 7 to 2

2. During exercise, Wendy's pulse for 10 seconds is 20 beats. What is the equivalent rate for 1 minute (60 seconds)?

   F. 10   **G.** 100   **H.** 120   **J.** 1200

3. A recipe for cookies calls for $2\frac{3}{4}$ cups of flour. If the recipe is doubled, how many cups of flour will be used?

   A. $4\frac{3}{4}$ c   **B.** $5\frac{1}{2}$ c   **C.** $3\frac{1}{2}$ c   **D.** $4\frac{1}{2}$ c

4. $\triangle ABC \sim \triangle DEF$. What is DE?

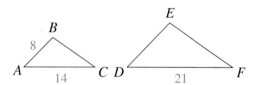

   F. $5\frac{1}{3}$ **G.** 12   **H.** 24   **J.** $36\frac{3}{4}$

5. Elisa is 5 feet tall and casts a 13-foot shadow. At the same time, a totem pole casts a 78-foot shadow. What is the pole's height?

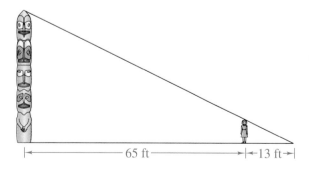

   A. 30 ft   **B.** 65 ft
   C. 78 ft   **D.** 202.8 ft

6. Diego plays on the Jordan High School basketball team. Diego is 6 ft 8 in. tall. How many inches is this?

   F. 68   **G.** 70   **H.** 80   **J.** 92

Please note that items 7–10 have *five* answer choices.

7. A computer program enlarges a scanned photo. The photo is 3 in. wide by 5 in. high. The enlargement can be at most 11 in. high. How wide will it be?

   A. $18\frac{1}{3}$ in.   **B.** 11 in.   **C.** $8\frac{1}{2}$ in.
   D. $6\frac{3}{5}$ in.   **E.** 5 in.

8. Anoki can build 3 tables in 5 hours. At this rate, how long will it take him to build 10 tables?

   F. $16\frac{2}{3}$ h   **G.** $11\frac{2}{3}$ h   **H.** 10 h
   J. 6 h   **K.** Not Here

9. The Kovaks are on a 400-mile trip. They have driven 220 miles in 4 hours. If they continue traveling at this rate, which proportion will give the total time T they travel?

   A. $\frac{400}{4} = \frac{220}{T}$ **B.** $\frac{220}{4} = \frac{400}{T}$

   C. $\frac{400}{180} = \frac{4}{T}$ **D.** $\frac{400}{220} = \frac{4}{T}$

   E. $\frac{400}{4} = \frac{180}{T}$

10. The Cubs have won 40 out of their first 100 games this year. Sixty-two games remain. If they keep winning at the same rate, what is a good estimate for how many of the 62 games they will win?

    F. 15   **G.** 25   **H.** 35
    J. 45   **K.** 55

6-8 Similarity and Indirect Measurement

What You'll Learn

▼ To measure distances indirectly using similar triangles

...And Why

You can use the length of a shadow to measure an object that is too tall to measure directly.

Here's How

Look for questions that
⚏ build understanding
✔ check understanding

THINK AND DISCUSS

You can measure some distances or lengths directly by using tools such as rulers or tape measures. Other distances or lengths, however, can only be measured by means of an **indirect measurement.** One common method of indirect measurement involves the use of similar triangles.

■ **EXAMPLE 1** *Real-World Problem Solving*

Measurement Jerome is 6 feet tall and casts a shadow 17 feet long. At the same time, a nearby tree casts a shadow 102 feet long. What is the height of the tree?

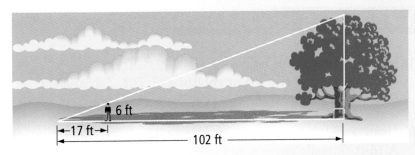

6 ft

├─17 ft─┤

102 ft

The rays of the sun, the shadows, and the heights form a pair of similar triangles. Set up a proportion.

Words • $\dfrac{\text{tree's height}}{\text{Jerome's height}} = \dfrac{\text{length of tree's shadow}}{\text{length of Jerome's shadow}}$

• Let h = tree's height

Proportion • $\dfrac{h}{6} = \dfrac{102}{17}$

$$17h = 6 \cdot 102 \qquad \longleftarrow \text{Write the cross products.}$$

$$h = \frac{6 \cdot 102}{17} = 36 \qquad \longleftarrow \begin{array}{l}\text{Divide each side by 17.}\\ \text{Then simplify.}\end{array}$$

The height of the tree is 36 ft.

1. ⚏*Look Back* What proportion would you use to solve the problem if Jerome were 5 feet 9 inches tall?

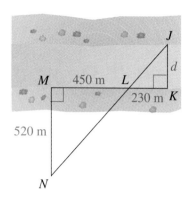

520 m

■ **EXAMPLE 2** *Real-World Problem Solving*

▦ *Surveying* A surveyor took the measurements shown in the figure at the left, where $\triangle JKL \sim \triangle NML$. Find d, the distance across the river.

Use the similar triangles to set up a proportion involving the lengths of corresponding sides.

$$\frac{JK}{NM} = \frac{KL}{ML} \qquad \longleftarrow \begin{array}{l} \overline{JK} \text{ corresponds to } \overline{NM}. \\ \overline{KL} \text{ corresponds to } \overline{ML}. \end{array}$$

$$\frac{d}{520} = \frac{230}{450} \qquad \longleftarrow \text{Substitute.}$$

$$450d = 520 \cdot 230 \qquad \longleftarrow \text{Write the cross products.}$$

$$d = \frac{520 \cdot 230}{450} \qquad \longleftarrow \text{Divide each side by 450.}$$

520 ✕ 230 ➗ 450 ▤ *265.77778*

The distance across the river is about 270 meters.

2. ✔ Try It Out If $NL = 688$ meters, find LJ.

EXERCISES *On Your Own*

1. In the figure at the right, $\triangle PQR \sim \triangle STR$.
   a. Write a proportion that relates PQ, QR, TR, and ST.
   b. Find d.

2. Draw and label similar triangles to illustrate this situation. A 15-ft flagpole casts a shadow 10 ft long. At the same time, a building that is 45 ft tall casts a shadow 30 ft long.

3. *Writing* Describe an everyday situation in which you might measure a distance indirectly.

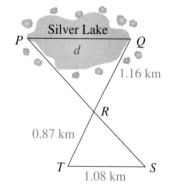

In each figure, use the similar triangles to find the unknown value.

4.
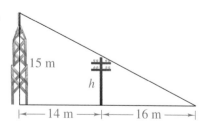

5.
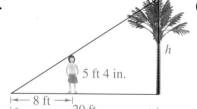

6.
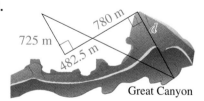

Use similar triangles to answer each question.

7. A girl $5\frac{1}{2}$ ft tall casts a shadow $8\frac{1}{4}$ ft long. She stands next to statue that has an 18-ft-long shadow. How tall is the statue?

8. *History* The Bunker Hill Monument in Charlestown, Massachusetts, is 221 ft tall. It casts a shadow 189 ft long at the same time that a nearby tree casts a shadow 29 ft long. To the nearest foot, how tall is the tree?

9. The tallest unsupported flagpole in the world is located in Vancouver, British Columbia. It casts a shadow 376 ft long at the same time that a man who is 6 ft tall casts a shadow 8 ft long. How tall is the flagpole?

10. Surveyors took the measurements below. In the diagram, $\triangle BDC \sim \triangle AEC$.

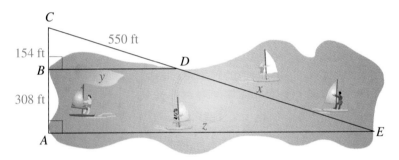

a. Use similar figures to find the value of x.
b. Use the Pythagorean theorem to find the value of y.
c. Use either similar triangles or the Pythagorean theorem to find the value of z.
d. Use the method that you did *not* choose in part (c) to show that the value of z checks.

11. *Critical Thinking* The figure at the right shows a method of indirect measurement involving a mirror. From optics, we know that $\angle YZX \cong \angle VZW$, and the triangles are similar.
a. Once you have placed the mirror on the floor, how do you determine where to stand?
b. State the similarity between the triangles.
c. Write a proportion you can use to find h.

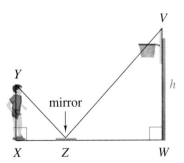

12. *Open-ended* Use the method illustrated in Exercise 11 to find the height of an object that is too tall for you to measure. Draw a diagram and describe your work.

Draw a figure with the given number of lines of symmetry. *(Lesson 4-9)*

13. four lines   **14.** no lines   **15.** five lines   **16.** three lines

Write the next two numbers in each pattern. *(Lessons 2-3 and 2-4)*

17. 576, 144, 36, 9, . . .   **18.** $-91, -76, -61, -46, . . .$ **19.** $-15, -14, -12, -9, . . .$

20. *Choose a Strategy* The number of infielders on a baseball team is one less than three times the number of pitchers. If there are eleven infielders, how many pitchers are there?

CHAPTER PROJECT

PROJECT LINK: ANALYZING

Select any two measurements on your scale model, and the two corresponding real-life dimensions of the object being modeled. Write a proportion using these four quantities. Then cross-multiply to verify that the proportion is true. Even if all of your work is accurate, the cross products may not be exactly equal. Explain why this is so.

✓ CHECKPOINT 2
Lessons 6-5 through 6-8

1. *Open-ended* Draw a triangle and label it $\triangle ABC$. Then draw its image under a dilation with center A and scale factor 2.

2. $\triangle XYZ$ has vertices $X(3, 0)$, $Y(6, -2)$, and $Z(0, -6)$. Find the coordinates of the vertices of its image after a dilation with center $(0, 0)$ and scale factor $\frac{1}{3}$.

3. **Choose A, B, C, or D.** On a map, two sites are 2 in. apart. The scale factor is 1 in. : 24 mi. What is the actual distance?

   A. 2 mi   **B.** 12 mi   **C.** 48 mi   **D.** $\frac{1}{2}$ mi

4. The scale of a model airplane is 1 in. : $3\frac{1}{2}$ ft. The wingspan of the plane is 35 ft. What is the wingspan of the model?

5. The triangles in the figure at the right are similar. Find the height h of the lighthouse.

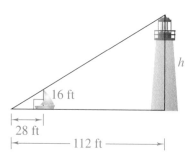

6-9

The Tangent Ratio

What You'll Learn

▼ **1** To find the tangent ratio

▼ **2** To solve problems using the tangent ratio

...And Why

You can use the tangent ratio to find measures indirectly.

Here's How

Look for questions that
- ⊞ build understanding
- ✔ check understanding

Work Together

Exploring the Tangent Ratio

1. a. Using graph paper and a protractor, draw ∠A, a 35° angle with one side on a horizontal line. Then choose vertical lines to draw segments $\overline{HG}$, $\overline{FD}$, and $\overline{CB}$ as shown.

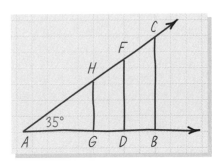

b. Use a centimeter ruler to measure the segments in the first two columns below to the nearest millimeter. Use a calculator to evaluate the ratios in the third column.

$BC =$ ■ $AB =$ ■ $\dfrac{BC}{AB} =$ ■

$DF =$ ■ $AD =$ ■ $\dfrac{DF}{AD} =$ ■

$GH =$ ■ $AG =$ ■ $\dfrac{GH}{AG} =$ ■

c. ⊞ **Patterns** What pattern do you notice in the ratios in the table? Compare the ratios you found with those of other members of your group.

2. Repeat Question 1, but this time, draw the figure so that $m\angle A = 62°$.

THINK AND DISCUSS

▼**1** *Finding the Tangent Ratio*

In the Work Together, you began the study of trigonometry, which comes from the Greek words meaning "triangle measurement." The ratio that you calculated is called the tangent ratio of ∠A. You discovered that the tangent ratio remains the same for any right triangle with the same measure of ∠A.

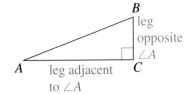

tangent of $\angle A = \dfrac{\text{length of leg opposite } \angle A}{\text{length of leg adjacent to } \angle A}$

You can abbreviate this equation as $\tan A = \dfrac{\text{opposite}}{\text{adjacent}}$.

EXAMPLE 1

In △RST at the right, find tan T.

$$\tan T = \frac{\text{length of leg opposite } \angle T}{\text{length of leg adjacent to } \angle T}$$

$$= \frac{36}{27}$$

$$= \frac{4}{3} = 1.\overline{3}$$

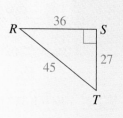

3. ✔ *Try It Out* Write tan R as a fraction and as a decimal.

4. ⠿ *Reasoning* How is tan R related to tan T?

You can use a calculator to find the tangent of any acute angle of a right triangle. To find tan 59°, use this key sequence.

59 TAN *1.6642794*   So, tan 59° ≈ 1.6643.

5. ⠿ *Calculator* Use a calculator to find each tangent. Round to the nearest ten-thousandth.
   a. tan 13°   **b.** tan 47°   **c.** tan 86°

▼2 *Solving Problems Using the Tangent Ratio*

You can use the tangent ratio to find measures indirectly.

■ EXAMPLE 2   *Real-World Problem Solving*

Rock Climbing In Yosemite National Park in California, a granite mass named El Capitan rises almost perpendicular to the valley floor. When you are standing 600 feet from the wall, you look up at an angle of 80° and see a rock climber near the top of El Capitan. Use indirect measurement to estimate the height of the climber.

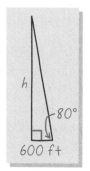

Draw a diagram to show the given measures. Let *h* represent the height of the climber.

$$\tan A = \frac{\text{opposite}}{\text{adjacent}} \quad \longleftarrow \text{Use the tangent ratio.}$$

$$\tan 80° = \frac{h}{600} \quad \longleftarrow \text{Substitute.}$$

$$h = 600(\tan 80°) \longleftarrow \text{Solve for } h.$$

600 ✕ 80 TAN ▤ *3402.7690*

The climber is about 3,400 feet above the ground.

6. ✔ *Try It Out* Find the value of *x* to the nearest tenth.

a.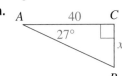

b.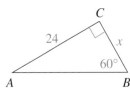

7. ▪ *Go a Step Further* Use your answers to Question 6 to find the length of the hypotenuse of each triangle. Round your answers to the nearest tenth.

EXERCISES *On Your Own*

1. Refer to $\triangle XYZ$ at the right.
   a. Which side is opposite $\angle X$? Opposite $\angle Z$?
   b. Which side is adjacent to $\angle X$? Adjacent to $\angle Z$?
   c. Find tan X and tan Z as fractions in simplest form and as decimals.
   d. What is the relationship between tan X and tan Z?

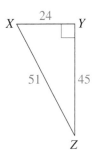

Use a calculator to find each tangent. Round to the nearest ten-thousandth.

2. tan $18°$

3. tan $85°$

4. tan $22°$

5. tan $45°$

Find tan *A* and tan *B* in each figure below. Express your answers as fractions in simplest form.

6.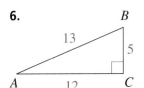

7.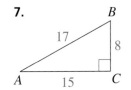

8.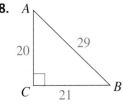

9.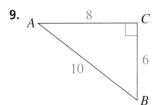

10. $\triangle PQR$ is a right triangle with $PQ = 25$, $PR = 60$, and $QR = 65$. Find tan Q as a fraction in simplest form and as a decimal. (*Hint:* The longest side of a right triangle is the hypotenuse.)

11. $\triangle ABC$ is a right triangle with $AB = 53$, $BC = 45$, and right angle C. Draw a diagram of $\triangle ABC$ and find tan A and tan B as fractions in simplest form. (*Hint:* Use the Pythagorean theorem.)

12. Refer to △RST at the right.

   a. Find *m* by writing and solving an equation involving tan *R*.

   b. Find *m* by writing and solving an equation involving tan *S*.

   c. *Writing* Which method do you prefer? Explain why.

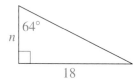

In each figure, find *n*. Round to the nearest tenth.

13.

14.

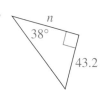

15.

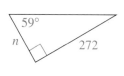

16.

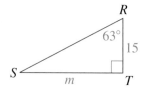

17. *Surveying* A surveyor stands at the end of a bridge across a canyon. The bridge is 20 feet long. The surveyor looks down at an angle of 68° to see the bottom of the canyon on the opposite side. Find the depth of the canyon to the nearest foot.

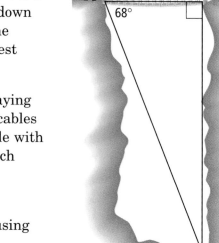

18. *Communications* A 200-m tower is to be built for relaying cellular phone signals. The tower is to be anchored by cables from the top of the tower that will each form a 65° angle with the ground. Find how far from the base of the tower each cable will be anchored. (*Hint:* Each cable forms the hypotenuse of a right triangle.)

19. *Open-ended* Make up a problem that you can solve using the tangent ratio. Write a solution for your problem.

Mixed Review

Graph each equation. *(Lesson 4-4)*

20. $y = 2x - 1$ **21.** $x + y = 12$ **22.** $x - y = 3$ **23.** $-x + 4y = 4$

Evaluate each expression mentally. *(Lesson 2-8)*

24. $-4 + 5 - 12 \times 2$ **25.** $25 \times 10 - 3$ **26.** $50 \times 50 - 50$ **27.** $3 + 2 \times 4 - 5$

28. *Gardening* Mercedes planted a row 8 feet long with carrots. For each foot planted, she should harvest $1\frac{3}{4}$ pounds of carrots. How many pounds of carrots should she be able to harvest? *(Lesson 5-7)*

6-10 The Sine and Cosine Ratios

What You'll Learn

▼ To find the sine and cosine ratios

▼ To solve problems using the sine and cosine ratios

...And Why

You can use the sine and cosine ratios to solve problems involving fire safety.

Here's How

Look for questions that
- build understanding
- ✔ check understanding

Work Together ___ Exploring Sine and Cosine Ratios

1. a. Using graph paper and a protractor, draw $\angle A$, a $40°$ angle with one side on a horizontal line. Then choose vertical lines to draw segments $\overline{HG}$, $\overline{FD}$, and $\overline{CB}$ as shown.

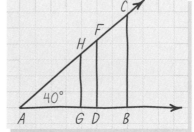

   b. Use a centimeter ruler to measure the segments in the first three columns below to the nearest millimeter. Use a calculator to find the ratios in the fourth and fifth columns.

   $BC = \blacksquare$ $AB = \blacksquare$ $AC = \blacksquare$ $\dfrac{BC}{AC} = \blacksquare$ $\dfrac{AB}{AC} = \blacksquare$

   $DF = \blacksquare$ $AD = \blacksquare$ $AF = \blacksquare$ $\dfrac{DF}{AF} = \blacksquare$ $\dfrac{AD}{AF} = \blacksquare$

   $GH = \blacksquare$ $AG = \blacksquare$ $AH = \blacksquare$ $\dfrac{GH}{AH} = \blacksquare$ $\dfrac{AG}{AH} = \blacksquare$

   c. **Patterns** Compare your ratios with those of other members of your group. What patterns do you find?

2. Repeat Question 1, but this time, use $m\angle A = 73°$.

THINK AND DISCUSS

▼ Finding the Sine and Cosine Ratios

The tangent ratio involves the lengths of the legs of a right triangle. The sine and cosine ratios involve the lengths of the hypotenuse and one of the legs. These three ratios are called **trigonometric ratios.**

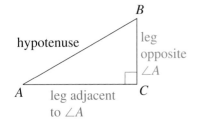

$$\textbf{sine } \text{of } \angle A = \frac{\text{length of leg opposite } \angle A}{\text{length of hypotenuse}}$$

$$\textbf{cosine } \text{of } \angle A = \frac{\text{length of leg adjacent to } \angle A}{\text{length of hypotenuse}}$$

These equations can be abbreviated.

$$\sin A = \frac{\text{opposite}}{\text{hypotenuse}} \qquad \cos A = \frac{\text{adjacent}}{\text{hypotenuse}}$$

■ EXAMPLE 1

Find sin G and cos G.

$$\sin G = \frac{\text{opposite}}{\text{hypotenuse}} = \frac{48}{52} = \frac{12}{13}$$

$$\cos G = \frac{\text{adjacent}}{\text{hypotenuse}} = \frac{20}{52} = \frac{5}{13}$$

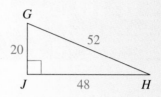

3. ✔ **Try It Out** Find sin H and cos H.

You can use a calculator to find the sine and cosine of any acute angle of a right triangle.

To find sin 41° and cos 41°, use these key sequences.

41 [SIN] 0.656059 So, sin 41° ≈ 0.6561.

41 [COS] 0.7547096 So, cos 41° ≈ 0.7547.

4. ⬢ **Calculator** Find sin 83° and cos 39° to the nearest ten-thousandth.

▼ Using the Sine and Cosine Ratios

You can use the sine and cosine ratios to solve problems.

■ EXAMPLE 2   *Real-World Problem Solving*

Fire Safety The longest ladder that a suburban fire department has is a 105-ft ladder mounted on top of a truck. For the safety of those on the ladder, the fire department does not want to extend the ladder to an angle greater than 75° with the roof of the truck. If the roof of the truck is 10 ft off the ground, find the highest point the ladder can reach.

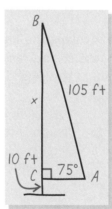

Draw a diagram to describe the problem.

Let x = the side opposite the 75° angle.

$$\sin A = \frac{\text{opposite}}{\text{hypotenuse}} \quad \longleftarrow \text{Use the sine ratio.}$$

$$\sin 75° = \frac{x}{105} \quad \longleftarrow \text{Substitute.}$$

$$x = \sin 75°(105) \quad \longleftarrow \text{Solve for } x.$$

75 [SIN] [×] 105 [=] 101.42221

So, $x \approx 101$. Since the roof of the truck is 10 feet off the ground, the highest the ladder can reach is 101 + 10, or 111 feet off the ground.

5. ✔ *Try It Out* Use the sine or cosine ratio to find x.

a.

b.

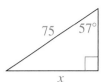

EXERCISES *On Your Own*

Write each trigonometric ratio as a fraction in simplest form.

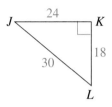

1. $\sin J$ **2.** $\cos J$ **3.** $\sin L$

4. $\cos L$ **5.** $\tan J$ **6.** $\tan L$

 Use a calculator to find each sine or cosine. Round to the nearest ten-thousandth.

7. $\sin 80°$ **8.** $\cos 4°$ **9.** $\sin 71°$ **10.** $\cos 19°$

11. $\sin 30°$ **12.** $\cos 60°$ **13.** $\cos 85°$ **14.** $\sin 45°$

Use the Pythagorean theorem to find n in each figure below. Then write $\sin X$, $\cos X$, and $\tan X$ as fractions in simplest form.

15.

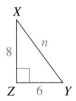

16.

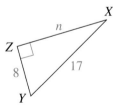

17.

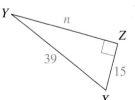

18.

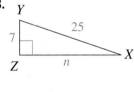

19. *Writing* Your friend is having trouble figuring out whether to use the sine, cosine, or tangent ratio to solve a problem. Write an explanation of how to choose an appropriate ratio. Give one example using each trigonometric ratio.

20. Choose A, B, C, or D. In $\triangle RST$ at the right, which equation can you use to find x?

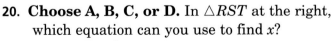

I. $\sin 61° = \dfrac{9}{x}$ **II.** $\cos 29° = \dfrac{x}{9}$ **III.** $\tan 29° = \dfrac{9}{x}$

A. I only   **B.** I or II only   **C.** II or III only   **D.** I, II, or III

21. Refer to △*ABC* at the right.

   a. Find *x* by writing and solving an equation that involves the sine ratio. Round to the nearest tenth.

   b. Find *x* by writing and solving an equation that involves the cosine ratio. Round to the nearest tenth.

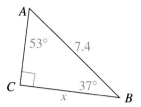

In each figure, find *t*. Round to the nearest tenth.

22. 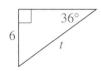 **23.**  **24.** 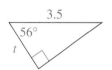 **25.**

26. *Water Parks* A slide at the Watermania Resort in Orlando, Florida, is called the Rainforest. It starts at a height of 20 ft and descends in a straight line that makes an angle of about 30° with the ground. About how long is the slide?

27. **a.** A 16-ft ladder rests against a building so that it forms a 75° angle with the ground. To the nearest tenth of a foot, what is the distance from the top of the ladder to the base of the building?

   b. To the nearest tenth of a foot, what is the distance from the bottom of the ladder to the base of the building?

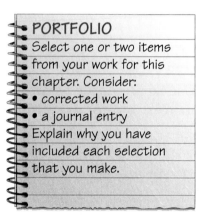

PORTFOLIO
Select one or two items from your work for this chapter. Consider:
• corrected work
• a journal entry
Explain why you have included each selection that you make.

Mixed Review

The points from each table lie on a line. Find the slope of the line. Then graph the line. *(Lesson 4-3)*

28.

x	1	2	3	4	5
y	2	4	6	8	10

29.

x	−2	−1	0	1	2
y	14	7	0	−7	−14

30.

x	−4	−2	0	2	4
y	−12	−6	0	6	12

Evaluate each expression. *(Lesson 2-7)*

31. $(-2)^2 + 10 \cdot 7$ **32.** $-2^2 + 8$ **33.** $9 - 6^2$ **34.** $(4 \cdot 3)^2 - 8$

35. *Choose a Strategy* A soccer club began the year with $35.00 in its treasury. Then 24 club members each paid $7.50 for dues. They spent $24.25 on postage and stationery, and $107.85 on equipment. Do they have enough money to pay a $50.00 deposit for a field to host a tournament?

CHAPTER
PROJECT

Build a Scale Model The Project Link questions on pages 289, 295, 300, and 312 should help you complete your project. Here is a checklist to help you gather the parts of your project together.

✔ the dimensions of the object you are modeling

✔ the scale

✔ the choice of material

✔ the finished scale model

Present your scale model to the class, and explain how you chose the item to model. Give the scale, and discuss the dimensions of both the model and the real-life object.

Reflect and Revise

Show your model to a friend. Is the model attractive? Are the dimensions to scale? If necessary, improve on your scale model.

Web Extension

Prentice Hall's Internet site contains information you might find helpful as you complete your project. Visit www.phschool.com/mgm3/ch6 for some links and ideas related to scale models.

Ratios, Rates, and Units of Measurement   6-1, 6-2

A **ratio** is a comparison of two quantities by division. A **unit rate** is a rate that has a denominator of 1.

In either the metric system or the customary system, it is important to choose appropriate units. **Dimensional analysis** is used to convert units of measure.

Write each ratio in simplest form.

  1. 16 : 48   **2.** $\frac{32}{8}$ **3.** 12 out of 45   **4.** 15 to 9

Write the unit rate.

  5. $42 for 1.5 h   **6.** 826 mi in 14 h   **7.** 150 km per 24 L   **8.** $1.98 for 3 cans

  9. Name an appropriate metric unit to   **10.** Name an appropriate customary unit to
      measure the volume of a pool.   to measure the length of a ladder.

Use dimensional analysis to find each missing value.

  11. 75 min = ▉ h   **12.** 36.8 ft/s = ▉ ft/min   **13.** 7900 km/h = ▉ m/s

Solving Proportions   6-3

To solve a proportion, write the cross products, and then solve.

Solve each proportion.

14. $\frac{4}{5} = \frac{y}{3.9}$ **15.** $\frac{x}{8} = \frac{3}{10}$ **16.** $\frac{9}{20} = \frac{2}{w}$ **17.** $\frac{8}{z} = \frac{5}{9}$

Similar Figures and Similarity Transformations   6-4, 6-5

Similar figures are figures that have the same shape but not necessarily the same size. Corresponding angles of similar polygons are congruent and corresponding sides are in proportion.

The image of a figure after a **dilation** is similar to the original figure. The **scale factor** of a dilation describes the size of the change from the original figure to its image.

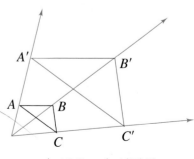

$\triangle ABC \sim \triangle A'B'C'$

In the figure at the right, △ACE ~ △BCD. Find each measure.

18. *AE*   **19.** *CE*   **20.** *DE*

21. *Writing* Suppose you know the coordinates of the vertices of a triangle. Explain how you would find the coordinates of the vertices of its image after a dilation with center (0, 0) and scale factor *r*.

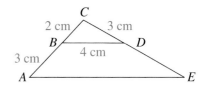

22. Use the figures at the right. Find the scale factor of a dilation that maps the red figure onto the blue figure.

Proportions, Diagrams, and Indirect Measurement   6-6, 6-7, 6-8

You can use proportions to solve scale-model problems and indirect-measurement problems.

23. The scale of an blueprint is 1 in. : 8 ft. A room will be 18 ft long by 14 ft wide. Find its dimensions on the blueprint.

24. Tai is 5 ft 6 in. tall and casts a 21-ft shadow. A building casts a 45-ft shadow at the same time. How high is the building?

Draw a diagram to solve the problem.

25. A dog owner has 12 sections of fence, each 1 yd long. How many different rectangular dog pens can she build using all of the fencing?

Tangent, Sine, and Cosine Ratios   6-9, 6-10

To find measures in a right triangle, use a **trigonometric ratio.**

$$\tan A = \frac{\text{opposite}}{\text{adjacent}}$$

$$\sin A = \frac{\text{opposite}}{\text{hypotenuse}} \qquad \cos A = \frac{\text{adjacent}}{\text{hypotenuse}}$$

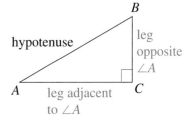

 In each figure, find *n*. Round to the nearest tenth.

26.
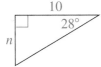

27.
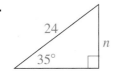

28.
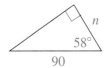

1. Write each ratio in simplest form.
   a. 6 : 36
   b. $\frac{54}{6}$
   c. 24 to 18
   d. 23 out of 92

2. Find each unit rate.
   a. 30 gal in 5 min
   b. $2.50 for 10 oz
   c. 210 mi in 4 h
   d. 96 words in 2 min

3. Use dimensional analysis to convert each measure.
   a. 4 h = ▧ s
   b. 448 in. = ▧ ft
   c. 23 qt = ▧ gal
   d. 22 wk = ▧ h

4. Use dimensional analysis to find an equal rate.
   a. $33/h = $▧ /min
   b. 186 ft/sec = ▧ ft/min

5. Solve each proportion.
   a. $\frac{3}{7} = \frac{6}{n}$
   b. $\frac{2}{8} = \frac{n}{36}$
   c. $\frac{25}{n} = \frac{100}{4}$
   d. $\frac{n}{5} = \frac{30}{13}$

6. A stock investment of 160 shares paid a dividend of $584. At this rate, what dividend would be paid on 270 shares of stock?

7. A 20-ft ladder leans against a tree and makes an angle of 40° with the ground. To the nearest tenth of a foot, what is the distance from the top of the ladder to the base of the tree?

8. △ABC has vertices A(1, 2), B(4, 3), and C(−2, 5). Find the coordinates of the image △A'B'C' after a dilation with center (0, 0) and scale factor 5.

9. You are given △ABC ~ △DEF, with BC = 90, EF = 72, and DE = 40. Find AB.

10. A scale drawing of a new office building uses a scale of 0.75 in. to 3 ft. A room measures 4.75 in. long on the drawing. What is the actual length of the room?

11. Copy △ABC. Draw △A'B'C', the image of △ABC after a dilation with center A and scale factor 4.

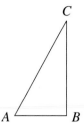

12. Use the Pythagorean theorem to find n. Then write each value as a fraction in simplest form.

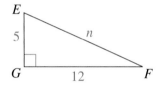

   a. sin E
   b. cos E
   c. tan E

13. In each figure, find n. Round to the nearest tenth.

   a.
   b.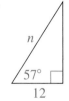

14. Latifa is 5 ft 3 in. tall and casts a shadow 16 ft long. At the same time of day, a telephone pole casts a shadow 90 ft long. What is the height of the pole?

15. *Writing* Explain what types of dilations are enlargements and what types are reductions. Give an example of each type and include its scale factor.

Choose the best answer.

1. Describe the relationship in the scatter plot at the right.

   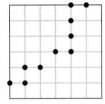

   A. no trend
   B. positive trend
   C. negative trend
   D. positive and negative trend

2. Which phrase cannot be written as $2n + 9$?

   A. nine more than twice n
   B. two times n, increased by nine
   C. double the sum of n and nine
   D. nine greater than twice n

3. $\triangle XYC$ is the image of $\triangle ABC$ after a dilation with center C. What is the scale factor?

   A. 2
   B. $\frac{1}{2}$
   C. $\frac{2}{3}$
   D. $\frac{3}{2}$

4. Using the diagram above, which equation is correct?

   A. $\tan A = \frac{12}{5}$
   B. $\cos A = \frac{5}{12}$
   C. $\tan A = \frac{4}{5}$
   D. $\sin A = \frac{4}{5}$

5. The LCD of $\frac{13}{21}$, $\frac{25}{12}$, and a third fraction is 84. Which cannot be the third fraction?

   A. $\frac{1}{6}$ B. $\frac{25}{28}$ C. $\frac{40}{49}$ D. $\frac{29}{14}$

6. If $2x + 3 = 13$, what is the value of x?

   A. 16   B. 10   C. 8   D. 5

7. What is the value of $-3 + x - y$ if $x = -8$ and $y = -4$?

   A. -7
   B. 7
   C. -15
   D. -9

8. When the temperature is $14°F$, it is a cold day. What is this temperature in degrees Celsius? Use the formula below.
   $$C = \tfrac{5}{9}(F - 32)$$

   A. about $26°C$
   B. $10°C$
   C. $-10°C$
   D. about $-26°C$

9. What set of ordered pairs describes the image of the vertices of $\triangle ABC$ after a translation 2 units left and 3 units down?

   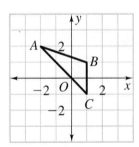

   A. $A'(-4, -1)$, $B'(-1, -2)$, $C'(-1, -4)$
   B. $A'(0, -1)$, $B'(3, -2)$, $C'(3, -4)$
   C. $A'(0, 5)$, $B'(3, 4)$, $C'(3, 2)$
   D. $A'(-4, 5)$, $B'(-1, 4)$, $C'(-1, 2)$

10. A triangle with three sides of equal length has a perimeter of $5\frac{1}{4}$ cm. What is the length of one side?

    A. $1\frac{1}{2}$ cm
    B. $1\frac{3}{4}$ cm
    C. $5\frac{3}{4}$ cm
    D. 15 cm
    E. $15\frac{3}{4}$ cm

7

Applications of Percent

WHAT YOU WILL LEARN IN THIS CHAPTER

- How to write fractions and decimals as percents
- How to use equations and proportions in percent problems
- How to create a circle graph

*I*nvest *in a* W*INNER*

Y ou've won! You entered a quiz
contest thinking you didn't have a
chance and now you're $5,000 richer!
You are looking for a way to double
your money in five years. Is this
possible?

Explore Ways to Invest Money For
your chapter project, you will explore
different investments, looking for the
best investment for your money. You
will prepare an oral and visual
presentation describing your investment
choice.

Steps to help you complete the project:

p. 341 Project Link: *Interviewing*
p. 346 Project Link: *Collecting Data*
p. 364 Project Link: *Displaying Data*
p. 369 *Finishing the Chapter Project*

• How to solve a
problem by making
a table

PROBLEM
SOLVING

327

Exploring Decimals

Before Lesson 7-1

Each digit in a decimal has both a place and a value. The value of any place is one tenth the value of the place to its left. A place value chart like the one at the right can help you read and write decimals.

ones	.	tenths	hundredths	thousandths	ten-thousandths	hundred-thousandths
0	.	3	8	5	2	6

■ EXAMPLE 1

a. Express 0.358 as a fraction with a power of 10 as a denominator.

The last digit, 8, is in the thousandths place.

So, $0.358 = \frac{358}{1000}$

b. Write *one* and *forty-two hundredths* as a decimal.

The hundredths place is two places to the right of the decimal point. So, the decimal will have two places after the decimal point.

The answer is 1.42.

■ EXAMPLE 2

Use a decimal square to model the following numbers.

a. 0.4   **b.** 0.76   **c.** 1.25

  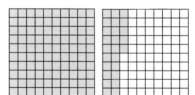

Express each decimal as a fraction with a multiple of 10 as a denominator.

1. 0.07   **2.** 0.3   **3.** 1.85   **4.** 0.006   **5.** 0.95   **6.** 2.056   **7.** 0.5

Write a decimal for the given words. Draw a decimal model for each.

8. six tenths   **9.** one and four hundredths   **10.** eight hundredths

11. fifty-five hundredths   **12.** one and two tenths   **13.** eleven hundredths

7-1 Fractions, Decimals, and Percents

What You'll Learn

▼ To write fractions and decimals as percents

▼ To write percents as fractions and decimals

...And Why

Statisticians use percents to report their survey results.

Here's How

Look for questions that
- build understanding
- ✔ check understanding

THINK AND DISCUSS

▼ Writing Fractions and Decimals as Percents

In a recent survey, one out of five, or one fifth, of those surveyed said they eat corn on the cob side-to-side. Four out of five, or four fifths, said they eat corn in circles.

Another way to express these fractions is to write them as percents. A **percent** is a ratio that compares a number to 100. To express a fraction as a percent, first write it as an equivalent fraction with denominator 100. Then express the fraction as a percent.

$$\frac{1}{5} = \frac{1 \cdot 20}{5 \cdot 20} = \frac{20}{100} = 20\% \qquad\qquad \frac{4}{5} = \frac{4 \cdot 20}{5 \cdot 20} = \frac{80}{100} = 80\%$$

You can use decimal models to show 20% and 80%.

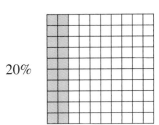

20%

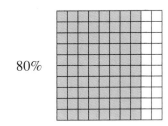

80%

1. **Modeling** Write each fraction as a percent. Then sketch a decimal model to show each percent.

   a. $\frac{2}{5}$ b. $\frac{3}{4}$ c. $\frac{17}{25}$ d. $\frac{12}{25}$

2. ✔ **Try It Out** Nineteen out of twenty people are born right-handed. Express this ratio as a percent.

When you cannot easily write a fraction as an equivalent fraction with denominator 100, use a proportion.

■ **EXAMPLE 1** *Real-World Problem Solving*

Government To be elected, a U.S. presidential candidate must receive more than 50% of the 538 electoral votes. In the 1996 presidential election, Bill Clinton received 379 votes. What percent of the votes did Bill Clinton receive?

$$\frac{379}{538} = \frac{x}{100} \quad \longleftarrow \text{Write a proportion.}$$

$$379 \cdot 100 = 538x \quad \longleftarrow \text{Write the cross products.}$$

$$\frac{37,900}{538} = x \quad \longleftarrow \text{Divide each side by 538.}$$

37,900 ⊟ 538 ⊟ 𝟽𝟶.𝟺𝟺𝟨𝟶𝟫𝟽

Bill Clinton received about 70.4% of the electoral votes.

3. ✔ Try It Out Bob Dole received 159 of the 538 electoral votes. What percent of the votes did he receive?

■ **EXAMPLE 2**

Write each decimal as a percent.

a. $0.12 = \frac{12}{100}$ **b.** $0.008 = \frac{8}{1000}$ **c.** $1.1 = \frac{11}{10}$

           $= 12\%$ $= \frac{8 \div 10}{1000 \div 10}$ $= \frac{11 \cdot 10}{10 \cdot 10}$

                                $= \frac{0.8}{100}$ $= \frac{110}{100}$

      $0.12 = 12\%$ $0.008 = 0.8\%$ $1.1 = 110\%$

4. ✔ Try It Out Change each decimal to a fraction with a denominator of 100 and then to a percent.

    a. 0.36   **b.** 0.015   **c.** 0.6   **d.** 1.75

Example 2 suggests the following rule for writing decimals as percents.

DECIMAL TO PERCENT

To write a decimal as a percent, move the decimal point two places to the right and write a percent sign.

Examples: 0.12 = 12%   0.008 = 0.8%   1.10 = 110%

A calculator can make it easy to convert fractions to decimals. Then you can change the decimal to a percent.

5. ✔ *Try It Out* Use a calculator to change each fraction to a decimal and then a percent.

a. $\frac{1}{8}$
b. $\frac{3}{500}$
c. $\frac{2}{3}$
d. $\frac{1}{2,000}$

❷ Writing Percents as Fractions and Decimals

To change a percent to a fraction, write the percent as a fraction with denominator 100, then simplify the fraction.

■ **EXAMPLE 3**   *Real-World Problem Solving*

Jewelry 18 karat gold is 75% pure gold, and 14 karat gold is $58\frac{1}{3}$% pure gold. Write each percent as a fraction in simplest form.

- $75\% = \frac{75}{100}$ ⟵ Write as a fraction with a denominator of 100.

  $= \frac{75 \div 25}{100 \div 25} = \frac{3}{4}$ ⟵ Divide the numerator and denominator by 25.

- $58\frac{1}{3}\% = \frac{58\frac{1}{3}}{100}$ ⟵ Write as a fraction with a denominator of 100.

  $= 58\frac{1}{3} \div 100$ ⟵ Rewrite the fraction as division.

  $= \frac{175}{3} \times \frac{1}{100}$ ⟵ Multiply by the reciprocal of 100.

  $= \frac{175 \div 25}{300 \div 25} = \frac{7}{12}$

18 karat gold is $\frac{3}{4}$ pure gold; 14 karat gold is $\frac{7}{12}$ pure gold.

PERCENT TO DECIMAL

To write a percent as a decimal, move the decimal point two places to the left and remove the percent sign.

Examples: $12\% = 0.12$ $00.8\% = 0.008$ $110\% = 1.1$

6. Write each of the percents in Example 3 as decimals.

7. ✔ *Try It Out* Write each percent as a decimal.
   a. 38%
   b. 0.5%
   c. 12.6%
   d. 200%

Choose Use a calculator, paper and pencil, or mental math. Write each fraction as a decimal and then as a percent. Round to the nearest tenth of a percent.

1. $\frac{3}{5}$ 2. $\frac{17}{20}$ 3. $\frac{1}{6}$ 4. $3\frac{1}{8}$ 5. $\frac{7}{15}$ 6. $\frac{6}{1000}$

7. $\frac{3}{200}$ 8. $\frac{7}{9}$ 9. $\frac{8}{5}$ 10. $\frac{12}{7}$ 11. $2\frac{2}{3}$ 12. $4\frac{3}{7}$

Mental Math Write each decimal as a percent.

13. 0.36   14. 0.04   15. 0.003   16. 5.2   17. 0.075   18. 1.12

19. 0.0025   20. 1.4   21. 0.989   22. 0.065   23. 0.25   24. 6.0

25. **Choose A, B, C, or D.** In which set are all three values equal?

   A. $52\%, 0.052, \frac{52}{100}$ B. $0.52\%, 0.52, \frac{52}{100}$ C. $52\%, 0.52, \frac{52}{100}$ D. $0.52\%, 0.0052, \frac{52}{100}$

26. **Data Analysis** *The First Really Important Survey of American Habits* reports responses to a national survey about habits. Express each of these survey results as a percent. Round your answers to the nearest percent.
   a. 73 out of 200 people sing in the shower.
   b. 69 out of 200 people plan what they will wear the next day.
   c. 145 out of 200 people squeeze the toothpaste from the top.
   d. 156 out of 200 people prefer showers to baths.

27. **Health** Did you know that in the age group 10 to 18 years, 1 in 7 youths is without health insurance? Express this fraction as a percent rounded to the nearest tenth.

Write each percent as a fraction or mixed number in simplest form.

28. 70%   29. 93%   30. 0.05%   31. 0.8%   32. 120%   33. $\frac{3}{4}\%$

34. 6%   35. 37.5%   36. 180%   37. $2\frac{1}{5}\%$ 38. 782%   39. 43.75%

Mental Math Write each percent as a decimal.

40. 40%   41. 20%   42. 16%   43. 8.3%   44. 9%   45. 0.1%

46. 5%   47. 134%   48. 106%   49. 600%   50. $4\frac{1}{2}\%$ 51. $5\frac{4}{5}\%$

52. *Data Analysis* The circle graph at the right shows what you find in U.S. landfills. Write each percent as a decimal and as a fraction in simplest form.

53. *Chemistry* BHA is a preservative that is added to foods to preserve freshness. A can of shelled walnuts, for example, contains 0.02% BHA. Express this percent as a fraction in simplest form.

54. *Nutrition* Emilio took a vitamin that supplied 835% of his minimum daily requirement of vitamin C. How many times his minimum daily requirement of vitamin C did he receive?

Trash In U.S. Landfills

Other Trash 19%
Paper 30%
Rubber & Leather 8%
Metal 8%
Food & Yard Waste 11%
Plastic 24%

Order each set of numbers from least to greatest.

55. $\frac{1}{3}$, 36%, 0.3, $\frac{3}{8}$

56. 125%, $1\frac{1}{2}$, $\frac{7}{5}$, 1.2

57. 0.01, 0.9%, $\frac{1}{99}$, 1.01%

58. 0.63, $\frac{25}{42}$, 0.6, $\frac{1}{2}$, $62\frac{1}{2}$%

59. $\frac{2}{9}$, $\frac{1}{4}$, 0.2, 20.9%

60. 150%, 150, $\frac{9}{5}$, 1.5%

61. *Writing* Explain why 0.05 is different from 0.05%.

62. *Research* Look in newspapers or magazines for examples of percents. Make a list of the percents you found. Change each percent to a decimal and to a fraction in simplest form.

Mixed Review

Express each quantity as a unit rate. *(Lesson 6-1)*

63. $16.80 for 14 gal

64. 5 lb of meat for $17.45

65. 292.5 mi in 6.5 h

Find each sum or difference. Write each answer as a fraction or a mixed number in simplest form. *(Lesson 5-5)*

66. $6\frac{4}{5} - 2\frac{1}{5}$

67. $3\frac{2}{10} + 1\frac{7}{10}$

68. $4\frac{2}{6} - 3\frac{3}{6}$

69. $9\frac{4}{15} + 7\frac{12}{15}$

70. $32\frac{1}{8} - 25\frac{3}{8}$

71. *Choose a Strategy* Five pads of paper cost $4.50, 10 pads cost $8.05, 20 pads cost $15.15, and 30 pads cost $22.25. If this pattern continues, how much should 50 pads cost?

Estimating with Percents

What You'll Learn

1 To estimate with percents by using compatible numbers

2 To estimate with percents by using multiples of 10% and 1%

...And Why

Shoppers estimate with percents every day as they calculate costs and savings.

Here's How

Look for questions that
- build understanding
- ✔ check understanding

Work Together — *Finding Commonly Used Percents*

Work with a partner. Display each set of commonly used fractions on a separate number line. Then write the percent equal to each fraction above the number line.

1. fifths: $\frac{1}{5}, \frac{2}{5}, \frac{3}{5}, \frac{4}{5}$
2. sixths, thirds, and halves: $\frac{1}{6}, \frac{1}{3}, \frac{1}{2}, \frac{2}{3}, \frac{5}{6}$
3. eighths, fourths, and halves: $\frac{1}{8}, \frac{1}{4}, \frac{3}{8}, \frac{1}{2}, \frac{5}{8}, \frac{3}{4}, \frac{7}{8}$

THINK AND DISCUSS

1 *Estimating Using Compatible Numbers*

You can find a percent of a number the same way you find a fraction of a number. For example, 50% of 18 is the same as $\frac{1}{2}$ of 18. You find $\frac{1}{2}$ of 18 by multiplying $\frac{1}{2}$ and 18.

You can estimate a percent of a number by using fractions and compatible numbers.

■ **EXAMPLE 1**   *Real-World Problem Solving*

Shopping Inez wants to buy a jacket that costs $64.95. Her parents will pay 25% of the cost. Estimate how much her parents will contribute.

25% of $64.95 ←—Write what you need to find.

$\frac{1}{4}$ of 64 ←— Replace 25% with an equal fraction. Replace 64.95 with an integer close to it in value and compatible with $\frac{1}{4}$.

$\frac{1}{4} \times 64 = 16$ ←—Multiply.

Inez estimates that her parents will contribute $16 towards the purchase of her jacket.

4. Inez's grandfather will pay 20% of the cost.
   a. **Think About It** What number would you use to replace $64.95 to estimate his contribution? Explain why.
   b. ✔ **Try It Out** Estimate her grandfather's contribution.

Another way to estimate a percent of a number is to replace the percent with a common fraction close to it in value.

■ **EXAMPLE 2**   *Real-World Problem Solving*

Music A band director claims that about 38% of his 88 students are "stars," those who practice for an hour or more a day. Estimate the number of stars.

38% of 88   ←—Write what you need to find.

$\frac{3}{8}$ of 88   ←—Since 8 is a factor of 88, a fraction in eighths is compatible with 88.
                    $38\% \approx 37.5\% = \frac{3}{8}$

$\frac{3}{8} \times \overset{11}{\underset{1}{88}} = 33$ ←—Multiply.

There are about 33 stars in the band.

5. ▪**Look Back** Explain how you can estimate the number of stars in Example 2 by replacing 38% with a different common fraction and by replacing 88 with a number compatible with that fraction.

▼2 *Estimating Using Multiples of 10% and 1%*

Another method you can use to estimate percents is to use multiples of 1% and 10%.

6. ✔ **Try It Out** Find 10% and 1% of each number.
    a. 120   **b.** 35   **c.** 58   **d.** 1800   **e.** 48.99

■ **EXAMPLE 3**   *Real-World Problem Solving*

Money The Chin family goes out to dinner. The bill is $29.70. They use estimation to compute a 15% tip. What is the estimate?

They can estimate 15% of $29.70 by first finding 10% of $30.00 and then finding 5% of $30.00. The sum of these two amounts is the estimated tip.

$10\% \text{ of } 30 = \frac{1}{10} \cdot 30 = 3$

$5\% \text{ of } 30 = \frac{1}{2} \cdot (10\% \text{ of } 30) = \frac{1}{2} \cdot 3 = 1.5$

The estimated tip is the sum of $3.00 and $1.50, or $4.50.

7. ✔ *Try It Out* Estimate 0.6% of 590 by finding 1% of 590 and taking half of your result.

8. ✔ *Try It Out* Estimate each of the following.
   a. 15% of $98.99
   b. 12% of $19
   c. 0.4% of 110
   d. 30% of 12

EXERCISES *On Your Own*

Estimate the given percent of each number. Explain why you chose the estimation strategy that you used.

1. 33% of 88
2. 65% of 242
3. 16.9% of 31
4. 0.4% of 175

5. 39% of 75
6. 270% of 109
7. 79% of 29
8. 4.9% of 81

9. 52% of 57.8
10. 9.8% of 139
11. 23% of 39
12. 41.9% of 413

Compare. Use >, <, or =.

13. 85% ▧ $\frac{5}{6}$
14. 65% ▧ $\frac{2}{3}$
15. 12.5% ▧ $\frac{1}{8}$
16. 225% ▧ $2\frac{1}{5}$

17. 45% ▧ $\frac{3}{8}$
18. 75% ▧ $\frac{3}{5}$
19. $83\frac{1}{3}$% ▧ $\frac{9}{10}$
20. $33\frac{1}{3}$% ▧ $\frac{2}{5}$

Shopping **The ad at the right shows the ticketed prices. Estimate each discounted price for the weekend sale.**

21. a jacket

22. a hat

23. a pair of jeans

24. a T-shirt

25. a pair of athletic shoes

Money **Estimate a 15% tip on each dinner bill.**

26. $9.85
27. $12.63
28. $18.20

29. $6.96
30. $24.38
31. $27.55

32. $37.02
33. $31.49
34. $48.37

This weekend only!
30% off all ticketed prices!
$15.00
$9.99
$44.99
$24.99
$29.99
Ticketed prices shown.

35. *Writing* Explain why it is important to estimate with percents even when you are using a calculator to find the exact answer.

36. *Shopping* Of the $14.1 billion spent on sports shoes in the United States in 1996, 21% was spent on basketball shoes. Estimate the amount spent on basketball shoes.

> **JOURNAL**
> Describe a real-world situation in which you have estimated a percent or you might need to estimate a percent.

Mixed Review

Solve each proportion. *(Lesson 6-3)*

37. $\frac{30}{15} = \frac{x}{5}$ **38.** $\frac{y}{4} = \frac{9}{1.2}$ **39.** $\frac{21}{9} = \frac{a}{3}$ **40.** $\frac{80}{b} = \frac{10}{3}$ **41.** $\frac{q}{6} = \frac{2.5}{4}$ **42.** $\frac{4}{p} = \frac{1.6}{1.8}$

Write each repeating decimal as a fraction or mixed number in simplest form. *(Lesson 5-3)*

43. $0.\overline{2}$ **44.** $0.\overline{3}$ **45.** $0.8\overline{3}$ **46.** $0.\overline{916}$ **47.** $0.\overline{6}$ **48.** $0.\overline{36}$

49. Carrie wants to buy a pen and pencil set for her father. Together they cost $15. The pen costs $10 more than the pencil. How much does the pencil cost? *(Lesson 3-6)*

Math at Work

MARINE BIOLOGIST

A marine biologist does research in a lab or on site. For example, a researcher might dive for specimens, bring them to the lab, and then observe them to collect various types of data. Marine biologists work on board large research ships, at aquariums, or in university or government research labs.

Marine biologists collect data, and interpret and analyze graphs, charts, and other types of statistical data. They need a solid mathematical background including calculus and statistics. The tasks of a marine biologist are quite varied. However, they are never boring!

For more information about careers in marine biology, visit the Prentice Hall Web site: www.phschool.com

7-3 Percents and Proportions

What You'll Learn

▼① To use a proportion to find part of a whole

▼② To use a proportion to find a whole amount

...And Why

You can use proportions to solve real-world problems involving taxes.

Here's How

Look for questions that
- build understanding
- ✔ check understanding

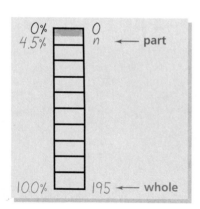

THINK AND DISCUSS

▼① *Finding Part of a Whole*

You can use a model to show the relationship between the part and the whole. The model below shows that 15 is 75% of 20.

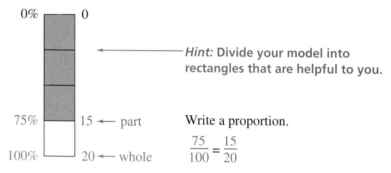

Hint: Divide your model into rectangles that are helpful to you.

Write a proportion.

$$\frac{75}{100} = \frac{15}{20}$$

Some of you may pay a state sales tax on things you buy. Like many other taxes, sales taxes are based on percents.

■ EXAMPLE 1   *Real-World Problem Solving*

▦ *Sales Tax* In Arkansas, the state sales tax is 4.5%. You want to buy a $195 bicycle in Arkansas. How much is the tax?

Write a proportion that compares the part represented by the tax to the whole represented by the cost of the bicycle.

$$\frac{4.5}{100} = \frac{n}{195} \quad \longleftarrow \text{Write a proportion.}$$

$$4.5 \cdot 195 = 100n \quad \longleftarrow \text{Write the cross products.}$$

$$\frac{195 \cdot 4.5}{100} = n \quad \longleftarrow \text{Divide each side by 100.}$$

$$8.775 = n \quad \longleftarrow \text{Simplify.}$$

The tax on the bicycle is $8.78.

Look Back 4.5% of $195 is about $\frac{1}{20}$ of $200, or $10. The answer is reasonable. ✔

1. ✔ *Try It Out* Write a proportion to solve each problem.
- **a.** Find 25% of $120.
- **b.** Find 85% of $150.
- **c.** Find 12.5% of $90.
- **d.** Find $5\frac{3}{4}$% of $1000.

▼2 Finding a Whole Amount

Sometimes you know the percent that a part represents, but you do not know the whole amount.

■ **EXAMPLE 2** *Real-World Problem Solving*

▦ *Education* Many students pay for their college education by working full time and going to school part time. In a recent year, there were 114,162 part-time college students in Massachusetts. Part-time students represented 34% of the state's college students. How many college students were there?

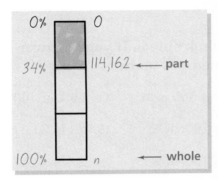

Make a percent model.
Then write a proportion.

$$\frac{34}{100} = \frac{114{,}162}{n}$$

$$34 \cdot n = 114{,}162 \cdot 100$$

$$n = \frac{114{,}162 \cdot 100}{34}$$

11,416,200 ⊟ 34 ▤ *335770.59*

There were 335,771 college students.

2. ▪ *Look Back* Use estimation to explain why the answer is reasonable.

The following table summarizes the three basic types of percent problems.

Percents and Proportions

Finding the Percent	Finding the Part	Finding the Whole
What percent of 8 is 2?	What number is 20% of 64?	5 is 30% of what number?
$\dfrac{\text{part} \longrightarrow}{\text{whole} \longrightarrow} \dfrac{n}{100} = \dfrac{2}{8}$	$\dfrac{\text{part} \longrightarrow}{\text{whole} \longrightarrow} \dfrac{20}{100} = \dfrac{n}{64}$	$\dfrac{\text{part} \longrightarrow}{\text{whole} \longrightarrow} \dfrac{30}{100} = \dfrac{5}{n}$

3. ✔ *Try It Out* Write a proportion for each percent problem.
   a. What percent of 16 is 12?   b. What is 24% of 160?
   c. Find 80% of 450.   d. 36 is 75% of what number?

Sales Tax The tables below show the 1995 sales tax in selected states. Find the amount of sales tax charged on a $49.99 cassette player. Then find the final cost.

	State	Sales Tax Rate
1.	California	6%
2.	Idaho	5%
3.	Texas	$6\frac{1}{4}\%$
4.	Virginia	3%

	State	Sales Tax Rate
5.	North Carolina	4%
6.	Utah	4.475%
7.	Mississippi	7%
8.	Kansas	4.9%

Use a proportion to solve each problem. If your answer is not an integer, round to the nearest tenth.

9. 80% of 72 is ■. 10. 60% of 355 is ■. 11. 85% of 400 is ■. 12. 30% of 48 is ■.

13. 2% of ■ is 1.4. 14. 70 is 20% of ■. 15. 29 is 20% of ■. 16. ■% of 30 is 18.

17. 15% of ■ is 18. 18. 33 is 15% of ■. 19. 2.4 is ■% of 60. 20. 0.9 is ■% of 180.

21. 63 is 29% of ■. 22. 78 is ■% of 50. 23. 45% of ■ is 224. 24. 4.5 is ■% of 300.

25. *Reading About Math* How many of the people surveyed chose blue toothbrushes? How many chose red? How many chose yellow?

26. *Data Analysis* There are about 50 million children ages 5 to 17 in the United States. Estimate how many children prefer blue toothbrushes.

27. *Writing* Explain why researchers often use percents to report their findings.

Teeth Are Big Business

People in the United States visit dentists almost 500 million times a year. Children ages 5 to 17 average about 2.4 visits per year.

Toothbrush manufacturers conduct market research to find out consumer likes and dislikes. In a recent survey of 500 people, the leading choice of toothbrush color was blue, at 23%. Red toothbrushes came in second, at

20%. Yellow toothbrushes came in third, at 16%.

In Exercises 28–30, choose the proportion that you can use to answer the question.

28. What percent is 17 of 42?

    A. $\dfrac{17}{42} = \dfrac{n}{100}$ **B.** $\dfrac{n}{42} = \dfrac{17}{100}$ **C.** $\dfrac{17}{n} = \dfrac{100}{42}$ **D.** $\dfrac{n}{17} = \dfrac{42}{100}$

29. What is 35% of 90?

    A. $\dfrac{35}{90} = \dfrac{n}{100}$ **B.** $\dfrac{n}{90} = \dfrac{35}{100}$ **C.** $\dfrac{35}{n} = \dfrac{90}{100}$ **D.** $\dfrac{n}{35} = \dfrac{100}{90}$

30. 92 is 80% of what number?

    A. $\dfrac{n}{92} = \dfrac{80}{100}$ **B.** $\dfrac{80}{n} = \dfrac{92}{100}$ **C.** $\dfrac{80}{92} = \dfrac{n}{100}$ **D.** $\dfrac{92}{n} = \dfrac{80}{100}$

31. **Geography** Rhode Island is the smallest state in the United States, with an area of 1,212 square miles. It accounts for only 0.03% of the country's area. Use this information to estimate the area of the United States in square miles.

32. **Budgets** A teacher spent $129.60 on supplies. This was 72% of his classroom budget. How much was his budget?

Mixed Review

33. In the diagram at the right, $\triangle ABC \sim \triangle PQR$. Find the values of x and y. *(Lesson 6-4)*

Solve each equation. *(Lesson 5-7)*

34. $\dfrac{1}{2}x = \dfrac{5}{8}$ 35. $-\dfrac{5}{3}y = 10$

36. $-\dfrac{9}{4}q = -6$ 37. $\dfrac{8}{9}a = -\dfrac{1}{3}$

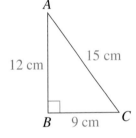

38. **Choose a Strategy** Of 120 computer programmers surveyed, 50 use the programming language C+, 30 use Pascal, and 15 use both. How many programmers use neither C+ nor Pascal?

CHAPTER PROJECT

PROJECT LINK: INTERVIEWING

Interview four adults. Take notes as you interview. Ask each person what kind of investments he or she has made in the past. Ask each to recommend a way you can invest your $5,000. Write a short report on your findings.

7-4 Percents and Equations

What You'll Learn

▼ To write and solve percent equations

▼ To use equations to solve percent problems

...And Why

You can use percent equations to solve problems involving commissions.

Here's How

Look for questions that
- build understanding
- ✔ check understanding

THINK AND DISCUSS

▼ Writing and Solving Percent Equations

In the steps shown below, the percent proportion is transformed into a percent equation. This gives you another method for solving percent problems.

$$\frac{\text{part}}{\text{whole}} = \frac{n}{100}$$

$$\frac{\text{part}}{\text{whole}} = P \quad \longleftarrow \text{Replace } \frac{n}{100} \text{ with } P, \text{ the percent expressed as a decimal.}$$

$$\text{part} = P \cdot \text{whole} \quad \longleftarrow \text{Multiply each side by the whole.}$$

■ EXAMPLE 1

What percent of 80 is 15?

$$\text{part} = P \cdot \text{whole} \quad \longleftarrow \text{Use the percent equation.}$$

$$15 = P \cdot 80 \quad \longleftarrow \text{Substitute.}$$

$$P = \frac{15}{80} = 0.1875 \quad \longleftarrow \text{Divide each side by 80.}$$

To change the decimal 0.1875 to a percent, move the decimal point two places to the right and add a % sign.

15 is 18.75% of 80.

The three basic types of percent problems are shown below.

Percent Equations

Finding the Percent	Finding the Part	Finding the Whole
part = P · whole	part = P · whole	part = P · whole
5 is what percent of 8?	What is 30% of 8?	12 is 25% of what?
5 = P × 8	n = 0.3 × 8	12 = 0.25 × n

1. ✔ **Try It Out** Write and solve an equation for each question.
   a. What is 75% of 18?
   b. 16 is 40% of what number?
   c. 28 is what percent of 72?
   d. What percent of 15 is 3?

2 ▼ *Using Equations to Solve Percent Problems*

Some sales jobs pay an amount based on how much you sell. This is called a *commission*.

■ **EXAMPLE 2**   *Real-World Problem Solving*

Real Estate Nekia sells real estate and receives a 3% commission on property she sells. How much money will she receive if she sells a house for $118,000?

Words   • amount of commission is 3% of 118,000

⬇

   • Let n = amount of commission

Equation • n = $0.03 \cdot 118,000$

$$n = 0.03 \cdot 118,000$$
$$n = 3,540 \qquad \longleftarrow \text{Multiply.}$$

Nekia receives a $3,540 commission.

2. ✔ Try It Out A salesperson receives a salary of $115 each week plus a 12.5% commission on all sales. In one week, his sales are $2,300. What does he earn?

■ **EXAMPLE 3**   *Real-World Problem Solving*

▦ *Environment* Over the past 200 years, Florida has lost about 9.3 million acres, or 46% of its wetland. About how many acres of wetland did Florida have 200 years ago?

Words   • 9.3 million is 46% of the wetland acres

⬇

   • Let n = number of wetland acres in millions

Equation • 9.3 = $0.46 \cdot n$

$$9.3 = 0.46 \cdot n$$
$$\frac{9.3}{0.46} = n \qquad \longleftarrow \text{Divide each side by 0.46.}$$

9.3 ➗ 0.46 🟰 *20.217391*

Florida had about 20.2 million acres of wetland 200 years ago.

Look Back $46\% \approx \frac{1}{2}$ and $9.3 \approx 10$. Since $\frac{1}{2}$ of 20 equals 10, the answer is reasonable. ✓

7-4 Percents and Equations   **343**

Tiger Woods hit a hole in one in the final round of the Greater Milwaukee Open, his first professional tournament.

3. ✔ *Try It Out* In a recent survey, 36 people, or 21% of the sample, said that they had never been out of the continental United States. How many people were in the sample?

The probability of an event occurring is a number from 0 to 1. You can also write this number as a percent from 0% to 100%.

■ EXAMPLE 4

▦ *Probability* The probability of a pro golfer getting a hole in one in one round on a PGA course is 1 out of 3,709. Express this probability as a percent.

Words • 1 is what percent of 3,709

↓ • Let P = the percent in decimal form

Equation • 1 = $P \cdot$ 3,709

$$1 = P \cdot 3{,}709$$

$$\frac{1}{3{,}709} = P \quad \longleftarrow \text{Divide each side by 3,709.}$$

1 ⊟ 3709 ⊟ 0.0002696

Move the decimal two places to the right and write a percent sign. Then, round your answer.

The probability of getting a hole in one is about 0.027%.

4. ⊞ *Think About It* Explain why it is reasonable that this percent is less than 1%.

5. ✔ *Try It Out* The probability of having identical twins is 1 in 274. Express this probability as a percent. Round to the nearest thousandth of a percent.

EXERCISES *On Your Own*

Match each problem with the equation that models it. P represents a percent in decimal form.

A. $9 = 0.12n$ **B.** $12 = P \times 9$ **C.** $n = 0.12 \times 9$ **D.** $9 = P \times 12$

1. 9 is what percent of 12?   **2.** What is 12% of 9?

3. 9 is 12% of what number?   **4.** 12 is what percent of 9?

Use an equation to solve each problem. Round to the nearest tenth.

5. What percent of 75 is 30?   6. 16.4 is what percent of 5?   7. Find 31% of 82.

8. 92% of what number is 6?   9. 4% of what number is 28?   10. What percent of 360 is 2?

11. 50 is what percent of 40?   12. 5 is 12% of what number?   13. Find 23% of 275.

14. What is 13% of 250?   15. 5% of what number is 3?   16. What number is 5% of 28?

17. *Entertainment* In a recent survey, 438 people, or 73% of the sample, chose popcorn as their favorite movie-theater snack. How many people were in the sample?

18. *Health* Calcium is important for bones and teeth. The RDA (recommended daily allowance) of calcium is set at 800 mg. If you consume 1500 mg of calcium, what percent of the RDA are you satisfying?

19. *Business* Jaron sells building supplies and earns a commission on his sales. Last week, he sold $3,735 worth of building supplies. What percent commission did he receive if he earned $672.30?

20. *Environment* Your class collected returnable bottles to raise money for the library. Your goal was to collect 80 bottles. You succeeded in collecting 100 bottles. What percent of your goal did you reach?

21. a. *Community Service* The Century Club set a fundraising goal of $500. They actually raised $758. What percent of their goal did they raise?
    b. *Writing* In part (a), the part (that is, the $758) is greater than the whole (the $500). Write and solve another real-world problem in which the part is greater than the whole.

22. *Probability* The probability of a pro bowler getting a perfect score of 300 in one year of bowling is 1 out of 4001. Express this probability as a percent. Round to the nearest thousandth of a percent.

23. *Open-ended* Write and solve a word problem for each of the three basic types of percent equations shown in the table at the bottom of page 342.

Mixed Review

Write each rational number in the form $\frac{a}{b}$. *(Lesson 5-2)*

24. -4 **25.** 0.35 **26.** 1.98 **27.** $5\frac{1}{2}$ **28.** -2.55 **29.** 17

Use a calculator to find each sine or cosine. Round to the nearest thousandth. *(Lesson 6-10)*

30. $\sin 5°$ **31.** $\cos 15°$ **32.** $\sin 85°$ **33.** $\cos 85°$ **34.** $\sin 17°$ **35.** $\cos 74°$

36. *Sports* The Eagles football team starts on their own 10 yd line. They gain 20 yd, lose 5 yd, gain 28 yd, and lose 6 yd. On what yard line are the Eagles after the 4 plays? *(Lesson 2-8)*

CHAPTER PROJECT

PROJECT LINK: COLLECTING DATA

Look in the business section of a newspaper for bank advertisements. List different banks and the interest rate each offers on a 5-year certificate of deposit (CD).

✓ CHECKPOINT 1

Lessons 7-1 through 7-4

Express each of the following as a decimal, a percent, and a fraction in simplest form.

1. 30% **2.** 0.12 **3.** 210% **4.** $\frac{5}{8}$ **5.** $\frac{3}{1000}$ **6.** 3.75

Estimate each of the following. Explain why you chose the strategy you used.

7. 15% of 198 **8.** 78% of 95 **9.** 32% of 145 **10.** 4.9% of 81 **11.** 9.8% of 139

Choose any method to solve each exercise. If your answer is not an integer, round to the nearest tenth.

12. What percent of 84 is 63?   **13.** What is 23% of 17?   **14.** 110 is 55% of what number?

15. What percent of 75 is 13?   **16.** What is 60% of 355?   **17.** 15 is 0.4% of what number?

18. In 1995, U.S. advertisers spent \$164 billion, 6.6% of which was on radio. How much was spent on radio advertising?

7-5 Creating Circle Graphs

What You'll Learn

▼ To create a circle graph

...And Why

Newspapers and magazines use circle graphs to display data.

Here's How

Look for questions that
⁝ build understanding
✔ check understanding

THINK AND DISCUSS

Food banks collect and distribute food to organizations that feed those in need. The circle graph below shows the ages of people in the United States who benefit from the work of food banks.

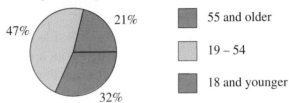

Ages of People Using Food Banks

47% 21% 32%

■ 55 and older
□ 19 – 54
■ 18 and younger

1. ⁝ **Reasoning** Explain why the sum of the percents in a circle graph is always 100%.

A **central angle** is an angle whose vertex is the center of a circle.

2. **a.** Use a protractor to measure each central angle above.
   b. ⁝ **Reasoning** Find the sum of the measures of all the angles. Explain why the sum should be about 360°.

You can find the measure of each central angle of a circle graph by multiplying the percent by 360°.

■ EXAMPLE 1

Suppose you want to make a circle graph showing the data in the table. Find the measure of the central angle of a circle graph that shows the percent of people who sleep 8 hours each night.

$$28\% = 0.28 \quad \longleftarrow \text{Change the percent to a decimal.}$$

$$0.28 \cdot 360° = 100.8° \quad \longleftarrow \begin{array}{l}\text{Multiply by 360° to find the measure}\\\text{of the angle.}\end{array}$$

Use 100.8° for the 8-hour category in your circle graph.

3. ✔ **Try It Out** Find the measures of the central angles for the four other categories.

Average Number of Hours Americans Sleep Per Night

Number of Hours	Percent
More than 8 h	3%
8 h	28%
7 h	30%
6 h	26%
Less than 6 h	12%

Source: Moore Research Center, Inc.

▦*Environment* According to the U.S. Department of the
Interior, 997 species of the world's animals are endangered.
Display the data shown in the table in a circle graph.

Endangered Species

Class	Number of Species	Class	Number of Species
Mammals	335	Birds	274
Fish	116	Reptiles	113
Clams	59	Insects	33
Other	67		

- Make a table to organize your work. Express each
  category as a fractional part of the total. Use a calculator
  to change each fraction to a percent in decimal form.
  Multiply each decimal by 360° to find the measure of each
  central angle. Round each measure to the nearest degree.

Class	Frequency	Fraction of Total	% (decimal)	Angle Measure
Mammals	335	$\frac{335}{997}$	0.336	121°
Birds	274	$\frac{274}{997}$	0.275	99°
Fish	116	$\frac{116}{997}$	0.116	42°
Reptiles	113	$\frac{113}{997}$	0.113	41°
Clams	59	$\frac{59}{997}$	0.059	21°
Insects	33	$\frac{33}{997}$	0.033	12°
Other	67	$\frac{67}{997}$	0.067	24°
Total	997	$\frac{997}{997}$	1.000	360°

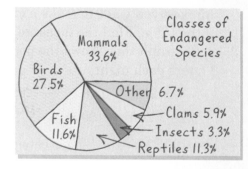

- Use a compass to
  draw a circle with any
  radius. Draw the
  central angles with a
  protractor.

- Label each section and
  add a title.

4. ⬡*Estimation* Explain how you could estimate the percents
   and the angle measures in Example 2.

Work Together

Work in a group to write a survey about how students in your class get to school. Categories might include school bus, walking, biking, public transportation, and car. Decide on three categories that are appropriate for your school. Use *other* as a fourth category to include all other possibilities. Survey your class and display the results in a circle graph.

EXERCISES *On Your Own*

Find the measure of the central angle that could represent each percent in a circle graph. Round your answer to the nearest degree.

1. 9%   **2.** 15%   **3.** 23.5%   **4.** 36%   **5.** 42.1%   **6.** 47.8%

7. 14%   **8.** 26%   **9.** 41.3%   **10.** 34.5%   **11.** 18%   **12.** 39.4%

13. *Health* A women's magazine conducted a survey on women's exercise habits. It found that 27.7% exercise frequently, 37.4% exercise occasionally, and 34.9% never exercise. Display the results in a circle graph.

14. *Nutrition* Health Focus Inc. surveyed consumers on whether they were buying more vegetables than they bought two years ago. Here are the responses.

more: 56.3%   the same: 40.1%

fewer: 1.9%   no response: 1.7%

Display the data in a circle graph.

15. *Writing* Explain why it is easier to make a circle graph for a budget if categories are given as percents rather than as dollar amounts.

16. *Food* Ella surveyed 81 students in the cafeteria about their favorite school lunch. Here is what they chose.

pizza: 35   spaghetti: 20

hamburger: 18   grilled cheese: 8

Display the survey results in a circle graph.

17. a. *Marketing* What color is your car? Employees of a company responded to this question. The results of the survey are shown in the bar graph at the right. Display the data in a circle graph.

b. Which graph do you think is more useful for the data? Explain.

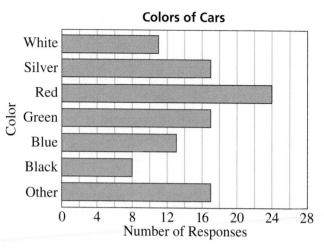

Colors of Cars

18. *Budgets* The spreadsheet below shows the budget for a museum field trip.

a. Copy and complete the spreadsheet.

b. Use the results to draw a circle graph.

	A	B	C	D
1	**Expense**	**Budgeted Amount**	**% of Total**	**Angle Measure**
2	Bus	$350	■	■
3	Admission	$250	■	■
4	Lunch	$175	■	■

19. *Open-ended* Choose a survey question. Write four possible responses. Use *other* for the fifth response. Predict the responses for a sample of 100 people. Display the data in a frequency table and then in a circle graph.

JOURNAL
Explain why you cannot always display the results of a survey question in a circle graph. Give an example.

Mixed Review

Write an inequality for each sentence. Solve and graph the solution on a number line. *(Lessons 3-8 and 3-9)*

20. 5 less than a number is greater than −9.　**21.** 2 more than a number is less than 14.

Write the prime factorization of each number. *(Lesson 5-1)*

22. 280　　**23.** 108　　**24.** 242　　**25.** 251　　**26.** 162　　**27.** 300

28. *Choose a Strategy* Patricia is going to exercise for 10 minutes today. She plans to increase her workout by 4 minutes each day. For how many minutes will she exercise on the sixth day?

7-6 Percent of Change

What You'll Learn

▼1 To solve problems that involve percent of decrease

▼2 To solve problems that involve percent of increase

...And Why

The U.S. Census Bureau uses percent of decrease and percent of increase to describe changes in population.

Here's How

Look for questions that
- build understanding
- ✔ check understanding

Work Together
Exploring Changes in Population

Population of Largest U.S. Cities

Rank and City	1950	1994
1. New York	7,891,957	7,333,253
2. Los Angeles	1,970,358	3,448,613
3. Chicago	3,620,962	2,731,743

1. a. Work with a partner to find the change in population for each city from 1950 to 1994. State whether the change is an increase or a decrease.

   b. Write the ratio $\frac{\text{change in population}}{1950 \text{ population}}$ for each city. Then write each ratio as a percent to the nearest tenth of a percent.

THINK AND DISCUSS

▼1 Solving Problems with the Percent of Decrease

The percent that a quantity increases or decreases from its original amount is the **percent of change.**

$$P = \frac{\text{amount of change}}{\text{original amount}}$$ ← *P* is the percent of change expressed in decimal form.

■ EXAMPLE 1

Estimation In 1970, Chicago's population was 3,369,357. Use the data from the Work Together table to estimate the percent of decrease in Chicago's population from 1970 to 1994.

$$\begin{aligned} \text{amount} \atop \text{of change} &= \text{population} \atop \text{in 1970} - \text{population} \atop \text{in 1994} \\ &= 3,400,000 - 2,700,000 \quad \leftarrow \text{Round to the nearest hundred thousand.} \\ &= 700,000 \quad \leftarrow \text{Subtract.} \end{aligned}$$

$$P = \frac{\text{amount of change}}{\text{original amount}} = \frac{700,000}{3,400,000} \approx \frac{7}{35} = \frac{1}{5} = 0.20$$

The percent of decrease is about 20% from 1970 to 1994.

2. ⁂ **Look Back** Compare the percent of decrease in Chicago's population from 1950 to 1994 with the percent of decrease from 1970 to 1994.

❷ Solving Problems with Percent of Increase

You can use the same approach to find the percent of increase.

■ **EXAMPLE 2**   *Real-World Problem Solving*

▦ *Population* Every ten years the United States government counts all the people in the country. The first U.S. census was taken in 1790. That year, the population was 3,929,200. In 1990, the population was 248,709,872. Find the percent of increase.

amount of change = 248,709,872 − 3,929,200
              = 244,780,672

$$P = \frac{244{,}780{,}672}{3{,}929{,}200} \quad \longleftarrow \text{ amount of change} \atop \longleftarrow \text{ original amount}$$

$P = 62.297840$ ← Use a calculator to divide.

$= 6{,}229.784\%$ ← Move the decimal point two places to the right to change the decimal to a percent.

The percent of increase is about 6,230%.

3. ⁂ **Look Back** Is the answer in Example 2 reasonable? Explain how you know it is.

When working with measures, be sure to express all measures in the same units.

■ **EXAMPLE 3**   *Real-World Problem Solving*

▦ *Entertainment* E.T. weighs $62\frac{1}{2}$ lb and is normally 3 ft tall. When he raises his neck, he is 4 ft 4 in. tall. Find the percent of increase in his height.

3 ft = 36 in.   ← Write measures in the same units.
4 ft 4 in. = 52 in.

amount of change = 52 − 36 = 16

$$P = \frac{16}{36} \quad \longleftarrow \text{ amount of change} \atop \longleftarrow \text{ original amount}$$

$P = 0.4444444$ ← Use a calculator.

E.T.'s height increases 44.4% when he raises his neck.

4. ✔ Try It Out Find each percent of change. Round to the nearest percent. Label *increase* or *decrease*.
    a. 4 h to 3 h 20 min   **b.** 12 lb to 16 lb 3 oz

EXERCISES *On Your Own*

Find each percent of decrease. Round your answer to the nearest tenth of a percent.

1. 105 to 83   **2.** 21 to 11.5   **3.** 90 to 45   **4.** 25 to 15

5. 8.5 km to 7 km   **6.** 190 cm to 52 cm   **7.** $4.95 to $4.49   **8.** 34 m to 31.7 m

9. *Environment* The city of Seattle is switching from rubbish collection and disposal at a cost of $105 a ton to recycling and processing at a cost of $50 a ton. Find the percent of decrease in the city's cost.

Find each percent of increase. Round your answer to the nearest tenth of a percent.

10. 75 to 110   **11.** 65 to 80   **12.** 15 to 95   **13.** 4 to 7.5

14. 7 h to 8.5 h   **15.** 55.2 m to 63 m   **16.** 1.35 km to 4.9 km   **17.** $74.00 to $79.99

18. 2 ft to 5 ft 8 in.   **19.** 4 h to 6 h 15 min   **20.** 9 mm to 18 cm   **21.** 3 lb 4 oz to 8 lb 2 oz

Mental Math **Use mental math to find each percent of change. Label your answer *increase* or *decrease*.**

22. 20 to 25   **23.** 40 to 30   **24.** 50 to 55   **25.** 80 to 70

26. 75 to 100   **27.** 5 to $2\frac{1}{2}$ **28.** 0.80 to 0.20   **29.** $\frac{1}{4}$ to $\frac{1}{2}$

30. *Money* In 1950 the minimum wage for nonfarm workers was $.75 per hour. In 1997, it was $5.25 per hour. Find the percent of increase.

31. *Sports* In the 1948 Olympics, Olga Gyarmati of Hungary won the women's long jump with a jump of 18 ft $8\frac{1}{4}$ in. In 1992, Heike Drechsler of Germany won with a jump of 23 ft $5\frac{1}{4}$ in. Find the percent of increase in the length of the jump.

32. *Writing* If you increase 100 by 20% and then decrease the result by 20%, do you get an answer of 100? Explain why or why not.

33. *Education* The Galvin Middle School increased its school day from 6 h 10 min to 6 h 25 min to meet the state education requirements. Find the percent of increase in the length of the school day.

Is Hollywood Nervous?

Although there are long lines for hit movies, people aren't going to the movies as much as they used to. There was a decline in movie attendance from 1930 to 1970. Since then, there has been a slight increase in movie theater attendance. Young people, who make up the largest portion of the movie audience, have more choices these days for their weekend entertainment.

U.S. Film Attendance

Year	Attendance (millions)
1930	3,900
1950	3,120
1960	2,080
1970	920
1980	1,022
1990	1,189
1995	1,263

Source: *The Universal Almanac,* 1997

Reading About Math **Find each percent of change in movie ticket sales. Round your answer to the nearest tenth of a percent. Label your answer *decrease* or *increase*.**

34. 1930 to 1950   **35.** 1930 to 1970   **36.** 1970 to 1995   **37.** 1990 to 1995

Mixed Review

The scale is 1 in. : 12 mi. Find the distance on a scale drawing for each actual distance. *(Lesson 6-6)*

38. 36 mi   **39.** 54 mi   **40.** 96 mi   **41.** 3 mi   **42.** 486 mi   **43.** 16 mi

44. A tree is 8 ft tall and casts a shadow of 9.6 ft. At the same time, a nearby plant casts a shadow 3.6 ft long. What is the height of the plant? *(Lesson 6-8)*

7-7 Markup and Discount

What You'll Learn

▼ To solve problems involving markup

▼ To solve problems involving discount

...And Why

Businesses use markups to make a profit and discounts to sell products quickly.

Here's How

Look for questions that
- build understanding
- ✔ check understanding

Need Help? For practice with multiplying decimals, see Skills Handbook page 604.

THINK AND DISCUSS

▼ Solving Problems Involving Markup

To make a profit, stores charge more for merchandise than they pay for it. The amount a price is increased is called the **markup.** The store's cost plus the markup equals the **selling price.**

■ **EXAMPLE 1** *Real-World Problem Solving*

Business The school store sells notebooks. Each notebook costs the store $.79. The store wants to mark up the price by 65%. At what price should the store sell each notebook?

Method 1: Find the markup first, then the selling price.

65% of $.79 equals the markup.

$$0.65 \times .79 = 0.5135 \quad \longleftarrow \text{Multiply to find the markup.}$$
$$\approx \$.52 \quad \longleftarrow \text{Round up to the nearest cent.}$$
$$\$.79 + \$.52 = \$1.31 \quad \longleftarrow \text{Store's cost + markup } = \textbf{selling price}$$

The school store should sell each notebook for $1.31.

Method 2: Find the selling price directly.

The selling price equals 100% of the cost plus 65% of the cost for the markup. So, the selling price is 100% + 65%, or 165% of the cost.

165% of $.79 equals the selling price.

$$1.65 \times 0.79 = 1.3035 \quad \longleftarrow \text{Multiply to find the selling price.}$$
$$\approx \$1.31 \quad \longleftarrow \text{Round up to the nearest cent.}$$

The school store should sell each notebook for $1.31.

1. **⬛Look Back** Which method do you prefer? Explain.

2. ✔ *Try It Out* Find the selling price. Round your answer up to the nearest cent.
   a. store's cost: $89
      markup rate: 60%
   b. store's cost: $134.98
      markup rate: 55%

When you know the selling price and the percent of markup, you can write an equation to find the store's cost.

■ **EXAMPLE 2**   *Real-World Problem Solving*

Retailing A store sells a jacket for $60. The markup rate is 25%. What is the store's cost for the jacket?

store's cost +   markup   = selling price

store's cost + 25% of store's cost = selling price

Let c = store's cost

$c + (0.25 \cdot c) = 60$ ←—Write an equation.

$\qquad\quad 1.25c = 60$ ←—Combine like terms: $c + 0.25c = 1.25c$.

$\qquad\qquad\quad c = \dfrac{60}{1.25}$ ←—Divide each side by 1.25.

$\qquad\qquad\quad c = 48$ ←—Simplify.

The cost of the jacket to the store is $48.

3. ▪ *Think About It* Explain how you can use a proportion to check the solution to Example 2.

4. ✔ *Try It Out* A store sells a coat for $105. The markup rate is 40%. What is the store's cost?

▼2 *Solving Problems Involving Discount*

When an item goes on sale, a store reduces its regular price to a sale price. The amount the price is reduced is called the **discount**. The regular price minus the discount equals the **sale price.**

■ **EXAMPLE 3**   *Real-World Problem Solving*

Retailing Save-More is having a 20%-off sale. What is the sale price of a CD player that regularly costs $159.98?

Method 1: Find the discount first, then the sale price.

20% of $159.98 equals the discount.

$\qquad\quad 0.20 \times 159.98 = 31.996$ ←—Multiply to find the discount.

$\qquad\qquad\qquad\quad \approx \$32.00$ ←—Round to the nearest cent.

$\$159.98 - \$32.00 = 127.98$ ←— regular price − discount = sale price

The sale price is $127.98.

Method 2: Find the sale price directly.

The sale price equals 100% of the cost minus 20% of the cost for the discount. So, the sale price is 100% − 20%, or 80%, of the cost.

80% of $159.98 equals the selling price.

$$0.80 \times 159.98 = 127.984 \quad \longleftarrow \text{Multiply.}$$
$$\approx \$127.98 \quad \longleftarrow \text{Round to the nearest cent.}$$

The sale price is $127.98.

5. ⚬ **Look Back** Is the solution to Example 3 reasonable? Explain how you know that it is.

6. ✔ **Try It Out** Find the sale price. Round up to the nearest cent.
   a. regular price: $180
      discount rate: 40%
   b. regular price: $35.50
      discount rate: 25%

When you know the sale price and the discount rate, you can write an equation to find the regular price.

■ **EXAMPLE 4** *Real-World Problem Solving*

Shopping Camila is going to a 40%-off sale. She is thinking about buying a pair of in-line skates at the sale price of $48. What is the regular price of the skates?

regular price − discount = sale price

regular price − 40% of regular price = sale price

Let n = regular price

$$n - (0.40 \cdot n) = 48 \quad \longleftarrow \text{Write an equation.}$$
$$0.60n = 48 \quad \longleftarrow \text{Combine like terms: } n - 0.40n = 0.60n$$
$$n = \frac{48}{0.60} \quad \longleftarrow \text{Divide each side by 0.60.}$$
$$n = 80 \quad \longleftarrow \text{Simplify.}$$

The regular price of the skates is $80.

7. ⚬ **Look Back** Explain how you can find the regular price in Example 4 by using another method.

8. ✔ **Try It Out** Find the regular price. Round up to the nearest cent.
   a. sale price: $125
      discount rate: 40%
   b. sale price: $28.95
      discount rate: 20%

EXERCISES *On Your Own*

Find the selling price. Round up to the nearest cent.

1. cost: $59.99
   markup rate: 60%

2. cost: $114.45
   markup rate: 55%

3. cost: $9.50
   markup rate: 35%

4. cost: $45.70
   markup rate: 70%

5. cost: $176.80
   markup rate: 45%

6. cost: $149.99
   markup rate: 20%

Find the store's cost. Round up to the nearest cent.

7. selling price: $180
   markup rate: 40%

8. selling price: $35.50
   markup rate: 25%

9. selling price: $29.99
   markup rate: 10%

10. selling price: $115.99
    markup rate: 150%

11. selling price: $74.49
    markup rate: 30%

12. selling price: $18.98
    markup rate: $33\frac{1}{3}$%

13. *Retailing* Zina buys book bags for $3.75 and sells them for $6.00. What is her percent of markup?

Find the sale price. Round up to the nearest cent.

14. regular price: $55.89
    discount: 30%

15. regular price: $76.29
    discount: 25%

16. regular price: $43.99
    discount: 45%

17. regular price: $19.45
    discount: 10%

18. regular price: $29.39
    discount: 20%

19. regular price: $154.95
    discount: $33\frac{1}{3}$%

20. *Shopping* Cassette tapes are on sale for 40% off the regular price of $8.99. Thelma has $35.00 to spend on cassettes. How many cassettes can she buy at the reduced price?

21. *Recreation* Eric bought a canoe for a sale price of $335.75. If he received a 20% discount off the regular price, what was the regular selling price?

22. *Writing* A street vendor buys T-shirts and marks them up 50%. When the T-shirts don't sell, he discounts them by 50% and they sell out. Does the vendor make any profit? Explain why or why not. Include sample prices in your answer.

23. Retailing The prices for different items and sizes are displayed in the matrix at the right. A *matrix* is a rectangular arrangement of numbers. The numbers are arranged in rows and columns. Each item in a matrix is called an *entry*.

Item Price

$$\begin{array}{c} & \text{Child} \quad \text{Junior} \quad \text{Miss} \\ \begin{array}{l} \text{Jeans} \\ \text{Shirt} \\ \text{Dress} \end{array} & \left[\begin{array}{ccc} 19.99 & 24.99 & 26.99 \\ 12.00 & 14.95 & 15.99 \\ 16.99 & 18.99 & 22.99 \end{array} \right] \end{array}$$

a. Multiply each entry of the matrix by 90% to get a matrix that shows the discounted prices for a 10%-off sale.

b. *Open-ended* Choose a different discount rate for the sale. Create a matrix to display the new discounted prices.

Mixed Review

Write the prime factorization of each number. *(Lesson 5-1)*

24. 51   **25.** 96   **26.** 225   **27.** 250   **28.** 91   **29.** 48

Compare. Use $>, <,$ **or** $=$**.** *(Lesson 5-4)*

30. $\frac{3}{5} \blacksquare 0.58$ **31.** $\frac{4}{7} \blacksquare 0.7$ **32.** $-1\frac{1}{2} \blacksquare -1.\overline{6}$ **33.** $0.4 \blacksquare 0.401$ **34.** $\frac{5}{8} \blacksquare 0.36$

35. What is the ratio of the number of minutes in an hour to the number of minutes in a day? *(Lesson 6-1)*

✓ CHECKPOINT 2   *Lessons 7-5 through 7-7*

1. The table at the right shows the Diaz family's budget. Display the data in a circle graph.

Family Budget

Expenses	Percent
Housing	33%
Transportation	10%
Food	25%
Clothing	18%
Savings	10%
Miscellaneous	4%

Find each percent of change to the nearest percent. Label your answer *decrease* **or** *increase*.

2. 52 to 65   **3.** 25 to 21.48

4. 135 lb to 130 lb   **5.** 30,859 to 82,226

6. 2.5 m to 4.5 m   **7.** 3 ft to 4 ft 8 in.

8. Ice skates regularly sell for $36.95 in Elsa's store. Find the sale price if Elsa offers a discount of 20%.

9. *Open-ended* Choose an item that you might want to sell if you were a street vendor. Estimate the initial cost of the item and a reasonable markup rate. Find your selling price.

7-8 Simple and Compound Interest

What You'll Learn

▼ To find simple interest

▼ To find compound interest

...And Why

Banks pay customers interest on savings and charge interest on loans.

Here's How

Look for questions that
- build understanding
- ✔ check understanding

THINK AND DISCUSS

▼ Finding Simple Interest

When you deposit money in a savings account, you allow the bank to use your money. In return, the bank pays you **interest** at a certain percentage rate called the **interest rate.** The money you initially deposit is called the **principal.** You can use the following formula to calculate simple interest. Simple interest is interest earned only on the principal.

SIMPLE INTEREST

$$I = p \cdot r \cdot t$$

where I is the interest, p is the principal,
r is the interest rate per year, and t is the time in years.

■ **EXAMPLE 1** *Real-World Problem Solving*

Career Education A student deposits $200 in an account at the school bank. The interest rate is 6% per year. How much simple interest will the account earn in three years?

$I = p \cdot r \cdot t$ ⟵ Use the simple interest formula.
$\quad = 200 \cdot 0.06 \cdot 3$ ⟵ Substitute. Use 0.06 for 6%.
$\quad = 36$ ⟵ Multiply.

The account earns $36 interest.

The **balance** in an account is the principal plus the interest earned.

1. **Look Back** Find the balance at the end of three years by adding the $200 principal to the answer in Example 1.

2. ✔ *Try It Out* Find the simple interest on $200 invested at 6% annual (yearly) interest for five years.

The students at Brockton High School in Brockton, Massachusetts run a school bank.

▼2 *Finding Compound Interest*

When a bank pays interest on both the principal and the interest that an account has already earned, the bank is paying **compound interest.**

EagleBank

Check out our
new rates on
savings accounts!

6%

Annual Interest Rate
Minimum balance is $200.

■ **EXAMPLE 2**   *Real-World Problem Solving*

Banking You deposit $200 in an account that earns 6% compounded annually. Use a spreadsheet to find the balance after three years.

	A	B	C	D	E
1	Year	Start of Year	Rate	Interest	End of Year
2	1st	$200.00	0.06	$12.00	$212.00
3	2nd	$212.00	0.06	$12.72	$224.72
4	3rd	$224.72	0.06	$13.48	$238.20

At the end of three years, the balance is $238.20.

3. ⬛ *Technology* In which cell of the spreadsheet would you find each formula?
  a. = B2 * C2   **b.** = B3 + D3

4. ✔ *Try It Out* Complete the spreadsheet for five years.

5. ⬛ *Explain* Why is the balance in Example 2 greater than the balance you found in Question 1?

6. ⬛ *Analyze* In each row of the spreadsheet, you multiplied the beginning balance by 0.06 and added the result to the beginning balance. Explain why this is the same as multiplying the beginning balance by 1.06.

Each year's beginning balance is 1.06 times the previous year's beginning balance. Another way to find the balance after five years is to multiply the beginning balance by 1.06 five times.

7. a. *Calculator* Simplify the following expression:
    $200 \cdot 1.06 \cdot 1.06 \cdot 1.06 \cdot 1.06 \cdot 1.06$
  b. Compare your answer to Question 4 with your answer to part (a).
  c. Explain how you can use the [yˣ] key on a scientific calculator to make your calculations in part (a) easier.

Question 7 suggests the following formula for compound interest.

COMPOUND INTEREST

$$B = p(1 + r)^t$$
where B is the final balance, p is the principal,
r is the interest rate per year, and t is the time in years.

■ **EXAMPLE 3**   *Real-World Problem Solving*

Investments Mrs. Tsiang does all her banking at the Banking Center in the local mall. She is going to invest $575 for 4 years at an annual interest rate of $6\frac{1}{4}\%$ compounded annually. What will be her balance at the end of this time?

$B = p(1 + r)^t$ ⟵ Use the compound interest formula.

$B = 575(1 + 0.0625)^4$ ⟵ Substitute: $p = 575$, $r = 6\frac{1}{4}\% = 0.0625$, $t = 4$.

575 ☒ 1.0625 ⟡ 4 ▤ *732.79685*

After 4 years, her balance will be $732.80.

8. a. ⚓ *Look Back* How much interest will Mrs Tsiang earn on the $575 she plans to invest in Example 3?
   b. Compare this amount with simple interest on $575 for 4 years at an annual rate of $6\frac{1}{4}\%$.

9. ✔*Try It Out* Find the final balance for each investment.
   a. $700 at 4% compounded annually for 2 years
   b. $1,600 at $5\frac{1}{2}\%$ compounded annually for 4 years

Work Together
Analyzing Investments

💻 *Technology* Work with a partner. Use either a spreadsheet or a calculator and *Guess and Test*.

10. You are investing $10,000 at 8% compounded annually. How long will it take you to double your investment? To triple your investment? To quadruple your investment?

▦ **Find the final balance for each account.**

1. $900 at 3% simple interest for 2 years

2. $500 at 5% simple interest for 6 years

3. $1,200 at 6.5% simple interest for 4 years

4. $198 at $5\frac{1}{2}$% simple interest for 3 years

5. $1,000 at 4% simple interest for $2\frac{1}{2}$ years

6. $3,500 at $6\frac{1}{4}$% simple interest for 5 years

7. Mr. Mazzeo is lending his daughter Christina $2,500 for a car. He is charging her 3% simple interest each year. She will pay him back in three years. How much interest will she pay?

▦ **Find the final balance for each account.**

8. $1,700 at 7% compounded annually for 2 years

9. $14,000 at 3% compounded annually for 3 years

10. $115 at 4% compounded annually for 2 years

11. $10,300 at 8% compounded annually for 5 years

12. $850 at $5\frac{1}{2}$% compounded annually for 4 years

13. $2,000 at $6\frac{1}{2}$% compounded annually for 3 years

14. *Consumer Issues* Bank accounts *pay* interest, but credit card companies *charge* interest. Deric buys a $350 set of encyclopedias with a credit card. He pays 1.5% monthly interest on any unpaid balance.
  a. At the end of the first month, Deric makes a $50 payment. After his payment is deducted, the interest is computed on his balance. How much interest is Deric charged?
  b. The interest is added to Deric's unpaid balance. How much does Deric now owe on his credit card?
  ▦ **c.** *Calculator* Deric plans to make a $50 payment each month. Use a spreadsheet to find out how long it will take him to pay for the books.
  d. *Writing* The books regularly sell for $450. Did Deric save money by buying the books on sale and using his credit card? Explain.

15. *Open-ended* Choose an amount of money to be invested and an interest rate. What is the value of the investment after 6 years if the interest is simple interest? If the interest is compound interest?

16. *Marketing* The advertisement at the right shows how $100 grew to $350 in 18 years. Use the *Guess and Test* strategy to find the annual interest rate that would allow $100 to increase to $350 over 18 years. Give your answer to the nearest tenth of a percent.

17. *Calculator* You have $500 in a savings account earning 4.25% compounded annually. Make a table showing the interest earned each year and the balance at the end of each year for three years.

WATCH IT GROW
Kohlberg Money Market Fund

The power of compound interest

1980   1998

18. Choose A, B, C, or D. Which of these interest rates will give you the most interest in 2 years?

 A. 4.25% simple interest   **B.** $3\frac{1}{2}$% compound interest
 C. $4\frac{1}{2}$% simple interest   **D.** 3.6% compound interest

Mixed Review

Use dimensional analysis to convert each measure.
(Lesson 6-2)

19. 3 h 25 min = ▧ min   **20.** 48.5 mi/hr = ▧ mi/min   **21.** 15 km/L = ▧ m/L

For each linear equation, make a table of solutions. Then find the slope and graph the line. *(Lesson 4-3)*

22. $y = x - \frac{2}{3}$ **23.** $y = 2x + 7$ **24.** $y = -\frac{1}{4}x - \frac{1}{2}$ **25.** $y = \frac{3}{5} + 3x$

26. *Choose a Strategy* Jeff travels 60 miles round-trip to work. He works 5 days a week. His car gets about 25 miles per gallon of gasoline. About how many gallons of gasoline does Jeff's car use during his weekly commute?

CHAPTER PROJECT

PROJECT LINK: DISPLAYING DATA

A principal invested at 3% annual interest compounded annually will more than quadruple in 50 years. Use the formula $B = p(1 + r)^t$ to prepare a chart showing the value of your $5,000 after 5 years of annual compounding at rates of 4%, 6%, and 10% annual interest. Display your results in a graph.

Choose the best answer.

1. What is 0.245 expressed as a percent?
   - **A.** 0.0245%
   - **B.** 2.45%
   - **C.** 24.5%
   - **D.** 245%

2. Miguel is getting a promotion and a 20% raise in pay. He earns $500 a week now. To find the amount of his raise, by which fraction should you multiply?
   - **F.** $\frac{1}{50}$
   - **G.** $\frac{1}{20}$
   - **H.** $\frac{1}{5}$
   - **J.** $\frac{1}{2}$

3. Tate bought 500 grams of hamburger. How many kilograms is this?
   - **A.** 0.05 kg
   - **B.** 0.5 kg
   - **C.** 5 kg
   - **D.** 50 kg

4. In 50 games, Kylah made 25 of 30 free throws. Which expression could you use to find the percent of shots she made?
   - **F.** $\frac{25}{30} \times 100$
   - **G.** $\frac{30}{50} \times 100$
   - **H.** $\frac{25}{50} \times 100$
   - **J.** $\frac{30}{75} \times 100$

5. Rosa and her friends are eating out for dinner. The bill is $45.80. They want to leave a 20% tip. What is a good estimate for the tip?
   - **A.** $5
   - **B.** $9
   - **C.** $23
   - **D.** $90

6. On a 5-item quiz, students got the following numbers of correct answers: 1, 5, 1, 3, 5, 4, 4, 5, 3, 2, 3, 3, 5, 2, 3, and 5. Which expression gives the percent of students who got 3 or more correct?
   - **F.** $\frac{1}{4} \times 100$
   - **G.** $\frac{5}{16} \times 100$
   - **H.** $\frac{5}{9} \times 100$
   - **J.** $\frac{3}{4} \times 100$

Please note that items 7–11 have *five* answer choices.

7. Julia bought 50 beads for $9.95. She can get a 10% discount if she buys more than 100 beads. What is a reasonable conclusion about the price of 200 beads?
   - **A.** It is between $10 and $20.
   - **B.** It is between $20 and $30.
   - **C.** It is between $30 and $40.
   - **D.** It is between $40 and $50.
   - **E.** It is more than $50.

8. A shirt at a discount store was marked down from $24 to $15. What was the percent of discount?
   - **F.** $12\frac{1}{2}\%$
   - **G.** 25%
   - **H.** $33\frac{1}{3}\%$
   - **J.** $37\frac{1}{2}\%$
   - **K.** 75%

9. In a recent school survey, 36% of students preferred dogs and 42% preferred cats. What is the difference between the percent that preferred cats and the percent that preferred dogs?
   - **A.** 78%
   - **B.** 64%
   - **C.** 58%
   - **D.** 16%
   - **E.** 6%

10. Two-hundred-pound Jonah is trying to gain weight so he can play football next year. If he gains 1 pound, what percent of his weight will he have gained?
    - **F.** 0.5%
    - **G.** 2%
    - **H.** 5%
    - **J.** 20%
    - **K.** 50%

11. In a beef roast, 45% of the calories are protein and 51% are fat. What percent of its calories are either protein or fat?
    - **A.** 4%
    - **B.** 6%
    - **C.** 49%
    - **D.** 55%
    - **E.** 96%

7-9

Make a Table

Problem Solving Strategies

Draw a Diagram
Guess and Test
Look for a Pattern
✔ Make a Table
Simulate the Problem
Solve a Simpler Problem
Too Much or Too Little
  Information
Use Logical Reasoning
Use Multiple Strategies
Work Backward
Write an Equation

THINK AND DISCUSS

When you need to look at many possibilities in order to solve a problem, you can organize the information in a table.

SAMPLE PROBLEM..

In Jefferson County, a local cable station produces a show called *Academic Challenge.* Each week a different middle school sends a team to try to win money for its school. Each team is asked ten questions. The team is awarded $50 for each correct answer, but has $25 subtracted from its winnings for each incorrect answer. If the team from Madison Middle School received $275, how many questions did the team answer correctly?

 READ

Read for understanding. Summarize the problem.

Read the problem carefully.

1. What information are you asked to find?

2. What information will you need to use to solve the problem?

PLAN

Decide on a strategy.

Make a table that shows the amount of money won for each possible combination of correct and incorrect answers. Making a table will allow you to account for all possibilities and help you avoid using the same combination more than once.

SOLVE

Try the strategy.

3. Copy and complete the table below.

Number Correct	0	1	2	3	4	5	6
Number Incorrect	10	9	8	7	6	■	■
Money Won	$0	$0	$0	$0	$50	■	■

4. How many questions did the team answer correctly?

LOOK BACK

Think about how you solved the problem.

5. What other strategies could you use to solve this problem?

6. Use the information about *Academic Challenge* to write and solve a new problem that has more than one solution.

EXERCISES *On Your Own*

Use the strategy *Make a Table* to solve each problem.

1. *Money* How many ways are there to make change for a half dollar, using only nickels, dimes, and quarters?

2. *Sports* In Erica Machut's first college basketball game, she scored nine points. How many different combinations of one-, two-, and three-point shots could she have scored?

3. *Consumer Issues* You have four 32-cent stamps and three 20-cent stamps. How many different amounts of postage could you stick onto a package?

4. *Number Theory* A palindrome is a number that reads the same forward and backward, such as 11 or 82,128. Single-digit numbers are not considered palindromes. How many palindromes are there between the numbers 0 and 300?

5. *Sports* Two teams are in the finals of a soccer tournament. The winner is the first team to win three out of five games. Both teams hope to win in three straight games. In how many *other* different ways can a team win the championship?

Use any strategy to solve each problem. If there is not enough information, state what information you need. Show all your work.

6. Mrs. Romero asks her math students to open their books to two facing pages that have a product of 2,756. What are the page numbers?

7. *Architecture* The Great Pyramid was erected at Giza by Pharaoh Khufu around 2580 B.C. The ratio of the perimeter of the base of the pyramid to its height was originally about 25 to 4. The perimeter of the base of the Great Pyramid was 3,024 ft. Estimate the original height of the Great Pyramid. Explain how you arrived at your estimate.

8. *Consumer Issues* Luther bought two tapes for $17.75. One tape sold for full price and the second for half price. If both tapes originally cost the same amount, how much did Luther pay for each tape?

9. *Sports* In the 1996 Summer Olympics, the United States won 38 more medals than Russia. Twenty-six of Russia's medals were gold medals. How many medals did Russia win?

10. *Money* Two friends received $95 for delivering advertising fliers. If Tani delivered 10 bundles and Rashad delivered 9 bundles, how much money should each receive?

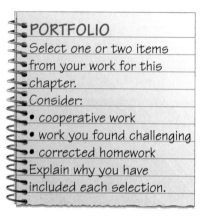

PORTFOLIO
Select one or two items from your work for this chapter.
Consider:
• cooperative work
• work you found challenging
• corrected homework
Explain why you have included each selection.

Mixed Review

Use any method to solve each problem. *(Lesson 7-3)*

11. What is 46% of 130?   12. 98 is what percent of 280?   13. 41 is 27% of what number?

Use the triangle at the right. Write each trigonometric ratio as a fraction in simplest form. *(Lesson 6-10)*

14. $\sin A$ 15. $\cos B$ 16. $\tan A$

17. $\sin B$ 18. $\cos A$ 19. $\tan B$

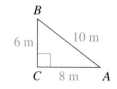

20. *Travel* On a map, the distance between Grapeland and Peachland is 16 cm. If the scale is 2 cm : 25 km, what is the actual distance? *(Lesson 6-6)*

CHAPTER PROJECT

Invest in a Winner

Explore Ways to Invest Money The Project Link questions on pages 341, 346, and 364 should help you complete your project. Here is a checklist to help you gather the parts of your project together.

✔ a report on your interviews with adults about investments

✔ a list of certificates of deposit and the interest rates offered by different banks

✔ an explanation of what investment you chose for your $5,000 and why

✔ a graph showing the projected growth over five years

Prepare an oral and visual presentation on your investment choice. Use your graph and actual calculations in your classroom presentation.

Reflect and Revise

Present your presentation to your family. If necessary, revise your explanation and graph before your classroom presentation.

Web Extension
Prentice Hall's Internet site contains information you might find helpful as you complete your project. Visit www.phschool.com/mgm3/ch7 for some links and ideas related to investments.

7 WRAP UP

Fractions, Decimals, and Percents   7-1

A **percent** is a ratio of a number to 100.

To write a fraction as a percent, use a proportion to find an equivalent fraction with a denominator of 100.

To write a decimal as a percent, write the decimal as a fraction with a denominator of 100. Or move the decimal point two places to the right and write a percent sign.

To write a percent as a decimal, move the decimal point two places to the left and remove the percent sign.

Write each percent as a fraction in simplest form.

1. 25%   2. 6.2%   3. 15%   4. 0.3%   5. 140%   6. $37\frac{1}{2}\%$

Write each decimal as a fraction and as a percent.

7. 0.36   8. 1.25   9. 0.7   10. 0.05   11. 2.75   12. 0.008

Estimating with Percents   7-2

When working with percents, it is helpful to estimate.

Estimate the percent of the number using any method. Explain why you chose the strategy you used.

13. 24% of 97   14. 15% of 61   15. 200% of 75   16. 68% of 89

Percents and Proportions, and Percents and Equations   7-3, 7-4

A percent problem can be solved using a proportion or an equation.

$$\frac{n}{100} = \frac{part}{whole} \qquad part = P \cdot whole$$

Solve each of the following. Round to the nearest tenth.

17. What percent of 5 is 4?   18. 30% of what number is 6?   19. 3 is $87\frac{1}{2}\%$ of what number?

20. Dinner for two friends costs $24.32. The pair wants to leave a 15% tip. How much should they leave for a tip?

A circle graph displays data that are parts of a whole.

21. Mia spent $3.75 for lunch, $2.25 for bus fare and $4 for a movie. Display the data in a circle graph.

The **percent of change** P can be expressed as a decimal.

$$P = \frac{\text{amount of change}}{\text{original amount}}$$

The amount a price is increased is the **markup.** The store's cost plus the markup equals the **selling price.**

The amount a price is decreased is the **discount.** The regular price minus the discount equals the **sale price.**

22. **Choose A, B, C, or D.** Which of the following changes represents a 25% increase?

    A. 75 to 100   **B.** 100 to 75   **C.** 30 to 40   **D.** 12 to 15

Find the final price.

23. regular price: $450, discount: 30%

24. store's cost: $60, markup: 75%

To find **simple interest,** use the formula $I = p \cdot r \cdot t$.

To find the final balance when interest is **compounded,** use the formula $B = p(1 + r)^t$.

Find the final balance for $1000 invested in each of the following ways.

25. 5% simple interest for 5 years

26. 7% compounded annually for 3 years

27. *Writing* Explain why compound interest produces a greater final amount than simple interest.

You can solve some problems by making a table.

28. Rick bought shirts for $18 each and socks for $1.75 a pair. If he spent $97, how many of each did he buy?

1. Compare. Use $>$, $<$, or $=$.
   a. 0.8% ▧ 0.8
   b. $\frac{5}{6}$ ▧ 85%
   c. 450% ▧ 4.5
   d. 0.625 ▧ $\frac{5}{8}$
   e. $-\frac{1}{3}$ ▧ -0.34
   f. -5.4 ▧ $-\frac{48}{9}$

2. **Choose A, B, C, or D.** In which set are all three values equal?
   A. $\frac{3}{5}$, 0.3, 30%
   B. $\frac{3}{5}$, 0.6, 6%
   C. $\frac{3}{5}$, 0.06, 6%
   D. $\frac{3}{5}$, 0.6, 60%

3. Find each percent of change to the nearest tenth of a percent. Label your answer as increase or decrease.
   a. 180 to 120
   b. 25 to 75
   c. 87.5 to 62.5
   d. $33\frac{1}{3}$ to $66\frac{2}{3}$

4. Estimate each of the following. Explain how you made your estimate and why.
   a. 76% of 48
   b. 250% of 29
   c. 21% of 36
   d. 0.5% of 498

5. Six million high school students in the United States play a scholastic sport. Only 92,000 college students receive sports scholarships. Estimate what percent of high school athletes receive scholarships to play college sports.

6. Solve using a proportion.
   a. What percent of 32 is 20?
   b. 18 is 30% of what number?
   c. Find 95% of 350.
   d. $12\frac{1}{2}$% of what number is 15?

7. Find the final price to the nearest cent after each markup or discount.
   a. $64.00, 25% discount
   b. $19.99, 15% markup
   c. $850.00, 10% markup
   d. $90.00, 33% discount

8. *Calculator* Find the final balance.
   a. $250 at 4% simple interest for 3 yr
   b. $4,500 at 6% compounded annually for 2 yr
   c. $8,000 at $6\frac{1}{2}$% compounded annually for 3 yr

9. Luis spent $22.50 on two CDs. This was 25% of his savings. How much had he saved?

10. Wendy purchased a pair of shoes for $40.80 during a 15%-off sale. What was the regular price?

11. Last year, Brett earned $5.00 per hour baby sitting. This year he earns $5.50 per hour. What is the percent of increase?

12. Make a circle graph to display the grading system shown in the table.

Assessment	Percent of Grade
Tests	40%
Quizzes	25%
Classwork	20%
Homework	15%

13. *Writing* The Drama Club bought nuts for $4 and sold them for $5. Ellen claims that the markup rate is 20% because $1 is 20% of $5. Explain what is wrong with Ellen's reasoning and give the correct markup rate.

14. Sue saves $30 a month and Lian saves $20 a month. In how many months will Sue have saved exactly $50 more than Lian has saved?

Choose the best answer.

1. Simplify 3.5×10^{-7}.

   A. 35,000,000　　B. 0.000035
   C. 0.0000035　　D. 0.00000035

2. Which pair of numbers has a GCF of 21?

   A. 14 and 21　　B. 84 and 105
   C. 630 and 126　　D. 42 and 84

3. An HO scale model railroad is $\frac{1}{87}$ scale, which means that 1 inch of an HO train is equal to 87 inches of a real train. What is the size of an HO boxcar if a real boxcar measures 50 feet?

   A. About 3.5 in.　　B. About 7 in.
   C. About 7 ft　　D. About 15 in.

4. Which value is the greatest?

   A. $\sin X$
   B. $\cos Y$
   C. $\tan X$
   D. $\tan Y$

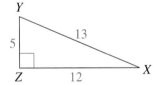

5. Which investment of $100 will give you the most money at the end of two years?

   A. 3.5% interest compounded yearly
   B. 4.5% simple interest
   C. 4% interest compounded yearly
   D. 6% simple interest

6. A jacket with a regular price of $79.99 is on sale for 35% off. Estimate the sale price of the jacket.

   A. $53　　B. $60　　C. $45　　D. $40

7. Which of these is *not* equal to 45%?

   A. 0.45　　B. $\frac{18}{40}$
   C. 9 out of 20　　D. 4.5

8. Solve $n - \frac{5}{6} = -\frac{1}{4}$.

   A. $-1\frac{1}{2}$　　B. $\frac{7}{12}$　　C. $\frac{3}{5}$　　D. $4\frac{1}{2}$

9. Solve $3x + 7 = -11$.

   A. -6　　B. -3　　C. 3　　D. 6

10. Simplify $64 - 4^2 \div 8$.

    A. 6　　B. 7.5　　C. 62　　D. 450

11. Add $-1\frac{3}{5} + 5\frac{1}{2}$.

    A. $3\frac{9}{10}$　　B. $4\frac{1}{10}$　　C. $3\frac{1}{10}$　　D. $4\frac{2}{3}$

12. Subtract $4\frac{2}{3} - \left(-3\frac{3}{4}\right)$.

    A. $-1\frac{1}{7}$　　B. $\frac{11}{12}$　　C. $7\frac{11}{12}$　　D. $8\frac{5}{12}$

13. Which could be the graph of $y = -3x + 2$?

    A.

    B.

    C.

    D.

14. A cube with numbers 1, 2, 3, 4, 5, and 6 on its faces is rolled once. Which of these probabilities is the least?

    A. P(multiple of 3)
    B. P(prime number)
    C. P(factor of 6)
    D. P(even number)

15. Fifteen is 12% of what number?

    A. 1.25　　B. 1.8
    C. 12.5　　D. 125

8

Patterns in Geometry

WHAT YOU WILL LEARN IN THIS CHAPTER

- How to use properties of figures to solve problems

- How to construct figures

- How to find the area of parallelograms, triangles, and circles

THEME:
LANDSCAPE
ARCHITECTURE

Great Escape.

As the summer sun goes down on another hot day, you just *have* to get outside. Where do you go? To the park! For generations, people in towns and cities have used parks as a place to escape. When properly planned, a park can be just the place to relax, meet friends, or skate, surrounded by natural beauty.

Design a Park For your chapter project, you will design a small park and be prepared to present your plan to the town council. Your final product will be a detailed plan of the park.

Steps to help you complete the project:

• **How to solve problems by looking for a pattern**

PROBLEM SOLVING

8-1

Look for a Pattern

Problem Solving Strategies

Draw a Diagram
Guess and Test
✔ Look for a Pattern
Make a Model
Make a Table
Simulate the Problem
Solve a Simpler Problem
Too Much or Too Little
    Information
Use Logical Reasoning
Use Multiple Strategies
Work Backward
Write an Equation

THINK AND DISCUSS

Sometimes the best way to solve a problem is to look for a pattern.

SAMPLE PROBLEM.............

The highest human pyramid ever built was created in Spain in the fall of 1981. The human pyramid had nine levels. How many people were in the pyramid?

 READ

Read for understanding. Summarize the problem.

1. Think about the information you are given and what you are asked to find.
   a. Is a human pyramid actually a pyramid? If not, what shape best describes it?
   b. How many people are in a two-level human pyramid? In a three-level pyramid?

 PLAN

Decide on a strategy.

A good strategy to use here is *Look for a Pattern*. Use dots to represent the people in a human pyramid.

 SOLVE

Try the strategy.

2. Make a table that shows the number of levels and the number of people in the human pyramid.

Levels	1	2	3	4
People	▪	▪	▪	▪

3. Look for a pattern. How is the number of people related to the number of levels?

4. Continue the table. How many people are in a nine-level pyramid?

Think about how you solved the problem.

When you look for a pattern and make a conjecture, you are using *inductive reasoning*. Because the conjectures you make are not always true, you should check your results whenever possible.

5. a. Amy analyzes the products $1 \times 2 \times 3$ and $2 \times 3 \times 4$ and concludes that the product of any three consecutive integers is even. Is her conjecture correct? Explain.

b. Amy also draws the conclusion that the product of any three consecutive integers is greater than any of the three integers. Is her conclusion correct? Explain.

EXERCISES *On Your Own*

1. *Writing* Darryl notices that 3, 5, and 7 are prime numbers. He concludes that all odd numbers are prime. Is his conjecture correct? Explain.

Look for a pattern to solve each problem. Show your work.

2. Find the next three numbers in the pattern.

1, 2, 3.5, 5.5, 8, ▪, ▪, ▪

3. Draw the sixth figure in the pattern.

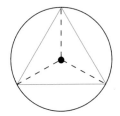 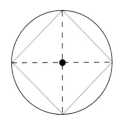 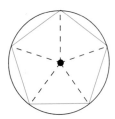

4. The houses on the north side of Hall Avenue are numbered in order with even numbers from 140 to 224. How many house numbers have at least one 6?

5. Onita drew $\angle RST$. She drew $\overrightarrow{SW}$ in the interior of the angle.
   a. How many angles can she name?
   b. Onita draws a second ray $\overrightarrow{SP}$ in the interior of $\angle RST$. How many angles can she name now?
   c. How many angles can Onita name after she draws a third ray? After she draws a sixth ray?

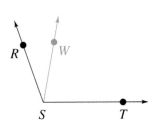

Use any strategy to solve each problem.

6. You are offered a job with an unusual pay rate. Your pay is $.15 for the first day. Each day after that, you earn twice as much as you did the day before. How many days will you need to earn more than $5 a day? More than $20 a day?

7. Jalissa's mother gave her a number puzzle. She told Jalissa to pick a number, add 7 to it, multiply the sum by 3, and then subtract 6. Jalissa did this and ended up with 45. What number did she start with?

8. *Restaurants* A local restaurant offers a breakfast buffet. The restaurant charges $8 for one person, $16 for two people, $23 for three, $29 for four, and so on.
   a. How much does a buffet breakfast for 7 cost? How much does the group save by eating together rather than alone?
   b. The buffet costs the restaurant $5 per person. What size group can the restaurant serve without losing money?

9. *Sports* Amal had made twice as many free throws as Rohan in the first games they had played together. In the next game, Amal made 2 free throws and Rohan made 5. In the following game Amal made no free throws and Rohan made 3. At that point they had made the same number of free throws. How many free throws had each player made before the last two games?

10. Four students are running for class president. How many different ways can they be listed on the ballot?

Mixed Review

Find the simple interest to the nearest cent. *(Lesson 7-8)*

11. $985 at 7.5% for 2 yr

12. $1,500 at 8% for 5 yr

13. $2,080 at 5.25% for 4 yr

14. $875 at 18% for 3 yr

15. $3,670 at 9% for 1.5 yr

16. $5,000 at 6.5% for 6 yr

Use the following data:
55, 65, 45, 63, 36, 52, 63, 64, 63, 57, 47, 39. *(Lesson 1-5)*

17. Display the data in a stem-and-leaf plot.

18. Find the median and the mode.

8-2 Pairs of Angles

What You'll Learn

1 To use adjacent angles and vertical angles

2 To use supplementary angles and complementary angles

...And Why

City planners use pairs of angles to design streets and parks.

Here's How

Look for questions that
- ⁙ build understanding
- ✔ check understanding

Work Together

Investigating Pairs of Angles

Two intersecting lines form four angles. Work in a group to explore the relationships among these angles.

1. **a.** Have each member of your group draw two intersecting lines. Number the angles as shown.
   b. Measure the angles. Record the results of your group in a table like the one shown below.

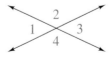

Member	$m\angle 1$	$m\angle 2$	$m\angle 3$	$m\angle 4$
Maria	130°	50°	▦	▦
Josh	▦	▦	▦	▦

2. Compare $m\angle 1$ and $m\angle 3$. Then compare $m\angle 2$ and $m\angle 4$. Make a conjecture about these pairs of angles.

3. **a.** Find the sum of $m\angle 1$ and $m\angle 2$.
   b. Find the sum of $m\angle 2$ and $m\angle 3$.
   c. ⁙*Patterns* Look for a pattern. Make a conjecture about these pairs of angles.

QUICKreview

The expression "$m\angle 1$" means "the measure of $\angle 1$."

THINK AND DISCUSS

1 *Adjacent Angles and Vertical Angles*

In this lesson you will learn to identify special pairs of angles.

Adjacent angles share a vertex and a side but have no common interior points.

Vertical angles are formed by intersecting lines. Vertical angles are congruent.

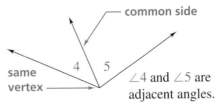

common side

same vertex

$\angle 4$ and $\angle 5$ are adjacent angles.

$\angle 1$ and $\angle 3$ are vertical angles, as are $\angle 2$ and $\angle 4$.

QUICKreview

You can name an angle by using a number, the vertex, or three letters.

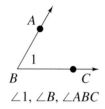

∠1, ∠B, ∠ABC

4. a. Are ∠ABE and ∠DBC vertical angles? Explain.
  b. Are ∠DBC and ∠DBE adjacent angles? Explain.

■ **EXAMPLE 1** *Real-World Problem Solving*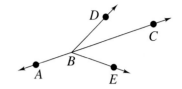

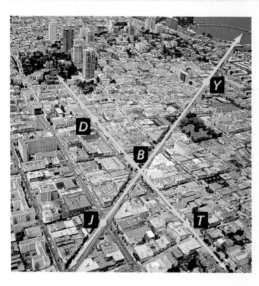

City Planning The streets in this photo of San Francisco intersect and form vertical angles. Identify a pair of vertical angles and a pair of adjacent angles.

∠DBY and ∠JBT are vertical angles.
∠DBJ and ∠JBT are adjacent angles.

5. ✔ Try It Out Identify another pair of vertical angles and another pair of adjacent angles.

6. ▪Look Back In Example 1, the measure of ∠DBY is 80°. Find the measures of ∠JBT, ∠DBJ, and ∠TBY.

❷ Supplementary Angles and Complementary Angles

Two angles are **supplementary** if the sum of their measures is 180°.

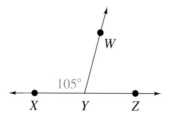

∠C and ∠WYZ are both supplements of ∠XYW.

Two angles are **complementary** if the sum of their measures is 90°.

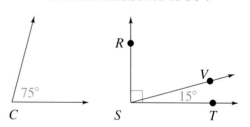

∠C and ∠VSR are both complements of ∠VST.

■ EXAMPLE 2

Algebra If $m\angle A = 42°$, find the measure of its complement.

$$x° + m\angle A = 90°$$ ← The sum of the measures of complementary angles is 90°.

$$x° + 42° = 90°$$ ← Substitute for $m\angle A$.

$$x° = 90° - 42°$$ ← Subtraction Property of Equality

$$x° = 48°$$

The measure of the complement of $\angle A$ is 48°.

7. ✔ **Try It Out** What is the measure of the supplement of $\angle A$ in Example 2?

■ EXAMPLE 3

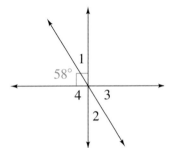

Find the measure of each numbered angle in the diagram at the left.

$$m\angle 1 = 90° - 58° = 32° \quad m\angle 2 = m\angle 1 = 32°$$

$$m\angle 3 = 58° \quad\quad\quad\quad m\angle 4 = 180° - 90° = 90°$$

EXERCISES *On Your Own*

Name a pair of vertical angles and a pair of adjacent angles in each figure. Find $m\angle 1$.

1.
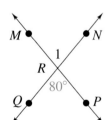

2.
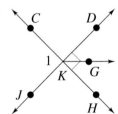

3.
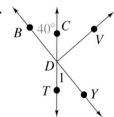

4.
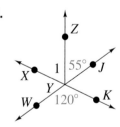

Use the diagram below for Exercises 5–9.

5. $\angle LBD$ and $\angle TBL$ are ▇ angles.

6. $\angle RBT$ and $\angle$▇ are vertical angles.

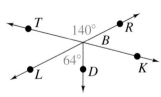

7. $m\angle KBL = $ ▇°   8. $m\angle DBK = $ ▇°

9. **Choose A, B, C, or D.** Find the measure of $\angle TBL$.
   A. 140°   **B.** 64°   **C.** 40°   **D.** 116°

10. **a.** *Map Reading* In the map at the right, find the measure of the angle formed by Route 43 and Devon Avenue.

    b. If you travel south on Route 43 and turn left onto Northwest Highway, at what angle do you turn?

11. **a.** *Writing* Can two supplementary angles have the same measure? Explain.

    b. Can two complementary angles have the same measure? Explain.

12. **a.** *Open-ended* Draw a pair of adjacent supplementary angles.

    b. Use a protractor to draw a pair of supplementary angles that are not adjacent. Label each angle measure.

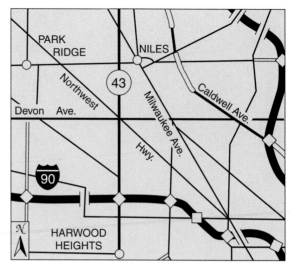

Route 43 is perpendicular to Devon Ave. Northwest Hwy. and Devon Ave. intersect at a 42° angle.

Find the measure of the complement and the supplement of each angle. If there is no complement, write *no complement*.

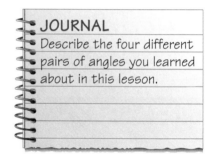

JOURNAL
Describe the four different pairs of angles you learned about in this lesson.

13. 39°   **14.** 42.3°   **15.** 74°   **16.** 85.9°   **17.** 24°

18. 78°   **19.** 116°   **20.** 139.5°   **21.** 179°   **22.** $x°$

Algebra **Complete each equation. Then solve for *x*.**

23. ■ = ■

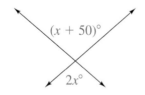

24. ■ + ■ = 180°

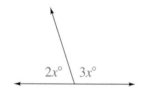

25. ■ + ■ = 90°

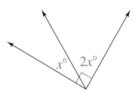

Mixed Review

Is a triangle with the given side lengths a right triangle? Explain. *(Lesson 5-10)*

26. 44 m, 483 m, 485 m   **27.** 51 m, 68 m, 85 m   **28.** 44 m, 240 m, 244 m

29. *Probability* What is the probability of choosing a red ball from a box containing ten white balls and two red balls? *(Lesson 1-11)*

Constructing Segments and Angles

What You'll Learn

1. To construct a segment congruent to a given segment
2. To construct an angle congruent to a given angle

...And Why

Architects and designers use constructions to create precise drawings.

Here's How

Look for questions that
- build understanding
- ✔ check understanding

QUICKreview

A segment is a part of a line. It consists of two points and all the points that are between the two points.

THINK AND DISCUSS

1 Constructing Congruent Segments

Do you think that $\overline{XY}$ or $\overline{UV}$ is longer?

Measure each segment. Although $\overline{UV}$ appears to be longer, $\overline{UV}$ and $\overline{XY}$ are actually the same length. Segments that have the same length are **congruent segments.** You can use a compass and a straightedge to construct congruent segments.

A **compass** is a tool used to draw circles or parts of circles called *arcs*. A **straightedge** is similar to a ruler but has no markings.

■ EXAMPLE 1

Construct segment $\overline{CD}$ congruent to $\overline{AB}$.

Step 1
Draw a ray with endpoint C.

Step 2
Open the compass to the length of $\overline{AB}$.

Step 3
Keep the compass open to the same width. Put the compass point on point C. Draw an arc intersecting the ray. Label the point of intersection D.

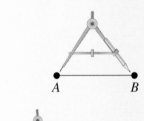

You have constructed $\overline{CD}$ congruent to $\overline{AB}$.

1. ✓ **Try It Out** Draw a segment $\overline{TR}$ that is 25 mm long. Then construct $\overline{SV}$ so that $\overline{SV}$ is congruent to $\overline{TR}$.

▼2 *Constructing Congruent Angles*

You can use a compass and straightedge to construct an angle congruent to a given angle.

■ **EXAMPLE 2**

Construct ∠*RST* congruent to ∠*XYZ*.

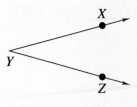

Step 1
Draw a ray. Label the endpoint *S*.

Step 2
Put the compass tip at *Y* and draw an arc that intersects both $\overrightarrow{YX}$ and $\overrightarrow{YZ}$.

Step 3
Keep the compass open to the same width. Put the tip at *S*. Draw an arc intersecting the ray at a point *T*.

Step 4
Adjust the compass width so that the tip and the pencil are at the points where the arc intersects $\overrightarrow{YX}$ and $\overrightarrow{YZ}$.

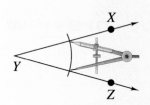

Step 5
Keeping the same compass width, put the tip at *T* and draw an arc that intersects the first arc. Label the point of intersection *R*. Draw $\overrightarrow{SR}$.

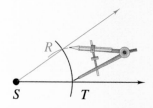

You have constructed ∠*RST* congruent to ∠*XYZ*.

2. Do you need to know the measure of an angle to construct a congruent angle? Explain.

3. a. ✓ *Try It Out* Draw an obtuse angle ∠G. Then construct ∠K congruent to ∠G.

b. Use a protractor to measure ∠G and ∠K. Compare your results. Explain any possible difference in measure.

EXERCISES *On Your Own*

Use $\overline{AB}$ and ∠C to construct each figure.

1. $\overline{EF}$ congruent to $\overline{AB}$

2. $\overline{GH}$ twice the length of $\overline{AB}$

3. ∠D congruent to ∠C

4. ∠B twice the measure of ∠C

5. △RST with an angle congruent to ∠C and two sides congruent to $\overline{AB}$

6. △XYZ with two angles congruent to ∠C

7. *Writing* Explain what a compass is used for in constructions.

8. Follow these steps to construct △EFG with all sides congruent to $\overline{AB}$.
Step ① Use a compass to construct $\overline{EF} \cong \overline{AB}$.
Step ② Using the same compass width, place the compass tip on point F and draw an arc above $\overline{EF}$.
Step ③ Using the same compass width, place the compass tip on point E and make another arc above $\overline{EF}$, intersecting the first arc. Label the point of intersection G.
Step ④ Draw $\overline{EF}$ and $\overline{FG}$ to form △EFG.

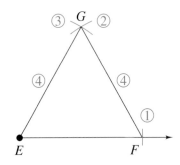

Mixed Review

Without graphing, state in which quadrant or on which axis you would find the points with these coordinates. *(Lesson 4-1)*

9. $(-3, 4)$ **10.** $(-3, -5)$ **11.** $(1, -6)$ **12.** $(3, 0)$ **13.** $(5, -5)$ **14.** $(-4, 0)$

15. *Choose a Strategy* Yoshi's mother is twice as old as Yoshi is. When Yoshi was 8 years old, her mother was 30 years old. How old is Yoshi now?

Angles and Parallel Lines

What You'll Learn

▼ **1** To find the measures of angles formed by parallel lines

▼ **2** To identify parallel lines

...And Why

Navigators use parallel lines to plot ship routes.

Here's How

Look for questions that

- ⬚ build understanding
- ✔ check understanding

Work Together
Exploring Parallel Lines

Navigation The pilot of a ship uses a navigational tool called a *parallel rule* to plot routes on charts. Recall that parallel lines lie in the same plane and do not intersect.

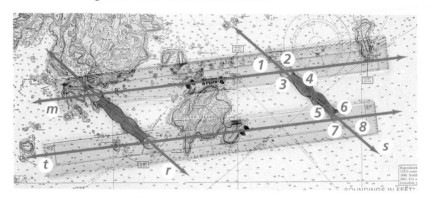

1. **a.** Which lines in the photo appear to be parallel?
   b. Use a protractor to measure the numbered angles.

2. **a.** ⬚ **Draw a Conclusion** Make a conjecture about the angles formed when a line intersects two parallel lines.
   b. Check your conjecture by measuring other angles in the diagram.

THINK AND DISCUSS

▼ **1** *Transversals and Angles*

A line that intersects two other lines in different points is a **transversal.**

3. How many angles are formed by two lines and a transversal?

In the diagram, $\overleftrightarrow{GH}$ is parallel to $\overleftrightarrow{JK}$. You can write this as $\overleftrightarrow{GH} \parallel \overleftrightarrow{JK}$.

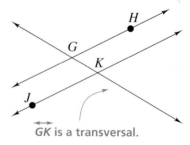

$\overleftrightarrow{GK}$ is a transversal.

Some pairs of angles formed by two lines and a transversal have special names.

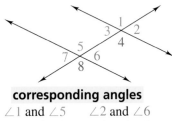

corresponding angles
∠1 and ∠5   ∠2 and ∠6
∠3 and ∠7   ∠4 and ∠8

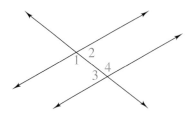

alternate interior angles
∠1 and ∠4   ∠2 and ∠3

■ **EXAMPLE 1**

Identify a pair of corresponding angles and a pair of alternate interior angles.

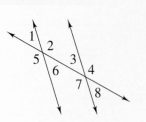

∠1 and ∠3 are corresponding angles.

∠2 and ∠7 are alternate interior angles.

4. ✓ *Try It Out* Identify three other pairs of corresponding angles and another pair of alternate interior angles.

You discovered in the Work Together that when a transversal intersects parallel lines,
• corresponding angles are congruent, and
• alternate interior angles are congruent.

■ **EXAMPLE 2**

In the diagram, $r \parallel s$.
If $m\angle 1 = 75°$,
find $m\angle 2$ and $m\angle 3$.

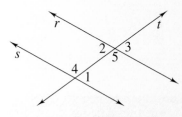

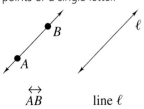
$m\angle 2 = m\angle 1 = 75°$ ⟵ Alternate interior angles are congruent.

$m\angle 3 = m\angle 1 = 75°$ ⟵ Corresponding angles are congruent.

5. ▪ *Look Back* Explain how you could find $m\angle 3$ in Example 2 in another way.

6. ✔ *Try It Out* Find the measures of ∠4 and ∠5 in the diagram for Example 2.

▼2 Identifying Parallel Lines

When a transversal intersects two parallel lines, some pairs of angles are congruent. The reverse is also true. If corresponding angles or alternate interior angles are congruent, the lines are parallel.

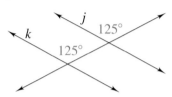

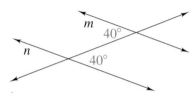

The corresponding angles are congruent, so $k \parallel j$.

The alternate interior angles are congruent, so $m \parallel n$.

■ **EXAMPLE 3**

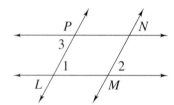

In the diagram at the left, $m\angle 1 = 65°$, $m\angle 2 = 65°$, and $m\angle 3 = 65°$. Explain why both pairs of opposite sides of $LMNP$ are parallel.

$\angle 1$ and $\angle 2$ are congruent corresponding angles. So $\overleftrightarrow{LP} \parallel \overleftrightarrow{MN}$.

$\angle 1$ and $\angle 3$ are congruent alternate interior angles. So $\overleftrightarrow{LM} \parallel \overleftrightarrow{NP}$.

QUICKreview

Perpendicular lines are lines that intersect to form right angles.

7. ▪*Reasoning* Transversal t is perpendicular to lines ℓ and m. Explain why $\ell \parallel m$.

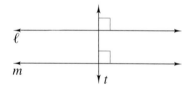

The reasoning used in Example 3 and Question 7 is called deductive reasoning. *Deductive reasoning* is a logical process of drawing conclusions from given facts.

EXERCISES *On Your Own*

Describe each pair of angles as *corresponding*, *alternate interior*, or *neither of these*.

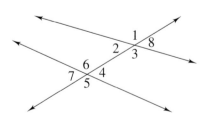

1. $\angle 6, \angle 3$ **2.** $\angle 8, \angle 4$ **3.** $\angle 2, \angle 1$

4. $\angle 2, \angle 4$ **5.** $\angle 1, \angle 5$ **6.** $\angle 2, \angle 7$

Line ℓ is parallel to line m. Find the measures of the numbered angles in each diagram.

7.

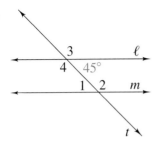

8.

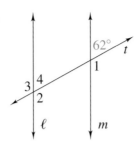

9.

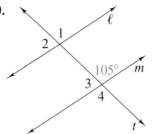

10.

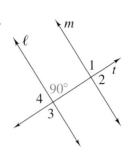

SUBDIVISION APPROVED

Want to live near the lake? Now may be your chance. The town has just approved the construction of a new subdivision near Veronica Lake. The subdivision will consist of forty houses situated on four parallel streets. According to the

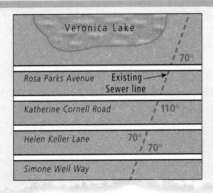

town engineer, Beth Michael, special attention will have to be paid to the drainage system of the development. "We don't want to pollute the lake with waste from the project. Town specifications require an additional sewer line."

11. **Reading About Math** Use the subdivision plan and what you learned in this lesson to explain how you know the streets are parallel.

12. To construct a line m parallel to line n, through point B, Aaron drew line t forming $\angle 1$. Then he constructed $\angle 2 \cong \angle 1$, as shown in the diagram. Explain why $n \parallel m$.

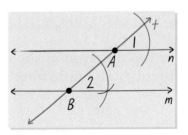

Determine which pairs of lines, if any, are parallel. Explain.

13.

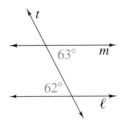

14.

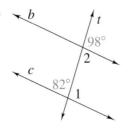

15.

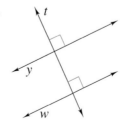

16.

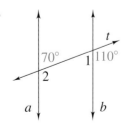

Mixed Review

Evaluate mentally. *(Lesson 2-8)*

17. $-5 + 8 \times 6$ **18.** $15 \div 3 - 2$ **19.** $24 - 20 \times 8$ **20.** $36 \div 9 \times 2 \div 4$

Find the GCF of each set of numbers. *(Lesson 5-1)*

21. $21, 14$ **22.** $72, 144$ **23.** $12, 24$ **24.** $12, 42$ **25.** $65, 95$ **26.** $15, 60$

27. *Choose a Strategy* Two corn muffins and a glass of milk cost $1.80. One corn muffin and a glass of milk cost $1.25. What is the cost of a glass of milk?

CHAPTER PROJECT

PROJECT LINK: DESIGNING

Design a small park. Use a fountain as its centerpiece. Include a path around the fountain and other walkways throughout the park. Create a scale drawing including dimensions and angle measures. Write a description of your plan using geometric terms from this chapter, such as *congruent* and *parallel*.

✓ CHECKPOINT 1

Lessons 8-1 through 8-4

In the diagram at the right, line ℓ is parallel to line m. Identify the following angles.

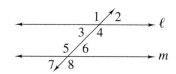

1. two pairs of vertical angles

2. two pairs of alternate interior angles

3. four pairs of corresponding angles   **4.** a pair of adjacent supplementary angles

5. If $m\angle 1$ is $152°$, find $m\angle 2$, $m\angle 3$, and $m\angle 4$.   **6.** Construct an angle congruent to $\angle 6$.

7. a. Find the next three numbers in the pattern.
     20.00, 19.75, 18.50, 16.25, 13.00, ■, ■, ■
   b. *Open-ended* Create your own number pattern. Explain the pattern in the numbers.

Parallel Lines and Similar Triangles

After Lesson 8-4

You can use dynamic geometry software to construct parallel lines and similar triangles.

1. a. Create $\triangle ABC$. Create a point D on $\overline{AB}$.

   b. Construct a line through point D parallel to $\overline{AC}$.

   c. Construct the point of intersection of the parallel line and $\overline{BC}$. Label the point E.

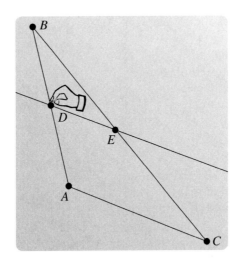

2. a. Using the computer program, find the measures of $\angle BAC$, $\angle BDE$, $\angle BCA$, and $\angle BED$.

   b. Explain why $\angle BAC \cong \angle BDE$ and $\angle BCA \cong \angle BED$.

3. a. Use the program to measure $\overline{BD}$, $\overline{BA}$, $\overline{BE}$, $\overline{BC}$, $\overline{DE}$, and $\overline{AC}$.

   b. Calculate the ratios $\frac{BD}{BA}$, $\frac{BE}{BC}$, and $\frac{DE}{AC}$.

   c. Identify a pair of similar triangles. Use your measurements to justify the similarity.

4. *Patterns* Move $\overleftrightarrow{DE}$ by dragging point D.

   a. What happens to the angles you measured in Question 2 when you move $\overleftrightarrow{DE}$?

   b. What happens to the calculated ratios in Question 3 when you move $\overleftrightarrow{DE}$?

   c. What remains true about $\triangle ABC$ and $\triangle DBE$ as you move $\overleftrightarrow{DE}$?

5. a. Complete the following conjecture.

   When a line intersects two sides of a triangle and is parallel to the third side, the triangles formed are ■.

   b. Test your conjecture by dragging point D and changing the shape of $\triangle ABC$.

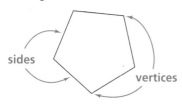

What You'll Learn

▼ **1** To identify corresponding parts of congruent polygons

▼ **2** To determine when two triangles are congruent

...And Why

Congruent triangles are used in the construction and design of many buildings and structures.

Here's How

Look for questions that
- ▪▪ build understanding
- ✔ check understanding

*QUICK*review

A polygon is a closed plane figure formed by three or more line segments.

sides

vertices

Work Together   *Investigating Congruent Triangles*

1. Have each member of your group form a triangle with sides 2, 4, and 5 toothpicks long. Compare your results. Are your triangles all the same size and shape?

THINK AND DISCUSS

1 *Identifying Corresponding Parts*

The triangles you formed in the Work Together are congruent. When two polygons are **congruent,** you can slide, flip or turn one so it fits exactly on the other one.

The matching angles and sides of congruent polygons are called corresponding parts. Matching vertices are corresponding vertices. When you name congruent polygons, always list the corresponding vertices in the same order.

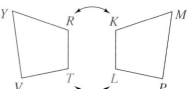

$\angle T$ corresponds to $\angle L$.
$\overline{YV}$ corresponds to $\overline{MP}$.
R corresponds to K.
$VTRY \cong PLKM$

■ **EXAMPLE 1**

$RSTW \cong LKJN$. List congruent corresponding parts.

$\overline{RS} \cong \overline{LK}$ $\overline{ST} \cong \overline{KJ}$
$\overline{TW} \cong \overline{JN}$ $\overline{WR} \cong \overline{NL}$
$\angle R \cong \angle L$ $\angle S \cong \angle K$
$\angle T \cong \angle J$ $\angle W \cong \angle N$

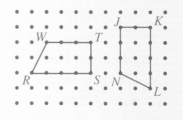

---

2. ▪▪**Look Back** Refer to the diagram for Example 1. Explain why each congruence statement is or is not correct.
   a. $STWR \cong LKJN$ b. $WRST \cong NLKJ$

3. ✔ *Try It Out* $\triangle CFH \cong \triangle DGM$. List congruent corresponding parts of the two triangles.

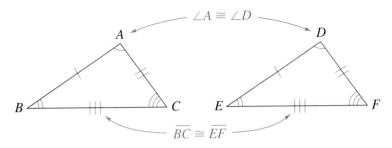

$\angle A \cong \angle D$

$\overline{BC} \cong \overline{EF}$

The tick marks in the diagram tell you which sides are congruent and the arcs tell you which angles are congruent.

4. Name a pair of congruent sides and a pair of congruent angles in the diagram.

You can use corresponding parts of congruent figures to find distances.

■ **EXAMPLE 2**   *Real-World Problem Solving*

Indirect Measurement
Jason drew this diagram so he could find the distance from A to B across the pond. $\triangle ABC$ is congruent to $\triangle EDC$. What is the distance AB?

Since corresponding parts of congruent triangles are congruent, $AB = ED = 82$ yd.

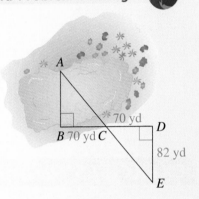

5. ✓ *Try It Out* List all the congruent corresponding parts for the pair of congruent triangles in Example 2.

❷ *Identifying Congruent Triangles*

In the Work Together you discovered that you do not need to know that *all* the corresponding parts are congruent to show that two triangles are congruent.

METHODS OF SHOWING THAT TRIANGLES ARE CONGRUENT

To show that two triangles are congruent, show that the following parts of one triangle are congruent to the corresponding parts of the other triangle.

Side-Side-Side | **Side-Angle-Side** | **Angle-Side-Angle**
(SSS) | (SAS) | (ASA)

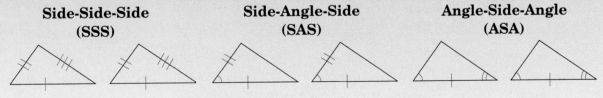

The order is important. For example, SSA or SAA do not show congruent triangles.

■ EXAMPLE 3

Is each pair of triangles congruent? If so, write the
congruence and tell why the triangles are congruent.

a.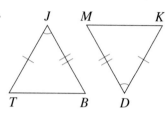

b.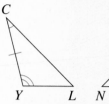

$\overline{TJ} \cong \overline{KD}$ **S**ide
$\angle J \cong \angle D$ **A**ngle
$\overline{BJ} \cong \overline{MD}$ **S**ide

$\triangle TJB \cong \triangle KDM$ by SAS.

$\angle C \cong \angle D$ **A**ngle
$\overline{CY} \cong \overline{DX}$ **S**ide
$\angle Y \cong \angle X$ **A**ngle

$\triangle CYL \cong \triangle DXN$ by ASA.

6. ⬤Reasoning The corresponding angles of two triangles are
congruent. Can you show that the triangles are congruent by
Angle-Angle-Angle? Draw figures to support your answer.

EXERCISES *On Your Own*

Given that $CRML \cong DNXT,$ **complete the following.**

1. $\angle R \cong$ ■

2. $\angle N \cong$ ■

3. $\angle M \cong$ ■

4. $m\angle C =$ ■°

5. $m\angle T =$ ■°

6. $\overline{TD} \cong$ ■

7. $\overline{NX} \cong$ ■

8. $RM =$ ■

9. $DN =$ ■

10. $CL =$ ■

11. $RMLC \cong$ ■

12. $LCRM \cong$ ■

13. $TXND \cong$ ■

14. $XTDN \cong$ ■

15. $RCLM \cong$ ■

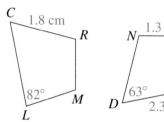

**Write a congruence statement for each pair of congruent
triangles.**

16.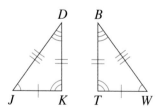

17.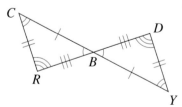

18.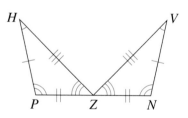

Is each pair of triangles congruent? If so, write the congruence and tell why the triangles are congruent.

19.

20.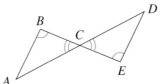

21.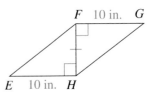

22.

23.

24.

25. Choose A, B, C, or D. Which triangle does not have to be congruent to the triangle at the right?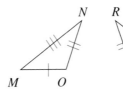

A.   B.   C.   D.

Explain why each pair of triangles is congruent. Then, find the missing measures in each diagram.

26.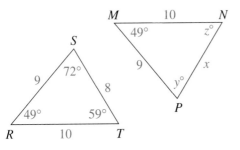

27.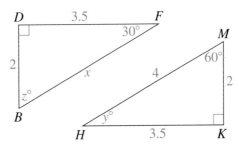

28. Construction Trace a pair of triangles that appear to be congruent in the scaffolding photo. Label your diagram and identify corresponding congruent parts.

29. Writing Explain why $\triangle ABC \cong \triangle DFE$.

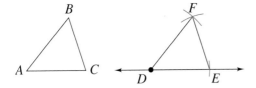

Solve each proportion mentally. *(Lesson 6-3)*

30. $\dfrac{36}{x} = \dfrac{8}{12}$ **31.** $\dfrac{32}{48} = \dfrac{4}{y}$ **32.** $\dfrac{z}{14} = \dfrac{6}{70}$ **33.** $\dfrac{13}{52} = \dfrac{a}{8}$ **34.** $\dfrac{35}{25} = \dfrac{b}{5}$ **35.** $\dfrac{c}{7} = \dfrac{24}{6}$

Determine whether each number is rational or irrational.
(Lesson 5-2)

36. -2.5 **37.** $\dfrac{7}{8}$ **38.** $\sqrt{5}$ **39.** $3.\overline{12}$ **40.** $4.1010010001\ldots$

41. *Choose a Strategy* In the first exercise class, students do
6 push-ups. The teacher tells the class that the number of
push-ups will increase by two each time they come to class.
How many push-ups will the class have to do on the ninth day?

Math at Work

DANCER

Music, movement, stories, and expression of
ideas can all be combined into an art form
known as dance. The career of a dancer is
strenuous and requires long hours of hard work
and practice. Many dancers perform in classical
ballet. Other types of dance, such as modern
dance, allow for more freedom of movement
and self-expression. Folk, ethnic, tap, and jazz
are all dance forms that complement other art
forms such as opera, Broadway shows, and
music videos.

You might wonder how mathematics can be
applied to dance. Often, dancers perform as a
group. The choreography, or the arranged movements of the
dance, consists of steps in repeating patterns. Knowledge of
patterns helps dancers remember the steps and keep in step.

Dancers from the show
Stomp use everyday objects
such as brooms for props.

For more information about different types of
dancing, visit the Prentice Hall Web site:
www.phschool.com

Extra Practice, Lesson 8-5, page 589

Quadrilaterals and Triangles

What You'll Learn

▼ To classify quadrilaterals

▼ To classify triangles by sides and by angles

...And Why

Architects use quadrilaterals and triangles in their designs.

Here's How

Look for questions that

▪ build understanding

✔ check understanding

QUICKreview

Segments are parallel if they lie in separate parallel lines.

THINK AND DISCUSS

1 Classifying Quadrilaterals

A **quadrilateral** is a polygon with four sides. A quadrilateral with two pairs of opposite sides parallel is a **parallelogram.** A quadrilateral with exactly one pair of parallel sides is a **trapezoid.**

Some parallelograms have special names. A parallelogram with four right angles is a **rectangle.** A parallelogram with four congruent sides is a **rhombus.** A parallelogram with four right angles and four congruent sides is a **square.** You can use a Venn diagram to show the relationships among quadrilaterals.

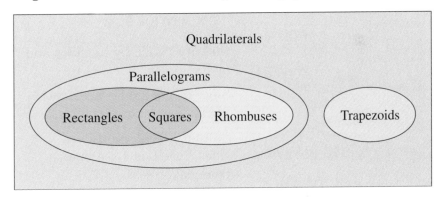

■ EXAMPLE 1

Judging by appearance, classify quadrilateral *DGHJ*.

It is a parallelogram because it has two pairs of parallel opposite sides. It is also a rhombus because all of its sides are congruent.

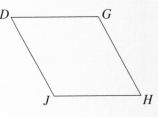

1. ▪ *Draw a Conclusion* Which name from Example 1 gives more information about *DGHJ*? Explain.

2. ▪ *Reasoning* Explain why *DGHJ* is not a square.

An acute angle measures less than 90°.

A right angle measures 90°.

An obtuse angle measures between 90° and 180°.

✌ *Classifying Triangles*

You can classify triangles by angle measures or by the number of congruent sides.

acute triangle

three acute angles

obtuse triangle

one obtuse angle

right triangle

one right angle

equilateral triangle

three congruent sides

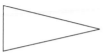

isosceles triangle

at least two
congruent sides

scalene triangle

no congruent sides

■ EXAMPLE 2

Classify △*JKL* by its sides and by its angles.

Since all its angles are acute, △*JKL* is an acute triangle.

Since it has no congruent sides, △*JKL* is a scalene triangle.

Therefore, △*JKL* is a scalene acute triangle.

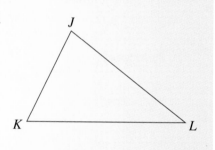

3. ✔ *Try It Out* Draw each figure.
   a. a scalene right triangle
   b. an isosceles obtuse triangle
   c. an equilateral triangle
   d. an isosceles right triangle

4. a. ⬥*Reasoning* Are all equilateral triangles isosceles? Explain.
   b. Are all isosceles triangles equilateral? Explain.
   c. Draw a Venn diagram to show the relationship between an isosceles triangle and an equilateral triangle.

5. ⬥*Analyze* Is it possible to draw an equilateral right triangle? Explain.

Work Together

Work with a partner to investigate quadrilaterals and triangles. Copy the table shown below. Make a parallelogram, a rectangle, a rhombus, and a square on a geoboard.

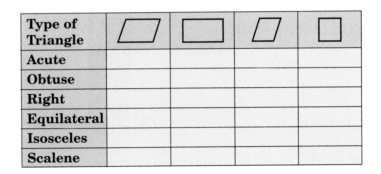

Type of Triangle				
Acute				
Obtuse				
Right				
Equilateral				
Isosceles				
Scalene				

6. Use a geoband to divide each quadrilateral into two triangles. Check off the types of triangles you can form. Compare your results with those of your classmates.

EXERCISES *On Your Own*

Judging by appearance, classify each quadrilateral. Name the congruent sides and angles.

1.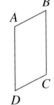

2.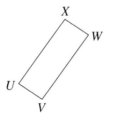

3.

4.

Draw and label a figure to fit each description.

5. an isosceles right triangle

6. a scalene obtuse triangle

7. an equilateral triangle

8. an isosceles trapezoid

9. a trapezoid with a right angle

10. a rhombus that is not square

Judging by appearance, name all the figures shown that fit each description.

11. parallelogram

12. isosceles triangle

13. right triangle

14. obtuse triangle

15. scalene triangle

16. acute triangle

17. rectangle

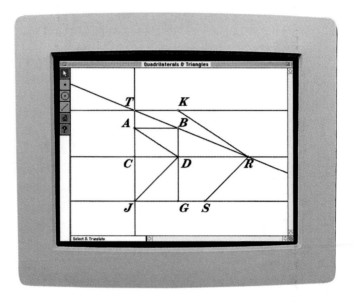

18. *Writing* Explain the relationships among rectangles, rhombuses, and squares. Use the words *all*, *some*, and *no*.

Mixed Review

Find each percent of change. Label your answer as an increase or a decrease. *(Lesson 7-6)*

19. 500 to 450   20. 11 to 15   21. 9.95 to 6.65   22. 12 to 13.5   23. 85 to 78

Compare. Use >, <, or =. *(Lesson 5-4)*

24. 0.04 ▊ 0.4   25. -3 ▊ -1 26. $-\frac{1}{2}$ ▊ -0.25 27. $-4\frac{3}{4}$ ▊ -4.8 28. 0.80 ▊ 0.8

29. *Choose a Strategy* Toni has $6.00, made up of quarters, dimes, and nickels. She has equal numbers of each type of coin. How many of each coin does she have?

CHAPTER PROJECT

PROJECT LINK: DRAWING

Sketch the locations for the various types of flowers, plants, or trees in your park. As part of your plan, describe the shapes of the flower beds using terms from this chapter, such as *triangle* and *trapezoid*.

8-7 Angles of Polygons

What You'll Learn

1 To find the sum of the measures of the angles of a polygon

2 To find the angle measure of each angle of a regular polygon

...And Why

Manufacturers and artists use polygons for tiles and mosaic patterns.

Here's How

Look for questions that
- build understanding
✔ check understanding

Polygon	Number of Sides
Pentagon	5
Hexagon	6
Heptagon	7
Octagon	8
Nonagon	9
Decagon	10

Work Together
Exploring Polygon Patterns

The diagram at the right shows in red all the possible *diagonals* that can be drawn from one vertex of a heptagon. Work in a group to explore how you can use triangles to find the sum of the measures of the angles of a polygon.

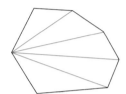

1. In your group draw a quadrilateral, a pentagon, and a hexagon. Then draw all the possible diagonals from one vertex of each figure and count the number of triangles formed.

2. Complete a table like the one shown below. Remember the sum of the measures of the angles of a triangle is 180°.

Polygon	Number of Sides	Number of Triangles Formed	Sum of All Angle Measures
Triangle	3	1	180°
Quadrilateral	4	2	360°
Pentagon	■	■	■
Hexagon	■	■	■

3. **Patterns** What happens to the sum of the angle measures as the number of sides of a polygon increases by 1? Explain.

4. **Reasoning** What relationship do you notice between the number of sides of a polygon and the number of triangles formed?

5. a. **Algebra** Suppose that a polygon has n sides. Write an expression for the number of triangles formed.
   b. Use your answer to part (a) to write an expression for the sum of the angle measures of a polygon with n sides.

THINK AND DISCUSS

▼1 *Angles of Polygons*

In the Work Together you discovered how to find the sum of the angle measures of any polygon.

POLYGON ANGLE SUM

The sum of the measures of the angles of a polygon with n sides is $(n - 2)180°$.

■ EXAMPLE 1

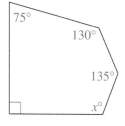

Algebra Find the missing angle measure in the pentagon at the left.

Find the sum of the angle measures of a pentagon.

$(n - 2)180° = (5 - 2)180°$ ←— Substitute 5 for n, since a pentagon has 5 sides.

$\qquad\qquad = 540°$ ←— Simplify.

Let x represent the missing angle measure.

$540° = 90° + 75° + 130° + 135° + x°$ ←— Write an equation.

$540° = 430° + x°$ ←— Add.

$110° = x°$ ←— Subtraction Property of Equality

6. ✓ *Try It Out* Find the sum of the measures of the angles of a polygon with the given number of sides.
   a. 10 sides   b. 9 sides   c. 7 sides   d. 20 sides

▼2 *Angles of Regular Polygons*

A regular polygon is a polygon with all the sides congruent and all the angles congruent.

7. a. How many sides does the polygon in the diagram have?
   b. How many angles does it have?
   c. ⚙ *Reasoning* Explain how you can find the measure of each angle of this regular polygon without measuring.

You can find the measure of each angle of a regular polygon by dividing the sum of the angle measures by the number of angles. A polygon with n sides has n angles.

■ **EXAMPLE 2**

Architecture The window in the photo is a regular octagon. Find the measure of each angle of a regular octagon.

Find the sum of the measures of the angles of the polygon.

$$(n - 2)180° = (8 - 2)180°$$ ←—Substitute 8 for n.

$$= 1080°$$ ←—Simplify.

Divide the sum of the measures of the angles of the polygon by the number of angles.

$$1080° ÷ 8 = 135°$$

Each angle of a regular octagon has a measure of 135°.

8. ✓ *Try It Out* Find the measure of each angle of a regular polygon with the given number of sides.
   a. 5 sides
   b. 6 sides
   c. 7 sides
   d. 10 sides

9. ✓ *Try It Out* What is the measure of each angle of a regular quadrilateral?

10. ▪ *Reasoning* What is another name for a regular quadrilateral?

EXERCISES *On Your Own*

Classify each polygon by the number of its sides.

1.
2.
3.
4.

5. *Writing* Describe the relationship between the number of sides of a polygon and the number of diagonals that can be drawn from one vertex.

Find the sum of the measures of the angles of a polygon with the given number of sides.

6. 11 sides   **7.** 12 sides   **8.** 15 sides   **9.** 24 sides   **10.** 30 sides

11. The measures of five angles of a hexagon are 145°, 115°, 152°, 87°, and 150°. Find the measure of the sixth angle.

12. The measures of six angles of a heptagon are 145°, 115°, 152°, 87°, 90°, and 150°. Find the measure of the seventh angle.

Find the measure of each angle of the given regular polygon.

13. pentagon   **14.** hexagon   **15.** octagon   **16.** decagon   **17.** nonagon

18. Choose A, B, C, or D. Which of the following variable expressions represents the measure of each angle of a regular polygon with n sides?

    A. $180° \cdot n$ **B.** $180°(n - 2)$ **C.** $180°$ **D.** $\dfrac{180°(n - 2)}{n}$

19. Mike and Laura both used calculators to find $m\angle 1$ in the diagram at the right. Look at the keystrokes they used.
    a. Explain why both methods work.
    b. Whose method do you prefer? Why?

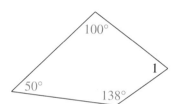

Mike

    360 $\boxminus$ 50 $\boxminus$ 100 $\boxminus$ 138 $\boxminus$ *72*

Laura

    50 $\boxplus$ 100 $\boxplus$ 138 $\boxminus$ *288*
    360 $\boxminus$ 288 $\boxminus$ *72*

20. Sports In the diagram of home plate at the right, $\angle 1 \cong \angle 2$. Find $m\angle 1$.

21. Writing Explain why you cannot find the measure of each angle in a *nonregular* polygon by dividing the sum of the measures of the angles by the number of angles.

22. *Probability* Hector placed the regular polygons shown at the right into a bag. Jill pulled out a polygon. What is the probability that the measure of an angle of the polygon is a multiple of 30?

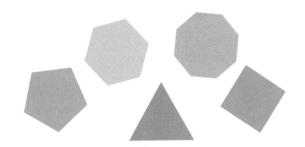

Mixed Review

Solve each inequality. Graph the solution. *(Lessons 3-9 and 3-10)*

23. $4 + x < 7$ **24.** $2y \geq -6$ **25.** $z - 4 \leq 0$ **26.** $0.75a > 1.5$

Graph each equation. *(Lesson 4-4)*

27. $2x + 3y = 3$ **28.** $2x - 6y = -4$ **29.** $3x - y = 0$ **30.** $4x + 4y = -2$

31. *Choose a Strategy* How many of the whole numbers between 100 and 1,000 contain only 3, 4, or 5 as digits?

✓ CHECKPOINT 2   *Lessons 8-5 through 8-7*

Quadrilateral $ABCD \cong KLMN$. **Complete the following.**

1. $\angle B \cong$ ■

2. $\angle N \cong$ ■

3. $m\angle N =$ ■°

4. $m\angle K =$ ■°

5. $\overline{AB} \cong$ ■

6. $\overline{MN} \cong$ ■

7. Choose A, B, C, or D. Look at the diagram above. Which congruence statement is correct?

   A. $ABDC \cong KLMN$ **B.** $LKMN \cong BACD$ **C.** $LMNK \cong BCDA$ **D.** $DBAC \cong LNMK$

Draw and label a figure to fit each description.

8. a scalene obtuse triangle

9. an isosceles trapezoid

Find the sum of the measures of the angles of a polygon with the given number of sides.

10. 4 sides   **11.** 8 sides   **12.** 12 sides   **13.** 18 sides

Choose the best answer.

1. △*ABC* is congruent to △*DBC*. How long is $\overline{AD}$?

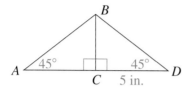

A. 4 in.　　　　　**B.** about 7 in.
C. 10 in.　　　　 **D.** 5 in.

2. Refer to the diagram for Question 1. What is the measure of ∠*ABC*?

F. 30°　　**G.** 45°　　**H.** 60°　　**J.** 90°

3. Which one of the polygons listed *cannot* have 4 right angles?

A. rectangle　　　**B.** rhombus
C. square　　　　**D.** trapezoid

4. What is the approximate circumference of circle *G*? (Use *π* ≈ 3.14.)

F. 15.7 in.　　　　**G.** 31.4 in.
H. 62.8 in.　　　　**J.** 78.5 in.

5. The drawing below shows how to

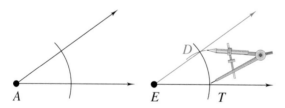

A. construct perpendicular lines.
B. construct congruent segments.
C. construct a circle.
D. construct congruent angles.

6. Triangle *EFG* is a right triangle. What is the length of $\overline{FG}$?

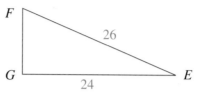

F. 10　　**G.** 18　　**H.** 12　　**J.** 15

Please note that items 7–8 have *five* answer choices.

7. Farmer Hoyle usually takes the shortcut across his rectangular field. How much distance does he save by taking the shortcut instead of walking along two sides of the field?

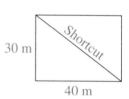

A. 50 m　　　**B.** 40 m　　　**C.** 30 m
D. 20 m　　　**E.** 10 m

8. Which expression would give the area of pentagon *ABCDE*?

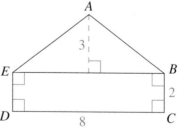

F. $\frac{1}{2} \cdot 3 + \frac{1}{2} \cdot 8 + 2 \cdot 8$
G. $\frac{1}{2} \cdot 3 \cdot 8 + 2 \cdot 8$
H. $2(3^2 + 4^2) + 2 \cdot 8$
J. $3 \cdot 8 + 2 \cdot 8$
K. Not Here

Polygons and Tessellations

What You'll Learn

▼ To identify and create a tessellation

...And Why

Tessellations can be found in art, in architecture, and in nature.

Here's How

Look for questions that

▪ build understanding

✔ check understanding

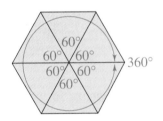

Work Together

Investigating Regular Polygons

The brick arrangement shown in the photo forms a repeating pattern. As you can see, the congruent rectangles cover a surface, or plane, with no gaps in between and no overlaps.

Cut out at least six congruent copies for each of the following regular polygons: triangle, quadrilateral, pentagon, hexagon, and octagon. Work in a group to discover which regular polygons can cover a plane. Then complete a table like the one below.

Regular Polygon	Measure of Each Angle	Factor of 360?	Covers the Plane?
Triangle	60°	yes	
Quadrilateral	90°		

1. ▪ **Patterns** Look for a pattern. Explain why some regular polygons cover a plane and others do not.

THINK AND DISCUSS

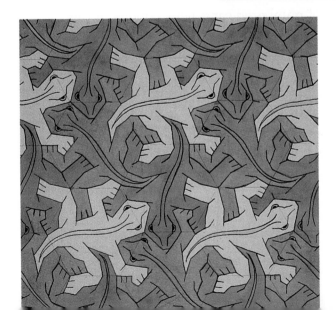

In the Work Together you discovered that some regular polygons tessellate and some do not. A **tessellation** is a repeated geometric design that covers a plane with no gaps or overlaps. The Dutch artist M. C. Escher (1898–1972) was famous for using tessellations in his art. Many of his designs are based on polygons that tessellate.

■ **EXAMPLE 1** *Real-World Problem Solving*

Art Identify the repeating figures found in the Zen pebble garden at the right.

Repeating figure

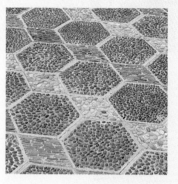

2. ✔ *Try It Out* Find a tessellation in your classroom. Identify the repeating figure.

Escher used translations, rotations, and reflections to create tessellating creatures. Follow the steps below to see how he used translations to make a parallelogram into a tessellating bird.

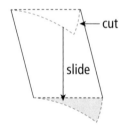

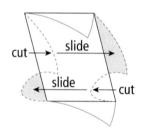

The reptile at the left is another tessellating creature found in Escher's artwork.

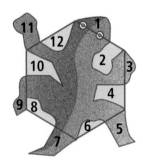

■ **EXAMPLE 2**

Identify six pairs of numbered congruent regions in the reptile diagram at the left.

1 and 12, 2 and 11, 3 and 6, 4 and 5, 7 and 10, 8 and 9

3. a. What polygon did Escher modify to form this reptile?

   b. ⚎ *Use What You Know* What transformations can you use to move each numbered region of the reptile onto its congruent region?

4. ✔ *Try It Out* Trace several copies of the reptile to create a tessellation.

Identify the repeating figure or figures that make up each tessellation.

1.

2.

3.

Make multiple copies of each figure on graph paper. Show how each figure tessellates.

4.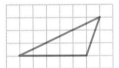

5.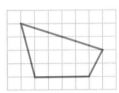

6.

7.

8.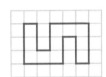

9.

10. Make multiple copies of the bird on page 408 and show how it tessellates.

List pairs of numbered congruent regions in each figure. Trace each figure and create a tessellation.

11.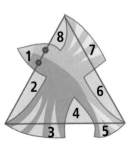

12.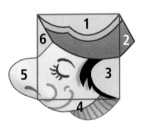

13.

14. *Writing* Explain why you cannot use a regular decagon to tessellate the plane.

15. Follow the steps below to create an Escher-like tessellation.

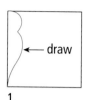 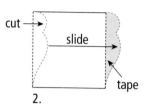 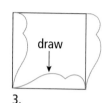 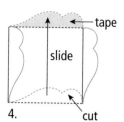 

1.   2.   3.   4.   5.

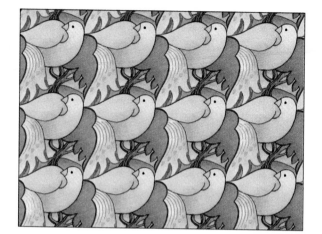

- Cut out a large square.

- On the left side, sketch a curve from the bottom vertex to the top vertex.

- Cut along this curve. Tape the cutout piece onto the right side of the square.

- Repeat this process, cutting off a piece from the bottom and taping it onto the top.

- Decorate the resulting figure. Use it to make a tessellation.

16. *Open-ended* Draw a parallelogram. Create your own Escher-like tessellation by following the instructions in Exercise 15. Use your imagination and decorate your tessellation using colored pencils.

> JOURNAL
> Describe three examples of a tessellation you have seen in your everyday life. Include a sketch of each example.

Mixed Review

Estimation **Use dimensional analysis to find a reasonable estimate for each quantity.** *(Lesson 6-2)*

17. $\frac{1}{2}$ mi = ▨ yd   **18.** 12 qt = ▨ gal   **19.** 2.5 pt = ▨ fl oz   **20.** 8 h = ▨ min

Rewrite each number as a decimal and as a percent.
(Lesson 7-1)

21. $5\frac{2}{5}$ **22.** $\frac{40}{45}$ **23.** $\frac{3}{8}$ **24.** $6\frac{3}{4}$ **25.** $\frac{54}{12}$ **26.** $\frac{7}{8}$

27. *Choose a Strategy* What three consecutive whole numbers have a sum of 702?

Areas of Parallelograms and Triangles

What You'll Learn

▼ To find the area of a parallelogram

▼ To find the area of a triangle

...And Why

Painters and construction workers use area to determine the amounts of the materials needed for a job.

Here's How

Look for questions that
- build understanding
- ✔ check understanding

THINK AND DISCUSS

▼ *Finding the Area of a Parallelogram*

Construction workers and painters use area to find the amounts of materials needed for a job.

You can find the area of a figure by counting the number of square units inside it. If the figure is a rectangle, you can use the formula $A = \ell w$ or $A = bh$. The diagram below shows how a parallelogram can be rearranged to form a rectangle.

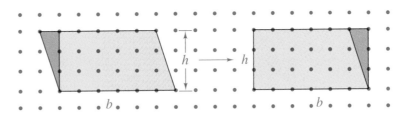

1. What is the area of the rectangle that is formed?

2. What was the area of the original parallelogram?

3. **a.** What are the base length b and the height h of the original parallelogram?
   b. ⊹ *Reasoning* How are b and h of the parallelogram related to the base length and height of the rectangle formed?

The formula for the area of a parallelogram follows from the formula for the area of a rectangle.

AREA OF A PARALLELOGRAM

The area of a parallelogram equals the product of any base length b and the corresponding height h.

$$A = bh$$

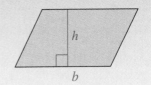

You can use the length of any side of a parallelogram as the base. The height is the perpendicular distance to the side parallel to the base.

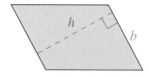

4. a. ✓ *Try It Out* Draw a parallelogram on graph paper. Identify a base and its corresponding height.

 b. Draw a copy of your parallelogram. Identify a different base and its corresponding height.

■ EXAMPLE 1

Find the area of each parallelogram.

a.

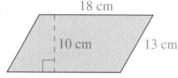

b.

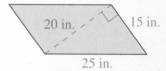

$A = bh$ ←— Area formula
$\ = (18)(10)$ ←— Substitute.
$\ = 180$ ←— Multiply.
The area is 180 cm^2.

$A = bh$ ←— Area formula
$\ = (15)(20)$ ←— Substitute.
$\ = 300$ ←— Multiply.
The area is 300 in.^{2}.

5. ✓ *Try It Out* Draw two different parallelograms on dot paper. Label the base length and height on each figure. Use the area formula to find the area of each.

▼2 *Finding the Area of a Triangle*

A diagonal of a parallelogram divides the figure into two congruent triangles.

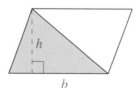 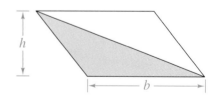

You can see that the area of a triangle is half the area of a parallelogram.

AREA OF A TRIANGLE

The area of a triangle equals half the product of any base length b and the corresponding height h.

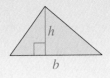

$$A = \frac{1}{2}bh$$

6. a. Find the area of the parallelogram at the right.

b. ⣿ *Visual Thinking* Draw a diagonal and then find the area of each congruent triangle formed.

■ **EXAMPLE 2** *Real-World Problem Solving*

Construction A builder wants to cover the front triangular section of a townhouse with cedar shingles. Find the area of the triangle.

The height of the triangle is 16 ft. The base length is 24 ft.

$A = \frac{1}{2}bh$ ←—triangle area formula

$= \frac{1}{2} \cdot 24 \cdot 16$ ←—Substitute.

$= 192$ ←—Multiply.

The area of the triangle is 192 ft^2.

7. a. ⣿ *Think About It* Shingles are sold in bundles. One bundle of cedar shingles covers 50 square feet. How many bundles are needed to cover the front triangular section of one of the townhouses?

b. Each bundle costs $43.50. What is the cost of the shingles?

8. ✔ *Try It Out* Find the area of the triangle at the right.

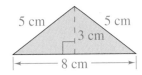

▦ **Find the area of each parallelogram.**

1.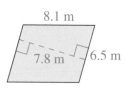
6 cm 5 cm
10 cm

2.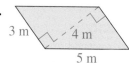
5 in.
8 in.

3.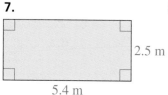
8 cm 10 cm
10 cm

4.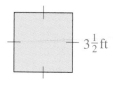
5 cm
12 cm

5.
8.1 m
7.8 m 6.5 m

6.
3 m 4 m
5 m

7.
2.5 m
5.4 m

8.
$3\frac{1}{2}$ ft

9. A parallelogram has an area of 63 m². One base length is 18 m. What is the corresponding height?

10. A square has an area of 81 m². What is its perimeter?

11. *Open-ended* Use graph paper to draw two different parallelograms with the same area. Identify the base length and corresponding height of each.

12. a. *Number Sense* The height of a parallelogram is doubled, but the base length is unchanged. How does this affect the area?
   b. The height of a parallelogram and its corresponding base length are both doubled. How does this affect the area?

13. *Engineering* Value Supermart is reviewing two plans for a new parking lot. One plan uses parallelograms for parking spaces and the other uses rectangles.
   a. Find the area of a parking space in each of the plans.
   b. Find the area of the unpaved sections in each plan.
   c. *Writing* Write a paragraph explaining why you would recommend one plan over the other.

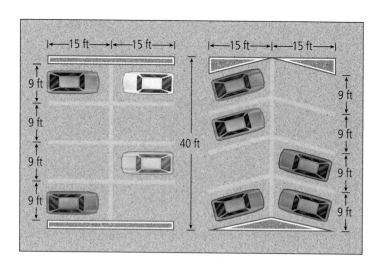

Find (a) the area of each parallelogram *ABCD* and (b) the area of each triangle *ADC*.

14.

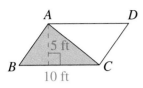

15.

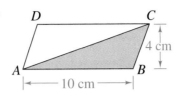

16.

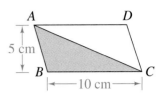

▦ *Choose* **Use a calculator, paper and pencil, or mental math to find the area of each triangle.**

17.

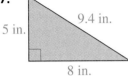

18.

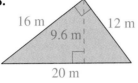

19.

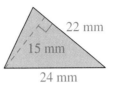

20.

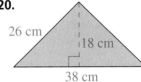

21.

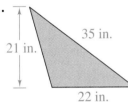

22.

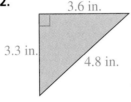

23.

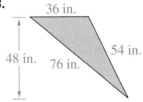

24.

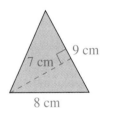

▦ **25. a.** *Geography* Use the map at the right to approximate the area of the state of Virginia.
   b. *Research* Compare your approximation with the actual area of Virginia.

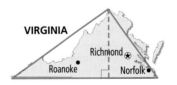

VIRGINIA

Richmond

Roanoke   Norfolk

1 cm = 170 km

Mixed Review

▦ **Find each square root.** *(Lesson 5-9)*

26. $\sqrt{81}$ **27.** $\sqrt{121}$ **28.** $\sqrt{625}$ **29.** $\sqrt{10,000}$ **30.** $\sqrt{169}$ **31.** $\sqrt{324}$

Rotate each point the given number of degrees about the origin. Give the coordinates of each image point. *(Lesson 4-10)*

32. $P(-5, 3)$; rotation of 90°   **33.** $A(7, -6)$; rotation of 270°   **34.** $M(3, -4)$; rotation of 180°

35. A painter needs 15 gallons of violet paint. The formula for mixing violet paint is 3 parts blue to 2 parts red. How many gallons of blue paint does the painter need? *(Lesson 6-3)*

What You'll Learn

▼ **1** To find the circumference of a circle

▼ **2** To find the area of a circle

...And Why

Circles are used in sports, designs, and graphs.

Here's How

Look for questions that

⊞ build understanding

✔ check understanding

THINK AND DISCUSS

1 Finding the Circumference of a Circle

The distance around a polygon is the *perimeter*. The **circumference** is the distance around a circle. The circumference is a little more than three times the diameter. **Pi** (π) is the special name for the ratio of the circumference (C) to the diameter (d).

$$\pi = \frac{C}{d}$$

If you solve this equation for C, you get $C = \pi d$, a formula for the circumference of a circle.

CIRCUMFERENCE OF A CIRCLE

The circumference of a circle is the product of π and the diameter d.

$$C = \pi d \text{ or } C = 2\pi r$$

---

1. ⊞ **Reasoning** Explain why πd is equivalent to $2\pi r$.

You can use $\frac{22}{7}$, 3.14, or a calculator $\boxed{\pi}$ key to approximate π, which is an irrational number.

■ **EXAMPLE 1** *Real-World Problem Solving*

▦ *Sports* The diameter of a basketball hoop is 45 cm. Find its circumference.

To find the circumference, use $C = \pi d$.

$\boxed{\pi}$ $\boxed{\times}$ 45 $\boxed{=}$ *141.37167*

The circumference is about 141 cm.

2. ✓ *Try It Out* Find the circumference of a circle with the given radius or diameter. Round to the nearest tenth.
   a. $d = 5$ cm **b.** $d = 25$ in. **c.** $r = 14$ yd

2 *Finding the Area of a Circle*

If you cut a pizza into equal pieces, you can form a figure that resembles a parallelogram.

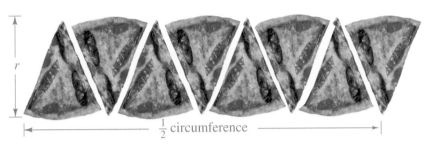

$\frac{1}{2}$ circumference

$A = \quad b \quad \cdot h \quad \longleftarrow$ parallelogram area formula
$= \frac{1}{2}(2\pi r) \cdot r \quad \longleftarrow$ Substitute $\frac{1}{2}(2\pi r)$ for b and r for h.
$= \pi r^2 \quad \longleftarrow$ Simplify. This is the circle area formula.

AREA OF A CIRCLE

The area of a circle is the product of π and the square of the radius r.

$$A = \pi r^2$$

■ EXAMPLE 2 *Real-World Problem Solving*

Food The diameter of a small pizza is 10 inches. Find its area.

The radius of the pizza is $10 \div 2$ or 5 inches. Now use the radius to find the area.

$A = \pi r^2 \quad \longleftarrow$ Use the area formula.
$= \pi(5)^2 \quad \longleftarrow$ Substitute 5 for r.

π ✕ 5 x^2 ▤ `78.539816`

The area of a small pizza is about 79 square inches.

3. a. The diameter of a large pizza is 14 inches. Find its area.
   b. A large pizza costs $9.99 and a small pizza costs $4.99. Which size is the better buy? Explain.

4. ✔ Try It Out Find the area of a circle with the given radius or diameter. Round your answer to the nearest hundredth.
   a. $d = 12$ in.   **b.** $r = 6\frac{1}{3}$ yd   **c.** $r = 1.8$ km

You can find the area of a circle if you know the circumference.

■ **EXAMPLE 3** *Real-World Problem Solving*

Recreation Luisa wants to
find how much water it will
take to fill a circular
swimming pool to different
depths. She knows she can
do this if she finds the area
of the bottom of the pool. She
measured the circumference
of the pool and found that it
was about 63 ft. What is the
area of the bottom?

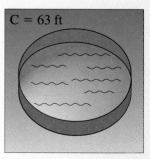

C = 63 ft

• Start by finding the radius.

$C = 2\pi r$ ⟵ Circumference formula

$63 = 2\pi r$ ⟵ Substitute 63 for C.

$\dfrac{63}{2\pi} = r$ ⟵ Divide each side by 2π.

63 ÷ (2 × π) = *10.026761*

• Now use this result in the area formula $A = \pi r^2$.

10.026761 x² × π = *315.84298* ⟵ Because the value of
r is on your screen,
square it and then
multiply by π.

The area of the bottom is about 316 ft².

5. ✔ *Try It Out* Find the approximate area of a circle with a
circumference of 48 ft.

EXERCISES *On Your Own*

Calculator **Use a calculator to find the circumference of
each circle. Round your answer to the nearest hundredth.**

1.
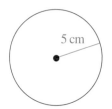
5 cm

2.
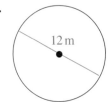
12 m

3.
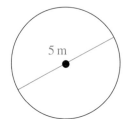
5 m

4.

4.5 cm

Mental Math **Find the circumference of a circle with the given diameter or radius. Use $\frac{22}{7}$ for π.**

5. $d = 21$ cm   **6.** $d = 28$ in.   **7.** $d = 14$ m   **8.** $r = 3.5$ m   **9.** $r = 7$ km

 Find the radius and the diameter of a circle with the given circumference. Round your answer to the nearest hundredth.

10. $C = 132$ cm   **11.** $C = 226$ in.   **12.** $C = 12.6$ m   **13.** $C = 62.8$ km   **14.** $C = 56.5$ m

15. Choose A, B, C, or D. Which of the following figures has a perimeter that is about the same as the circumference of a circle with a radius 10?

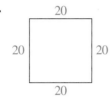

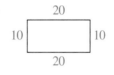

Calculator Use a calculator to find the area of each circle. Round your answer to the nearest hundredth.

16.

14 in.

17.

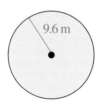

9.6 m

18.

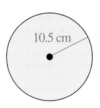

10.5 cm

19.

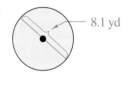

8.1 yd

Mental Math **Find the approximate circumference and area of a circle with the given diameter or radius. Use $\pi \approx 3$.**

20. $d = 2$ cm   **21.** $d = 10$ in.   **22.** $d = 4$ m   **23.** $r = 30$ cm   **24.** $r = 6$ km

25. $r = 1$ in.   **26.** $r = 5$ cm   **27.** $d = 20$ km   **28.** $r = \frac{1}{2}$ in.   **29.** $r = \frac{1}{3}$ yd

30. *Writing* Explain how to find the area of the shaded ring at the right.

31. a. What is the radius of a circle with an area of 225π square units?
   b. Find the circumference of the circle in part (a). Round your answer to the nearest tenth.

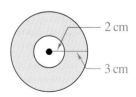

32. Data Analysis The circle graph at the right shows the average number of hours Americans sleep each night. The radius of the circle is 1.2 cm.

a. Find the area of the circle.

b. Find the area of each wedge of the graph.

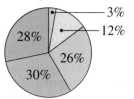
33. Look at circle P below.

a. $\angle QPS$ has a measure 120°. What fractional part of the circle is the shaded wedge?

b. Find the area of circle P.

c. Find the area of the shaded wedge.

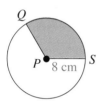

PORTFOLIO
For your portfolio, select an item from your work for this chapter. Here are some possibilites.
• a construction
• a challenging problem
Explain why you have included each selection.

Mixed Review

Write each answer as a fraction or mixed number in simplest form and as a decimal. *(Lessons 5-6 and 5-7)*

34. $\frac{3}{8} \div \left(-\frac{1}{2}\right)$
35. $\frac{4}{14} \cdot 2\frac{3}{4}$
36. $\frac{6}{8} + 5\frac{7}{12}$
37. $\frac{1}{11} - \frac{16}{22}$
38. $\frac{1}{2} \times \left(-\frac{4}{9}\right)$

39. Choose a Strategy Jorge is working on his family tree. Going back one generation, he has 2 parents. Going back two generations he has 4 grandparents. Going back three generations, he has 8 great-grandparents. How many ancestors does he have if he goes back 8 generations?

CHAPTER PROJECT

PROJECT LINK: CALCULATING

For the purpose of ordering materials such as sod, soil, or bricks, be sure that your plan shows the width of each walkway. Find the area of each walkway. Also, find the areas of the other regions in your park such as flower beds, and include all this information in your plan.

Design a Park The Project Link questions on pages 390, 400, and 420 should help you complete your project. Here is a checklist to help you gather the parts of your project together.

✔ the dimensions of the various parts of the park

✔ the placement of the fountain and all walkways

✔ the locations and the shapes of flower beds

✔ the areas of the walkways and other regions

Plan your proposal for the town council. Be sure that your design is neat and clear, and that the dimensions are reasonable. A brief written description of the parts of the park and their sizes should accompany your designs. Your goal is to have your plan approved.

Reflect and Revise

Present your plan to a friend. Is the plan complete? Are your choices reasonable? If necessary, make changes to improve your project.

Web Extension
Prentice Hall's Internet site contains information you might find helpful as you complete your project. Visit www.phschool.com/mgm3/ch8 for some links and ideas related to parks.

Look for a Pattern

8-1

Identifying patterns can be helpful in solving problems.

1. You are in an elevator on the seventh floor. Go down 4 floors. Go up 8 floors. Go down 3 floors. Go up 9 floors. Following this pattern, what floor will you be on if the elevator goes down again and you step off?

2. *Geometry* You can divide a circle into two parts with one straight line. With two lines you can get four parts. Three lines will result in a maximum of seven parts. What is the maximum number of parts you can get with five lines?

Pairs of Angles

8-2, 8-4

Special relationships exist between certain pairs of angles. **Vertical angles** are congruent. The sum of the measures of a pair of **supplementary angles** is 180°. The sum of the measures of a pair of **complementary angles** is 90°.

If two parallel lines are cut by a **transversal,** the **corresponding angles** are congruent, and the **alternate interior angles** are congruent.

Find the measures of ∠1 and ∠2 in each diagram.

3.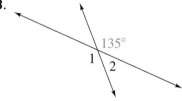

4.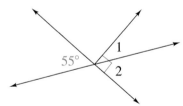

5.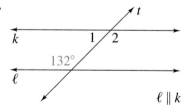

$\ell \parallel k$

Constructing Segments and Angles

8-3

You can construct congruent segments or congruent angles by using two geometric tools, a **compass** and a **straightedge.**

6. Use a ruler to draw $\overline{AB}$ with a length of 2.5 cm. Then construct $\overline{RS}$, so that $\overline{RS} \cong \overline{AB}$.

7. Use a protractor to draw ∠T with a measure of 115°. Then construct ∠K, so that ∠K ≅ ∠T.

Triangles and Quadrilaterals 8-5, 8-6

Polygons with the same size and shape are **congruent.** You can use **SAS**, **ASA**, or **SSS** to show that two triangles are congruent.

You can classify triangles by angles and by sides. Some types of quadrilaterals have special names.

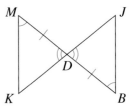

8. Are the triangles at the right congruent? If so, write a congruence statement and explain why.

9. *Writing* Explain why all squares are rectangles but not all rectangles are squares.

Polygons and Tessellations 8-7, 8-8

The sum of the measures of the angles of a polygon equals the product of 180° and two less than the number of sides.

The measure of each angle of a **regular polygon** equals the sum of the angle measures divided by the number of angles.

A **tessellation** is a repeated geometric design that covers a plane with no gaps and no overlaps. Certain regular polygons tessellate.

Find the sum of the angle measures for each polygon.

10. pentagon **11.** nonagon **12.** decagon **13.** octagon **14.** heptagon

15. a. Find the measure of each angle of a regular hexagon.
　　b. *Writing* Explain why a regular hexagon tessellates.

Measuring Polygons and Circles 8-9, 8-10

Area formulas: parallelogram: $A = bh$
　　　　　　triangle: $A = \frac{1}{2} bh$
　　　　　　circle: $A = \pi r^2$

The distance around a circle is the **circumference** of the circle.
$C = \pi d$ or $C = 2\pi r$

Find the area of each figure. If necessary, round your answer to the nearest hundredth.

16.

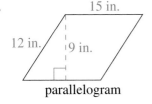

parallelogram

17.

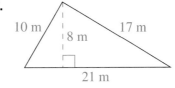

18.

19. Estimate the circumference of a circle with a radius of 8 cm.

8 ASSESSMENT

1. A quadrilateral has two diagonals. How many diagonals does an octagon have?

2. Describe each pair of angles as *alternate interior, corresponding, adjacent, vertical,* or *none of these.*
   a. ∠2, ∠4   **b.** ∠1, ∠5   **c.** ∠1, ∠3
   d. ∠3, ∠4   **e.** ∠4, ∠6   **f.** ∠3, ∠6

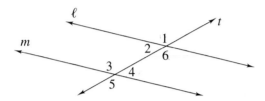

3. **a.** Find the measures of the numbered angles in the diagram below.

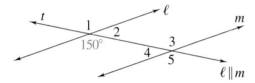

   b. Construct an angle congruent to ∠1.

4. Use a ruler to draw $\overline{AB}$ with a length of 3.5 cm. Then construct $\overline{BC}$ so that $\overline{BC} \cong \overline{AB}$.

5. The measure of ∠D is 68°.
   a. Find the measure of its supplement.
   b. Find the measure of its complement.

6. Write *true* or *false.* Explain.
   a. An equilateral triangle is always an isosceles triangle.
   b. An obtuse triangle can be a right triangle.
   c. A scalene triangle can be obtuse.
   d. A rhombus can have four right angles.

7. What is the sum of the measures of the angles of a decagon?

8. What is the measure of each angle of a regular pentagon?

9. **Writing** How are a rectangle and a parallelogram alike? How are they different?

10. Determine whether each pair of triangles must be congruent. If so, write a congruence statement and tell why they are congruent.

   a.
   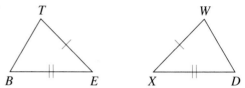

   b.
   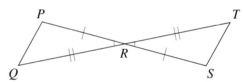

Find the area of each figure.

11.
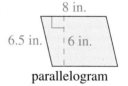
parallelogram

12.
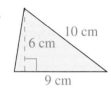

13. Use a calculator to find the area and circumference of a circle with a diameter of 15 cm. Round your answer to the nearest tenth.

14. **Choose A, B, C, or D.** Which of these figures does *not* tessellate?
   A. regular hexagon
   B. regular triangle
   C. regular pentagon
   D. rectangle

Choose the best answer.

1. Which square root lies between the whole numbers 11 and 12?

   A. $\sqrt{135}$ B. $\sqrt{144}$
   C. $\sqrt{120}$ D. $\sqrt{101}$

2. Aleisha can read four pages in 12 min. Which proportion can be used to figure out how long it will take her to read an 18-page chapter?

   A. $\frac{4}{12} = \frac{x}{18}$ B. $\frac{4}{18} = \frac{12}{x}$

   C. $\frac{12}{18} = \frac{4}{x}$ D. $\frac{4}{x} = \frac{18}{12}$

3. Write $3\frac{1}{2}\%$ as a fraction in simplest form.

   A. $\frac{7}{2}$ B. $\frac{7}{20}$

   C. $\frac{7}{200}$ D. $\frac{3.5}{100}$

4. Which conclusion is correct?

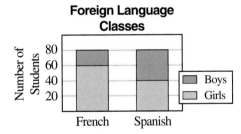

   Foreign Language Classes

   A. Eighty boys take French.
   B. More boys than girls take Spanish.
   C. More girls take French than Spanish.
   D. The total number of students studying Spanish and French is 150.

5. What is the circumference of a circle whose area is 36π square inches?

   A. 12π inches
   B. 18π inches
   C. 36π inches
   D. 6π inches

6. Which is equivalent to $5^3 \times 5^2$?

   A. 25^6 B. 25^5
   C. 5^6 D. 5^5

7. Choose a pair of corresponding angles.

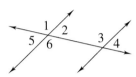

   A. $\angle 1$ and $\angle 6$ B. $\angle 3$ and $\angle 6$
   C. $\angle 1$ and $\angle 4$ D. $\angle 2$ and $\angle 4$

8. A job pays \$160 for 25 hours. What would it pay for 40 hours?

   A. \$216   B. \$256
   C. \$640   D. \$1000

9. Which variable expression is *not* equivalent to $2(x + 5)$?

   A. $2(x) + 2(5)$ B. $(x + 5) + (x + 5)$
   C. $2(5 + x)$ D. $5 + 2x$

10. $S'(-3, -2)$ is the image point after a translation of 6 units to the left and 2 units up. What are the coordinates of the original point?

    A. $(9, -2)$ B. $(3, 2)$
    C. $(1, 2)$ D. $(3, -4)$

11. Choose the step you should complete first to construct $\overline{EF} \cong \overline{MN}$.

    A. Open the compass to the length of $\overline{MN}$.
    B. Draw a ray with end point E.
    C. Measure $\overline{MN}$ with a ruler.
    D. Draw points E and F.

Geometry and Measurement

9

A BETTER Way

S top by at the cereal section of your local supermarket. There are dozens of brands! Now check out the packaging. Most cereals are packaged in pretty much the same way: cardboard, folded into rectangular boxes which are high and wide, but not deep.
Is this a waste of cardboard? Can you design a better package? You can . . . because now, you're in charge!

Design Packaging for Cereal For your chapter project, redesign the packaging of your favorite cereal. Your final product will be a new cardboard package which holds the same volume as the original.

• **How to apply multiple strategies to solve problems**

PROBLEM SOLVING

What You'll Learn

▼ 1 To identify pyramids, prisms, cones, and cylinders, and their parts

▼ 2 To identify three-dimensional figures in the real world

...And Why

Builders and carpenters combine common three-dimensional objects to create buildings, furniture, and other useful products.

Here's How

Look for questions that
▪ build understanding
✔ check understanding

QUICKreview

Types of Polygons

Number of Sides	Name of Polygon
5	Pentagon
6	Hexagon
7	Heptagon
8	Octagon
9	Nonagon
10	Decagon

THINK AND DISCUSS

▼ 1 *Naming Three-Dimensional Figures*

The figures below are common **three-dimensional figures,** also called **space figures** or solids.

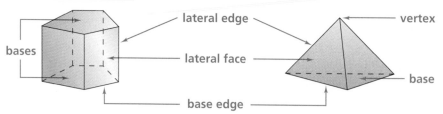

Prism

A **prism** is a space figure with two bases that are parallel and congruent to each other. The lateral faces are parallelograms. A prism is named for the shape of its bases. The prism above is a pentagonal prism.

Pyramid

A **pyramid** is a space figure with exactly one base. The base is a polygon. The lateral faces are triangles that meet at a vertex. A pyramid is named for the shape of its base. The pyramid above is a triangular pyramid.

Cylinder

The two bases of a **cylinder** are congruent circles that are parallel to each other.

Cone

A **cone** has only one base, and the base is a circle.

1. a. ▪ *Reasoning* How are prisms and cylinders alike?
   b. How are cylinders and cones alike?
   c. How are cylinders and cones different?
   d. How can you tell the difference between the bases and the lateral faces of a prism?

■ **EXAMPLE 1**

For each figure, describe the base(s) of the figure, name the figure, and name the part labeled $\overline{RL}$.

a.
b.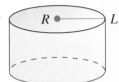
c.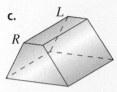

a. The only base is a circle. The figure is a cone. $\overline{RL}$ is a diameter.

b. The two bases are circles. The figure is a cylinder. $\overline{RL}$ is a radius.

c. The two bases are trapezoids and the lateral faces are parallelograms, so it is a trapezoidal prism. $\overline{RL}$ is a lateral edge.

This photo was taken in downtown Houston, Texas. Which of these buildings are prisms? Which are not?

When every face of a prism is a rectangle, any pair of opposite faces can be the bases.

2. a. ✔Try It Out
Describe the bases.
b. Name the figure.
c. Name the part labeled $\overline{AB}$.

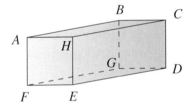

Lines in space that do not intersect and are not parallel are called **skew** lines. In the figure for Question 2, $\overline{AH}$ and $\overline{CD}$ are skew because the lines that contain them do not intersect and are not parallel.

3. ✔ Try It Out Refer to the diagram for Question 2. Name all the lines that when paired with $\overleftrightarrow{FG}$ are skew.

4. Refer to the diagram for Question 2. Decide whether each pair of lines intersects, is parallel, or is skew.
a. $\overleftrightarrow{AH}, \overleftrightarrow{DG}$ **b.** $\overleftrightarrow{CH}, \overleftrightarrow{EF}$ **c.** $\overleftrightarrow{FG}, \overleftrightarrow{AF}$

A three-dimensional figure with a polygon for each of its faces is called a **polyhedron.**

5. ⣿ **Think About It** Which figures in this lesson are polyhedrons?

② *Identifying Three-Dimensional Figures*

Some common objects are made up of different space figures.

■ **EXAMPLE 2**   *Real-World Problem Solving*

Crafts Which three-dimensional figures would you use to make this birdhouse?

The box is a pentagonal prism. The perch is a cylinder. The knob at the end of the perch is a sphere.

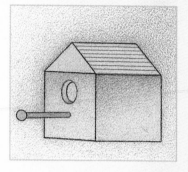

6. ✔*Try It Out* Name the three-dimensional figure or figures that make up the door of your classroom.

EXERCISES *On Your Own*

For each figure, describe the base(s) of the figure, name the figure, and name the part labeled $\overline{PQ}$.

1.
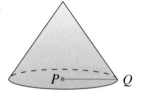

2.

3.
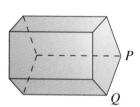

4.
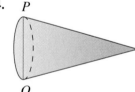

5.
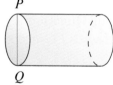

6.
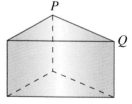

7.
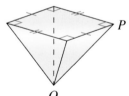

8.
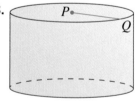

Choose the most precise name for each figure.

9. The figure has four lateral faces that are triangles.

10. The figure has three lateral faces that are rectangles.

11. The figure has four lateral faces that are squares.

12. The figure has one lateral surface and one base.

Name the three-dimensional figure or figures that make up each object.

13.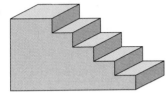

14.

15.

16.

17.

18.

19. **Writing** Kenji says that the figure at the right is a trapezoidal prism. Ester says that it is a triangular prism and rectangular prism combined. Who is correct? Explain.

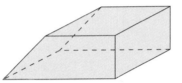

20. Refer to Exercises 1–8. Which figures are polyhedrons?

Use the rectangular pyramid at the right. State whether each pair of lines is *intersecting, parallel,* or *skew.*

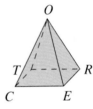

21. $\overleftrightarrow{CO}$, $\overleftrightarrow{CE}$ 22. $\overleftrightarrow{OR}$, $\overleftrightarrow{CE}$ 23. $\overleftrightarrow{CT}$, $\overleftrightarrow{ER}$

24. $\overleftrightarrow{EO}$, $\overleftrightarrow{TR}$ 25. $\overleftrightarrow{EO}$, $\overleftrightarrow{ER}$ 26. $\overleftrightarrow{OT}$, $\overleftrightarrow{ER}$

Mixed Review

Describe each pattern. *(Lesson 8-1)*

27. 100, 50, 25, 12.5, . . .   28. 1, 11, 21, 31, . . .   29. −1, −8, −27, −64, . . .

Solve for *y* in terms of *x*. *(Lesson 3-7)*

30. $x - y = 0$ 31. $2 + y = x$ 32. $-4y = x$ 33. $4 + y = 3x$ 34. $3x + y = \frac{1}{3}$

35. **Choose a Strategy** Varsha earned $39 baby-sitting this week. On Saturday she worked one more hour than twice the number of hours she worked on Friday. If she earns $3 per hour, how many hours did she work each day?

Drawing Three-Dimensional Figures

What You'll Learn

▼ To draw a base plan

▼ To draw top, front, and right views

...And Why

Architects and builders use different views to analyze a structure.

Here's How

Look for questions that

🔹 build understanding

✔ check understanding

Work Together

Exploring Different 3-D Views

Work with a partner to explore different views of three-dimensional objects.

1. Position ten cubes as shown in the photo. Have one person face the front side and the other person face the right side.

2. Describe the shape and dimensions of the front side and right side of the figure.

3. Suppose you describe the figure with *pictures* of its faces and no words or numbers. Would showing four lateral sides be enough to communicate the shape of the figure? Explain.

4. a. 🔹*Draw a Conclusion* What is the least number of faces needed to describe the figure?
   b. Which faces are they? Draw and label them.

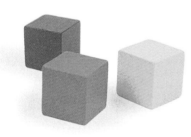

5. Now use the ten cubes to make a stack of four cubes, a stack of three cubes, a stack of two cubes, and one cube alone. Arrange them according to the diagram.

4	2
3	1

Right

Front

6. a. Look at the figure from the right side. Draw a figure that shows the shape of the right side.
   b. Repeat part (a) for the front side and top side of the figure.
   c. 🔹*Draw a Conclusion* Suppose you gave your three drawings to someone and asked them to re-create the figure by using cubes. Should they be able to? Explain.

▼ *Drawing a Base Plan*

In Lesson 4-8, you sketched a three-dimensional figure by drawing one base, translating it, and then connecting the two figures.

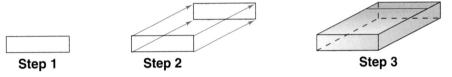

Step 1   **Step 2**   **Step 3**

In this lesson you will learn three other methods for drawing figures. These methods are used by architects, engineers, and designers.

A **base plan** shows the shape of the base and the height of each part. It is an efficient way to represent a three-dimensional figure made with cubes. In Question 5 of the Work Together, you stacked cubes according to a given base plan.

■ **EXAMPLE 1**

Draw the base plan for the stacked cubes in the photo.

Draw a square for each stack, and write the number of cubes in the stack inside each square. Label the front and right sides.

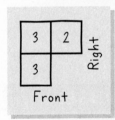

7. ✔ *Try It Out* Draw a base plan for the figure in Question 1 of the Work Together.

▼ *Drawing Top, Front, and Right Views*

Architects and builders use a **top view,** a **front view,** and a **right view** to help them analyze a three-dimensional structure.

They also use isometric views. An **isometric view** is a corner view of a figure. Sometimes it is drawn on isometric dot paper.

■ EXAMPLE 2

Draw the top, front, and right views of each figure. Assume that no blocks are hidden from view.

a.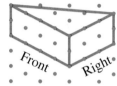

b.

a.
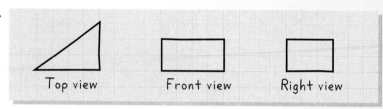

Top view Front view Right view

b.
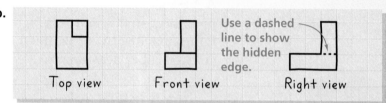

Use a dashed line to show the hidden edge.

Top view Front view Right view

8. ✔*Try It Out* Draw the top, front, and right views of the figure.

EXERCISES *On Your Own*

Draw the base plan for the stacked cubes.

1.

2.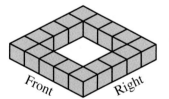

3.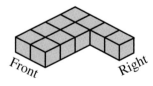

4.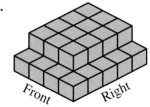

5.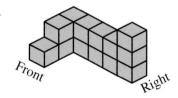

6.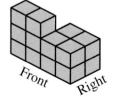

7. *Reasoning* Draw the top, front, and right views of the figure represented by this base plan.

3	2	2
2	1	

Front

8. a. *Open-ended* Build a 7-cube structure and draw a base plan for it.

b. Draw the top, front, and right views for your structure.

Draw the top, front, and right views of each figure.

9.
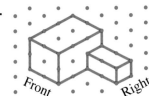

10.
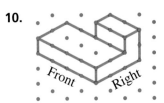

11.

12.
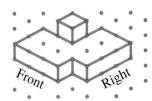

13.

14.
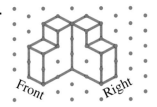

15. *Writing* Describe a situation in which drawing a base plan would be useful.

16. *Architecture* Architects use the top, front, and right views to show the layout of a house. Draw a base plan for this house that shows how many stories tall each part of the house is.

□ = 9 SQUARE FEET

Find the measure of the complement and the supplement of each angle. If there is no complement, write *no complement*. *(Lesson 8-2)*

17. $m\angle A = 35°$ **18.** $m\angle P = 45°$ **19.** $m\angle Y = 124°$ **20.** $m\angle 2 = 71°$ **21.** $m\angle 3 = 88°$

Write a proportion and solve it. *(Lesson 6-3)*

22. 36% of what number is 72?

23. 105 is what percent of 30?

24. Katrina scored 15 points less than twice the lowest score. If her score was 95, what was the lowest score? *(Lesson 3-4)*

CHAPTER PROJECT

PROJECT LINK: ANALYZING

Choose a box of your favorite cereal. Describe the shape, and give its precise dimensions. Then name at least two shapes from this chapter other than a rectangular prism. Tell how practical those shapes would be as cereal boxes, and why.

Math at Work

LANDSCAPE ARCHITECT

Landscape architects are involved in planning and designing residential areas, parks, shopping centers, golf courses, and college campuses. The landscape architects make a detailed plan that includes the location of buildings, roads and walkways, and the arrangement of shrubs, trees, and flowers. A knowledge of geometry helps them in preparing sketches and models of a proposed site. They also use their mathematical skills to estimate the costs for the project.

For current information about landscape architecture, visit the Prentice Hall Web site: www.phschool.com

What You'll Learn

▼ To identify nets of three-dimensional figures

▼ To identify three-dimensional figures from nets

...And Why

Nets are used in many industries—especially the packaging industry.

Here's How

Look for questions that
- build understanding
✔ check understanding

Work Together

Investigating Nets

1. Look at the patterns below. How are they alike? How are they different?

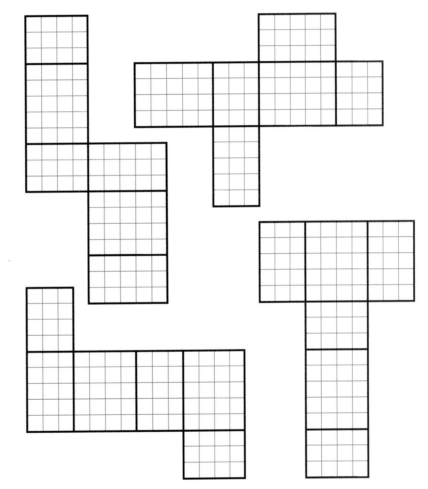

2. Have each person in your group copy a different one of the four patterns onto graph paper.

3. Cut out the patterns and fold them along the inside segments. Then tape the edges together to form a solid. Compare the figures. What do you notice?

Activity continued on next page.

4. Predict the figure each pattern makes. Then copy, cut, fold, and tape the patterns. Which shape does each make?

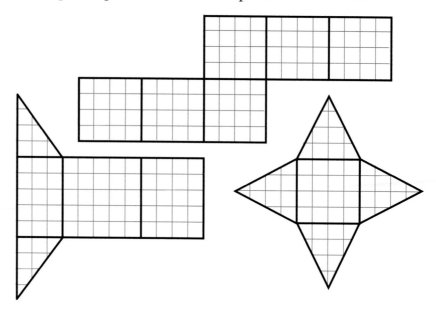

THINK AND DISCUSS

▼ *Identifying Nets of Space Figures*

Many items are packaged in common space figures. In the Work Together, you made figures from flat patterns, or **nets.**

■ **EXAMPLE 1**   *Real-World Problem Solving*

Packaging Match each package with its net.

a.

b.

I.

II.

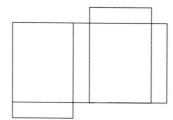

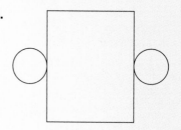

a. The oatmeal container is a cylinder. The net showing two circles and one rectangle is Figure II.

b. The rice box is a rectangular prism. The net showing six rectangles is Figure I.

5. ✔ *Try It Out* Sketch a net for a hexagonal pyramid.

6. a. ⁂ *Think About It* How do the sides of an actual cardboard box adhere to each other?

b. Does the net of the box allow for all the cardboard needed to make the box? Explain.

▼2 *Identifying Space Figures from Nets*

People who work in packaging warehouses can save space by storing empty packaging as nets.

■ **EXAMPLE 2**

Identify the figure that can be made from each net.

a. 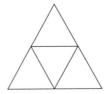 **b.**

a. The net shows three congruent triangles and a fourth triangle, so it is a triangular pyramid.

b. The net shows a rectangle with no fold lines, so it is a cylinder without bases.

7. ✔ *Try It Out* Describe the figure for a net with four triangles and one rectangle.

 Hector Rojas, from La Paz, Bolivia, folded plain paper to make these kangaroos. Then he colored them. The art of paper folding, known as origami, originated in Japan.

EXERCISES *On Your Own*

Describe the net for each figure. List the shapes that make up the net and write the number of each shape used.

1. triangular prism

2. hexagonal pyramid

3. cylinder

4. rectangular prism

5. cone

6. rectangular pyramid

Packaging **Match each container with the correct net.**

A. 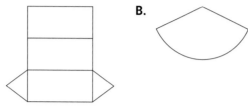   B.   C.   D.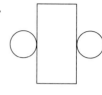

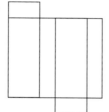

7.    8.    9.    10.

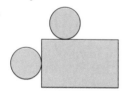

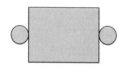

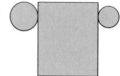

11. **Choose A, B, C, or D.** Which of the following could be a net for a cylinder?

A.   B.   C.   D.

12. Draw a net for a rectangular box that is 8 cm long, 6 cm wide, and 4 cm tall. Label the net with the appropriate dimensions.

13. Draw a net for a cylinder whose height is 8 cm and whose radius is 4 cm.

14. *Reasoning* Is it possible to have different nets that fold to form the same prism? Explain.

15. *Writing* A net for a rectangular prism and a net for a rectangular pyramid are next to each other. How can you tell them apart?

16. *Reasoning* A cylinder has a diameter of 10 cm and a height of 10 cm. The sides of a cube are each 10 cm. Would either figure fit inside the other? Explain.

17. *Open-ended* Draw a net for an object you can find in your house or school.

QUICKreview

A cube is a rectangular prism with six square sides.

Name the space figure for each net.

18.

19.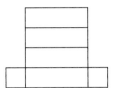

20.

21.

22.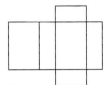

23.

24.

25.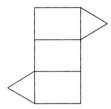

Mixed Review

Find the slope of the line that contains the points. *(Lesson 4-3)*

26. $P(5, 0)$, $M(0, -5)$ **27.** $H(9, 7)$, $G(4, 3)$ **28.** $A(-4, 7)$, $B(3, 11)$ **29.** $K(1, -4)$, $L(-1, 4)$

30. Draw a segment $\overline{DE}$. Construct a quadrilateral $DEFG$ that has three sides of length DE. *(Lesson 8-3)*

31. *Choose a Strategy* A jet left Boston at 6:55 A.M. EST and reached Seattle at 10:47 A.M. PST after a 24-min stop in Chicago. What was the total flying time of the jet?

✓ CHECKPOINT 1   *Lessons 9-1 through 9-3*

Use the figure below for Exercises 1–3.

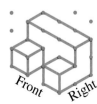

1. Name the figure.

2. Name the vertex.

3. Name the diameter.

4. Draw the base plan for the figure at the right.

5. Draw the top, front, and right views of the figure at the right.

6. Name the space figure for this net.

9-4

Precision and Significant Digits

What You'll Learn

▼1 To find and compare the precision of measurements

▼2 To use significant digits

...And Why

Surveyors, builders, and scientists all work with precision in planning and measuring.

Here's How

Look for questions that
- ▪▪ build understanding
- ✔ check understanding

THINK AND DISCUSS

▼1 Using Precision in Measurements

You may measure the distance between the library and your home to the nearest mile. Your dentist may measure teeth or gums to the nearest tenth of a millimeter. Your dentist measures with more accuracy, or precision, because with teeth there is less room for error.

1. ▪▪ *Number Sense* Decide which requires more precision.
   a. threading a needle or walking down a hallway
   b. watering a potted plant or watering a lawn
   c. packing a lunch or packing light bulbs
   d. traveling to Mexico or traveling to Mexico City

The **precision** of a measurement is determined by the size of the units used. The marks on a scale or other instrument tell you the precision that is possible.

■ **EXAMPLE 1** *Real-World Problem Solving*

Nutrition Some people measure the size of food servings. What is the greatest precision possible with this scale?

Each mark represents $\frac{1}{2}$ ounce. Measurements made using this scale will be precise to the nearest half ounce.

When comparing measurements, the measurement that uses the smaller units is more precise. To show precision, you do not write fractional measurements in simplest form.

■ EXAMPLE 2

Choose the more precise measurement.

a. $2\frac{2}{8}$ c, 2 c

Since eighth cups are smaller than whole cups, the measurement $2\frac{2}{8}$ c is more precise.

b. 26.1 m, 26.09 m

Since hundredths of a meter are smaller than tenths of a meter, the measurement 26.09 m is more precise.

2. ⁑ *Number Sense* Explain why the measurement $2\frac{4}{8}$ in. is more precise than $2\frac{1}{2}$ in.

3. ✔ *Try It Out* Choose the more precise measurement.
    a. $\frac{3}{4}$ h, $\frac{1}{2}$ h   **b.** 4 L, 3.8 L   **c.** 3.8 m, 383 cm

When you add or subtract measurements, round your answer to match the precision of the least precise measurement.

■ EXAMPLE 3

Compute. Round your answer to match the less precise measurement.

a. 20.08 km + 5.2 km

$20.08 + 5.2 = 25.28$ ← Since 5.2 is less precise than 20.08, round to the nearest tenth.
The total is 25.3 km.

b. 36 g − 12.3 g

$36 - 12.3 = 23.7$ ← Since 36 is less precise than 12.3, round to the nearest whole unit.
The result is 24 g.

Need Help? For practice with adding and subtracting decimals, see Skills Handbook page 603.

4. ✔ *Try It Out* Compute. Round your answer to match the less precise measurement.
    a. $4,102 + $3,862.16   **b.** $6\frac{4}{8}$ yd − $2\frac{1}{4}$ yd

5. ⁑ *Reasoning* How would you add 63 min and $2\frac{1}{2}$ h so that your answer has the correct precision?

▼2 *Using Significant Digits*

Suppose your height is 64 inches, using a tape measure. Using an electronic ruler, your height is 64.23 inches. The second measurement contains more significant digits. **Significant digits** are digits that represent an actual measurement.

Nonzero digits (1–9) are always significant. To decide if a zero digit (0) is significant, you should check its position in relation to the decimal point and other digits.

Counting Significant Digits

Type of Number	Which Digits to Count	Example
decimal numbers between 0 and 1	all digits, *except* zeros between the decimal point and a nonzero digit	2 significant digits ↓ 0.0080 ↑ not significant digits
positive integers	all digits, *except* zeros between the decimal point and a nonzero digit	4 significant digits ↓ 306,200 ↑ not significant digits
noninteger decimal numbers greater than 1	all digits	7 significant digits ↓ 420.0190

6. ✔ *Try It Out* How many significant digits are in each measurement?

   a. 0.035 mm   **b.** 1,820 mi   **c.** 34.002 L

When you multiply or divide measurements, round your answer to match the least number of significant digits in the problem.

■ **EXAMPLE 4**   *Real-World Problem Solving*

Surveying Find the area of a rectangular lot that measures 115.6 ft by 81.2 ft.

   115.6   •   81.2   =   9386.72 ←—Multiply.
     ↑   ↑
4 significant digits   3 significant digits

The area is 9,390 ft². ←————— Since the least number of significant digits is 3, round the answer to 3 significant digits.

Need Help? For practice with multiplying decimals, see Skills Handbook page 604.

7. ✔*Try It Out* Compute. Use significant digits to round each answer.
  a. 38.07 ÷ 2.1   **b.** 0.20 · 0.015

EXERCISES *On Your Own*

Choose the more precise unit of measure.

1. second, hour   **2.** quart, cup   **3.** inch, yard   **4.** ton, pound   **5.** pint, gallon

What precision is possible with each scale shown?

6.   **7.**   **8.**

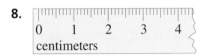

Choose the more precise measurement.

9. 4.3 km, 4 km **10.** 41.2 s, 41 s **11.** $31, $31.45 **12.** $4\frac{1}{8}$ in., 4 in. **13.** $\frac{3}{16}$ mi, $\frac{1}{4}$ mi

14. 26 mo, 2 y **15.** 0.5 g, 505 mg **16.** 17 oz, 1 lb **17.** 9 days, 1 wk **18.** 1 tbsp, 4 tsp

19. Choose A, B, C, or D. Which is more precise than 53 min?

  A. $\frac{9}{10}$ h   **B.** 50 min   **C.** $53\frac{1}{2}$ min   **D.** 1 h

Compute each sum or difference. Round your answer to match the less precise measurement.

20. 16.2 mm + 12 mm   **21.** 5,300 gal + 463 gal   **22.** $4\frac{1}{2}$ yd $-\frac{7}{8}$ yd

23. 51° − 12.8°   **24.** 9.221 m − 4.7 m   **25.** $12\frac{1}{2}$ in. + 1 ft

26. *Writing* Galvin says that because 12 in. = 1 ft, the measurements 36 in. and 3 ft are equally precise. Do you agree? Explain.

27. *Biology* Last week a plant leaf measured 3.4 cm. This week the same leaf measures 4.08 cm. How much did the leaf grow?

28. *Pets* A kitten weighed 14.3 oz when he arrived at an animal shelter. Over the next ten weeks, he gained 3 lb 7 oz. What did he weigh then?

How many significant digits are in each number?

29. 2.05   **30.** 0.00312   **31.** 0.2045   **32.** 4,280   **33.** 601

Round each number to two significant digits.

34. 1,295   **35.** 4,090   **36.** 25.16   **37.** 1.087   **38.** 223.5

39. *Open-ended* Use the digits 0, 1, and 4 to write a number with exactly three significant digits.

Compute each product or quotient. Use significant digits.

40. $1,400 \cdot 2$ **41.** $0.0801 \cdot 11$ **42.** $119.5 \div 7$ **43.** $282.3 \cdot 24.2$

44. $0.011 \div 3$ **45.** $12.1 \cdot 450$ **46.** $15,000 \div 12$ **47.** $19.4 \div 0.086$

48. *Geometry* Use significant digits to compute the area of a rectangle whose sides measure 4.2 cm and 40.1 cm.

Mixed Review

Identify each statement as *true* or *false*. *(Lesson 8-5)*

49. If $\triangle LMN \cong \triangle RST$, then $\angle L \cong \angle T$.   **50.** If $\triangle EFG \cong \triangle UVW$, then $\overline{FG} \cong \overline{VW}$.

Order each set of numbers from least to greatest. *(Lesson 5-4)*

51. $-\frac{1}{2}, -\frac{2}{3}, \frac{1}{4}$ **52.** $-1.5, -\frac{4}{3}, -1\frac{1}{4}$ **53.** $-9.7, -9\frac{7}{12}, -9\frac{3}{4}$ **54.** $-4.12, -4.22, -4.05$

55. *Choose a Strategy* Bianca has $564.78 in her checking account. Suppose she writes checks for $42.12 for groceries, $23.64 for utilities, and $87.98 for telephone charges and then deposits $429.56. What is her new balance?

CHAPTER PROJECT

PROJECT LINK: DRAWING

Propose different packaging for the cereal box from the Project Link on page 436. The shape can be a rectangular prism with different dimensions, or it can be an entirely different shape. Describe the proposed packaging. Then sketch top, front, and right views of your new package.

EXPLORATION

MATH TOOLBOX

Greatest Possible Error

After Lesson 9-4

Measurement is not exact. To the nearest half inch, each line segment at the right measures $1\frac{1}{2}$ inches. When a measurement is rounded to the nearest half inch, it can vary from the actual length by as much as one fourth inch. We say that one fourth inch is the greatest possible error of the measurement.

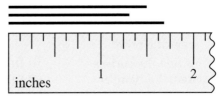

The **greatest possible error** of a measurement is half the unit of measure to which the measurement has been rounded.

■ EXAMPLE

Find the greatest possible error for each measurement.

a. 28.3 L   The measurement is rounded to the nearest tenth of a liter. Since $\frac{1}{2} \cdot 0.1 = 0.05$, the greatest possible error is 0.05 L.

b. $2\frac{1}{4}$ ft   The measurement is rounded to the nearest quarter foot. Since $\frac{1}{2} \cdot \frac{1}{4} = \frac{1}{8}$, the greatest possible error is $\frac{1}{8}$ ft.

c. 800 kg   The measurement is rounded to the nearest hundred kilograms. So, the greatest possible error is 50 kg.

Find the greatest possible error for each measurement.

1. 12 qt   **2.** 15.5 mL   **3.** 4.27 km   **4.** $6\frac{7}{8}$ in.   **5.** 7 g   **6.** $18\frac{1}{2}$ oz

7. $1\frac{1}{4}$ c   **8.** 2.1 mm   **9.** $5\frac{3}{8}$ gal   **10.** 15.38 m   **11.** 255 ft   **12.** 35.375 mg

13. 400 mi (rounded to nearest 100 mi)   **14.** 60 lb (rounded to nearest 10 lb)

15. 32,000 mi (rounded to nearest 1,000 mi)   **16.** 3.40 ft (rounded to nearest 0.01 ft)

17. *Manufacturing* Suppose a bolt is to be manufactured with a diameter of 18 mm ±0.2 mm (read as *18 mm plus or minus 0.2 mm*). Find the least diameter and the greatest diameter that will be acceptable.

18. *Writing* How does the precision of a measurement relate to the greatest possible error of a measurement? Give examples.

Math Toolbox   **447**

What You'll Learn

▼ 1 To find the surface area of a prism

▼ 2 To find the surface area of a cylinder

...And Why

You use the surface area of a prism in order to cover your school books or make a gift box out of cardboard.

Here's How

Look for questions that

⊞ build understanding

✔ check understanding

GEOLOGY Crystals that are longer than they are tall or wide are called "prismatic" crystals. This crystal has six rectangular faces, and hexagonal bases on both ends.

THINK AND DISCUSS

▼ 1 *Finding the Surface Area of a Prism*

To find the surface area of a prism, find the area of each face and add the areas together.

■ **EXAMPLE 1**

Find the surface area of the triangular prism to the nearest ten cm^2.

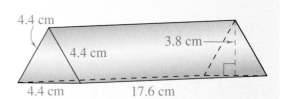

The surfaces of the prism consist of two congruent triangles and three congruent rectangles, so the total surface area is as follows.

$$\text{S.A.} = 2 \cdot \text{area of triangle} + 3 \cdot \text{area of rectangle}$$
$$= 2 \cdot \tfrac{1}{2}bh \qquad\qquad + 3 \cdot bh$$
$$= 2 \cdot \tfrac{1}{2}(4.4)(3.8) \qquad + 3 \cdot (17.6)(4.4) \quad \longleftarrow \text{Substitute.}$$
$$= 249.04 \qquad\qquad\qquad\qquad \longleftarrow \text{Simplify.}$$

To the nearest ten cm^2, the surface area of the prism is 250 cm^2.

1. ✔ *Try It Out* Find the surface area of this rectangular prism.

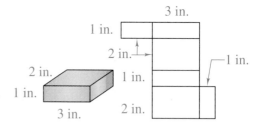

2. **a.** How many lateral faces does an octagonal prism have?
   b. ⊞ *Reasoning* Must all the lateral faces be congruent to each other? Explain.
   c. How many different shapes would the faces of a *regular* octagonal prism have? Describe them.

▼2 *Finding the Surface Area of a Cylinder*

If you cut a label from
a can, you will see that
the label is a rectangle.

The height of the rectangle is the height of the can. The base
length of the rectangle is the circumference of the can. The area
of the rectangle is the *lateral area* of the can.

To find the surface area of a cylinder, add the areas of the two
circular bases to the lateral area.

■ **EXAMPLE 2**   *Real-World Problem Solving*

▦ *Packaging* Find the area
of aluminum needed to
make the cylindrical can.
Give your answer to the
nearest cm^2.

7 cm

11.5 cm

The surfaces of the cylinder consist of two circles and one
rectangle, so the total surface area is as follows.

$$
\begin{aligned}
\text{S.A.} &= 2 \cdot \text{area of circle} + \text{area of rectangle}\\
&= 2 \cdot \pi r^2 && + bh\\
&= 2 \cdot \pi r^2 && + (2\pi r)h && \leftarrow b = C = 2\pi r\\
&= 2 \cdot \pi(3.5)^2 && + 2\pi(3.5)(11.5) && \leftarrow \text{Substitute.}\\
&= 24.5\pi + 80.5\pi && && \leftarrow \text{Simplify.}\\
&= 105\pi = 329.86723
\end{aligned}
$$

To the nearest cm^2, the area of the aluminum needed for
the can is 330 cm^2.

3. ✔ *Try It Out* Find
the surface area of
this cylinder to the
nearest whole unit.

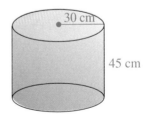

30 cm

45 cm

4. a. ⊞ *Reasoning* If you know the radius and height of a
cylinder, how can you find its lateral area?
   b. How can you find the area of the base of the cylinder?
   c. How can you find the total surface area of the cylinder?

Work Together

Some solids have holes in them. Work in groups to find the total surface area of a three-dimensional figure with a hole in it.

5. The figure at the right is a rectangular prism with a smaller rectangular prism removed from it. How many faces does the figure have altogether?

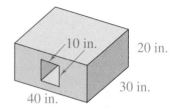

6. Copy and complete the table by counting the number of different faces.

Outside Faces	How Many?	Inside Faces	How Many?
20 in. × 40 in. face with a 10 in. × 10 in. hole	■	10 in. × 30 in. face	■
20 in. × 30 in. face	■		
40 in. × 30 in. face	■		

7. How can you find the area of a 20 in. × 40 in. face with a 10 in. × 10 in. hole in it?

8. ⬦ *Draw a Conclusion* What is the surface area of the entire figure?

9. The rectangular prism at the right has a triangular prism removed from it.

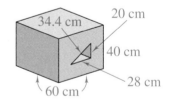

   a. How many faces does the figure have?
   b. List the different dimensions of the faces of the figure and the number of faces with those dimensions.
   c. Find the total surface area.

10. a. ⬦ *What If . . .* What would the surface area of the rectangular prism in Question 9 be if it were completely solid (without the hole)?
    b. Is the surface area of the solid prism greater than or less than the prism with the hole in it?

Find the surface area of the solid represented by each net.
Give your answer to the nearest whole unit.

1.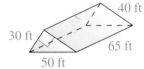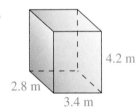
26.6 cm   26.6 cm
84 cm
86.8 cm

2.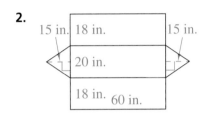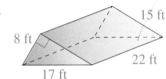
15 in.   18 in.   15 in.
20 in.
18 in.   60 in.

3.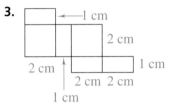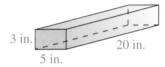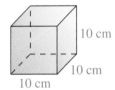
1 cm
2 cm
2 cm   1 cm
2 cm 2 cm
1 cm

4. *Writing* Which figure has more differently shaped faces, a rectangular prism or a triangular prism with an isosceles triangle base? Explain.

Find the surface area of each prism.

5.
40 ft
30 ft
65 ft
50 ft

6.
5 cm
3 cm
15.5 cm
4 cm

7.
3 in.
20 in.
5 in.

8.
4.2 m
2.8 m
3.4 m

9.
15 ft
8 ft
22 ft
17 ft

10.
10 cm
10 cm
10 cm

11. a. *Painting* An oil tank is 32 ft tall with a diameter of 84 ft. If the entire outside of the tank were painted, how much surface area would the paint cover?
b. One gallon of paint covers 325 ft². How many gallons of paint are needed?

12. *Reasoning* The surface area of a cube is 486 cm². What is the length of each edge?

13. *Packaging* Which box will require more cardboard to make, a box 9 in. by 5.5 in. by 11.75 in., or a box 8 in. by 6.25 in. by 10.5 in.? Explain.

Find the surface area of each cylinder. Give your answer to the nearest tenth of a unit.

14. 1 m / 2 m

15. 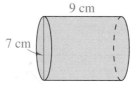 9 cm / 7 cm

16. 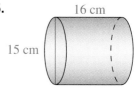 16 cm / 15 cm

17. Choose A, B, C, or D. Which is the best estimate for the ratio of the surface area of the square prism to the surface area of the cylinder?

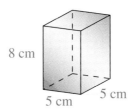

8 cm / 5 cm / 5 cm

10 cm / 5 cm

    A. 1 : 1   **B.** 2 : 1
    C. 1 : 2   **D.** 3 : 2

18. Find the surface area of the largest cylinder that can fit into a cube with a side of 10 cm.

Each figure below has a hole in it. Find the total surface area of each figure. Give your answer to the nearest whole unit.

19. 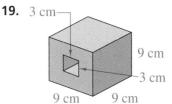 3 cm / 9 cm / 3 cm / 9 cm / 9 cm

20. 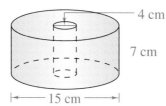 4 cm / 7 cm / 15 cm

21. 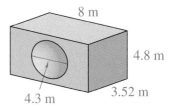 8 m / 4.8 m / 3.52 m / 4.3 m

---

Mixed Review

Solve each inequality. Graph the solution. *(Lessons 3-9 and 3-10)*

22. $a - 2 \le 9$ **23.** $-5 > b - 1$ **24.** $-4x \le -16$ **25.** $6 < -9y$ **26.** $2p \ge -7$

Find the simple interest to the nearest cent. *(Lesson 7-8)*

27. $500 at 3.25% for 2 yr   **28.** $4,500 at 4.75% for 1 yr   **29.** $8,000 at 5.5% for 3 yr

30. Mark bikes to his friend's house and then returns home. In order to get there he goes 3 blocks east, 2 blocks northwest, 3 blocks west, and then returns home. Name the geometric figure that represents his path. *(Lesson 8-6)*

Surface Areas of Pyramids and Cones

What You'll Learn

1 To find the surface area of pyramids

2 To find the surface area of cones

...And Why

Painters use surface area to estimate the amount of paint needed.

Here's How

Look for questions that
- build understanding
- ✔ check understanding

THINK AND DISCUSS

▼ Finding Surface Area of Pyramids

The height of a pyramid can be confused with the height of one of its lateral faces. For this reason, the height of the lateral face is called the **slant height** and is indicated by the symbol ℓ.

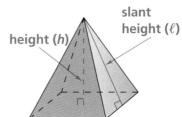

To find the surface area of a pyramid, add the areas of the lateral faces to the area of the base.

■ EXAMPLE 1

Find the surface area of this square pyramid.

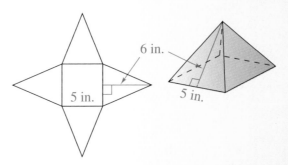

S.A. = area of square + 4 · area of triangle

$= s^2 \qquad + 4 \cdot \frac{1}{2} bh$

$= 5^2 \qquad + 4 \cdot \frac{1}{2}(5)(6)$ ◀— Substitute.

$= 25 \qquad + 60$ ◀— Simplify.

$= 85$ ◀— Add.

So the surface area of the pyramid is 85 in.^{2}.

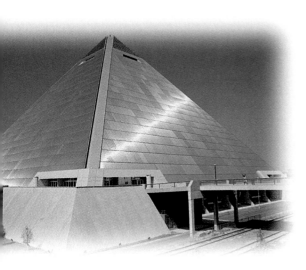

The Pyramid Arena Facility in Memphis, Tennessee, was built in the shape of the Great Pyramid of Khufu in Egypt. The arena is 290 feet tall.

1. ✔ **Try It Out** Find the surface area of the square pyramid.

16 cm

12 cm   12 cm

■ **EXAMPLE 2** *Real-World Problem Solving*

Painting As a community service project, you and your friends are going to paint the outside of the playhouse in Sunburst Park. How many square feet do you need to paint, including the areas of the door and windows?

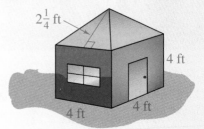

The area to be painted includes the four congruent rectangular walls and the four congruent triangles that make up the roof. Make a table of the different faces.

Shape and Dimensions	How Many?	Total Area
Square: 4 by 4	4	$4(4 \cdot 4) = 64$
Triangle: $b = 4, h = \ell = 2\frac{1}{4}$	4	$4\left(\frac{1}{2} \cdot 4 \cdot 2\frac{1}{4}\right) = 18$

The total surface area to be painted is $64 + 18 = 82$ ft^2.

2. ✔ *Try It Out* Find the total surface area of a playhouse with double the dimensions of the playhouse in Example 2.

▽2 *Finding Surface Area of Cones*

The curved surface of a cone is its lateral area. The net of a cone may remind you of a triangle with a height ℓ and a base equal to the circumference of the circular base. If you substitute the circumference $2\pi r$ for b, and ℓ for h in the triangle area formula, the result is the formula for the lateral area of a cone.

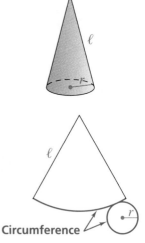

$A = \frac{1}{2}bh$ ⟵ triangle area formula

$\quad = \frac{1}{2}C\ell$ ⟵ Substitute C for b and ℓ for h.

$\quad = \frac{1}{2}(2\pi r)\ell$ ⟵ $C = 2\pi r$

$A = \pi r\ell$ ⟵ Simplify. The result is the formula for the lateral area of a cone.

Circumference

SURFACE AREA OF A CONE

The surface area (S.A.) of a cone is the sum of the base area and the lateral area, or S.A. $= \pi r^2 + \pi r \ell$.

■ **EXAMPLE 3**

Find the surface area of this cone to the nearest ten ft^2.

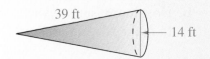
39 ft   14 ft

$$S.A. = \pi r^2 + \pi r \ell \qquad \leftarrow \text{cone surface area formula}$$
$$= \pi(7)^2 + \pi(7)(39) \qquad \leftarrow \text{Substitute for } r \text{ and } \ell.$$
$$= 49\pi + 273\pi \qquad \leftarrow \text{Multiply.}$$
$$= 322\pi \qquad \leftarrow \text{Add the areas.}$$

The surface area of the cone is 322π, or about 1,010 ft^2.

3. ✔ *Try It Out* Find the surface area of a cone if the radius is 12 ft and the lateral area is 204.1 ft^2.

4. ▪ *Reasoning* Can the slant height and the height of a cone ever be the same length? Explain.

EXERCISES *On Your Own*

Find the surface area of each square pyramid.

1.
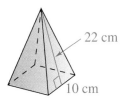
22 cm
10 cm

2.
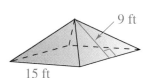
9 ft
15 ft

3.
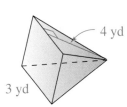
4 yd
3 yd

4.
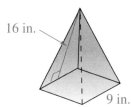
16 in.
9 in.

5.
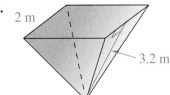
2 m
3.2 m

6.
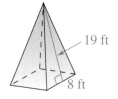
19 ft
8 ft

7. How can you find the slant height of a square pyramid if all you know are the base edge length and the height?

8. *Writing* Describe how to find the total surface area of a square pyramid whose base edge length is 9 cm and whose slant height is 6 cm.

9. *Tents* The top of the tent pictured is a square pyramid with slant height $2\frac{1}{3}$ yd. The area of the base is $\frac{100}{9}$ yd^2.
   a. What is the length of each base edge?
   b. How many square yards of canvas are needed to make the top of the tent?

Find the surface area of each cone. Give your answer to the nearest tenth of a unit.

10.
14.14 m — 10 m

11.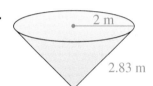
2 m
2.83 m

12.
$3\frac{1}{2}$ ft   1 ft

13.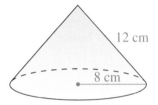
12 cm
8 cm

14.
12 in.
12 in.

15.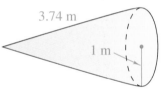
3.74 m
1 m

Find the surface area of each solid. Give your answer to the nearest tenth of a unit.

16.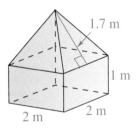
1.7 m
1 m
2 m   2 m

17.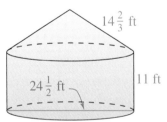
$14\frac{2}{3}$ ft
$24\frac{1}{2}$ ft
11 ft

18.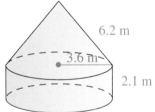
6.2 m
3.6 m
2.1 m

19. *Algebra* Amir uses the formula S.A. = $\pi r(r + \ell)$ to find the surface area of a cone. Will this always work? Explain.

20. *Food* The slant height of a frozen yogurt cone is 4.5 in. and its diameter is 2 in. How much surface area does it have?

21. *Research* Find out about ancient Mexican and Egyptian pyramids. How are they alike? How are they different? Summarize your findings in a short report.

JOURNAL
Write a brief description of how to find the surface area of any solid having two or more surfaces.

Mixed Review

State whether each statement is *true* or *false*. *(Lesson 8-6)*

22. All squares are rhombuses.

23. All parallelograms are rectangles.

24. All trapezoids are rectangles.

25. A square is both a rhombus and a rectangle.

Rewrite each number in scientific notation or in standard form. *(Lesson 2-11)*

26. 840,000   **27.** 1.586×10^6 **28.** 5,220,000   **29.** 2.5×10^{10} **30.** 20 billion

31. *Choose a Strategy* Gail spent half her money for dinner and half of what remained for a pair of earrings. If she now has $4 left, how much did she spend for dinner?

✓ CHECKPOINT 2   *Lessons 9-4 through 9-6*

Name the more precise measurement.

1. 1 h or 57 min

2. 4 qt or 1 gal

3. 12 in. or 1 ft

4. 2.5 cm or 2.55 cm

5. $\frac{1}{2}$ in. or $\frac{7}{16}$ in.

6. 47 cm or 4.7 m

Find the area of each figure. Use significant digits.

7. circle with a radius of 4.12 m

8. square whose sides are 3.5 in. long

9. *Open-ended* Use three zeros, a 2, and a 5 to write a number with exactly three significant digits.

Find the surface area of each figure. If an answer is not a whole number, round to the nearest tenth of a unit.

10. a cone with a diameter of 9.5 cm and a slant height of 22.1 cm

11. a cylinder with a radius of 32 cm and a height of 8 cm

12. a square pyramid with a base edge of 12 in. and a slant height of 9 in.

13. a rectangular prism with dimensions 5 in., 9 in., and 10 in.

14. **Choose A, B, C, or D.** What is the surface area of a prism that is 4 cm tall, 9 cm wide, and 6 cm long?

    A. 216 cm^2 **B.** 192 cm^2 **C.** 228 cm^2 **D.** 168 cm^2

Spheres

After Lesson 9-6

Sometimes an experiment can lead to a mathematical formula.

■ EXAMPLE

Cut an orange in half and use one half to trace the circumference of the orange *twice* on a sheet of paper. Peel half of the orange. Cut the peel into pieces about 1 centimeter square. Estimate the surface area of the half by placing the pieces into the circles that you drew.

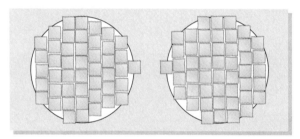

You should discover that the surface area of half the orange is about twice the area of one circle. So, the surface area of the orange is about 4 times the area of one circle. Since the area of the circle is πr^2, the surface area of the orange is $4\pi r^2$.

SURFACE AREA OF A SPHERE

The surface area S.A. of a sphere with radius r is given by the formula S.A. $= 4\pi r^2$.

Find the surface area of the sphere with the given dimensions. Round your answer to the nearest tenth.

1. radius = 10 m

2. radius = 4 in.

3. diameter = 4 in.

4. diameter = 2 in.

5. circumference = 3π units

6. circumference = 100 mm

7. *Writing* What happens to the surface area of a sphere when the radius is doubled? When the radius is tripled? Give specific examples to support your answers.

Volumes of Prisms and Cylinders

What You'll Learn

▼ To find the volume of prisms

▼ To find the volume of cylinders

...And Why

Volume tells you how much material fits inside the figure.

Here's How

Look for questions that

▪ build understanding

✔ check understanding

Work Together _____ *Investigating Area and Volume*

Use unit cubes to explore area and volume.

1. ▪*Open-ended* Make a rectangular prism with six or more cubes.

2. Record your data in a table like this one.

Base Dimensions	Base Area (square units)	Height	No. of Cubes in Prism
■ × ■	■	■	■

3. a. ▪*Open-ended* Make a new prism with different dimensions.
   b. Record its data in your table.

4. a. ▪*Patterns* Continue making different prisms and recording data until you notice a pattern in the table.
   b. How do the height and the area of the base relate to the total number of cubes in the prism?
   c. Summarize your findings in one sentence.

THINK AND DISCUSS

▼ *Finding the Volume of a Prism*

The number of unit cubes, or cubic units, in a space figure is its **volume.** You can abbreviate a unit of volume such as cubic centimeters as cm^3.

In the Work Together you discovered that for a rectangular prism, the area of the base multiplied by the height results in the number of unit cubes in the prism.

VOLUME OF A PRISM

The volume V of a prism is the product of the base area B and the height h.

$$V = Bh$$

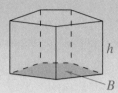

5. Which area formula does this volume formula resemble?

6. ⊞*Reasoning* How is finding volume different from finding surface area?

To find the volume of a prism, start by finding the area of its base.

■ EXAMPLE 1

Find the volume of the prism. Give your answer to the nearest cubic centimeter.

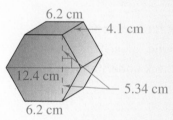

6.2 cm
4.1 cm
12.4 cm
5.34 cm
6.2 cm

The base consists of two congruent trapezoids.

$$\begin{aligned} A &= 2 \cdot \text{area of trapezoid} \\ &= 2 \cdot \tfrac{1}{2}h(b_1 + b_2) \quad \longleftarrow \text{trapezoid area formula} \\ &= h(b_1 + b_2) \quad \longleftarrow \text{Simplify.} \\ &= 5.34(6.2 + 12.4) \quad \longleftarrow \text{Substitute for } h, b_1, \text{ and } b_2. \\ &= 99.324 \quad \longleftarrow \text{Simplify.} \end{aligned}$$

Now use the area to find the volume.

$$\begin{aligned} V &= Bh \quad \longleftarrow \text{prism volume formula} \\ &= 99.324 \cdot 4.1 \quad \longleftarrow \text{Substitute for } B \text{ and } h. \\ &= 407.2284 \quad \longleftarrow \text{Multiply.} \end{aligned}$$

To the nearest cubic centimeter, the volume is 407 cm³.

7. ✔ *Try It Out* The area of the base of a prism is 42 in.², and its height is 51 in. Find the volume.

8. ⊞*Explain* Suppose you know the volume, height, and width of a rectangular prism. How would you find the length?

▼2 *Finding the Volume of a Cylinder*

To create a formula for the volume of a cylinder, substitute the area formula for a circle for *B* in the formula *V = Bh*.

> ### VOLUME OF A CYLINDER
>
> The volume of a cylinder is the product of the base area *B* and the height, *h*.
>
> $$V = Bh, \text{ or } V = \pi r^2 h$$

■ **EXAMPLE 2** *Real-World Problem Solving*

Baking Wedding cakes are often made using cylindrical baking pans. The top layer of this wedding cake has a 12-inch diameter and is 5 inches tall. Find the volume of the top layer of the cake.

$$
\begin{aligned}
V &= \pi r^2 h &&\longleftarrow \text{cylinder volume formula} \\
&= \pi \cdot 6^2 \cdot 5 &&\longleftarrow \text{Substitute for } r \text{ and } h. \\
&= 565.48668 &&\longleftarrow \text{Use a calculator to simplify.}
\end{aligned}
$$

The volume of the top layer is about 570 in.^{3}.

9. ✔**Try It Out** Find the volume of a layer of the cake that is 6 inches tall and has a diameter of 18 inches.

EXERCISES *On Your Own*

Find the volume of each prism.

1.
4 cm
1.5 cm
6.5 cm

2.
10 cm
20 cm
12 cm

3.
15 ft
8 ft
17 ft
22 ft

4.
20 cm
12 cm
15 cm

5.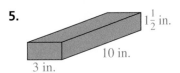
$1\frac{1}{2}$ in.
10 in.
3 in.

6.
6 m
6 m
8 m

7. a. *Gardening* You need to add 4 in. of topsoil to a garden area 12 ft by 3 ft. How many cubic feet of topsoil do you need?

b. *Calculator* If topsoil costs $1.79/ft^3, how much will all of the topsoil cost?

8. *Algebra* If e is the length of each edge of a cube, what is the formula for the volume of the cube?

Find the volume of each cylinder. Give your answer to the nearest tenth of a unit.

9.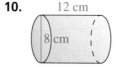
6 in.
8 in.

10.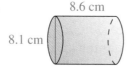
12 cm
8 cm

11.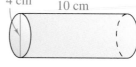
4 cm   10 cm

12.
4 m   4 in.
5.5 in.

13.
8.6 cm
8.1 cm

14.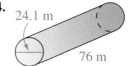
24.1 m
76 m

15. a. *Reading About Math* What was the volume of the box of salt described in the article?

b. If each cylinder of salt has a radius of 4 cm and a height of 13.5 cm, what is its volume?

c. Which shape would you buy? Explain.

16. What is the most space-efficient way to place the cylindrical containers from Exercise 15 in a space that is 30 cm wide, 1 m long, and 14 cm high? Draw a diagram to show your answer.

Salt of the Earth

Salt always comes in cylinders — or does it?

Cylindrical cartons for salt were introduced in the early 1900s. They had the advantage of being stronger than boxes. A cylinder of salt can support a person standing on it.

Years after cylinders became the standard for salt containers, the Leslie Salt Co. decided to put its salt into boxes measuring 9 cm by 15cm by 15 cm. They touted the fact that their container was a more efficient use of shelf space. Old habits die hard, though. The cylinders of salt sold out, while the boxes sat on the shelves.

17. **Choose A, B, C, or D.** Which is most likely to have a volume closest to 150 cm^3?

   A. coffee mug   **B.** cereal box   **C.** classroom   **D.** Lake Superior

18. *Writing* Describe how you would find the radius of a cylinder with a height of 20 in. and a volume of 628 in.^{3}.

19. *Science* One milliliter of water occupies 1 cm^3 of space. A typical straw is 19.4 cm high with a diameter of 0.6 cm. How much water can be contained in a straw?

20. *Estimate* Estimate the volume of the cylinder at the right.

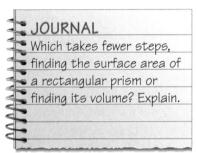

Mental Math **Use mental math to find the volume of each rectangular prism with the given dimensions.**

21. 25 cm by 8 cm by 4 cm   22. 1.2 m by 1.2 m by 10 m

23. An air traffic control center may monitor an area covering 100,000 mi^2 of Earth's surface. If most air traffic is at or below an altitude of 8 mi, draw a cylinder with dimensions that approximate this airspace.

> JOURNAL
> Which takes fewer steps, finding the surface area of a rectangular prism or finding its volume? Explain.

Mixed Review

Use dimensional analysis to convert each measure.
(Lesson 6-2)

24. 42 in. = ▧ ft   25. 8 days = ▧ h   26. 2 mi = ▧ ft   27. 3 gal = ▧ c   28. 430 min = ▧ h

Estimate the percent of each number. *(Lesson 7-2)*

29. 48% of 162   30. 18.5% of 39   31. 195% of 285   32. 0.87% of 415

33. A clock has a minute hand 8 in. long. What is the distance traveled by the tip of the minute hand in one day? *(Lesson 8-10)*

CHAPTER PROJECT

PROJECT LINK: CALCULATING

Find the surface area and the volume of the original cereal box. Then adjust the dimensions of your proposed package so that the volume is about the same, but it uses less cardboard. Calculate the surface area and the volume for your new design. Build a model of your proposed package.

9-8 Proportions and Changing Dimensions

What You'll Learn

▼ To see how change in dimensions affects surface area and volume

...And Why

You can design a set of matching containers of different sizes.

Here's How

Look for questions that
⁙ build understanding
✔ check understanding

QUICKreview

To double a number, multiply the number by 2.
To triple a number, multiply the number by 3.
To quadruple a number, multiply the number by 4.

Work Together _____ *Exploring Changing Dimensions*

Work in groups to explore how changing dimensions affects surface area and volume.

1. What is the surface area of a cube with dimensions $1 \times 1 \times 1$?

2. What is the volume of the cube?

3. The cube with dimensions $1 \times 1 \times 1$ is your original cube. Copy the table below. Record your data in the table.

Cube	Dimensions	Surface Area	Volume
Original	$1 \times 1 \times 1$	■	■
Double	■ × ■ × ■	■	■
Triple	■ × ■ × ■	■	■
Quadruple	■ × ■ × ■	■	■

4. a. Double each dimension of the original cube. Find and record the new surface area and volume.
   b. Triple and quadruple the dimensions of the original cube. Find and record the new surface areas and volumes.

5. Copy and complete the table of ratios shown below. Use information from your other table to find each ratio. Write each ratio in simplest form.

Ratio	Dimensions	Surface Areas	Volumes
Original : Double	$1 : 2$	■ : ■	■ : ■
Original : Triple	■ : ■	■ : ■	■ : ■
Original : Quadruple	■ : ■	■ : ■	■ : ■

6. a. ⁙*Patterns* What patterns do you notice in your table?
   b. Predict the next row of data. Then test your prediction.

THINK AND DISCUSS

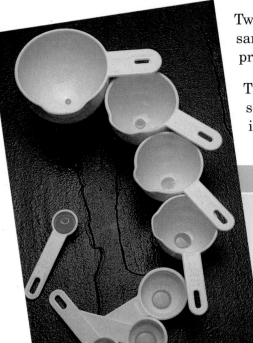

Two space figures are **similar space figures** if they have the same shape and if all of their corresponding dimensions are proportional.

The prisms you created in the Work Together were similar solids. You discovered the following property of similar solids in the Work Together.

SURFACE AREA AND VOLUME OF SIMILAR SOLIDS

If the ratio of corresponding dimensions of two similar solid figures is $a : b$, then

- the ratio of their surface areas is $a^2 : b^2$
- the ratio of their volumes is $a^3 : b^3$

The patterns above can save you time in computing surface area and volume.

■ EXAMPLE 1

The surface area of a prism is 26 ft^2, and its volume is 24 ft^3. Find the surface area and volume of a similar prism whose dimensions are tripled.

The ratio of the dimensions is 1 : 3, so the ratio of the surface areas is $1^2 : 3^2$, or 1 : 9.

$$\frac{\text{surface area of smaller prism}}{\text{surface area of larger prism}} = \frac{1}{9} \quad \longleftarrow \text{Write a proportion.}$$

$$\frac{26}{\text{S.A.}} = \frac{1}{9} \quad \longleftarrow \text{Substitute.}$$

$$\text{S.A.} = 234 \quad \longleftarrow \text{cross product property}$$

Since the ratio of the dimensions is 1 : 3, the ratio of the volumes is $1^3 : 3^3$, or 1 : 27.

$$\frac{\text{volume of smaller prism}}{\text{volume of larger prism}} = \frac{1}{27} \quad \longleftarrow \text{Write a proportion.}$$

$$\frac{24}{V} = \frac{1}{27} \quad \longleftarrow \text{Substitute.}$$

$$V = 648 \quad \longleftarrow \text{cross product property}$$

The surface area is 234 ft^2 and the volume is 648 ft^3.

7. ✓ *Try It Out* Find the surface area and volume of the figure whose dimensions are double those of the figure given in Example 1.

You can also apply the property of similar solids to cylinders.

■ **EXAMPLE 2**   *Real-World Problem Solving*

Pottery Derry designed a cylindrical pitcher with a diameter of 6 inches. Now he is designing a matching creamer to hold $\frac{1}{8}$ what the pitcher holds. What will the creamer's diameter be?

The ratio of the volumes is $1 : 8$, or $1^3 : 2^3$. Therefore, the ratio of the dimensions is $1 : 2$.

$$\frac{\text{diameter of creamer}}{\text{diameter of pitcher}} = \frac{1}{2} \qquad \longleftarrow \text{Write a proportion.}$$

$$\frac{d}{6} = \frac{1}{2} \qquad \longleftarrow \text{Substitute.}$$

$$2d = 6 \qquad \longleftarrow \text{cross product property}$$

$$d = 3 \qquad \longleftarrow \text{Divide each side by 2.}$$

The diameter of the creamer will be 3 inches.

8. ✓ *Try It Out* If Derry designs a matching ice bucket with a volume 27 times that of the creamer, what will the diameter of the bucket be?

If the dimensions of two similar figures have a ratio $1 : a$, then a is called the **scale factor.**

9. What scale factor did Derry use to make the creamer from the pitcher in Example 2?

EXERCISES *On Your Own*

The surface area and volume of a prism are given. Find the surface area and volume of a prism with (a) double and (b) triple the dimensions of the given prism.

1. S.A. = 23 ft^2
    $V = 12$ ft^3

2. S.A. = 64.21 cm^2
    $V = 22.4$ cm^3

3. S.A. = 39 in.^{2}
    $V = 16\frac{1}{2}$ in.^{3}

4. S.A. = 103 yd^2
    $V = 51$ yd^3

5. S.A. = 81.9 m^2
    $V = 60.4$ m^3

6. S.A. = 111 ft^2
    $V = 81$ ft^3

7. S.A. = 61.7 m^2
    $V = 28.2$ m^3

8. S.A. = 24 cm^2
    $V = 8$ cm^3

9. **Choose A, B, C, or D.**
Which of these prisms
contains about half as much
water as the prism at the
right?

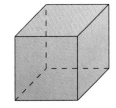

I.
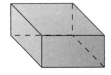

II.
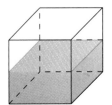

III.
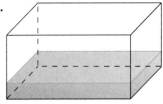

A. I only **B.** I and II only **C.** I and III only **D.** I, II, and III

10. *Writing* The
graph at the
right is misleading.
Use what you have
learned in this lesson
to explain why.

11. *Ceramics* Two similar
ceramic cylindrical
vases have diameters
6 in. and 8 in.
   a. What is the ratio of
   their surface areas?
   b. What is the ratio of
   their volumes?

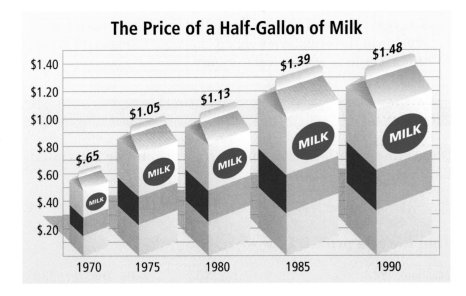

The Price of a Half-Gallon of Milk

12. a. *Patterns* What happens to the volume of a rectangular
   prism with dimensions 2 cm, 5 cm, and 8 cm when you
   double *one* dimension?
   b. What happens when you double *two* dimensions?
   c. What happens when you double all *three* dimensions?
   d. What happens to the volume when you multiply one
   dimension by *n*? Two dimensions by *n*? Three dimensions
   by *n*?

13. *Sports* A regulation-size table tennis ball has a
circumference of $4\frac{1}{2}$ inches. The volume of a regulation-size
baseball is 8 times that of a table tennis ball. What is the
circumference of a baseball?

14. *Architecture* An architect creates a model of an office building with a scale factor of 1 : 200. The surface area of the scale model is 0.31 ft^2. What is the surface area of the actual building?

15. A cube has a surface area of 126 cm^2.
    a. What is the length of each side?
    b. What is the volume of the cube?

16. Find the length of each edge of a cube that has a volume twice that of the cube shown. Give your answer to the nearest tenth of a centimeter. (*Hint*: Use *Guess and Test* and a calculator.)

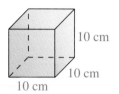

10 cm
10 cm
10 cm

17. *Art* A sculptor made a small version of his next art piece. The real piece will be 10 times taller than the model. How much will the sculpture weigh if the model weighs 42 lb? (*Hint*: Weight is proportional to volume.)

Mixed Review

Determine whether each number is rational or irrational. Explain. (*Lesson 5-9*)

18. $-\frac{1}{2}$ 19. $\sqrt{44}$ 20. 0.85   21. $-\sqrt{5}$ 22. 1.5   23. 2.11111 . . .

Find the sale price. (*Lesson 7-7*)

24. book: $48
    discount rate: 15%

25. sweater: $55
    discount rate: 22%

26. toaster: $36
    discount rate: 5%

27. shoes: $83
    discount rate: 44%

28. The sum of the measures of the angles of a regular polygon is 1,080°. What is the measure of each angle? (*Lesson 8-7*)

CHAPTER PROJECT

PROJECT LINK: WRITING

What shape of rectangular prism uses the least cardboard to enclose a given volume? Explain why you think cereal packages don't use that shape. Then explain why you chose the shape you did, addressing issues such as surface area, volume, convenience, shipping, and advertising.

9-9

Use Multiple Strategies

Problem Solving Strategies

Draw a Diagram
Guess and Test
Look for a Pattern
Make a Table
Simulate the Problem
Solve a Simpler Problem
Too Much or Too Little
 Information
Use Logical Reasoning
✔ Use Multiple Strategies
Work Backward
Write an Equation

THINK AND DISCUSS

Sometimes you need to use more than one problem solving strategy to solve a problem. Consider the following problem.

SAMPLE PROBLEM..

You can cut square corners off a piece of cardboard measuring 9 inches by 12 inches to make a pattern for an open box. What size squares should you cut from each corner to get the greatest volume? Give your dimensions to the nearest half inch.

READ

Read for understanding. Summarize the problem.

1. Think about the information given in the problem and what you are asked to find.
   a. What is the original size of the rectangle?
   b. What shape will you cut from the corners?
   c. What kind of three-dimensional figure is to be formed?
   d. What dimensions will you need to find its volume?

PLAN

Decide on a strategy.

To solve, you will use multiple strategies. *Draw a diagram* to help you plan your solution. *Make a table* to organize the results. Then test all possible solutions. You may, however, shorten your work if you *look for a pattern*.

SOLVE

Try the strategy.

2. Draw a diagram. Let x be the length of each side of the square you cut from each corner.
   a. In terms of x, what will be the length, width, and height of the box?
   b. What is the maximum value of x? Why?
   c. What values of x should you use to solve the problem?

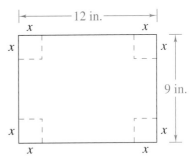

3. Find the volumes for different values of x. Make a table to organize your results. Look for a pattern.

x	Length	Width	Height	Volume
$\frac{1}{2}$ in.	▣ in.	▣ in.	▣ in.	▣ in.^{3}

4. **a.** What value of x, to the nearest half inch, will give the greatest volume?
   b. What are the three dimensions of the box?
   c. What is the greatest volume?

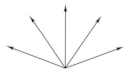

LOOK BACK

Think about how you solved the problem.

5. What patterns helped you to complete the table?

6. Find the value of x, to the nearest *quarter* inch, that will give the greatest volume.

EXERCISES *On Your Own*

Use multiple strategies to solve each problem. Show all of your work.

1. Suppose you cut square corners off a piece of cardboard with dimensions 16 in. by 20 in. to make a pattern for an open box. To the nearest half inch, what lengths for the sides of the squares will give the greatest volume?

2. *Pets* A dog owner wants to use 200 ft of fencing to fence the greatest possible area for her dog. She wants the fenced area to be rectangular. What dimensions should she use?

3. How many diagonals can be drawn in a regular decagon?

4. *Consumers* A customer gives you a $100 bill for a $64 purchase. In what ways can you give change if the customer will accept no more than six $1 bills? (Assume that you have no $2 bills.)

5. Each face of a cube can be painted either blue or yellow. How many different-looking cubes are possible?

6. How many angles are in the figure at the right?

7. The square root of the sum of the consecutive odd integers $1, 3, 5, \ldots, n$ is 10. What is the value of n?

Use any strategy or combination of strategies to solve each problem. Show all your work.

8. The computer game Tetris involves "pieces" made of four squares that each share at least one side with another square. How many different Tetris pieces are there? Draw them all.

9. *Calculator* A circle and a square each have area 144 cm^2. Is the circumference of the circle less than, greater than, or equal to the perimeter of the square?

10. The figure at the right shows a $3 \times 3 \times 3$ cube.
    a. How many $1 \times 1 \times 1$ cubes are there?
    b. How many $2 \times 2 \times 2$ cubes are there?
    c. How many $3 \times 3 \times 3$ cubes are there?
    d. How many cubes are there in all?
    e. How many cubes are there in a $4 \times 4 \times 4$ cube?

11. *Hiking* A hiker will walk 60 mi in three days. On Monday he walks 50% of the distance. Tuesday he walks 25% of the remaining distance. How far must he walk on Wednesday?

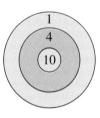

12. *Games* Four darts are thrown at the target shown at the right. If each dart lands on the target, how many different point totals are possible?

Mixed Review

Determine whether each figure tessellates. *(Lesson 8-8)*

13. regular triangle   14. regular hexagon   15. regular pentagon   16. square

Find the slope and the *y*-intercept. Graph each equation. *(Lesson 4-3)*

17. $y = 3x - 5$ 18. $y = -\frac{1}{2}x + 2$ 19. $y = 3 - x$ 20. $y + 2x = 5$ 21. $y + 0.75x = 0$

22. *Restaurants* Marvin is a waiter at a family restaurant. In one hour on Friday night, he waited on 5 tables. The bills for the 5 tables came to $24.30, $28.60, $34.50, $38.65, and $29.80. If Marvin's customers left the customary 15% tip, estimate his tips for the 5 tables. *(Lesson 7-2)*

Volumes of Pyramids and Cones

What You'll Learn

1 To find the volume of a pyramid

2 To find the volume of a cone

...And Why

Some jewelry is designed with cones and pyramids.

Here's How

Look for questions that

⬛ build understanding

✔ check understanding

THINK AND DISCUSS

1 *Finding the Volume of a Pyramid*

The volume of a pyramid is related to the volume of a prism with a congruent base and double the height of the pyramid.

Look at the cube at the right. Suppose the point in the center of the cube is connected to each vertex of the cube as shown. Six congruent square pyramids fit inside the cube. So the volume of each pyramid is $\frac{1}{6}$ the volume of the cube, or $\frac{1}{3}$ the volume of half of the cube.

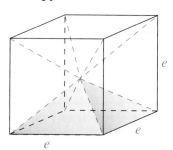

VOLUME OF A PYRAMID

The volume V of a pyramid is one third the product of the base area B and height h.

$$V = \tfrac{1}{3}Bh$$

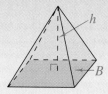

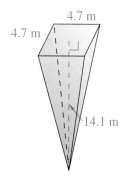

4.7 m
4.7 m
14.1 m

■ EXAMPLE 1

Find the volume of the square pyramid at the left.

First, find the area of the base.

$A = s^2$ ←—area formula for square

$\quad = 4.7^2$ ←—Substitute.

$\quad = 22.09$ ←—Simplify.

Now use the area to find the volume.

$V = \tfrac{1}{3}Bh$ ←—volume formula for pyramid

$\quad = \tfrac{1}{3}(22.09)(14.1)$ ←—Substitute 22.09 for B and 14.1 for h.

$\quad = 103.823$ ←—Simplify.

So the volume is about 104 m^3.

1. ✔ *Try It Out* Find the volume of a square pyramid whose base edge is 15 in. and whose height is 11 in.

▼2 *Finding the Volume of a Cone*

The cone and cylinder at the right have congruent bases and equal heights. If you filled the cone with sand three times and poured it into the cylinder, the cylinder would be filled. So the volume of the cone is $\frac{1}{3}$ that of the cylinder.

VOLUME OF A CONE

The volume V of a cone is one third the product of the base area B and the height h.

$$V = \frac{1}{3}Bh, \text{ or } V = \frac{1}{3}\pi r^2 h$$

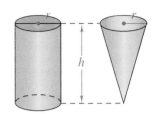

■ EXAMPLE 2

What is the radius of a cone with volume 1,508 cm^3 and height 10 cm?

$V = \frac{1}{3}\pi r^2 h$ ←—volume formula for cone

$1{,}508 = \frac{1}{3}\pi r^2(10)$ ←—Substitute for V and h.

$4{,}524 = \pi r^2(10)$ ←—Multiply each side by 3.

$144.003 \approx r^2$ ←—Divide each side by 10π.

$12 \approx r$ ←—Take the square root of each side.

So the radius of the cone is about 12 cm.

2. ✔ *Try It Out* Find the height of a cone with radius 6 ft and volume 264 ft^3.

3. ⬥ *Open-ended* Suppose you are asked to design a frozen yogurt cone for a state fair. What would be its dimensions? Explain why you chose the dimensions you did.

The first ice cream cone was made on September 22, 1896, in New York City by Italo Marchioni. He was granted a patent for his special mold in 1903.

Jewelry Trina designed a pendant made from two cones as shown. Each cubic centimeter requires 7.92 grams of gold amalgam. How much amalgam will she use to make the pendant?

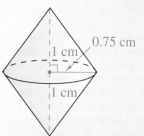

$V = 2 \cdot$ volume of cone

$= 2 \cdot \frac{1}{3}\pi r^2 h$ ←—volume formula for cone

$= 2 \cdot \frac{1}{3}\pi (0.75)^2 (1)$ ←—Substitute for *r* and *h*.

≈ 1.178 ←—Simplify.

Now use the volume to find the amount of gold amalgam.

$\dfrac{7.92 \text{ g}}{1 \text{ cm}^3} = \dfrac{x \text{ g}}{1.178 \text{ cm}^3}$ ←—Write a proportion.

$9.32976 \approx x$ ←—cross product property

So Trina needs about 9.33 grams of gold amalgam.

4. ✔ *Try It Out* How much gold would Trina use if the radius were changed to 0.7 centimeters?

EXERCISES *On Your Own*

Find the volume of each pyramid or cone. If an answer is not a whole number, round it to the nearest whole unit.

1.
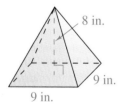
8 in.
9 in.
9 in.

2.
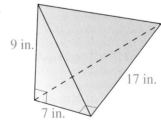
9 in.
17 in.
7 in.

3.
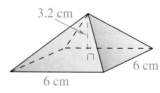
3.2 cm
6 cm
6 cm

4.
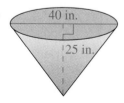
40 in.
25 in.

5.
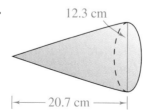
12.3 cm
20.7 cm

6.

24 m
8 m

▦ *Choose* **Use mental math, paper and pencil, or a calculator to find each volume to the nearest cubic unit.**

7. pyramid: base 5 m × 6 m, *h* = 9 m

8. cone: *d* = 16.8 cm, *h* = 22.4 cm

Estimation **Estimate the volume of each cone.**

9. *r* = 10 cm, *h* = 10 cm

10. *r* = 2 in., *h* = 5 in.

11. *d* = 10 cm, *h* = 4 cm

Find the volume of each figure to the nearest tenth.

12.
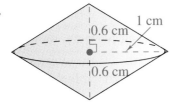
1 cm
0.6 cm
0.6 cm

13.
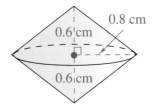
0.8 cm
0.6 cm
0.6 cm

14.
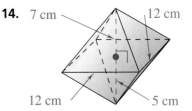
7 cm
12 cm
12 cm
5 cm

15. *Writing* Explain how you might use the area formulas for rectangles and triangles to help you remember the volume formulas for pyramids, cones, prisms, and cylinders.

16. *Reasoning* The volume of a cone is 900 in.^{3}. Andy wants to know the volume of a cylinder with the same size base and height. Vi suggests that he just multiply the volume of the cone by 3. Is this correct? Explain.

17. What happens to the volume of a cone when you double its diameter and height?

PORTFOLIO
Select one or two items
from your work for this
chapter. Consider:
  • corrected work
  • work you found challenging
  • a journal entry
Explain why you have
included each selection
that you make.

Mixed Review

Use the Pythagorean theorem to find the length of the hypotenuse of a right triangle with legs of the given lengths. *(Lesson 5-10)*

18. 7, 24   **19.** 9, 12   **20.** 9, 40   **21.** 16, 63   **22.** 2, 13   **23.** 8, 24

Find each percent of change. Label each answer as an increase or decrease. *(Lesson 7-6)*

24. $26 to $20   **25.** 8 in. to 8.45 in.   **26.** 25 mi to 55 mi   **27.** $3.99 to $2.39

28. How many different lunches can you make from a choice of 3 different sandwiches, 4 drinks, and 2 pieces of fruit? *(Lesson 1-11)*

Choose the best answer.

1. How many faces does a pentagonal prism have?

   A. 5   **B.** 6   **C.** 7   **D.** 8

2. Which of these *cannot* be a name for the figure?

   F. cube   **G.** rectangular prism
   H. square prism   **J.** square pyramid

3. If a triangular prism and a plane intersect, which of the following figures *cannot* describe the intersection?

   A. point   **B.** line segment
   C. triangle   **D.** ray

4. A box of corn flakes has dimensions 2 in. by 7 in. by 10 in. How much does the box hold?

   F. 104 in.^3 **G.** 108 in.^3
   H. 140 in.^3 **J.** 208 in.^3

5. Ignoring overlap, tell how much cardboard was used to make the cereal box in Exercise 4.

   A. 104 in.^2 **B.** 108 in.^2
   C 140 in.^2 **D.** 208 in.^2

6. Which of these is precise to the nearest meter?

   F. 20.2 m   **G.** 21 m
   H. 3.4 m   **J.** 450 cm

7. Which of these is precise to the nearest hundredth of a centimeter?

   A. 6.07 cm   **B.** 8.1 cm
   C. 12.235 cm   **D.** 75 cm

Please note that items 8–11 have *five* answer choices.

8. Ruth packages a box measuring 2 in. by 3 in. by 3 in. inside a gift box that is a 4-inch cube. How much space is left inside the gift box for packing material?

   F. 4 in.^3 **G.** 20 in.^3 **H.** 46 in.^3
   J. 58 in.^3 **K.** 82 in.^3

9. A table is 36 in. by 88 in. Beth wants to buy a tablecloth with a 9-in. overhang on all four sides. What size tablecloth should she buy?

   A. 18 in. by 70 in.   **B.** 27 in. by 79 in.
   C. 44 in. by 96 in.   **D.** 45 in. by 97 in.
   E. 54 in. by 106 in.

Use this diagram of Max's garden for Exercises 10 and 11.

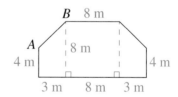

10. What is the length of $\overline{AB}$ in Max's garden?

   F. 3 m   **G.** 4 m
   H. 5 m   **J.** About 7.4 m
   K. Not Here

11. Which of these expressions gives the area (in m^2) of Max's garden?

   A. $\frac{1}{2} \cdot 3(4 + 8) + 8 \cdot 8 + \frac{1}{2} \cdot 3(4 + 8)$

   B. $\frac{1}{2} \cdot 3(4 \cdot 8) + 8 \cdot 8 + \frac{1}{2} \cdot 3(4 \cdot 8)$

   C. $\frac{1}{2} \cdot 8(8 + 14)$

   D. $2 \cdot 3 \cdot 8 + 8 \cdot 8$

   E. Not Here

CHAPTER PROJECT

A BETTER Way

Design Packaging for Cereal The Project Link questions on pages 436, 446, 463, and 468 should help you complete your project. Here is a checklist to help you gather the parts of your project together.

✔ the dimensions of your favorite cereal box

✔ the surface area and volume of your favorite cereal box

✔ the shape, dimensions, surface area, and volume of your proposed packaging

✔ a model of your proposed packaging

Pretend you have a chance to present your proposal for new packaging to the president of a cereal company. Convince your audience to switch to your design. Include convincing arguments related to appearance, the environment, cost, and so on. You want to win your case!

Reflect and Revise

Discuss your proposal with a friend or a relative, and listen to that person's comments or concerns. Is your proposal well reasoned? If necessary, make changes to improve your design.

Web Extension

Prentice Hall's Internet site contains information you might find helpful as you complete your project. Visit www.phschool.com/mgm3/ch9 for some links and ideas related to packaging.

Three-Dimensional Figures 9-1, 9-3

Figures that do not lie in a plane are **three-dimensional figures**, or **space figures**. Some common space figures are **prisms**, **cylinders**, **cones**, and **pyramids**. Patterns that can be folded into space figures are called **nets**.

1. **Choose A, B, C, or D.** Which of the following nets will *not* fold to form a three-dimensional figure?

A.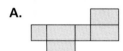
B.
C.
D.

2. *Writing* Compare cylinders and cones to each other.

Drawing Three-Dimensional Figures 9-2

A **base plan** shows the shape of the base and the height of each part of a figure made of cubes. The **top view**, **front view**, and **right view** together communicate the shape of a figure.

Draw a base plan and top, front, and right views for each figure.

3.

4.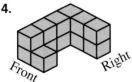

Precision and Significant Digits 9-4

The more **precise** of two measurement is the one with the smaller unit of measure. To multiply or divide with **significant digits**, round the answer to match the number of significant digits in the least precise number.

Compute each product or quotient. Use significant digits.

5. $190.2 \cdot 16$
6. $51.2 \div 0.12$
7. $0.008 \cdot 4$
8. $356 \div 12.1$

Surface Areas of Prisms, Cylinders, Pyramids, and Cones 9-5, 9-6

The surface area of a space figure is the sum of the areas of all the surfaces.

Find each surface area. If an answer is not a whole number, give it to the nearest tenth of a unit.

9.
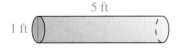
5 ft
1 ft

10.
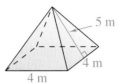
5 m
4 m
4 m

11.
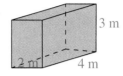
3 m
2 m
4 m

Volumes of Prisms, Cylinders, Pyramids, and Cones 9-7, 9-10

The **volume** of a space figure is the number of cubic units needed to fill the figure. The volume of a prism or cylinder is the area of the base times the height. The volume of a cone or a pyramid is $\frac{1}{3}$ the area of the base times the height.

12. How much potting soil is needed to fill a flower box that is 33 in. long, 6 in. wide, and 8 in. high?

13. Find the height of a cone with a volume of 377 cm^3 and diameter 8 cm. Give your answer to the nearest cm.

Proportions and Changing Dimensions 9-8

If all dimensions of a space figure are multiplied by n, the surface area is multiplied by n^2 and the volume is multiplied by n^3.

Find the new volume and surface area of each figure if all dimensions are doubled.

14. a rectangular prism with a volume of 24 cm^3 and a surface area of 52 cm^2

15. a cylinder with a volume of 785 in.^3 and a surface area of 219.8 in.^2

Use Multiple Strategies 9-9

To solve a problem, you may need to use more than one strategy.

16. How many different rectangular prisms can be built using 12 unit cubes? What are the dimensions of the rectangular prism with the largest surface area? The smallest surface area?

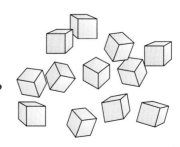

1. Draw a top, front, and right view of each figure.
   a. triangular prism
   b. square pyramid
   c. cone

2. Draw a net for a triangular pyramid.

3. *Open-ended* Use the digits 0, 7, 8, and 9 to write a number with exactly three significant digits.

4. Find the surface area of each figure. If an answer is not a whole number, round to the nearest tenth.
   a. a cube with an edge length of 10 cm
   b. a rectangular prism with height 9 cm and base dimensions 6 cm by 8.5 cm
   c. a cone with slant height 7 in. and diameter 8 in.
   d. a cylinder with height 7.2 cm and diameter 5 cm

5. Find the surface area and volume of each figure. If an answer is not a whole number, round to the nearest tenth.

   a.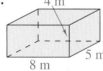

   b.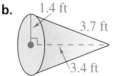

   c.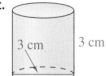

   d.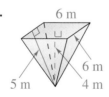

6. *Writing* Explain how the volume formulas for pyramids and cones relate to the volume formulas for prisms and cylinders.

7. **Choose A, B, C, or D.** Which of these figures has the greatest volume?
   A. a square pyramid with base edge length 6 cm and height 6 cm
   B. a cone with radius 4 cm and height 9 cm
   C. a cylinder with radius 4 cm and height 4 cm
   D. a rectangular prism with a base 5 cm by 5 cm and a height of 6 cm

8. **Choose A, B, C, or D.** The length of each edge of a prism is tripled. How many times greater is the volume of the new prism than the volume of the original prism?
   A. 3 times   B. 6 times
   C. 9 times   D. 27 times

9. Elaine is painting the walls of a room that is 18 ft long by 12 ft wide by 8 ft high. There are two rectangular windows, each 3 ft by 4 ft, and one door 3 ft by 7 ft. If Elaine paints at a rate of 100 ft² per hour, how long will the job take? Write your answer to the nearest half hour.

10. What is the greatest precision that can be achieved with this ruler?

11. Find the surface area of a prism whose dimensions are triple those of a prism with surface area 94 cm².

12. Find the volume of a cylinder whose dimensions are double those of a cylinder with volume 110 cm³.

Choose the best answer.

1. What is the probability that a day of the week selected at random begins with the letter *T*?

   A. $\frac{1}{26}$ B. $\frac{1}{7}$ C. $\frac{7}{26}$ D. $\frac{2}{7}$

2. Estimate the shaded area.

   A. 7 units^2
   B. 17 units^2
   C. 27 units^2
   D. 0.7 units^2

   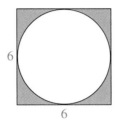

3. Round 5.0672 to the nearest hundredth.

   A. 5.1   B. 5.07
   C. 5.067   D. 5.06

4. Katia wants to buy the bread-making machine that makes the largest loaf by volume. Which model should she buy?

   A. Model A makes a cylindrical loaf with diameter 8 in. and height 10 in.
   B. Model B makes a prism-shaped loaf 6 in. by 6 in. by 11 in.
   C. Model C makes a prism-shaped loaf 6 in. by 8 in. by 11 in.
   D. Model D makes a prism-shaped loaf 7 in. by 7 in. by 10 in.

5. Which object is *not* an example of a prism?

   A. a shoe box   B. a domino
   C. a file cabinet   D. a soup can

6. What is the length of a rectangular garden whose perimeter is 32 ft and whose width is 7 ft?

   A. 25 ft   B. 9 ft
   C. 13 ft   D. 18 ft

7. Of the first 50 customers to visit Daily Bagels, 11 ordered a bagel. If Daily Bagels normally has about 880 customers per day, how many bagels should they expect to sell?

   A. about 16 dozen
   B. about 80
   C. about 8 dozen
   D. about 110

8. Which set of rational numbers is ordered from least to greatest?

   A. 0.38, $\frac{3}{8}$, $\frac{1}{2}$, 0.65
   B. $\frac{12}{27}$, 0.58, $\frac{3}{7}$, 0.89
   C. -0.1, -0.74, $\frac{-2}{3}$, $\frac{-9}{11}$
   D. 0.16, $\frac{2}{5}$, 0.86, $\frac{19}{20}$

9. A cubit was a measure used in ancient times. There are about 2 cubits in a yard. Which of these is about equal to a cubit?

   A. 1 ft   B. 12 in.
   C. 18 in.   D. 2 ft

10. In which set are all three values equal?

    A. 0.5, 5%, $\frac{50}{100}$
    B. $\frac{3}{8}$, 38%, 0.38
    C. 35%, 0.35, $\frac{35}{100}$
    D. 3, 300%, $\frac{3}{100}$

11. Which figure has the least volume?

    A. a cube with edge length 6 cm
    B. a cylinder with radius 3 cm and height 6 cm
    C. a cone with radius 2 cm and height 6 cm
    D. a rectangular prism with dimensions 6 cm × 3 cm × 2 cm

Functions and Polynomials

WHAT YOU WILL LEARN IN THIS CHAPTER

- How to describe number patterns
- How to display functions as rules, tables, and graphs
- How to use polynomials to find perimeter and area

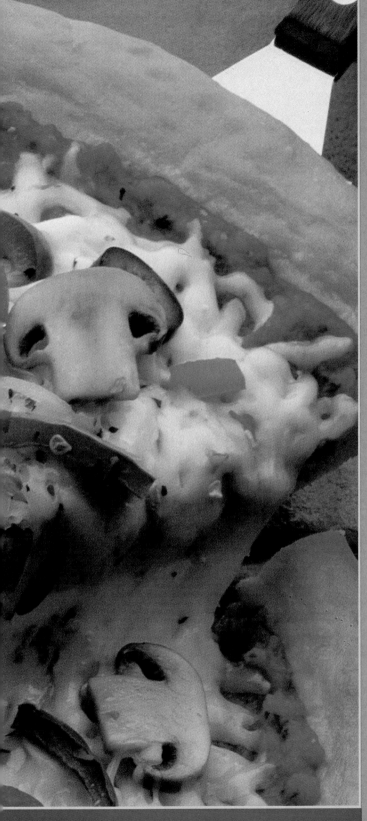

How Much Dough?

How much should a pizza cost? Many merchants sell pizzas in a variety of sizes and styles, with many kinds of toppings. So there are many different prices. Do merchants base prices on what they feel customers will pay? Or do they take a mathematical approach and figure costs using area formulas?

Set Prices for a Product For your chapter project, you will investigate prices for a product that is available in many sizes. You will look for patterns in the prices and describe the patterns mathematically. Finally, you will analyze prices and decide on prices for new products.

Steps to help you complete the project:

• How to solve a problem by first solving a simpler problem

PROBLEM SOLVING

483

10-1

Patterns and Sequences

What You'll Learn

▼ To describe number patterns that represent arithmetic or geometric sequences

▼ To use an algebraic expression to write a sequence

...And Why

You can use sequences to describe participation in sports tournaments.

Here's How

Look for questions that
▪ build understanding
✔ check understanding

Work Together

Exploring Sequences

Work with a partner. Suppose you've just paid $25 to join a baseball-card club for a year. To receive your cards, you must choose one of the three options below.

Option A	Option B	Option C
Receive 230 cards the first month, 250 the second month, 270 the third month, and so on for 12 months.	Receive 1 card the first month, 2 cards the second month, 4 cards the third month, 8 cards the fourth month, and so on for 12 months.	Receive a total of 4,000 cards when you join.

1. ▪ *Analyze* How many cards would you receive in one year if you chose Option A? Option B? Option C?

2. ▪ *Choose* Which option would you choose? Explain your answer. Compare your answer with others in your class.

THINK AND DISCUSS

▼ *Describing Number Patterns*

A **sequence** is a set of numbers that follows a pattern. When you know the pattern, you can find more numbers in the sequence. Each number in a sequence is called a **term.**

■ EXAMPLE 1

Write a rule to describe the sequence 2, 5, 8, 11, ... Then find the next three terms in the sequence.

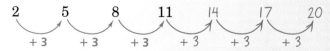

The rule for the sequence is *Start with 2 and add 3 repeatedly.* The next three terms are 14, 17, and 20.

You pronounce arithmetic sequence as ar ith MEH tik SEE kwens.

The sequence in Example 1 is an arithmetic sequence. Each term of an **arithmetic sequence** is found by *adding* a fixed number (called the **common difference**) to the previous term.

3. ▪**Look Back** What is the common difference in the sequence in Example 1?

The common difference in a sequence may be negative. For example, in the sequence 30, 25, 20, 15, . . . , the rule is *Start with 30 and add −5 repeatedly.*

4. ✔ *Try It Out* Identify the common difference in each arithmetic sequence. Then find the next three terms.
  a. 3, 4, 5, 6, 7, . . . **b.** 6, 4, 2, 0, −2, . . . **c.** 9, $8\frac{1}{2}$, 8, $7\frac{1}{2}$, . . .

▪ **EXAMPLE 2** *Real-World Problem Solving*

Sports A state soccer tournament begins with 128 teams. The next rounds have 64 teams, 32 teams, 16 teams, and so on. Write a rule to describe this sequence. Then find the next three terms.

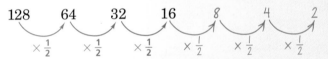

128 64 32 16 8 4 2

$\times\frac{1}{2}$ $\times\frac{1}{2}$ $\times\frac{1}{2}$ $\times\frac{1}{2}$ $\times\frac{1}{2}$ $\times\frac{1}{2}$

The rule for the sequence is *Start with 128 and multiply by $\frac{1}{2}$ repeatedly.*

The sequence in Example 2 is a geometric sequence. Each term of a **geometric sequence** is found by *multiplying* the previous term by a fixed number (called the **common ratio**).

5. ✔ *Try It Out* Identify the common ratio in each geometric sequence.
  a. 1, 3, 9, 27, . . .
  b. 100, 10, 1, $\frac{1}{10}$, . . .
  c. 5, 10, 20, 40, . . .

6. ✔ *Try It Out* Write a rule to describe each sequence. Then find the next three terms in the sequence.
  a. 3, 6, 12, 24, . . .
  b. 24, 21, 18, 15, . . .
  c. 625, 125, 25, . . .

② *Writing a Sequence*

Not every sequence is arithmetic or geometric. You can use an algebraic expression to describe the terms of many different sequences.

■ **EXAMPLE 3** *Real-World Problem Solving*

Gardening When gardening space is limited, you can use small plots in which each square foot is assigned to a plant. The expression $n(n + 1)$ describes the area of each plot shown below.

  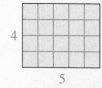

a. Write the terms of a sequence that gives the areas of the first five plots.

$n(n + 1)$ ← Evaluate the expression
$1(1 + 1) = 1 \cdot 2 = 2$ $n(n + 1)$ for
$2(2 + 1) = 2 \cdot 3 = 6$ $n = 1, 2, 3, 4,$ and 5.
$3(3 + 1) = 3 \cdot 4 = 12$
$4(4 + 1) = 4 \cdot 5 = 20$
$5(5 + 1) = 5 \cdot 6 = 30$

The sequence is 2, 6, 12, 20, 30.

b. Find the area of the tenth plot in the sequence.

$n(n + 1)$ ← Evaluate the
$10(10 + 1) = 10 \cdot 11 = 110$ expression $n(n + 1)$
for $n = 10.$

The area is 110 square feet.

7. **⁑Think About It** Explain why the sequence in Example 3 is neither arithmetic nor geometric.

8. ✔ **Try It Out** Evaluate each expression for $n = 1, 2, 3, 4,$ and 5. Tell whether the sequence formed is *arithmetic, geometric,* or *neither.*
   a. $5n + 8$ **b.** $n^2 + 3$ **c.** $3 \cdot 2^n$ **d.** $20 - 4n$

9. **⁑Patterns** Write a rule to describe the sequence 1, 3, 6, 8, 16, 18, ... Then find the next three terms of the sequence.

Write a rule to describe each sequence. Then find the next three terms in the sequence.

1. 6, 4, 2, 0, . . .

2. 800, 400, 200, 100, . . .

3. 8, 8, 8, 8, . . .

4. $1, \frac{1}{2}, \frac{1}{4}, \frac{1}{8}, \ldots$

5. 4, 7, 10, 13, 16, . . .

6. 80, 50, 20, -10, . . .

Identify the common difference in each arithmetic sequence.

7. 11, 15, 19, 23, . . .

8. 20, 12, 4, -4, . . .

9. $-60, -49, -38, -27, \ldots$

10. *Writing* *True* or *false*: An arithmetic sequence that has a negative common difference will always contain negative numbers. Justify your answer.

Identify the common ratio in each geometric sequence.

11. 750, 75, 7.5, 0.75, . . .

12. 3, 6, 12, 24, . . .

13. 0.12, 0.36, 1.08, . . .

14. *Open-ended* Describe a situation that represents a geometric sequence. Write a sequence of numbers for the situation and identify the common ratio.

15. *Patterns* In the Fibonacci sequence 1, 1, 2, 3, 5, 8, . . . , you can find each term (after the first two terms) by adding certain terms together. Find the pattern and use it to write the next three terms of the sequence.

Identify each sequence as *arithmetic, geometric,* or *neither*. Find the next three terms of the sequence.

16. 2.0, 2.3, 2.6, 2.9, . . .

17. 2, 5, 10, 17, . . .

18. 21, 15, 9, 3, . . .

19. 2, 6, 18, 54, . . .

20. 2, 1, 0.5, 0.25, . . .

21. 1.1, 1.01, 1.001, . . .

Tell whether each situation produces an *arithmetic sequence*, a *geometric sequence*, or *neither*.

22. The temperature falls at the rate of 0.5 degrees per hour.

23. The number of bacteria in a lake doubles every day.

24. A baby gains 2 oz every day.

25. The number of minutes a person exercises each day varies between 30 and 45.

26. *Movies* In the 1957 movie *The Incredible Shrinking Man*, the main character mysteriously starts shrinking. Suppose his original height is 6 ft and he shrinks 3 in. every day.
  a. How tall is the man at the end of one week?
  b. How many days would it take for the man to shrink to half his original height?
  c. Does this represent an arithmetic or geometric sequence?
  d. Describe one way the man's height could change to represent a geometric sequence.

Evaluate each expression for $n = 1, 2, 3, 4,$ and 5. Is the sequence formed *arithmetic, geometric,* or *neither*?

27. $5n$

28. $n(n + 5)$

29. $35 - 5n$

30. 2^n

31. n^2

32. $400 \cdot \left(\frac{1}{2}\right)^n$

33. *Time* A clock gains 3 minutes every day. How many minutes fast will the clock be at the end of 60 days?

34. *Geometry* Look at the pattern shown at the right. Each side of the pentagons is one unit in length.
  a. Write a sequence of numbers showing how the perimeter of the figure changes with each step.
  b. What is the perimeter of a row of ten regular pentagons? Explain how you found your answer.

35. Choose A, B, C, or D. Myra is beginning an exercise program. She starts by walking 2 mi the first day and increases her distance by 0.3 mi each day. Which expression represents her distance on the sixth day?
  A. $2(0.3)^6$ **B.** $2 + 6(0.3)$ **C.** $2 + 5(0.3)$ **D.** $0.3 + (2)^5$

Mixed Review

Find the measure of the complement and the supplement of each angle. If there is no complement, write *no complement*. *(Lesson 8-2)*

36. $168°$ **37.** $29°$ **38.** $47°$ **39.** $111°$ **40.** $140.8°$ **41.** $86.3°$

42. At a copy center, Maureen paid $6.60 for 12 copies of a magazine article. How much would she pay for 25 copies of the article? *(Lesson 6-6)*

Exploring Sequences

After Lesson 10-1

■ EXAMPLE 1

Use a graphing calculator. Find the first five terms of the sequence
with the rule *Start with 100 and multiply by 0.9 repeatedly.*

Step 1 Press 100 ENTER

Step 2 Press ✕ 0.9 ENTER

Step 3 Press ENTER repeatedly.

The first five terms are 100, 90, 81, 72.9, 65.61.

```
100
                      100
Ans*0.9
                       90
                       81
                     72.9
                    65.61
```

You can also use a formula to make a sequence.

■ EXAMPLE 2

Find the sequence of y-values when $y = 3x + 2$ and
$x = 1, 2, 3, 4, 5$. Then write a rule for the sequence.

Step 1 Enter the formula.

```
Y1 ■ 3X + 2
Y2 =
Y3 =
Y4 =
Y5 =
Y6 =
Y7 =
Y8 =
```

Step 2 Set the TABLE feature.

```
TABLE SETUP
  TblMin=1
  ΔTbl=1
  Indpnt: Auto  Ask
  Depend: Auto  Ask
```

Step 3 View the table.

```
 X        Y1
 1         5
 2         8
 3        11
 4        14
 5        17
 6        20
 7        23
X=1
```

The sequence of y-values is 5, 8, 11, 14, 17. The rule is *Start
with 5 and add 3 repeatedly.*

Find the first five terms of each sequence.

1. Start with -3.5; add 0.7 repeatedly.

2. Start with 900; subtract 83 repeatedly.

3. Start with 250; multiply by 0.8 repeatedly.

4. Start with 10; multiply by 1.5 repeatedly.

**For each formula, find the sequence of y-values when
$x = 1, 2, 3, 4, 5$. Then write a rule for the sequence.**

5. $y = x + 4$

6. $y = 5x$

7. $y = -4x + 30$

8. $y = 2x + 4$

9. $y = 2^x$

10. $y = 5 \cdot 3^x$

11. $y = \left(\frac{1}{2}\right)^x$

12. $y = 1{,}000 \cdot 0.98^x$

What You'll Learn

▼ To represent functions with equations and tables

▼ To use function notation

...And Why

A function rule that relates cost to telephone use allows you to predict the amount of a monthly bill.

Here's How

Look for questions that
▪ build understanding
✔ check understanding

THINK AND DISCUSS

▼ Representing Functions

To encourage recycling, many states require a nickel deposit on drink containers. The total deposit you pay depends on the number of containers you buy. You can describe this relationship using an equation with two variables.

$d = \$.05n$ ←— input variable: n = number of containers

output variable: d = deposit

A **function** describes the relationship between two variables called the *input* and the *output*.

■ **EXAMPLE 1**   *Real-World Problem Solving*

Recycling Complete the table of input/output pairs for the function $d = \$.05n$.

Input n (Number of Containers)	Output d (Deposit)	
6	▪	←—$\$.05 \times 6 = \$.30$
12	▪	←—$\$.05 \times 12 = \$.60$
24	▪	←—$\$.05 \times 24 = \$1.20$

1. ▪ **Look Back** Suppose the deposit is $2.00. Use the function $d = \$.05n$ to find the number of containers bought.

2. ✔ **Try It Out** The table at the right shows a function that relates the number of people who sign up for a hockey league to the number of teams that are formed. Complete the table of input/output pairs.

$t = n \div 11$

Input n (Number Who Sign Up)	Output t (Number of Teams)
44	▪
132	▪
▪	15

In a function, each input value has only one output value. This means that a function predicts the output for any given input.

■ **EXAMPLE 2**

Does each situation represent a function? Explain.

a. **Input:** the number of $6 tickets you buy
   Output: the total cost of tickets

   Yes; if you know the number of tickets you buy, you can predict the total cost. You say that the total cost is a function of the number of tickets bought.

b. **Input:** the amount of your allowance
   Output: the time you get to school

   No; there is no relationship between the two variables.

c. **Input:** the number of people a car will hold
   Output: the cost of the car

   No; one car that holds five people may cost $15,000. Another car holding five people may cost $25,000. You cannot predict the output (cost) based on the input (number of people).

3. ✔ *Try It Out* Look at the ad at the left. Suppose the input is the number of tires and the output is the price. Does this situation represent a function? Explain.

▼2 *Using Function Notation*

Function notation is another way to show a function. It is closely related to a word description.

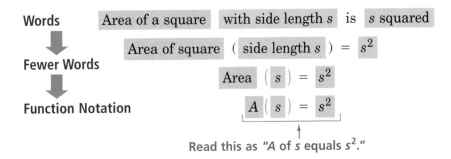

So, $A(4)$ means *Area of a square with side length 4.* The notation $A(4)$ represents the output of the function when the input value is 4.

The letter f is often used to name functions. For example, $f(3)$ represents the output of function f when the input value is 3.

■ **EXAMPLE 3**   *Real-World Problem Solving*

Energy The function $f(x) = 0.23x$ describes the number of kilowatt-hours of power used in x hours by a color television. Find $f(20)$. What does it represent?

$$f(x) = 0.23x$$
$$f(20) = 0.23(20) \quad \longleftarrow \text{Substitute 20 for } x.$$
$$= 4.6 \quad \longleftarrow \text{Simplify.}$$

$f(20)$ represents the output 4.6 kilowatt-hours, which occurs when the input is 20 hours. In other words, if the television is on for 20 hours, it will use 4.6 kilowatt-hours of power.

4. ✔ *Try It Out* Use the function $f(x) = 3x + 4$. Find each output.
   a. $f(2)$ **b.** $f(10)$ **c.** $f(0)$ **d.** $f(-5)$

■ **EXAMPLE 4**   *Real-World Problem Solving*

Aquariums Suppose you buy several dwarf gourami fish at $2 each. The total cost depends on how many you buy. Use function notation to show this relationship. Identify the variables you use.

Words • total cost = $2 · number of fish bought

⬇ • Let n = number of fish bought ⟵ input
   • Let $f(n)$ = total cost ⟵ output

Function • $f(n) = 2n$

5. ✔ *Try It Out* Use function notation to describe this relationship: The area of a circle with radius r equals π times the radius squared.

Here is a summary of function notation, using the function from Example 4.

input
$$f(n) = 2n$$
output (read as "function of n" or "f of n") rule for the function

Complete the table of input/output pairs for each function.

1. $y = 4x$

Input x	Output y
5	■
7	■
9	■
11	■

2. $d = 50t$

Input t	Output d
1	■
2	■
3	■
■	200

3. $y = 20 - 5x$

Input x	Output y
0	■
1	■
■	10
■	5

4. $y = x \div 3$

Input x	Output y
12	■
21	■
57	■
■	45

Does each situation represent a function? Explain.

5. Input: the number of pens at $.79 each
Output: the total cost

6. Input: the time of day you buy gas
Output: the cost of filling the gas tank

7. Input: the number of words to be typed
Output: the time it takes if you can
type 30 words/min

8. Input: the power of a stereo you buy
Output: the amount of money it costs

Does each table represent a function? Explain.

9.

x	0	1	2	3	4
y	2	6	10	14	18

10.

x	1	2	2	3	3
y	1	3	6	9	12

11.

x	2	3	4	5	6
y	5	5	5	5	5

12.

x	-2	-1	0	1	2
y	$\frac{1}{4}$	$\frac{1}{2}$	1	2	4

Use the function $f(x) = 2x + 3$. Find each output.

13. $f(0)$ **14.** $f(-2)$ **15.** $f(2)$ **16.** $f(10)$ **17.** $f(5.5)$ **18.** $f(100)$

Use the function $f(x) = 3x^2 - 7$. Find each output.

19. $f(0)$ **20.** $f(-2)$ **21.** $f(2)$ **22.** $f(10)$ **23.** $f(5.5)$ **24.** $f(100)$

25. *Energy* The function $f(x) = 0.12x$ describes the number of kilowatt-hours of power used in x hours by a television.
   a. Find $f(0)$ and $f(15)$. What does each output represent?
   b. *Writing* The *domain* of a function is all possible input values. The *range* is all possible output values. Which variable represents the domain? Explain.
   c. What domain value produces a range value of 2.4?

Find $f(-5)$ and $f(5)$ for each function.

26. $f(n) = 10n$ **27.** $f(x) = x - 10$ **28.** $f(a) = a^2$ **29.** $f(a) = |a|$

Reasoning **For each function, find $f(1)$, $f(2)$, $f(3)$, and $f(4)$. What type of sequence do these outputs form?**

30. $f(n) = 100 - 4n$ **31.** $f(n) = n(4 - n)$ **32.** $f(n) = 3 \cdot 0.1^n$ **33.** $f(n) = -20 + 2n$

Use function notation to show each relationship. Identify the variable you use.

34. The amount of money you can make equals $4 multiplied by the number of cars you wash.

35. Suppose you have $15 on Monday. The amount of money you have left during the week equals $15 minus $2.50 times the number of lunches you buy.

JOURNAL

Find several solutions of the equation $y = 3x - 2$. Explain how these solutions are related to input/output pairs for the function $f(x) = 3x - 2$. Show how to write each solution in the form $f(\blacksquare) = \blacksquare$.

Mixed Review

Find the volume of each rectangular prism. *(Lesson 9-7)*

36. 16 m by 12 m by 20 m   **37.** 2 cm by 1 cm by 35 cm   **38.** 4 yd by 3 yd by 10 yd

Use an equation to solve each of the following. *(Lesson 7-4)*

39. What percent of 60 is 54?   **40.** Find 68% of 12,400.   **41.** 45% of what number is 40.5?

42. *Fishing* When Imran goes fishing, he catches large fish 5% of the time, medium fish 60% of the time, small fish 25% of the time and no fish 10% of the time. Make a circle graph for these data. *(Lesson 7-5)*

CHAPTER PROJECT

PROJECT LINK: COLLECTING DATA

In newspapers or magazines, find ads for groups of items that differ from each other only in size (tires, picture frames, lumber, carpets, construction materials, or similar items). What patterns, if any, can you find in the prices that are charged for different-size items?

Graphing Linear Functions

Grandparents provide child care for 15.8% of the children under age five whose mothers are employed.

Source: *Statistical Abstract of the United States*

THINK AND DISCUSS

▼ *Using a Table to Graph a Function*

To graph a function, use the coordinate plane. Place input values along the horizontal axis (*x*-axis) and output values along the vertical axis (*y*-axis).

■ **EXAMPLE 1** *Real-World Problem Solving*

Earnings Carlos charges $3 per hour for baby-sitting, plus an extra $5 if he prepares a meal. He has a baby-sitting job every Saturday that includes making dinner. If the parents stay home, they still pay him $5 for reserving the time.

a. Make a table to describe what Carlos earns (output) as a function of time (input).

Input, x Time (hours)	0	1	2	3	4	5
Output, y Earnings ($)	5	8	11	14	17	20

b. Graph the function.

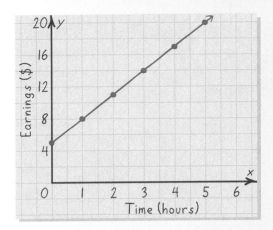

1. a. Why does the graph show only the first quadrant?
   b. ⊞ *Think About It* Should the graph have a highest or a lowest point? Explain.

2. ✔ *Try It Out* Suppose your average speed on a car trip is 40 miles per hour. The distance you cover (output) depends on the time you spend on the road (input). Make a table. Then graph the function.

QUICKreview

In the linear equation $y = mx + b$, m represents the slope and b represents the y-intercept.

2 *Using a Rule to Graph a Function*

Points of a **linear function** lie on a line. You can write a linear function in the form $f(x) = mx + b$. Then you can use the slope and the y-intercept to graph the function.

■ EXAMPLE 2

Graph the linear function $f(x) = 2x - 3$.

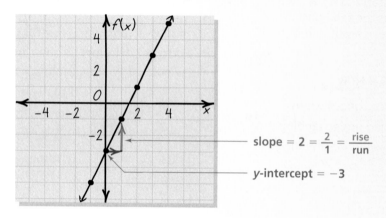

$$\text{slope} = 2 = \frac{2}{1} = \frac{\text{rise}}{\text{run}}$$

$$y\text{-intercept} = -3$$

3. ✔ *Try It Out* Graph each function.
  a. $f(x) = x - 1$  **b.** $f(x) = -\frac{3}{2}x + 3$ **c.** $f(x) = 5x$

Sometimes the points on the graph of a function should not be connected. For example, suppose you are buying concert tickets at $20 each. Since you cannot buy part of a ticket, the graph should show outputs only for inputs that are whole numbers.

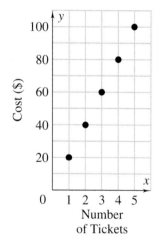

4. ▪ *Look Back* Why is it appropriate to connect the points in the graph for Question 2 above?

5. ✔ *Try It Out* Tell whether the graph of each function should consist of disconnected points or a line. Then draw the graph.
  a. The function $f(x) = 75 + 20x$ predicts the temperature of an oven (in °F) as a function of the time x (in minutes) that the oven has been on.
  b. The function $f(x) = 2.19x$ represents the cost (in dollars) of x gallon containers of milk.

Work Together

6. Have each person in your group write a rule for an arithmetic sequence or a geometric sequence.

7. For each sequence, find the first five terms. Then complete the table by replacing the boxes with the terms you found.

x (Term Number)	1	2	3	4	5
y (Term)	▪	▪	▪	▪	▪

8. For each sequence, graph the ordered pairs from Question 7 on a coordinate plane.

9. ⁛*Analyze* What do you notice about the graph of each arithmetic sequence? Of each geometric sequence?

EXERCISES *On Your Own*

Make a table of input/output pairs for each function. Then graph the function. Show only the portion of the graph that makes sense for each situation.

1. A rock climber is 200 feet above the base of a cliff. She is climbing at a rate of 10 feet per minute. Her height above the base of the cliff (output) is a function of the number of minutes that pass (input).

2. On a car trip, Ian averages 50 mi/h. The distance he covers (output) is a function of time (input).

3. Suppose you earn $5.50 per hour. The number of hours you work (input) determines your pay (output).

4. Suppose you have $30. The amount of money you spend (input) decreases the amount you have left (output).

5. *Science* The height of a burning candle shows how much time has passed since it was lit. For one type of candle, the function $t = 8 - \frac{1}{2}h$ gives the time t the candle has burned (in hours) as a function of the candle height h (in cm).
   a. Graph the function.
   b. What was the original height of the candle?
   c. What is the greatest amount of time the candle can burn?

Graph each linear function.

6. $f(x) = -2x + 5$ **7.** $f(x) = \frac{2}{3}x - 1$ **8.** $f(x) = -\frac{3}{2}x - 2$ **9.** $f(x) = 4$

10. $f(x) = 4x$ **11.** $f(x) = x + 4$ **12.** $f(x) = 5x + 3$ **13.** $f(x) = 12 - \frac{2}{3}x$

14. *Open-ended* Give an example of a real-life situation that you could model with a linear function. Make a table and a graph for the function.

15. *Writing* When should you not connect the points on the graph of a function? Give examples.

Make a table for each function. Decide if the points on the graph should be connected. Then graph the function.

16. *Money* You have $40. Cassettes cost $11 each. The money you have left (output) depends on how many cassettes you buy (input).

17. *Parachuting* A parachutist is 4,000 ft above the ground and falling at 600 ft/min. His height (output) is a function of time (input).

18. *Sales* You sell magazine subscriptions and earn a $3 commission for each sale. The money you earn (output) depends on how many subscriptions you sell (input).

19. *Oceans* The deeper a diver descends, the more pressure he or she feels. The function $f(x) = 1 + 0.3x$ represents the pressure (in atmospheres) at x feet below sea level.

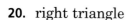

Mixed Review

Judging by appearance, identify an example of each type of triangle. Use the diagram at the right. *(Lesson 8-6)*

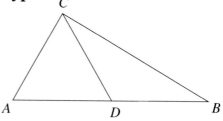

20. right triangle

21. obtuse triangle

22. acute triangle

23. scalene triangle

24. equilateral triangle

25. isosceles triangle

Compute. Use significant digits. *(Lesson 9-4)*

26. $0.908 \cdot 21$ **27.** $7.1 \div 0.040$ **28.** $0.025 \cdot 11.1$ **29.** $68,800 \div 4.2$

30. *Choose a Strategy* Kavitha, Bianca, Doreen, and Manisha competed in a talent contest. Kavitha competed after Doreen but before Bianca. Manisha competed just before Bianca. Doreen competed first. In what order did the girls compete?

10-4 Writing Rules for Linear Functions

What You'll Learn

▼ To write a function rule from words

▼ To write a function rule from a table or graph

...And Why

You can use a function rule to summarize the relationship between inputs and outputs.

Here's How

Look for questions that
- build understanding
- ✔ check understanding

THINK AND DISCUSS

▼ *Writing a Rule from Words*

You have seen that functions can be described in words, in a table, in a graph, or by writing a rule in function notation.

■ **EXAMPLE 1**   *Real-World Problem Solving*

Communications   The rate for basic monthly phone service is $7.42 plus $.055 per message unit. Write a rule to show how the bill depends on the number of message units used.

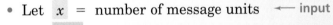

Words   •   monthly bill = $7.42 + $.055 × number of message units

•   Let x = number of message units ← input
•   Let $f(x)$ = monthly bill ← output

Function   • $f(x) = 7.42 + 0.055x$ ← function notation

1. a. ■ *Look Back* Write the function rule in Example 1 in the form $f(x) = mx + b$.

b. What is the slope of the function? What is the y-intercept?

c. Find $f(100)$ and $f(101)$. By how much do these two outputs differ? Explain.

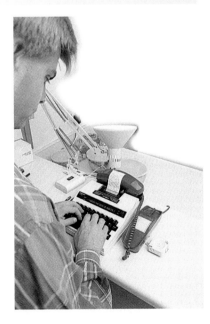

A telecommunications device for the deaf (TDD) allows a hearing-impaired person to use a telephone. It includes a keyboard and a visual display of the conversation.

2. ✔ *Try It Out* A school orchestra is buying music stands. The group has $298 in its treasury. Each stand costs $32.
  a. Write a function rule f to show how the balance in the treasury depends on the number of stands bought.
  b. Find $f(8)$. What does this output represent?

▼2 *Writing a Rule from a Table or Graph*

When do data in a table represent a linear function? You can tell by looking at the changes in inputs and outputs.

■ EXAMPLE 2

Do the data in the table represent a linear function? If so, write the function rule.

						Find the changes in inputs.
	+2	+2	+2	+2		

x	0	2	4	6	8
$f(x)$	10	7	4	1	-2

$-3 \quad -3 \quad -3 \quad -3$ ← Find the changes in outputs.

$\dfrac{\text{change in } f(x)}{\text{change in } x} \qquad \dfrac{-3}{2} \quad \dfrac{-3}{2} \quad \dfrac{-3}{2} \quad \dfrac{-3}{2}$ ← Compare the changes as ratios.

Since each ratio is the same, the function is linear.

The point $(0, 10)$ lies on the graph of the function, so the y-intercept is 10. The slope is $-\frac{3}{2}$.

$f(x) = mx + b$ ← Substitute in the slope-intercept form.

$f(x) = -\frac{3}{2}x + 10$

The function rule is $f(x) = -\frac{3}{2}x + 10$.

3. ■ *Go a Step Further* Use the data in the table at the right.

x	0	1	2	3	4
$f(x)$	1	2	4	5	8

  a. Find the changes in inputs and outputs. Compare them as ratios. Then use the ratios to explain why the data do *not* represent a linear function.
  b. Graph the data in the table. Use the graph to explain why the data do not represent a linear function.

4. ✔ *Try It Out* Do the data in each table represent a linear function? If so, write the function rule.

a.

x	0	1	2	3	4
f(x)	2	4	7	8	10

b.

x	−2	0	2	4	6
f(x)	3	2	1	0	−1

5. ⬟ *Visual Thinking* Write a linear function rule for each graph. Use the slope and y-intercept.

a.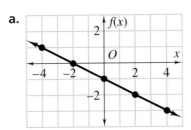

b.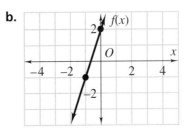

Work Together

Writing Rules from Patterns

Work with a partner to play "What's My Rule?" The object of the game is to guess the function rule your partner is using.

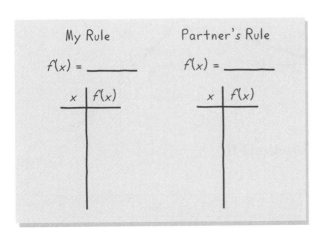

6. Set up your paper as shown at the left. Write your own function rule. Do not show the rule to your partner.

7. Give your partner an input. Your partner will tell you the output, using his or her rule. Record the input/output pair in the appropriate table.

8. Take turns giving inputs. When you have enough pairs to figure out your partner's rule, write the rule.

EXERCISES *On Your Own*

Write a linear function rule for each situation. Identify the input and output variables.

1. *Ecology* Water flows over a dam at a rate of 500 gallons per minute. The amount of water over the dam is a function of the number of minutes that have passed.

2. *Sales* Mrs. Savin receives a base salary of $200, plus a commission of $800 on each car that she sells. Her total pay depends on how many cars she sells.

3. **Art** At a fair, Bob Silva draws caricatures. He pays the fair $30 for space to set up his table, and $2 for each drawing that he sells.
   a. Let x = the number of drawings he sells. Write a function rule to represent his total payment to the fair as a function of the number of drawings he sells.
   b. **Reasoning** What input is paired with the output $54? What does this input represent? Express the input/output pair in the form $f(\blacksquare) = \blacksquare$.

4. Prices at Rub-a-Dub Laundry are $.75 per load of wash and $.75 for 30 minutes of dryer time. An average load takes 1 hour to dry.
   a. Let n = the number of loads of wash. Write a function rule to describe the total cost of washing and drying as a function of the number of loads.
   b. Find $f(3)$. What does this output represent?

For each graph, find the slope and y-intercept. Use the values to write a function rule.

5.
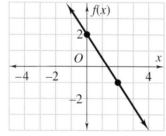

6.
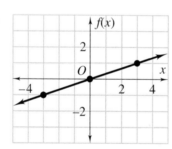

7.
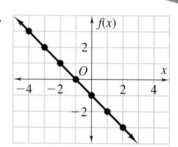

Do the data in each table represent a linear function? If so, write the function rule.

8.
x	0	1	2	3	4
$f(x)$	8	6	4	2	0

9.
x	0	1	2	3	4
$f(x)$	3	5	7	10	13

10.
x	0	3	6	9	12
$f(x)$	0	1	3	6	10

11.
x	-2	-1	0	1	2
$f(x)$	8	5	2	-1	-4

12.
x	-3	-2	-1	0	1
$f(x)$	9	4	1	0	1

13.
x	-10	-5	0	5	10
$f(x)$	0	3	6	9	12

14. **Writing** Explain how to determine if a function is linear by analyzing an input/output table.

Mixed Review

Find the surface area of each figure to the nearest whole unit. *(Lesson 9-5)*

15.
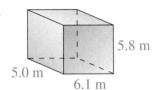
5.8 m
5.0 m
6.1 m

16.
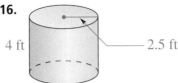
4 ft
2.5 ft

17.
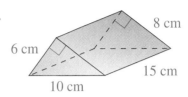
8 cm
6 cm
15 cm
10 cm

Write each percent as a decimal and as a fraction. *(Lesson 7-1)*

18. 18%   **19.** 75%   **20.** 130%   **21.** 94%   **22.** 37%   **23.** 3%

24. *Choose a Strategy* Joan sold three jackets at $29.95 each, plus 15 souvenir pins. She collected a total of $119.10. How much did one souvenir pin cost?

CHAPTER PROJECT

PROJECT LINK: DISPLAYING DATA

Use the data you gathered in the Project Link on page 494. Display the sizes and prices of each group of items in a table. Then graph the function values from your table.

✓ CHECKPOINT 1   *Lessons 10-1 through 10-4*

Identify each sequence as *arithmetic, geometric,* or *neither*. Find the next three terms of the sequence.

1. 1, 4, 9, 16, . . .   **2.** 12, 6, 3, 1.5, . . .   **3.** 125, −25, 5, −1, . . .   **4.** 12, 23, 34, 45, . . .

Use the function rule $f(x) = -3x - 2$. Find each output.

5. $f(-1)$ **6.** $f(5)$ **7.** $f(0)$ **8.** $f\left(-\frac{1}{2}\right)$ **9.** $f(10)$ **10.** $f(-10)$

11. Choose A, B, or C. Which rule represents the data in the table at the right?

x	−3	0	3	6
$f(x)$	−7	−1	5	11

   A. $f(x) = 2x + 1$ **B.** $f(x) = 2x - 1$ **C.** $f(x) = 3x - 1$

12. Suppose a town has 5,000 residents and that the population increases by 400 residents per year. Write and graph a linear function that represents the population as a function of time.

Extra Practice, Lesson 10-4, page 591

10-5 Solve a Simpler Problem

THINK AND DISCUSS

Sometimes when you are faced with a complicated problem situation, it helps to break the problem into simpler steps and look for a pattern.

SAMPLE PROBLEM ....

How many squares of different sizes are there on a standard checkerboard? Consider each small square as 1 square unit.

1 unit^2

 READ

Read for understanding. Summarize the problem.

1. Read the problem carefully. What is the problem about?

2. What are you asked to find?

 PLAN

Decide on a strategy.

Make up a simpler problem that is similar to the given problem. Then solve the simpler problem. Use the same reasoning to solve the given problem.

What different-size squares do you see on the checkerboard? For example, there are squares 1 unit by 1 unit, and there are squares 2 units by 2 units.

 SOLVE

Try the strategy.

Think of simpler situations that are similar to the problem you want to solve.

Number of 1×1 squares	1	4	9	16
Number of 2×2 squares	0	1	4	9
Number of 3×3 squares	0	0	1	4
Number of 4×4 squares	0	0	0	1
Totals	1	5	14	30

3. a. What is the simplest board on which you can count multiple squares? How many squares are on this board?

b. What is the next simplest situation? How many squares are there in this situation?

4. Describe the pattern in the table.

5. Use the pattern to find the number of squares on the checkerboard.

➤ **LOOK BACK**

*Think about how you
solved the problem.*

6. What other strategies did you use to solve the checkerboard problem?

7. Is the number of squares a function of n? Explain.

EXERCISES *On Your Own*

Use the strategy of solving a simpler problem.

1. a. What is the total number of small triangles in the figure?

b. Suppose you extend the figure to ten rows. How many small triangles will there be in the complete figure?

c. Suppose you extend the figure to show a total of n rows. What will be the total number of small triangles?

d. Is the total number of small triangles a function of the number of rows? If so, write the rule in function notation.

Row
1
2
3
4
5
6
7

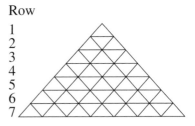

2. *Sports* In a tennis tournament, each participant plays one game against each of the other players. There are 10 participants. How many games will be played?

3. How many different arrangements of children by age can there be in families with a total of five children? (*Hint:* boy-girl-girl-girl-boy is different from boy-boy-girl-girl-girl.)

4. A rancher wishes to fence a square lot with dimensions 40 yards by 40 yards. He will install a fence post every 5 yards. How many fence posts will he need?

Use any strategy to solve the problem. Show your work.

5. *Consumer Issues* The Community Youth Club bought booster buttons at a wholesale price of 3 for $1. They sold the buttons for $.50 each. How much profit did the club make on the sale of 5 dozen buttons?

6. A writer has just finished typing the manuscript for a book and is numbering the pages.
   a. The book is 354 pages long. How many times will the number 3 appear in the page numbers?
   b. There will be one illustration on every thirtieth page of the book, starting on page 1. How many illustrations are planned?

7. *Sports* Regina scored 16 points, 22 points, and 24 points in three basketball games. What is the least number of points she must score in her next game to average at least 20 points per game for the four games?

8. *Jobs* Malcolm sells magazine subscriptions. He earns $15 a week plus $3 for each subscription he sells. How many subscriptions must he sell to earn $90 in one week?

9. Paper plates come in packages of 15 or 20. Karl bought 10 packages and had a total of 170 plates. How many of each size package did he buy?

10. A Creole gumbo recipe calls for 1 tsp of thyme and 10 oz of okra. Suppose you use $1\frac{1}{4}$ lb of okra. How many tsp of thyme should you use?

Mixed Review

Find the area of each triangle to the nearest tenth. *(Lesson 8-9)*

11.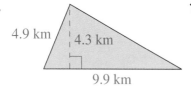

12.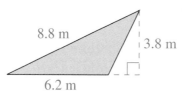

13.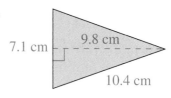

Find each percent of change. Label each answer as an increase or decrease. Round to the nearest tenth. *(Lesson 7-6)*

14. 35 to 45   15. 80 to 65   16. 20 to 25   17. 130 to 95   18. 45.5 to 62

19. *Choose a Strategy* Toshio made a flower bed in the shape of an equilateral triangle. Then he divided the triangle, using all possible lines of symmetry. If he plants one daisy in each of the newly formed triangles, how many daisies will he need?

10-6 Relating Graphs to Events

What You'll Learn

▼ To interpret a graph of a real-world situation

▼ To sketch a graph for a real-world situation

...And Why

Drawing graphs helps you to visualize relationships and interpret data.

Here's How

Look for questions that

⬛ build understanding

✔ check understanding

THINK AND DISCUSS

▼ Interpreting a Graph

A graph can show complex relationships between variables in a simple, visual way.

⬛ **EXAMPLE 1**   *Real-World Problem Solving*

Transportation The graph shows the speed of a commuter train as it makes a morning run.

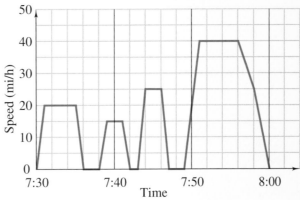

a. How long did the trip take?

   Time is shown on the *x*-axis. The trip lasted 30 minutes, from 7:30 to 8:00.

b. Between which two times did the speed of the train change the most? What was the change?

   Between 7:49 and 7:51, the speed increased from 0 to 40 miles per hour.

1. a. ✔ *Try It Out* What was the train's fastest speed?
   b. How many stops did it make between 7:30 and 8:00?
   c. How long did it travel at 20 miles per hour?
   d. At 7:57, was the train speeding up or slowing down?

▼2 Sketching a Graph

When you draw a graph without actual data, you are making a sketch. A sketch can help you visualize relationships.

■ **EXAMPLE 2**   *Real-World Problem Solving*

Aerobics An athlete measures her pulse rate during a 50-min workout. The workout includes a 10-min warm-up period and a 5-min cool-down period. Sketch and label a graph showing her pulse rate during her workout.

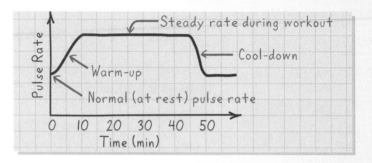

2. ✔ *Try It Out* Suppose you walk from your home to a theater. For 10 min, you walk at a steady pace. For 5 min, you watch a ball game in the park. For the last 5 min, you run so you won't miss the beginning of the movie. Sketch a graph showing the distance you traveled during that 20 min.

Work Together
_____ *Making and Interpreting a Graph*

Work with a partner to explore the relationship between time and the number of steps you take while jogging in place.

3. ⁂ *Data Collection* While you jog, count the total number of steps you take. Your partner should record the number of steps after 15 s, 30 s, 45 s, and so on for two minutes. Then reverse roles. You record the data while your partner jogs.

4. ⁂ *Data Analysis* For each partner, make a table showing *time* in the first column and *total steps taken* in the second.

5. ⁂ *Visual Thinking* Make a double line graph of the data.

6. a. ⁂ *Draw a Conclusion* Did you speed up or slow down during the activity? How can you tell from the graph?
   b. During which 15-s interval did you take the most steps?

EXERCISES *On Your Own*

1. *Olympics* The graph shows the average weekly swimming distances in the 26-week training period before the Olympics.

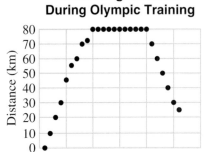

Swimming Distance During Olympic Training

a. For how many weeks is the peak training level of 80 km/wk maintained?

b. How many weeks does it take to reach the peak training level?

c. Between which two weeks does the greatest increase in swimming distance happen? What is the increase?

d. What is the change in the average swimming distance between weeks 24 and 25?

2. **Choose A, B, or C.** A student walks home from school, stopping at a friend's house on the way. Which graph could describe the total distance walked?

A.
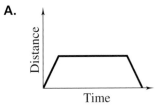

B.
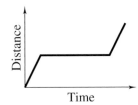

C.
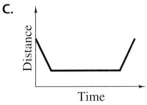

3. *Data Analysis* The graph at the right shows parking fees at a city garage.

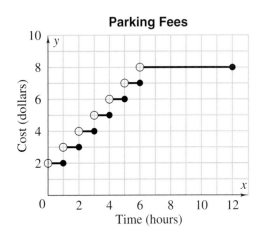

Parking Fees

a. What is the rate for the first hour?

b. What is the cost to park for $3\frac{1}{2}$ hours?

c. What is the maximum cost for up to 12 hours?

d. What is the cost for each additional hour between 1 and 6 hours?

4. *Open-ended* The graph in Exercise 3 is called a *step graph*. Think of another situation that can be represented using a step graph.

a. How would you label the axes?

b. Sketch a graph for the situation.

Sketch a graph of each relationship.

5. You throw a ball into the air. It lands 4 seconds later. Sketch the height of the ball during this time.

6. In a 24-hour period, air temperatures rise during the day and cool off at night. Sketch the temperature during this time.

What a Difference!

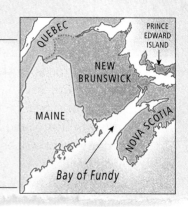

The tides in the Bay of Fundy are world famous. The difference between the water level at low tide and at high tide averages 39.4 ft, but can be as much as 70 ft. Situated between New Brunswick and Nova Scotia, the Bay of Fundy is about 180 mi long and has an average width of 35 mi. Scientists believe that the bay's long, narrow shape accounts for its extreme tidal range.

7. **a.** *Writing* Explain how the graph at the right describes the water level between low tides at the Bay of Fundy.
   b. Suppose low tide occurs at 3:30 P.M. At what time will the tide have risen 30 ft?

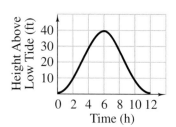

8. *Aviation* An airplane flew from Boston to New York in 50 min. The plane took 20 min to reach its cruising altitude. It took 15 min to descend into New York. Sketch a graph that shows the plane's altitude during the flight.

9. *Recreation* A boat moves at low speed for 3 min while leaving a harbor. Then it moves at cruising speed for 15 min. Finally, it moves at low speed for 5 min into another harbor. Sketch a graph that shows the boat's speed during the trip.

Mixed Review

The surface area of a prism is 54 cm^2 and its volume is 60 cm^3. Find the surface area and volume of each similar prism. *(Lesson 9-8)*

10. a prism with dimensions double the dimensions of the given prism

11. a prism with dimensions triple the dimensions of the given prism

Find each sum or difference. Write each answer as a fraction or mixed number in simplest form. *(Lesson 5-5)*

12. $-\frac{3}{8} + \frac{7}{8}$

13. $-5 - 4\frac{11}{13}$

14. $\frac{7}{9} - \left(-\frac{5}{9}\right)$

15. $3\frac{9}{10} - 9\frac{3}{10}$

16. $-13\frac{4}{5} + \left(-8\frac{1}{5}\right)$

17. *Sales* Compact discs are marked down 30% below the regular price of $11.99. Estimate the sale price of the compact discs. *(Lesson 7-2)*

Extra Practice, Lesson 10-6, page 591

What You'll Learn

1. To write a quadratic function from a table
2. To graph a quadratic function

...And Why

You can describe area relationships using a quadratic function.

Here's How

Look for questions that
- build understanding
- ✓ check understanding

Work Together

Finding Areas

Suppose your class is going to plant a rectangular garden against one wall of the school. You have 20 feet of fencing for the other three sides. How do the dimensions you choose affect the area?

1. Suppose the width is 2 feet.
   a. Find the length of the garden.
   b. Find the area of the garden.

2. Complete the table.

Width x	Length	Area $f(x)$
1	18	18
2	▪	▪
3	▪	▪
4	▪	▪
5	▪	▪
6	▪	▪
7	▪	▪
8	▪	▪
9	▪	18

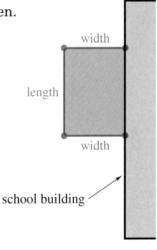

3. ▪ *Visual Thinking* Make a graph showing the area of the garden (output) as a function of the width of the garden (input). Connect the points that you plot with a smooth curve.

4. a. ▪ *Draw a Conclusion* What inputs yield a garden with an area of 42 ft^2?
   b. Estimate the inputs that yield a garden of 25 ft^2.
   c. What input yields the largest garden?

THINK AND DISCUSS

▼ *Writing a Quadratic Function*

When values in a table do not represent a linear function, you can sometimes find a pattern based on squaring the input numbers.

■ EXAMPLE 1

In the table at the right, the outputs are related to the squares of the inputs. Write a rule for the function.

x	$f(x)$
0	3
2	7
3	12
5	28

Input x	(Input)^2 x^2	Output $f(x)$
0	0	3
2	4	7
3	9	12
5	25	28

←— Compare each output to (input)^2. Each output is greater than (input)^2 by 3.

Words • output = (input)^2 + 3

Function • $f(x) = x^2 + 3$

When a function rule is based on squaring the input variable, it is a **quadratic function.** In a quadratic function, the greatest power of the variable is 2.

5. ✔ Try It Out Write a rule for each quadratic function.

a.

x	0	1	2	3	4
$f(x)$	0	2	8	18	32

b.

x	−3	−1	0	2	4
$f(x)$	7	−1	−2	2	14

6. ⬚ Visual Thinking Make a table of input/output pairs from the graph at the right. Then write a function rule that correctly describes the table and the graph.

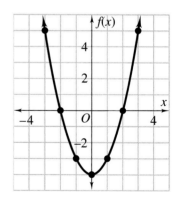

▼2 *Graphing a Quadratic Function*

The graph of a quadratic function is a U-shaped curve called a **parabola** that opens upward or downward. After you plot several points on the graph, connect them with a smooth curve.

■ **EXAMPLE 2**

Graph the quadratic function $f(x) = 4x - x^2$. Use integers from -1 to 5 for inputs.

Make a table.

x	$4x - x^2$						= $f(x)$
-1	$4(-1) - (-1)^2$	=	$-4 - 1$		=		-5
0	$4(0) - (0)^2$	=	$0 - 0$		=		0
1	$4(1) - (1)^2$	=	$4 - 1$		=		3
2	$4(2) - (2)^2$	=	$8 - 4$		=		4
3	$4(3) - (3)^2$	=	$12 - 9$		=		3
4	$4(4) - (4)^2$	=	$16 - 16$		=		0
5	$4(5) - (5)^2$	=	$20 - 25$		=		-5

Draw the graph.

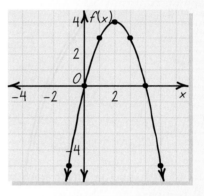

The path of the oranges is a parabola.

7. ✔ *Try It Out* Graph each quadratic function.

a. $f(x) = 2x^2 - 5$ **b.** $f(x) = -x^2 + x$

EXERCISES *On Your Own*

Write a rule for each quadratic function.

1.

x	0	1	2	3	4
$f(x)$	5	6	9	14	21

2.

x	0	1	2	3	4
$f(x)$	0	-2	-8	-18	-32

3.

x	-2	-1	0	1	4
$f(x)$	0	-3	-4	-3	12

4.

x	-10	-5	0	5	10
$f(x)$	20	5	0	5	20

Tell whether the ordered pair (2, 5) lies on the graph of each function. Explain.

5. $f(x) = x^2 + 1$ **6.** $f(x) = 2x^2 - 1$ **7.** $f(x) = 2x^2 - 3$ **8.** $f(x) = x^2 + x - 1$

9. *Gardening* Suppose you have 12 yards of fencing to enclose a garden plot. Complete the table to show area as a function of the garden's width. Graph the function.

Width x	Length	Area $f(x)$
1	5	■
2	4	■
3	■	■
4	■	■
5	■	■

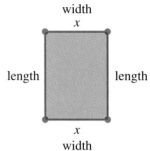

10. *Writing* Suppose $f(x) = 2x^2 - 7$. Explain why $f(3) = f(-3)$.

For each quadratic function, copy and complete the table. Then draw the graph.

11. $f(x) = x^2 - 2$

x	$x^2 - 2 = f(x)$
−2	■
−1	■
0	■
1	■
2	■

12. $f(x) = x^2 - 4x$

x	$x^2 - 4x = f(x)$
0	■
1	■
2	■
3	■
4	■

13. $f(x) = 6x - 2x^2$

x	$6x - 2x^2 = f(x)$
−1	■
0	■
1	■
2	■
3	■

Make a table of values for each function. Use integers from −3 to 3 for inputs. Then graph the function.

14. $f(x) = x^2$ 15. $f(x) = -2x^2$ 16. $f(x) = x^2 - x$ 17. $f(x) = 6x - x^2$

18. *Farming* The number of bushels of walnuts that a tree produces (ouput) is a function of the number of trees planted per acre (input). The function rule is $f(x) = -0.01x^2 + 0.8x$.
   a. Evaluate the function for 10, 20, 30, 40, 50, and 60 trees per acre. Then graph the function.
   b. *Writing* Write a paragraph describing how the number of trees planted per acre affects walnut production.

19. *Open-ended* Write a quadratic function of your own choosing. Graph the function.

20. *Patterns* Consider the pattern of dots at the right.
   a. Let n = the number of dots in the top row of a figure. Write a function rule that describes the total number of dots in that figure.
   b. Describe how you determined the function rule.

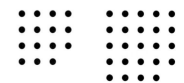

Draw the top, right, and front view of each figure. *(Lesson 9-2)*

21.

22.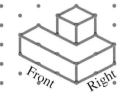

23.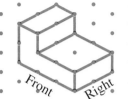

24. *Choose a Strategy* An express bus travels at a speed of 50 mi/h. If Sandeep takes the 9:00 A.M. bus to travel 45 miles, at what time will he reach his destination?

CHAPTER PROJECT

PROJECT LINK: MODELING DATA

Write a function rule that gives the area of a circular pizza as a function of its diameter. Choose five diameters and make a table of values for the function. Then use the table to graph the function. See back of book.

Math at Work

MUSICIAN

Many people think only of rock bands when they think of musicians. Actually, a career as a musician can involve playing an instrument, singing, composing, arranging, conducting, or teaching.

Whether symphony or jazz, musicians use mathematical skills in their profession. Knowledge of patterns helps composers create and structure complex rhythms. Conductors need to read and count the beats of a musical piece. Songwriters today, however, can get help from computers. Programs are now available that produce the musical notation that the musician plays on the keyboard.

For more information about a career as a musician, visit the Prentice Hall Web site: www.phschool.com

Choose the best answer.

1. What is 38.56 rounded to the nearest tenth?

   A. 39   **B.** 38.6   **C.** 38.5   **D.** 38

2. What numbers come next in this pattern?
   $$-27, 9, -3, 1, \ldots$$

   F. $\frac{1}{3}, -\frac{1}{9}, \frac{1}{27}$ **G.** $-1, \frac{1}{3}, -\frac{1}{9}$

   H. $3, -1, \frac{1}{3}$ **J.** $-\frac{1}{3}, \frac{1}{9}, -\frac{1}{27}$

3. A nickel weighs about 5 grams. About how much would 20 nickels weigh?

   A. 0.01 kg   **B.** 0.1 kg
   C. 1 kg   **D.** 10 kg

4. Which of these measurements is precise to the nearest centimeter?

   F. 23.46 cm   **G.** 2.66 cm
   H. 61.5 cm   **J.** 83 cm

5. What is the circumference of a circle with a 3-inch radius? Use $\pi = 3.14$.

   A. 113.04 in.   **B.** 28.26 in.
   C. 18.84 in.   **D.** 9.42 in.

6. What expression comes next in this pattern?
   $$2x, 6x^2, 18x^3, 54x^4, \ldots$$

   F. $108x^5$ **G.** $128x^3$ **H.** $148x^3$ **J.** $162x^5$

7. Which construction does the diagram show?

   A. perpendicular line
   B. bisector of a segment
   C. perpendicular bisector
   D. angle bisector

Use the table for Exercises 8–9.

How Long Students Studied Last Night

Number of Hours	Less than 1	1	2	3	More than 3
Number of Students	15	12	8	3	5

8. How many students were surveyed?

   F. 15   **G.** 33   **H.** 43   **J.** 53

9. How many studied 1 hour or less?

   A. 35   **B.** 27   **C.** 15   **D.** 12

Please note that items 10–13 have *five* answer choices.

10. A photo 3 in. by 5 in. is surrounded by a border 1 in. wide. What is the area of the border?

   F. 5 in.^{2} **G.** 7 in.^{2} **H.** 10 in.^{2}
   J. 15 in.^{2} **K.** 20 in.^{2}

11. The perimeter of a square is 21.6 cm. How long is one side?

   A. 4.6 cm   **B.** 4.9 cm   **C.** 5.4 cm
   D. 6.3 cm   **E.** 7.2 cm

The weight of 5 packages ranges from 1.5 lb to 4.5 lb.

12. What is a reasonable mean weight for the packages?

   F. less than 1.5 lb
   G. between 1.5 lb and 2.5 lb
   H. between 2.1 lb and 3.9 lb
   J. between 3.5 lb and 4.5 lb
   K. more than 4.5 lb

13. What is a reasonable total weight for the packages?

   A. 5 lb   **B.** 7.5 lb   **C.** 8 lb
   D. 15 lb   **E.** 22.5 lb

Other Nonlinear Functions

What You'll Learn

▼ To use tables, rules, and graphs with functions having curved graphs

...And Why

The time to complete a task can be described by a function with a curved graph.

Here's How

Look for questions that
▪ build understanding
✔ check understanding

THINK AND DISCUSS

You have seen that the graph of any linear function is a line. The graph of any quadratic function is a U-shaped curve. Other types of functions also have curved graphs.

▪ **EXAMPLE 1**   *Real-World Problem Solving*

Environment It will take a total of 60 hours of work to clean wildlife damaged by an oil spill. With more people, the time each person must work decreases. Make a table that shows the time each person must work as a function of the number of people. Then graph the data.

Use the relationship 60 hours ÷ $\dfrac{\text{number of}}{\text{people}}$ = $\dfrac{\text{hours per}}{\text{person}}$.

Number of People, x	Hours per Person, $f(x)$
3	60 ÷ 3 = 20
4	60 ÷ 4 = 15
5	60 ÷ 5 = 12
6	60 ÷ 6 = 10
10	60 ÷ 10 = 6
12	60 ÷ 12 = 5
15	60 ÷ 15 = 4
20	60 ÷ 20 = 3

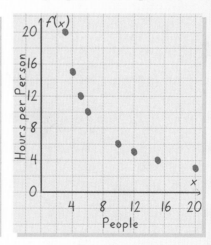

1. ▪ **Look Back** The function rule $f(x) = \dfrac{60}{x}$ describes the relationship in Example 1.
   a. Find $f(8)$. What does it represent?
   b. Does an input of 7.5 make sense in Example 1? Explain.
   c. Is this a linear function? Explain.

2. ✔ *Try It Out* Suppose you must travel 200 miles. The function $f(t) = \frac{200}{t}$ relates the time for the trip (in hours) to the speed (in miles per hour). Make a table and a graph for the function. Draw a curve through the points on the graph.

Some function rules use the input variable as an exponent.

■ EXAMPLE 2

Make a table and a graph for the function $f(x) = 2^x$.

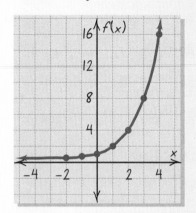

x	$2^x = f(x)$
-2	$2^{-2} = \frac{1}{4}$
-1	$2^{-1} = \frac{1}{2}$
0	$2^0 = 1$
1	$2^1 = 2$
2	$2^2 = 4$
3	$2^3 = 8$
4	$2^4 = 16$

3. ▪ *Look Back* The outputs in the table for Example 2 form a geometric sequence. What is the common ratio?

Work Together _____ *Comparing Function Graphs*

▣ *Technology* Use a computer or graphing calculator.

4. Work with a partner. Take turns making graphs of the functions in each group shown below. Keep a record of the functions and their graphs.

   a. $y = \frac{12}{x}$ $y = \frac{12}{x} + 3$ $y = \frac{12}{x} - 2$
   b. $y = x$ $y = x + 3$ $y = x - 2$
   c. $y = x^2$ $y = x^2 + 3$ $y = x^2 - 2$
   d. $y = 2^x$ $y = 2^x + 3$ $y = 2^x - 2$

5. ▪ *Visual Thinking* Identify the shape of each group of graphs. What characteristics affect the shape of the graph?

6. ▪ *Summarize* In what ways are the graphs within each group different? In what ways are they the same?

Complete the table for each function. Then graph the function. Draw a curve through the points on the graph.

1. $f(x) = \frac{18}{x}$

x	$\frac{18}{x} = f(x)$
2	▓
3	▓
6	▓
9	▓

2. $f(x) = \frac{10}{x} + 3$

x	$\frac{10}{x} + 3 = f(x)$
1	▓
2	▓
5	▓
10	▓

3. $f(x) = 27\left(\frac{1}{3}\right)^x$

x	$27\left(\frac{1}{3}\right)^x = f(x)$
0	▓
1	▓
2	▓
3	▓

4. $f(x) = 3 \cdot 2^x$

x	$3 \cdot 2^x = f(x)$
−1	▓
0	▓
1	▓
2	▓
3	▓

5. $f(x) = 3^x - 2$

x	$3^x - 2 = f(x)$
−1	▓
0	▓
1	▓
2	▓
3	▓

6. $f(x) = \frac{16}{x}$

x	$\frac{16}{x} = f(x)$
1	▓
2	▓
4	▓
8	▓
16	▓

Graph each function. Use positive integers as inputs. Draw a curve through the points on the graph.

7. $f(x) = \frac{10}{x}$

8. $f(x) = \frac{8}{x}$

9. $f(x) = \frac{20}{x}$

10. $f(x) = \frac{100}{x}$

11. $f(x) = 80\left(\frac{1}{2}\right)^x$

12. $f(x) = 48\left(\frac{1}{2}\right)^x$

13. $f(x) = 3^x$

14. $f(x) = 5 \cdot 2^x$

15. Does the point $(3, 5)$ lie on the graph of each function?
   a. $f(x) = 3x - 4$ **b.** $f(x) = 5 \cdot 3^x$ **c.** $f(x) = x^2 - 4$ **d.** $f(x) = \frac{15}{x}$

16. *Money* Suppose you put $50 in an account that pays 12% interest compounded annually. The function $f(x) = 50(1.12)^x$ describes the amount of money in the account after x years.
   a. Find $f(2)$. What does it represent?
   b. Graph the function for input values from 0 to 7.
   c. Estimate when the balance will first exceed $100.

17. *Design* An artist creates a design for the cover of a compact disk. The design uses rectangles with areas of 12 cm^2.
   a. Make a table of possible lengths and widths in the design.
   b. Does your table represent a linear function? Explain.
   c. Graph the data in your table. Place lengths along the x-axis and widths along the y-axis.

18. Choose A, B, or C. The function table at the right describes the distance in feet that a stone falls over time. Which graph best describes the information?

A.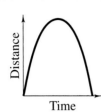

B.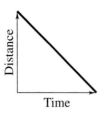

C.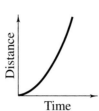

Time (s)	Distance (ft)
0	0
0.5	4
1	16
1.5	36
2	64

Mixed Review

Find the surface area of each figure. Use $\pi \approx \frac{22}{7}$. *(Lesson 9-6)*

19. cone with diameter 6 m and slant height 14 m

20. square pyramid with base edge 4 in. and slant height 4 in.

21. *Choose a Strategy* Kenji and Terrill will work 30 hours each this month. Kenji has already worked 5 more hours than Terrill, who has worked 18 hours. How many more hours does Kenji need to work?

> **JOURNAL**
> Write a function that yields an arithmetic sequence when evaluated for x = 1, 2, 3, ... Write a function that yields a geometric sequence.

✓ CHECKPOINT 2

Write a quadratic function rule for each table.

1.

x	0	1	2	3	4
$f(x)$	-3	-2	1	6	13

2.

x	-4	-2	0	2	4
$f(x)$	8	2	0	2	8

Make a table and a graph for each function.

3. $f(x) = x^2 + 4x$

4. $f(x) = 10 - x^2$

5. $f(x) = \frac{15}{x}$

6. $f(x) = 60 \left(\frac{1}{2}\right)^x$

7. *Consumer Issues* A computer system sells for a regular price of $1,200. During a sale in August, the system sells for 25% off its regular price. During sales in December and April, the system sells for 15% off its regular price.

  a. How much does the system sell for during the August sale? During the December sale?

  b. Make a graph showing the selling price of the computer system over a 12-month period.

8. *Open-ended* Write and graph a nonlinear function.

Extra Practice, Lesson 10-8, page 591

Graphing Inequalities

After Lesson 10-8

The graph of an inequality with two variables is a region of the coordinate plane.

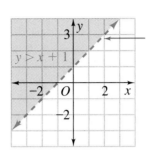

Each point on a *dashed* boundary line is not a solution.

Each point on a *solid* boundary line is a solution.

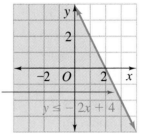

■ EXAMPLE

A football team gains x yards by passing (throwing the ball) and y yards by rushing (running with the ball). The plan for a game calls for the team to gain at least 300 yards. Show the possible combinations of passing and rushing by graphing $x + y \geq 300$.

Graph the boundary line $x + y = 300$. Use a solid line.

Test a point. Use (0, 0).

$$x + y \geq 300$$
$$0 + 0 \geq 300$$
$$0 \geq 300 \quad \longleftarrow \text{False}$$

The inequality is false for (0, 0). Shade the region that does *not* contain (0, 0).

Each point in the shaded region is a solution of the inequality. For instance, (250, 100) represents 250 yards rushing and 100 yards passing.

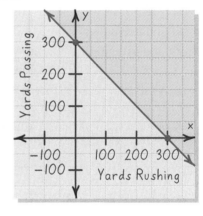

Tell whether (3, −2) is a solution of each inequality.

1. $y < 2x - 5$ 2. $x + y \geq 4$ 3. $y \leq x^2 - 12$ 4. $y > -2x^2$

Graph each inequality.

5. $y > \frac{1}{2}x + 1$ 6. $y \geq -2x + 3$ 7. $x + 3y \leq 6$ 8. $3x - 4y > 24$

9. $20x + 25y < 200$ 10. $y \leq -\frac{5}{2}x + 10$ 11. $y < x^2$ 12. $y \geq \frac{1}{2}x^2 - 2$

13. To raise at least $600 for a yearbook, students sell ads at $20 each and yearbooks at $15 each. Write and graph an inequality to show various ways they can achieve their goal.

What You'll Learn

1. To model a polynomial with algebra tiles

2. To simplify a polynomial by combining like terms

...And Why

You can use polynomials to investigate number relationships.

Here's How

Look for questions that
- build understanding
- ✔ check understanding

Work Together

Reviewing Algebra Tiles

1. **Modeling** Use algebra tiles to model each step of the number trick below. Begin with an x-tile to represent the number chosen in Step 1.

   Step 1 Choose a number.
   Step 2 Multiply the chosen number by 3.
   Step 3 Add 4 to the result.
   Step 4 Multiply the result by 2.
   Step 5 Subtract 2 from the result.
   Step 6 Divide the result by 6.

2. **Analyze** How is the number chosen in Step 1 related to the result in Step 6?

3. Create a similar number trick. Use tiles to show how it works.

THINK AND DISCUSS

1 Modeling a Polynomial

You have already used algebra tiles to represent expressions like $2x + 5$ and $3x - 2$. You can use the tiles shown below to model expressions that contain terms like $2x^2$ or $-4x$.

represents 1.   represents x.   represents x^2.

represents -1.   represents $-x$.   represents $-x^2$.

■ EXAMPLE 1

Write a variable expression for each model.

a.

$2x^2 + x + 3$

b.

$-x^2 + 3x - 4$

Recall that a term is a part of a variable expression. The expression $-2x^2 + 3x + 2$ has three terms, $-2x^2$, $3x$, and 2. A **polynomial** is one term or the sum or difference of two or more terms. A term that does not contain a variable, such as 3, is a **constant.**

▼2 *Simplifying a Polynomial*

To simplify a polynomial, combine like terms. Recall that like terms are modeled with tiles that are the same size.

■ EXAMPLE 2

Use tiles to simplify the polynomial $2x^2 - 3x - x^2 + 2x + 5$.
Model each term.

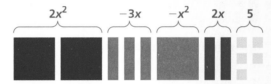

Group tiles of the same size together. Remove zero pairs. Then write an expression for the result.

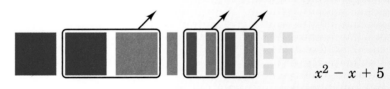

$x^2 - x + 5$

4. ⬝**Look Back** Explain why $2x^2$ and $-3x$ are not like terms.

You can also use properties to simplify polynomials.

■ EXAMPLE 3

Simplify the polynomial $3x^2 + 6x - 2x^2 - 9$.

$3x^2 + 6x - 2x^2 - 9$
$= 3x^2 - 2x^2 + 6x - 9$ ⟵ commutative property
$= (3x^2 - 2x^2) + 6x - 9$ ⟵ associative property
$= (3 - 2)x^2 + 6x - 9$ ⟵ distributive property
$= x^2 + 6x - 9$ ⟵ All like terms are combined.

5. ✔ *Try It Out* Simplify each polynomial.
   a. $4x^2 - 5x - 2x^2 + 7x$ b. $-3x^2 + 3x - x + 7$

QUICKreview

Opposite tiles form a zero pair.
Examples:

$= 0$
x^2 $-x^2$

$= 0$
x $-x$

$= 0$
1 -1

EXERCISES On Your Own

Write a variable expression for each model.

1.

2.

3.

Use tiles to model each polynomial.

4. $-3x^2 + 2x - 7$ 5. $x^2 + x + 1$ 6. $x^2 - x - 1$ 7. $2x^2 - 4x + 5$

Write and simplify the polynomial represented by each model.

8.

9.

Choose **Use tiles or properties to simplify each polynomial.**

10. $x^2 + x^2 + 3x + 2x + 1$

11. $3x^2 + x + x - 4$

12. $3x^2 - 2x^2 + 3x - 2x + 3 - 2$

13. $3x^2 - x^2 + 7x - 5x$

14. $3x^2 - 5x^2 + 2x - 4x - 8 + 3$

15. $3x^2 - 4x + 6x - 2$

16. $2x^2 + 3x^2 - 7x + 3 + 2x$

17. $4x^2 - 7x - 3x^2 + 9x - 1$

Mixed Review

Use the graph for Exercises 18–20. *(Lesson 1-2)*

18. About how many hours per week do women age 18–24 watch television?

19. Which age group shows the least difference between men and women? Which age group shows the greatest difference?

20. *Writing* Who watches television more, men or women? Explain.

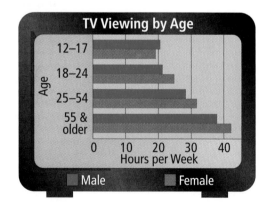

21. Is each function *linear* or *quadratic?* *(Lesson 10-7)*
    a. $f(x) = 3x + 1$ b. $f(x) = x^2 - 2x + 1$ c. $f(x) = 7$

   Extra Practice, Lesson 10-9, page 591

Adding and Subtracting Polynomials

Work Together _____ *Adding Polynomials with Tiles*

1. Work with a partner. Represent the polynomials $x^2 + 5x - 3$ and $2x^2 - 3x + 1$ with algebra tiles.

2. Combine the two groups of tiles. Remove zero pairs and record the result.

3. Copy and complete each addition problem.
   a. $1 + 2$ **b.** $5 - 3$ **c.** $-3 + 1$

4. ⚏ *Think About It* How are the addition problems in Question 3 related to your addition using algebra tiles?

5. ⚏ *Summarize* Summarize your work. Copy and complete the addition problem shown at the right.

$$\begin{array}{r} x^2 + 5x - 3 \\ + \ 2x^2 - 3x + 1 \\ \hline \blacksquare x^2 + \blacksquare x - \blacksquare \end{array}$$

THINK AND DISCUSS

▼1 *Adding Polynomials*

Adding two polynomials is just like simplifying one polynomial. You find and combine the like terms. To combine like terms quickly, you can add the coefficients in the like terms. A **coefficient** is the numerical factor in any term of a polynomial.

$$-2x^2 + x - 3 \qquad\qquad -x^2 + 0x + 5$$
$$\uparrow \quad \uparrow \quad \uparrow \qquad\qquad \uparrow \quad \uparrow \quad \uparrow$$
coefficients: $-2 \quad 1 \ -3 \qquad\qquad -1 \quad 0 \quad 5$

6. Name the coefficients in each polynomial.
   a. $2x^2 + 3x - 1$ **b.** $x^2 - x + 5$ **c.** $-x^2 - 2x + 1$

Coefficients can be positive, negative, or zero. When you add coefficients, you must use the addition rules for signed numbers.

7. ⚏ *Number Sense* Find each sum.
   a. $-7 + 3$ **b.** $-5 + (-4)$ **c.** $12 + (-5)$

■ **EXAMPLE 1**

Add: $(3x^2 - 4x + 2) + (x^2 + 6x - 5)$.

$(3x^2 - 4x + 2) + (x^2 + 6x - 5)$

$= (3x^2 + x^2) + (-4x + 6x) + (2 - 5)$ ←— Group like terms.

$= (3 + 1)x^2 + (-4 + 6)x + (2 - 5)$ ←— distributive property

$= 4x^2 + 2x - 3$ ←— Add and subtract.

8. ✔ *Try It Out* Add.

a. $\begin{array}{r} x^2 + 3x - 1 \\ + \ 2x^2 + 4x + 3 \\ \hline \end{array}$

b. $\begin{array}{r} x^2 + 3x - 1 \\ + \ -4x^2 - \ x + 7 \\ \hline \end{array}$

c. $(5x^2 + x - 8) + (-3x^2 - x - 2)$

▼2 Subtracting Polynomials

You can use algebra tiles to subtract polynomials.

■ **EXAMPLE 2**

Use tiles to model $(3x^2 - 2x) - (x^2 + 3x)$.

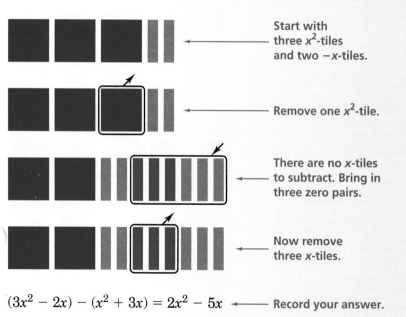

Start with three x^2-tiles and two $-x$-tiles.

Remove one x^2-tile.

There are no x-tiles to subtract. Bring in three zero pairs.

Now remove three x-tiles.

$(3x^2 - 2x) - (x^2 + 3x) = 2x^2 - 5x$ ←— Record your answer.

In Chapter 2, you learned that to subtract an integer, you add its opposite. To subtract a polynomial, you add the opposite of each term in the polynomial.

9. **♣ Number Sense** Write the opposite of each term in the given polynomial.

    a. $3x^2 - 4x + 1$ **b.** $-x^2 + 2x + 2$

■ EXAMPLE 3

Subtract: $(x^2 - 2x + 5) - (2x^2 + x - 4)$.

$(x^2 - 2x + 5) - (2x^2 + x - 4)$

  $= (x^2 - 2x + 5) + (-2x^2 - x + 4)$ ← Add the opposite of each term in the polynomial to be subtracted.

  $= (x^2 - 2x^2) + (-2x - x) + (5 + 4)$ ←Group like terms.

  $= (1 - 2)x^2 + (-2 - 1)x + (5 + 4)$ ←distributive property

  $= -x^2 - 3x + 9$ ←Add and subtract.

10. **✔ Try It Out** Subtract.

    a. $(3x^2 + 5x + 7) - (2x^2 + 4x + 6)$

    b. $(4x^2 - 3x + 1) - (6x^2 - 3x + 3)$

EXERCISES *On Your Own*

Write the addition problem modeled in each exercise.
Then find the sum.

1.    **2.**

Add.

3. $3x - 7$
    $+ \ 5x + 9$

4. $x^2 - 4x$
    $+ \ 3x^2 + x$

5. $3x^2 - 2x + 1$
    $+ \ 5x^2 + 4x - 4$

6. $7x^2 + x - 3$
    $+ -6x^2 \quad\ + 3$

7. $(x^2 + 3x) + (3x^2 - 2x)$

8. $(2x^2 + x - 3) + (2x^2 - x - 3)$

9. $(x^2 + 7x - 6) + (-x^2 - 5x + 3)$

10. $(3x^2 - 7) + (2x^2 + 7x)$

Geometry **Find the perimeter of each figure.**

11.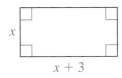
   x
      $x + 3$

12.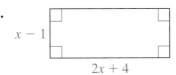
   $x - 1$
      $2x + 4$

13.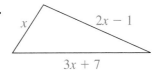
   x $2x - 1$
      $3x + 7$

Choose **Use tiles or coefficients to subtract.**

14. $(3x^2 + 7x) - (2x^2 + 5x)$

15. $(2x^2 + 5x + 7) - (x^2 + 3x + 4)$

16. $(2x^2 + 5x + 7) - (3x^2 + 7x + 8)$

17. $(2x^2 + 5x + 7) - (x^2 - 3x - 1)$

18. $(x^2 + 7) - (3x^2 + 2x + 1)$

19. $(3x^2 - 4x - 1) - (2x^2 + x - 4)$

20. $(3x^2 + 4x - 2) - (3x^2 + 2x - 4)$

21. $(5x^2 + 7x + 3) - (9x - 8)$

22. *Business* The polynomial $13x + 400$ represents the expense of producing x items. The polynomial $25x - 30$ represents the income from x items.
   a. Subtract the two polynomials to find a polynomial that represents the profit on x items.
   b. Evaluate each of the three polynomials for $x = 100$. Verify that profit = income − expenses.

23. *Writing* How is the process for adding two polynomials like the process for adding two integers? How is it different?

24. *Error Analysis* Simon rewrote $(6x^2 + 4x - 2) - (3x^2 - x)$ as $6x^2 + 4x - 2 - 3x^2 - x$. What mistake did he make?

25. **Choose A, B, C, or D.** Add $(3x^2 - 8) + (2x^2 - 3x)$.
   A. $5x^2 - 11x$ **B.** $5x^2 + 3x - 8$ **C.** $5x^2 + 5x$ **D.** $5x^2 - 3x - 8$

26. *Open-ended* Write a polynomial addition problem. Use two different methods to find the sum.

Mixed Review

Find the volume of each figure. *(Lesson 9-10)*

27. pyramid with base area 20 in.^{2} and height 12 in.

28. cone with diameter 6 cm and height 12 cm

Use the function $f(x) = 2x^2 + 5$. Find each output. *(Lesson 10-2)*

29. $f(2)$ **30.** $f(-2)$ **31.** $f(12)$ **32.** $f(0.5)$ **33.** $f(-3.5)$ **34.** $f(0)$

35. *Choose a Strategy* Gina wants to buy a home video system that costs $469. She has $250 in a savings account. She saves $30 from her paycheck every week. In how many weeks will she have enough money to buy the system?

10-11 Multiplying Polynomials

What You'll Learn

1 To use an area model for multiplication

2 To multiply polynomials

...And Why

You can multiply polynomials to find the area of geometric figures.

Here's How

Look for questions that
- build understanding
- ✔ check understanding

THINK AND DISCUSS

1 *Using an Area Model*

The area of each algebra tile is based on the familiar formula for the area of a rectangle: *length × width = area*.

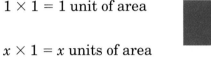

$1 \times 1 = 1$ unit of area

$x \times 1 = x$ units of area

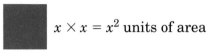

$x \times x = x^2$ units of area

Suppose a rectangle is $3x$ units long and $2x + 3$ units wide. You can use tiles to find its area.

■ EXAMPLE 1

Find the area of the rectangle.

Count tiles to find the area.

There are six x^2-tiles.

There are nine x-tiles.

The area is $6x^2 + 9x$.

So $3x(2x + 3) = 6x^2 + 9x$.

1. ✔ *Try It Out* Find the area of the front view of the construction. The length is $2x + 5$ and the width is $2x$.

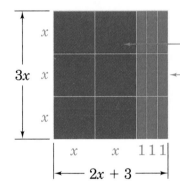

2. ▪ *Visual Thinking* Draw a tile model to find the area of a rectangle with length $3x$ and width $x + 2$.

▼2 *Multiplying Polynomials*

A polynomial that has only one term is called a **monomial.** To multiply monomials, multiply the coefficients and use the properties of exponents.

3. ▪ *Number Sense* Use the properties of signed numbers to explain the sign of each answer.

    a. $(3x)(2x) = 6x^2$ **b.** $(-3x)(2x) = -6x^2$

    c. $(3x)(-2x) = -6x^2$ **d.** $(-3x)(-2x) = 6x^2$

4. ▪ *Mental Math* Simplify each expression.

    a. $2^5 \cdot 2^3$ **b.** $x^5 \cdot x^3$ **c.** $x^5 \cdot x$

QUICKreview

To multiply numbers or variables with the same base, add the exponents.

■ **EXAMPLE 2**

Multiply $-5x^2$ by $4x^3$.

$$(-5x^2)(4x^3) = (-5) \cdot 4 \cdot x^2 \cdot x^3 \quad \longleftarrow \text{Rearrange factors.}$$
$$= -20 \cdot x^2 \cdot x^3 \quad \longleftarrow \text{Multiply coefficients.}$$
$$= -20x^5 \quad \longleftarrow \text{Add exponents.}$$

5. ✔ *Try It Out* Multiply.

    a. $(4x^3)(-3x^2)$ **b.** $(-6x)(-2x)$ **c.** $(-2x^3)(x)$

A polynomial that has two terms is called a **binomial.** You can use the distributive property to find the product of a monomial and a binomial.

■ **EXAMPLE 3**

Multiply $3x$ by $2x^2 - 1$.

$$3x(2x^2 - 1) = 3x(2x^2) + 3x(-1) \quad \longleftarrow \text{distributive property}$$
$$= 6x^3 - 3x \quad \longleftarrow \text{Multiply monomials.}$$

6. ▪ *Go a Step Further* Use the distributive property to multiply $3x(2x^2 - 5x + 1)$.

7. ✔ *Try It Out* Find each product.

    a. $2x(3x^2 - 5)$ **b.** $2x(-3x^2 + 5x + 1)$

    c. $3x^2(x + 2)$ **d.** $-5x(x^2 - 2x - 3)$

8. ⚬ *Visual Thinking*
Use the tile model to
find the product
$(2x + 3)(x + 2)$.

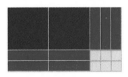

9. ⚬ *Patterns* Study how the distributive property can be used
to multiply two polynomials. Match each product shown in
red to a region of the tile model.

$$(2x + 3)(x + 2) = 2x(x + 2) + 3(x + 2)$$
$$= 2x^2 + 4x + 3x + 6$$
$$= 2x^2 + 7x + 6$$

10. ✔ *Try It Out* Find the product $(x + 4)(3x + 2)$ by using
tiles. Then find it by using the distributive property.

EXERCISES *On Your Own*

Find the area of each rectangle.

1.
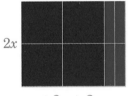
$2x$
$2x + 2$

2.

$x + 4$
$2x + 3$

3.
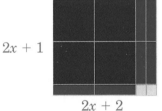
$2x + 1$
$2x + 2$

Draw a tile model to find the area of each rectangle.

4. length = x
width = $x + 3$

5. length = x
width = $2x + 1$

6. length = $2x$
width = $x + 2$

7. length = $3x + 4$
width = $2x + 3$

Multiply.

8. $x^5 \cdot x$

9. $5x \cdot 3x$

10. $(-5x)(3x)$

11. $(-3x^2)(-4x^3)$

12. $4x^4 \cdot 3x^3$

13. $(-x^3)(6x^2)$

14. $(7x^2)(-2x^3)$

15. $(10x^2)(-4x)$

Use the distributive property to find each product.

16. $x(x - 3)$

17. $2x(x + 7)$

18. $7(3x^2 - 2x + 1)$

19. $-3x(x^2 - 6x)$

20. $2x^2(5x - 1)$

21. $-3x^2(x^2 + 2x - 4)$

Find the area of each figure.

22.

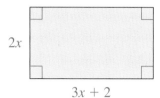

$2x$

$3x + 2$

23.

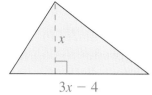

x

$3x - 4$

24.

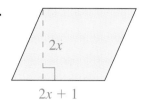

$2x$

$2x + 1$

25. *Writing* Explain how to model the product $(2x + 5)(x + 1)$ with tiles. Write the product as a polynomial in simplest form.

26. **Choose A, B, C, or D.** What is the product of $-3x$ and $x^2 - 2x + 3$?

   A. $-3x^3 + 6x^2 - 9x$ **B.** $-3x^2 - 6x + 9$

   C. $-3x^2 + 6x - 9$ **D.** $-3x^2 - 2x + 3$

Mixed Review

Describe the net for each figure. State how many surfaces the figure has and what shapes they are. *(Lesson 9-3)*

27. rectangular prism

28. pentagonal pyramid

29. triangular pyramid

30. *Sales* You estimate that you can make candles for $.75 each. Advertising will cost $15.00. You sell the candles for $2.00 each. Write and graph equations to represent income and expenses. Find the break-even point. *(Lesson 4-7)*

31. A dining room is a rectangle 10 ft long and 8 ft wide. A table 2 ft long and 3 ft wide will be put inside the room. How many square feet of space will be left around the table? *(Lesson 8-9)*

CHAPTER PROJECT

PROJECT LINK: ANALYZING DATA

Use ads or go to a store to collect prices for several sizes of one brand of pizza. Analyze the prices you find. Suggest a pricing scheme for new sizes of pizza that is based only on the area of the pizza. Suggest another scheme that encourages people to buy larger sizes. Use functions to support your reasoning.

CHAPTER PROJECT

How Much Dough?

Set Prices for a Product The Project Link questions on pages 494, 503, 515, and 532 should help you complete your project. Here is a checklist to help you gather the parts of your project together.

- ✔ prices for various sizes of a product
- ✔ a table and a graph of the prices as a function of size
- ✔ a function for pizza area
- ✔ prices of pizza from a store
- ✔ two ways to set new pizza prices

Organize your proposal for setting pizza prices. Include all of your work from the project and the reasons behind your decisions.

Reflect and Revise

Show your competed project to a friend or someone in your family. Does the person find your reasoning and presentation clear and convincing? Which pricing scheme does your friend favor? If necessary, revise your work.

Web Extension
Prentice Hall's Internet site contains information you might find helpful as you complete your project. Visit www.phschool.com/mgm3/ch10 for some links and ideas related to pricing.

Patterns and Sequences

You find each term of an **arithmetic sequence** by adding a fixed number (called the **common difference**) to the previous term. You find each term of a **geometric sequence** by multiplying the previous term by a fixed number (called the **common ratio**).

Identify each sequence as *arithmetic, geometric,* or *neither*. Find the next three terms.

1. 1600, 400, 100, 25, . . .   2. 14, 21, 28, 35, . . .   3. $-40, -39, -37, -34, . . .$

Functions

A **function** describes the relationship between two variables called the input and the output. In a function, each input value has only one output value. In function notation, $f(3)$ represents the output of function f when the input is 3.

x	$f(x)$
1	5
2	10
2	15
3	20

4. Does the table at the right represent a function? Explain.

Use the function rule $f(x) = 4x - 7$. Find each output.

5. $f(3)$ 6. $f(0)$ 7. $f(-5)$ 8. $f(-1)$ 9. $f\left(\frac{1}{2}\right)$ 10. $f(100)$

Linear Functions

A **linear function** has the form $f(x) = mx + b$. Its graph is a line.

Do the data in each table represent a linear function? If so, write the function rule.

11.

x	0	1	2	3	4
$f(x)$	10	7	4	1	-2

12.

x	-4	-2	0	2	4
$f(x)$	-1	0	1	2	3

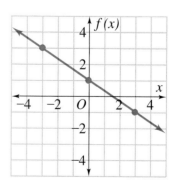

Make a table of values. Then graph each function.

13. $f(x) = \frac{2}{3}x$ 14. $f(x) = -x + 3$ 15. $f(x) = 7$

16. Write a function rule for the graph at the right.

Sometimes you can solve a complicated problem by first solving a simpler problem. You can use graphs to describe real-world situations.

17. The digits in the number 235 have a sum of 10. How many numbers between 0 and 300 have digits with a sum of 10?

18. *Writing* Describe a situation that could be represented by each of the following graphs.

a.

b.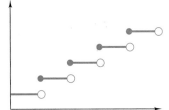

Quadratic Functions and Other Nonlinear Functions   10-7, 10-8

A **quadratic function** is a function in which the highest power of the variable is 2. Its graph is a U-shaped curve called a **parabola.** Other functions also have curved graphs.

Make a table of values. Then graph each function.

19. $f(x) = 2x^2 - 4$ **20.** $f(x) = x^2 - 2x$ **21.** $f(x) = x^2 - 3$ **22.** $f(x) = -x^2 + 2$

Polynomials   10-9, 10-10, 10-11

An expression like $2x^2 + 3x - 5$ is a **polynomial.** To simplify a polynomial, combine like terms. To add or subtract polynomials, use the rules for signed numbers as you combine like terms.

A polynomial with only one term is a **monomial.** To multiply monomials, rearrange factors and use properties of exponents. To multiply polynomials, use the distributive property.

Add, subtract, or multiply.

23. $(8x^2 - 7x + 3) + (3x^2 + x - 5)$

24. $(-4x^2 + 7x) + (x^2 - 7x + 3)$

25. $(8x - 4) - (9x + 3)$

26. $(2x^2 - 4x + 8) - (x^2 - 5x + 3)$

27. $(-6x)(3x^3)$ **28.** $(-2x)(-7x)$

29. $-x(3x - 2)$ **30.** $5x(x^2 - 3x + 2)$

1. Tell whether each situation produces an arithmetic or a geometric sequence. State the common difference or ratio.
   a. A house gains $2,000 in value each year.
   b. A clock loses 30 seconds each hour.
   c. The number of bacteria in a pond triples each day.

2. Write the next three terms in the sequence with a common ratio of $\frac{4}{5}$ and a first term of 125.

3. If $f(x) = -x^2 - 3x$, find each output.
   a. $f(-6)$ b. $f(3)$ c. $f(0)$

4. a. Make a table to display the taxi fare described by $f(x) = 2.4x + 3$. The dollar fare is $f(x)$ and the distance in miles is x.
   b. Find the fare for a trip of $2\frac{1}{2}$ miles.

5. Graph each function. For part (d) use only positive integers as input values.
   a. $f(x) = \frac{1}{2}x - 3$ b. $f(x) = x^2$
   c. $f(x) = 2^x$ d. $f(x) = \frac{12}{x} + 2$

6. Twenty points are placed around a circle. How many segments are needed to join each point to every other point?

7. Match each function with its graph.
   a. $y = -x - 1$ b. $y = x^2 + 1$
   c. $y = x - 1$ d. $y = \frac{1}{2}x$

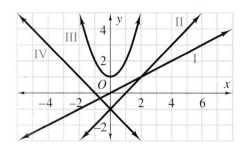

8. *Writing* The graph shows the afternoon route of a school bus. Write a story describing its trip.

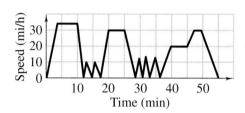

9. Write a quadratic function rule for the table below.

x	-2	-1	0	1	2
$f(x)$	5	2	1	2	5

10. Write and simplify the polynomial represented by the model below.

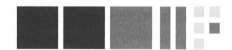

11. Add or subtract.
    a. $(5x^2 + 4x - 2) + (3x^2 - 3x - 5)$
    b. $(7x^2 - x + 2) - (x^2 + 4x - 1)$
    c. $(x^2 - 3x + 5) + (-x^2 + 4x - 4)$

12. Multiply.
    a. $(-9x)(2x)$
    b. $x(3x + 5)$
    c. $2x(x^2 - 6x + 4)$

13. Find the perimeter and the area of the figure below.

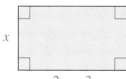

Choose A, B, C, or D.

1. You have a set of data with five items. The median is 14, the mean is 14.8, the mode is 14, and the range is 4. Which could be the correct data set?

    A. 14, 14, 14, 16, 18
    B. 12, 14, 14, 15, 20
    C. 13, 14, 14, 16, 17
    D. 12, 13, 14, 16, 16

2. Which number could *not* be a value of $f(x)$ if $f(x) = 2x^2 - 3$?

    A. 5　　B. -3　　C. 15　　D. -5

3. Which inequality is represented by the graph below?

    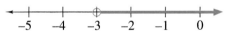

    A. $-\frac{x}{3} < 1$　　　　B. $6z > 18$
    C. $2 + y \le -1$　　　D. $-2w \ge -6$

4. Which proportion could *not* be represented by the model below?

    A. $\frac{12}{15} = \frac{8}{10}$　　　B. $\frac{2}{8} = \frac{3}{12}$
    C. $\frac{3}{10} = \frac{2}{15}$　　　D. $\frac{4}{5} = \frac{8}{10}$

5. Ervin has art class every 6th day of school. How often does he have art class on Monday?

    A. every week
    B. every 5th week
    C. every 6th week
    D. every 7th week

6. In 1937, it cost $1.5 million to make the film *Snow White and the Seven Dwarfs*. In 1992, it cost $85 million to make *Aladdin*. Which expression could you use to find the percent of increase in the cost of making an animated film?

    A. $\frac{1.5 + 85}{85}$　　　B. $\frac{1.5 + 85}{1.5}$
    C. $\frac{85 - 1.5}{1.5}$　　　D. $\frac{85 - 1.5}{85}$

7. Which set of numbers could be the sides of a right triangle?

    A. 15, 12, 9
    B. 9, $\sqrt{15}$, 10
    C. 8, 14, 22
    D. 28, 6, 30

8. The distance light travels in a year, 1 light-year, is about 5,880,000,000,000 miles. What is this number written in scientific notation?

    A. 5.88×10^{12}　　B. 5.88×10^{13}
    C. 58.8×10^{13}　　D. 588×10^{12}

9. How much profit does a store make on a T-shirt that costs $4.87 and has a selling price of $15.95?

    A. $11.02　　　B. $11.08
    C. $11.18　　　D. $20.82

10. Find the surface area of the square pyramid below.

    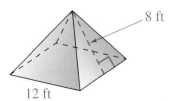

    A. 192 ft^2　　　B. 240 ft^2
    C. 336 ft^2　　　D. 528 ft^2

Probability

WHAT YOU WILL LEARN IN THIS CHAPTER

- How to apply probability concepts

- How to distinguish between types of probability

- How to use probability to analyze games and make decisions

THEME:
SPORTS

Start with the Stats

There are fifteen seconds to go in a close basketball game. Should you foul intentionally? What is the probability that the player you foul will make both free throws? Statistics are everywhere in sports: field goal percentages, batting averages, and so on. Coaches and players use these statistics to assess probabilities and make decisions.

Prepare a Stat Sheet Supply the new basketball coach with all the data she'll need about last year's team. Help her get off to a great start! Pick a team —school, professional, even fictional. Present a statistical report that summarizes last year's team.

- **How to use simulation to solve problems**

PROBLEM SOLVING

What You'll Learn

▼ To use tree diagrams and the counting principle to find the number of possible outcomes

...And Why

You can find the number of different possibilities available when buying clothes or meals.

Here's How

Look for questions that
⁙ build understanding
✔ check understanding

THINK AND DISCUSS

Do you want large, medium, or small? Plain or patterned? Every time you go shopping, you have to make choices. The possibilities seem endless—but are they? The topics in this chapter will help you to figure out the number of possibilities.

■ **EXAMPLE 1** *Real-World Problem Solving*

Shopping Suppose a clothing store sells 3 sizes of shirts (small, medium, and large) in 2 styles (loose-fitting and tailored). Each style comes in 2 colors (white and blue). How many choices of shirts are there?

You can use a tree diagram to solve the problem.

Decision 1	**Decision 2**	**Decision 3**
First, you choose a size.	Then you choose a style.	Then you choose a color.

```
                        loose ─── white
        small  ───────                blue
                        fitted ─── white
                                     blue

                        loose ─── white
        medium ───────                blue          ← Each branch
                        fitted ─── white                represents
                                     blue               one choice.

                        loose ─── white
        large  ───────                blue
                        fitted ─── white
                                     blue
```

There are 12 choices of shirts available.

1. ✔ *Try It Out* Suppose the shirts in Example 1 also come in black. How many choices of shirts are there?

2. ⁙ *Reasoning* Multiply $3 \times 2 \times 2$. How does this calculation relate to the tree diagram in the Example?

The tree diagram shows how the counting principle is used.

THE COUNTING PRINCIPLE

If there are *m* ways of making one choice and *n* ways of making a second choice, then there are $m \times n$ ways of making the first choice followed by the second.

■ **EXAMPLE 2** *Real-World Problem Solving*

Nutrition Suppose the school cafeteria has two choices of sandwiches and three choices of drinks. If you have one sandwich and one drink, in how many different ways can you choose your lunch?

sandwiches	drinks
2	3 ⟵ number of choices available

$2 \times 3 = 6$ ⟵ Use the counting principle.

There are 6 different ways you can choose your lunch.

3. ⣿*Look Back* Draw a tree diagram for Example 2.

4. ⣿*Think About It* Does the order in which you list the decisions make a difference? Explain.

You can use the counting principle when a tree diagram would be too large to draw.

■ **EXAMPLE 3** *Real-World Problem Solving*

License Plates In some states, license plates for cars display three digits followed by three letters. How many different license plates are possible using this system?

There are 10 choices of digits and 26 choices of letters.

digit	digit	digit	letter	letter	letter
10	· 10	· 10	· 26	· 26	· 26 = 17,576,000

There are 17,576,000 different possible license plates.

5. ✔*Try It Out* In other states, license plates display three letters, two digits, and one letter. Which system offers more possible license plate numbers? Explain.

1. A diner advertises a make-your-own meal for $8.99.
   a. Copy and complete the tree diagram below to show all the different meals that can be made by choosing one item from each category.
   b. How many different make-your-own meals can you make?

Make-Your-Own Meal

Entree	Side 1	Side 2
Ham	Peas	Potatoes
Chicken	Corn	Rice
Fish	Carrots	

Entree   **Side 1**   **Side 2**

```
                                        ── potatoes
                        peas ──────────── rice
          ham ────────── corn
                        carrots

chicken


fish
```

2. Sarina has 2 necklaces, 3 pairs of earrings, and 2 bracelets. Use a tree diagram to show the number of ways she can wear one of each.

3. *Photography* You need a roll of film for your 35-mm camera. Choices are given at the right.
   a. How many decisions must you make?
   b. Draw a tree diagram to show the choices for a roll of film. How many different kinds of film can you buy?
   c. The store is sold out of slide film in 12 exposures. How many choices does this eliminate? Explain.

Color Film Available

Speed	100, 200, or 400
Exposures	12, 24, or 36
Type	Print or slide

4. *Communications* U.S. radio station call letters begin with either the letter K or W and are either 3 or 4 letters long.
   a. How many different 3-letter stations can there be?
   b. How many more stations are there that have 4 call letters than have 3?

5. *Technology* A spreadsheet has rows labeled 1−9 and columns labeled A−Z. Each cell in the spreadsheet is identified by a letter and a number, such as D3. Use the counting principle to find the total number of cells in the spreadsheet.

	A	B	C	D
1				
2				
3				
4				

6. **a.** *Reasoning* Refer to Example 3. How could the state increase the number of possible license plates?

   b. *Writing* Which license plate system provides more possible outcomes, one with five letters or one with seven digits? Explain.

7. *Research* Find out what system your state uses for license plates. How many different plates are possible in your state? Are any combinations not allowed?

8. *Shopping* Refer to the chart at the right. How many types of jeans are available?

Jeans at the Style Shop

Sizes	28, 30, 32, 34, and 36
Styles	Regular, slim, and relaxed
Colors	Black and blue

9. *Marketing* A car dealership offers three styles of car: sedan, hatchback, and wagon. Each style comes with either manual or automatic transmission, and is available in 8 different colors. How many different kinds of car does a potential buyer have to consider?

10. *Dining* A 4-course dinner special consists of soup or salad, a main dish, dessert, and coffee or tea. If there are 8 different main dishes and 5 different desserts to choose from, how many different dinner specials can be ordered?

11. *U.S. Postal Service* The first ZIP (Zone Improvement Program) codes, introduced on July 1, 1963, consisted of 5 digits. Current ZIP codes consist of 9 digits: a 5-digit number followed by a 4-digit number, such as 12345-6789. How many more codes are there with a 9-digit code than with a 5-digit code?

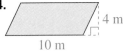

JOURNAL
When is it better to use the counting principle? A tree diagram? Both? Give some examples.

Mixed Review

Geometry **Find the area of each figure. If an answer is not a whole number, round to the nearest tenth.** (*Lessons 8-9 and 8-10*)

12.

50 m

13.

9 m

14 m

14.

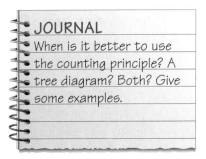

4 m

10 m

15. *Money* The sales tax in some states is 5%. How much would you pay in all for two $12 books and three $15 books?
    (*Lesson 7-7*)

What You'll Learn

▼ To find the number of permutations of a set of objects

▼ To use permutation notation

...And Why

You can use permutations to find the number of possible arrangements of winners in a competitive event.

Here's How

Look for questions that
⚬ build understanding
✔ check understanding

Work Together
Counting Arrangements of People

1. For a school-wide game show, each class chooses one contestant and one alternate. How many ways can you choose a contestant from your class?

2. Once a contestant is chosen, how many choices are there for an alternate from your class?

3. Using the counting principle, find the number of ways to choose two students from your class.

4. A class selects Raquel as the contestant and Matt as the alternate. To represent this, they write (Raquel, Matt). What, then, do you think (Matt, Raquel) represents?

THINK AND DISCUSS

▼ *Exploring Permutations*

Sometimes, the order of objects in an arrangement is important. A **permutation** is an arrangement of a set of objects in a particular order.

■ **EXAMPLE 1**

In how many ways can Matt, Raquel, and Jordan line up?

Matt ⟨ Raquel —— Jordan ① (M, R, J)
　　　 Jordan —— Raquel ② (M, J, R)

Raquel ⟨ Matt —— Jordan ③ (R, M, J)
　　　　 Jordan —— Matt ④ (R, J, M)

Jordan ⟨ Matt —— Raquel ⑤ (J, M, R)
　　　　 Raquel —— Matt ⑥ (J, R, M)

Matt, Raquel, and Jordan can line up in six different ways.

5. ✔*Try It Out* In how many ways can 5 people form a line?

You can also use the counting principle to help you find the number of permutations of a set.

■ **EXAMPLE 2** *Real-World Problem Solving*

Communication Suppose you have to write thank-you notes to seven people. In how many ways can you choose the order in which to write the notes?

There are seven ways to select the first note to write, six ways to select the second, and so on.

$$7 \cdot 6 \cdot 5 \cdot 4 \cdot 3 \cdot 2 \cdot 1 = 5,040$$ ← Use the counting principle.

There are 5,040 different orders in which to write the notes.

The solution to Example 2 involves the product of all the whole numbers from 7 to 1. You can use **factorial** notation to write this expression. The symbol for factorial is an exclamation point. The expression "7!" is read "7 factorial."

$$7! = 7 \cdot 6 \cdot 5 \cdot 4 \cdot 3 \cdot 2 \cdot 1$$

6. ✔ *Try It Out* Many CD players can shuffle the order in which the songs play. Your favorite CD has 9 songs.
   a. Write the factorial expression for the number of different orders in which the songs could play.
   b. *Calculator* Evaluate the factorial expression.

CALCULATOR HINT

Some calculators have a factorial key. For example, to evaluate 4! press 4 $\boxed{x!}$.

▼2 Using Permutation Notation

A class of fifteen students must choose a president and a vice-president. There are 15 possible choices for the president. Then there are 14 possible choices for the vice-president. Therefore there are 15 · 14 possible ways to choose a president and a vice-president from 15 students. You can write this as $_{15}P_2$.

$$_{15}P_2 = 15 \cdot 14 = 210$$

fifteen objects   groups of two

CALCULATOR HINT

Some calculators have a permutation key. To calculate $_5P_2$ press

5 $\boxed{nPr}$ 2 $\boxed{=}$.

PERMUTATION NOTATION

The expression $_nP_r$ stands for the number of permutations of n objects chosen r at a time.

You can use permutations to find the number of ways to choose first, second, and third place in competitions.

■ **EXAMPLE 3** *Real-World Problem Solving*

Horse Shows At a horse show, ribbons are given for first, second, third, and fourth place. There are 20 horses in the show. How many different arrangements of four winning horses are possible?

20 horses Choose 4.

$$_{20}P_4 = 20 \cdot 19 \cdot 18 \cdot 17 = 116,280$$

1st place 2nd place 3rd place 4th place

There are 116,280 different arrangements of four winning horses.

7. ⬚*Open-ended* Write a problem you could solve by evaluating $_{20}P_5$. Solve your problem.

8. ✔*Try It Out* The eighth-grade class of 144 students selects a president, vice-president, and treasurer. Explain why you would use $_{144}P_3$ to find the number of possible outcomes.

EXERCISES *On Your Own*

1. Four students are in line to see the school nurse. In how many different ways can the students form the line?

2. Use a tree diagram to show all the 2-digit numbers that can be formed with the digits 1, 3, 5, 7, and 9, if no digit is repeated.

3. An awards ceremony has five categories. How many ways are there to arrange the order of awarding the prizes?

4. a. Explain what is meant by 13!.
   b. Describe two different ways you can use a calculator to compute 8!.

5. How many different ways can you arrange 6 friends in a row for a photograph?

6. In how many ways can you arrange the digits 1, 2, 3, and 4, if no digit is repeated?

7. Each spring the Country Middle School holds a speech contest. There are seven finalists this year. In how many different orders can the speeches be given?

8. Suppose you rent three movies from your local video store. In how many different orders can you watch the three movies?

Choose Use a calculator, paper and pencil, or mental math to evaluate each factorial.

9. $4!$ **10.** $7!$ **11.** $5!$ **12.** $8!$ **13.** $10!$ **14.** $\frac{5!}{3!}$

15. $1!$ **16.** $10! - 5!$ **17.** $2! \times 4!$ **18.** $2! + 6!$ **19.** $\frac{6!}{5!}$ **20.** $3! \times 2!$

21. *Reasoning* How would having repeated letters in your name affect the number of possible arrangements of the letters of your name?

Find the value of each expression.

22. $_{25}P_3$ **23.** $_{18}P_2$ **24.** $_{32}P_3$ **25.** $_8P_4$ **26.** $_{400}P_2$

27. $_{12}P_5$ **28.** $_{52}P_3$ **29.** $_6P_6$ **30.** $_{10}P_4$ **31.** $_{14}P_3$

32. *Surveys* From a list of 10 artists, students were asked to list their favorite four in order of preference. How many different arrangements are possible?

33. Twenty-five dogs enter a dog show. Prizes are awarded for 1st, 2nd, and 3rd place. How many different arrangements of 3 winning dogs are possible?

34. Suppose an ATM password consists of 4 different digits. How many different passwords can there be?

35. A swim meet consists of 12 swimmers. In how many ways can you choose the 1st-, 2nd-, 3rd-, and 4th-place winners?

36. Suppose you have five books. In how many different orders can you read three of the five books?

37. There are 10 differently colored blocks in a bag. In how many different orders can you select 5 blocks?

Mixed Review

Geometry Find the surface area of each cylinder to the nearest square unit. *(Lesson 9-5)*

38. $r = 11$ in., $h = 5$ in. **39.** $d = 24$ cm, $h = 10$ cm **40.** $r = 9$ m, $h = 8$ m

41. *Open-ended* Draw two lines and a transversal. Label a pair of alternate interior angles $\angle 1$ and $\angle 2$. Then label the angle that corresponds to $\angle 1$ as $\angle 3$ and the angle that corresponds to $\angle 2$ as $\angle 4$. *(Lesson 8-4)*

42. For the function $f(x) = 4x^2 - 3$, make a table that includes the following values for x: -2, -1, $-\frac{1}{2}$, 0, $\frac{1}{2}$, 1, and 2. Sketch the graph. *(Lesson 10-3)*

Combinations

What You'll Learn

▼ To find the number of combinations of a set of objects

▼ To solve problems involving combinations

...And Why

You can find the number of possible combinations of team or committee members.

Here's How

Look for questions that
- build understanding
- ✔ check understanding

THINK AND DISCUSS

▼ *Exploring Combinations*

The pair Amber and Dimitri is the same as the pair Dimitri and Amber. They form the same combination. A **combination** is a group of items in which the order of the items is *not* considered.

■ **EXAMPLE 1**   *Real-World Problem Solving*

Committees The school committee has five members. The superintendent wants to form a subcommittee of two. How many different groups of two can be formed from the five school committee members?

Let A, B, C, D, and E represent each of the five committee members.

Make a list of all the possible committees.

AB	AC	AD	AE
BA	BC	BD	BE
CA	CB	CD	CE
DA	DB	DC	DE
EA	EB	EC	ED

Cross out any group that is a duplicate of another.

AB	AC	AD	AE
~~BA~~	BC	BD	BE
~~CA~~	~~CB~~	CD	CE
~~DA~~	~~DB~~	~~DC~~	DE
~~EA~~	~~EB~~	~~EC~~	~~ED~~

For example, since BA is the same as AB, cross it out.

Count the groups that remain. The superintendent can form 10 different subcommittees, each having two members.

1. Which is greater, the number of combinations or the number of permutations of a set of objects? Explain.

2. ✔*Try It Out* From a group of six students, your teacher selects three tutors. How many combinations are possible?

You can write the number of combinations of five committee members taken two at a time as $_5C_2$. In Example 1, you found $_5C_2$ by using a list. When the number of objects is large, you can use permutations as a first step to find the number of combinations.

2 Solving Problems Using Combinations

To find $_5C_3$, start by finding the number of permutations of five objects, chosen three at a time. $_5P_3 = 5 \cdot 4 \cdot 3 = 60$. Since order is not important in combinations, a group with the same objects as another is considered a duplicate group. The number of permutations of 3 objects is 3!, or 6. So, the number of combinations is one sixth the number of permutations.

$$_5C_3 = \frac{1}{3!} \cdot {}_5P_3 = \frac{1}{6} \cdot (5 \cdot 4 \cdot 3) = 10$$

COMBINATION NOTATION

$$_nC_r = \frac{1}{r!} \cdot {}_nP_r$$

■ EXAMPLE 2

Find $_6C_2$.

$$_6C_2 = \frac{1}{2!} \cdot {}_6P_2 \qquad \longleftarrow \text{Substitute into the notation.}$$

$$= \frac{1}{2} \cdot (6 \cdot 5) = 15 \quad \longleftarrow \text{Simplify, then multiply.}$$

3. ✔Try It Out Find $_7C_4$.

■ EXAMPLE 3 *Real-World Problem Solving*

Fishing In deep-sea fishing, several fishing lines are put off the back of the boat at one time. The boat *Lady Jane* uses 5 lines. Each holds one lure, and there are 12 different lures. How many different combinations of lures can be used at one time?

Find the number of ways you can choose 5 lures from 12.

$$_{12}C_5 = \frac{1}{5!} \cdot {}_{12}P_5$$

$$= \frac{1}{120} \cdot (12 \cdot 11 \cdot 10 \cdot 9 \cdot 8) = 792$$

There are 792 different combinations of 5 out of 12 lures.

4. ⁑Think About It Explain why the number of permutations of 5 lures from a total of 12 lures is multiplied by $\frac{1}{5!}$.

5. ⁑Look Back If the Lady Jane uses 7 lines rather than 5 lines, are more combinations possible? Explain.

Work in pairs. Decide if each situation describes a permutation or a combination. Then find the number of possible outcomes.

6. Arrange all 4 children in a line for a family picture.

7. Choose 3 items from 10 at a salad bar.

8. Start 5 basketball players from a team of 15 players.

9. Choose 6 cards from a pack of 52.

10. Ten people form a line at a bank.

EXERCISES *On Your Own*

List all possible outcomes for each situation. Then find the number of combinations.

1. You have six pens, one each of the colors purple, green, black, red, yellow and orange. Choose two pens.

2. Four friends pair up so that each person plays a game of tennis with each of the other three friends.

3. Choose 2 different letters from the word CLEAR.

4. Choose 2 people from a group of 8. (Name the 8 people A through H.)

Find each number of combinations.

5. $_7C_4$

6. $_3C_1$

7. $_9C_6$

8. $_8C_5$

9. $_6C_2$

10. $_{16}C_4$

11. $_{10}C_9$

12. $_{10}C_1$

13. $_{13}C_{12}$

14. $_{13}C_1$

15. $_7C_3$

16. $_7C_2$

17. $_{11}C_2$

18. $_{12}C_7$

19. $_5C_3$

20. $_8C_4$

21. $_{20}C_{19}$

22. $_{16}C_{10}$

23. Write an expression for each situation in Exercises 1–4 in combination notation.

24. *Reasoning* Are there more combinations or permutations of 2 people chosen from a total of 4? Explain.

25. A president and a vice-president are to be elected from 52 members of a club. How many outcomes are possible?

26. How many different groups of 3 birthday cards can you choose from a group of 10?

27. *Design* A graphic designer must choose 4 colors from the palette below for the logo at the right. How many combinations of 4 colors are possible?

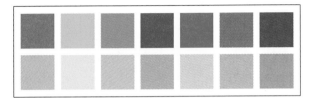

28. *Sports* From a girls' softball team of 18 players, a coach needs to select two girls as co-captains. How many different pairs can the coach select?

29. *Writing* Describe a problem that you can solve using combinations. Then change the problem so you can solve it using permutations.

30. *Travel* A group of six tourists arrives at the airport 15 min before flight time. At the gate they learn there are only two seats left on the airplane. How many different groups of two could get on the airplane? How many different groups of four could *not* get on the airplane?

31. *Music* Sixteen listeners called a radio station to request that a song be played. No song was requested by more than one person. The disc jockey had time to play 10 more songs. How many different sets of 10 songs could the disc jockey play?

32. *Games* Twenty people enter a chess tournament. Each person plays every other person once. How many matches are necessary?

33. **Choose A, B, C, or D.** Which situation has $_{10}C_2$ possible outcomes?
   A. Select two digits from 0 to 9 for a secret code number.
   B. Choose a pair from ten friends for a tournament.
   C. Choose a winner and a runner-up from ten finalists.
   D. Arrange ten books on two shelves.

34. *Education* At the beginning of the year, your teacher gives you a list of 10 projects, of which you must choose 2 to do. In how many possible ways can you make your selections?

Mixed Review

Write a function rule for each table. *(Lesson 10-4)*

35.

x	-5	-4	-3	-2
y	-2	-1	0	1

36.

x	-2	-1	0	1
y	-6	-3	0	3

37.

x	-2	-1	0	1
y	5	4	3	2

38. *Geometry* The surface area of a jewelry box is 62 cm^2. The volume is 30 cm^3. If each dimension is doubled, what will be the new surface area and volume? *(Lesson 9-8)*

✓ CHECKPOINT 1

Lessons 11-1 through 11-3

Evaluate each of the following.

1. $7!$

2. $_5P_4$

3. $_5C_4$

4. $_8P_3$

5. $\dfrac{9!}{8!}$

6. A pizza parlor offers 2 choices of crust, 2 choices of tomato sauce, 3 choices of meat, and 4 choices of vegetable. How many different pizzas can you order, making one selection from each category?

7. Choose A, B, C, or D. A menu has a list of 7 appetizers. Your party will choose 3. Which of the following represents the number of possible choices?

A. $\dfrac{7!}{3!}$ **B.** $_7P_3$ **C.** $_7C_3$ **D.** $7! - 3!$

Math at Work

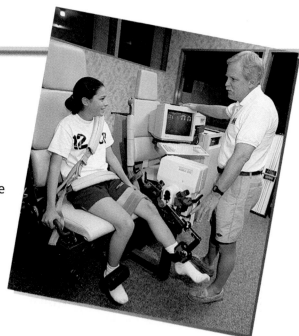

SPORTS THERAPIST

Sports therapists work to improve mobility, relieve pain, and limit disabilities from injuries. They also test an athlete's strength and range of motion. Problem solving skills and logical reasoning help the sports therapist diagnose and prescribe a course of treatment. Therapists also need to analyze test results and data in a patient's medical history.

For more information about sports medicine, visit the Prentice Hall Web site: www.phschool.com

EXPLORATION

Pascal's Triangle

After Lesson 11-3

The structure of Pascal's triangle is described below.

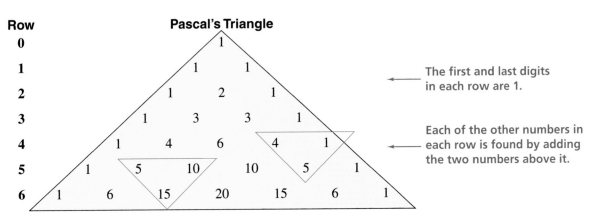

Row — **Pascal's Triangle**

The first and last digits in each row are 1.

Each of the other numbers in each row is found by adding the two numbers above it.

You can use Pascal's triangle to find a number of combinations.

■ EXAMPLE

Find $_5C_2$ using Pascal's triangle.

Row 5 of Pascal's triangle gives all combinations of the form $_5C_n$.

1	5	10	10	5	1	← row 5

$_5C_0 \quad _5C_1 \quad _5C_2 \quad _5C_3 \quad _5C_4 \quad _5C_5$ ← combinations in the form $_5C_n$

$$_5C_2 = 10$$

1. Copy Pascal's triangle. Complete two more rows.

2. **a.** Find the sum of the numbers in each row of the triangle. Write each sum as $2^{\blacksquare}$.
   b. The sum of the numbers in row n is $2^{\blacksquare}$.

Use Pascal's triangle to find each combination.

3. $_5C_3$ 4. $_6C_4$ 5. $_3C_2$ 6. $_4C_4$ 7. $_2C_2$ 8. $_7C_4$

9. *Reasoning* To find $_{24}C_8$, would you use Pascal's triangle or the combination formula and a calculator? Explain.

11-4 Theoretical and Experimental Probability

What You'll Learn

▼ To find the experimental probability of an event

▼ To compare experimental and theoretical probabilities

...And Why

You can find the probability of an event by studying past events.

Here's How

Look for questions that
▪ build understanding
✔ check understanding

Work Together   *Investigating Experimental Probability*

1. Drop a paper cup from a height of about 3 feet. How does it land?

2. Repeat this experiment 20 times. Copy and complete the table at the right.

3. Which event occurs more often than the others?

Outcome	Number of Occurrences
Rim up	▪
Rim down	▪
On its side	▪

4. Compare your results to those of your classmates. Did all the groups in your class get the same results? Why do you think this is so?

THINK AND DISCUSS

▼ *Finding Experimental Probability*

Experiments can help you determine probability. Probability based on experimental data is called **experimental probability.**

■ **EXAMPLE 1**   *Real-World Problem Solving*

Biology Gregor Mendel (1822–1884) is famous for his work in developing the laws of heredity. Mendel crossbred green-seed pea plants and yellow-seed pea plants. Out of 8,023 crosses, 6,022 had yellow seeds and 2,001 had green seeds. Based on these data, find the probability that a plant had green seeds.

$$P(\text{green}) = \frac{\text{number of plants with green seeds}}{\text{number of plants}}$$

$$= \frac{2,001}{8,023} \qquad \longleftarrow \text{Substitute.}$$

$$\approx 0.249 \ \approx \ 25\% \quad \longleftarrow \text{Divide.}$$

The probability that a pea plant will have green seeds is about 25%.

5. ✔**Try It Out** Use Mendel's data to find $P(\text{yellow})$.

EXPERIMENTAL PROBABILITY

$$P(\text{event}) = \frac{\text{number of times an event happens}}{\text{number of trials done}}$$

■ EXAMPLE 2

Aki tosses two pennies 20 times. She records her results in a table as shown at the right. What is the experimental probability that the next toss will produce 2 heads?

Outcome	Number of Occurrences
1 head/1 tail	11
2 heads	2
2 tails	7

$$P(2 \text{ heads}) = \frac{\text{number of times tosses produced 2 heads}}{\text{number of tosses}}$$
$$= \frac{2}{20} = 0.1 = 10\%$$

According to the experimental data, the probability that the next toss will produce 2 heads is 0.1, or 10%.

QUICKreview

You can write a probability as a fraction, a decimal, or a percent.

6. ✔**Try It Out** Use Aki's data to find each probability.
   a. $P(1 \text{ head and } 1 \text{ tail})$ b. $P(2 \text{ tails})$

7. ✔**Try It Out** Make a tree diagram to show the sample space for this experiment. Find $P(2 \text{ heads})$ from your diagram. How does this compare to $P(2 \text{ heads})$ in Example 2?

2 *Comparing Probabilities*

To answer Question 7, you found a probability by finding the ratio of favorable outcomes to the total number of outcomes. This type of probability is called **theoretical probability.**

In Example 2, you saw that experimental probability and theoretical probability are different. However, the larger the number of trials you perform, the more likely it is that the experimental probability will be close to the theoretical probability.

8. Refer to Example 2. Suppose Aki tossed both coins 10,000 times. How do you think $P(2 \text{ heads})$ would differ from her results using only 20 tosses? Explain.

9. ⁂*Explain* Why might the experimental probability of an event not equal the theoretical probability of the event?

■ **EXAMPLE 3**   *Real-World Problem Solving*

Elections Read the newspaper article at the left. Does the article describe experimental or theoretical probability?

The reported probability is based on the results from a town survey, so it is an experimental probability.

10. ✔**Try It Out** A bag contains two red marbles and three white marbles. $P(\text{red})$ is $\frac{2}{5}$. Which type of probability is this?

Recall that probabilities range from 0 to 1.

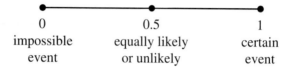

0	0.5	1
impossible	equally likely	certain
event	or unlikely	event

The **complement** of an event is the opposite of that event. For example, in choosing one person at random from a group of people, $P(\text{male})$ and $P(\text{female})$ are complements.

11. ▪*Open-ended* Give another example of a pair of complementary events.

The probability of an event plus the probability of the complement of that event is always equal to 1 or 100%.

$$P(A) + P(\text{not } A) = 1$$
$$\text{or}$$
$$P(\text{not } A) = 1 - P(A)$$

■ **EXAMPLE 4**

Find the probability of *not* rolling a 6 with a number cube.

$P(\text{not } 6) = 1 - P(6)$ ←—definition of complement

$\quad\quad = 1 - \frac{1}{6}$ ←— The probability of rolling a 6 is 1 out of 6.

$\quad\quad = \frac{5}{6}$ ←—Subtract.

The probability of *not* rolling a 6 is $\frac{5}{6}$.

12. ✔**Try It Out** What is $P(\text{not 1 or 6})$? Explain.

13. **a.** You have a spinner with red and other colors on it. Write an expression for the probability that the pointer will not land on red.
    b. If $P(\text{red})$ is 30%, find $P(\text{not red})$.

1. *Data Collection* Toss a coin 50 times. Record your results in a table.
   a. Use your data to find $P(\text{heads})$ and $P(\text{tails})$.
   b. Are heads and tails equally likely outcomes based on your results? Explain.

A surveyor asked a group of children what time they went to bed. The results are shown at the right. Find each experimental probability.

2. $P(9{:}30)$ 3. $P(8{:}00)$ 4. $P(7{:}30-8{:}30)$

5. $P(\text{not } 9{:}00)$ 6. $P(\text{after } 8{:}30)$ 7. $P(\text{before } 9{:}30)$

What's Your Bedtime?

Time	Number
7:30	24
8:00	31
8:30	38
9:00	42
9:30	36
10:00	27

8. Choose a paragraph from any book. Count the number of times each vowel appears. Display your results in a table.
   a. Find $P(a)$, $P(e)$, $P(i)$, $P(o)$, and $P(u)$.
   b. Choose another paragraph about equal in length to the first. Find each probability again.
   c. How do the probabilities found in part (a) compare to the probabilities found in part (b)?

9. *Chemistry* Currently, there are 109 elements in the periodic table. The first 12 are listed at the right. Notice that most of the first 12 elements in the periodic table end with the letter *m* or *n*.
   a. If you select one of the first 12 elements at random, what is the probability that it ends with *m* or *n*?
   b. Is this experimental or theoretical probability?
   c. How could you get experimental data for this problem?

The First Twelve Elements

hydrogen
helium
lithium
beryllium
boron
carbon
nitrogen
oxygen
flourine
neon
sodium
magnesium

10. A bag contains 13 red marbles, 32 green marbles, and 25 blue marbles. Suppose one marble is selected from the bag.
    a. Find $P(\text{red})$, $P(\text{green})$, and $P(\text{blue})$. Which type of probability is this? Explain.
    b. *Writing* Describe an experiment you could conduct to find an experimental probability for this situation.

11. A school survey reports that 55% of students do their homework after dinner. If you choose a student at random, there is a 55% chance that he does his homework after dinner. Is this experimental or theoretical probability?

Use the spinner at the right for Exercises 12 and 13.

12. Find the probability of each outcome for the spinner shown at the right.

    a. P(not orange)   b. P(not red)

    c. P(not yellow)   d. P(not red or yellow)

13. The *odds* in favor of an event are $\dfrac{\text{number of favorable outcomes}}{\text{number of unfavorable outcomes}}$.

    a. What are the odds in favor of spinning red?

    b. What are the odds in favor of spinning a color other than orange?

    c. *Open-ended* Design a spinner so that the odds in favor of your spinning green are 7 : 5.

Mixed Review

In $\triangle ABC$, $m\angle A = 90°$ and $m\angle B = 32°$. **Find each of the following to the nearest hundredth.** (*Lessons 6-9 and 6-10*)

14. $\cos B$ 15. $\tan C$ 16. AB if $AC = 32$ 17. BC if $AB = 12$

Write each sum or difference as a fraction or mixed number in simplest form. (*Lesson 5-6*)

18. $\dfrac{14}{15} - \dfrac{1}{30}$ 19. $\dfrac{5}{12} + \left(-\dfrac{7}{8}\right)$ 20. $-\dfrac{5}{9} - \dfrac{8}{27}$ 21. $\dfrac{6}{17} - \left(-\dfrac{25}{34}\right)$ 22. $7\dfrac{3}{8} + \left(-3\dfrac{1}{2}\right)$

23. *Choose a Strategy* Anitha and Pearl share a bedroom. Anitha's alarm is set for 6:30 A.M. It has a snooze alarm that goes off every 9 minutes. Pearl's alarm is set for 6:50 A.M. Its snooze alarm goes off every 5 minutes. If both of them wake up and hit the snooze alarm several times in one morning, at what time would both alarms go off together?

CHAPTER PROJECT

PROJECT LINK: COLLECTING DATA

Choose a basketball team, and compile statistics from last year. What was the won-lost record? The winning percentage? What was the average number of points scored per game? The average number of points allowed per game? List any significant winning streaks or losing streaks. Include this and other information in your report to the new coach.

What You'll Learn

▼ To find the probability of independent events

▼ To find the probability of dependent events

...And Why

You can use probability to figure out your chances of winning a game or drawing.

Here's How

Look for questions that

⬛ build understanding

✔ check understanding

Work Together
Comparing Types of Events

Use ten tiles. Mark X on five tiles and O on five tiles. Put the tiles in a bag.

1. **a.** Choose a tile at random from the bag. What is $P(X)$?
    b. Choose an X-tile. Then put it back in the bag. Has $P(X)$ changed? Explain. Conduct several trials if you need to.

2. Select an X-tile from the bag. This time, don't put it back in the bag. Has $P(X)$ changed? Explain.

THINK AND DISCUSS

▼ Finding Probability of Independent Events

When you choose a tile and then put it back, $P(X)$ does not change. When the outcome of one event does not affect the outcome of a second event, the events are **independent.**

INDEPENDENT EVENTS

If A and B are independent events,
$P(A \text{ and } B) = P(A) \times P(B)$.

⬛ EXAMPLE 1

A drawer contains 4 red marbles and 6 blue marbles. You draw a marble at random, replace it, and draw another marble. Find the probability that both marbles are blue.

Since the first marble is replaced, these are independent events.

$P(\text{blue and blue}) = P(\text{blue}) \times P(\text{blue})$ ◄—Use the formula.

$\qquad = \dfrac{6}{10} \times \dfrac{6}{10}$ ◄ Substitute. 6 of the 10 marbles are blue.

$\qquad = \dfrac{36}{100} = \dfrac{9}{25}$ ◄—Multiply and simplify.

The probability of choosing two blue marbles is $\dfrac{9}{25}$, or 0.36.

Need Help? For practice writing equivalent fractions, see Skills Handbook page 610.

3. ✔*Try It Out* Refer to Example 1. Find each probability.
   a. P(two red marbles)   **b.** P(two different colors)

▼2 *Finding Probability of Dependent Events*

In Question 2, when you chose a tile and didn't put it back, $P(\text{X})$ changed. When the outcome of one event *does* affect the outcome of a second event, the events are **dependent.**

DEPENDENT EVENTS

If A and B are dependent events, then
$P(A, \text{ then } B) = P(A) \times P(B \text{ after } A)$.

■ **EXAMPLE 2**   *Real-World Problem Solving*

Raffles Two girls and three boys enter a raffle. Two names are selected at random. Find the probability that both winners are girls.

Since the winner of the first drawing cannot win the second drawing, the two events are dependent.

1st drawing $P(\text{girl}) = \dfrac{2}{5}$ ← Of 5 entrants, 2 are girls.

2nd drawing $P(\text{girl after girl}) = \dfrac{1}{4}$ ← Of 4 entrants left, 1 is a girl.

$P(\text{girl, then girl}) = P(\text{girl}) \times P(\text{girl after girl})$ ← Use the formula.

$\qquad\qquad = \dfrac{2}{5} \times \dfrac{1}{4}$ ← Substitute.

$\qquad\qquad = \dfrac{2}{20} = \dfrac{1}{10}$ ← Multiply and simplify.

The probability that both winners are girls is $\dfrac{1}{10}$, or 0.1.

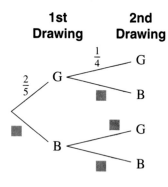

1st Drawing   **2nd Drawing**

The tree diagram at the left displays the sample space for Example 2. The probability is written along each branch that leads to the outcome "girl, then girl." To find $P(\text{girl, then girl})$, multiply the probabilities on the two branches leading to that outcome.

4. ✔*Try It Out* Copy and complete the tree diagram. Find each probability.
   a. P(girl, then boy)   **b.** P(boy, then boy)

You can use area models to solve some probability problems.

■ **EXAMPLE 3**

A mouse is placed in the maze at the left. The mouse selects a path at random at each intersection. Find the probability that the mouse will find the cheese on its first attempt through the maze.

Draw a rectangle to represent the sample space.

The mouse must first make a choice between two paths.

The left path splits into two paths. The right path splits into three paths.

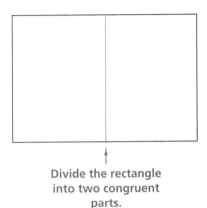

Divide the rectangle into two congruent parts.

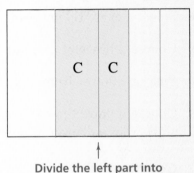

Divide the left part into 2 congruent parts and the right part into 3 congruent parts.

The areas labeled C represent the mouse finding the cheese. The fraction of the total area that is shaded represents *P*(mouse finds cheese). Find the total shaded area.

$$\frac{1}{4} + \frac{1}{6} = \frac{5}{12} \approx 0.42 = 42\%$$

The mouse has a 42% chance of finding the cheese.

5. Why are the choices in the maze dependent events?

EXERCISES *On Your Own*

Each of a set of 26 cards is marked with a letter of the alphabet. One card is chosen at random and then replaced. Then a second card is chosen. Find each probability.

1. *P*(I and a vowel)

2. *P*(Z and a consonant)

3. *P*(a vowel and a consonant)

4. *P*(2 vowels)

5. *P*(2 consonants)

6. *P*(2 R's)

7. *P*(A and B)

8. *P*(C and X)

9. *P*(2 like letters)

Suppose you roll a number cube and spin the spinner at the right. Find each probability.

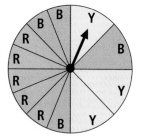

10. $P(3 \text{ and red})$

11. $P(\text{an even number and red})$

12. $P(5 \text{ and yellow})$

13. $P(\text{a number less than 3 and blue})$

14. $P(\text{prime and blue})$

15. $P(8 \text{ and yellow})$

Are the events dependent or independent? Explain.

16. Toss a coin. Then roll a number cube.

17. Select a card. Replace it. Then select another card.

18. Select a card. Do not replace it. Then select another card.

19. Choose a bracelet and put it on. Choose another bracelet.

20. Pick one flower from a garden, and then pick another flower.

21. Choose a pair of pants from a closet of pants. Then choose a shirt from a drawer of shirts.

22. *Geometry* Use an area model to find the probability of a mouse finding the cheese on its first attempt in the maze below. Assume the mouse selects a path at random at each intersection.

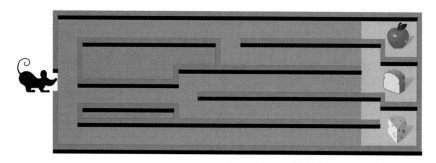

23. *Packaging* A manufacturer packages 6 mini-boxes of sweetened cereal and 8 mini-boxes of unsweetened cereal together. You select 2 boxes at random from a package. Draw a tree diagram that shows the probability of each possible outcome.

24. A pack of juice boxes contains 4 apple, 4 cherry, 4 orange, and 4 grape boxes. If you and a friend each select a juice box at random, what is the probability that you will both get grape?

25. There are six black socks and four blue socks in a drawer.
  a. Copy and complete the tree diagram at the right.
  b. If you take two socks from the drawer, find P(two blue).

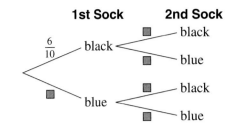

1st Sock   2nd Sock
$\frac{6}{10}$ black — black
            black — blue
            blue — black
            blue — blue

Biology **Use the colorblindness data at the right.**

26. If a person is chosen at random, find P(colorblind male).

27. *Writing* Are colorblindness and gender independent or dependent events? Explain.

28. Of 100 people selected at random, how many would you expect to be colorblind?

29. *Calculator* A rectangular jigsaw puzzle has 200 pieces.
  a. You take four puzzle pieces from the box. What is the probability that all four are corner pieces?
  b. The first 100 pieces you take are not corner pieces. What is the probability that the next piece is a corner piece?

30. *Reasoning* Suppose, when doing a jigsaw puzzle, you like to put together edge and corner pieces first. You take one piece at a time from the box. If it is a corner or edge piece, you place it in a pile. If it is neither, you put it back in the box. Describe the disadvantage of doing a puzzle in this way.

**Colorblindness (CB) Data
for Males and Females
Selected at Random**

Outcome	Male	Female
CB	40	2
Not CB	460	498
Total	500	500

JOURNAL
Use your own words to explain the difference between dependent and independent events. Give examples.

Mixed Review

Simplify each polynomial. *(Lesson 10-9)*

31. $3 - 2x + 3x^2 + 7 - 2x^2$

32. $4x^2 - 2x^2 - 13 + 2 - 7x$

Banking **For Exercises 33 and 34, find the final balance in each account.** *(Lesson 7-8)*

33. $500 at 5.5% compounded annually for 2 years

34. $3,000 at 6.25% compounded annually for 3 years

35. *Choose a Strategy* Two whole numbers have a sum of 15 and a product of 54. What are the two numbers?

11-6 Simulate the Problem

THINK AND DISCUSS

You can estimate the solutions to many probability problems by simulating the problem. You develop a model, complete a number of trials to generate data, and then use the data to analyze the problem.

SAMPLE PROBLEM..

At a street fair, a clown plays a game with three paper cups turned upside down. He puts a small ball under one cup and tells you that if you can guess where it is, you win a prize. The clown moves the cups around so fast that you lose track of the ball. So you make a guess. The clown, knowing the location of the ball, lifts up one of the empty cups. He asks if you want to stay with your first choice or switch to the remaining cup. What should you do, stay or switch?

READ

Read for understanding. Summarize the problem.

1. **a.** State in your own words what you are asked to decide.
   b. Do you need to find and compare two probabilities?

2. Is the fact that the clown knows the location of the ball important to the problem? Explain.

3. If you were playing the game and did not have much time to think about it, would you stay or switch? Explain.

PLAN

Decide on a strategy.

Instead of actually playing this game, you can simulate it by using one marked index card and two unmarked cards. Fold each card so that it can stand. The marked side should face the "clown." Have one player turn away while the "clown" player moves the cards around.

4. Use a table like the one at the right to record the results. Each time you play the game, place a tally mark in the table. Play 12 times using the stay strategy. Then switch roles and play 12 times using the switch strategy.

Strategy	Win	Lose
Stay	■	■
Switch	■	■

5. Combine your data with those of your classmates. Why might you want to increase the number of trials?

 SOLVE
Try the strategy.

6. a. Use the data to find the experimental probability of winning if the player stays with the original choice.
   b. Find the experimental probability of winning if the player switches to the other choice.

7. Should you stay or switch in this game? Why?

 LOOK BACK
Think about how you solved the problem.

Does the answer surprise you? Does it seem reasonable? Are you convinced that your solution to this problem is valid?

8. Think back to your answer in Question 3. Explain what was right or wrong about your reasoning at that point.

9. ⁂*Reasoning* Besides giving you an answer to the problem, did the simulation give you any insight on the problem and its solution?

10. Can you solve this problem without using simulation? Explain.

EXERCISES *On Your Own*

1. *Writing* Write a paragraph explaining what it means to "simulate a problem."

Solve by simulating the problem. Show all your work.

2. You and a friend play a game in which you toss a single coin. You score a point for each heads and your friend scores a point for each tails. The first person to score ten points wins. The score is 8 to 6 in your favor when the bell rings and you must stop. If you continue the game the next day, what is the probability that your friend will win?

3. *Entertainment* A TV game show, *The Choice is Yours,* offers contestants the chance to win a prize hidden behind one of 4 doors. After a contestant chooses a door, the host opens one of the doors without prizes. The contestant can then switch to one of the remaining closed doors or stay with the original choice. Which method—switching or staying—gives the contestant a better chance of winning? Explain.

Use any strategy to solve each problem. Show your work.

4. *Number Sense* The numbers 1, 2, and 3 are placed at the vertices of the triangle at the right. Use the numbers 4, 5, 6, 7, 8, and 9 only once. Find at least one way to place two numbers on each side of the triangle so that the sum of all four numbers on each side is equal to 17.

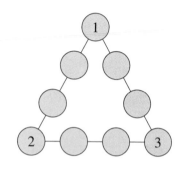

5. *Testing* A multiple-choice test has 6 questions. Each question has 4 possible answers. Find the probability of answering all the questions correctly if you guess on all six of them.

6. *Camping* A weather forecaster reports that the probability of sunny weather for each of the next three days is 75%. You begin a three-day camping trip. Find the probability of three sunny days in a row.

7. A teacher at a day-care center looks out a window and counts 15 children riding tricycles or bicycles. "There are 42 wheels in motion," she comments. How many children are riding tricycles?

8. Find the sum of the whole numbers from 1 to 999.

9. A farmer wishes to fence in a square lot with dimensions 70 yards by 70 yards. She will install a fence post every 5 yards. How many fence posts will she need?

Mixed Review

Tell whether each function is linear or quadratic. *(Lesson 10-7)*

10. $f(x) = 3x^2 - x$ **11.** $f(x) = 8$ **12.** $f(x) = 4x + \frac{1}{2}$ **13.** $f(x) = 3x - x^2$

Simplify each polynomial. *(Lesson 10-9)*

14. $4x^2 - 5x^2 + x + 6x$ **15.** $-x^2 - 3x + 4 - 2x^2$ **16.** $9x^2 + x - 4 - 9x^2 + 5$

17. This morning, Waneta began walking to school at a normal pace. After 2 minutes, she stopped to talk to a neighbor. She then walked quickly for 1 minute, arriving at school 7 minutes after leaving home. Sketch a graph that shows the distance she traveled on her way to school. *(Lesson 10-6)*

✓ CHECKPOINT 2   *Lessons 11-4 through 11-6*

1. You toss 3 coins. Find $P(3 \text{ heads})$.

2. You roll a number cube. Find $P(\text{not } 4 \text{ or } 5)$.

3. A local news station surveyed 145 people on an upcoming referendum. The station reported that the referendum had about a 55% chance of being rejected. Was this report based on experimental or theoretical probability?

4. You place 10 cards marked with the digits 0–9 in a box and select one at random. You put it aside and select another card at random from the box. Find $P(3, \text{ then } 0)$, $P(3, \text{ then } 3)$, and $P(5, \text{ then an even number})$.

5. Find the probability of guessing exactly 4 correct answers on a 5-question true-false quiz. *(Hint: Simulate the Problem.)*

CHAPTER PROJECT

PROJECT LINK: WRITING

Suppose a team has a winning record of 0.580. What is the probability that the team will win its next game? Suppose that a player makes 70% of her free throws. What is the probability that her next free throw will score? Explain your answers, and include a discussion of experimental probability.

Using Random Numbers

After Lesson 11-6

Random numbers can help you simulate some situations. You can use a graphing calculator or a computer to generate random numbers.

The command "rand" generates a group of 10 random digits on a graphing calculator. To get this command, press [MATH] ◄ 1.

Each time you press [ENTER] you will get a different group of ten random digits.

Rand	
	.2209784733
	.3694814382
	.0078387869
	.9351587791
	.1080114624
	.0062633066

■ EXAMPLE

Weather Suppose the weather forecast says there is a 40% chance of rain on each of the next 3 days. Find the probability that it will rain on exactly two of the next three days.

Use your calculator to generate random numbers. Record the first three digits of each number.

Since there is a 40% chance of rain on each day, let the digits 1, 2, 3, and 4 represent rain. Let 5, 6, 7, 8, 9, and 0 represent no rain.

907	966	<u>191</u>	925
<u>271</u>	9<u>32</u>	8<u>12</u>	458
569	683	431	257
<u>393</u>	027	556	488
730	113	537	989

Any group with exactly two of the digits 1, 2, 3, or 4 represents rain on exactly two of the three days.

Based on 20 trials, the probability that it will rain on exactly two of the three days is $\frac{5}{20}$, or 25%.

Choose **Use the random numbers in the Example above or generate your own to simulate each problem.**

1. One fifth of the students in a class have blonde hair. What is the probability that at least 1 of the first 3 students to enter the class will have blonde hair?

2. A survey revealed that 30% of the people polled preferred Brand X toothpaste. What is the probability that exactly 2 of next 3 people you see use Brand X toothpaste?

3. *Writing* Write a probability problem that can be solved using a random number table. Solve it.

Choose the best answer.

1. Barret bought 5 plum, 5 yellow, and 10 red tomato plants. What is the probability that any plant selected at random will be a plum tomato?

    A. $\frac{1}{5}$ B. $\frac{1}{4}$ C. $\frac{1}{3}$ D. $\frac{1}{2}$

2. The sides of a square are 4.2 cm long. What is the perimeter?

    F. 16.8 cm   G. 17.64 cm
    H. 168 cm   J. 176.4 cm

3. The Fashion Place stocks women's blouses in 3 different sizes, 8 different colors, and 2 different styles (short sleeve and long sleeve). How many different blouses does the store have to keep in stock?

    A. 13   B. 36   C. 48   D. 96

4. What is the approximate length of $\overline{AB}$?

    A ●━━━━━━━━━━━━━● B

    F. 6 mm   G. 6 km
    H. 6 cm   J. 6 m

5. The length of a paper clip would most likely be expressed in which units?

    A. inches   B. feet
    C. yards   D. miles

Please note that items 6–10 have *five* answer choices.

6. Jamar wears either tall or regular pants with either a 30, 32, or 34 waist. He takes one of each to the dressing room. What is the probability that the first pair he tries on will be the best-fitting pair?

    F. $\frac{1}{6}$ G. $\frac{1}{5}$ H. $\frac{1}{3}$
    J. $\frac{2}{3}$ K. $\frac{1}{1}$

Dion polled his customers to see which brand of salsa they preferred.

Preference	No. of Votes
Brand X	92
Brand Y	80
Brand Z	120
No preference	108
Total	400

7. What is the probability that a customer chosen at random will choose Brand Z?

    A. $\frac{1}{4}$ B. $\frac{3}{10}$ C. $\frac{1}{2}$
    D. $\frac{3}{4}$ E. $\frac{5}{8}$

8. If Dion does not stock Brand Y, what percent of his customers will not be able to select a salsa they like?

    F. 20%   G. 25%   H. 40%
    J. 50%   K. 80%

A poll was taken to predict the outcome of a school election.

Candidate	No. of Votes
Fran	45
Marco	30
Marisa	75
Total	150

9. If 750 students vote in the election, how many votes can Marisa expect to get?

    A. 75   B. 150   C. 375
    D. 500   E. 750

10. What percent of the votes cast can Marco expect to get?

    F. 20%   G. 30%   H. 40%
    J. 50%   K. 75%

What You'll Learn

▼ **1** To use simulation to determine the fairness of games

▼ **2** To use a sample space to determine the fairness of a game

...And Why

You can use probability to decide if a game is fair or unfair.

Here's How

Look for questions that
▪ build understanding
✔ check understanding

Work Together
Is the Game Fair?

1. A game is **fair** if the players are equally likely to win. Read the directions below for the game Doubles or Nothing. Do you think this game is fair or unfair? Explain.

DOUBLES OR NOTHING

- Decide who is Player A and who is Player B.

- Each player rolls two number cubes. If the four cubes show *exactly* one set of doubles, Player A scores one point. Otherwise, Player B scores one point.

- The player with more points after 30 rounds wins.

2. Play Doubles or Nothing with a partner. Now do you think this game is fair? Explain.

THINK AND DISCUSS

▼ **1** *Using Simulation to Analyze a Game*

You can use random digits to simulate a problem or a game.

Random Number Table

23948	71477	12573	05954
65628	22310	09311	94864
41261	09943	34078	70481
34831	94515	41490	93312
09802	09770	11258	41139
66068	74522	15522	49227
00458	48800	33785	67694
45713	06400	87143	19586
57648	49551	40424	72908
21397	31604	84615	40513

■ **EXAMPLE 1**

Use the random number table at the left to simulate the game Doubles or Nothing. Determine if the game is fair or unfair.

Let the digits 1–6 in the table represent the result of one roll of a number cube. Ignore the digits 0, 7, 8, and 9. You need four digits to represent the rolls of four number cubes (one round of the game). The first 10 rounds are shown below.

2341 4125 3554 6562 2231 3114 6441 2614 3344 1343

B   B   A   A   A   A   A   B   B   A

After 30 rounds, Player A wins 21 points and Player B wins 9. This simulation indicates that the game is likely unfair.

3. ⬝Analyze Explain why Player A did not win the ninth trial.

4. ✔ Try It Out Use the random number feature on a graphing calculator to simulate another game of Doubles or Nothing. How do these results compare to those in Example 1?

▼2 Using Sample Space to Analyze a Game

You can also analyze a game by looking at the sample space.

5. Read the directions below for the game Three's a Crowd. Do you think this game is fair or unfair? Explain your reasoning.

THREE'S A CROWD

- Decide who is Player A and who is Player B.
- Each player tosses two coins. If the four coins show exactly three heads or three tails, Player A scores one point. Otherwise, Player B scores one point.
- The player with more points after 30 rounds wins.

■ EXAMPLE 2

Find the sample space of outcomes to decide if Three's a Crowd is fair or unfair.

List all the possible outcomes from tossing four coins. Then determine the winner of each toss.

TTTT (B)	TTTH (A)	TTHT (A)	THTT (A)
HTTT (A)	TTHH (B)	THTH (B)	THHT (B)
HTHT (B)	HHTT (B)	HTTH (B)	THHH (A)
HTHH (A)	HHTH (A)	HHHT (A)	HHHH (B)

Player A wins 8 points while Player B wins 8 points.
So, Three's a Crowd is a fair game.

6. ⬝Go a Step Further How could you change the rules of Three's a Crowd so it becomes an unfair game?

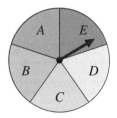

The game Spin Around uses a spinner like the one at the left. Read the rules of the game and answer the questions that follow.

SPIN AROUND

● Decide who is Player A and who is Player B.

● Each player spins the spinner once. If the spinner lands on the same letter both times, Player A scores a point. If it lands on different letters, Player B scores a point.

● The player with the more points after 20 spins wins.

7. a. ✓ Try It Out List all of the possible outcomes.
  b. How many outcomes are there?
  c. What is the probability that Player A will win?
  d. Is the game Spin Around fair or unfair? Explain.

EXERCISES *On Your Own*

1. *Reasoning* Greta created a fair game for two players, A and B. What do you know about P(A wins) and P(B wins)?

2. Suppose you want to use a list of random digits to simulate Three's a Crowd in Example 2. You will use all the digits 0–9. Explain how you would conduct your simulation. Be sure to explain which digits represent heads and which represent tails.

3. *Writing* Describe how you can use the list of random digits on page 570 to simulate Spin Around.

4. *Open-ended* Create a game for two people that can be simulated using a random number table.

5. Andy played a game 10 times and decided it was unfair. Sam used random digits to simulate the same game 100 times and decided that it was fair. With whom do you agree? Explain.

6. *Reasoning* John uses a simulation to determine if a game is fair. Lunette lists the sample space to determine if the same game is fair. Who can be more certain of the results? Explain.

To learn how to use a graphing calculator to produce random digits, see page 568.

Read the directions given for the games Rolling Thunder and Good Times.

ROLLING THUNDER	GOOD TIMES
● Choose Player A and Player B.	● Choose Player A and Player B.
● Each player rolls 2 number cubes. Player A finds the product of his or her 2 numbers. Player B finds the sum of all 4 numbers. Player B wins if the sum is greater than the product; otherwise, Player A wins.	● Players take turns rolling 2 number cubes and finding the product of the numbers rolled.
	● If the product is even, Player A scores 1 point. If the product is odd, Player B scores 1 point.
● The player with more points after 30 rounds wins.	● The player with more points after 20 rounds wins.

7. Use random digits to determine if the game Rolling Thunder is fair or unfair. If it seems unfair, which player is more likely to win?

8. Simulate the game Good Times. Based on your simulations, is the game fair or unfair? Explain how you simulated the problem.

9. a. Use a sample space to decide if Good Times is fair or unfair. If it is unfair, which player is more likely to win?
   b. *Reasoning* If the game is unfair, how can you change the rules to make it fair?

10. Based on your simulations in Exercises 7 and 8, decide whether Rolling Thunder or Good Times is more unfair. Explain.

Mixed Review

▦ *Geometry* **Find the volume of each pyramid or cone. Round your answer to the nearest unit.** *(Lesson 9-10)*

11. $B = 20$ m^2, $h = 10$ m   **12.** $d = 8$ m, $h = 12$ m   **13.** $B = 50$ m^2, $h = 3.5$ m

Does (−2, 6) lie on the graph of each function? *(Lesson 10-8)*

14. $f(x) = \dfrac{12}{x}$ **15.** $f(x) = 2^x + 4$ **16.** $f(x) = 2x^2 - 2$ **17.** $f(x) = \dfrac{6}{x} + 9$ **18.** $f(x) = 3^x + 15$

19. *Choose a Strategy* Elise bought $3\frac{1}{2}$-inch floppy diskettes for $1.19 each and special labels for $0.59 per package. If she spent $15.44, how many of each did she buy?

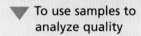

11-8 Making Decisions with Probability

What You'll Learn

▼ To use samples to analyze quality

...And Why

You can use sampling and probability to predict the number of defective samples in a batch.

Here's How

Look for questions that
⊞ build understanding
✔ check understanding

THINK AND DISCUSS

The Flyer Company makes plastic flying disks. The disks must sail smoothly through the air when thrown. Quality control workers inspect a few disks from each batch.

1. A worker inspects 500 disks. Ten are defective. Based on these data, what is the probability that a disk chosen at random is defective?

2. After the company adjusts the manufacturing process, 800 disks are inspected. Two are defective. Has the quality changed? Explain.

3. The company then produces 10,000 disks each week. Predict the number of defective disks produced each week.

You can use a chart to display data collected during a process.

■ **EXAMPLE**   *Real-World Problem Solving*

Production The chart shows the masses of 12 flying disks selected at random. What is the ideal mass of a disk? How many disks have a mass greater than the ideal? How many are defective?

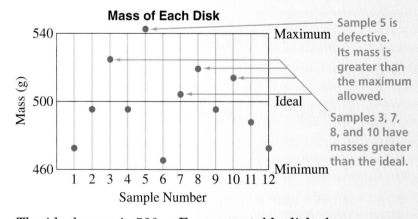

Mass of Each Disk

Sample 5 is defective. Its mass is greater than the maximum allowed.

Samples 3, 7, 8, and 10 have masses greater than the ideal.

The ideal mass is 500 g. Four acceptable disks have a mass greater than 500 g. Of the twelve disks, one is defective.

4. ✔ *Try It Out* Suppose the company in the Example produces 12,500 disks. Based on the samples in the Example, how many can they expect to be defective?

If a chart shows too many defective samples, or if it shows an upward or downward trend, you may want to adjust the process.

5. Describe any trends in the charts below.

a.

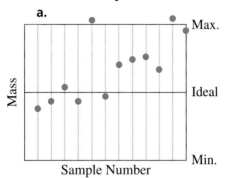

b.

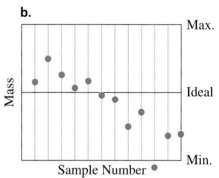

EXERCISES *On Your Own*

1. About 25 out of 1000 heaters need repairs in the first five years of service. In one week, a store sells 120 heaters. Predict how many will need repairs in the next five years.

2. *Measurement* From each lot of 50 buttons, six are measured before they are accepted. The measurement taken on the sample is the diameter of the button. The measurements of 25 samples are shown at the right. The target value is 1.06 cm. The minimum and maximum values are 0.94 cm and 1.18 cm.
  a. Make a chart to display the data.
  b. How many have a diameter greater than 1.18 cm?
  c. How many are defective?
  d. Suppose the company produces 145,750 buttons each week. Based on the data in the table, predict the number of defective buttons produced each week.

Width (cm)				
1.00	0.95	0.98	1.01	1.03
1.06	1.10	1.11	1.12	1.04
0.98	0.96	1.01	1.06	1.06
0.99	0.92	1.00	1.01	1.04
1.11	1.06	1.03	0.98	1.00

3. *Writing* What are the benefits of using charts like the one in this lesson?

4. A dinnerware company sampled 35 plates and found 3 defective. Predict how many plates out of 450 were *not* defective.

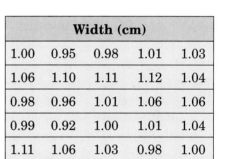

5. The target value for the output voltage of a battery is 3.5 V. The company requires that the output voltage of a battery fall within 0.1% of the mean. Find the maximum and minimum allowed values.

Describe any trend shown in each chart.

6.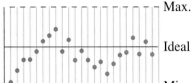

7.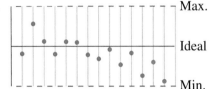

> **PORTFOLIO**
> Choose two or three topics from this chapter that you enjoyed studying. Summarize the concepts and list two or three real-world applications of each.

Mixed Review

Simplify each expression. *(Lesson 10-11)*

8. $3r^5 \cdot 3r^{10}$ **9.** $4x^5 \cdot 4x^3$ **10.** $(-5x^2)(2x^5)$ **11.** $2x(2x^2 - 3x + 3)$

Calculator Find each value. *(Lessons 11-2 and 11-3)*

12. $12!$ **13.** $_7P_3$ **14.** $_{20}C_7$ **15.** $_{11}P_4$ **16.** $_{15}C_{12}$ **17.** $_9P_6$

18. *Cars* On a highway, a driver sets a car's cruise control for a constant speed of 55 mi/h. Sketch a graph that shows the distance the car travels over time, and another graph that shows the speed of the car over time. *(Lesson 10-6)*

CHAPTER PROJECT

PROJECT LINK: COLLECTING DATA

List the five key players from last year, and decide which individual statistics you will include in your report. Categories could include field-goal percentage, free-throw percentage, minutes played per game, and others. Include these statistics in your report to the new coach.

Prepare a Stat Sheet The Project Link questions on pages 558, 567, and 576 should help you complete your project. Here is a checklist to help you gather the parts of your project together.

✔ the data on last year's team

✔ the data on the five key players from last year

✔ a discussion of how a coach might use experimental probability

Suppose you are hired as the team statistician for a basketball team. A new coach has been hired, and it's your job to give her all the information she'll need about last year's team. Be thorough, and be accurate!

Reflect and Revise

Show your stat sheet to a basketball player or coach. Get his or her reaction, and if necessary make improvements to your statistical report.

Web Extension

Prentice Hall's Internet site contains information you might find helpful as you complete your project. Visit www.phschool.com/mgm3/ch11 for some links and ideas related to sports.

WRAP UP

Counting Outcomes
11-1

Use the **counting principle** to find the number of outcomes for two or more events. Multiply the number of outcomes for each event.

1. Max has 3 hats, 4 ties, 2 shirts, and 5 pairs of pants. How many different outfits does Max have?

2. A phone company offers 4 styles of phones with a choice of 5 colors. How many different phones can a customer choose?

Permutations and Combinations
11-2, 11-3

A **permutation** is an arrangement of a set of objects in a particular order. The number of permutations of 5 things can be written 5! (read "5 factorial").

$$5! = 5 \cdot 4 \cdot 3 \cdot 2 \cdot 1$$

The number of permutations of nine things chosen four at a time can be written $_9P_4$.

$$_9P_4 = 9 \cdot 8 \cdot 7 \cdot 6$$

A **combination** is a group of items in which the order of the items is not important. The number of combinations of nine things taken four at a time, $_9C_4$, is $_9P_4$ multiplied by $\frac{1}{4!}$.

$$_9C_4 = \frac{1}{4!} \cdot {_9P_4}$$

3. By using the whole numbers 1 to 5 without repeating a digit, how many different 3-digit numbers can you write?

4. How many different ways can you choose 2 magazines from a shelf of 10 magazines in a convenience store?

5. If 12 people are playing in a tournament and each person plays every other person, how many games will be played?

6. How many different ways can you choose 6 baseball cards at random to trade from a set of 25 cards?

Theoretical and Experimental Probability
11-4

You can find the **experimental probability** of an event by using this formula.

$$P(\text{event}) = \frac{\text{number of times an event happens}}{\text{total number of trials done}}$$

You can find the **theoretical probability** of an event by using this formula.

$$P(\text{event}) = \frac{\text{number of favorable outcomes}}{\text{total number of possible outcomes}}$$

Toss two coins 30 times. Use your data to find each probability.

7. P(head and tail)

8. P(two tails)

9. P(not two tails)

Independent and Dependent Events   11-5

When the outcome of one event *does not* affect the outcome of a second event, the events are **independent**. You can find the probability of two independent events by using this formula.

$$P(A \text{ and } B) = P(A) \times P(B)$$

If the outcome of one event *does* affect the outcome of a second event, the events are **dependent**. You can find the probability of two dependent events by using this formula.

$$(A, \text{ then } B) = P(A) \times P(B \text{ after } A)$$

Are the events dependent or independent?

10. Roll a number cube. Then roll it again.

11. Elect 2 class officials from a group of 12 students.

12. *Writing* Give an example of two independent and two dependent events.

Simulate the Problem, and Analyzing Games   11-6, 11-7

Many probability problems can be solved by simulating the problem. You can simulate some problems by tossing a coin, rolling a number cube, or using a random number table.

A game is **fair** if the players have an equal chance of winning.

13. Use the random number table to simulate the probability of guessing correctly exactly 3 out of 5 true-false questions.

14. Roll 4 number cubes. Player A wins if all numbers are 5 or less, and otherwise Player B wins. Is this game fair?

15. Two players are tossing three coins. Player A gets 1 point for each head that is tossed. Player B gets 3 points for tossing 3 heads or 3 tails. The player with the most points after 10 turns wins. Is this a fair game? Explain why or why not.

Random Number Table

16730	88055	14218	61907
15027	18164	63881	99740
04039	17261	74067	35810
96769	45016	11989	68048
94965	29302	23006	64650
75820	03019	50777	06225
50993	75783	64703	73486
31050	91506	34814	35296
67304	02236	67217	66214

Making Decisions with Probability   11-8

Companies use samples and product inspection for quality control.

16. A toy company sampled 10 toys and found 3 defective ones. Predict how many toys out of 250 will not be defective.

1. A stationery store sells paper and envelopes separately. Both come in cream, purple, and peach colors, and in two styles. How many different paper and envelope combinations are there?

2. Which license plate system provides more possible license numbers: two digits and three letters, or seven digits?

3. **Choose A, B, C, or D.** A basketball team is choosing a forward, a center, and a guard. There are 12 people on the team. Which expression best describes the number of possible outcomes?

   A. $_{12}P_2$ **B.** $_{12}P_3$
   C. 12! **D.** 3!

4. Find each value.
   a. 8!
   b. $_4P_3$
   c. $_{18}C_2$
   d. $\frac{6!}{2!}$
   e. $P(\text{not } E)$ if $P(E) = 0.53$

5. Is each expression equivalent to $_{12}C_3$? Write *yes* or *no*. Explain.
   a. $_{12}C_9$ b. $\frac{12!}{9!}$
   c. $\frac{12 \cdot 11 \cdot 10}{3!}$ d. $_{12}P_3$

6. Lucinda has a box with 5 yellow blocks, 3 blue blocks, and 2 green blocks. She picks one block at a time and does not replace it. Find $P(\text{yellow, then blue})$.

7. Find the probability of tossing 2 heads and 2 tails in four tosses of a coin.

A number from 0–999 is selected at random. Find each probability by calculating it or by using the random number table on page 579. Explain how you arrived at your answer.

8. Find $P(\text{odd number})$.

9. Find $P(\text{number ending with 1})$.

10. Find $P(\text{all even digits})$.

11. Find $P(\text{number containing a 4})$.

12. Two players each roll one standard number cube. Player A wins if the sum does not include the digit 1 and is even. Otherwise Player B wins. Is this a fair game? Explain.

13. Caitlin used 10 trials to simulate a game between two players, A and B. She found that $P(\text{A wins}) = 0.55$. Can she conclude that this game is fair or unfair? Explain.

14. *Writing* For each chart, identify any trends. Explain.

    a.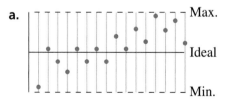

    b.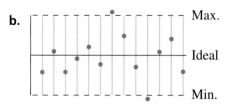

15. Jasper's Welding Shop found that out of 126 fenders it had welded, 7 had cracks. Predict the number of fenders with cracks out of a total of 198 fenders.

Choose the best answer.

1. If $a < b$, which of these statements is always true?

   I. $b > a$ II. $\frac{a}{c} < \frac{b}{c}$

   III. $a - c < b - c$

   A. I only   B. II only
   C. I and III only   D. I, II, and III

2. In the figure below, the triangles are similar. Find the unknown length h.

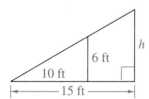

   A. 6 ft   B. 9 ft   C. 3 ft   D. 30 ft

3. Which expression is *not* equivalent to $\frac{6^3}{6^7}$?

   A. $6^3 \times 6^{-7}$ B. $6^3 \div 6^7$
   C. 6^{-4} D. 6^{10}

4. Each angle of a regular polygon has measure $140°$. Find the number of sides.

   A. 7   B. 8   C. 10   D. 9

5. In how many different orders can 5 out of 8 people be seated in a row of 5 chairs?

   A. 6,720   B. 56
   C. 40,320   D. 120

6. Find the area of the figure at the right.

   A. 26 mm^2
   B. 41 mm^2
   C. 45 mm^2
   D. 20 mm^2

   5 mm
   9 mm
   7 mm
   3 mm

7. Which quantity does not equal the others?

   A. 60% of 80
   B. 80% of 60
   C. 80 decreased by 40%
   D. 40 increased by 80%

8. If you start with a number, multiply by $\frac{3}{4}$, subtract 3, and then divide by 12, the result is 2. What is the number?

   A. 36   B. 108   C. 6   D. 27

9. What is the next term in the sequence 4, 12, 36, 108, . . . ?

   A. 111   B. 216   C. 2,916   D. 324

10. 4,449,875 people live in the Dallas-Fort Worth metropolitan area. 2,957,910 live in the Dallas area. Estimate the number of people who live in the Fort Worth area.

    A. About 7 million
    B. Over 6 million
    C. About 2 million
    D. About 1.5 million

11. Jim had $500 in his account on Monday. He wrote checks for $200 and $400 on Tuesday and Wednesday. Which of these represents the amount of money in his account on Thursday?

    A. $1100   B. $300
    C. $100   D. −$100

12. Which of the following expressions has a value of 12?

    A. $12 \div (6 + 2) \cdot 5$
    B. $(12 \div 6 + 2) \cdot 5$
    C. $12 \div 6 + 2 \cdot 5$
    D. $12 \div (6 + 2 \cdot 5)$

Use the data at the right to make each type of graph.   ■ LESSONS 1-1, 1-2

1. sliding bar graph
2. stacked bar graph
3. line graph with a break symbol to show total enrollment
4. multiple line graph

School Enrollment

Pupils	Grade 6	Grade 7	Grade 8
Boys	85	78	82
Girls	74	88	81

For Exercises 5 and 6, use the following temperature data.   ■ LESSONS 1-3, 1-4

High temperatures (°F): 88, 76, 93, 81, 76, 79, 85, 81, 94, 68, 87

5. Choose intervals to group the data. Then make a frequency table and a histogram.
6. Find the mean, the median, and the mode of the data.

Use the stem-and-leaf plot below for Exercises 7 and 8.   ■ LESSONS 1-5, 1-6

7. Find the mean, median, mode, and range of the data.
8. Make a box-and-whisker plot for the data.

```
7 | 0 3 4
8 | 2 5
9 | 3 6 7 8
   7 | 0 means 7.0
```

Describe the trend in each scatter plot.   ■ LESSON 1-7

9.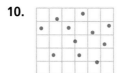

10.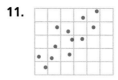

11.

Choose the type of graph that would best display each kind of data.   ■ LESSON 1-8

12. parts of a monthly budget
13. change in temperature in one week
14. the number of girls and boys in three kindergartens
15. a comparison of years in school and literacy rates

Rewrite each question as a closed-option question.   ■ LESSON 1-9

16. What is your favorite snack?
17. How much homework do you do each night?

Suppose a coin is tossed twice. Find each probability.   ■ LESSON 1-11

18. P(no heads)
19. P(exactly one head)
20. P(at least one head)

Compare. Write $<$, $>$, or =. ■ LESSON 2-1

1. -7 ■ 7
2. 32 ■ $|-32|$
3. $|-9|$ ■ -3
4. $|-8|$ ■ $|-6|$

Evaluate each expression for $n = 2$, $m = 3$, and $t = 5$. ■ LESSON 2-2

5. $3t - 4n$
6. $13 - (m + n)$
7. $\dfrac{m + t}{n}$
8. $7 + mt$

Find each sum or difference. ■ LESSONS 2-3, 2-4

9. $-6 + 4$
10. $-4 + (-5)$
11. $-2 - 6$
12. $-8 - (-5)$
13. $15 - (-8)$

Find each product or quotient. ■ LESSON 2-5

14. $(-3) \cdot 4$
15. $(-15)(5)$
16. $-45 \div -5$
17. $|-36| \div 9$
18. $5 \cdot (-45 \div 9)$

Write each expression with a single exponent. ■ LESSON 2-6

19. $3^2 \cdot 3^3$
20. $2^5 \cdot 2$
21. $(-4^3)(-4^{10})$
22. $m^6 \cdot m^7$
23. $(-p^4)(p^5)$
24. $5^0 \cdot 5^{10}$

Evaluate. ■ LESSON 2-7

25. $-3^2 - (-8)$
26. $3 + 4^2 - 15$
27. $(-2)^3 + 4 \div 2 - 3$
28. $(3 - 4)^5 - 17 + 1^0$
29. $2r^2 + 6r + 3$ for $r = -6$
30. $|c| + (-c)^2$ for $c = 4$
31. $-c^3 + 2c^2 - c + 8$ for $c = -3$
32. $-3a + 4b$ for $a = 3$ and $b = -2$

Explain which property is illustrated by each equation. ■ LESSON 2-8

33. $2(11) + 2(4) = 2(11 + 4)$
34. $(3 + 4) - 5 = 3 + (4 - 5)$
35. $2n + p = p + 2n$

Simplify each expression. Use only positive exponents. ■ LESSON 2-10

36. $\dfrac{4^7}{4^5}$
37. $\dfrac{12m^6}{5m^6}$
38. $3n^4 \div n^4$
39. $8(3y)^{-2}$
40. $\dfrac{8^2}{8^4}$
41. $5^{-3}h^3$

Write each number in scientific notation. ■ LESSON 2-11

42. $400{,}000{,}000$
43. $8{,}570{,}000$
44. 0.0000009
45. 0.000592

Write each number in standard form.

46. 1.286×10^3
47. 2.05×10^4
48. 6.488×10^{-3}
49. 5.6×10^6

Extra Practice

Simplify each expression.　　　　　　　　　　　　■ **LESSON 3-1**

1. $6x + 4 - 3x$　　　2. $7(h - 5)$　　　3. $2(x + 1) + 5$　　　4. $-5 + 3p - p$

Solve each equation.　　　　　　　　　　　　　　■ **LESSONS 3-2, 3-3**

5. $x - 6 = -15$　　6. $-12 = m + 8$　　7. $1.5 = m - 3.2$　　8. $x + 10 = 10$

9. $\frac{b}{7} = 9$　　10. $-3w = 360$　　11. $144 = -6k$　　12. $20 = \frac{h}{-10}$

Solve each equation.　　　　　　　　　　　　　　■ **LESSONS 3-4, 3-6**

13. $6n + 3 = 21$　　14. $10 = \frac{m}{5} + 2$　　15. $-b + 2 = -\frac{1}{2}$　　16. $9g - 4g = 10$

17. $5(d + 2) = 25$　　18. $-10 = 2w + 3w$　　19. $5k = -k + 18$　　20. $5x - 2 = x + 8$

21. Five less than three times a number is 16 more than two times the number. Write and solve an equation to find the number.

22. Solve the formula $V = \frac{1}{3}Bh$ for h.　　　　　　■ **LESSON 3-7**

23. Find the perimeter and area of a rectangle with base 14 cm and height 5 cm.

Define a variable and write an inequality to describe each　■ **LESSON 3-8**
situation.

24. You must be at least 18 years old to vote in an election.

25. The maximum weight you can carry in a 15-ft canoe is 450 lb.

Write an inequality for each graph.

26. ⟵─┼─┼─┼─●─┼─┼─┼─┼─→
　　　-3 -2 -1 0 1 2 3

27. ⟵─┼─┼─◯─┼─┼─┼─┼─┼─→
　　　　-3 -2 -1 0 1 2 3

Solve each inequality. Graph each solution on a number　■ **LESSONS 3-9, 3-10**
line.

28. $x + 3 > 4$　　29. $h - 2 \le -5$　　30. $9 < t - 7$　　31. $0 \ge k + 12$

32. $-t < 6$　　33. $12m \ge -72$　　34. $20 > -5w$　　35. $-16 \le \frac{x}{4}$

Name the point with the given coordinates. ■ **LESSON 4-1**

1. $(4, 1)$ 2. $(-2, 2)$ 3. $(2, -2)$ 4. $(0, -1)$

Name the coordinates of each point. In which quadrant does the point lie?

5. C 6. D 7. K 8. M

The points from each table lie on a line. Find the slope. ■ **LESSON 4-3**

9.

x	0	1	2	3	4
y	1	3	5	7	9

10.

x	-2	0	2	4	6
y	10	7	4	1	-2

11.

x	-4	-1	2	5	8
y	-5	0	5	10	15

Identify the slope and the *y*-intercept. Then graph each line. ■ **LESSONS 4-2, 4-4**

12. $y = 3x - 2$ 13. $y = x + 5$ 14. $y = \frac{2}{3}x$ 15. $y = -\frac{3}{4}x + 6$

Use *x*- and *y*-intercepts to graph each line. ■ **LESSON 4-6**

16. $3x + 5y = 15$ 17. $2x - 7y = 28$ 18. $x + y = 7$ 19. $4x - 3y = -12$

20. The table represents the altitude of two weather balloons. Graph the data and estimate when the balloons are at the same altitude. ■ **LESSON 4-7**

Altitude (thousands of feet)

Time (min)	0	5	10	15	20	25
Balloon A	4	5	6	7	8	9
Balloon B	10	8.5	7	5.5	4	2.5

In Exercises 21–23, copy the figure shown below. Then draw its image after the given transformation. ■ **LESSONS 4-8, 4-9, 4-10**

21. translation 3 units right and 1 unit down

22. reflection over the *y*-axis

23. rotation $270°$ about the origin

24. Does the figure shown above have reflectional symmetry? If so, state how many lines of symmetry it has.

25. Does the figure shown above have rotational symmetry? If so, give the angle of rotation.

Extra Practice

Use the prime factorization to find the GCF of each set of numbers. ■ LESSON 5-1

1. 9, 33 **2.** 7, 15 **3.** 6, 24 **4.** 9, 30 **5.** 4, 18

Write each fraction as a decimal. Write each decimal as a fraction or mixed number in simplest form. ■ LESSONS 5-2, 5-3

6. 0.725 **7.** 3.54 **8.** -0.3475 **9.** $\frac{7}{3}$ **10.** $0.\overline{8}$

11. $-2.\overline{6}$ **12.** $\frac{3}{16}$ **13.** $\frac{14}{15}$ **14.** $5.1\overline{6}$ **15.** $-7.\overline{1}$

16. $\frac{-3}{8}$ **17.** $\frac{5}{18}$ **18.** $1\frac{7}{20}$ **19.** $-2\frac{5}{12}$ **20.** $4\frac{4}{11}$

Compare. Use >, <, or =. ■ LESSON 5-4

21. $\frac{25}{36}$ ■ $0.69\overline{4}$ **22.** 2.7 ■ $\frac{10}{3}$ **23.** -4.3 ■ -4.2 **24.** $-\frac{17}{3}$ ■ -15.9

Find each sum or difference. Write your answer as a fraction or mixed number in simplest form. ■ LESSONS 5-5, 5-6

25. $-\frac{3}{8} + \frac{7}{8}$ **26.** $-\frac{15}{18} + \left(-\frac{3}{18}\right)$ **27.** $12\frac{1}{3} - 6\frac{2}{3}$ **28.** $\frac{7}{12} - \left(-\frac{11}{12}\right)$

29. $-\frac{5}{8} + \left(-\frac{7}{12}\right)$ **30.** $-\frac{6}{7} + \frac{8}{14}$ **31.** $6\frac{2}{5} - 7\frac{1}{3}$ **32.** $\frac{3}{4} - \frac{16}{24}$

Find each product or quotient. Write your answer as a fraction or mixed number in simplest form. ■ LESSON 5-7

33. $-\frac{3}{7} \cdot \frac{5}{9}$ **34.** $-4\frac{5}{24} \cdot (-6)$ **35.** $-\frac{1}{2} \div 6$ **36.** $-25 \div \frac{5}{7}$ **37.** $\frac{2}{3} \div \left(-\frac{8}{9}\right)$

Find each square root. If a number is not a perfect square, approximate the square root to the nearest tenth. ■ LESSON 5-9

38. $\sqrt{196}$ **39.** $\sqrt{225}$ **40.** $\sqrt{307}$ **41.** $\sqrt{650}$ **42.** $\sqrt{4,525}$

State whether each number is rational or irrational.

43. $1.020304\ldots$ **44.** $2.4444\ldots$ **45.** $5.63\overline{63}$ **46.** $0.9090090009\ldots$

47. How high can you build your tree house if you have a 12-ft ladder that must be placed 3 ft from the tree for stability? ■ LESSON 5-10

Find each unit rate.

■ LESSON 6-1

1. 240 mi on 8 gal   **2.** $3.50 for 10 oz   **3.** 450 mi in 9 h   **4.** $18 for 12 cans

Use dimensional analysis to find each unknown value.

■ LESSON 6-2

5. 3.5 mi = ■ ft   **6.** 7.2 km = ■ m   **7.** 80 oz = ■ lb   **8.** 120 fl oz = ■ gal

Solve each proportion.

■ LESSON 6-3

9. $\frac{4}{7} = \frac{x}{21}$ **10.** $\frac{3}{x} = \frac{18}{9}$ **11.** $\frac{x}{10} = \frac{8}{15}$ **12.** $\frac{3}{5} = \frac{2}{x}$

Each pair of polygons is similar. Find the value of each variable.

■ LESSON 6-4

13.   **14.**   **15.**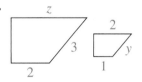

16. Graph $\triangle ABC$ with vertices $A(-1, 2)$, $B(-1, -1)$, and $C(1, -1)$. Then graph its image after a dilation with center $(0, 0)$ and scale factor 4.

■ LESSON 6-5

17. The scale of a map is 1 in. : 30 mi. What is the actual distance between two cities that are $2\frac{3}{4}$ in. apart on the map? Give your answer to the nearest tenth of a mile.

■ LESSON 6-6

18. A telephone pole has a sign attached to it 6 ft above the ground. The pole casts a shadow 26 ft long. The shadow of the portion up to the sign is 8 ft long. How tall is the pole?

■ LESSON 6-8

Write each answer as a fraction in simplest form.

■ LESSONS 6-9, 6-10

19. $\sin A$ **20.** $\cos A$

21. $\tan B$ **22.** $\sin B$

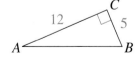

23. The top of a fallen tree rests against the side of a house. The base of the tree is 18 ft from the house and the tree forms a $60°$ angle with the ground. Find the length of the tree.

Extra Practice

Write each number as a decimal, a fraction, and a percent.   ■ LESSON 7-1

1. $\frac{1}{3}$ 2. 21%   3. 3.47   4. 0.00042   5. $\frac{3}{20}$ 6. 215.4%

Estimate the percent of the number. Explain why you   ■ LESSON 7-2
chose the estimation strategy that you used.

7. 28% of 54   8. 0.7% of 93   9. 17.9% of 32   10. 125% of 84

Solve each problem.   ■ LESSONS 7-3, 7-4

11. 18% of 36 is ■.   12. 44 is ■% of 32.   13. 145 is 15% of ■.

14. 0.4 is ■% of 5.   15. 0.09% of 1,024 is ■.   16. 215% of 20 is ■.

For Exercises 17–20, use the data at the right.   ■ LESSON 7-5

17. Express each item in the table as a percent of the total.

18. Add a column to the table to show what each item's central angle would be in a circle graph.

19. Display the data shown in the table in a circle graph.

20. Which item is more than a third of the budget?

Monthly Budget

Rent	$450
Utilities	$80
Food	$200
Insurance	$70
Transportation	$50
Other	$150

Find each percent of change. Round your answer to the   ■ LESSON 7-6
nearest tenth of a percent.

21. 16 to 20   22. 320 to 542   23. 1 to 0.4   24. 80 to 55   25. 0.002 to 0.003

26. **a.** Daniel ordered $18.00 sunglasses for his store. He   ■ LESSON 7-7
      marked them up 50%. What is the selling price?
   b. Unfortunately, they weren't selling, so he marked the
      glasses down to $22.95. What was the discount rate?

27. A salesperson gets 8% of the marked price as a commission.
   How much does she sell if she earns $94.40 in commission?

Find the final balance for each account.   ■ LESSON 7-8

28. $1,650 at 4.5% simple interest for $2\frac{1}{2}$ yr   29. $3,500 at $5\frac{1}{4}$% compounded annually for 3 yr

For Exercises 1–5, use the diagram at the right. ■ LESSON 8-2

1. ∠MKL and ∠■ are complementary angles.

2. ∠LPM and ∠■ are vertical angles.

3. m∠LPM = ■° **4.** m∠MPN = ■° **5.** m∠PLM = ■°

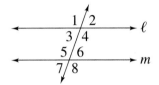

6. Use a protractor to draw ∠A with a measure ■ LESSON 8-3
   of 120°. Then construct ∠B so that ∠B ≅ ∠A.

In the diagram at the right, ℓ ∥ m. ■ LESSON 8-4

7. Name a pair of alternate interior angles and a pair of
   corresponding angles.

8. If m∠1 = 110°, find the measure of each numbered angle.

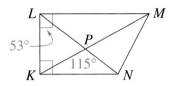

Are the following triangles congruent? If so, state the ■ LESSON 8-5
congruence and the reason why.

9. 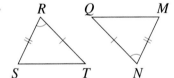 10.   11.

Judging by appearance, name the following figures. ■ LESSON 8-6

12.   13.   14.   15.

Find the sum of the angle measures for each polygon. ■ LESSON 8-7

16. rhombus **17.** hexagon **18.** triangle **19.** pentagon **20.** trapezoid

21. Create a tessellation that involves two different shapes. ■ LESSON 8-8

Find the area of each figure. If an answer is not a whole ■ LESSONS 8-9, 8-10
number, round to the nearest tenth.

22. parallelogram: b = 6 m, **23.** triangle: b = 8 cm, **24.** circle: d = 5.5 in.
    h = 12 m h = 15 cm

Name each figure described.   ■ LESSON 9-1

1. a three-dimensional figure with two circular, parallel, and congruent bases

2. a three-dimensional figure with one circular base and one vertex

3. a three-dimensional figure with one square base and four triangular faces

Draw the top, front, and right view of each figure.   ■ LESSON 9-2

4.

5.

6.

Draw a net for each figure.   ■ LESSON 9-3

7. cube   8. cone   9. cylinder   10. square pyramid

Compute to the least precise measurement.   ■ LESSON 9-4

11. $22.6 \text{ m} + 2.56 \text{ m}$ 12. $52.4 \text{ m} - 29 \text{ m}$ 13. $3\frac{1}{2} \text{ yd} - 2\frac{7}{8} \text{ yd}$ 14. $\$215.18 + \$3,276$

Find (a) the surface area and (b) the volume of each figure. If   ■ LESSONS 9-5, 9-7
an answer is not a whole number, round to the nearest tenth.

15. cube with edge length 1.2 m

16. rectangular prism 10 cm × 15 cm × 18 cm

17. cylinder with radius 1 ft and height 8 ft

18. cylinder with diameter and height 4 in.

Find (a) the surface area and (b) the volume of each figure. If   ■ LESSONS 9-6, 9-10
an answer is not a whole number, round to the nearest tenth.

19. square pyramid, with 4-in. height, 5-in. slant height, and 6 in.-by-6 in. base

20. square pyramid, with 3-ft height, 5.8-ft slant height, and 10 ft-by-10 ft base

21. cone with diameter 12 cm, height 8 cm, and slant height 10 cm

22. cone with radius 2.8 m, height 4.6 m, and slant height 5.4 m

The surface area and volume of a prism are given. Find the   ■ LESSON 9-8
surface area and volume of a prism with (a) double and
(b) triple the dimensions of the given prism.

23. S.A. = 248 cm^2
    V = 240 cm^3

24. S.A. = 84 m^2
    V = 36 m^3

25. S.A. = 216 m^2
    V = 216 m^3

26. S.A. = 10.88 cm^2
    V = 1.44 cm^3

Extra Practice

Identify each sequence as *arithmetic, geometric,* or *neither*. Find the next three terms.

■ LESSON 10-1

1. 4, 16, 64, . . .   **2.** $-5, -3, -1, 1, . . .$ **3.** $1, \frac{5}{6}, \frac{2}{3}, \frac{1}{2}, . . .$ **4.** 12, 6, 3, . . .

Use the function rule $f(x) = \frac{1}{2}x^2 - 3x$. Find each output.

■ LESSON 10-2

5. $f(2)$ **6.** $f(4)$ **7.** $f(10)$ **8.** $f(0)$ **9.** $f(-2)$ **10.** $f(5)$

Make a table of values. Then graph each function.

■ LESSON 10-3

11. $f(x) = 3x$ **12.** $f(x) = -2x + 3$ **13.** $f(x) = \frac{3}{5}x + 1$ **14.** $f(x) = 4$

Do the data in each table represent a linear function? If so, write the function rule.

■ LESSON 10-4

15.

x	0	1	2	3	4
f(x)	8	6	4	2	0

16.

x	-3	-1	1	3	5
f(x)	0	1	2	3	4

17.

x	0	3	6	9	12
f(x)	0	2	4	7	10

Match each situation with the appropriate graph.

■ LESSON 10-6

18. the altitude of an airplane during one flight

19. the fee for an overdue book

20. distance traveled when driving to the library

21. the speed of a school bus during its morning route

A.

time

B.

time

C.

time

D.

time

Make a table of values for each function. Use integers from 1 to 4 for inputs. Then graph the function.

■ LESSONS 10-7, 10-8

22. $f(x) = \frac{10}{x}$ **23.** $f(x) = 2^x$ **24.** $f(x) = \frac{12}{x}$ **25.** $f(x) = 32 \cdot \left(\frac{1}{2}\right)^x$

Simplify, add, subtract, or multiply.

■ LESSONS 10-9, 10-10, 10-11

26. $x^2 - 3x^2 - 5x + 3x + 4$

27. $-x^2 + 2x^2 - 6x - 3x + 3 - 2$

28. $(2x^2 - x + 1) - (4x^2 + 5x - 3)$

29. $(-x^2 + 2x - 6) + (x^2 + 2x - 2)$

30. $(-4x^2)(3x^4)$ **31.** $(6x)(-2x)$ **32.** $4x^2(2x - 7)$ **33.** $3x(-x^2 + 3x - 4)$

Extra Practice

1. A furniture store sells a style of sofa that can be ordered in 6 different lengths, with 3 different arm styles, and in 10 different fabric choices. How many different sofas can be ordered ?

■ LESSON 11-1

Find the value of each expression.

■ LESSONS 11-2, 11-3

2. $_6P_3$

3. $_7P_2$

4. $\dfrac{9!}{7!\,3!}$

5. $\dfrac{100!}{99!}$

6. $_4P_4$

7. $_5C_3$

8. $_7C_4$

9. $_6C_2$

10. $_9C_7$

11. $_4C_2$

Suppose one spinner has the letters of the alphabet on it and another has the digits 0 through 9. Find each value when both are spun. (Vowels are a, e, i, o, and u only.)

■ LESSON 11-4

12. P(M and 2)

13. P(C and prime)

14. P(F and 5)

15. P(vowel and even)

16. P(consonant and 4)

17. P(vowel and not prime)

State whether the events are dependent or independent.

■ LESSON 11-5

18. Take a box of cookies off a shelf. Do not replace it. Take another box.

19. Select a type of cereal. Then select a carton of juice.

20. Choose a coin from your wallet. Spend it. Choose another coin.

21. Two number cubes are rolled. Player A wins if the sum is less than 8, and Player B wins if the sum is greater than or equal to 8. Is this a fair game? Explain.

■ LESSON 11-7

Use the chart at right.

■ LESSON 11-8

22. A widget manufacturer selected 11 samples at random. The chart shows the mass of each widget selected.
   a. What is the ideal mass of a widget?
   b. What is the maximum mass allowed? The minimum mass allowed?
   c. How many widgets are defective?
   d. What is the probability that a widget chosen at random is defective?
   e. Predict how many widgets out of a batch of 2600 will not be defective.

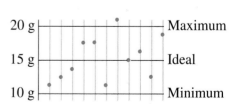

Tables

TABLE 1 *Measures*

Metric

Length

10 millimeters (mm) = 1 centimeter (cm)

100 cm = 1 meter (m)

1,000 m = 1 kilometer (km)

Area

100 square millimeters (mm^2) = 1 square centimeter (cm^2)

10,000 cm^2 = 1 square meter (m2)

Volume

1,000 cubic millimeters (mm^3) = 1 cubic centimeter (cm^3)

1,000,000 cm^3 = 1 cubic meter (m^3)

Mass

1,000 milligrams (mg) = 1 gram (g)

1,000 g = 1 kilogram (kg)

Volume

1,000 milliliters (mL) = 1 liter (L)

Customary

Length

12 inches (in.) = 1 foot (ft)

3 feet = 1 yard (yd)

36 in. = 1 yd

5,280 ft = 1 mile (mi)

1,760 yd = 1 mi

Area

144 square inches ($in.^2$) = 1 square foot (ft^2)

9 ft^2 = 1 square yard (yd^2)

4,840 yd^2 = 1 acre

Volume

1,728 cubic inches ($in.^3$) = 1 cubic foot (ft^3)

27 ft^3 = 1 cubic yard (yd^3)

Weight

16 ounces (oz) = 1 pound (lb)

2,000 lb = 1 ton (T)

Volume

8 fluid ounces (fl oz) = 1 cup (c)

2 c = 1 pint (pt)

2 pt = 1 quart (qt)

4 qt = 1 gallon (gal)

Time

1 minute (min) = 60 seconds (s)

1 hour (h) = 60 min

1 day (d) = 24 h

1 year (yr) = 365 d

TABLE 2   *Symbols*

$>$	is greater than	A'	image of A, A prime
$<$	is less than	A	Area
$\geq$	is greater than or equal to	b_1, b_2	base lengths of a trapezoid
$\leq$	is less than or equal to	b	base length
$=$	is equal to	h	height
$\neq$	is not equal to	P	perimeter
$\approx$	is approximately equal to	ℓ	slant height, length
$\stackrel{?}{=}$	is this statement true?	w	width
$+$	plus (addition)	C	circumference
$-$	minus (subtraction)	S.A.	surface area
$\pm$	plus or minus	B	area of a base
$\times, \cdot$	times (multiplication)	V	volume
$\div, \sqrt{\ }$	divide (division)	r	rate, radius
$\sqrt{x}$	nonnegative square root of x	$\odot A$	circle with center A
$^\circ$	degrees	$\overline{AB}$	segment AB
$\%$	percent	$\overrightarrow{AB}$	ray AB
$(\ )$	parentheses for grouping	$\overleftrightarrow{AB}$	line AB
$|a|$	absolute value of a	$\triangle ABC$	triangle with vertices A, B, and C
$a : b, \frac{a}{b}$	ratio of a to b	$\angle A$	angle with vertex A
(a, b)	ordered pair with x-coordinate a and y-coordinate b	$\angle ABC$	angle with sides $\overrightarrow{BA}$ and $\overrightarrow{BC}$
$\cong$	is congruent to	$m\angle ABC$	measure of angle ABC
$\not\cong$	is not congruent to	AB	length of segment $\overline{AB}$
$\sim$	is similar to	$\sin A$	sine of $\angle A$
$\perp$	is perpendicular to	$\cos A$	cosine of $\angle A$
$\parallel$	is parallel to	$\tan A$	tangent of $\angle A$
π	pi, an irrational number approximately equal to 3.14	$P(\text{event})$	probability of an event
$f(n)$	function value at n, f of n	$n!$	n factorial
b	y-intercept	$_nP_r$	permutations of n things taken r at a time
m	slope of a line	$_nC_r$	combinations of n things taken r at a time
$\begin{bmatrix} 1 & 2 \\ 3 & 4 \end{bmatrix}$	matrix	$\wedge$	raised to a power (in a spreadsheet formula)
$-a$	opposite of a	$*$	multiply (in a spreadsheet formula)
$\frac{1}{a}$	reciprocal of a	$/$	divide (in a spreadsheet formula)
a^n	nth power of a		
d	distance, diameter		

TABLE 3 *Properties of Real Numbers*

Unless otherwise stated, a, b, c, and d are real numbers.

Identity Properties

Addition $\quad a + 0 = a$ and $0 + a = a$

Multiplication $\quad a \cdot 1 = a$ and $1 \cdot a = a$

Commutative Properties

Addition $\quad a + b = b + a$

Multiplication $\quad a \cdot b = b \cdot a$

Associative Properties

Addition $\quad (a + b) + c = a + (b + c)$

Multiplication $\quad (a \cdot b) \cdot c = a \cdot (b \cdot c)$

Inverse Properties

Addition

$a + (-a) = 0$ and $-a + a = 0$

Multiplication

$a \cdot \dfrac{1}{a} = 1$ and $\dfrac{1}{a} \cdot a = 1$ $(a \neq 0)$

Distributive Properties

$a(b + c) = ab + ac \quad (b + c)a = ba + ca$

$a(b - c) = ab - ac \quad (b - c)a = ba - ca$

Properties of Equality

Addition $\quad$ If $a = b$, then $a + c = b + c$.

Subtraction $\quad$ If $a = b$, then $a - c = b - c$.

Multiplication $\quad$ If $a = b$, then $a \cdot c = b \cdot c$.

Division $\quad$ If $a = b$, and $c \neq 0$, then
$\dfrac{a}{c} = \dfrac{b}{c}$.

Substitution $\quad$ If $a = b$, then b can replace a in any expression.

Reflexive $\quad a = a$

Symmetric $\quad$ If $a = b$, then $b = a$.

Transitive $\quad$ If $a = b$ and $b = c$, then $a = c$.

Cross Product Property

$\dfrac{a}{b} = \dfrac{c}{d}$ is equivalent to $ad = bc$.

Zero-Product Property

If $ab = 0$, then $a = 0$ or $b = 0$.

Closure Property

$a + b$ is a unique real number.

ab is a unique real number.

Density Property

Between any two rational numbers, there is a least one other rational number.

Properties of Inequality

Addition $\quad$ If $a > b$, then $a + c > b + c$.

$\quad$ If $a < b$, then $a + c < b + c$.

Subtraction $\quad$ If $a > b$, then $a - c > b - c$.

$\quad$ If $a < b$, then $a - c < b - c$.

Multiplication

If $a > b$ and $c > 0$, then $ac > bc$.

If $a < b$ and $c > 0$, then $ac < bc$.

If $a > b$ and $c < 0$, then $ac < bc$.

If $a < b$ and $c < 0$, then $ac > bc$.

Division

If $a > b$, and $c > 0$, then $\dfrac{a}{c} > \dfrac{b}{c}$.

If $a < b$, and $c > 0$, then $\dfrac{a}{c} < \dfrac{b}{c}$.

If $a > b$, and $c < 0$, then $\dfrac{a}{c} < \dfrac{b}{c}$.

If $a < b$, and $c < 0$, then $\dfrac{a}{c} > \dfrac{b}{c}$.

Transitive $\quad$ If $a > b$ and $b > c$, then $a > c$.

Comparison $\quad$ If $a = b + c$ and $c > 0$, then
$a > b$.

Properties of Exponents

For any nonzero number a and any integers m and n:

Zero Exponent $\quad a^0 = 1$

Negative Exponent $\quad a^{-n} = \dfrac{1}{a^n}$

Product of Powers $\quad a^m \cdot a^n = a^{m+n}$

Quotient of Powers $\quad \dfrac{a^m}{a^n} = a^{m-n}$

Tables

TABLE 4   *Geometric Formulas*

Perimeter and Circumference

Rectangle

$P = 2\ell + 2w$

Circle

$C = \pi d$ or $C = 2\pi r$

Area

Square

$A = s^2$

Parallelogram and Rectangle

$A = bh$

Triangle

$A = \frac{1}{2}bh$

Trapezoid

$A = \frac{1}{2}h(b_1 + b_2)$

Circle

$A = \pi r^2$

Triangle Formulas

Pythagorean Theorem

In a right triangle with legs of lengths a and b and hypotenuse of length c, $a^2 + b^2 = c^2$.

Trigonometric Ratios

$$\text{tangent of } \angle A = \frac{\text{length of leg opposite } \angle A}{\text{length of leg adjacent to } \angle A}$$

$$\text{sine of } \angle A = \frac{\text{length of leg opposite } \angle A}{\text{length of hypotenuse}}$$

$$\text{cosine of } \angle A = \frac{\text{length of leg adjacent to } \angle A}{\text{length of hypotenuse}}$$

Triangle Angle Sum

For any $\triangle ABC$,
$m\angle A + m\angle B + m\angle C = 180°$.

Surface Area

Rectangular Prism

$\text{S.A.} = 2\ell w + 2wh + 2\ell h$

Cylinder

$\text{S.A.} = 2\pi rh + 2B$

Square Pyramid

$\text{S.A.} = 2s\ell + s^2$

Cone

$\text{S.A.} = \pi r\ell + \pi r^2$

Sphere

$\text{S.A.} = 4\pi r^2$

Volume

Prism

$V = Bh$

Cylinder

$V = Bh$ or $V = \pi r^2 h$

Pyramid

$V = \frac{1}{3}Bh$

Cone

$V = \frac{1}{3}Bh$ or $V = \frac{1}{3}\pi r^2 h$

Sphere

$V = \frac{4}{3}\pi r^3$

TABLE 5 *Geometric Constructions*

Congruent Segments and Congruent Angles

For instructions on how to construct congruent segments and congruent angles, see Chapter 8, pages 383–384.

Perpendicular Bisector

Construct the perpendicular bisector of $\overline{AB}$.

Angle Bisector

Construct the angle bisector of $\angle P$.

Step 1

Open the compass to more than half the length of $\overline{AB}$. Put the tip of the compass at A and draw an arc intersecting $\overline{AB}$.

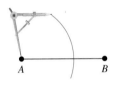

Step 1

Put the tip of the compass at P and draw an arc that intersects the sides of $\angle P$. Label the points of intersection S and T.

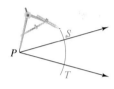

Step 2

Keeping the compass open to the same width, put the tip at B and draw another arc intersecting $\overline{AB}$. Label the points of intersection of the arcs C and D.

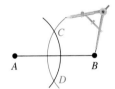

Step 2

With the compass tip at S and then at T, and with the same compass opening, draw intersecting arcs. Label the point where the arcs intersect X.

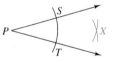

Step 3

Draw $\overleftrightarrow{CD}$. Label the intersection of $\overline{AB}$ and $\overleftrightarrow{CD}$ point M.

$\overleftrightarrow{CD}$ is the perpendicular bisector of $\overline{AB}$. Point M is the midpoint of $\overline{AB}$.

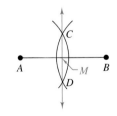

Step 3

Draw $\overrightarrow{PX}$.

$\overrightarrow{PX}$ is the bisector of $\angle SPT$.

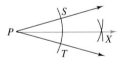

Other Constructions

Equilateral triangle, page 385, Exercise 8

Parallel lines, page 389, Exercise 20

Congruent triangles, page 395, Exercise 29

TABLE 6   Squares and Square Roots

N	N^2	$\sqrt{N}$	N	N^2	$\sqrt{N}$
1	1	1	51	2,601	7.141
2	4	1.414	52	2,704	7.211
3	9	1.732	53	2,809	7.280
4	16	2	54	2,916	7.348
5	25	2.236	55	3,025	7.416
6	36	2.449	56	3,136	7.483
7	49	2.646	57	3,249	7.550
8	64	2.828	58	3,364	7.616
9	81	3	59	3,481	7.681
10	100	3.162	60	3,600	7.746
11	121	3.317	61	3,721	7.810
12	144	3.464	62	3,844	7.874
13	169	3.606	63	3,969	7.937
14	196	3.742	64	4,096	8
15	225	3.873	65	4,225	8.062
16	256	4	66	4,356	8.124
17	289	4.123	67	4,489	8.185
18	324	4.243	68	4,624	8.246
19	361	4.359	69	4,761	8.307
20	400	4.472	70	4,900	8.367
21	441	4.583	71	5,041	8.426
22	484	4.690	72	5,184	8.485
23	529	4.796	73	5,329	8.544
24	576	4.899	74	5,476	8.602
25	625	5	75	5,625	8.660
26	676	5.099	76	5,776	8.718
27	729	5.196	77	5,929	8.775
28	784	5.292	78	6,084	8.832
29	841	5.385	79	6,241	8.888
30	900	5.477	80	6,400	8.944
31	961	5.568	81	6,561	9
32	1,024	5.657	82	6,724	9.055
33	1,089	5.745	83	6,889	9.110
34	1,156	5.831	84	7,056	9.165
35	1,225	5.916	85	7,225	9.220
36	1,296	6	86	7,396	9.274
37	1,369	6.083	87	7,569	9.327
38	1,444	6.164	88	7,744	9.381
39	1,521	6.245	89	7,921	9.434
40	1,600	6.325	90	8,100	9.487
41	1,681	6.403	91	8,281	9.539
42	1,764	6.481	92	8,464	9.592
43	1,849	6.557	93	8,649	9.644
44	1,936	6.633	94	8,836	9.695
45	2,025	6.708	95	9,025	9.747
46	2,116	6.782	96	9,216	9.798
47	2,209	6.856	97	9,409	9.849
48	2,304	6.928	98	9,604	9.899
49	2,401	7	99	9,801	9.950
50	2,500	7.071	100	10,000	10

TABLE 7 Trigonometric Ratios

Angle	Sine	Cosine	Tangent	Angle	Sine	Cosine	Tangent
1°	0.0175	0.9998	0.0175	46°	0.7193	0.6947	1.0355
2°	0.0349	0.9994	0.0349	47°	0.7314	0.6820	1.0724
3°	0.0523	0.9986	0.0524	48°	0.7431	0.6691	1.1106
4°	0.0698	0.9976	0.0699	49°	0.7547	0.6561	1.1504
5°	0.0872	0.9962	0.0875	50°	0.7660	0.6428	1.1918
6°	0.1045	0.9945	0.1051	51°	0.7771	0.6293	1.2349
7°	0.1219	0.9925	0.1228	52°	0.7880	0.6157	1.2799
8°	0.1392	0.9903	0.1405	53°	0.7986	0.6018	1.3270
9°	0.1564	0.9877	0.1584	54°	0.8090	0.5878	1.3764
10°	0.1736	0.9848	0.1763	55°	0.8192	0.5736	1.4281
11°	0.1908	0.9816	0.1944	56°	0.8290	0.5592	1.4826
12°	0.2079	0.9781	0.2126	57°	0.8387	0.5446	1.5399
13°	0.2250	0.9744	0.2309	58°	0.8480	0.5299	1.6003
14°	0.2419	0.9703	0.2493	59°	0.8572	0.5150	1.6643
15°	0.2588	0.9659	0.2679	60°	0.8660	0.5000	1.7321
16°	0.2756	0.9613	0.2867	61°	0.8746	0.4848	1.8040
17°	0.2924	0.9563	0.3057	62°	0.8829	0.4695	1.8807
18°	0.3090	0.9511	0.3249	63°	0.8910	0.4540	1.9626
19°	0.3256	0.9455	0.3443	64°	0.8988	0.4384	2.0503
20°	0.3420	0.9397	0.3640	65°	0.9063	0.4226	2.1445
21°	0.3584	0.9336	0.3839	66°	0.9135	0.4067	2.2460
22°	0.3746	0.9272	0.4040	67°	0.9205	0.3907	2.3559
23°	0.3907	0.9205	0.4245	68°	0.9272	0.3746	2.4751
24°	0.4067	0.9135	0.4452	69°	0.9336	0.3584	2.6051
25°	0.4226	0.9063	0.4663	70°	0.9397	0.3420	2.7475
26°	0.4384	0.8988	0.4877	71°	0.9455	0.3256	2.9042
27°	0.4540	0.8910	0.5095	72°	0.9511	0.3090	3.0777
28°	0.4695	0.8829	0.5317	73°	0.9563	0.2924	3.2709
29°	0.4848	0.8746	0.5543	74°	0.9613	0.2756	3.4874
30°	0.5000	0.8660	0.5774	75°	0.9659	0.2588	3.7321
31°	0.5150	0.8572	0.6009	76°	0.9703	0.2419	4.0108
32°	0.5299	0.8480	0.6249	77°	0.9744	0.2250	4.3315
33°	0.5446	0.8387	0.6494	78°	0.9781	0.2079	4.7046
34°	0.5592	0.8290	0.6745	79°	0.9816	0.1908	5.1446
35°	0.5736	0.8192	0.7002	80°	0.9848	0.1736	5.6713
36°	0.5878	0.8090	0.7265	81°	0.9877	0.1564	6.3138
37°	0.6018	0.7986	0.7536	82°	0.9903	0.1392	7.1154
38°	0.6157	0.7880	0.7813	83°	0.9925	0.1219	8.1443
39°	0.6293	0.7771	0.8098	84°	0.9945	0.1045	9.5144
40°	0.6428	0.7660	0.8391	85°	0.9962	0.0872	11.4301
41°	0.6561	0.7547	0.8693	86°	0.9976	0.0698	14.3007
42°	0.6691	0.7431	0.9004	87°	0.9986	0.0523	19.0811
43°	0.6820	0.7314	0.9325	88°	0.9994	0.0349	28.6363
44°	0.6947	0.7193	0.9657	89°	0.9998	0.0175	57.2900
45°	0.7071	0.7071	1.0000				

Tables

Decimals and Place Value

Each digit in a whole number or a decimal has both a place and a value. The value of any place is one tenth the value of the place to its left. The chart below can help you read and write decimals.

billions	hundred millions	ten millions	millions	hundred thousands	ten thousands	thousands	hundreds	tens	ones	.	tenths	hundredths	thousandths	ten-thousandths	hundred-thousandths	millionths
2	4	0	1	2	6	2	8	3	0	.	7	5	0	1	9	1

■ **EXAMPLE**

a. **What is the value of the digit 8 in the number above?**

The digit 8 is in the hundreds place.
So, its value is 8 hundreds.

b. **Write 2.006 in words.**

The digit 6 is in the thousandths place.
The answer is two and six thousandths.

c. **Write five and thirty-four ten-thousandths as a decimal.**

Ten-thousandths is 4 places to the right of the decimal point.
So, the decimal will have 4 places after the decimal point.
The answer is 5.0034.

EXERCISES *On Your Own*

Use the chart above. Write the value of each digit.

1. the digit 9
2. the digit 7
3. the digit 5

4. the digit 6
5. the digit 4
6. the digit 3

Write a decimal for the given words.

7. forty-one ten-thousandths
8. eighteen and five hundred four thousandths

9. eight millionths
10. seven and sixty-three hundred-thousandths

11. twelve thousandths
12. sixty-five and two hundred one thousandths

Write each decimal in words.

13. 0.06
14. 4.7
15. 0.00011
16. 0.9

17. 0.012
18. 0.000059
19. 0.0042
20. 6.029186

Comparing and Ordering Decimals

To compare two decimals, use the symbols > (is greater than),
< (is less than), or = (is equal to). When you compare, start at
the left and compare the digits.

■ EXAMPLE 1

Use >, <, or = to compare the decimals.

a. 0.1 ■ 0.06
1 tenth > 0 tenths, so
0.1 > 0.06

b. 2.4583 ■ 2.48
5 hundredths < 8 hundredths,
so 2.4583 < 2.48

c. 0.30026 ■ 0.03026
3 tenths > 0 tenths, so
0.30026 > 0.03026

■ EXAMPLE 2

Draw number lines to compare the decimals.

a. 0.1 ■ 0.06

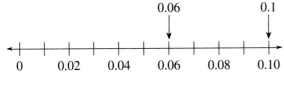

0.1 > 0.06

b. 2.4583 ■ 2.48

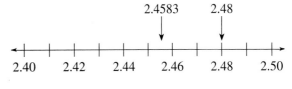

2.4583 < 2.48

EXERCISES *On Your Own*

**Use >, <, or = to compare the decimals. Draw number
lines if you wish.**

1. 0.003 ■ 0.02   **2.** 84.2 ■ 842   **3.** 0.162 ■ 0.106   **4.** 0.0659 ■ 0.6059

5. 2.13 ■ 2.99   **6.** 3.53 ■ 3.529   **7.** 02.01 ■ 02.010   **8.** 0.00072 ■ 0.07002

9. 0.458 ■ 0.4589   **10.** 8.627 ■ 8.649   **11.** 0.0019 ■ 0.0002   **12.** 0.19321 ■ 0.19231

Write the decimals in order from least to greatest.

13. 2.31, 0.231, 23.1, 0.23, 3.21

14. 1.02, 1.002, 1.2, 1.11, 1.021

15. 0.02, 0.002, 0.22, 0.222, 2.22

16. 55.5, 555.5, 55.555, 5.5555

17. 0.07, 0.007, 0.7, 0.71, 0.72

18. 2.78, 2.7001, 2.701, 2.71, 2.7

19. 7, 7.3264, 7.3, 7.3246, 7.0324

20. 0.0101, 0.0099, 0.011, 0.00019

Rounding

When you round to a particular place, look at the digit to the right of that place. If it is 5 or more, the digit in the place you are rounding to will increase by 1. If it is less than 5, the digit in the place you are rounding to will stay the same.

■ EXAMPLE

a. **Round 1.627 to the nearest whole number.**
   The digit to the right of the units place is 6, so 1.627 rounds up to 2.

b. **Round 12,034 to the nearest thousand.**
   The digit to the right of the thousands place is 0, so 12,034 rounds down to 12,000.

c. **Round 2.7195 to the nearest hundredth.**
   The digit to the right of the hundredths place is 9, so 2.7195 rounds up to 2.72.

d. **Round 0.060521 to the nearest thousandth.**
   The digit to the right of the thousandths place is 5, so 0.060521 rounds up to 0.061.

EXERCISES *On Your Own*

Round to the nearest thousand.

1. 105,099
2. 10,400
3. 79,527,826
4. 79,932
5. 4,312,349

Round to the nearest whole number.

6. 135.91
7. 3.001095
8. 96.912
9. 101.167
10. 299.9

Round to the nearest tenth.

11. 82.01
12. 4.67522
13. 20.397
14. 399.95
15. 129.98

Round to the nearest hundredth.

16. 13.458
17. 96.4045
18. 0.699
19. 4.234
20. 12.09531

Round to the place of the underlined digit.

21. 7.0$\underline{6}$15
22. $\underline{5}$.77125
23. 1,5$\underline{2}$2
24. 0.919$\underline{5}$2
25. 4.$\underline{2}$43

26. 2$\underline{3}$6.001
27. $\underline{3}$52
28. 3.4953$\underline{6}$6
29. 8.0$\underline{7}$092
30. $\underline{0}$.6008

31. 4$\underline{0}$9
32. 23,9$\underline{5}$1,888
33. 2.5$\underline{7}$84
34. 8$\underline{6}$2
35. 19.$\underline{3}$2

36. $\underline{9}$18
37. 7,$\underline{7}$35
38. 25.66$\underline{0}$47
39. 9$\underline{8}$3,240,631
40. $\underline{2}$7

41. 0.0037$\underline{7}$1
42. 0.$\underline{0}$649
43. 12.$\underline{7}$77
44. 1,759$\underline{2}$30
45. 2$\underline{0}$,908

Adding and Subtracting Decimals

You add or subtract decimals just as you do whole numbers. You line up the decimal points and then add or subtract. If you wish, you can use zeros to make the columns even.

■ **EXAMPLE**

Find each sum or difference.

a. **37.6 + 8.431**

$$
\begin{array}{r} 37.6 \\ + \ 8.431 \\ \hline \end{array} \rightarrow
\begin{array}{r} 37.600 \\ + \ 8.431 \\ \hline 46.031 \end{array}
$$

b. **8 − 4.593**

$$
\begin{array}{r} 8 \\ -4.593 \\ \hline \end{array} \rightarrow
\begin{array}{r} 8.000 \\ -4.593 \\ \hline 3.407 \end{array}
$$

c. **8.3 + 2.99 + 17.5**

$$
\begin{array}{r} 8.3 \\ 2.99 \\ +17.5 \\ \hline \end{array} \rightarrow
\begin{array}{r} 8.30 \\ 2.99 \\ +17.50 \\ \hline 28.79 \end{array}
$$

EXERCISES *On Your Own*

Find each sum or difference.

1.
$$\begin{array}{r} 39.7 \\ -36.03 \\ \hline \end{array}$$

2.
$$\begin{array}{r} 1.08 \\ -0.9 \\ \hline \end{array}$$

3.
$$\begin{array}{r} 6.784 \\ +0.528 \\ \hline \end{array}$$

4.
$$\begin{array}{r} 5.01 \\ -0.87 \\ \hline \end{array}$$

5.
$$\begin{array}{r} 13.02 \\ +23.107 \\ \hline \end{array}$$

6.
$$\begin{array}{r} 8.634 \\ +1.409 \\ \hline \end{array}$$

7.
$$\begin{array}{r} 2.1 \\ -0.5 \\ \hline \end{array}$$

8.
$$\begin{array}{r} 8.23 \\ -3.1 \\ \hline \end{array}$$

9.
$$\begin{array}{r} 1.05 \\ +12.9 \\ \hline \end{array}$$

10.
$$\begin{array}{r} 2.6 \\ +0.003 \\ \hline \end{array}$$

11.
$$\begin{array}{r} 0.1 \\ 58.21 \\ + \ 1.9 \\ \hline \end{array}$$

12.
$$\begin{array}{r} 12.2 \\ 3.06 \\ + \ 0.5 \\ \hline \end{array}$$

13.
$$\begin{array}{r} 9.42 \\ 3.6 \\ +21.003 \\ \hline \end{array}$$

14.
$$\begin{array}{r} 15.22 \\ 7.4 \\ + \ 8.125 \\ \hline \end{array}$$

15.
$$\begin{array}{r} 3.7 \\ 20.06 \\ +16.19 \\ \hline \end{array}$$

16. 76.39 − 8.47

17. 8.7 + 17.03

18. 32.403 + 12.06

19. 20.5 + 11.45

20. 8.9 − 4.45

21. 1.245 + 5.8

22. 3.9 + 6.57

23. 14.81 − 8.6

24. 11.9 − 2.06

25. 3.45 + 4.061

26. 8.29 + 4.3

27. 7.06 − 4.235

28. 6.02 + 4.005

29. 7.05 − 3.5

30. 1.18 + 3.015

31. 2.304 − 0.87

32. 5.002 − 3.45

33. 6.8 + 3.57

34. 0.23 + 0.091

35. 0.5 − 0.18

36. 8.3 + 2.99 + 17.52

37. 9.5 + 12.32 + 6.4

38. 4.521 + 1.8 + 3.07

39. 3.602 + 9.4 + 24

40. 11.6 + 8.05 + 5.13

41. 7.023 + 1.48 + 3.9

42. 57 + 0.6327 + 189.007

43. 741 + 6.08 + 0.0309

44. 0.045 + 16.32 + 8.6

45. 4.27 + 6.18 + 0.91

46. 3.856 + 14.01 + 1.72

47. 11.45 + 3.79 + 23.861

Multiplying Decimals

Multiply decimals as you would whole numbers. Then place the decimal point in the product. To do this, add the number of decimal places in the factors.

■ EXAMPLE 1

Multiply 0.068 × 2.3.

Step 1: Multiply.

```
  0.068
× 2.3
  204
+1360
 1564
```

Step 2: Place the decimal point.

```
  0.068  ←—three decimal places
× 2.3    ←—one decimal places
  204
+1360
 0.1564  ←—four decimal places
```

■ EXAMPLE 2

Find each product.

a. **3.12 × 0.9**

```
  3.12
× 0.9
```

b. **5.75 × 42**

```
   5.75
×    42
  11 50
+230 00
```

c. **0.964 × 0.28**

```
   0.964
×   0.28
   7712
+19280
```

EXERCISES *On Your Own*

Multiply.

1.
```
  1.48
× 3.6
```

2.
```
  191.2
×   3.4
```

3.
```
  0.05
×   43
```

4.
```
  0.27
×    5
```

5.
```
  1.36
× 3.8
```

6.
```
  6.23
×0.21
```

7.
```
  0.512
× 0.76
```

8.
```
  0.04
×    7
```

9.
```
  0.136
×   8.4
```

10.
```
     3
×0.05
```

11. 2.07×1.004

12. 0.12×6.1

13. 3.2×0.15

14. 0.74×0.23

15. 2.6×0.14

16. 0.77×51

17. 9.3×0.706

18. 71.13×0.4

19. 0.42×98

20. 6.3×85

21. 45×0.028

22. 76×3.3

23. 9×1.35

24. 4.56×7

25. 5×2.41

26. 704×0.3

27. 8.003×0.6

28. 42.2×0.9

29. 0.6×30.02

30. 0.05×11.8

Zeros in a Product

When you multiply with decimals, you may have to write one or more zeros to the left of a product before you can place the decimal point.

■ **EXAMPLE 1**

Multiply 0.06 × 0.015.

Step 1: Multiply.	**Step 2:** Place the decimal point.
0.015	0.015
× 0.06	× 0.06
90	0.00090

The product should have 5 decimal places, ← so you must write three zeros before placing the decimal point.

■ **EXAMPLE 2**

a. **0.02 × 1.3**

1.3
×0.02

b. **0.012 × 2.4**

2.4
×0.012
48
+240

c. **0.022 × 0.051**

0.051
×0.022
102
+1020

EXERCISES *On Your Own*

Multiply.

1. 0.03
× 0.9

2. 0.06
× 0.5

3. 2.4
×0.03

4. 7
×0.01

5. 0.05
×0.05

6. 0.016
× 0.12

7. 0.031
× 0.08

8. 0.03
× 0.2

9. 0.27
×0.033

10. 0.014
× 0.25

11. 0.003 × 0.55

12. 0.01 × 0.74

13. 0.47 × 0.08

14. 0.76 × 0.1

15. 0.3 × 0.27

16. 0.19 × 0.05

17. 0.018 × 0.04

18. 0.43 × 0.2

19. 0.03 × 0.03

20. 4.003 × 0.02

21. 0.5 × 0.08

22. 0.06 × 0.7

23. 0.047 × 0.008

24. 0.05 × 0.06

25. 0.03 × 0.4

26. 0.05 × 0.036

27. 0.4 × 0.23

28. 0.3 × 0.017

29. 0.3 × 0.24

30. 0.67 × 0.09

31. 3.02 × 0.006

32. 0.31 × 0.08

33. 0.14 × 0.05

34. 0.07 × 0.85

Dividing Decimals by Whole Numbers

When you divide a decimal by a whole number, the decimal point in the quotient goes directly above the decimal point in the dividend. You may need extra zeros to place the decimal point.

■ EXAMPLE 1

Divide 2.432 ÷ 32.

Step 1: Divide.

```
       76
32)2.432
  -2 24
    192
   -192
      0
```

Step 2: Place the decimal point.

```
    0.076     ← You need two extra
32)2.432        zeros to get the decimal
  -2 24         point in the correct place.
    192
   -192
      0
```

■ EXAMPLE 2

a. **37.6 ÷ 8**

```
    4.7
8)37.6
 -32
   5 6
  -5 6
     0
```

b. **39.33 ÷ 69**

```
     0.57
69)39.33
  -34 5
    4 83
   -4 83
       0
```

c. **4.482 ÷ 54**

```
     0.083
54)4.482
  -4 32
    162
   -162
      0
```

EXERCISES *On Your Own*

Divide.

1. $7)\overline{17.92}$

2. $5)\overline{16.5}$

3. $9)\overline{6.984}$

4. $6)\overline{91.44}$

5. $4)\overline{35.16}$

6. $56)\overline{8.848}$

7. $22)\overline{2.42}$

8. $26)\overline{1723.8}$

9. $83)\overline{15.272}$

10. $39)\overline{26.91}$

11. $14.49 \div 7$

12. $10.53 \div 9$

13. $17.52 \div 2$

14. $37.14 \div 6$

15. $0.1352 \div 8$

16. $0.0324 \div 9$

17. $0.0882 \div 6$

18. $0.8682 \div 6$

19. $12.342 \div 22$

20. $29.792 \div 32$

21. $22.568 \div 26$

22. $11.340 \div 36$

23. $45.918 \div 18$

24. $79.599 \div 13$

25. $59.7 \div 15$

26. $74.664 \div 12$

27. $2.1 \div 84$

28. $89.378 \div 67$

29. $0.0672 \div 48$

30. $171.031 \div 53$

Multiplying and Dividing by Powers of Ten

You can use shortcuts to multiply or divide by powers of ten.

When you multiply by	Move the decimal point	When you divide by	Move the decimal point
10,000	4 places to the right	10,000	4 places to the left
1,000	3 places to the right	1,000	3 places to the left
100	2 places to the right	100	2 places to the left
10	1 place to the right	10	1 place to the left
0.1	1 place to the left	0.1	1 place to the right
0.01	2 places to the left	0.01	2 places to the right
0.001	3 places to the left	0.001	3 places to the right

■ EXAMPLE

Multiply or divide.

a. **0.7×0.001**
Move the decimal point 3 places to the left.
0.000.7
$0.7 \times 0.001 = 0.0007$

b. **$0.605 \div 100$**
Move the decimal point 2 places to the left.
0.00.605
$0.605 \div 100 = 0.00605$

EXERCISES *On Your Own*

Multiply or divide.

1. $10,000 \times 0.056$
2. 0.001×0.09
3. 5.2×10
4. $0.03 \times 1,000$

5. $236.7 \div 0.1$
6. $45.28 \div 10$
7. $0.9 \div 1,000$
8. $1.07 \div 0.01$

9. 100×0.08
10. $1.03 \times 10,000$
11. 1.803×0.001
12. 4.1×100

13. $13.7 \div 0.001$
14. $203.05 \div 0.01$
15. $4.7 \div 10$
16. $0.05 \div 100$

17. 23.6×0.01
18. $1,000 \times 0.12$
19. 0.41×0.001
20. 0.01×6.2

21. $42.3 \div 0.1$
22. $0.4 \div 10,000$
23. $5.02 \div 0.01$
24. $16.5 \div 100$

25. $0.27 \div 0.01$
26. 1.05×0.001
27. 10×0.04
28. $2.09 \div 100$

29. 0.65×0.1
30. $0.03 \div 100$
31. $2.6 \div 0.1$
32. $12.6 \times 10,000$

33. $0.3 \div 1,000$
34. 0.01×6.7
35. 100×0.158
36. $23.1 \div 10$

Dividing Decimals by Decimals

To divide with a decimal divisor, multiply it by the smallest power of ten that will make the divisor a whole number. Then multiply the dividend by that same power of ten.

■ **EXAMPLE**

Find each quotient.

a. **3.348 ÷ 6.2**
 Multiply by 10.

$$
\begin{array}{r}
0.54 \\
6.2\overline{)3\,3.48} \\
-3\,1\,0 \\
\hline
2\,48 \\
-2\,48 \\
\hline
0
\end{array}
$$

b. **2.4885 ÷ 0.35**
 Multiply by 100.

$$
\begin{array}{r}
7.11 \\
0.35\overline{)2\,48.85} \\
-2\,45 \\
\hline
3\,8 \\
-3\,5 \\
\hline
35 \\
-35 \\
\hline
0
\end{array}
$$

c. **0.0576 ÷ 0.012**
 Multiply by 1,000.

$$
\begin{array}{r}
4.8 \\
0.012\overline{)0\,057.6} \\
-48 \\
\hline
9\,6 \\
-9\,6 \\
\hline
0
\end{array}
$$

EXERCISES *On Your Own*

Divide.

1. $3.2\overline{)268.8}$ 2. $1.9\overline{)123.5}$ 3. $0.3\overline{)135.6}$ 4. $2.3\overline{)170.2}$ 5. $7.9\overline{)252.8}$

6. $5.7\overline{)10.26}$ 7. $2.3\overline{)71.53}$ 8. $3.1\overline{)16.12}$ 9. $7.8\overline{)24.18}$ 10. $6.3\overline{)14.49}$

11. $134.42 \div 5.17$ 12. $89.96 \div 3.46$ 13. $160.58 \div 5.18$ 14. $106.59 \div 6.27$

15. $62.4 \div 3.9$ 16. $260.4 \div 8.4$ 17. $316.8 \div 7.2$ 18. $162.4 \div 2.9$

19. $1.512 \div 0.54$ 20. $3.225 \div 0.43$ 21. $2.484 \div 0.69$ 22. $511.5 \div 5.5$

23. $0.992 \div 0.8$ 24. $4.53 \div 0.05$ 25. $3.498 \div 0.06$ 26. $59.2 \div 0.8$

27. $2.198 \div 0.07$ 28. $14.28 \div 0.7$ 29. $1.98 \div 0.5$ 30. $26.36 \div 0.04$

31. $3.922 \div 7.4$ 32. $23.52 \div 0.98$ 33. $71.25 \div 7.5$ 34. $114.7 \div 3.7$

35. $0.832 \div 0.52$ 36. $1.125 \div 0.09$ 37. $9.666 \div 2.7$ 38. $1.456 \div 9.1$

39. $0.4374 \div 1.8$ 40. $2.3414 \div 0.46$ 41. $0.07224 \div 0.021$ 42. $0.1386 \div 0.18$

43. $0.16926 \div 0.091$ 44. $0.6042 \div 5.3$ 45. $2.3374 \div 0.62$ 46. $1.0062 \div 0.078$

Zeros in Decimal Division

When you are dividing by a decimal, sometimes you need to use extra zeros in the dividend or the quotient, or both.

■ **EXAMPLE 1**

Divide 0.045 ÷ 3.6.

Step 1: Multiply by 10.

$$3.6\overline{)0.0.45}$$

Step 2: Divide.

$$
\begin{array}{r}
125 \\
3.6\overline{)0.0.4500} \\
-36 \\
\hline
90 \\
-72 \\
\hline
180 \\
-180 \\
\hline
0
\end{array}
$$

Step 3: Place the decimal point.

$$
\begin{array}{r}
0.0125 \\
3.6\overline{)0.0.4500} \\
-36 \\
\hline
90 \\
-72 \\
\hline
180 \\
-180 \\
\hline
0
\end{array}
$$

■ **EXAMPLE 2**

Find each quotient.

a. **0.4428 ÷ 8.2**
Multiply by 10.

$$
\begin{array}{r}
0.054 \\
8.2\overline{)0.4.428}
\end{array}
$$

b. **0.00434 ÷ 0.07**
Multiply by 100.

$$
\begin{array}{r}
0.062 \\
0.07\overline{)0.00.434}
\end{array}
$$

c. **0.00306 ÷ 0.072**
Multiply by 1,000.

$$
\begin{array}{r}
0.0425 \\
0.072\overline{)0.003.0600}
\end{array}
$$

EXERCISES *On Your Own*

Divide.

1. $0.05\overline{)0.0023}$

2. $0.02\overline{)0.000162}$

3. $0.12\overline{)0.009}$

4. $2.5\overline{)0.021}$

5. $0.0019 \div 0.2$

6. $0.9 \div 0.8$

7. $0.000175 \div 0.07$

8. $0.142 \div 0.04$

9. $0.0017 \div 0.02$

10. $0.003 \div 0.6$

11. $0.0105 \div 0.7$

12. $0.034 \div 0.05$

13. $0.00056 \div 0.16$

14. $0.0612 \div 7.2$

15. $0.217 \div 3.1$

16. $0.052 \div 0.8$

17. $0.000924 \div 0.44$

18. $0.05796 \div 0.63$

19. $0.00123 \div 8.2$

20. $0.0954 \div 0.09$

21. $0.0084 \div 1.4$

22. $0.259 \div 3.5$

23. $0.00468 \div 0.52$

24. $0.104 \div 0.05$

25. $0.00063 \div 0.18$

26. $0.011 \div 0.25$

27. $0.3069 \div 9.3$

28. $0.00045 \div 0.3$

29. $0.6497 \div 8.9$

30. $0.00246 \div 0.06$

31. $0.00168 \div 0.3$

32. $0.00816 \div 3.4$

Writing Equivalent Fractions

If you multiply or divide both numerator and denominator of a fraction by the same number, you get an equivalent fraction.

■ **EXAMPLE 1**

a. **Find the missing number in $\frac{5}{6} = \frac{20}{\blacksquare}$.**

$$\overset{\times 4}{\frac{5}{6} = \frac{20}{\blacksquare}}$$

$$\underset{\times 4}{\frac{5}{6} = \frac{20}{24}}$$

b. **Find the missing number in $\frac{12}{30} = \frac{\blacksquare}{15}$.**

$$\overset{\div 2}{\frac{12}{30} = \frac{\blacksquare}{15}}$$

$$\underset{\div 2}{\frac{12}{30} = \frac{6}{15}}$$

To write a fraction in simplest form, divide both numerator and denominator by the greatest common factor.

■ **EXAMPLE 2**

a. **Write $\frac{6}{15}$ in simplest form.**

3 is the greatest common factor.

$$\frac{6}{15} = \frac{6 \div 3}{15 \div 3} = \frac{2}{5}$$

The simplest form of $\frac{6}{15}$ is $\frac{2}{5}$.

b. **Write $\frac{36}{42}$ in simplest form.**

6 is the greatest common factor.

$$\frac{36}{42} = \frac{36 \div 6}{62 \div 6} = \frac{6}{7}$$

The simplest form of $\frac{36}{42}$ is $\frac{6}{7}$.

EXERCISES *On Your Own*

Find each missing number.

1. $\frac{1}{3} = \frac{\blacksquare}{6}$

2. $\frac{3}{4} = \frac{\blacksquare}{16}$

3. $\frac{18}{30} = \frac{6}{\blacksquare}$

4. $\frac{2}{3} = \frac{\blacksquare}{21}$

5. $\frac{3}{4} = \frac{9}{\blacksquare}$

6. $\frac{3}{10} = \frac{9}{\blacksquare}$

7. $\frac{4}{5} = \frac{\blacksquare}{30}$

8. $\frac{2}{3} = \frac{8}{\blacksquare}$

9. $\frac{33}{55} = \frac{\blacksquare}{5}$

10. $\frac{27}{72} = \frac{9}{\blacksquare}$

11. $\frac{2}{3} = \frac{\blacksquare}{24}$

12. $\frac{11}{12} = \frac{55}{\blacksquare}$

13. $\frac{3}{5} = \frac{18}{\blacksquare}$

14. $\frac{60}{72} = \frac{10}{\blacksquare}$

15. $\frac{7}{8} = \frac{\blacksquare}{24}$

Write each fraction in simplest form.

16. $\frac{12}{36}$

17. $\frac{25}{30}$

18. $\frac{14}{16}$

19. $\frac{27}{36}$

20. $\frac{21}{35}$

21. $\frac{40}{50}$

22. $\frac{24}{40}$

23. $\frac{32}{64}$

24. $\frac{15}{45}$

25. $\frac{27}{63}$

26. $\frac{44}{77}$

27. $\frac{45}{75}$

28. $\frac{60}{72}$

29. $\frac{77}{84}$

30. $\frac{12}{24}$

31. $\frac{24}{32}$

32. $\frac{7}{21}$

33. $\frac{18}{42}$

34. $\frac{35}{49}$

35. $\frac{18}{81}$

36. $\frac{6}{18}$

37. $\frac{28}{56}$

38. $\frac{10}{25}$

39. $\frac{16}{28}$

Mixed Numbers and Improper Fractions

A fraction, such as $\frac{10}{7}$, in which the numerator is greater than or equal to the denominator is an improper fraction. You can write an improper fraction as a mixed number that shows the sum of a whole number and a fraction.

Sometimes it is necessary to do the opposite and write a mixed number as an improper fraction.

■ EXAMPLE

a. Write $\frac{11}{5}$ as a mixed number.

$$\frac{11}{5} \rightarrow \begin{array}{r} 2 \\ 5\overline{)11} \\ -10 \\ \hline 1 \end{array}$$

$\leftarrow$ whole number

$\leftarrow$ remainder

$\frac{11}{5} = 2\frac{1}{5}$ $\quad\leftarrow$ whole number $+ \dfrac{\text{remainder}}{\text{denominator}}$

b. Write $2\frac{5}{6}$ as an improper fraction.

$$2\frac{5}{6} = 2 + \frac{5}{6}$$
$$= \frac{12}{6} + \frac{5}{6} \quad\leftarrow \text{Write 2 as } \frac{12}{6}.$$
$$= \frac{12 + 5}{6} \quad\leftarrow \text{Add the numerators.}$$
$$2\frac{5}{6} = \frac{17}{6}$$

EXERCISES *On Your Own*

Write each improper fraction as a mixed number.

1. $\frac{7}{5}$ 2. $\frac{9}{2}$ 3. $\frac{13}{4}$ 4. $\frac{21}{5}$ 5. $\frac{13}{10}$ 6. $\frac{49}{5}$

7. $\frac{21}{8}$ 8. $\frac{13}{7}$ 9. $\frac{17}{5}$ 10. $\frac{49}{6}$ 11. $\frac{17}{4}$ 12. $\frac{5}{2}$

13. $\frac{27}{5}$ 14. $\frac{12}{9}$ 15. $\frac{30}{8}$ 16. $\frac{37}{12}$ 17. $\frac{8}{6}$ 18. $\frac{19}{12}$

19. $\frac{45}{10}$ 20. $\frac{15}{12}$ 21. $\frac{11}{2}$ 22. $\frac{20}{6}$ 23. $\frac{34}{8}$ 24. $\frac{21}{9}$

Write each mixed number as an improper fraction.

25. $1\frac{1}{2}$ 26. $2\frac{2}{3}$ 27. $1\frac{1}{12}$ 28. $3\frac{1}{5}$ 29. $2\frac{2}{7}$ 30. $4\frac{1}{2}$

31. $2\frac{7}{8}$ 32. $1\frac{2}{9}$ 33. $5\frac{1}{5}$ 34. $4\frac{7}{9}$ 35. $9\frac{1}{4}$ 36. $2\frac{3}{8}$

37. $7\frac{7}{8}$ 38. $1\frac{5}{12}$ 39. $3\frac{3}{7}$ 40. $6\frac{1}{2}$ 41. $3\frac{1}{10}$ 42. $4\frac{6}{7}$

Adding and Subtracting Fractions with Like Denominators

When you add or subtract fractions with the same denominator, add or subtract the numerators and then write the answer over the denominator.

■ EXAMPLE 1

Add or subtract. Write the answers in simplest form.

a. $\frac{5}{8} + \frac{7}{8}$

$$\frac{5}{8} + \frac{7}{8} = \frac{5+7}{8} = \frac{12}{8} = 1\frac{4}{8} = 1\frac{1}{2}$$

b. $\frac{11}{12} - \frac{2}{12}$

$$\frac{11}{12} - \frac{2}{12} = \frac{11-2}{12} = \frac{9}{12} = \frac{3}{4}$$

To add or subtract mixed numbers, add or subtract the fractions first. Then add or subtract the whole numbers.

■ EXAMPLE 2

Add or subtract. Write the answers in simplest form.

a. $3\frac{4}{6} + 2\frac{5}{6}$

$$3\frac{4}{6}$$
$$+\ 2\frac{5}{6}$$
$$\overline{5\frac{9}{6}} = 5 + 1 + \frac{3}{6} = 6\frac{1}{2}$$

b. $6\frac{1}{4} - 1\frac{3}{4}$

$$6\frac{1}{4} \qquad 5\frac{5}{4} \quad \longleftarrow \text{ Rewrite 1 unit as as } \frac{4}{4} \text{ and add it to } \frac{1}{4}.$$
$$-\ 1\frac{3}{4} \quad \longrightarrow \quad -\ 1\frac{3}{4}$$
$$\overline{\qquad} \qquad \overline{4\frac{2}{4}} = 4\frac{1}{2}$$

EXERCISES *On Your Own*

Add or subtract. Write the answers in simplest form.

1. $\frac{4}{5} + \frac{3}{5}$
2. $\frac{2}{6} - \frac{1}{6}$
3. $\frac{2}{7} + \frac{2}{7}$
4. $\frac{7}{8} + \frac{2}{8}$
5. $1\frac{2}{5} - \frac{1}{5}$

6. $\frac{3}{6} - \frac{1}{6}$
7. $\frac{6}{8} - \frac{3}{8}$
8. $\frac{2}{9} + \frac{1}{9}$
9. $\frac{4}{5} - \frac{1}{5}$
10. $\frac{5}{9} + \frac{7}{9}$

11. $9\frac{1}{3} - 8\frac{1}{3}$
12. $8\frac{6}{7} - 4\frac{2}{7}$
13. $3\frac{1}{10} + 1\frac{3}{10}$
14. $2\frac{2}{9} + 3\frac{4}{9}$

15. $4\frac{5}{12} - 3\frac{1}{12}$
16. $9\frac{5}{9} + 6\frac{7}{9}$
17. $5\frac{7}{8} + 2\frac{3}{8}$
18. $4\frac{4}{7} - 2\frac{1}{7}$

19. $9\frac{3}{4} + 1\frac{3}{4}$
20. $8\frac{2}{3} - 4\frac{1}{3}$
21. $8\frac{7}{10} + 2\frac{3}{10}$
22. $1\frac{4}{5} + 3\frac{3}{5}$

23. $7\frac{1}{5} - 2\frac{3}{5}$
24. $4\frac{1}{3} - 1\frac{2}{3}$
25. $4\frac{3}{8} - 3\frac{5}{8}$
26. $5\frac{1}{12} - 2\frac{7}{12}$

Multiplying and Dividing Fractions

To multiply fractions, multiply the numerators and the denominators. To divide fractions, multiply by the reciprocal of the divisor.

Multiply. Write the answers in simplest form.

a. $\dfrac{8}{9} \times \dfrac{3}{10} = \dfrac{\overset{4}{\cancel{8}}}{\underset{3}{\cancel{9}}} \times \dfrac{\overset{1}{\cancel{3}}}{\underset{5}{\cancel{10}}} = \dfrac{4}{15}$

b. $3\dfrac{1}{8} \times 1\dfrac{3}{4} = \dfrac{25}{8} \times \dfrac{7}{4}$

$= \dfrac{175}{32} = 5\dfrac{15}{32}$ ← Rewrite as a mixed number.

Divide. Write the answers in simplest form.

c. $\dfrac{2}{3} \div \dfrac{4}{5} = \dfrac{2}{3} \times \dfrac{5}{4}$

$= \dfrac{\overset{1}{\cancel{2}}}{3} \times \dfrac{5}{\underset{2}{\cancel{4}}} = \dfrac{5}{6}$

d. $3\dfrac{1}{8} \div 1\dfrac{3}{4} = \dfrac{25}{8} \div \dfrac{7}{4}$

$= \dfrac{25}{\underset{2}{\cancel{8}}} \times \dfrac{\overset{1}{\cancel{4}}}{7} = \dfrac{25}{14} = 1\dfrac{11}{14}$ ← Rewrite as a mixed number.

EXERCISES *On Your Own*

Multiply. Write the answers in simplest form.

1. $\dfrac{3}{4} \times \dfrac{3}{5}$
2. $\dfrac{2}{3} \times \dfrac{3}{4}$
3. $6 \times \dfrac{2}{3}$
4. $\dfrac{3}{4} \times \dfrac{5}{6}$
5. $\dfrac{5}{8} \times \dfrac{2}{3}$

6. $\dfrac{9}{16} \times \dfrac{2}{3}$
7. $\dfrac{3}{10} \times \dfrac{2}{15}$
8. $\dfrac{3}{4} \times \dfrac{1}{6}$
9. $\dfrac{1}{4} \times \dfrac{5}{20}$
10. $\dfrac{9}{10} \times \dfrac{1}{3}$

11. $1\dfrac{1}{3} \times 2\dfrac{2}{3}$
12. $\dfrac{3}{5} \times 2\dfrac{3}{4}$
13. $2\dfrac{1}{4} \times 3\dfrac{1}{3}$
14. $\dfrac{1}{4} \times 3\dfrac{1}{3}$

15. $6\dfrac{1}{4} \times 7$
16. $1\dfrac{3}{4} \times 2\dfrac{1}{5}$
17. $2\dfrac{3}{4} \times \dfrac{1}{2}$
18. $3\dfrac{4}{5} \times 2\dfrac{1}{3}$

Divide. Write the answers in simplest form.

19. $\dfrac{5}{8} \div \dfrac{5}{7}$
20. $\dfrac{5}{7} \div \dfrac{5}{8}$
21. $\dfrac{3}{4} \div \dfrac{6}{11}$
22. $\dfrac{1}{9} \div \dfrac{1}{9}$
23. $\dfrac{1}{9} \div 9$

24. $\dfrac{9}{10} \div \dfrac{3}{5}$
25. $\dfrac{2}{3} \div \dfrac{1}{9}$
26. $\dfrac{4}{5} \div \dfrac{5}{6}$
27. $\dfrac{1}{5} \div \dfrac{8}{9}$
28. $\dfrac{7}{8} \div \dfrac{1}{3}$

29. $4\dfrac{1}{5} \div 2\dfrac{2}{5}$
30. $6\dfrac{1}{4} \div 4\dfrac{3}{8}$
31. $2\dfrac{1}{3} \div 5\dfrac{5}{6}$
32. $1\dfrac{1}{2} \div 4\dfrac{1}{2}$

33. $15\dfrac{2}{3} \div 1\dfrac{1}{3}$
34. $10\dfrac{1}{3} \div 2\dfrac{1}{5}$
35. $6\dfrac{1}{4} \div 1\dfrac{3}{4}$
36. $6\dfrac{2}{3} \div 3\dfrac{1}{8}$

Working with Integers

Quantities less than zero can be written using negative integers. For example, a temperature of 5 degrees below zero can be written as −5. Positive integers are used for quantities greater than zero.

■ EXAMPLE 1

Write an integer for each situation.

   a. 10 degrees above zero   **b. a loss of $20**   **c. 15 yards lost**

     +10, or 10   −20   −15

A number line can be used to compare integers. The integer to the right is greater.

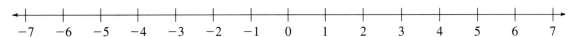

■ EXAMPLE 2

Compare. Use >, <, or =.

  a. 0 ■ −3   **b. −2 ■ −6**   **c. −7 ■ 3**

   0 is to the right, so   −2 is to the right,   −7 is to the left,
   it is greater.   so it is greater.   so it is less.
   0 > −3   −2 > −6   −7 < 3

EXERCISES *On Your Own*

Write an integer for each situation.

  1. 6 yards gained   **2.** 10 yards lost   **3.** 5 steps forward   **4.** 4 steps backward

  5. find $3   **6.** lose $8   **7.** 12 floors up   **8.** 4 floors down

Compare. Use >, <, or =.

  9. 0 ■ −1   **10.** −9 ■ 0   **11.** −3 ■ 3   **12.** 7 ■ −3   **13.** 0 ■ 1

  14. 3 ■ 0   **15.** 1 ■ −4   **16.** −2 ■ −9   **17.** 6 ■ −1   **18.** 3 ■ −10

  19. −7 ■ 3   **20.** 4 ■ 6   **21.** −16 ■ −25   **22.** −15 ■ −12   **23.** 7 ■ −8

  24. 2 ■ 3   **25.** −7 ■ −8   **26.** 35 ■ −40   **27.** −30 ■ −20   **28.** 25 ■ −25

  29. 9 ■ −9   **30.** −6 ■ −5   **31.** −23 ■ −15   **32.** −17 ■ −19   **33.** −15 ■ −25

Raising a Power to a Power

After Lesson 2-10

To raise a power to a power, think of the meaning of exponents. Study the following examples.

■ EXAMPLE

Simplify each expression.

a. $(2^4)^3 = 2^4 \cdot 2^4 \cdot 2^4$
$\qquad = 2^{4+4+4}$ ←── Follow the rule for multiplying. ──→
$\qquad = 2^{4 \cdot 3}$
$\qquad = 2^{12}$ ←── Simplify. ──→

b. $(x^7)^2 = x^7 \cdot x^7$
$\qquad = x^{7+7}$
$\qquad = x^{7 \cdot 2}$
$\qquad = x^{14}$

The examples above suggest the following rule:
To raise a number or variable with an exponent to a power, multiply the exponents.

Arithmetic	**Algebra**
$(4^3)^5 = 4^{3 \cdot 5} = 4^{15}$	$(a^m)^n = a^{mn}$

EXERCISES *On Your Own*

Simplify each expression.

1. $(d^6)^4$
2. $(3^3)^7$
3. $(9^2)^5$
4. $(h^4)^2$

5. $(y^3)^5$
6. $(4^3)^2$
7. $(7^9)^3$
8. $(v^7)^3$

9. $(p^6)^6$
10. $(b^4)^8$
11. $(5^2)^5$
12. $(8^3)^7$

13. $(2^5)^9$
14. $(6^3)^3$
15. $(x^{10})^3$
16. $(3^8)^3$

Write each expression using a single exponent.

17. $x \cdot (x^4)^4$
18. $3^3 \cdot (3^3)^3$
19. $(y \cdot y^4)^2 \cdot y^3$
20. $(m^3)^2 \cdot m^6$

21. $5^7 \cdot (5^4)^3$
22. $(8^2 \cdot 8^3)^2 \cdot 8^3$
23. $(6^5)^4 \cdot 6^{12}$
24. $k^{10} \cdot (k^6 \cdot k^2)^2$

Evaluate each expression for the given value.

25. $(w^2)^3$ for $w = 3$
26. $(a^4)^2$ for $a = 2$

27. $(h \cdot h^2)^3$ for $h = 2$
28. $(t^2)^2$ for $t = 4$

Compound Inequalities

Just as compound sentences use the words *and* and *or*, so do compound inequalities. Two inequalities joined by the word *and* or the word *or* are called **compound inequalities.**

A solution of a compound inequality joined by the word *and* is any number that makes both inequalities true. A solution of a compound inequality joined by the word *or* is any number that makes either inequality true.

$x \geq -1$ and $x < 4$

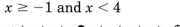

$x < -1$ or $x \geq 4$

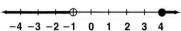

■ EXAMPLE 1

Graph the compound inequality on a number line.

a. $n > -8$ and $n \leq 2$

b. $r < -1$ or $r > 5$

c. $a > 0$ or $a < 3$

All numbers satisfy this compound inequality.

d. $b \leq -2$ and $b > 6$

No numbers satisfy this compound inequality.

■ EXAMPLE 2

a. Solve $n - 4 > -3$ or $3n \leq 0$. Graph the solution on a number line.

$$n - 4 > -3 \qquad \text{or} \qquad 3n \leq 0 \quad \longleftarrow \text{Solve each inequality.}$$

$$n - 4 + 4 > -3 + 4 \qquad \frac{3n}{3} \leq \frac{0}{3}$$

$$n > 1 \qquad \text{or} \qquad n \leq 0$$

The solution is $n > 1$ or $n \leq 0$.

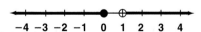

On the graph above, the solution is those values which satisfy *either* inequality, indicated by both parts of the graphs.

b. Solve $x + 3 < 9$ and $-5x \le -20$. Graph the solution on a number line.

$$x + 3 < 9 \qquad \text{and} \qquad -5x \le -20$$
$$x + 3 - 3 < 9 - 3 \qquad \qquad \left(-\tfrac{1}{5}\right)(-5x) \ge \left(-\tfrac{1}{5}\right)(-20) \quad \longleftarrow \quad \text{When you multiply by a}$$
$$x < 6 \qquad \text{and} \qquad x \ge 4 \qquad \qquad \text{negative number, reverse the}$$
direction of the inequality.

The solution is $x < 6$ and $x \ge 4$.

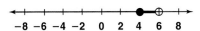

On the graph above, the solution is those values which satisfy *both* inequalities, indicated by those parts of the two graphs which overlap.

EXERCISES *On Your Own*

Graph the compound inequality on a number line.

1. $j < -3$ or $j \ge 2$ **2.** $b \le -6$ or $b > 0$ **3.** $m < 3$ and $m > -4$

4. $v > -3$ and $v \le 7$ **5.** $c \le 0$ or $c > -4$ **6.** $x \ge -9$ and $x < -5$

Write a compound inequality that each graph could represent.

7.

8.

9.

10.

Solve each inequality and graph the solutions on a number line.

11. $x + 7 < 4$ or $3x \ge 6$ **12.** $-\dfrac{1}{4}w > 1$ and $2w > -12$

13. $x - 7 > -5$ or $2x \le 6$ **14.** $3a \ge 15$ or $a + 4 < -4$

15. $5 + r > -3$ and $-6r \le 18$ **16.** $5 + k > 4$ or $4k \le -20$

17. $-3 \le 3h$ or $7h > 28$ **18.** $x - 9 > 0$ or $2x \le 8$

19. $d + 5 > 3$ and $\dfrac{1}{3}d < -2$ **20.** $x - 7 \ge 0$ or $x - 1 < 4$

21. $n - 6 > -5$ and $n + 3 < 6$ **22.** $j - 5 \ge -3$ and $-j > -4$

23. $-b < -8$ or $b + 2 \le -1$ **24.** $5m \ge 10$ and $3m \le 12$

Conversion Between Measurement Systems

After Lesson 6-2

When we measure anything we normally work within the metric system or the U.S. Customary system. For some tasks, however, it is convenient to know how to convert units from one system to the other.

The table at the right shows several common conversion factors between systems.

Conversion Factors
Length
1 in. = 2.54 cm
1 km ≈ 0.62 mi
Capacity
1 L ≈ 1.06 qt
Weight
1 oz ≈ 28 g
1 kg ≈ 2.2 lb

■ EXAMPLE 1

Use dimensional analysis to convert 17 in. to the nearest centimeter.

$$17 \text{ in.} = \frac{17 \text{ in.}}{1} \cdot \frac{2.54 \text{ cm}}{1 \text{ in.}}$$ ← Use $\frac{2.54 \text{ cm}}{1 \text{ in.}}$ since conversion is to centimeters. Cancel matching units.

$$= (17)(2.54) \text{ cm}$$ ← Simplify.

$$= 43.18 \text{ cm}$$ ← Multiply. Round to a whole number.

$$= 43 \text{ cm}$$

■ EXAMPLE 2

Use dimensional analysis to convert 13 qt to the nearest liter.

$$13 \text{ qt} \approx \frac{13 \text{ qt}}{1} \cdot \frac{1 \text{ L}}{1.06 \text{ qt}}$$ ← Multiply by $\frac{1 \text{ L}}{1.06 \text{ qt}}$ since conversion is to liters. Cancel matching units.

$$\approx \frac{13 \text{ L}}{1.06}$$ ← Simplify.

$$\approx 12 \text{ L}$$ ← Round to a whole number.

■ EXAMPLE 3

The school cafeteria buys cans of corn that weigh five lb each. How many grams per can is this?

$$5 \text{ lb} \approx \frac{5 \text{ lb}}{1} \cdot \frac{16 \text{ oz}}{1 \text{ lb}} \cdot \frac{28 \text{ g}}{1 \text{ oz}}$$ ← Convert pounds to ounces, then ounces to grams. Cancel matching units.

$$\approx (5)(16)(28) \text{ g}$$ ← Simplify.

$$\approx 2,240 \text{ g}$$

EXERCISES *On Your Own*

Use dimensional analysis to convert each measure. Round to the nearest unit.

1. 32 in. ≈ ■ cm

2. 700 g ≈ ■ oz

3. 3 km ≈ ■ mi

4. 66 cm ≈ ■ in.

5. 24 lb ≈ ■ kg

6. 42 oz ≈ ■ g

7. 15 kg ≈ ■ lb

8. 6 L ≈ ■ qt

9. 40 mi ≈ ■ km

10. 1,608 g ≈ ■ oz

11. 102 in. ≈ ■ cm

12. 14 qt ≈ ■ L

13. 8 ft = ■ cm

14. 2 mi ≈ ■ m

15. 10 gal ≈ ■ L

16. 60 lb ≈ ■ kg

17. 15.5 km ≈ ■ mi

18. 18 L ≈ ■ gal

Estimation **Which of the two measurements is greater?**

19. 300 km or 100 mi

20. 45 lb or 16 kg

21. 90 qt or 102 L

22. 35.2 oz or 800 g

23. 64 cm or 40 in.

24. 29.5 mi or 60,000 m

25. 1,000 L or 200 gal

26. 5 ft or 200 cm

27. 3,000 mL or 6 qt

28. 600 cm or 10 yd

29. *Distance* When the sign says, "Montreal, 483 km," about how many miles would you drive to get there?

30. *Analyze* At a hardware store, pipe is measured and separated into bins. If a pipe is 8 in. or longer, it goes into Bin A. If it is shorter than 8 in., it goes into Bin B. A customer needs a pipe that is 20 cm long. In which bin will it be found?

31. *Sports* Vadim moved from Europe to America. He said he was 188 cm tall. How many inches tall should the basketball program list for him?

32. *Baking* Amy's recipe for brownies calls for 448 g of chocolate chips. How many ounces of chocolate chips does she need?

33. *Recreation* A backyard swimming pool contains 8,600 gal of water. How many liters of water does the pool contain?

Taxes

Generally when people talk about taxes, they use the term *tax* to refer to the part, *rate* to refer to the percent, and *base* to refer to the item's price. So, a corresponding equation is **tax = rate · base.** You can use this equation in the problems that follow.

After Lesson 7-4

part = P · whole

tax = rate · base

■ EXAMPLE 1

Find the total cost of a $35 jacket if the sales tax is $6\frac{3}{4}$%.

$$\text{tax} = \text{rate} \cdot \text{base}$$ ⟵ Use the tax equation to find the sales tax.
$$t = 0.0675 \cdot 35$$ ⟵ Substitute. Let t = tax.
$$t = 2.36$$ ⟵ Multiply.

The sales tax is $2.36.
$35.00 + $2.36 = $37.36 ⟵ Add to find the total cost.

The total cost of the jacket is $37.36.

■ EXAMPLE 2

The sales tax on a $150 VCR is $12.75. Find the tax rate.

$$\text{tax} = \text{rate} \cdot \text{base}$$ ⟵ Use the tax equation.
$$12.75 = r \cdot 150$$ ⟵ Substitute. Let r = rate.
$$\frac{12.75}{150} = r$$ ⟵ Divide.
$$r = 0.085 = 8.5\%$$ ⟵ Change the decimal to a percent.

The tax rate is 8.5%.

■ EXAMPLE 3

Find the selling price of a sweater if the tax rate is 7% and the tax is $1.75.

$$\text{tax} = \text{rate} \cdot \text{base}$$ ⟵ Use the tax equation.
$$1.75 = 0.07 \cdot b$$ ⟵ Substitute. Let b = base.
$$\frac{1.75}{0.07} = b$$ ⟵ Divide.
$$b = 25$$

The selling price of the sweater is $25.

Real-estate taxes are based on the value of a home or property, as determined by an assessor. Usually there are four or more taxing bodies such as public schools or libraries that receive the taxes.

■ EXAMPLE 4

Find the total amount of real-estate taxes on a home with assessed valuation of $148,000 using the tax rates shown.

Figure each tax separately, or add the tax rates first.

$$0.02\% + 0.82\% + 0.18\% + 1.13\% + 0.12\% = 2.27\% = 0.0227$$
$$t = 0.0227 \cdot 148{,}000 = 3{,}359.6$$

The real-estate taxes are $3,359.60.

Taxing Body	Tax Rate
state	0.02%
county	0.82%
township	0.18%
school district	1.13%
library	0.12%

EXERCISES *On Your Own*

Find the missing amount(s).

	Item	Selling Price	Sales Tax Rate	Sales Tax	Total Cost
1.	bicycle	$200	7.5%	▦	▦
2.	TV	▦	6.25%	$16.25	▦
3.	car	$12,000	$5\frac{3}{4}\%$	▦	▦
4.	sofa	$375	▦	$30.00	▦
5.	groceries	$22.40	2.5%	▦	▦
6.	lamp	$60	▦	$3.75	▦
7.	boat	▦	$6\frac{3}{4}\%$	$573.75	▦
8.	watch	$119	4%	▦	▦
9.	camera	$349.99	▦	▦	$369.24
10.	CD	$14.50	▦	$.87	▦

Solve each problem.

11. *Government*   The state income tax in one state is 7.5%, while it is only 4.75% in a neighboring state. What is the difference in taxes on an annual taxable income of $32,000?

12. *Real Estate*   Taxes for a $16,000 vacant lot are levied as follows: state—0.025%, county—0.65%, township—0.24%, school district—1.4%, and library—0.15%.
a. Find the amount of tax for the school district.
b. Find the total amount of tax.

Glossary / Study Guide

A

Absolute value (p. 61) A number's distance from zero on the number line is called its absolute value. You write "the absolute value of -3" as $|-3|$.

The absolute value of -3 is 3 because -3 is 3 units from zero on the number line.

Acute angle (p. 290) An acute angle is any angle that measures less than $90°$.

Example: $0° < m\angle 1 < 90°$

Acute triangle (p. 398) An acute triangle is a triangle with three acute angles.

Example: $\angle 1$, $\angle 2$, and $\angle 3$ are acute.

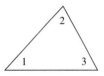

Addition Property of Equality (p. 121) If the same number is added to each side of an equation, the two sides remain equal.

If $a = b$, then $a + c = b + c$.

Additive inverses (p. 69) Two numbers whose sum equals zero are called additive inverses.

23 is the additive inverse of -23 because $-23 + 23 = 0$.

Adjacent angles (p. 379) Two angles that share a vertex and a side but have no common interior points are called adjacent angles.

Example: $\angle 1$ and $\angle 2$ are adjacent angles.

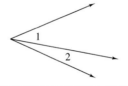

Alternate interior angles (p. 383) Pairs of nonadjacent angles, both interior, on opposite sides of the transversal, are called alternate interior angles.

Example: $\angle 2$ and $\angle 3$ are alternate interior angles. $\angle 1$ and $\angle 4$ are also alternate interior angles.

Angle (p. 290) An angle is made up of two rays with a common endpoint.

Example: $\angle 1$ is made up of $\overrightarrow{GP}$ and $\overrightarrow{GS}$ with common endpoint G.

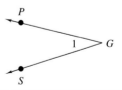

Area (p. 142) The area of a figure is the amount of space that it encloses.

Example: $\ell = 6$ ft, and $w = 4$ ft, so the area is 24 ft^2.

Each square equals 1 ft^2.

Examples

Arithmetic sequence (p. 482)   A sequence of numbers in which each term is the result of adding the same number (called the common difference) to the preceding term is called an arithmetic sequence.

The sequence 4, 10, 16, 23, 29, 35, . . . is an arithmetic sequence. The common difference is 6.

Associative Properties of Addition and Multiplication (p. 91)   Changing the grouping of the addends or factors does not change the sum or product.

$(a + b) + c = a + (b + c)$

$(a \cdot b) \cdot c = a \cdot (b \cdot c)$

B

Balance (p. 360)   The balance in an account is the principal plus the earned interest.

See *Compound interest, Simple interest.*

Bar graph (pp. 4, 5)   A bar graph compares amounts.

See *Stacked bar graph, Sliding bar graph.*

Base (p. 82)   When a number is written in exponential form, the repeated factor is the base.

$5^4 = 5 \cdot 5 \cdot 5 \cdot 5$
5 is the base.

Bases of two-dimensional figures (p. 412, 413, 142)   See *Parallelogram, Triangle,* and *Trapezoid.*

Bases of three-dimensional figures (p. 428)   See *Cone, Cylinder, Prism,* and *Pyramid.*

Base plan (p. 433)   A base plan shows the shape of the foundation and the height of each part of a three-dimensional figure.

Example: The first drawing is a base plan; the second is an isometric drawing using the base plan.

Biased question (p. 43)   A biased question is an unfair question worded so that one answer seems better than another.

"Do you like healthy food or junk food?"

Binomial (p. 530)   A binomial is a polynomial with two terms.

$3x^2 - 1$ is a binomial.

Box-and-whisker plot (p. 27)   A box-and-whisker plot shows the distribution of data in each quartile, that is, in each 25% of the data.

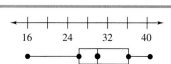

Example: The box-and-whisker plot uses these data: 16   19   26   26   27   29   30   31   34   34   38   39   40.

The lower quartile is 26. The median is 30.
The upper quartile is 36.

C

Central angle (p. 347) A central angle is an angle whose vertex is the center of the circle.

Example: In circle O, $\angle AOB$ is a central angle.

Circle (p. 347) A circle is the set of points in a plane that are all the same distance from a given point, called the center.

Example: Circle O

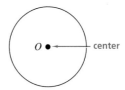

Circle graph (p. 37) A circle graph shows the parts of a whole. The total must be 100% or 1.

Example: This circle graph represents the different types of plays William Shakespeare wrote.

Shakespeare's Plays

Histories 26%
Tragedies 26%
Romances 13%
Comedies 35%

Circumference (p. 416) Circumference is the distance around a circle. You calculate the circumference of a circle by multiplying the diameter by π.

Example: The circumference of a circle with a diameter of 10 cm is approximately 31.4 cm.

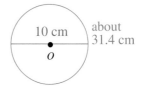

10 cm about 31.4 cm
O

Closed-option question (p. 43) A closed-option question for a survey has a limited number of choices.

Is your favorite juice orange juice or cranberry juice?

Coefficient (p. 525) The numerical factor in a term containing a variable.

In the expression $2x + 3y - 16$, 2 is the coefficient of x and 3 is the coefficient of y.

Combination (p. 548) A combination is a group of items in which the order of the items is *not* considered.

The combination (pots and pans) is the same as the combination (pans and pots).

Common difference (p. 485) See *Arithmetic sequence.*

Common ratio (p. 485) See *Geometric sequence.*

Commutative Properties of Addition and Multiplication (p. 91) Changing the order of the addends or factors does not change the sum or product.

$a + b = b + a$

$ab = ba$

Compass (p. 383) A compass is a geometric tool used to draw circles and arcs.

Glossary/Study Guide

Examples

Compatible numbers (p. 283) Compatible numbers are numbers close in value to the numbers you want to multiply or divide. Estimating products or quotients is easier when you use compatible numbers. Compatible numbers are easy to multiply or divide mentally.

Estimate $151 \div 14.6$.
$151 \approx 150$
$14.6 \approx 15$
$150 \div 15 = 10$
$151 \div 14.6 \approx 10$

Complement of an event (p. 556) The complement of an event is all the other possible events for that situation. The probability of an event plus the probability of its complement equals 1.

The event *no rain* is the complement of the event *rain*.

Complementary angles (p. 380) Two angles are complementary if the sum of their measures is 90°.

Example: ∠*BCA* and ∠*CAB* are complementary angles.

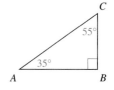

Composite number (p. 221) A whole number greater than 1 that has more than two factors is called a composite number.

24 is a composite number that has 1, 2, 3, 4, 6, 8, 12, and 24 as factors.

Compound inequality (p. 616) Two inequalities that are joined by *and* or *or*.

x > 2 and x < 4
x < −14 or x ≥ 3

Compound interest (p. 361) Compound interest is interest paid on both the principal and the interest earned in previous interest periods. You can use the formula $B = p(1 + r)^t$ where B is the balance in the account, p is the principal, r is the annual interest rate, and t is the time in years that the account earns interest.

You deposit $500 in an account earning 5% annual interest.
The balance after six years is $500(1 + 0.05)^6$ or $670.05.

Cone (p. 428) A cone is a space figure with one circular base and one vertex.

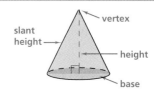

Congruent angles (p. 291) Angles that have the same measure are congruent.

Example: ∠*B* ≅ ∠*C*

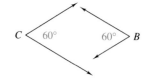

Congruent figures (p. 291) Figures that have the same size and shape are congruent. Congruent polygons have congruent corresponding sides and congruent corresponding angles.

Example: $\overline{AB} \cong \overline{QS}$, $\overline{CB} \cong \overline{RS}$ and $\overline{AC} \cong \overline{QR}$
$\angle A \cong \angle Q$, $\angle C \cong \angle R$, and $\angle B \cong \angle S$. Triangles ABC and QSR are congruent. $\triangle ABC \cong \triangle QSR$

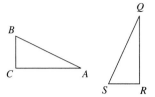

Congruent segments (p. 383) Segments that have the same length are congruent.

Example: $\overline{AB} \cong \overline{WX}$

Constant term (p. 523) A term that has no variable factor is a constant term.

In the expression $4x - 13y + 17$, 17 is the constant term.

Coordinate plane (p. 169) A coordinate plane is formed by the intersection of a horizontal number line called the x-axis and a vertical number line called the y-axis. The x- and y-axes divide the coordinate plane into four quadrants.

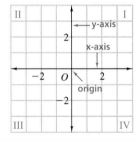

Coordinates (p. 168) Each point on the coordinate plane is identified by a unique ordered pair of numbers (x, y) called its coordinates. The x-coordinate (the first coordinate) tells how far from the origin to move along the x-axis. The y-coordinate (the second coordinate) tells how far from the origin to move along the y-axis.

Example: The ordered pair $(-2, 1)$ describes the point that is 2 units to the left of the y-axis and one unit above the x-axis.

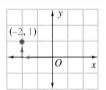

Corresponding angles (p. 388) Pairs of nonadjacent angles, one interior angle and one exterior angle, both on the same side of the transversal, are called corresponding angles.

Example: $\angle 1$ and $\angle 3$ are corresponding angles.
$\angle 2$ and $\angle 4$ are also corresponding angles.

Corresponding angles of polygons (p. 291) The matching angles of similar or congruent figures are corresponding angles.

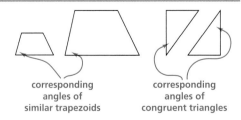

corresponding angles of similar trapezoids

corresponding angles of congruent triangles

Glossary/Study Guide

Examples

Corresponding sides of polygons (p. 291) The matching sides of similar or congruent figures are corresponding sides.

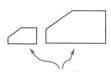

corresponding sides of similar polygons

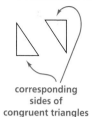

corresponding sides of congruent triangles

Cosine ratio (p. 317) In a right triangle, the cosine of an acute angle is the ratio of the length of the side adjacent to the angle to the length of the hypotenuse.

See *Trigonometric ratios.*

Counting principle (p. 541) The number of outcomes for an event is the product of the number of outcomes for each stage of the event.

Flip a coin and roll a number cube. The total number of possible outcomes is $2 \times 6 = 12$.

Cross products (p. 286) In a proportion, cross products are the product of the numerator of the first ratio and the denominator of the second ratio, as well as the product of the denominator of the first ratio and the numerator of the second ratio. These products are equal.

$\frac{3}{4} = \frac{6}{8}$

The cross products are $3 \cdot 8$ and $4 \cdot 6$.

$3 \cdot 8 = 24$ and $4 \cdot 6 = 24$

Cube (p. 440) A cube is rectangular prism with six square faces.

face

Cylinder (p. 428) A cylinder is a space figure with two circular, parallel, and congruent bases.

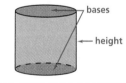

bases

height

D

Decagon (p. 401) A decagon is a polygon with ten sides.

See *Polygon.*

Dependent events (p. 560) Events are dependent if the outcome of the first event affects the outcome of the second event.

When a marble is drawn from a bag containing red and blue marbles, and not returned, the events (red, then blue) are dependent.

Diagonal (p. 401) A diagonal of a polygon is a segment that connects two vertices that are not next to each other.

Example: $\overline{BD}$ is a diagonal of quadrilateral *ABCD*.

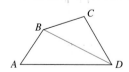

Examples

Diameter (p. 416) A diameter is a segment that passes through the center of a circle and has both endpoints on the circle.

Example: $\overline{RS}$ is a diameter of circle O.

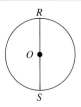

Dilation (p. 296) A dilation is a similarity transformation with a center and a scale factor. The scale factor r describes the size of the change from the original figure to its image. If $r > 1$, the dilation is an enlargement. If $r < 1$, the dilation is a reduction.

Example: The blue triangle is an enlargement of the red triangle. The red triangle is a reduction of the blue triangle.

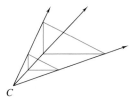

Dimensional analysis (p. 282) Dimensional analysis is the conversion of units of measure by multiplying by a ratio equal to 1.

$0.5 \text{ mi} = \frac{0.5 \text{ mi}}{1} \times \frac{5280 \text{ ft}}{1 \text{ mi}} = 2{,}640 \text{ ft}$

Discount (p. 356) The amount a price is reduced is called the discount.

A $10 book is reduced by 15%. The discount is $1.50.

Distributive property (p. 93) If a, b, and c are any numbers, then $a(b + c) = ab + ac$ and $a(b - c) = ab - ac$.

$2(3 + \frac{1}{2}) = 2 \cdot 3 + 2 \cdot \frac{1}{2}$
$8(5 - 3) = 8(5) - 8(3)$

Divisible (p. 220) One number is divisible by another number if the second number divides into the first with no remainder.

15 and 20 are both divisible by 5, because $15 \div 5 = 3$ and $20 \div 5 = 4$.

Division Property of Equality (p. 126) If both sides of an equation are divided by the same nonzero number, the two sides remain equal.

If $a = b$ and $c \neq 0$, then $\frac{a}{c} = \frac{b}{c}$.

E

Edge (p. 428) The intersection of two faces of a polyhedron is called an edge.

See *Polyhedron*.

Enlargement (p. 298) An enlargement is a dilation with scale factor greater than 1.

See *Dilation*.

Equation (p. 120) A mathematical sentence that contains an equal sign, =, is an equation. The left side of the equal sign has the same value as the right side.

$2(6 + 17) = 46$

Examples

Equilateral triangle (p. 398) An equilateral triangle is a triangle with three congruent sides.

Example: $\overline{SL} \cong \overline{LW} \cong \overline{WS}$

Evaluate an expression (p. 65) To evaluate an expression, replace each variable with a number. Then follow the order of operations.

To evaluate the expression $3x + 2$ for $x = 4$, substitute 4 for x.

$3x + 2 = 3(4) + 2 = 12 + 2 = 14$

Event (p. 49) An event is a result or several results of an experiment.

In a game that includes tossing a coin and rolling a standard number cube, "heads and a 2" is an event.

Experimental probability (p. 554) You find the experimental probability of an event by repeating an experiment many times and using this ratio.

$$P(\text{event}) = \frac{\text{number of times an event happens}}{\text{number of times the experiment is done}}$$

Suppose a basketball player makes 19 baskets in 28 attempts. The experimental probability that she makes a basket is $\frac{19}{28} \approx 68\%$.

Exponent (p. 82) An exponent expresses how many times a base is used as a factor.

$3^4 = 3 \cdot 3 \cdot 3 \cdot 3$

F

Face (p. 428) A surface of a polyhedron is called a face.

See *Polyhedron*.

Factor (p. 220) One number is a factor of a second number if it divides that number with no remainder.

1, 2, 3, 4, 6, 9, 12, and 36 are factors of 36.

Factorial notation (p. 545) The expression $n!$ is the product of all natural numbers starting with n and counting backward to 1.

$5! = 5 \cdot 4 \cdot 3 \cdot 2 \cdot 1$

Fair game (p. 570) A game is fair if the players are equally likely to win.

Tossing a coin is a fair game, since heads and tails are equally likely to appear.

Formula (p. 142) A formula is a statement of a mathematical relationship.

The formula $P = 4s$ gives the perimeter of a square in terms of a side, s.

Frequency table (p. 14) A frequency table lists items together with the number of times, or frequency, that they occur.

Example: This frequency table shows the number of household telephones for a class of students.

Household Telephones

Phones	Tally	Frequency
1	ЖⅢ Ⅲ	8
2	ЖⅢ Ⅰ	6
3	ⅢⅠ	4

Front-end estimation (p. 19)   You can use front-end estimation to estimate a sum. First add the front-end digits. Then adjust by estimating the sum of the remaining digits. Add the two values.

Estimate $3.49 + $2.29.

$3 + 2 = 5$

$0.49 + 0.29 \approx 1$

$\$3.49 + \$2.29 \approx \$5 + \$1 = \$6$

Function (p. 490)   A function is a relationship in which each member of one set is paired with exactly one member of a second set. It describes the relationship between two variables called the input and the output.

Earned income is a function of the number of hours worked (w). If you earn $5/h, then your income is expressed by the function $f(w) = 5w$.

G

Geometric sequence (p. 485)   A sequence of numbers in which each term is the result of multiplying the preceding term by the same number (called the common ratio) is called a geometric sequence.

The sequence 1, 3, 9, 27, 81, . . . is a geometric sequence. The common ratio is 3.

Greatest possible error (p. 447)   The greatest possible error of a measurement is half the unit of measure to which the measurement has been rounded.

The measurement 400 kg is rounded to the nearest hundred kilograms. So, the greatest possible error is 50 kg.

Greatest common factor (GCF) (p. 222)   The number that is the greatest factor of two or more numbers is the greatest common factor (GCF).

The greatest common factor (GCF) of 12 is 30 and 6.

H

Height of two-dimensional figures (pp. 142, 411)
See *Parallelogram, Triangle,* and *Trapezoid.*

Height of three-dimensional figures (p. 449)
See *Cylinder* and *Prism.*

Heptagon (p. 401)   A heptagon is a polygon with seven sides.

See *Polygon.*

Hexagon (p. 401)   A hexagon is a polygon with six sides.

See *Polygon.*

Histogram (p. 16)   A histogram is a bar graph used to show the frequency of data. There are no spaces between bars and the height of each bar gives the frequency of the data.

Example: This histogram gives the frequency of board game purchases at a local toy store.

Board Game Purchases

Examples

Hypotenuse (p. 263) In a right triangle, the hypotenuse is the side opposite the right angle.

See *Right triangle*.

I

Identity Properties of Addition and Multiplication (p. 91) The sum of any number a and 0 is a. The product of 1 and any number a is a.

$a + 0 = a$
$a(1) = a$

Image (p. 198) A point, line, or figure that has been transformed to a new set of coordinates is the image of the original point, line, or figure.

See *Transformation*.

Improper fraction (p. 225) An improper fraction has a numerator that is greater than or equal to the denominator.

$\frac{24}{15}$ and $\frac{16}{16}$ are improper fractions.

Independent events (p. 559) Events are independent if the outcome of one event does not affect the outcome of a second event.

When a number cube is rolled twice, the events (6, then 3) are independent.

Indirect measurement (p. 309) Indirect measurement is a method of determining length or distance when direct measurement is impossible.

Example: By using the distances shown in the diagram and using properties of similar figures, you can find the height of the taller tower.

$\frac{240}{540} = \frac{x}{1,192} \rightarrow x \approx 530$ ft

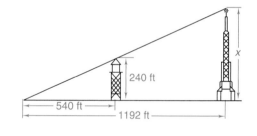

Inequality (p. 147) An inequality is a comparison of two expressions that uses one of the symbols $<$, $\leq$, $>$, or $\geq$.

$0 \leq 2, k > -3, 10 < t$

Integer (p. 60) The integers are the set of whole numbers and their opposites.

The numbers $-45, 0$, and 289 are all integers.

Interest (p. 360) See *Compound interest, Simple interest*.

Irrational number (p. 259) A number that is represented by a nonrepeating, nonterminating decimal is called an irrational number.

The number π, 3.141592653 . . . , is an irrational number.

Isosceles triangle (p. 398) An isosceles triangle is a triangle with at least two congruent sides.
Example: $\overline{LM} \cong \overline{LB}$
$\triangle MLB$ is an isosceles triangle.

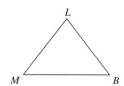

K

Examples

Key (p. 4)   A key or legend identifies categories in a graph.

Example: You can use the key of this graph to find the number of boys and girls in grades 6, 7, and 8.

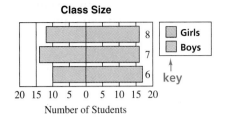

L

Least common denominator (LCD) (p. 235)   The least common denominator of two or more fractions is the least common multiple (LCM) of their denominators.

The least common denominator (LCD) for the fractions $\frac{3}{8}$ and $\frac{7}{10}$ is $2 \cdot 2 \cdot 2 \cdot 5$, or 40.

Least common multiple (LCM) (p. 234)   The least number that is a common multiple of two or more numbers is the least common multiple (LCM).

The least common multiple (LCM) of 15 and 6 is 30.

Legs of a right triangle (p. 263)   The two shorter sides of a right triangle form a right angle and are called the legs of the triangle.

See *Right triangle.*

Like terms (p. 117)   Terms with the same variable(s), raised to the same power, are like terms.

Example: $3b$ and $12b$ are like terms. Like terms can be combined using the distributive property:

$$3b + 12b = 3 \cdot b + 12 \cdot b$$
$$= (3 + 12)b$$
$$= 15b$$

Line graph (p. 6)   A line graph shows changes over time.

Example: This line graph shows the amount of time a student spends reading each night for a week.

Example: This multiple line graph represents seasonal air conditioner and snow blower sales (in thousands) for a large chain of stores.

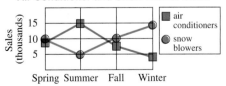

Line of reflection (p. 204)   A line over which a figure is reflected is a line of reflection.

See *Reflection.*

Glossary/Study Guide

Line of symmetry (p. 206)   When the reflection of a figure coincides with the original figure, the line of reflection is a line of symmetry.

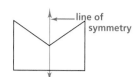

Line plot (p. 14)   A line plot shows data on a number line by placing an $\times$ for each response above the category of the response.

Example: The line plot shows the heights in inches of a classroom of girls.

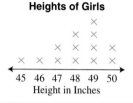

Linear equation (p. 174)   An equation is a linear equation when the graph of all of its solutions lies on a line.

Example: $y = \frac{1}{2}x + 3$ is linear because the graph of its solutions lies on a line.

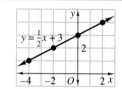

Linear function (p. 496)   A linear function is a function whose points lie on a line.

Example: $f(x) = \frac{1}{2}x + 2$ is a linear function.

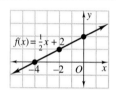

Lower quartile (p. 27)   The lower quartile is the median of the lower half of a data set.

See *Box-and-whisker plot*.

M

Mean (p. 20)   The mean of a set of numbers is the sum of the numbers divided by the number of data items.

The mean temperature (°F) for the set of temperatures 44, 52, 48, 55, 61, 67 and 58:

$$\frac{44 + 52 + 48 + 55 + 61 + 67 + 58}{7} = 55°F$$

Measures of central tendency (p. 20)   The statistics mean, median, and mode are measures of central tendency.

See *Mean*, *Median*, and *Mode*.

Median (p. 20)   The median is the middle number in a set of ordered data. If there is an even number of data items, the median is the mean of the two middle items.

Temperatures (°F) for one week arranged in numerical order are 44, 48, 52, 55, 58, 61, and 67. 55 is the median because it is the middle number in the set of data.

Mixed number (p. 225)   A mixed number shows the sum of a whole number and a fraction.

$3\frac{11}{16}$ is a mixed number.
$3\frac{11}{16} = 3 + \frac{11}{16}$

Mode (p. 20)   The mode of a set of numbers is the data item that occurs the most often.

The mode of the set of prices $2.50, $3.75, $3.60, $2.75, $2.75, and $3.70 is $2.75.

Monomial (p. 530)   A polynomial that has only one term is a monomial.

$5x$, -4, y^3 are all monomials.

Multiple (p. 234)   A multiple of a number is the product of that number and any nonzero whole number.

The multiples of 13 are 13, 26, 39, 52, and so on.

Multiple line graph (p. 6)   A multiple line graph shows more than one category changing over time.

See *Line graph.*

Multiplication Property of Equality (p. 128)   If each side of an equation is multiplied by the same number, the two sides remain equal.

If $a = b$, then $a \cdot c = b \cdot c$.

Multiplicative inverse (p. 309)   The reciprocal of a number is also called its multiplicative inverse.

The multiplicative inverse of $\frac{4}{9}$ is $\frac{9}{4}$.

N

Net (p. 438)   A net is a pattern that can be folded to form a space figure.
Example: This net can be folded to make a cube.

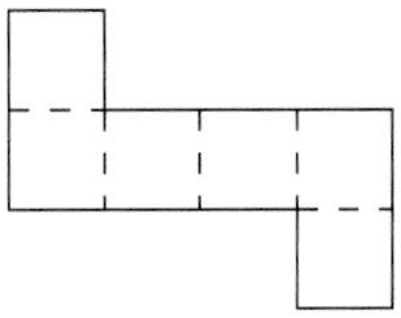

Nonagon (p. 401)   A nonagon is a polygon with nine sides.

See *Polygon.*

O

Obtuse angle (p. 290)   An obtuse angle has measure greater than 90° but less than 180°.

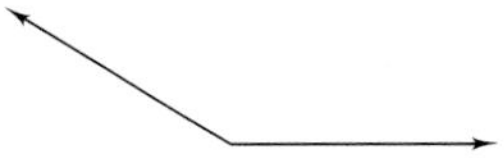

Obtuse triangle (p. 398)   An obtuse triangle is a triangle with one obtuse angle.
Example: $\triangle NJX$ is an obtuse triangle, since $\angle J$ is an obtuse angle.

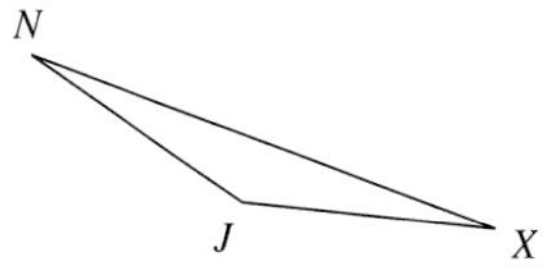

Octagon (p. 401)   An octagon is a polygon with eight sides.

See *Polygon.*

Open-option question (p. 43)   An open-option question for a survey allows free responses.

What is your favorite color?

Opposites (p. 60)   Numbers that are the same distance from zero on the number line but in opposite directions are opposite numbers.

-17 and 17 are opposite numbers because they are both 17 units from zero on the number line.

Glossary/Study Guide

Examples

Order of operations (p. 65)
1. Do all operations within parentheses.
2. Do all work with exponents.
3. Multiply and divide in order from left to right.
4. Add and subtract in order from left to right.

$2^3(7 - 4) = 2^3(3) = 8 \cdot 3 = 24$

Ordered pair (p. 169)   An ordered pair is a pair of numbers that describe the location of a point on a coordinate plane. The first value is called the x-coordinate and the second value is called the y-coordinate.

See *Coordinates.*

Origin (p. 169)   The intersection of the axes is called the origin. The ordered pair that describes the origin is $(0, 0)$.

See *Coordinate plane.*

Outcomes (p. 49)   Outcomes are the possible results or consequences of an action.

See *Probability of an event.*

Outlier (p. 22)   An item of data that is much higher or lower than the rest of the data is an outlier.

An outlier in the list 1, 1, 2, 3, 4, 4, 6, 7, 7, 52 is 52.

P

Parabola (p. 512)   A parabola is a U-shaped graph of an equation like $y = x^2 - 2$.

Example: This parabola is the graph of the equation $y = x^2 - 2$.

Parallel lines (p. 386)   Parallel lines are lines in the same plane that do not intersect. Parallel segments are segments of parallel lines.

$\overleftrightarrow{EF} \parallel \overleftrightarrow{HI}$

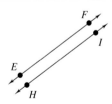

Parallelogram (p. 397)   A parallelogram is a quadrilateral with two pairs of opposite sides parallel.

Example: $KVDA$ is a parallelogram.
$\overline{KV} \parallel \overline{AD}$ and $\overline{AK} \parallel \overline{DV}$.

Pentagon (p. 401)   A pentagon is a polygon with five sides.

See *Polygon.*

Percent (p. 329)   A percent is a ratio that compares a number to 100. The symbol for percent is %.

$\frac{50}{100} = 50\%$

Percent of change (p. 351)   Percent of change is the percent something increases or decreases from its original measure or amount.

If a school's population increased from 500 to 520 students, the percent of change would be $\frac{520 - 500}{500} = 4\%$.

Perfect square (p. 258)   The square of a whole number is a perfect square.

$3^2 = 9$. The number 9 is a perfect square.

Perimeter (p. 142)   The perimeter of a figure is the distance around it. To find the perimeter of a polygon, find the sum of the lengths of all its sides.

Example: The perimeter of *ABCD* is 12 ft.

Permutation (p. 544)   A permutation is an arrangement of a set of objects in a particular order. You can use the notation $_nP_r$ to express the number of permutations of n objects chosen r at a time.

The seating plans (Judith, Ann, Adrian) and (Ann, Judith, Adrian) are two different permutations.

Perpendicular lines (p. 204)   Perpendicular lines are lines that intersect to form right angles.

$\overleftrightarrow{DE} \perp \overleftrightarrow{RS}$

Pi (p. 416)   Pi (π) is the special name for the ratio of the circumference, C, to the diameter, d, of a circle.

$\pi = \dfrac{C}{d}$

Polygon (p. 291)   A polygon is a closed plane figure with at least three sides, each of which is a segment.

Polyhedron (p. 429)   A space figure whose faces are all polygons is called a polyhedron.

Polynomial (p. 523)   A polynomial is one term or the sum or difference of two or more terms.

$4x^2 - 3x + 7$ is a polynomial.

Population (p. 42)   A population is any group of objects or people.

See *Sample*.

Power (p. 82)   Any expression in the form a^n is a power.

5^4 and x^2 are both powers.

Glossary/Study Guide

Examples

Precision in measurement (p. 442) The precision of a number refers to its degree of exactness. A measurement cannot be more precise than the precision of the measuring tool used.

A ruler divided into centimeters cannot be used to measure in millimeters.

Prime factorization (p. 221) Writing a composite number as the product of its prime factors is called prime factorization.

The prime factorization of 30 is $2 \cdot 3 \cdot 5$.

Prime number (p. 221) A whole number greater than 1 that has exactly two factors, 1 and the number itself, is a prime number.

13 is a prime number because its only factors are 1 and 13.

Principal (p. 360) Your original deposit in an account is your principal.

See *Simple interest.*

Prism (p. 428) A prism is a space figure with two parallel and congruent polygonal faces, called bases. A prism is named by the shape of its base.

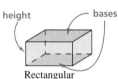
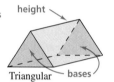

Rectangular   Triangular

Probability of an event (p. 49) When all outcomes are equally likely, the probability that an event E will happen is

$P(E) = \dfrac{\text{number of favorable outcomes}}{\text{number of possible outcomes}}$.

The probability of getting a 4 on a number cube is $\frac{1}{6}$.

Proportion (p. 286) A proportion is an equation stating that two ratios are equal.

$\frac{3}{12} = \frac{12}{48}$ is a proportion.

Pyramid (p. 428) A pyramid is a space figure with triangular faces that meet at one point and a base that is a polygon. A pyramid is named for the shape of its base.

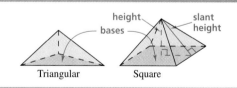

Triangular   Square

Pythagorean theorem (p. 264) In any right triangle, the sum of the squares of the lengths of the legs (a and b) is equal to the square of the length of the hypotenuse (c): $a^2 + b^2 = c^2$.

Example: The right triangle shown has legs 3 and 4 and hypotenuse 5, so $3^2 + 4^2 = 5^2$.

Q

Quadrants (p. 169) The x- and y-axes divide the coordinate plane into four regions, called quadrants.

See *Coordinate plane.*

Examples

Quadratic function (p. 512) In a quadratic function, the greatest power of the variable is 2. The graph of a quadratic function is a U-shaped curve.

$f(x) = -\frac{1}{2}x^2 + 2x$

Quadrilateral (p. 397) A quadrilateral is a polygon with four sides.

See *Polygon*.

Quartiles (p. 27) Quartiles divide a data set into four equal parts.

See *Box-and-whisker plot*.

R

Radius (plural is radii) (p. 416) A radius is any segment with one endpoint at the center and the other endpoint on the circle.

Example: $\overline{OA}$ is a radius of circle O.

Random sample (p. 42) If each member of a population has an equal chance of being chosen for a sample, then the sample is a random sample.

For the population "customers at a mall," a random sample would be every 20th customer at each entrance for a 2-hour period.

Range (p. 25) The range of a set of numerical data is the difference between the greatest and least values in the set.

A group of students spent the following number of hours a week exercising: 7 9 15 3 18 2 16 14 14 20.

The range of the data is $20 - 2 = 18$.

Rate (p. 277) A rate is a ratio that compares two quantities measured in different units.

A student typed 1,100 words in 50 min. The student's typing rate is 1,100 words per 50 min, or 22 words/min.

Ratio (p. 276) A ratio is a comparison of two numbers by division.

You can write a ratio three different ways: 72 to 100, 72 : 100, and $\frac{72}{100}$.

Rational number (p. 225) A rational number is a number that can be written in the form $\frac{a}{b}$ where a is an integer and b is any nonzero integer.

$\frac{3}{5}$, -8, 8.7, 0.333 . . . , $-5\frac{3}{11}$, 0, and $\frac{17}{4}$ are all rational numbers.

Ray (p. 290) A ray is a part of a line. It consists of one endpoint and all the points of the line on one side of the endpoint.

$\overrightarrow{SW}$ represents a ray.

— endpoint of $\overrightarrow{SW}$

Real number (p. 260) The rational numbers and irrational numbers together form the set of real numbers.

3, -5.25, 3.141592653 . . . , and $\frac{7}{8}$ are real numbers.

Glossary/Study Guide

Examples

Reciprocal (p. 250) Two numbers whose product is 1 are called reciprocals.

$-\frac{4}{9}$ and $-\frac{9}{4}$ are reciprocals.

$-\frac{4}{9} \cdot \left(-\frac{9}{4}\right) = 1$

Rectangle (p. 397) A rectangle is a parallelogram with four right angles.

$RSWH$ is a rectangle.

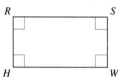

Reduction (p. 298) A dilation with a scale factor less than 1 is called a reduction.

See *Dilation*.

Reflection (p. 204) A reflection flips a figure across a line. The line is called the line of reflection.

Example: $K'L'M'N'$ is a reflection of $KLMN$ over the y-axis. The y-axis is the line of reflection.

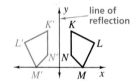

Reflectional symmetry (p. 206) A figure has reflectional symmetry if it can be reflected over a line so that its image matches the original figure. The line is called the line of symmetry.

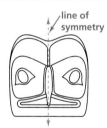

Regular polygon (p. 402) A regular polygon is a polygon with all its sides congruent and all its angles congruent.

Example: $ABDFEC$ is a regular hexagon.

Repeating decimal (p. 229) A repeating decimal is a nonterminating decimal in which a digit or a sequence of digits keeps repeating. The symbol for a repeating decimal is a bar over the digit or digits that repeat.

$0.8888 \ldots$, or $0.\overline{8}$

Rhombus (p. 397) A rhombus is a parallelogram with four congruent sides.

Example: $GHJI$ is a rhombus.
$GH = HJ = IJ = GI$

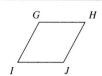

Right angle (p. 290)   A right angle is an angle with a measure of 90°.

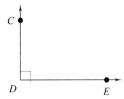

Right triangle (p. 398)   A right triangle is a triangle with one right angle.

Example: △*ABC* is a right triangle, since ∠*B* is a right angle.

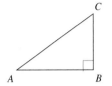

Rotation (p. 209)   A rotation is a transformation that turns a figure about a fixed point, called the center of rotation.

Example: The image of △*STR* after a 180° rotation about the origin is △*S'T'R'*. The origin is the center of rotation.

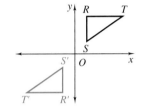

Rotational symmetry (p. 210)   A figure has rotational symmetry when an image after a rotation of 180° or less fits exactly on top of the original figure.

Example: This figure has a 60° rotational symmetry.

S

Sample (p. 42)   A sample is a small subset of the population, which is any collection of objects. A random sample is a sample in which each object in the population has an equal chance of being selected. The number of objects in the sample is called the sample size.

A class of 25 students is a sample of a school population. The sample size is 25.

Sample space (p. 50)   The set of all possible outcomes of a situation is called the sample space.

The sample space for tossing two coins is HH, HT, TH, TT.

Scale factor (p. 296)   The scale factor of a dilation describes the size of the change from the original figure to its image.

Example: This dilation has center *C* and scale factor 3.

Scale model (p. 302)   A scale model represents an actual object.

A map is a two-dimensional scale model.

Glossary/Study Guide

Scalene triangle (p. 398)   A scalene triangle is a triangle with no congruent sides.

Example: △*NPO* is a scalene triangle.

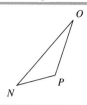

Scatter plot (p. 32)   A scatter plot displays data from two sets as ordered pairs.

Example: The scatter plot displays the amount various companies spent on advertising (in dollars) versus product sales (in thousands of dollars).

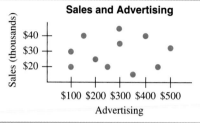

Scientific notation (p. 103)   A number is expressed in scientific notation when it is written as the product of a number greater than or equal to 1 and less than 10, and a power of 10.

37,000,000 is written as 3.7×10^7 in scientific notation.

Segment (p. 383)   A segment is part of a line. It consists of two points, called endpoints, and all the points on the line that are between the two points.

$\overline{CB}$ represents a segment.

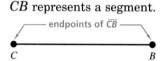

Sequence (p. 484)   A sequence is a set of numbers that follows a pattern. Each number in a sequence is a term of the sequence.

2, 2.3, 2.34, 2.345, . . .

Side (pp. 290, 291)   See *Angle, Polygon*.

Significant digits (p. 444)   Significant digits are digits that represent an actual measurement.

Similar polygons (p. 291)   Polygons whose corresponding angles are congruent and the length of whose corresponding sides have equal ratios are similar polygons.

Example: △*ABC* ∼ △*RTS*

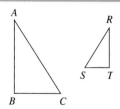

Simple interest (p. 360)   Simple interest is interest calculated on the principal, the initial amount of money invested or borrowed.

The simple interest on $1,000 at 5% for 2 years is $100.

The balance after 2 years is $1,000 plus $100 or $1,100.

Simplest form of a fraction (p. 225)   A fraction is in simplest form when the only factor common to both the numerator and the denominator is 1.

$\frac{3}{4}$ is the simplest form of the fraction $\frac{15}{20}$.

Simulation (p. 570)   A simulation is a model of a real-world situation.

A baseball team has an equal chance of winning or losing its next game. You can toss a coin to simulate the situation.

Sine ratio (p. 31)   In a right triangle, the sine of an acute angle is the ratio of the length of the side opposite the angle to the length of the hypotenuse.

See *Trigonometric ratios.*

Skew lines (p. 429)   Skew lines are lines in space that do not intersect and are not parallel.

$\overline{AH}$ and $\overline{CD}$ are skew lines.

Slant height (p. 453)   See *Cone, Pyramid.*

Sliding bar graph (p. 5)   A sliding bar graph displays two categories as bars graphed in opposite directions. Sliding bar graphs can be used to compare amounts or frequencies.

Example: The sliding bar graph represents class sizes for grades 6, 7, and 8 for both boys and girls.

Class Size

Girls
Boys

20 15 10 5   0   5   10 15 20
Number of Students

Slope (pp. 176, 177)   Slope is a number that describes the steepness of a line. Slope $= \dfrac{\text{rise}}{\text{run}} = \dfrac{\text{vertical change}}{\text{horizontal change}}$

Example: The slope of the given line $= \dfrac{2}{4} = \dfrac{1}{2}.$

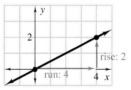

Slope-intercept form of an equation (p. 182)   The slope-intercept form of an equation is $y = mx + b$ where m is the slope and b is the y-intercept of the line.

The equation $y = 2x + 1$ is written in slope-intercept form with $m = 2$ and $b = 1.$

Solution (pp. 120, 147, 172)   A solution is any value or values that make an equation or an inequality true.

4 is the solution of $x + 5 = 9.$

$(8, 4)$ is a solution of $y = -x + 12$ because $4 = -(8) + 12.$

-4 is a solution of $2x < -3,$ because $2 \cdot -4 < -3.$

$(-1, 3)$ is a solution of $y > x - 4,$ because $3 > -1 - 4.$

Space figures (p. 428) Three-dimensional figures are called space figures or solids.

Example: A cylinder, a cone, and a prism are all space figures.

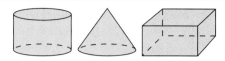

Sphere (p. 430) A sphere is the set of all points in space that are the same distance from a given point called the center.

Square (p. 397) A square is a parallelogram with four right angles and four congruent sides.

Example: $QRTS$ is a square.
$\angle Q$, $\angle R$, $\angle T$, and $\angle S$ are right angles.
$QR = RT = TS = SQ$

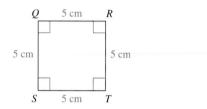

Square root (p. 258) The square root of a number is a number that when multiplied by itself equals the given number. The symbol for a square root is $\sqrt{\ }$.

$\sqrt{25} = 5$ because $5^2 = 25$.

Stacked bar graph (p. 4) A stacked bar graph has bars divided into categories. Each bar represents a total. Stacked bar graphs can be used to compare amounts or frequencies.

Example: This stacked bar graph represents class sizes for grades 6, 7, and 8.

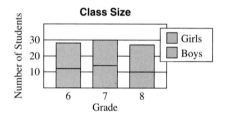

Stem-and-leaf plot (p. 24) A display that shows data in order of place value is a stem-and-leaf plot. A leaf is a data item's last digit on the right. A stem represents the digits to the left of the leaf.

Example: This stem-and-leaf plot displays recorded times in a race. The stem records the whole number of seconds. The leaves represent tenths of a second. So, 27 | 7 represents 27.7 seconds.

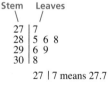

Subtraction Property of Equality (p. 120) If the same number is subtracted from each side of an equation, the two sides remain equal.

If $a = b$, then $a - c = b - c$.

Supplementary angles (p. 380) Two angles are supplementary if the sum of their measures is 180°.

Example: $\angle A$ and $\angle D$ are supplementary.

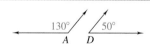

Surface area (pp. 448, 449, 453, 455, 458, 465)   The surface area of a space figure is the number of square units that covers the outside surface of the figure.

Example: The surface area of a prism is the sum of the areas of the faces.
$$4 \cdot 12 + 2 \cdot 9 = 66 \text{ in.}^2$$

Each square $= 1 \text{ in.}^2$

Symmetry (p. 206)   A figure is symmetrical when one side of a figure is the mirror image of the other side.

See *Reflectional symmetry, Rotational symmetry*.

 T

Tangent ratio (p. 313)   In a right triangle, the tangent of an angle is the ratio of the length of the side opposite the angle to the length of the side adjacent to the angle.

See *Trigonometric ratios*.

Term (p. 117)   A term is a number, a variable, or the product of a number and a variable.

The expression $7x + 12 + (-9y)$ has three terms: $7x$, 12, and $-9y$.

Terminating decimal (p. 229)   A terminating decimal is a decimal that stops, or terminates.

Both 0.6 and 0.7265 are terminating decimals.

Tessellation (p. 407)   A tessellation is a repeated geometric design that covers a plane without gaps or overlaps.

Example: This tessellation consists of small and large squares.

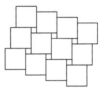

Theoretical probability (p. 555)   Theoretical probability describes how likely it is that an event will happen based on all the possible outcomes. The ratio for the probability of an event occurring is P(event).

$$P(\text{event}) = \frac{\text{number of favorable outcomes}}{\text{number of possible outcomes}}$$

The probability of spinning the number 4 is $\frac{1}{8}$.

Three-dimensional figures (p. 428)   Figures, such as buildings, that do not lie in a plane are three dimensional. The dimensions are length, width, and height.

See *Space figures*.

Transformation (p. 198)   A transformation is a change of position, shape, or size of a figure. Four types of transformations are dilations, translations, reflections, and rotations.

Example: $K'L'M'N'$ is a reflection of $KLMN$ over the y-axis.

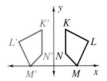

Glossary/Study Guide

Translation (p. 198)   A translation slides a figure.

Example: $A'B'C'D'$ is the image of $ABCD$ after a translation.

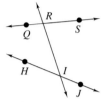

Transversal (p. 386)   A transversal is a line that intersects two other coplanar lines in different points.

Example: $\overleftrightarrow{RI}$ is a transversal of $\overleftrightarrow{QS}$ and $\overleftrightarrow{HJ}$.

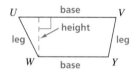

Trapezoid (p. 397)   A trapezoid is a quadrilateral with exactly one pair of parallel sides.

Example: $UVYW$ is a trapezoid.
   $\overleftrightarrow{UV} \parallel \overleftrightarrow{WY}$.

Tree diagram (p. 540)   A tree diagram displays all the possible outcomes of an event.

Example: There are 4 possible outcomes for tossing 2 coins: HH, HT, TH, TT.

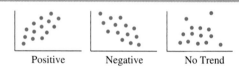

Trend (p. 34)   Two sets of related data show a positive trend if, in general, as the values of one set of data increase, the values of the other set increase also. Two sets of related data show a negative trend if, in general, as the values of one set increase, the values of the other set decrease. Two sets of data show little or no trend if the data show no relationship.

Trend line (p. 33)   A line that closely fits the data points in a scatter plot is a trend line.

Triangle (p. 391)   A triangle is a polygon with three sides.   See *Polygon.*

Trigonometric ratios (p. 317)   In $\triangle ABC$ with right $\angle C$,

$$\cos A = \frac{\text{length of leg adjacent to } \angle A}{\text{hypotenuse}},$$

$$\sin A = \frac{\text{length of leg opposite } \angle A}{\text{hypotenuse}},$$

$$\tan A = \frac{\text{length of leg opposite } \angle A}{\text{length of leg adjacent to } \angle A}$$

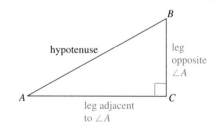

U

Unit rate (p. 277)   A unit rate is a rate that has a denominator of 1.

If you drive 165 mi in 3 h, your unit rate of travel is 55 mi in 1 h or 55 mi/h.

Upper quartile (p. 27)   The upper quartile is the median of the upper half of a data set.

See *Quartiles*.

V

Variable (p. 64)   A variable is a letter or symbol that represents a number.

x is a variable in the equation $9 - x = 3$.

Variable expression (p. 64)   A variable expression is a group of numbers, variables, and operations.

$7 + x$, $2y - 4$, $\frac{3}{5}g$, $\frac{7}{k}$

Venn diagram (p. 187)   A Venn diagram is a diagram that illustrates the relationship between sets.

Example: The Venn diagram shows the activities of 67 music students.

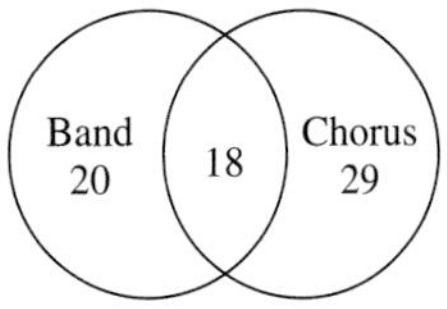

Band 20 | 18 | Chorus 29

Vertex (pp. 290, 428)   See *Angle, Polygon, Polyhedron.*

Vertical angles (p. 379)   Two pairs of vertical angles are formed by intersecting lines. Vertical angles are congruent.

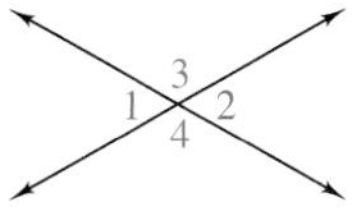

$\angle 1$ and $\angle 2$ are vertical angles, as are $\angle 3$ and $\angle 4$.

Volume (p. 459)   The volume of a space figure is the number of unit cubes or cubic units needed to fill the space inside the figure.

Example: The volume of the rectangular prism is 36 in.^{3}.

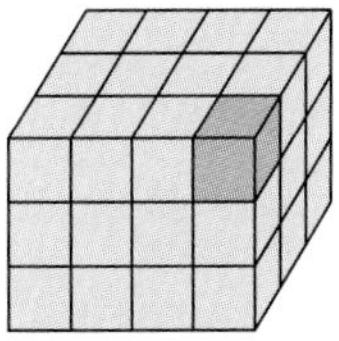

each cube = 1 in.^{3}

X

x-axis (p. 169)   The x-axis is the horizontal number line that, together with the y-axis, forms the coordinate plane.

See *Coordinate plane*.

x-coordinate (p. 169)   The x-coordinate shows the location of a point in the coordinate plane along the x-axis.

See *Coordinates*.

x-intercept (p. 191)   The x-intercept of a line is the x-coordinate of the point where the line crosses the x-axis.

The x-intercept is 2. The y-intercept is -3.

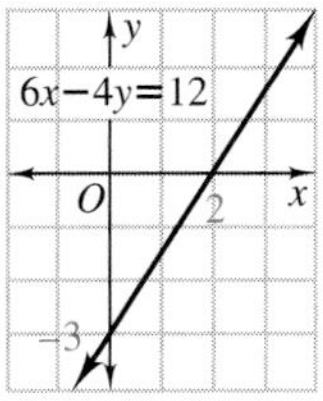

$6x - 4y = 12$

Y

y-axis (p. 169)   The *y*-axis is the vertical number line that, together with the *x*-axis, forms the coordinate plane.

See *Coordinate plane.*

y-coordinate (p. 169)   The *y*-coordinate shows the location of a point in the coordinate plane along the *y*-axis.

See *Coordinates.*

y-intercept (p. 169)   The *y*-intercept of a line is the *y*-coordinate of the point where the line crosses the *y*-axis.

See *x-intercept.*

Z

Zero pair (p. 122)   A positive tile and a negative tile make a zero pair.

◻ ◼ ◄—— a zero pair

Selected Answers

TOOLS FOR PROBLEM SOLVING

The Four-Step Approach page xxii

ON YOUR OWN   1. 9 ways   **3.** 1   **5.** 12 years
7. 147, 148, 149, 150

Using Strategies page xxv

ON YOUR OWN   1. $1.75   **3.** 78 squares

Working Together page xxvii

ON YOUR OWN   1a. The numerator of each is the
repeated digit following the decimal.   **b.** Each
numerator is repeated every 2 decimal places after
the decimal.   **c.** Each numerator is repeated every
3 decimal places after the decimal.   **3a.** 14.4 L;
100.8 L; 5,256 L   **b.** 69 d 10 h 40 min

Preparing for Standardized Tests page xxix

ON YOUR OWN   1. A   **3.** A   **5.** D   **7.** B

CHAPTER 1

Lesson 1-1 pages 4–8

ON YOUR OWN

1.

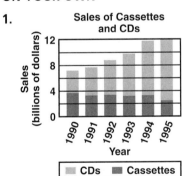

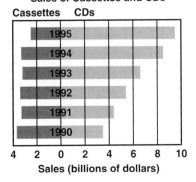

3.

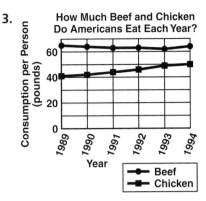

5.

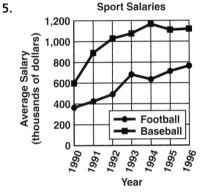

7. about 30 million tons

9.

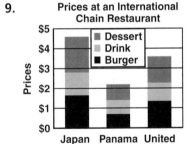

MIXED REVIEW   11. 1,100   **13.** 6   **15.** about
110,000 leagues; about 4 times

Lesson 1-2 pages 9–12

ON YOUR OWN   1a. *Geographic Life*
b. *Reader's World*

3. Circulation of Four Magazines

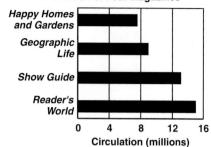

5. Recycling of Soft Drink Containers

MIXED REVIEW **7.** bar graph **9.** 1,500; 1,462
11. 400; 392

Problem Solving Practice — page 13

1. B **3.** A **5.** D **7.** C

Lesson 1-3 — pages 14–18

ON YOUR OWN **1.** Quiz Grades

```
                      X
              X   X   X   X
  X   X   X   X   X   X   X
 70  75  80  85  90  95 100
```

3. Cost of a Movie

```
                        X
  X     X     X         X
  X     X     X         X       X
$5.00 $5.50 $6.00 $6.50 $7.00 $7.50
```

7a. 15–19, 20–24, 25–29, 30–34, 35–39, 40–44
b. 51–60, 61–70, 71–80, 81–90, 91–100 **13a.** 9–11
b. 17 students **c.** between 123 and 157 books

MIXED REVIEW **17.**

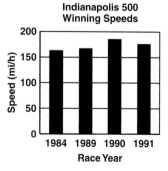

Indianapolis 500 Winning Speeds

---

19. 720 **21.** 500

CHECKPOINT

1. Weekly Leisure Time

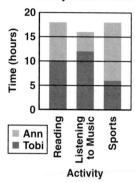

Weekly Leisure Time

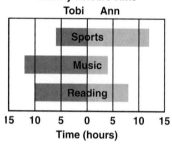

Toolbox — page 19

1. 3,100 **3.** 18,000 **5.** $88 **7.** 1,200 **9.** 280
11. 56 **13.** 8,000

Lesson 1–4 — pages 20–23

ON YOUR OWN **1.** 1; 1; 0 **3.** about $1.48; $1.35;
$1.25 and $1.75 **5a.** In each case, there are 5
data items and the sum of the data is 40. **b.** 10
7. B **13.** Mode; you can only find the most
common response among nonnumerical data.

MIXED REVIEW

17.

Number	Frequency
28	1
30	4
31	7

19.

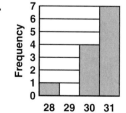

ON YOUR OWN   **1.** 20, 21, 22, 23   **3.** 11   **5.** They would each be multiplied by 10.

7.
```
0 | 2 6 9
1 | 3 3 7 8 9
2 | 4 6 7 7
3 | 0 2 5

   0 | 2 means 2
```

9.
```
6 | 8
7 | 0 5 5 7 8 9
8 | 2 2 3 7 7

   6 | 8 means 68

78.5; 75, 82, and 87; 19
```

11. 16 mi/gal   **13.** highway driving   **15.** Yes; a stem with no leaves accurately reflects the distribution of the data.

ON YOUR OWN   **1.** 85   **3.** 90   **5.** 50   **7.** Find the mean of the two middle numbers in the lower half of the data.   **9.** The middle two quarters of the data are distributed over a great range.   **11.** The distance from the median to the lower quartile $(1703 - 1038 = 665)$ is greater than the distance from the median to the upper quartile $(2181 - 1703 = 478)$.

15. Median Age at First Marriage   **17.** A

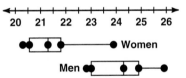

Men when they first get married tend to be older than women when they first get married. The lowest point for men is greater than the upper quartile for women.

MIXED REVIEW

19.
```
3 | 1 2 3 8
4 | 5 5 5
5 | 0 0 2

   3 | 3 means 33
```

21. 45

23.

Interval	Frequency
30–34	3
35–39	1
40–44	0
45–49	3
50–54	3

25. 450 T

ON YOUR OWN

1.

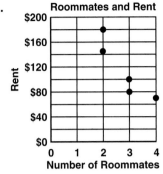

Roommates and Rent

3.

What's a Car Worth?

5a. about 47°F
b. about 34° North

7.

Roommates and Rent

9.

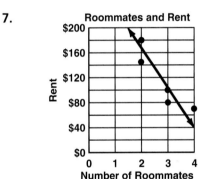

What's a Car Worth?

11. negative
13. positive
17. Negative; the warmer it is outside, the fewer layers you wear.   **19.** A

21.

Number of U.S. Farms

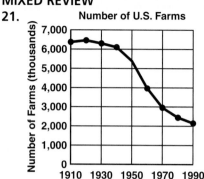

23. 100; 99
25. 100; 102
27. 12; 12.2
29. 60; 57.6

7. B

Percent of Eye-Chart Symbols Identified

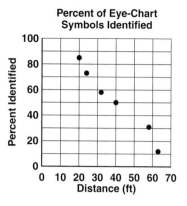

Lesson 1-8 — pages 37–41

ON YOUR OWN **1.** purchase price **3.** gas, oil, and maintenance **5.** $5,500 **7.** $27 **9.** Scatter plot; there are two sets of numeric data. **11.** Bar graph; you are comparing only one set of numeric data.

13. scatter plot

When Do Students Wear Jackets?

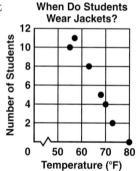

17. box-and-whisker plot

MIXED REVIEW **19.** < **21.** > **23.** 6:15 A.M.

CHECKPOINT **1.** about 94.5 **2.** 90 **3.** 88 **4.** 30
5.

```
 ◄─┼─┼─┼─┼─┼─┼─┼─┼─┼─┼─┼─┼─┼─┼─┼─┼─►
   80  84  88  92  96  100 104 108 112
```

6.
```
11 │ 0 5 6 7
12 │ 0 5 9 9
13 │ 2 5 5
```

            12 | 5 means 125

Lesson 1-9 — pages 42–45

ON YOUR OWN **1.** No; you may be surveying only teenagers who do go to movies or only teenagers who like the particular movie. **3.** No; not every teenager has a chance to be surveyed. **5.** Open-option; is your favorite music group rock, soul, or alternative? **7.** Open-option; how much money do you spend on lunch each week: less than $5, between $5 and $10, between $10 and $15, or more than $15? **9.** The question makes kittens seem more desirable than puppies.

MIXED REVIEW **13.** $21; $23.03 **15.** $3.50; about $3.47 **17a.** 70 **b.** 85 **c.** 34 **d.** 66

Lesson 1-10 — pages 46–48

ON YOUR OWN **1.** You need to know either how much time Priya spent in the bakery or how long she walked. **3.** You need to know the regular price of the rolls. **5.** 9 quarters and 12 dimes **7.** yes **9.** 294 chairs **11.** 5 ways

MIXED REVIEW **13.** $\frac{2}{3}$ **15.** $\frac{1}{6}$ **17.** $\frac{1}{25}$ **19.** $\frac{4}{5}$
21. bar graph

Typical Heights of Trees after 15 Years

Lesson 1-11 — pages 49–52

ON YOUR OWN **1a.** 61% **b.** 10% **c.** 78% **3.** $\frac{3}{8}$

5. 1   **7.** 0   **9.** $\frac{3}{8}$ **11.** $\frac{1}{4}$ **13.** $\frac{3}{16}$ **15.** $\frac{1}{4}$

17a.

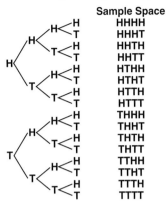

Sample Space
HHHH
HHHT
HHTH
HHTT
HTHH
HTHT
HTTH
HTTT
THHH
THHT
THTH
THTT
TTHH
TTHT
TTTH
TTTT

b. $\frac{1}{16}$ **c.** $\frac{1}{4}$

d. $\frac{3}{8}$ **e.** $\frac{1}{4}$

19. No; numbers between 0 and 1, inclusive; probability cannot be greater than 1 because the number of favorable outcomes cannot be greater than the total number of outcomes.

MIXED REVIEW   **21.** C   **23.** A

Wrap Up   **pages 54–55**

1.

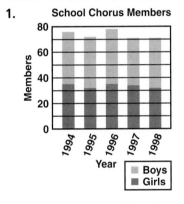

School Chorus Members

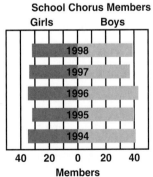

2. School Chorus Members

4. about 67.2; 66.5; 78

6.

6	3 5 7
7	2 5 8 8 9 9 9
8	5 5 9
9	0 9

9 | 0 means 90

7. Juice Prices (cents)

8. Length and Water Flow of U.S. Rivers

9. B
11a. HHH, HHT, HTH, HTT, THH, THT, TTH, TTT   **b.** $\frac{3}{8}$
c. $\frac{1}{2}$ **d.** $\frac{1}{8}$
12. You need to know how long Minowa stopped for breakfast.

CUMULATIVE REVIEW   **1.** C   **3.** D   **5.** D   **7.** D
9. B   **11.** C

CHAPTER 2

Lesson 2-1   **pages 60–63**

ON YOUR OWN   **1.** +3   **3.** +1,000   **5.** +50
7. −129   **9.** 52   **11.** 0   **13.** 10   **15.** =
17. >   **19.** >   **21.** <   **23.** yes   **25.** Alaska
27. −16, −13, −6, −4, 2, 7, 11   **29.** U **31.** T
35. oxygen   **37.** D

Lesson 2-2 — pages 64–68

ON YOUR OWN **1.** $27 + n$ **3.** $2n$ **5.** $-4n$
7. $n \div -10$, or $\frac{n}{-10}$ **9.** $|n| + 7$ **11.** $0.75x$
13. $3c$ **15.** $n + 3$ **17.** $241n$ **19.** 27 **21.** 64
23. -1 **25.** 13 **27.** 36 **29.** 12 **31.** 12 **33.** 7
41. E **43.** C **45a.** 450 ft **b.** 15 min

MIXED REVIEW **49.** $\frac{47}{10}$ **51.** $\frac{58}{7}$ **53.** $\frac{121}{16}$
55. $20.46 **57.** $3.70 **59.** 1,599 people

Lesson 2-3 — pages 69-72

ON YOUR OWN **1.** $(-6) + 4 = -2$
3. $(-30) + 35 = 5$ **5.** $6 + (-10) = -4$
7.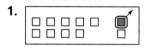

9. ■ ■ ■ + □ □ □ □ □ = □ □

11. $-53 + 28$ **13.** $-24 + 8$ **15.** -112 **17.** -48
19. -12 **21.** -70 **23.** 100 **25.** -31
27. positive **29.** positive **31.** -9 **33.** 74
35. 29,028 ft

MIXED REVIEW **37.** $>$ **39.** $<$ **41.** $n + 7$
43. circle graph

Lesson 2-4 — pages 73-76

ON YOUR OWN
1. [diagram] 10 **3.** [diagram] -3

5. negative **7.** positive **9.** positive **11.** negative
13. $27 + (-52); -25$ **15.** $-10 + 8; -2$
17. $|-12| + (-17); -5$ **19.** $-28 + 28; 0$
21. $-36 + (-|29|); -65$ **23.** $-55 + (-21); -76$
25. $56 + (-28); 28$ **27.** $95 + 39; 134$ **29.** $6, -1,$
$-8, -15$ **31.** $-14, -21, -28, -35$ **33.** $10, 4, 8, 3$
35. $97 **37.** 2 **39.** 1 **41.** 0 **43.** -1 **45.** -5

MIXED REVIEW **49.** 18 **51.** $.84

CHECKPOINT **1.** $<$ **2.** $<$ **3.** $>$ **4.** $=$ **5.** $<$

6. $-3n$ **7.** $n \div 12$, or $\frac{n}{12}$ **8.** -19 **9.** -7
10. -21 **11.** 28 **12.** 37 **13.** -6 **14.** 21
15. 30 **16.** -5

Lesson 2-5 — pages 77-81

ON YOUR OWN **1.** positive **3.** positive
5. -18 **7.** -70 **9.** -60 **11.** -45 **13.** -14

---

15. $-54 \div 18 = -3; -54 \div (-3) = 18$
17. $-12 \div 3 = -4; -12 \div (-4) = 3$ **19.** negative
21. positive **23.** negative **25.** -10 **27.** -8
29. 4 **31.** -3 **33.** 9 **35.** -1 and -4
37. $.80 per day average gain **39.** 7 **41.** -6
43. 75 **45a.** $-40,230$ **b.** 8 mi **47.** -24 **49.** 25

MIXED REVIEW **51.** -9 **53.** -6 **55.** -7
61. 2,555 h

Lesson 2-6 — pages 82-85

ON YOUR OWN **1.** 7^4 **3.** $(-x)^4$ **5.** $3 \cdot 3$
7. $-(7 \cdot 7)$ **9.** $b \cdot b$ **11.** 9 **13.** -64 **15.** 343
17. No; $3^4 = 3 \cdot 3 \cdot 3 \cdot 3$, or 81 and $4^3 = 4 \cdot 4 \cdot 4$,
or 64. Since $81 \neq 64$, $3^4 \neq 4^3$. **19.** 64 **21.** 81
23. a^8 **25.** $(-5)^9$ **27.** b^{10} **29.** 2 **31.** $2; 4$
33. -64 **35.** $531,441$ **37.** 125
39. 144 cm^2

MIXED REVIEW **41.**

1	6
2	3 5 9
3	2 5 5 6
4	1 5
5	
6	7

2 | 5 represents 25

43. line graph **45.** $n \div (-2)$, or $\frac{n}{-2}$ **47.** $56.91

Toolbox — page 86

1a. 53 **b.** 125 **c.** 85 **3a.** 10 **b.** -210
c. $-1,692$

Lesson 2-7 — pages 87-90

ON YOUR OWN **1.** 69 **3.** 41 **5.** 8 **7.** 69
9. -35 **11.** $-2,160$ **13.** 7 **15.** $\frac{9}{4}$, or 2.25
17. 4 **19.** 43 **21.** 10.625 **23.** 620
25. $-39,062.5$ **27.** -1 **29.** 6.25 **31.** $A = 4s^2$
33. $3,391.2$ cm^3 **35.** 0 **37.** 8 **39.** 30

MIXED REVIEW **41.** 20 **43.** $28.4; 31; 14$
45. $15.4; 15; 15$ **47.** $h - 6$ **49.** $s + 12,500$

Lesson 2-8 — pages 91-95

ON YOUR OWN **1.** 10 **3.** 0 **5.** 0 **7.** 833
9. 718 **11.** $24,500$ **13.** 320 **15.** 126
17. $-11,600$ **19.** $(2 - 0.2)(5); 9$
21. $(100 + 3)(22); $2,266 **23.** false **25.** false
27. $4.96 **29.** 1001 **31a.** 20 **b.** associative
property **33.** $2.44 **35.** $8.63

MIXED REVIEW **37.** $n + 5$ **39.** 12 **41.** 4
43. 6, 7, 20

CHECKPOINT **1.** -416 **2.** 4 **3.** -72 **4.** -27
5. 20 **6.** 13 **7.** -4 **8.** 32 **9.** -20 **10.** B

Lesson 2-9 **pages 96–98**

ON YOUR OWN **1.** 1st day: 900 m; 2nd day:
1,150 m **3.** 12 girls; 14 boys **5.** 500 mi **7a.** no
b. 6 combinations **9.** 64 players

MIXED REVIEW **11.** 21,000 **13.** 14,000

Lesson 2-10 **pages 99-102**

ON YOUR OWN **1.** 1 **3.** 27 **5.** -27 **7.** m^7
9. s^4 **11.** false; $4^0 = 1$ and $4^1 = 4$ **13.** false;
$1^{-5} = 1$ and $(-1)^5 = -1$ **15.** $\frac{-1}{125}$ **17.** $\frac{1}{16}$ **19.** -1
21. $\frac{1}{x^4}$ **23.** $\frac{y^2}{4}$ **25.** $\frac{1}{4}$ **27.** 2 **29.** $\frac{1}{y^5}$ **31.** 7
33. 8 **35.** -8 **37.** -3 **39.** 10 **43.** when a is
negative; when a is positive **45.** 10^{-4} **47.** 10^{-8}

MIXED REVIEW
49.

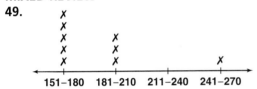

X		
X		
X	X	
X	X	
X	X	X
151–180	181–210	211–240	241–270

51. -13 **53.** 1 **55.** 16 years old

Lesson 2-11 **pages 103–107**

ON YOUR OWN **1.** 4.56×10^4 **3.** 8×10^7
5. 9.81×10^{-4} **7.** 1.01×10^{-2} **9.** 6.25×10^6
11. D **13.** -3 **15.** 6.37 **17.** 3.008
19. 5×10^{-4} **21.** 1×10^{-5} **23.** 136,200,000
25. 4,000 **27.** 0.95 **29.** 0.0005 **31.** 0.0036
33. 9×10^{-4}; the exponent is greater. **35.** C
37. $3.1 \times 10^3, 5.7 \times 10^3, 8.6 \times 10^3, 9.5 \times 10^3$
39. $4.2 \times 10^{-8}, 2.15 \times 10^{-7}, 3.1 \times 10^{-5}$,
5.678×10^{-5} **41.** 7.892×10^{-10};
0.0000000007892 **43.** 4.9×10^{-12};
0.0000000000049 **45.** 3.491×10^7; 34,910,000
47. 5×10^{12} red blood cells **49.** The number is
greater than 1; the number is between 0 and 1.

MIXED REVIEW **51.** 3 **53.** 13 **55.** 6.25; 3.125;
1.5625; 0.78125 **57.** 2 **59.** 4,500

Problem Solving Practice **page 108**

1. B **3.** A **5.** C **7.** C **9.** E **11.** B

Wrap Up **pages 110–111**

1. $<$ **2.** $<$ **3.** $>$ **4.** $=$ **5.** -12 **6.** 5 **7.** -6
8. -11 **9.** -54 **10.** 17 **11.** -28 **12.** -5
14. $b + 7$ **15.** $w - 8$ **16.** $2y + 3$ **17.** 6
18. 27.5 **19.** 4.21 **20.** -10 **21.** $-16,800$
22. 1,094 **23.** 172 **24.** -13 **25.** width: 5 m,
length: 11 m **26.** 13 squares, 17 triangles
27. 32 **28.** -14 **29.** t^{-2}, or $\frac{1}{t^2}$ **30.** 64 **31.** $\frac{1}{4}$
32. 2.956×10^2 **33.** 8.3×10^{-3}
34. 9.056×10^4 **35.** 3×10^{-2}
36. 5.987×10^{-1}

Cumulative Review **page 113**

1. B **3.** A **5.** B **7.** C **9.** D **11.** B

CHAPTER 3

Lesson 3-1 **pages 116–119**

ON YOUR OWN **1.** $2x + 3$ **3.** $x - 6$ **5.** $5z$
7. $-3t$ **9.** $-3j$ **11.** $-h$ **13.** $3k$ **15.** q
17. $-9j$ **19.** $8x$ **21.** z; 6; z; 3; 18 **23.** $9m + 63$
25. $2x + 4y$ **27.** $5q + 5$ **29.** $5r - 1$ **31.** $3x - 2y$
33. $-2b + c + 5$ **35.** $-3b + 32$ **37.** 6

MIXED REVIEW

41a.

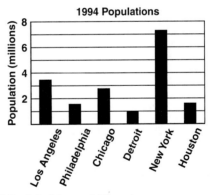

1994 Populations

b. Philadelphia and Houston
c. New York
d. Detroit

Lesson 3-2 **pages 120–124**

ON YOUR OWN **1.** $x + 1 = 4$; 3 **3.** $x + 2 = -4$;
-6 **5.** 30 **7.** -2 **9.** $7\frac{1}{2}$ **11.** -422 **13.** -1.2
15. 28 **17.** 1,355 **19.** -4.3 **21.** 5 **23.** 27
25. 21 **27.** -14 **29.** $18,700 = a - 13,900$;
$32,600 **31.** $34 - 16 = x$; 18 tooth extractions
33. -7 **35.** 9.09 **37.** $4\frac{1}{2}$ **39.** 20.75

41. -10.07 **43.** -20 **47.** $-3, 3$ **49.** 0 **51.** $-3, 1$ **53.** 57 **55.** 17 **57.** -5

MIXED REVIEW

59.

Data	Tally	Frequency
22	II	2
23	II	2
24	I	1
25	III	3
26	II	2
27	II	2

61. -3 **63.** -14 **65.** 431×52

Toolbox   **page 125**

1. $-5; -3; 3$ **3.** $-4; 5; 17; -1; 2$ **5.** Yes; the sum for each row is also multiplied by -2.

Lesson 3-3   **pages 126–130**

ON YOUR OWN **1.** $2x = -10; -5$ **3.** $4x = 12; 3$ **5.** -5 **7.** -4 **9.** 6 **11.** -12 **13.** 50 **15.** -23 **17.** $\frac{1}{3}$ **19a.** $9x = 180; \$20$ **b.** $12y = 180; 15$ wk **21.** -24 **23.** -8 **25.** -40 **27.** 7 **29.** -6 **31.** -18 **33.** -20 **35.** $8p = 9.84; \$1.23$ **37.** $a = 8 \cdot 8; 64\%$ **39.** yes; $\frac{15}{(-5)} = -3$ **41.** yes; $10 = -2(-5)$ **45.** 5.6 **47.** 0.0029 **49.** $3n + 5$

Lesson 3-4   **pages 131–134**

ON YOUR OWN **1.** 4 **3.** -8 **5.** 40 **7.** 3 **9.** -324 **11.** 31 **13.** -1 **15.** -30 **17.** 1 **19.** 0 **21.** 44 **23.** 5 **25.** C **27.** $\$7$ **29.** 309 orders

MIXED REVIEW **33.** $\frac{1}{3}$ **35.** $\frac{1}{36}$ **37.** 30 **39.** 20 **41.** 66

CHECKPOINT **1.** $9d + 36$ **2.** $-8m + 4$ **3.** $6h - 20$ **4.** $3x + 3y$ **5.** 11 **6.** -8 **7.** 1453 **8.** 3 **9.** 3.5 **10.** 36 **11.** 15 **12.** 26 **13.** 7 pencils

---

Lesson 3-5   **pages 135–137**

ON YOUR OWN **1.** $(7 - 5)x = 35; 7$ mi **3.** $4x - 4 = 60; 16$ V/m **5.** $64, 65$ **7.** $\$78$ **9.** 22 h

MIXED REVIEW **13.** 0.0035 **15.** 0.359 **17.** 0.1426 **19.** 15 and $-27, 27$ and -15

Lesson 3-6   **pages 138–141**

ON YOUR OWN **1.** 2 **3.** -2 **5.** 9 **7.** 2 **9.** 7 **11.** 5 **13.** $\frac{-2}{5}$ **15.** -5 **17.** 33 **19.** 46 g **21.** -1 **23.** -3 **25.** 3.2 **27.** 5 **29.** 9 **31.** 4

---

33. $4m + 5 = 21; 4$

MIXED REVIEW **37.** 216 **39.** 1 **41.** -64

Lesson 3-7   **pages 142–145**

ON YOUR OWN **1.** 36 cm **3.** 18 ft **5.** 20 m^2 **7.** 15 in.^{2} **9.** 0.25 cm^2 **11.** 12 m **13.** You must isolate the variable to solve; the solution may contain another variable. **15.** $n = 4(F - 37)$, or $n = 4F - 148$ **17.** $t = \frac{d}{r}$ **19.** $d_2 = \frac{2A}{d_1}$ **21.** $\ell = \frac{P - 2w}{2}$ **23.** $b = y - mx$ **25a.** $h = \frac{2A}{b_1 + b_2}$ **b.** 9.5 ft

MIXED REVIEW **27.** $2{,}030{,}000$ **29.** 0.00324 **31.** 0.0798 **33.** 102.5 **35.** 25 of each coin

---

Toolbox   **page 146**

1. $=$A2 $+$ B2 $+$ C2 **3.** $= 0.5*$A2$*$B2 **5.** $40; 44;$ $48; 52; 56; 60$ **7.** It decreases; it increases.

Lesson 3-8   **pages 147–151**

ON YOUR OWN **1.** no; $-4 < -1$ **3.** yes; $0 > -1$ **5.** no; $-1 = -1$ **7.** $k \leq 0$ **9.** $p \leq 40$ **11.** $s =$ number of stops; $s > 85$ **13.** $h =$ height in in.; $h \geq 50$ **15.** $s =$ number of students; $s \leq 400$ **17.** $s =$ number of students; $s \leq 65$ **19.** $x > -1$ **21.** $x \geq -2$

23. **25.**

35. $<$ **37.** B **41.** $t \geq 90°$ **43a.** $s =$ number of schools; $s > 95{,}000.$ **b.** $d =$ dollars spent; $d >$ $200{,}000{,}000{,}000.$ **c.** $u =$ number of colleges and universities; $u \leq 4000.$ **d.** $n =$ number of part-time U.S. college students; $n \leq 7{,}000{,}000.$

MIXED REVIEW **45.** mean: 72.25; median: 75.5 **47.** $<$ **49.** $=$

Problem Solving Practice   **page 152**

1. A **3.** C **5.** C **7.** D

Lesson 3-9   **pages 153–156**

ON YOUR OWN **1.** 2 **3.** 8

5a. $x < -2$

c. $(-2) + 7 < 5$ is false, so -2 is not a solution.

d. Solve the inequality and substitute numbers from each side of the solution number as well as the number itself.

7. $s \geq -19$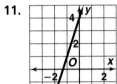

9. $y > 1,300$

1,100   1,300   1,500   1,700

19. $9 + 8 + 10 + 9 + x \geq 45$; $x \geq 9$; Amy must score at least 9 points.

MIXED REVIEW **35.** 372.4 **37.** 14 **39.** 50

CHECKPOINT **1.** -3 **2.** 3 **3.** -1

4. $n < 5$

1   3   5   7

5. $b \geq -2$

-4 -2 0   2

6. $k \geq -9$

-11 -9 -7 -5

7. 48 mi/h **8.** A **9.** 127 mi

Lesson 3-10   pages 157–160

ON YOUR OWN

1. $p > 7$

5   7   9   11

3. $b > 4$

2   4   6   8

33. $n \geq 2$ **35.** $b \leq 20$ **37.** $3x \geq 150$; $x \geq 50$; each earned at least \$50. **39.** 7 tapes

MIXED REVIEW **41.** 1 **43.** -20 **45.** 35, 42, 49 **47.** 45, 55, 65 **49.** 45

Wrap Up   pages 162–163

1. $11x - 12$ **2.** $8a + 1$ **3.** $x - 9$ **4.** 30 **5.** 1.5 **6.** -9.6 **7.** 9 **8.** 20 **9.** -8.4 **10.** -3.2 **11.** 74 **12.** 12 **13.** -3.6 **14.** -15 **15.** -10.8 **16.** -4 **17.** 5 **18.** 3.2 **19.** Combine x and $-5x$ on the right side, and distribute 4 on the left side, so $4x - 20 = 4 - 4x$. Add $4x$ and 20 to each side, so $8x = 24$. Then divide each side by 8, so $x = 3$. **20.** 8 bagels **21.** \$12 **22.** 32 ft; 55 ft^2 **23.** 45 mi/h **24.** A **25.** $x =$ money needed; $x \geq 150$

26. $x > -5$

-7 -5 -3 -1

27. $t \geq 24$

20   24   28   32

---

1. C **3.** A **5.** B **7.** B **9.** C **11.** C

CHAPTER 4

Lesson 4-1   pages 168–171

ON YOUR OWN **1.** E **3.** M **5.** I **7.** $(0, -5)$ **9.** $(-5, 0)$ **11.** $(1, -2)$ **13.** I **15.** II **17.** III **19.** y-axis **21.** II **23.** II

MIXED REVIEW **37a.** 17 in. **b.** age 10 **39.** 6 **41.** -20 **43.** 3

Lesson 4-2   pages 172–175

ON YOUR OWN **1.** yes; no; yes **3.** -4 **5.** 96 **7.** -38 **9.** \$36

11. 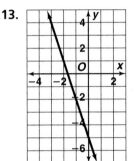 **13.**

MIXED REVIEW **23.** 1.56 **25.** 10.12 **27.** 47 **29.** 340

Lesson 4-3   pages 176–180

ON YOUR OWN **1.** 2 **3.** $-\frac{2}{3}$ **5.** Since $\frac{5}{3} > \frac{3}{5}$, the roof with a rise of 5 and a run of 3 is steeper.

7. $\frac{2}{3}$;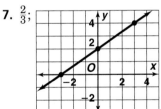

9. 1;

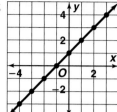

11. 2   **13.** $-\frac{3}{2}$ **15.** 1; each hour the amount of snow increases by 1 in.   **17.** 10; each month the amount in savings increases $10.

MIXED REVIEW   **19.** -11 **21.** 37
23. 1,800 words

Toolbox   *page 181*

1.

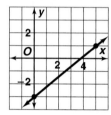

x	y
-3	-5.4
-2	-4.6
-1	-3.8
0	-3
1	-2.2
2	-1.4
3	-0.6

3.

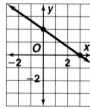

x	y
-3	4
-2	$3.\overline{3}$
-1	$2.\overline{6}$
0	2
1	$1.\overline{3}$
2	$0.\overline{6}$
3	0

Lesson 4-4   *pages 182–186*

ON YOUR OWN   **1.** 3; -2 **3.** -2; -8

5.

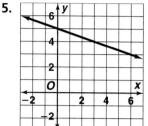

7.

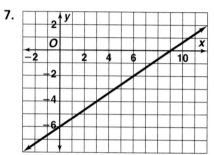

13. 1; 0; the equation can be written $y = 1x + 0$.   **15.** Subtract $3x$ from both sides of the equation. Then divide both sides of the equation by 2.   **17.** $y = \frac{4}{3}x - 2$ **19.** $y = -x + 2$

23. intersecting

MIXED REVIEW

25.

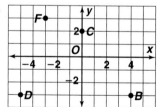

27.   **29.** 180 times

CHECKPOINT

1–4.

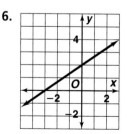

5.   **6.**

8. a: 0; b: $\frac{3}{2}$; c: -1

ON YOUR OWN

1.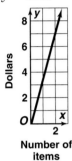

Factors of 30   Factors of 40

3   6   1   2   4   8
15   5   10   20
    30   40

1, 2, 5, 10; 10

3. 12 students   **5.** 12 boys   **7.** row 14

MIXED REVIEW   **9.** $\frac{3}{4}$ **11.** $\frac{1}{125}$ **13.** $\frac{3}{8}$ **15.** m^3

17. 17   **19.** 64

ON YOUR OWN

1. $y = 3.5x$ **3.** $y = -x + 24$

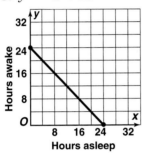

5. $3,000   **7.** $\frac{1}{10}$; $50 profit; there is $1 profit for every $10 in sales.   **9a.** $y = 2x + 20$ **b.** $56 **c.** 16 customers

11. 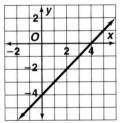   **13.**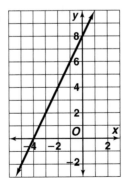

ON YOUR OWN   **1.** Loss; expenses are greater than income.   **3.** 20 key chains   **5a.** $y = 3x$ **b.** 3   **c.** $3   **7.** $50   **9.** 10 shirts cost $80 and bring $80 income.   **11a.** Balloon A: $y = 100x + 1,000$; Balloon B: $y = -200x + 2,500$ **b.** (5, 1,500); in 5 min both balloons will be at 1,500 ft.

MIXED REVIEW   **13.** $9x + 2$ **15.** $3y + 5$

CHECKPOINT   **1.** 5 students

2a.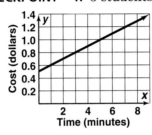

3. (20, 200); 20 caps cost $200 to make and provide $200 income.

ON YOUR OWN   **1.** $S'(-5, -2)$, $T'(1, -2)$, $U'(2, -5)$, $V'(-4, -5)$ **3.** $S'(-8, 8)$, $T'(-2, 8)$, $U'(-1, 5)$, $V'(-7, 5)$ **5.** (1, 5)

7.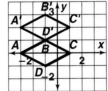

9. 6 units right   **11.** $(x, y) \rightarrow (x - 5, y)$
13. $(x, y) \rightarrow (x + 3, y - 4)$ **15.** $(x, y) \rightarrow (x + 7, y + 11)$ **17.** Move right 6 units and up 14 units; the x-value changes $3 + 7 - 4$, or 6 units, and the y-value changes $5 + 11 - 2$, or 14 units.

MIXED REVIEW

19.

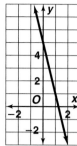

21.

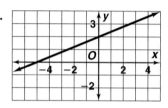

23. 56   **25.** −8   **27.** 5   **29.** 2:30 P.M.

Problem Solving Practice   *page 203*

1. D   **3.** B   **5.** A   **7.** C

Lesson 4-9   *pages 204–208*

ON YOUR OWN

7.

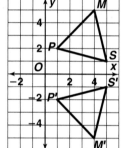

9.

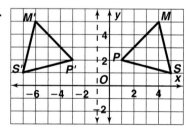

11a–b.

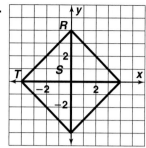

c. square with its diagonals   **13.** no

15.

17.

CODE

21. COD, DECK, DOE   **23a.** Find the perpendicular bisector of $\overline{TT'}$.   **b.** $y = x$

MIXED REVIEW   **29.** −10   **31.** 9

33. $n \leq -6$

35. $s > -15$

37a.

b. mean: 27; median: 25; mode: 20; range: 24

Lesson 4-10   *pages 209–212*

ON YOUR OWN   **1.** 270°   **3.** 180°

5.

7.

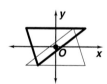

9. $M'(-2, 4)$ **11.** $P'(-4, 0)$ **13.** A   **15.** no
17. yes; 180°

MIXED REVIEW   **21.** 3   **23.** 15   **25.** 1
27. −24.5   **29.** −5

Wrap Up   *pages 214–215*

1. A   **2.** F   **3.** G   **4.** B   **5.** $(-3, -2)$
6. $(-2, 3)$ **7.** $(1, -2)$ **8.** $(-2, -3)$

9. 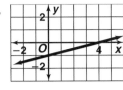 **10.**

13. IV **14.** slope: $\frac{3}{4}$; y-intercept: 6 **15.** slope: 2; y-intercept: 1 **16.** slope: -2; y-intercept: 3

17. 2 **18.** -1 **19.** $-\frac{3}{2}$ **20.** Since the graphs have the same slope and $1 > -3$, the graph of $y = -7x - 3$ is below the graph of $y = -7x + 1$.
21. 50 students

22a.

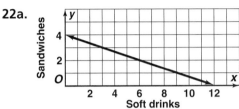

23a. expenses: $y = 2x + 10$; income: $y = 4x$

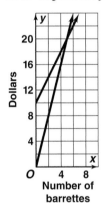

b. $(5, 20)$ **24.** 90° rotation **25.** translation right 1 unit, down 2 units **26.** reflection over the x-axis **27.** reflection over the line $y = 1$

Cumulative Review　　　　**page 217**

1. A **3.** C **5.** B **7.** B **9.** D **11.** D

CHAPTER 5

Lesson 5-1　　　　**pages 220–224**

ON YOUR OWN **1.** 1, 2, 3, 5, 6, 10, 15, 30 **3.** 1, 5, 11, 55 **5.** 1, 2, 4, 13, 26, 52 **7.** 1, 2, 3, 4, 6, 8, 12, 16, 24, 32, 48, 96 **9.** 1, 3, 5, 9, 15, 45 **11.** 1, 53 **13.** composite; 1, 3, 7, 21 **15.** composite; 1, 3, 31, 93 **17.** prime **19.** prime **21.** composite; 1, 3, 29, 87 **23.** composite; 1, 2, 3, 6, 9, 11, 18, 22, 33, 66, 99, 198 **25.** $2 \cdot 3^3$ **27.** $3^2 \cdot 5^2$ **29.** $3^3 \cdot 23$

31. $2^6 \cdot 3 \cdot 7$ **33.** $2^3 \cdot 3^2 \cdot 11$ **39.** 4 **41.** 42 **43.** 14 **45.** 15 **47.** 5 **49a.** 6 classes **b.** 20 paint brushes, 13 boxes of markers, 4 packs of paper, 9 sets of watercolors

MIXED REVIEW **51.** -2 **53.** -9 **55.** -8 **57.** 2 **59.** yes **61.** no **63.** no **65.** 420 people

LESSON 5-2　　　　*pages 225–228*

ON YOUR OWN **1.** $\frac{5}{8}$ **3.** $-\frac{2}{9}$ **5.** $-\frac{2}{5}$ **7.** $-\frac{7}{10}$ **9.** $\frac{4}{5}$ **11.** B **13.** $-\frac{2}{3}$ **15.** $\frac{5}{6}$ **17.** $1\frac{1}{5}$ **19.** -20.5 **21.** -12 **43.** integer, rational number

45. rational number **47.** rational number

49. rational number **51.** $\frac{4}{5}$; $\frac{4}{5}$ **53.** 0.6; -0.6

55. $\frac{1}{3}$; $\frac{1}{3}$

MIXED REVIEW **57.**

59.

LESSON 5-3　　　　*pages 229–233*

ON YOUR OWN **1.** $0.58\overline{3}$ **3.** $0.\overline{6}$ **5.** -0.8 **7.** 1.875 **9.** $-0.\overline{3}$ **11.** 4.4 **13.** -18.75 **15.** $-0.\overline{7}$ **17.** -0.15 **19.** 0.125, 0.25, 0.375, 0.5, 0.625, 0.75, 0.875; $0.1\overline{6}$, $0.\overline{3}$, 0.5, $0.\overline{6}$, $0.8\overline{3}$; 0.2, 0.4, 0.6, 0.8 **23.** $0.\overline{142857}$ **25.** $0.31\overline{4}$ **27.** $5.\overline{27}$

29. $\frac{4}{9}$ **31.** $23\frac{4}{33}$ **33.** $-1\frac{7}{9}$ **35.** $2\frac{8}{9}$ **37.** $1\frac{34}{99}$

MIXED REVIEW **41.** $y = 2x + 3$; 2, 3 **43.** $y = 1.5x - 5$; 1.5, -5 **45.** $y = 4x - 2$; 4, -2 **47.** $y = 4x - 1$; 4, -1

CHECKPOINT **1.** prime **2.** composite; 1, 2, 19, 38 **3.** composite; 1, 3, 19, 57 **4.** prime **5.** composite; 1, 5, 73, 365 **6.** $2^5 \cdot 5$ **7.** $2^2 \cdot 3^3$ **8.** $7 \cdot 11^2$ **9.** $3^2 \cdot 59$ **10.** $2 \cdot 5^2 \cdot 13$ **11.** 0.75 **12.** $-4.\overline{6}$

13. -0.625 **14.** 6.35 **15.** -12.8 **16.** $\frac{2}{5}$ **17.** $-3\frac{4}{25}$ **18.** $24\frac{1}{8}$ **19.** $\frac{6}{11}$ **20.** $1\frac{8}{9}$

Lesson 5-4　　　　*pages 234–238*

ON YOUR OWN **1.** 30 **3.** 72 **5.** 80 **7.** 120 **9.** 192 **11.** 300 **13.** 400 **15.** 1,296 **19.** > **21.** = **23.** > **25.** < **27.** = **29.** = **31.** C **33.** June 16

MIXED REVIEW **35.** 30–39 **37.** < **39.** = **41.** > **43.** 97,531

Lesson 5-5 — pages 240–243

ON YOUR OWN 1. $1\frac{1}{2}$ 3. $\frac{1}{2}$ 5. $-1\frac{1}{2}$ 7. $-1\frac{1}{3}$
9. $1\frac{1}{2}$ 11. $-10\frac{4}{5}$ 13. $-2\frac{1}{3}$ 15. $-11\frac{1}{3}$ 17. $-9\frac{1}{2}$
19. $8\frac{3}{5}$ 21. 1 23. no

MIXED REVIEW
35. $x \le -5$ 37. $r > -6\frac{1}{2}$

$-8 \quad -6 \quad -4 \quad -2$ $-10 \quad -8 \quad -6 \quad -4$

39. -2 41. -30 43. -13

Lesson 5-6 — pages 244–248

ON YOUR OWN 1. $\frac{7}{8}$ 3. $\frac{1}{8}$ 5. $\frac{1}{6}$ 7. $1\frac{1}{3}$ 9. $-1\frac{1}{6}$
11. $-1\frac{7}{12}$ 13. $-10\frac{3}{20}$ 15. $-3\frac{8}{15}$ 17. $2\frac{5}{8}$
19. $16\frac{7}{10}$ 21a. $19\frac{5}{8}$ in. b. $4\frac{3}{8}$ in. 23. $25\frac{1}{8}$
25. $-\frac{3}{4}$, -0.75 27. $-\frac{5}{6}$, $-0.8\overline{3}$ 29. $-11\frac{7}{10}$, -11.7
31. $-\frac{5}{12}$ 33. $1\frac{1}{8}$ 35. $-1\frac{1}{4}$ 37. 3.6 39. $-3\frac{2}{3}$
41. $-4\frac{3}{10}$ or -4.3 43. 3 in. 45. A 47. $1\frac{1}{2}$
49. 0, 2 51. 0, 1 53. 1

MIXED REVIEW 55. $\frac{2}{3}$ 57. $\frac{7}{9}$ 59. 5 61. 8 63. 1

Lesson 5-7 — pages 249–253

ON YOUR OWN 1. $-\frac{2}{3}$ 3. $-\frac{3}{5}$ 5. $-10\frac{7}{8}$ 7. 9
9. $12\frac{1}{2}$ 11. 4 13. $8\frac{3}{4}$ yd 15. -16 17. $-7\frac{1}{2}$
19. -3 21. $-\frac{5}{64}$ 23. $5\frac{1}{3}$ 25. $1\frac{1}{4}$ 27. $-2\frac{1}{2}$
29. -11 31. $\frac{1}{2}$ 33. 20 35. Yes; the box has $10\frac{2}{3}$ c
of cereal and you need just 6 c of cereal for four
dozen muffins. 39. $7\frac{1}{2}$ in., $3\frac{33}{64}$ in.^{2} 41. $6\frac{2}{5}$ in.,
$2\frac{14}{25}$ in.^{2}

MIXED REVIEW 43. $7w$ 45. $x + 2$ 47. yellow
square, blue circle, green triangle

CHECKPOINT 1. < 2. < 3. = 4. < 5. >
6. $\frac{2}{3}$ 7. $-5\frac{11}{15}$ 8. $1\frac{2}{3}$ 9. $\frac{7}{20}$ 10. -2 11. $-1\frac{5}{12}$
12. $-1\frac{7}{24}$ 13. $-\frac{15}{16}$ 14. $-\frac{1}{9}$ 15. C

Lesson 5-8 — pages 254–256

ON YOUR OWN 1a. 108 b. Multiplication,
subtraction, division, and addition; they are the
inverse operations of those mentioned in the
problem. 3. 220 pens 5. white house, yellow door
7a. 1, $\frac{1}{2}$, 2 b. $-\frac{2}{3}$, $-\frac{2}{9}$, $-\frac{2}{27}$ 9a. 14 b. 1 quarter,
3 dimes, 2 nickels

MIXED REVIEW 11. left 5, down 8 13. -12, -8,
-6, -2, 4, 10 15. -98, -85, 2, 18, 23, 24
17. -38, -22, -15, -2, 16 19. 44 ft below the
surface of the water

Toolbox — page 257

1. $1\frac{1}{24}$ 3. $\frac{3}{10}$ 5. $2\frac{1}{2}$ 7. $4\frac{4}{9}$ 9. $\frac{17}{20}$ 11. $\frac{31}{42}$ 13. $36\frac{3}{4}$
15. $3\frac{1}{3}$ 17. $1\frac{1}{2}$ 19. 16 21. $1\frac{7}{20}$ 23. 45 25. $1\frac{1}{3}$

Lesson 5-9 — pages 258–262

ON YOUR OWN 1. 13 3. -9.4 5. 52 7. 17
9. 0.5 11. 55 13. 7 15. 11 17. 12 19. 10
21. 9 23. 10 25. 9 in.^{2} 27. Irrational; 12 is not
a perfect square. 29. irrational 31. rational
33. real number, rational number 35. real
number, rational number 37. real number,
rational number 39. real number, rational
number, integer 41. real number, irrational
number 43. 10, -10 45. 13, -13 47. 25, -25
49a. $\sqrt{10}$; 3.2 b. $\sqrt{18}$; 4.2 c. $\sqrt{16}$; 4 d. $\sqrt{36}$; 6
e. $\sqrt{75}$; 8.7 f. $\sqrt{100}$; 10

MIXED REVIEW 51. 28 53. $-\frac{1}{9}$ 55. 5
63. 9 letters and 1 postcard

Lesson 5-10 — pages 263–267

ON YOUR OWN 1. $\overline{EF}$; $\overline{DE}$, $\overline{DF}$ 3. $\overline{KB}$; $\overline{KT}$, $\overline{TB}$
5. 17 cm 7. 5.3 m 9. 5.3 units 11. 10.8 ft
13. 9.9 in. 15. 13.3 mi 19. $\sqrt{50}$ 21. $\sqrt{41}$
23. 17.3 m 25. no; $15^2 + 35^2 \ne 40^2$ 27. yes;
$2.8^2 + 4.5^2 = 5.3^2$ 29. yes; $(\sqrt{56})^2 + 5^2 = 9^2$
31. yes; $3^2 + (\sqrt{15})^2 = (\sqrt{24})^2$

MIXED REVIEW 33. 1.0×10^8; 100,000,000
35. 1.6×10^7; 16,000,000 37. 9.9999×10^{10};
99,999,000,000 39. 29 and 17

Problem Solving Practice — page 268

1. A 3. B 5. A 7. C 9. B 11. D 13. C

Wrap Up — pages 270–271

1. 4; 80 2. 45; 90 3. 28; 56 4. 5; 300 5. 12; 72
6. $2^3 \cdot 3^2 \cdot 5$ 7. $2^2 \cdot 5^2 \cdot 7$ 8. $2^5 \cdot 3^2 \cdot 5$
9. $2 \cdot 3^3 \cdot 7$ 10. $2^2 \cdot 3^3 \cdot 5 \cdot 13$ 11. < 12. >
13. < 14. = 20. $\frac{9}{25}$ 21. -0.9 22. 0.8
23. $-4.\overline{6}$ 24. $1\frac{13}{20}$ 25. $0.\overline{36}$ 26. -1.625

27. $-0.\overline{6}$ **28.** $1\frac{1}{3}$ **29.** $6\frac{8}{33}$ **30.** $-\frac{1}{8}$ **31.** $-1\frac{1}{2}$
32. $-1\frac{2}{9}$ **33.** $-\frac{2}{3}$ **34.** $\frac{1}{2}$ **35.** $\frac{1}{16}$ **36.** $3\frac{1}{4}$
37. $-2\frac{1}{10}$ **38.** $-\frac{1}{4}$ **39.** 14 **40.** $-\frac{5}{6}$ **41.** 7.5
42. 1.3 **43.** 15 **44.** 16 ft

| *Cumulative Review* | page 273 |

1. D   **3.** C   **5.** A   **7.** D   **9.** D   **11.** C

CHAPTER 6

| *Lesson 6-1* | pages 276–280 |

ON YOUR OWN   **5.** $1:7$ **7.** 5 out of 8   **9.** 3 to 2
11. 11 out of 17   **13.** 2 to 9   **15.** 1 to 3
17. 1 to 6   **19.** 1 to 6   **21a.** $4:3$ **b.** no; $\frac{18}{14} = \frac{9}{7}$
c. ratio becomes less   **23.** $\frac{11}{9}$, 1.22 **25.** $\frac{11}{20}$, 0.55
27. 5 gal/min   **29.** 9.09 m/s   **31.** 12 people/room
33. 52 mi/h   **35.** \$8.25/h   **37.** carton of twelve
39. $35:1$

MIXED REVIEW   **43.** $2^5 \cdot 3 \cdot 5^2$ **45.** $2 \cdot 457$
47. $2^4 \cdot 3^2$ **49.** III   **51.** IV   **53.** y-axis

| *Lesson 6-2* | pages 281–285 |

ON YOUR OWN   **1.** in.   **3.** fl oz   **5.** gal   **7.** fl oz
9. t   **11.** m   **13.** g   **15.** cm or m   **17.** g
19. $2\frac{2}{3}$ **21.** $3,000$ **23.** 900 **25.** $7,920$
27. 4.25 **29.** 176 **31.** about 387,786 per day;
16,158 per h; 269 per min; 4 per s   **33.** about
158,333 h/business day   **35.** 7.5 **37.** 0.5
39. $5,280$ **41.** 504 **43.** $1,500$ **45.** $4\frac{3}{8}$ gal
47. 12 **49.** 8 **51.** 8

MIXED REVIEW

53.   **55.**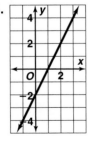

65. 3×10^{-4} in.

| *Lesson 6-3* | pages 286–289 |

ON YOUR OWN   **3.** 7 **5.** 9 **7.** 6 **9.** 27 **13.** 12
15. 3 **17.** 38 **19.** 42 **21.** 16.5 **23.** 12.6

25. 80 **27.** 3.1 **29.** 14 **33.** $\frac{6}{1.00} = \frac{28}{x}$; \$4.67
35. $\frac{1.08}{18} = \frac{x}{40}$; \$2.40   **37.** $\frac{0.5582}{1} = \frac{350}{x}$; about 627
marks

MIXED REVIEW   **39.** $3\frac{8}{9}$ **41.** $\frac{1}{3}$ **43.** $\frac{2}{3}$ **45.** 18
47. 16 **49.** \$12

| *Toolbox* | page 290 |

1. $110°$; obtuse   **3.** $60°$; acute

5. 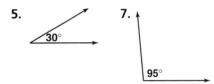   **7.**

| *Lesson 6-4* | pages 291–295 |

ON YOUR OWN   **1.** no   **3.** yes; $\triangle PQN \sim \triangle LMN$
5. yes; $XYZQ \sim FTRL$ **7.** $x = 4.5$, $y = 7.5$
9. $a = 11.25$, $b = 7.5$, $c = 5.625$ **11.** $x = 80$,
$y = 45$ **13.** yes

MIXED REVIEW   **17.** $=$ **19.** $>$ **21.** $>$
23. $-1; 4$ **25.** $-2; -16$

CHECKPOINT   **1.** \$4.75/page   **2.** 40,040 ft/min
3. liter   **4.** pound   **5.** 6 **6.** 2.8 **7.** 3.75
8. $n = 6$, $y = 1.7\overline{3}$

| *Lesson 6-5* | pages 296–300 |

ON YOUR OWN   **7.** $A'(-4, -2)$, $B'(4, 0)$, $C'(4, 4)$,
$D'(-2, 4)$ **9.** $A'(0, 3)$, $B'(6, 9)$, $C'(3,12)$, $D'(-3, 6)$
11. $\frac{1}{2}$; reduction   **13.** $1\frac{1}{2}$; enlargement   **15.** $\frac{1}{5}$;
reduction   **17.** $\frac{2}{3}$; reduction   **19.** 55% **21a.** 2
b. 9cm, 16cm   **c.** 24cm, 48cm
MIXED REVIEW

23. 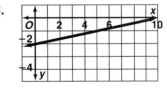   **25.**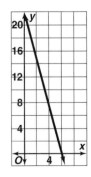

27. $\frac{2}{3}$ **29.** 1 **31.** \$425

Lesson 6-6   pages 302–304

ON YOUR OWN   **1a.** 30 in.   **b.** 6 in.   **c.** 12.5 in., 2.5 in.   **d.** 1 in. : 3.75 ft   **3.** $17\frac{1}{2}$ ft   **5.** HO   **7.** N
9. 1 in. : 36 ft   **11.** 560 km   **13.** $11\frac{7}{8}$ ft long, 5.9375 ft wide, and 5 ft tall

MIXED REVIEW
15.

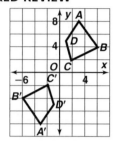

17. 10   **19.** 20   **21.** 15

Lesson 6-7   pages 305–307

ON YOUR OWN   **1.** 7th   **3.** (0, 0) to (−1, −3) to (−2, −2) to (−4, −7)   **5a.** A; B   **b.** 2 gal/min
7a. 2 to sand, 5 to attach, and 3 to paint
b. 60 trucks

MIXED REVIEW   **9.** yes; $8^2 + 15^2 = 17^2$
11. yes; $12^2 + 16^2 = 20^2$ **13.** (4, −11)

Problem Solving Practice   page 308

1. B   **3.** B   **5.** A   **7.** D   **9.** B

Lesson 6-8   pages 309–312

ON YOUR OWN   **1a.** $\frac{PQ}{ST} = \frac{QR}{TR}$ **b.** 1.44 km
5. 13 ft 4 in.   **7.** 12 ft   **9.** 282 ft

MIXED REVIEW
17. 2.25, 0.5625   **19.** −5, 0

CHECKPOINT   **2.** $X'(1, 0)$, $Y'(2, -\frac{2}{3})$, $Z'(0, -2)$
3. C   **4.** 10 in.   **5.** 64 ft

Lesson 6-9   pages 313–316

ON YOUR OWN   **1a.** $\overline{YZ}$; $\overline{XY}$ **b.** $\overline{XY}$; $\overline{YZ}$
c. $\frac{15}{8}$, 1.875; $\frac{8}{15}$, $0.5\overline{3}$ **d.** $\tan X = \frac{1}{\tan Z}$ **3.** 11.4301
5. 1.0000   **7.** $\frac{8}{15}$, $\frac{15}{8}$ **9.** $\frac{3}{4}$, $\frac{4}{3}$

11. $\frac{45}{28}$, $\frac{28}{45}$

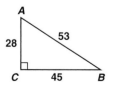

13. 3.4   **15.** 163.4   **17.** 50 ft

MIXED REVIEW
21.

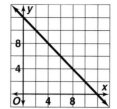

23.

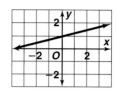

25. 247   **27.** 6

Lesson 6-10   pages 317–320

ON YOUR OWN   **1.** $\frac{3}{5}$ **3.** $\frac{4}{5}$ **5.** $\frac{3}{4}$ **7.** 0.9848
9. 0.9455   **11.** 0.5000   **13.** 0.0872
15. 10; $\frac{3}{5}$, $\frac{4}{5}$, $\frac{3}{4}$ **17.** 36; $\frac{12}{13}$, $\frac{5}{13}$, $\frac{12}{5}$
21a. $x = 7.4 \sin 53°$; 5.9   **b.** $x = 7.4 \cos 37°$; 5.9
23. 2.0   **25.** 60.0   **27a.** 15.5 ft   **b.** 4.1 ft

MIXED REVIEW
29. −7;

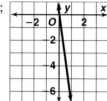

31. 74   **33.** −27
35. yes

Wrap Up   pages 322–323

1. 1 : 3   **2.** $\frac{4}{1}$ **3.** 4 out of 15   **4.** 5 to 3   **5.** $28/h
6. 59 mi/h   **7.** 6.25 km/L   **8.** $0.66/can   **9.** L
10. ft   **11.** 1.25   **12.** 2,208   **13.** $2,194.\overline{4}$ **14.** 3.12
15. 2.4   **16.** $4\frac{4}{9}$ **17.** $14\frac{2}{5}$ **18.** 10 cm
19. 7.5 cm   **20.** 4.5 cm   **22.** 3   **23.** $2\frac{1}{24}$ in. long × $1\frac{3}{4}$ in. wide   **24.** 11.8 ft   **25.** 3   **26.** 5.3   **27.** 13.8
28. 47.7

Cumulative Review   page 325

1. B   **3.** C   **5.** C   **7.** A   **9.** A

CHAPTER 7

Toolbox   page 328

1. $\frac{7}{100}$ **3.** $\frac{185}{100}$ **5.** $\frac{95}{100}$ **7.** $\frac{5}{10}$

9. 1.04

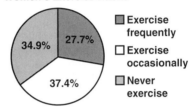

11. 0.55

Lesson 7-1 — pages 329–333

ON YOUR OWN **1.** $0.\overline{6}$; 60% **3.** $0.1\overline{6}$; 16.7%
5. $0.4\overline{6}$; 46.7% **7.** 0.015; 1.5% **9.** $1.\overline{6}$; 160%
11. $2.\overline{6}$; 266.7% **13.** 36% **15.** 0.3% **17.** 7.5%
19. 0.25% **21.** 98.9% **23.** 25% **25.** C
27. 14.3% **29.** $\frac{93}{100}$ **31.** $\frac{1}{125}$ **33.** $\frac{3}{400}$ **35.** $\frac{3}{8}$
37. $\frac{11}{500}$ **39.** $\frac{7}{16}$ **41.** 0.2 **43.** 0.083 **45.** 0.001
47. 1.34 **49.** 6.00 **51.** 0.058 **53.** $\frac{1}{5000}$
55. $0.3, \frac{1}{3}, 36\%, \frac{3}{8}$ **57.** $0.9\%, 0.01, 1.01\%, \frac{1}{99}$
59. $0.2, 20.9\%, \frac{2}{9}, \frac{1}{4}$

MIXED REVIEW **63.** \$1.20 /gal **65.** 45 mi/h
67. $4\frac{9}{10}$ **69.** $17\frac{1}{15}$ **71.** \$36.45

Lesson 7-2 — pages 334–337

ON YOUR OWN **1.** 30 **3.** 4.5 **5.** 30 **7.** 24
9. 30 **11.** 10 **13.** > **15.** = **17.** > **19.** <
21. \$30 **23.** \$16 **25.** \$20 **27.** \$1.85 **29.** \$1.05
31. \$4.20 **33.** \$4.80

MIXED REVIEW **37.** 10 **39.** 7 **41.** 3.75 **43.** $\frac{2}{9}$
45. $\frac{83}{99}$ **47.** $\frac{2}{3}$ **49.** \$2.50

Lesson 7-3 — pages 338–341

ON YOUR OWN **1.** \$3; \$52.99 **3.** \$3.12; \$53.11
5. \$2; \$51.99 **7.** \$3.50; \$53.49 **9.** 57.6 **11.** 340
13. 70 **15.** 145 **17.** 120 **19.** 4 **21.** 217.2
23. 497.8 **25.** 115; 100; 80 **29.** B
31. Sample: 4,000,000 sq mi

MIXED REVIEW **33.** 8, 10 **35.** −6 **37.** $-\frac{3}{8}$

Lesson 7-4 — pages 342–346

ON YOUR OWN **1.** D **3.** A **5.** 40% **7.** 25.4
9. 700 **11.** 125% **13.** 63.3 **15.** 60 **17.** 600
19. 18% **21a.** 151.6%

MIXED REVIEW **25.** $\frac{35}{100}$ **27.** $\frac{11}{2}$ **29.** $\frac{17}{1}$
31. 0.966 **33.** 0.087 **35.** 0.276

CHECKPOINT **1.** 0.3; 30%; $\frac{3}{10}$ **2.** 0.12; 12%; $\frac{3}{25}$
3. 2.1; 210%; $\frac{21}{10}$ **4.** 0.625; 62.5%; $\frac{5}{8}$ **5.** 0.003;
0.3%; $\frac{3}{1,000}$ **6.** 3.75; 375%; $\frac{15}{4}$ **7.** 30 **8.** 75 **9.** 50
10. 4 **11.** 14 **12.** 75% **13.** 3.9 **14.** 200
15. 17.3% **16.** 213 **17.** 3,750 **18.** \$10.824 billion

Lesson 7-5 — pages 347–350

ON YOUR OWN **1.** 32° **3.** 85° **5.** 152° **7.** 50°
9. 149° **11.** 65°
13.

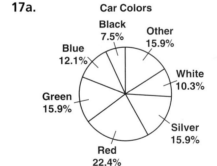

Women's Exercise Habits

- ■ Exercise frequently
- ☐ Exercise occasionally
- ☐ Never exercise

34.9% 27.7% 37.4%

17a.

Car Colors

Black 7.5%, Other 15.9%, Blue 12.1%, White 10.3%, Green 15.9%, Silver 15.9%, Red 22.4%

MIXED REVIEW **21.** $x + 2 < 14$

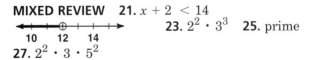

10 12 14

23. $2^2 \cdot 3^3$ **25.** prime
27. $2^2 \cdot 3 \cdot 5^2$

Lesson 7-6 — pages 351–354

ON YOUR OWN **1.** 21.0% **3.** 50% **5.** 17.6%
7. 9.3% **9.** 52.4% **11.** 23.1% **13.** 87.5%
15. 14.1% **17.** 8.1% **19.** 56.3% **21.** 150%
23. 25% decrease **25.** 12.5% decrease **27.** 50%
decrease **29.** 100% increase **31.** 25.4% **33.** 4.1%
increase **35.** 76.4% decrease **37.** 6.2% increase

MIXED REVIEW **39.** 4.5 in. **41.** $\frac{1}{4}$ in. **43.** $1\frac{1}{3}$ in.

ON YOUR OWN   **1.** $95.99   **3.** $12.83
5. $256.36   **7.** $128.58   **9.** $27.27   **11.** $57.30
13. 60%   **15.** $57.22   **17.** $17.51   **19.** $103.30
21. $419.69
23a.

	child	junior	miss
jeans	17.99	22.49	24.29
shirt	10.80	13.46	14.39
dress	15.29	17.09	20.69

MIXED REVIEW   **25.** $2^5 \cdot 3$ **27.** $2 \cdot 5^3$ **29.** $2^4 \cdot 3$
31. <   **33.** <   **35.** 1 : 24

CHECKPOINT
1.

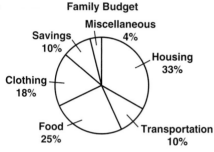

Family Budget
Miscellaneous 4%
Savings 10%
Housing 33%
Clothing 18%
Food 25%
Transportation 10%

2. 25% increase
3. 14% decrease
4. 4% decrease
5. 166% increase
6. 80% increase

7. 56% increase   **8.** $29.56

ON YOUR OWN   **1.** $954   **3.** $1,512   **5.** $1,100
7. $225   **9.** $15,298.18   **11.** $15,134.08
13. $2,415.90

MIXED REVIEW   **19.** 205   **21.** 15,000

23.

x	y
−2	3
0	7
2	11

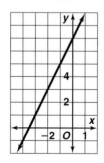

25.

x	y
−1	$-2\frac{2}{5}$
0	$\frac{3}{5}$
1	$3\frac{3}{5}$

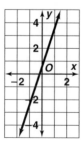

1. C   **3.** B   **5.** B   **7.** C   **9.** E   **11.** E

ON YOUR OWN   **1.** 10 ways   **3.** 19 different
amounts   **5.** 9 different ways   **7.** 480 ft.
MIXED REVIEW   **11.** 59.8   **13.** 151.85   **15.** $\frac{3}{5}$
17. $\frac{4}{5}$ **19.** $\frac{4}{3}$

1. $\frac{1}{4}$ **2.** $\frac{31}{500}$ **3.** $\frac{3}{20}$ **4.** $\frac{3}{1,000}$ **5.** $\frac{7}{5}$ **6.** $\frac{3}{8}$ **7.** $\frac{9}{25}$;
36%   **8.** $\frac{5}{4}$; 125%   **9.** $\frac{7}{10}$; 70%   **10.** $\frac{1}{20}$; 5%   **11.** $\frac{11}{4}$;
275%   **12.** $\frac{1}{125}$; 0.8%   **13.** 25   **14.** 9   **15.** 150
16. 63   **17.** 80%   **18.** 20   **19.** 3.4   **20.** $3.60
21.

Mia's Spending Budget
Movie 40%
Lunch 37.5%
Bus Fare 22.5%

22. D   **23.** $315
24. $105
25. $1,250
26. $1,225.04
28. 5 shirts, 4 pairs of socks

1. D   **3.** B   **5.** D   **7.** D   **9.** A   **11.** A   **13.** B
15. D

CHAPTER 8

ON YOUR OWN   **1.** No; 9 is not a prime number.
3.

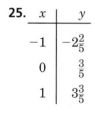

5a. 3 angles   **b.** 6 angles
c. 10 angles; 28 angles
7. 10   **9.** Rohan: 6 free throws;
Amal: 12 free throws

MIXED REVIEW   **11.** $147.75   **13.** $436.80
15. $495.45

17.

```
3 | 6 9
4 | 5 7
5 | 2 5 7
6 | 3 3 3 4 5
```

6 | 3 means 63

Lesson 8-2   pages 379–382

ON YOUR OWN   **5.** adjacent   **7.** 140   **9.** C
11a. Yes; two 90° angles are supplementary.
b. Yes; two 45° angles are complementary.
13. 51°, 141°   **15.** 16°, 106°   **17.** 66°, 156°
19. no complement, 64°   **21.** no complement, 1°
23. $2x = x + 50$; 50   **25.** $x + 2x = 90$; 30

MIXED REVIEW   **27.** yes; $51^2 + 68^2 = 85^2$ **29.** $\frac{1}{6}$

Lesson 8-3   pages 383–385

ON YOUR OWN
1.    **3.**

MIXED REVIEW   **9.** II   **11.** IV   **13.** IV
15. 22 years old

Lesson 8-4   pages 386–390

ON YOUR OWN   **1.** alternate interior
3. neither   **5.** neither   **7.** $m\angle 1 = 45°$;
$m\angle 2 = 135°$; $m\angle 3 = 135°$; $m\angle 4 = 135°$
9. $m\angle 1 = 105°$; $m\angle 2 = 75°$; $m\angle 3 = 75°$;
$m\angle 4 = 105°$ **13.** no parallel lines   **15.** $y \parallel w$;
corresponding angles are congruent.

MIXED REVIEW   **17.** 43   **19.** -136 **21.** 7   **23.** 12
25. 5   **27.** $.70

CHECKPOINT   **5.** 28°; 28°; 152°   **7a.** 8.75, 3.50,
-2.75

Toolbox   page 391

3c. $\triangle ABC$ and $\triangle DBE$ **5a.** similar

Lesson 8-5   pages 392–396

ON YOUR OWN   **1.** $\angle N$ **3.** $\angle X$ **5.** 82°   **7.** $\overline{RM}$
9. CR **11.** $NXTD$ **13.** $LMRC$ **15.** $NDTX$
17. $\triangle CRB \cong \triangle YDB$ **19.** $\triangle ABC \cong \triangle KHG$ by SAS
21. not congruent   **23.** not congruent

25. C   **27.** SAS or ASA; $x = 4$ in.; $y = 30°$; $z = 60°$

MIXED REVIEW   **31.** 6   **33.** 2   **35.** 28
37. rational   **39.** rational   **41.** 22 push-ups

Lesson 8-6   pages 397–400

ON YOUR OWN   **1.** parallelogram;
$\overline{AB} \cong \overline{DC}$, $\overline{AD} \cong \overline{BC}$; $\angle A \cong \angle C$, $\angle B \cong \angle D$
3. rhombus; $\overline{EH} \cong \overline{FG} \cong \overline{GH} \cong \overline{HE}$; $\angle E \cong \angle G$,
$\angle F \cong \angle H$ **11.** $ABDC, CDGJ, DRSL, ABGJ$
13. $\triangle ABD, \triangle ACD, \triangle BDR, \triangle DCJ, \triangle DGJ$,
$\triangle TAB, \triangle TCR$ **15.** $\triangle TKR, \triangle TAB, \triangle TCR$,
$\triangle ABD, \triangle ACD, \triangle BDR, \triangle ADJ$ **17.** $ABDC$,
$CDGJ, ABGJ$

MIXED REVIEW   **19.** 10% decrease   **21.** about 33%
decrease   **23.** about 8% decrease   **25.** <   **27.** >
29. 15 coins of each kind

Lesson 8-7   pages 401–405

ON YOUR OWN   **1.** hexagon   **3.** octagon
7. 1,800°   **9.** 3,960°   **11.** 71°   **13.** 108°   **15.** 135°
17. 140°   **21.** The angle measures in a nonregular
polygon may not be all equal.

MIXED REVIEW
23. $x < 3$ **25.** $z \le 4$ **31.** 27

CHECKPOINT   **1.** $\angle L$ **2.** $\angle D$ **3.** 90   **4.** 69
5. $\overline{KL}$ **6.** $\overline{CD}$ **7.** C   **10.** 360°   **11.** 1,080°
12. 1,800°   **13.** 2,880°

Problem Solving Practice   page 406

1. C   **3.** D   **5.** D   **7.** D

Lesson 8-8   pages 407–410

ON YOUR OWN   **11.** 1 and 4, 2 and 3, 5 and 8, 6
and 7   **13.** 1 and 3, 2 and 6, 5 and 4

MIXED REVIEW   **17.** 880   **19.** 40   **21.** 5.4; 540%
23. 0.375; 37.5%   **25.** 4.5; 450%   **27.** 233, 234,
and 235

Lesson 8-9   pages 411–415

ON YOUR OWN   **1.** 50 cm^2 **3.** 80 cm^2
5. 50.7 m^2 **7.** 13.5 m^2 **9.** 3.5 m   **13a.** Each area
is 135 ft^2.   **b.** Each area is 120 ft^2.
15. 40 cm^2; 20 cm^2 **17.** 20 in.^{2} **19.** 165 mm^2
21. 231 in.^{2} **23.** 864 in.^{2} **25a.** 104,000 km^2

b. The actual area is 109,624 km^2.

MIXED REVIEW **27.** 11 **29.** 100 **31.** 18
33. $(-6, -7)$ **35.** 9 gal

Lesson 8-10   **pages 416–420**

ON YOUR OWN **1.** 31.42 cm **3.** 15.71 m
5. 66 cm **7.** 44 m **9.** 44 km **11.** 35.97 in.;
71.94 in. **13.** 9.99 km; 19.99 km **15.** C
17. 289.53 m^2 **19.** 51.53 yd^2 **21.** 30 in.; 75 in.^{2}
23. 180 cm; 2,700 cm^2 **25.** 6 in.; 3 in.^{2}
27. 60 km; 300 km^2 **29.** 2 yd; $\frac{1}{3}$ yd^2 **31a.** 15 units
b. 94.2 units **33a.** $\frac{1}{3}$ **b.** about 201 cm^2
c. about 67 cm^2

MIXED REVIEW **35.** $\frac{11}{14}$ **37.** $-\frac{7}{11}$
39. 256 ancestors

Wrap Up   **pages 422–423**

1. 15th floor **2.** 16 parts **3.** 135°; 45°
4. 35°; 55° **5.** 48°; 132°
6.

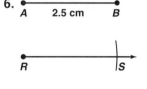

7.

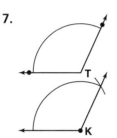

8. $\triangle MDK \cong \triangle BDJ$ by ASA **10.** 540° **11.** 1,260°
12. 1,440° **13.** 1,080° **14.** 900° **15a.** 120°
b. The measure of each angle is a factor of 360.
16. 135 in.^{2} **17.** 84 m^2 **18.** 50.27 cm^2
19. about 48 cm

Cumulative Review   **page 425**

1. A **3.** C **5.** A **7.** D **9.** D **11.** B

CHAPTER 9

Lesson 9-1   **pages 428–431**

ON YOUR OWN **1.** circle; cone; radius
3. pentagons; pentagonal prism; base edge
5. circles; cylinder; diameter **7.** rectangle;
rectangular pyramid; lateral edge **9.** rectangular
pyramid **11.** rectangular prism or cube
13. several rectangular prisms **15.** 3 cylinders
17. cylinder, cone, rectangular prism, and

triangular prism **21.** intersecting **23.** parallel
25. intersecting

MIXED REVIEW **27.** Start with 100, then
multiply by $\frac{1}{2}$ repeatedly. **31.** $y = x - 2$
33. $y = 3x - 4$ **35.** 4 h on Friday and 9 h on
Saturday

Lesson 9-2   **pages 432–436**

ON YOUR OWN
1. **3.**

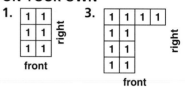

9.

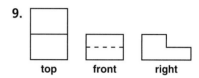

11.

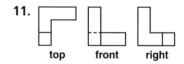

MIXED REVIEW
17. 55°; 145° **19.** no complement; 56° **21.** 2°;
92° **23.** 350%

Lesson 9-3   **pages 437–441**

ON YOUR OWN **1.** 5 surfaces; 2 triangles and
3 rectangles **3.** 3 surfaces; 1 rectangle and
2 circles **5.** 2 surfaces; 1 circle and 1 circular
sector **7.** D **9.** A **11.** B **13.**

19. cube **21.** triangular pyramid
23. rectangular prism **25.** triangular prism

MIXED REVIEW **27.** $\frac{4}{5}$ **29.** -4 **31.** 6 h 28 min

CHECKPOINT **1.** cone **2.** P **3.** $\overline{MN}$

4.
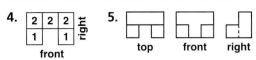

5.

| top | front | right |

6. cube

Lesson 9-4   *pages 442–446*

ON YOUR OWN **1.** second **3.** inch **5.** pint
7. 2 lb **9.** 4.3 km **11.** \$31.45 **13.** $\frac{3}{16}$ mi
15. 505 mg **17.** 9 days **19.** C **21.** 5,800 gal
23. 38° **25.** 2 ft **27.** 0.7 cm **29.** 3 digits
31. 4 digits **33.** 3 digits **35.** 4,100 **37.** 1.1
41. 0.88 **43.** 6,830 **45.** 5,400 **47.** 230

MIXED REVIEW **49.** false **51.** $-\frac{2}{3}, -\frac{1}{2}, \frac{1}{4}$
53. $-9\frac{3}{4}, -9.7, -9\frac{7}{12}$ **55.** \$840.60

Toolbox   *page 447*
---

1. $\frac{1}{2}$ qt **3.** 0.005 km **5.** $\frac{1}{2}$ g **7.** $\frac{1}{8}$ c **9.** $\frac{1}{16}$ gal
11. $\frac{1}{2}$ ft **13.** 50 mi **15.** 500 mi **17.** 17.8 mm;
18.2 mm

Lesson 9-5   *pages 448–452*

ON YOUR OWN **1.** 8,403 cm^2 **3.** 16 cm^2
5. 9,000 ft^2 **7.** 350 in.^{2} **9.** 1,000 ft^2 **11a.** about
13,986 ft^2 **b.** 43 gal **13.** 9 in. $\times$ 5.5 in. $\times$ 11.75 in.;
this box has the greater surface area. **15.** 274.9 cm^2
17. A **19.** 576 cm^2 **21.** 185 m^2

MIXED REVIEW

23. $b < -4$

25. $y < -\frac{2}{3}$

27. \$32.50 **29.** \$1,320.00

Lesson 9-6   *pages 453–457*

ON YOUR OWN **1.** 540 cm^2 **3.** 33 yd^2
5. 16.8 m^2 **7.** Use the Pythagorean theorem.
9a. $3\frac{1}{3}$ yd **b.** $15\frac{5}{9}$ yd^2 **11.** 30.3 m^2
13. 502.7 cm^2 **15.** 14.9 m^2 **17.** 1,882.5 ft^2
19. Yes; use the distributive property to get
$\pi r^2 + \pi r \ell$.

MIXED REVIEW **23.** false **25.** true
27. 1,586,000 **29.** 25,000,000,000 **31.** \$8

CHECKPOINT **1.** 57 min **2.** 4 qt **3.** 12 in.
4. 2.55 cm **5.** $\frac{7}{16}$ in. **6.** 47 cm **7.** 53.3 m^2

8. 12.3 in.^{2} **9.** sample: 0.0250 **10.** 400.7 cm^2
11. 8,042.5 cm^2 **12.** 360 in.^{2} **13.** 370 in.^{2}
14. C

Toolbox   *page 458*
---

1. 1,256.6 m^2 **3.** 50.3 in.^{2} **5.** 28.3 units^2

Lesson 9-7   *pages 459–463*

ON YOUR OWN **1.** 39 cm^3 **3.** 1,320 ft^3
5. 45 in.^{3} **7a.** 12 ft^3 **b.** \$21.48 **9.** 904.8 in.^{3}
11. 125.7 cm^3 **13.** 443.2 cm^3 **15a.** 2,025 cm^3
b. about 678.6 cm^3 **c.** The box; if each container
is the same price, the box is the better buy.
17. A **19.** about 5.5 mL **21.** 800 cm^3
23. The airspace is defined by a cylinder 8 mi tall
with a radius of about 178 mi.

MIXED REVIEW **25.** 192 **27.** 48 **29.** 80
31. 570 **33.** about 1,206.4 in.

Lesson 9-8   *pages 464–468*

ON YOUR OWN **1a.** 92 ft^2; 96 ft^3 **b.** 207 ft^2;
324 ft^3 **3a.** 156 in.^{2}; 132 in.^{3} **b.** 351 in.^{2};
445.5 in.^{3} **5a.** 327.6 m^2; 483.2 m^3 **b.** 737.1 m^2;
1,630.8 m^3 **7a.** 246.8 m^2; 225.6 m^3 **b.** 555.3 m^2;
761.4 m^3 **9.** D **11a.** 9 : 16 **b.** 27 : 64 **13.** 9 in.
15a. about 4.6 cm **b.** about 97 cm^3 **17.** 42,000 lb

MIXED REVIEW **19.** irrational **21.** irrational
23. rational **25.** \$42.90 **27.** \$46.48

Lesson 9-9   *pages 469–471*

ON YOUR OWN **1.** 3 in. **3.** 35 diagonals
5. 10 cubes **7.** 19 **9.** less **11.** 22.5 mi

MIXED REVIEW **13.** yes **15.** no **17.** 3; -5
19. -1; 3

Lesson 9-10   *pages 472–475*

ON YOUR OWN **1.** 216 in.^{3} **3.** 38 cm^3
5. 820 cm^3 **7.** 90 m^3 **9.** 1,000 cm^3
11. 100 cm^3 **13.** 0.8 cm^3 **17.** The volume is
multiplied by 8.

MIXED REVIEW **19.** 15 **21.** 65 **23.** about 25.3
25. 6% increase **27.** 40% decrease

Problem Solving Practice   *page 476*
---

1. C **3.** D **5.** D **7.** A **9.** E **11.** A

Selected Answers

1. C

3.

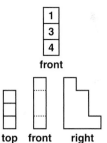

4.

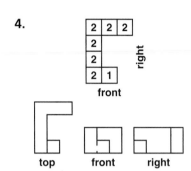

5. 3,000   **6.** 430   **7.** 0.03   **8.** 29.4   **9.** 17.3 ft^2
10. 56 m^2 **11.** 52 m^2 **12.** 1,584 in.^{3}
13. 22.5 cm   **14.** 192 cm^3; 208 cm^2
15. 6,280 in.^{3}; 879.2 in.^{2}
16. 4 prisms; $1 \times 1 \times 12$; $2 \times 2 \times 3$

1. D   **3.** B   **5.** D   **7.** A   **9.** C   **11.** C

CHAPTER 10

ON YOUR OWN   **1.** Start with 6 and add -2
repeatedly; -2, -4, -6.   **3.** Answers may vary.
Start with 8 and add 0 repeatedly or start with 8
and multiply by 1 repeatedly; 8, 8, 8.   **5.** Start
with 4 and add 3 repeatedly; 19, 22, 25.   **7.** 4

9. 11   **11.** $\frac{1}{10}$ **13.** 3   **15.** 13, 21, 34   **17.** neither;
26, 37, 50   **19.** geometric; 162; 486; 1,458
21. neither; 1.0001, 1.00001, 1.000001
23. geometric   **25.** neither   **27.** 5, 10, 15, 20, 25;
arithmetic   **29.** 30, 25, 20, 15, 10; arithmetic
31. 1, 4, 9, 16, 25; neither   **33.** 180 min   **35.** C

MIXED REVIEW   **37.** 61°; 151°   **39.** no complement;
69°   **41.** 3.7°; 93.7°

1. -3.5, -2.8, -2.1, -1.4, -0.7 **3.** 250; 200; 160;
128; 102.4   **5.** 5, 6, 7, 8, 9; start with 5 and add 1
repeatedly.   **7.** 26, 22, 18, 14, 10; start with 26
and add -4 repeatedly.   **9.** 2, 4, 8, 16, 32;
start with 2 and multiply by 2 repeatedly.
11. $\frac{1}{2}$, $\frac{1}{4}$, $\frac{1}{8}$, $\frac{1}{16}$, $\frac{1}{32}$; start with $\frac{1}{2}$ and multiply by $\frac{1}{2}$
repeatedly.

ON YOUR OWN

1.

x	5	7	9	11
y	20	28	36	44

3.

x	0	1	2	3
y	20	15	10	5

5. Yes; if you know the number of pens to buy, you
can predict the cost.   **7.** Yes; if you know the
number of words to be typed, you can predict the
amount of time.   **9.** Yes; each input has only one
output.   **11.** Yes; each input has only one output.
13. 3   **15.** 7   **17.** 14   **19.** -7 **21.** 5   **23.** 83.75
25a. 0, 1.8; 0 kilowatt-hours in 0 hours, 1.8
kilowatt-hours in 15 h   **b.** x; since x represents
input values, it represents the domain.   **c.** 20
27. -15; -5 **29.** 5; 5   **31.** 3; 4; 3; 0; neither
arithmetic nor geometric   **33.** -18; -16; -14;
-12; arithmetic   **35.** $r(\ell) = 15 - 2.5\ell$;
ℓ represents the number of lunches, and $r(\ell)$ is
the amount of money remaining.

MIXED REVIEW   **37.** 70 cm^3 **39.** 90%   **41.** 90

ON YOUR OWN

1. 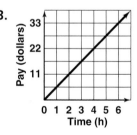   **3.**

5a. 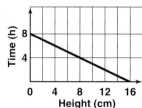   **b.** 16 cm   **c.** 8 h

7.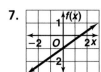

9.

12. $f(x) = 400x + 5{,}000$

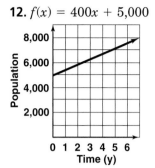

17.

Time	Height
0	4,000
1	3,400
2	2,800
3	2,200
4	1,600

19.

Depth	Pressure
0	1
10	4
20	7
30	10
40	13

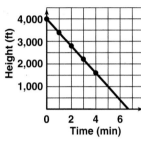

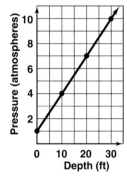

MIXED REVIEW **21.** $\triangle BCD$ **23.** $\triangle ABC$
25. $\triangle BCD$ or $\triangle ACD$ **27.** 180 **29.** 16,000

Lesson 10-4 pages 499–503

ON YOUR OWN **1.** $f(x) = 500x$; x is the time in
min; $f(x)$ is the amount of water in gal.
3a. $f(x) = 2x + 30$ **b.** 12; 12 drawings sold;

$f(12) = 54$ **5.** $f(x) = -\frac{3}{2}x + 2$ **7.** $f(x) = -x - 1$

9. no **11.** yes; $f(x) = -3x + 2$ **13.** yes;

$f(x) = \frac{3}{5}x + 6$

MIXED REVIEW **15.** 190 m^2 **17.** 408 cm^2

19. 0.75; $\frac{3}{4}$ **21.** 0.94; $\frac{47}{50}$ **23.** 0.03; $\frac{3}{100}$

CHECKPOINT **1.** neither; 25, 36, 49 **2.** geometric;
0.75, 0.375, 0.1875 **3.** geometric; 0.2, -0.04,

0.008 or $\frac{1}{5}$, $-\frac{1}{25}$, $\frac{1}{125}$ **4.** arithmetic; 56, 67, 78

5. 1 **6.** -17 **7.** -2 **8.** $-\frac{1}{2}$ **9.** -32 **10.** 28 **11.** B

Lesson 10-5 pages 504–506

ON YOUR OWN **1a.** 49 small triangles
b. 100 small triangles **c.** n^2 small triangles
d. yes; $f(n) = n^2$ **3.** 32 different arrangements
5. $10.00 **7.** 18 points **9.** 6 packages of 15,
4 packages of 20

MIXED REVIEW **11.** 21.3 km^2 **13.** 34.8 cm^2
15. 18.8% decrease **17.** 26.9% decrease
19. 6 daisies

Lesson 10-6 pages 507–510

ON YOUR OWN **1a.** 11 wk **b.** 10 wk **c.** weeks
4 and 5; about 16 km **d.** about 10 km **3a.** $2
b. $5 **c.** $8 **d.** $1
5.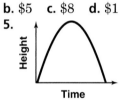

7a. The graph shows that
the water rises 40 ft, and
then returns to low tide
after 12 h. **b.** 7:30 P.M.

9.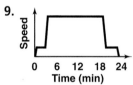

MIXED REVIEW **11.** 486 cm^2; 1620 cm^3

13. $-9\frac{11}{13}$ **15.** $-5\frac{2}{5}$ **17.** $8

Lesson 10-7 pages 511–515

ON YOUR OWN **1.** $f(x) = x^2 + 5$ **3.** $f(x) = x^2 - 4$
5. yes; $(2)^2 + 1 = 5$ **7.** yes; $2(2)^2 - 3 = 5$

9.

x	Length	$f(x)$
1	5	5
2	4	8
3	3	9
4	2	8
5	1	5

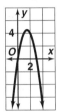

11.

x	−2	−1	0	1	2
$f(x)$	2	−1	−2	−1	2

13.

x	−1	0	1	2	3
$f(x)$	−8	0	4	4	0

15.

x	−3	−2	−1	0	1	2	3
$f(x)$	−18	−8	−2	0	−2	−8	−18

17.

x	−3	−2	−1	0	1	2	3
$f(x)$	−27	−16	−7	0	5	8	9

MIXED REVIEW

21.
Top Right Front

23.
Top Right Front

Problem Solving Practice **page 516**

1. B **3.** B **5.** C **7.** A **9.** B **11.** C **13.** D

On Your Own

1.

x	$f(x)$
2	9
3	6
6	3
9	2

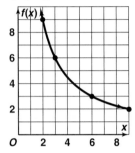

3.

x	$f(x)$
0	27
1	9
2	3
3	1

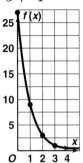

7.

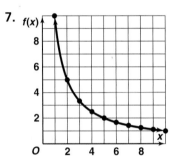

9.

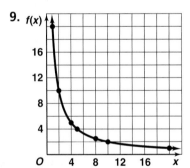

15a. yes;
$3(3) - 4 = 5$
b. no; $5 \cdot 3^{(3)} \neq 5$
c. yes; $(3)^2 - 4 = 5$
d. yes; $\frac{15}{(3)} = 5$

17a.

length	width
1	12
2	6
3	4
4	3
6	2
12	1

b. No; the ratios of $\frac{\text{change in length}}{\text{change in width}}$ are not the same for each pair of data.

c.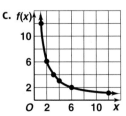

MIXED REVIEW 19. 160 m^2 **21.** 7 h

CHECKPOINT 1. $f(x) = x^2 - 3$ **2.** $f(x) = \frac{x^2}{2}$

3.

x	-4	-2	-1	0	1
$f(x)$	0	-4	-3	0	5

4.

x	-2	-1	0	1	2	3
$f(x)$	6	9	10	9	6	1

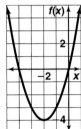
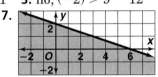

7a. $900; $1,020

b.
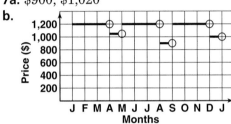

Toolbox   **page 521**

1. yes; $(-2) < 2(3) - 1$ **3.** no; $(-2) > 9 - 12$

5.
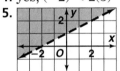
7.

13.
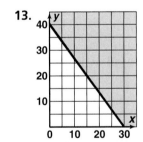

$20x + 15y \geq 600$
or $y \geq -\frac{4}{3}x + 40$

Lesson 10-9   **pages 522–524**

ON YOUR OWN 1. $2x^2 - 2x + 3$ **3.** $-3x^2 + x - 2$

5.
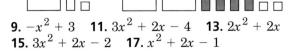
7.

9. $-x^2 + 3$ **11.** $3x^2 + 2x - 4$ **13.** $2x^2 + 2x$
15. $3x^2 + 2x - 2$ **17.** $x^2 + 2x - 1$

MIXED REVIEW 19. 12–17; 55 and older
21a. linear **b.** quadratic **c.** linear

Lesson 10-10   **pages 525–528**

ON YOUR OWN 1. $(2x^2 - 2x + 3) + (-x^2 + x + 2)$;
$x^2 - x + 5$ **3.** $8x + 2$ **5.** $8x^2 + 2x - 3$
7. $4x^2 + x$ **9.** $2x - 3$ **11.** $4x + 6$ **13.** $6x + 6$
15. $x^2 + 2x + 3$ **17.** $x^2 + 8x + 8$ **19.** $x^2 - 5x + 3$
21. $5x^2 - 2x + 11$ **25.** D

MIXED REVIEW 27. 80 in.^{3} **29.** 13 **31.** 293
33. 29.5 **35.** 8 weeks

Lesson 10-11   **pages 529–532**

ON YOUR OWN 1. $4x^2 + 4x$ **3.** $4x^2 + 6x + 2$
5. $2x^2 + x$ **7.** $6x^2 + 17x + 12$ **9.** $15x^2$ **11.** $12x^5$
13. $-6x^5$ **15.** $-40x^3$ **17.** $2x^2 + 14x$
19. $-3x^3 + 18x^2$ **21.** $-3x^4 - 6x^3 + 12x^2$

23. $\frac{3}{2}x^2 - 2x$

MIXED REVIEW 27. 6 rectangles **29.** 4 triangles
31. 74 ft^2

Wrap Up   **pages 534–535**

1. geometric; 6.25, 1.5625, 0.390625
2. arithmetic; 42, 49, 56 **3.** neither; $-30, -25, -19$
4. No; the input 2 has two different outputs.
5. 5 **6.** -7 **7.** -27 **8.** -11 **9.** -5 **10.** 393

11. yes; $f(x) = -3x + 10$ **12.** yes; $f(x) = \frac{x}{2} + 1$

13.

x	-6	-3	0	3	6
$f(x)$	-4	-2	0	2	4

14.

x	-1	0	1	2	3
$f(x)$	4	3	2	1	0

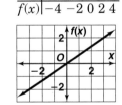
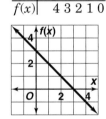

16. $f(x) = -\frac{2}{3}x + 1$ **17.** 28 numbers

19.

x	-2	-1	0	1	2
$f(x)$	4	-2	-4	-2	4

20.

x	-2	-1	0	1	2	3
$f(x)$	8	3	0	-1	0	3

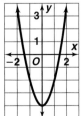
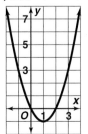

23. $11x^2 - 6x - 2$ **24.** $-3x^2 + 3$ **25.** $-x - 7$
26. $x^2 + x + 5$ **27.** $-18x^4$ **28.** $14x^2$
29. $-3x^2 + 2x$ **30.** $5x^3 - 15x^2 + 10x$

1. C   **3.** A   **5.** C   **7.** A   **9.** B

CHAPTER 11

ON YOUR OWN

1a.

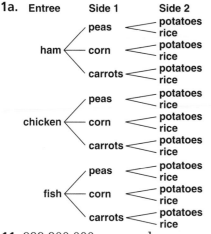

b. 18 meals
3a. 3 decisions
b. 18 kinds of film
c. 3 choices; there are 3 speed choices for a 12-exposure roll of slide film.
5. 234 cells
9. 48 kinds of cars

11. 999,900,000 more codes

MIXED REVIEW   13. 63 m^2 **15.** $72.45

ON YOUR OWN   1. 24 ways   **3.** 120 ways
5. 720 ways   **7.** 5,040 orders   **9.** 24   **11.** 120
13. 3,628,800   **15.** 1   **17.** 48   **19.** 6   **21.** The number of possible arrangements would decrease.
23. 306   **25.** 1,680   **27.** 95,040   **29.** 720
31. 2,184   **33.** 13,800 arrangements   **35.** 11,880 ways   **37.** 30,240 orders

MIXED REVIEW   39. 1,659 cm^2

ON YOUR OWN   1. purple = p, green = g, black = b, red = r, yellow = y, orange = o: pg, pb, pr, py, po, gb, gr, gy, go, br, by, bo, ry, ro, yo; 15 combinations   **3.** CL, CE, CA, CR, LE, LA, LR, EA, ER, AR; 10 combinations   **5.** 35   **7.** 84   **9.** 15
11. 10   **13.** 13   **15.** 35   **17.** 55   **19.** 10   **21.** 20
23. $_6C_2$; $_4C_2$; $_5C_2$; $_8C_2$ **25.** 2,652 outcomes
27. 1,001 possible combinations   **31.** 8,008 sets
33. B

MIXED REVIEW   35. $y = x + 3$ **37.** $y = -x + 3$

CHECKPOINT   1. 5,040   **2.** 120   **3.** 5   **4.** 336
5. 9   **6.** 48 pizzas   **7.** C

1. 1 7 21 35 35 21 7 1

1 8 28 56 70 56 28 8 1   **3.** 10   **5.** 3   **7.** 1

ON YOUR OWN   3. about 16%   **5.** about 79%
7. about 68%   **9a.** $\frac{11}{12}$ or about 92%   **b.** theoretical probability   **11.** experimental probability
13a. 1 : 1   **b.** 5 : 3

MIXED REVIEW   15. 1.60   **17.** 14.15
19. $-\frac{11}{24}$ **21.** $1\frac{3}{34}$ **23.** 7:15 A.M.

ON YOUR OWN   1. 0.7%   **3.** 15.5%   **5.** 65.2%
7. 0.1%   **9.** 3.8%   **11.** 15.6%   **13.** 10.4%   **15.** 0
17. independent   **19.** dependent   **21.** independent
23.

$P(\text{SS}) = \frac{15}{91}$; $P(\text{SU}) = \frac{24}{91}$;
$P(\text{US}) = \frac{24}{91}$; $P(\text{UU}) = \frac{28}{91}$

25a.

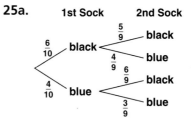

b. $\frac{4}{30}$
27. Dependent; the chances of a random person being colorblind depends on whether the person is male or female.

29a. about 0.0000015%   **b.** 4 %

MIXED REVIEW   31. $x^2 - 2x + 10$ **33.** $556.51
35. 9 and 6

ON YOUR OWN   5. $\frac{1}{4,096}$ or about 0.02%   **7.** 12 children on tricycles   **9.** 56 fence posts

MIXED REVIEW **11.** linear **13.** quadratic
15. $-3x^2 - 3x + 4$ **17.**

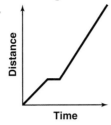

CHECKPOINT **1.** $\frac{1}{8}$ or 12.5% **2.** $\frac{2}{3}$

3. experimental probability **4.** $\frac{1}{90}$ or about 1.1%;

0 or 0%; $\frac{1}{18}$ or 5.6%

Problem Solving Practice   *page 569*

1. B **3.** C **5.** A **7.** B **9.** C

Lesson 11-7   *pages 570–573*

ON YOUR OWN **1.** $P(A) = P(B)$ **9a.** The game is
unfair; 27 out of the 36 possible products favor
player A.

MIXED REVIEW **11.** 67 m^3 **13.** 58 m^3 **15.** no
17. yes **19.** 10 diskettes and 6 packages of labels

Lesson 11-8   *pages 574–576*

ON YOUR OWN **1.** 3 heaters **5.** 3.5035 V; 3.4965 V
7. downward trend, with no defective samples

MIXED REVIEW **9.** $16x^8$ **11.** $4x^3 - 6x^2 + 6x$
13. 210 **15.** 7,920 **17.** 60,480

Wrap Up   *pages 578–579*

1. 120 outfits **2.** 20 phones **3.** 60 numbers
4. 45 ways **5.** 66 games **6.** 177,100 ways
10. independent **11.** dependent **16.** 175 toys

Cumulative Review   *page 581*

1. C **3.** D **5.** A **7.** D **9.** D **11.** D

EXTRA PRACTICE

CHAPTER 1
1.

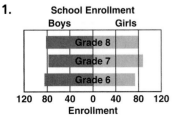
School Enrollment

3.

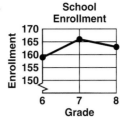

5.

Temperature	Frequency
66–70	1
71–75	0
76–80	3
81–85	3
86–90	2
91–95	2

7. 8.5, 8.5, no mode, 2.8 **9.** strong negative
11. weak positive **13.** line **15.** scatterplot **19.** $\frac{1}{2}$

CHAPTER 2 **1.** $<$ **3.** $>$ **5.** 7 **7.** 4 **9.** -2
11. -8 **13.** 23 **15.** -75 **17.** 4 **19.** 3^5
21. 4^{13} **23.** $-p^9$ **25.** -1 **27.** -9
29. 39 **31.** 56 **33.** distributive **35.** commutative
property of addition **37.** $\frac{12}{5}$ **39.** $\frac{8}{9y^2}$ **41.** $\frac{h^3}{5^3}$
43. 8.57×10^6 **45.** 5.92×10^{-4} **47.** 20,500
49. 5,600,000

CHAPTER 3 **1.** $3x + 4$ **3.** $2x + 7$ **5.** -9
7. 4.7 **9.** 63 **11.** -24 **13.** 3 **15.** $2\frac{1}{2}$ **17.** 3
19. 3 **21.** $3x - 5 = 16 + 2x$; 21 **23.** 38 cm;
70 cm^2 **27.** $x < -2$

29. $h \le -3$ **31.** $k \le -12$

CHAPTER 4 **1.** A **3.** H **5.** $(-3, 1)$; II
7. $(3, -2)$; IV **9.** 2 **11.** $\frac{5}{3}$
13. 1; 5;   **15.** $-\frac{3}{4}$; 6

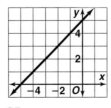 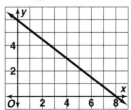

25. no

CHAPTER 5 **1.** 3 **3.** 6 **5.** 2 **7.** $3\frac{27}{50}$ **9.** $2.\overline{3}$
11. $-2\frac{2}{3}$ **13.** $0.9\overline{3}$ **15.** $-7\frac{1}{9}$ **17.** $0.2\overline{7}$
19. $-2.41\overline{6}$ **21.** $=$ **23.** $<$ **25.** $\frac{1}{2}$ **27.** $5\frac{2}{3}$

29. $-1\frac{5}{24}$ **31.** $-\frac{14}{15}$ **33.** $-\frac{5}{21}$ **35.** $-\frac{1}{12}$
37. $-\frac{3}{4}$ **39.** 15 **41.** 25.5 **43.** irrational
45. rational **47.** 11.6 ft

CHAPTER 6 **1.** 30 mi/gal **3.** 50 mi/h **5.** 18,480
7. 5 **9.** 12 **11.** $5\frac{1}{3}$ **13.** 10.5 **15.** $y = 1.5, z = 4$
17. 82.5 mi **19.** $\frac{5}{13}$ **21.** $\frac{12}{5}$ **23.** 36 ft

CHAPTER 7 **1.** $0.\overline{3}$, 33.3% **3.** $\frac{347}{100}$, 347%
5. 0.15, 15% **7.** 15 **9.** 6 **11.** 6.48 **13.** 966.67
15. 0.9216 **17.** 45%, 8%, 20%, 7%, 5%, 15%
19.

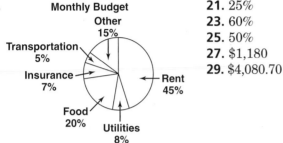

Monthly Budget
Other 15%
Transportation 5%
Insurance 7%
Rent 45%
Food 20%
Utilities 8%

21. 25%
23. 60%
25. 50%
27. $1,180
29. $4,080.70

CHAPTER 8 **1.** $\angle LMK$ or $\angle MKN$ **3.** 115° **5.** 37°
9. yes; $\triangle RST \cong \triangle NMQ$; SAS **11.** no
13. trapezoid **15.** rectangle **17.** 720° **19.** 540°
23. 60 cm^2

CHAPTER 9 **1.** cylinder **3.** rectangular pyramid
11. 25.2 m **13.** $-\frac{1}{4}$ yd **15a.** 8.6 m^2 **b.** 1.7 m^3
17a. 56.5 ft^2 **b.** 25.1 ft^3 **19a.** 96 in.^{2} **b.** 48 in.^{3}
21a. 301.6 cm^2 **b.** 301.6 cm^3 **23.** 992 cm^2,
1,920 cm^3; 2,232 cm^2,6,480 cm^3 **25.** 864 m^2,
1,728 m^3; 1,944 m^2, 5,832 m^3

CHAPTER 10 **1.** geom.; 256, 1024, 4096
3. arith.; $\frac{1}{3}$, $\frac{1}{6}$, 0 **5.** -4 **7.** 20 **9.** 8
11.

x	$f(x)$
0	0
1	3
2	6
3	9

13.

x	$f(x)$
0	1
1	1.6
2	2.2
3	2.8

15. yes; $f(x) = -2x + 8$
17. no **19.** B
21. C
27. $x^2 - 9x + 1$
29. $4x - 8$

31. $-12x^2$ **33.** $-3x^3 + 9x^2 - 12x$

CHAPTER 11 **1.** 180 **3.** 42 **5.** 100 **7.** 10
9. 15 **11.** 6 **13.** $\frac{1}{65}$ **15.** $\frac{5}{52}$ **17.** $\frac{3}{26}$
19. independent **21.** no

SKILLS HANDBOOK

PAGE 600 **1.** hundred-thousandths
3. hundredths **5.** hundred millions **7.** 0.0041
9. 0.000008 **11.** 0.012 **13.** six hundredths
15. eleven hundred-thousandths **17.** twelve
thousandths **19.** forty-two ten-thousandths

PAGE 601 **1.** < **3.** > **5.** < **7.** = **9.** < **11.** >
13. 0.23, 0.231, 2.31, 3.21, 23.1 **15.** 0.002, 0.02,
0.22, 0.222, 2.22 **17.** 0.007, 0.07, 0.7, 0.71, 0.72
19. 7, 7.0324, 7.3, 7.3246, 7.3264

PAGE 602 **1.** 105,000 **3.** 79,528,000
5. 4,312,000 **7.** 3 **9.** 101 **11.** 82.0 **13.** 20.4
15. 130.0 **17.** 96.40 **19.** 4.23 **21.** 7.06 **23.** 1,520
25. 4.2 **27.** 400 **29.** 8.1 **31.** 410 **33.** 2.58
35. 19 **37.** 7,700 **39.** 980,000,000 **41.** 0.00377
43. 12.8 **45.** 21,000

PAGE 603 **1.** 3.67 **3.** 7.312 **5.** 36.127 **7.** 1.6
9. 13.95 **11.** 60.21 **13.** 34.023 **15.** 39.95
17. 25.73 **19.** 31.95 **21.** 7.045 **23.** 6.21
25. 7.511 **27.** 2.825 **29.** 3.55 **31.** 1.434
33. 10.37 **35.** 0.32 **37.** 28.22 **39.** 37.002
41. 12.403 **43.** 747.1109 **45.** 11.36 **47.** 39.101

PAGE 604 **1.** 5.328 **3.** 2.15 **5.** 5.168
7. 0.38912 **9.** 1.1424 **11.** 2.07828 **13.** 0.48
15. 0.364 **17.** 6.5658 **19.** 41.16 **21.** 1.26
23. 12.15 **25.** 12.05 **27.** 4.8018 **29.** 18.012

PAGE 605 **1.** 0.027 **3.** 0.072 **5.** 0.0025
7. 0.00248 **9.** 0.00891 **11.** 0.00165 **13.** 0.0376
15. 0.081 **17.** 0.00072 **19.** 0.0009 **21.** 0.04
23. 0.000376 **25.** 0.012 **27.** 0.092 **29.** 0.072
31. 0.01812 **33.** 0.007

PAGE 606 **1.** 2.56 **3.** 0.776 **5.** 8.79 **7.** 0.11
9. 0.184 **11.** 2.07 **13.** 8.76 **15.** 0.0169
17. 0.0147 **19.** 0.561 **21.** 0.868 **23.** 2.551
25. 3.98 **27.** 0.025 **29.** 0.0014

PAGE 607 **1.** 560 **3.** 52 **5.** 2,367 **7.** 0.0009
9. 8 **11.** 0.001803 **13.** 13,700 **15.** 0.47
17. 0.236 **19.** 0.00041 **21.** 423 **23.** 502 **25.** 27
27. 0.4 **29.** 0.065 **31.** 26 **33.** 0.0003 **35.** 15.8

PAGE 608 **1.** 84 **3.** 452 **5.** 32 **7.** 31.1 **9.** 3.1
11. 26 **13.** 31 **15.** 16 **17.** 44 **19.** 2.8 **21.** 3.6
23. 1.24 **25.** 58.3 **27.** 31.4 **29.** 3.96 **31.** 0.53
33. 9.5 **35.** 1.6 **37.** 3.58 **39.** 0.243 **41.** 3.44
43. 1.86 **45.** 3.77

PAGE 609 **1.** 0.046 **3.** 0.075 **5.** 0.0095
7. 0.0025 **9.** 0.085 **11.** 0.015 **13.** 0.0035
15. 0.07 **17.** 0.0021 **19.** 0.00015 **21.** 0.006

23. 0.009   **25.** 0.0035   **27.** 0.033   **29.** 0.073   **31.** 0.0056

PAGE 610   **1.** 2   **3.** 10   **5.** 12   **7.** 24   **9.** 3   **11.** 16   **13.** 30   **15.** 21   **17.** $\frac{5}{6}$ **19.** $\frac{3}{4}$ **21.** $\frac{4}{5}$ **23.** $\frac{1}{2}$ **25.** $\frac{3}{7}$ **27.** $\frac{3}{5}$ **29.** $\frac{11}{12}$ **31.** $\frac{3}{4}$ **33.** $\frac{3}{7}$ **35.** $\frac{2}{9}$ **37.** $\frac{1}{2}$ **39.** $\frac{4}{7}$

PAGE 611   **1.** $1\frac{2}{5}$ **3.** $3\frac{1}{4}$ **5.** $1\frac{3}{10}$ **7.** $2\frac{5}{8}$ **9.** $3\frac{2}{5}$ **11.** $4\frac{1}{4}$ **13.** $5\frac{2}{5}$ **15.** $3\frac{3}{4}$ **17.** $1\frac{1}{3}$ **19.** $4\frac{1}{2}$ **21.** $5\frac{1}{2}$ **23.** $4\frac{1}{4}$ **25.** $\frac{3}{2}$ **27.** $\frac{13}{12}$ **29.** $\frac{16}{7}$ **31.** $\frac{23}{8}$ **33.** $\frac{26}{5}$ **35.** $\frac{37}{4}$ **37.** $\frac{63}{8}$ **39.** $\frac{24}{7}$ **41.** $\frac{31}{10}$

PAGE 612   **1.** $1\frac{2}{5}$ **3.** $\frac{4}{7}$ **5.** $1\frac{1}{5}$ **7.** $\frac{3}{8}$ **9.** $\frac{3}{5}$ **11.** 1   **13.** $4\frac{2}{5}$ **15.** $1\frac{1}{3}$ **17.** $8\frac{1}{4}$ **19.** $11\frac{1}{2}$ **21.** 11   **23.** $4\frac{3}{5}$ **25.** $\frac{3}{4}$

PAGE 613   **1.** $\frac{9}{20}$ **3.** 4   **5.** $\frac{5}{12}$ **7.** $\frac{1}{25}$ **9.** $\frac{1}{16}$ **11.** $3\frac{5}{9}$ **13.** $7\frac{1}{2}$ **15.** $43\frac{3}{4}$ **17.** $1\frac{3}{8}$ **19.** $\frac{7}{8}$ **21.** $1\frac{3}{8}$ **23.** $\frac{1}{81}$ **25.** 6   **27.** $\frac{9}{40}$ **29.** $1\frac{3}{4}$ **31.** $\frac{2}{5}$ **33.** $11\frac{3}{4}$ **35.** $3\frac{4}{7}$

PAGE 614   **1.** 6   **3.** 5   **5.** 3   **7.** 12   **9.** >   **11.** <   **13.** <   **15.** >   **17.** >   **19.** <   **21.** >   **23.** >   **25.** >   **27.** <   **29.** >   **31.** <   **33.** >

ADDITIONAL TOPICS

PAGE 615   **1.** d^{24} **3.** 9^{10} **5.** y^{15} **7.** 7^{27} **9.** p^{36} **11.** 5^{10} **13.** 2^{45} **15.** x^{30} **17.** x^{17} **19.** y^{13} **21.** 5^{19} **23.** 6^{32} **25.** 729   **27.** 512

PAGE 617

1.

3.

5.

7. $p < -5$ or $p > -1$

9. $t > -3$ and $t < 0$ **11.** $x < -3$ or $x \ge 2$;
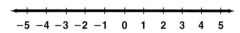

13. all numbers;

15. $r > -8$ and $r \ge -3$;

17. $h \ge -1$ or $h > 4$;

19. no solution;

21. $n > 1$ and $n < 3$;

23. $b \le -3$ or $b > 8$;

PAGE 619   **1.** 81   **3.** 2   **5.** 11   **7.** 33   **9.** 65   **11.** 259   **13.** 244   **15.** 38   **17.** 10   **19.** 300 km   **21.** 102 L   **23.** 40 in.   **25.** 1,000 L   **27.** 6 qt   **29.** ≈299 mi   **31.** ≈74 in.   **33.** ≈32,453 L

PAGE 621   **1.** $15, $215   **3.** $690, $12,690   **5.** $0.56, $22.96   **7.** $8,500, $9,073.75   **9.** $5\frac{1}{2}$%, $19.25   **11.** $880

Index

Index

defined, 169
distances in, 267
graphing, 168–171, 214
graphing equations in, 173–175, 190–193, 194–197
inequalities in, 521
ordered pairs, 169, 172, 174, 175, 214, 224, 513
origin, 169, 185, 297
plotting points, 168–171, 214
polygons in, 199–202, 204–212
quadrant, 169, 170, 495
reflections in, 204–208, 215
slope-intercept form, 182–186, 214, 233
transformations. *See* Transformations
translations in, 198–202, 215, 408
x-axis, 169, 495
x-coordinate, 169, 214
y-axis, 169, 495
y-coordinate, 169, 214
See also Graph; Graphing

Corresponding angles, 291–293, 387–389, 422

Corresponding parts
of congruent triangles, 392–395
of similar triangles, 291, 309–311

Corresponding sides, 291–293, 322

Cosine, 317–320

Counting
tree diagram for, 540–542
using multiplication, 540–543

Counting principle, 541, 542, 578

Critical Thinking, 311. *See also* Reasoning exercises

Cross product, 286–287, 595

Cube
edges of, 462, 468
net of, 441
surface area of, 451, 452, 464
volume of, 85, 464, 468

Cumulative Reviews, 57, 113, 165, 217, 273, 325, 373, 425, 481, 537, 581

Customary system of measurement, 281–285, 593

Cylinder
base of, 428–430, 449, 461
defined, 428
height of, 449, 461
net of, 438–440
surface area of, 449, 451, 452, 547, 596
volume of, 90, 461–463, 466, 479, 596

Data
in bar graph, 4–8, 54
in box–and-whisker plot, 27–30, 54–55
choosing appropriate graph for, 38–41
in circle graph, 37–40, 232, 240, 347–350, 371
collecting, 34, 35, 508, 557
comparing, 28, 30
on computer spreadsheet, 31, 32, 146, 361, 542
in decision making, 574–576, 579
in double bar graph, 8, 31
frequency, 14
in frequency table, 14–18
graphing with spreadsheet program, 31
in histogram, 15–18, 54
in line graph, 6, 54
in line plot, 14–15, 16, 54
in multiple line graph, 6, 54
organizing and displaying, 4–8
population, 42
quartile, 27
random sample, 42, 55
range of, 25, 26, 54, 181
reading on graph, 9–12
sample, 42, 55
scale of, 10–12
in stem-and-leaf plot, 24–26, 54–55, 273
in survey, 42–45, 55
trends in, 33–34, 35, 36, 55

Data analysis
average. *See* Mean
comparison, 28, 30, 38
Cooperative learning, 20
decision making with probability, 574–576, 579
interpreting and making graphs and tables, 4–18
interpreting probabilities, 49–52
making predictions, 32–36, 55
misleading information, 9, 467
problems involving, 6, 8, 20, 25, 28, 62, 232, 240, 420, 508, 509
surveys, 42–45, 55
trends, 33–34, 35, 36, 55

Decagon, 401, 404, 409, 428

Decimals
adding, 603
comparing, 236, 237, 601
dividing by, zero in, 609
dividing by decimal, 608
dividing by whole number, 606
estimating with, 351
modeling, 328, 329
multiplying, 604

ordering, 601
place value of, 328, 600
as rational number, 226–229, 236, 237, 270
repeating, 230–233, 270, 289
rounding, 130, 278
in scientific notation, 104, 105, 106, 107
subtracting, 603
terminating, 229, 231, 232, 270
writing as fraction, 230–233, 270, 328
writing as percent, 329–333, 370
writing fraction as, 229–230, 231, 270, 410, 420
writing mixed number as, 231, 420
writing percent as, 137, 331–333, 370, 503

Decimal patterns, 230, 231, 328

Decision making
choosing appropriate graph, 38–41
mean, median, or mode, 20–23, 54
with probability, 574–576, 579
using data in, 574–576, 579

Decoding, 14

Decrease, percent of, 351–354, 371, 400, 475, 506

Deductive reasoning, 388

Denominator, 225, 226, 229, 235, 328, 331
adding and subtracting fractions, 240–248
common, 235
comparing to numerator, 239
least common, 235
like, 240–243, 612
multiplying and dividing fractions, 249–253
unlike, 244–246, 271

Density property, 595

Dependent events, 560–563, 579

Diagonal
of parallelogram, 412
of regular polygon, 401, 403

Diagram
drawing, xxiv, 305–307, 323
as problem solving strategy, xxiv, 305–307, 323
tree, 51, 52, 540–542, 560
Venn, 63, 187–188, 222, 234, 260, 398

Diameter, 416, 417, 419

Difference
common, 485, 487, 534
evaluating mentally, 91–92
sign of, 73, 110
See also Subtraction

Digit
nonzero, 444

evaluating sums and differences, 91–92, 94, 111

fractions, 231, 237, 288, 295

with percents, 63, 332, 353

solving equations, 123, 129

using properties, 91–95, 111

volume, 463

Message decoding, 14

Metric system, units of measurement in, 281–285, 593, 618–619

Misleading information, 9, 467

Mixed numbers, 611

adding and subtracting, 241–243

like denominators, 241–243, 271

multiplying and dividing, 250–253

as rational numbers, 225, 249

repeating decimal to, 232

simplifying, 232, 242, 246, 247, 253, 420

writing as decimals, 230–231, 420

writing as improper fractions, 226, 242, 250

Mixed Reviews, 8, 12, 18, 23, 26, 30, 36, 41, 45, 48, 52, 63, 68, 72, 76, 81, 85, 90, 95, 98, 102, 107, 119, 124, 130, 134, 137, 141, 145, 151, 156, 160, 171, 175, 180, 186, 189, 193, 197, 202, 208, 212, 224, 228, 233, 238, 243, 248, 253, 256, 262, 267, 280, 285, 289, 295, 300, 304, 307, 312, 316, 320, 333, 337, 341, 346, 350, 354, 359, 364, 368, 378, 382, 385, 390, 396, 400, 405, 410, 415, 420, 431, 436, 441, 446, 452, 457, 463, 468, 471, 475, 488, 494, 498, 503, 506, 510, 515, 520, 524, 528, 532, 543, 547, 552, 558, 563, 567, 573, 576

Mode, 20–23, 54, 378

Model

algebraic. *See* Algebra tiles

nets, 438–441, 451, 454, 478

number line. *See* Number line

scale, 275, 289, 295, 300, 302–304, 312, 321, 323, 466, 468

train, 303

verbal. *See* Verbal models, phrases, and descriptions

Modeling

addition, 69–70, 71

area, 529–530, 561, 562

decimals, 328, 329

exercises that use, 71, 75, 118, 121, 122, 126, 128, 131, 138, 139, 140, 329

expressions, 69–70, 71, 116, 118

factors, 220

integers, 69–71

percents, 334

polynomials, 522–524

ratios, 278

simplifying variable expressions, 118

solving equations, 120, 122, 126, 131, 138, 139

subtraction, 73, 75

variable expressions, 116, 118

Money

exchange rate for, 287, 289

making change, xxii, 256, 470

principal and interest, 360–364, 371, 378, 452

real-world applications of, xxii, 48, 64, 66, 79, 108, 121, 129, 154, 194, 256, 287, 289, 335, 336, 353, 367, 368, 498, 519, 620–621

unit price, 277, 280

Monomial

defined, 530, 535

multiplying, 530, 535

Multiple

common, 234, 237

defined, 234

least common, 234–235, 237, 270

of 10% and 1%, 335–336

Multiple line graph, 6, 54

Multiple strategies, 469–471, 479

Multiplication

of binomials, 530–531

of decimals, 604

estimating products, 239

exponents and, 83–84

of fractions, 613

of integers, 77–78, 79, 80–81, 110

of measures, 444, 446

mental math and, 92–93, 94

of mixed numbers, 250–253

modeling, 531, 532

of polynomials, 530–532, 535

by powers of ten, 607

of powers with same base, 83–84, 530, 595

in problems involving percents, 334–336

properties of, 91, 92, 93

of rational numbers, 249–253, 271

in ratios and proportions, 286–288, 338–341

in scientific notation, 103–107

sign of, 77–78, 80, 110

for solving equations, 128–130, 162, 250

for solving inequalities, 159–160, 163

of unlike fractions, 249–253, 271

verbal phrases and descriptions for, 95, 129, 192, 249

Multiplication properties

of equality, 128, 595

for inequalities, 159, 595

Multiplicative inverse, 250, 595

Multi-step equation

solving, 138–141

solving using distributive property, 139

Natural numbers, 260

Negative exponent, 100–102, 595

Negative number, 60, 75. *See also* Integers

Negative slope, 177–179

Negative square root, 258

Negative trend, 34, 36

Net, 438–441, 451, 454, 478, 532

Nonagon, 401, 428

Nonlinear equation, 511–515, 517–520

Nonlinear function, 511–515, 517–520, 535

graphing, 517–520

quadratic, 511–515, 535

Nonzero digit, 444

Notation

arrow, 199

combination, 548, 549

factorial, 545

function, 491–494, 534

permutation, 545–547

scientific, 103–107, 111, 267, 457

Number line

absolute value, 61

decimals on, 236

estimating on, 239

fractions on, 236, 239, 334

graphing inequalities on, 148–151, 163, 228, 350,

integers on, 61, 69, 72

line plots, 14–15

opposites on, 60

quartiles on, 27, 29

rational numbers on, 228, 236

Number pattern, 256, 377, 390, 484–488

Numbers

classifying, 63, 260

comparing, 61–63, 235–238, 270

compatible, 283, 334–335

composite, 221, 223, 233

factoring, 220–224

irrational, 259–262, 271, 468

natural, 260

cosine, 317–320, 599
defined, 276, 322
equivalent, 226
of measures of similar polygons,
    291, 292, 309, 310, 322, 391
of measures of similar three-
    dimensional figures, 464–468, 479
modeling, 278
in problem solving, 277
rate. *See* Rate
reciprocal of, 283, 595
scale factors, 296, 297, 298, 299,
    300, 301, 322, 466, 468
simplest form of, 276–277, 278, 322
sine, 317–320, 323
slope as, 176–177
tangent, 313–316, 323, 599
trigonometric, 313–316, 317–320,
    323, 599
writing rational number as, 227, 270

Rational numbers, 225–228, 285,
    346
adding and subtracting, 240–248,
    271
comparing and ordering, 235–238,
    270
as decimals, 225–228, 236, 237
defined, 225, 260, 270
dividing, 251–252, 271
equivalent, 226
identifying, 225–228, 468
multiplying, 249–253, 271
on number line, 228, 236
opposites of, 228
reciprocal of, 250, 595
simplest form of, 225, 227, 270
solving equations with, 245–248
in Venn diagram, 260
writing as ratios, 227, 270
See also Decimals, Fractions,
    Integers, Mixed numbers, Whole
    numbers

Ray, 383, 384

Reading about Math, 81, 133, 150,
    180, 247, 279, 340, 354, 389, 462

Real numbers
classifying, 259–262
properties of, 595
in Venn diagram, 260

Real-world applications. *See*
Connections to real-world
applications

Reasoning
demonstrate understanding, 23, 49,
    102, 107, 119, 123, 124, 150, 200,
    221, 259, 403, 435, 443, 494, 502,
    540, 543, 565, 572
develop a formula or a procedure,
    26, 195, 208, 233, 255, 278, 449,
    451, 553

justify or rationalize conclusions,
    36, 94, 195, 224, 244, 262, 283,
    285, 302, 347, 388, 394, 397, 398,
    402, 416, 440, 448, 455, 475, 563,
    572
make comparisions, 7, 25, 179, 314,
    401, 411, 428, 460, 550
make conjectures, 207, 402, 547,
    573
See also Draw a Conclusion;
    Deductive reasoning; Inductive
    reasoning; Logical reasoning;
    Spatial reasoning; Think About It

Reciprocal, 250, 283, 331

Recorder, xxvii

Rectangle
area of, 411, 529–530, 531, 596
congruent, 292
defined, 397
modeling factors in, 220
perimeter of, 143–146, 596
surface area of, 552
vertex of, 171

Rectangular prism
net of, 439, 441
surface area of, 448, 450–452
volume of, 459, 461–463, 494, 596

Rectangular pyramid, volume of,
143

Reduction, 298, 299, 300

Reflection
in coordinate plane, 204–208, 215
defined, 204
graphing, 204–208
line of, 204
line symmetry and, 206–208

Reflectional symmetry, 206–208,
215

Reflexive property of equality, 595

Regular polygon
angles of, 402–405
defined, 402, 423
patterns in, 407
tiling with, 407–410, 423, 471

Repeated addition, 77

Repeating decimal, 229–233, 270,
289, 337

Research, 18, 30, 68, 145, 202, 284,
333, 415, 543

Researcher, xxvii

Reviews. *See* Chapter Wrap Ups,
Checkpoints, Cumulative Reviews,
Extra Practice, Math Toolboxes,
Mixed Reviews, Quick Reviews

Rhombus, 397

Right angle, 290, 398

Right triangle, 307

defined, 263, 398
hypotenuse of, 263–266, 475
identifying, 265–267
legs of, 263–266, 313, 314, 317, 318
Pythagorean theorem and,
    263–267, 271, 311, 319, 475
ratio of side lengths of, 313–316,
    317–320, 323
trigonometric ratios, 313–316,
    317–320, 323, 599

Right view, 433–435, 478

Rojas, Hector, 439

Rotation, 209–212, 215
center of, 209
defined, 209
graphing, 209–212, 415

Rotational symmetry, 210–212, 215

Rounding, 602
compatible numbers, 283
decimals, 130, 602
exercises that use, 98, 130, 316,
    446, 458, 474–475
fractions, 239
percents, 332, 353

Sale price, 356–359, 371, 468

Sales tax, 620–621

Sample
defined, 42, 55
random, 42, 55

Sample space, 50–52, 55, 571–573

Scale
on graph, 10–12
of model, 302, 303, 312, 468

Scale factor
defined, 296, 322, 466
finding, 298, 299, 300, 301, 466, 468

Scale model, 302–304, 468
building, 275, 289, 295, 300, 312,
    321
defined, 302

Scalene triangle, 398

Scatter plot, 32–36, 55
best-fit (trend) line, 33–34, 35, 36, 55
defined, 32, 55
finding trends with, 33–34, 35, 36
making, 32
predictions and, 33–36, 55

Scientific calculator, 257

Scientific notation, 103–107, 111,
267
on calculator, 105, 106
changing to standard form,
    104–105, 106, 267, 457
defined, 103, 111
using, 103–104, 111

Index

evaluating, 65–68, 75, 86, 110, 111
with exponent, 88–90, 615
like terms in, 117–119, 138
modeling with algebra tiles, 116, 118
monomials, 530, 535
polynomials, 522–532, 535, 563, 567
simplifying, 101–102, 116–119
terms in, 117–119, 138, 522–523
verbal model for, 64–67, 130, 253
writing, 64, 66, 90, 111

Venn diagram, 63, 187–188, 260, 398
classifying quadrilaterals in, 397
identifying greatest common factor, 222
identifying least common multiple, 234
of numbers, 63, 260
organizing information in, 187–188

Verbal models, phrases, and descriptions
for addition, 69, 71, 95
for division, 129
for inequality, 147–149, 160, 350
for integers, 60–62
for multiplication, 91, 95, 129, 249
for variable expressions, 64–67, 130, 253
for writing equations, 135–137, 163, 192, 194–195
for writing linear equations, 194–195
for writing rules in function notation, 499–500

Vertex
of angle, 290
of rectangle, 171
of three-dimensional figure, 428, 472
of triangle, 199, 201, 204, 206, 207, 392

Vertical angle, 379–382, 422

Vertical line, graph of, 184

Vertical method for adding or subtracting rational numbers, 241

Views of three-dimensional figures, 432–435, 478, 515

front, 433–435, 478
isometric, 433
right, 433–435, 478
top, 433–435, 478

Visualizing three-dimensional figures, nets for, 437–438

Visual thinking, 11, 176, 182, 190, 194, 199, 413, 501, 508, 511, 512, 518, 530, 531

Volume
area and, 459
of composite shapes, 474, 475
of cone, 473–475, 479, 573, 596
of cube, 85, 464, 468
of cylinder, 90, 461–463, 466, 479, 596
defined, 459, 479
of prism, 459–463, 465, 466, 479, 510
of pyramid, 143, 472–475, 479, 573, 596
of rectangular prism, 459, 463, 494, 596
of similar solids, 464–469, 479
of sphere, 596
units of, 281, 282, 593

Web Extension. *See* Internet

Weight, units of, 281, 282, 593, 618–619

What If, 190, 199

Whisker, 27

Whole amount
finding, 339–341
finding part of, 339

Whole numbers
defined, 228
dividing decimals by, 606

Work Backward **problem solving strategy,** 254–256, 271

Work Together. *See* Cooperative learning

Write an Equation **problem solving strategy,** xxv, 135–137, 163

Writing exercises, 8, 11, 18, 23, 26, 30, 31, 36, 40, 44, 52, 55, 56, 63, 68, 72, 75, 80, 84, 89, 94, 102, 107, 110, 112, 119, 123, 125, 129, 133, 140, 144, 150, 155, 159, 162, 164, 171, 175, 179, 181, 185, 196, 202, 207, 208, 212, 215, 216, 223, 227, 232, 233, 237, 242, 247, 252, 261, 266, 272, 280, 284, 288, 294, 299, 303, 310, 316, 319, 323, 324, 333, 337, 340, 345, 349, 354, 358, 363, 371, 372, 377, 382, 385, 395, 400, 403, 404, 409, 414, 419, 423, 424, 431, 435, 440, 445, 447, 451, 456, 458, 463, 467, 475, 478, 480, 487, 493, 498, 502, 510, 514, 524, 528, 532, 535, 536, 543, 551, 557, 563, 565, 568, 572, 575, 579, 580. *See also* Journal, Portfolio

***x*-axis,** 169, 495

***x*-coordinate,** 169, 199–200, 214

***x*-intercept,** 191–193, 300

***y*-axis,** 169, 495

***y*-coordinate,** 169, 199–200, 214

***y*-intercept,** 182–185, 191–193, 214, 295, 300
slope and, 182–186

Zero
in decimal division, 609
as exponent, 100, 595
in product, 605

Zero pair, 122, 131, 523

Zero-product property, 595

Zero slope, 178

Cover Design: Bruce Bond; Martucci Studio

Cover Photos: Martucci Studio

Book Design: Olena Serbyn; Brown Publishing Network

Page Design and Design Management: Brown Publishing Network

Technical Illustration: GTS Graphics; Brown Publishing Network

ILLUSTRATION

Annie Bissett: 7, 232, 264, 309, 316, 357, 360, 463, 467

Dan Brawner: 193, 240, 254, 354, 541, 545, 564

Daniel Collins: 88, 426

Andrea Golden: 200, 224, 252, 551

Tom Klare: 79, 93, 139, 452

Tom Lochray: 28, 329, 561, 562

Karen Minot: 62, 74, 158, 198, 389, 404, 405, 406, 410, 510

Michael Moran: 172, 259, 332, 335

Ortelius Design: 304, 411

Outlook/ANCO: 177

Steve Pica: 96

Matthew Pippin: 529

Gary Torrisi: 106, 431

Camille Venti: 18, 34, 156, 175, 300, 491, 519, 524

Rose Zgodzinski: 8, 12, 29, 66, 95, 294

PHOTOGRAPHY

Photo Research: Brown Publishing Network

Front Matter

vii, Bob Daemmrich/The Image Works; **viii,** Paul Conklin/Photo Edit; **ix,** Ed Elbertfield/Uniphoto; **x,** Bob Daemmrich/The Image Works; **xi,** Superstock; **xii,** Viviane Holbrooke/Stock Market; **xiii,** Steve Munday/Allsport; **xiv,** Richard Wood/The Picture Cube; **xv,** Jean Higgins/Envision; **xvi,** Michael Newman/Photo Edit; **xvii,** Superstock; **xviii,** Lawrence Migdale; **xix c,** Prentice Hall photo by Irene Perlman; **xix t,** Bob Daemmrich/The Image Works; **xx,** Bill Horseman/Stock Boston; **xxiii,** Chris Luneski/Index Stock; **xxiv,** Bob Daemmrich; **xxvi,** **xxix,** Edith G. Haun/Stock Boston

Chapter One

2–3, J. W. Meyers/Stock Boston; **5,** Bob Daemmrich/ Image Works; **9,** Superstock; **11,** Stefan Meyers/Earth Scenes; **14,** UPI-Corbis/Bettmann; **17,** William Sallas/Duomo; **20,** Prentice Hall photo by Ken O'Donoghue; **22,** Prentice Hall photo by Russ Lappa; **24,** Hershkowitz/Monkmeyer; **25,** Prentice Hall photo by Ken O'Donoghue; **33,** Prentice Hall photo by Ken O'Donoghue; **34,** Joe Carini/The Image Works; **37,** Burns/Monkmeyer; **38,** Bob Daemmrich; **40,** Frank Siteman/Tony Stone Images; **43,** Bob Daemmrich/ The Image Works; **45,** Richard Nowitz/Photo Researchers; **47,** Al Tielemans/Duomo; **49,** Prentice Hall photo by Ken O'Donoghue; **51,** Dale Durfee/Tony Stone Images

Chapter Two

58–59, Art Wolfe/Tony Stone Images; **60,** David Young-Wolff/Photo Edit; **62,** Dave Davis/FPG; **65,** D. & I. MacDonald/The Picture Cube; **67,** Superstock; **68,** David Young-Wolff/Photo Edit; **73,** Art Wolfe; **76,** Ed Carlin/The Picture Cube; **81,** Bob Abraham/ Pacific Stock; **83,** Prentice Hall photo by Russ Lappa; **84,** Rick Scott/The Picture Cube; **88,** Mark Richards Photo Edit; **99,** Photo Researchers; **101,** R. F. Head/Animals, Animals; **103,** Stock Market; **105,** Paul Conklin/Photo Edit

Chapter Three

114–115, Stock Market; **116,** Ed Elbertfeld/Uniphoto; **119,** Esbin-Anderson/The Image Works; **121,** Tess Codrington/Tony Stone Images; **123,** Andrew Sacks/Tony Stone Images; **127,** Terry Wachter/Photo Researchers; **129,** Katherine Lambert; **130,** Billy E. Barnes/Stock Boston; **133,** Cameron Hervet/Tony Stone Images; **135,** Bernard Wolf/Monkmeyer; **136,** Dick Blume/The Image Works; **141,** Bob Daemmrich/The Image Works; **143,** Jeff Schultz/Alaska Stock; **144,** Okapia-Frank/Photo Researchers; **147a,** David Young-Wolff/Photo Edit; **147b,** Dick Blume/The Image Works; **147c,** Michael Newman/Photo Edit; **154,** R. Hutchings/Photo Edit

Chapter Four

166–167, Bob Daemmrich/The Image Works; **169,** Kobal Collection; **170,** Four by Five/Superstock; **177,** Art Wolfe; **178,** David Young-Wolff/Photo Edit; **183,** Jim Steinberg/ Photo Researchers; **186,** Bob Daemmrich/Stock Boston; **191,** Bob Daemmrich/ Image

Works; **195,** Mark Richards/Photo Edit; **196,** Prentice Hall photo by Ken O'Donoghue; **202,** Prentice Hall photo by Russ Lappa; **204,** Prentice Hall photo by Russ Lappa; **206,** Prentice Hall photo by Russ Lappa; **207l,** Nuridsany et Perennou/Photo Researchers; **207r,** Prentice Hall photo by Russ Lappa; **208,** Rod Williams/Bruce Coleman

Chapter Five

218–219, Superstock; **220,** Prentice Hall photo by Russ Lappa; **222,** Chromosohm/Sohm/Photo Researchers; **225,** Courtesy Bun Boy Restaurant; **227,** Viola's Photo Visions; **229,** Topps, photo by Russ Lappa; **230,** Prentice Hall photo by Russ Lappa; **234,** Bob Daemmrich/Stock Boston; **237,** K. McGlynn/The Image Works; **240,** Prentice Hall photo by Russ Lappa; **243,** Arthur Grace/Stock Boston; **244,** Prentice Hall photo by Russ Lappa; **247,** David Ball/Picture Cube; **249,** Superstock; **251,** Bob Daemmrich/The Image Works; **261,** Comstock; **264,** Deborah Davis/Photo Edit; **273,** Superstock

Chapter Six

274–275, Dave Bartruff; **277,** Randi Anglin/Image Works; **280,** Byron/ Monkmeyer; **283,** Stuart Westmorland/Photo Researchers; **284,** Uniphoto; **287,** DeRichmond/The Image Works; **289,** George Haling/Photo Researchers; **294,** Kobal Collection; **298,** Viviane Holbrooke/Stock Market; **302,** Cameramann/Image Works; **306,** J. Pickerell/Image Works; **314,** Uniphoto; **318,** David Lassman/Image Works

Chapter Seven

326–327, Prentice Hall photo by Tracy Wheeler; **329,** David Young-Wolff/Photo Edit; **331,** Tom McCarthy/Photo Edit; **335,** Nicole Bergiveno/ Matrix; **336,** Superstock; **337,** Superstock; **339,** Jim Zipp/Photo Researchers; **340,** Steve Munday/Allsport; **345,** David Grossman/Photo Researchers; **347,** Uniphoto; **348,** Fotos International/Archive Photo; **350,** John Berry/Image Works; **357,** John Boykin; **356,** Courtesy Don Calla, Brockton High School/Photo Edit; **360,** Michael Newman/Photo Edit; **362,** Bill Bachmann/Photo Edit

Chapter Eight

374–375, Bill Horseman/Stock Boston; **376,** John Elk III/Stock Boston; **378,** Kindra Clineff/The Picture Cube; **380,** David Frazier; **384,** Prentice Hall photo by Jon Chomitz; **386t,** Prentice Hall photo by Mark Thayer; **386b,** Richard Wood/The Picture Cube; **393,** Angela Sciaraffa; **395,** Photo Researchers; **396,** *Stomp,* photo by Junichi Takanashi; **399,** Prentice Hall photo by Russ Lappa; **400,** Prentice Hall photo by Russ Lappa; **403,** Robert Finken/The Picture Cube; **404,** Ed Bock/ Stock Market; **407t,** Superstock; **407b,** M. C. Escher's "Symmetry Drawing E25" ©1997 Cordon Art-Baarn-Holland. All rights reserved; **408,** Jayne R. Phillips/The Picture Cube; **409l,** Thomas W. Martin/Photo Researchers; **409r,** Corel; **413,** Joyce Photographics/Photo Researchers; **417l,** Carol Lee/The Picture Cube; **417r,** Carol Lee/The Picture Cube

Chapter Nine

426–427, Prentice Hall photo by Ken O'Donoghue; **429,** Superstock; **432,** Prentice Hall photos by Russ Lappa; **433,** Prentice Hall photo by Russ Lappa; **436,** David Young-Wolff/Photo Edit; **442,** Bob Daemmrich/The Image Works; **445,** Jean Higgins/Envision; **448,** Breck Kent/Animals, Animals; **451,** Will & Deni McIntyre/Photo Researchers; **453,** Crandall/The Image Works; **459,** Prentice Hall photo by Russ Lappa; **461,** Brady/Monkmeyer; **462,** Prentice Hall photo by Tracy Wheeler; **465,** Schaefer/Monkmeyer; **473,** Superstock

Chapter Ten

482–483, Nawrocki/Picture Perfect; **485,** Superstock; **486,** David Young-Wolff/Photo Edit; **488,** Kobal Collection; **492,** Robert Brenner/Photo Edit; **497,** Duomo; **499,** Michael Newman/Photo Edit; **500,** Michael Newman/ Photo Edit; **507,** Superstock; **509,** Superstock; **513,** Prentice Hall photo by Ken O'Donoghue; **515,** Mimi Forsyth/Monkmeyer; **517,** Superstock

Chapter Eleven

538–539, Todd Warshaw/Allsport; **546,** Frank Siteman/The Picture Cube; **548,** Prentice Hall photo by Russ Lappa; **552,** David Young-Wolff/Photo Edit; **554,** Fred R. Palmer/Stock Boston; **566,** Superstock; **571,** Prentice Hall photo by Ken O'Donoghue; **572,** Prentice Hall photo by Russ Lappa; **574,** Prentice Hall photo by Russ Lappa